TOWARDS
THE MYSTICAL
EXPERIENCE
OF MODERNITY

THE MAKING
OF RAV KOOK,
1865-1904

Jewish Thought, Jewish History: New Studies
Series Editor: Gregg Stern, PhD

TOWARDS THE MYSTICAL EXPERIENCE OF MODERNITY

THE MAKING OF RAV KOOK, 1865-1904

YEHUDAH MIRSKY

BOSTON
2021

Library of Congress Cataloging-in-Publication Data

Names: Mirsky, Yehudah, author.
Title: Towards the Mystical Experience of Modernity: The Making of Rav Kook, 1865-1904 / Yehudah Mirsky.
Description: Boston : Academic Studies Press, 2019. | Series: Jewish thought,
    Jewish history: new studies | Identifiers: LCCN 2019019117 (print) | LCCN 2019020852 (ebook) | ISBN
    9781618119544 (adobe PDF) | ISBN 9781618119537 (hardcover) | ISBN 9781618119551
    (pbk.)
Subjects: LCSH: Kook, Abraham Isaac, 1865-1935. | Rabbis--Europe,
    Eastern--Biography. | Jewish philosophy. | Religious Zionism--Philosophy.
    | Europe, Eastern--Biography.
Classification: LCC BM755.K66 (ebook) | LCC BM755.K66 M577 2019 (print) | DDC
    296.8/32092 [B] --dc23
LC record available at https://lccn.loc.gov/2019019117

9781618119537 hardback
9781618119544 ebook PDF
9781618119551 paperback
9781644695302 ePub

Book design by Lapiz Digital Services
Cover design by Ivan Grave

Published by Academic Studies Press
1577 Beacon Street
Brookline, MA 02446, USA
press@academicstudiespress.com
www.academicstudiespress.com

In Memory of My Teachers

Rabbi Yehudah Amital
הרב יהודה עמיטל
(1924–2010)

Rabbi Emanuel Rackman
הרב מנחם רקמן
(1910–2020)

Rabbi David Mirsky
אבי מורי הרב דוד מירסקי
(1921–1982)

הגיד לך אדם מה טוב ומה ד׳ דורש ממך כי אם עשות משפט ואהבת חסד והצנע לכת עם אלהיך

(מיכה ו:ח)

He has told you, human, what is good, and what God seeks from you, but
doing justice and lovingkindness and walking in humility with your God.

(Micah 6:8)

Contents

To the Reader viii

Abbreviations and Acronyms xi

Note on Translation and Transliteration xiii

Introduction 1

1. Childhood and Early Years: Between Mitnagdism, Hasidism, and Haskalah ... 41

2. All in the Mind: The Writings of the Zeimel Period 90

3. Boisk: Turning Inward at the Crossroads of Mussar and *Tiqqun* ... 140

4. *ʿEyn Ayah*: Intellect, Imagination, Self-Expression, Prophecy ... 183

5. The Turn Towards Nationalism: Between Ideology and Utopia, or, Ethics and Eschatology ... 233

6. "The New Guide of the Perplexed" and "The Last in Boisk": Making Sense of Heresy en Route to Zion ... 278

Conclusion 329

Acknowledgments 348

Bibliography 351

Index 381

To the Reader

This volume seeks to understand how one extraordinary, and extraordinarily influential, thinker and public figure, Avraham Yitzhak Ha-Cohen Kook, came to be who he was, amid the dynamic, intellectual, spiritual, and political currents of Jewish Eastern Europe of the fin-de-siècle. Though much has, and continues to be, written on him, relatively little has been done on the nearly four decades of his life before his arrival in Palestine in 1904, and there is no comprehensive intellectual biography of him in any language. This book seeks to start filling that gap, telling a story of both the ideas and the man.

The volume traces an arc of development in his thinking, whose points of reference in the currents of Jewish intellectual history are Lithuanian Talmudism and Kabbalah, the heritage of medieval Jewish philosophy, and modern thought, as filtered through the Eastern European Jewish culture of the time. Our sociohistorical points of reference are Lithuanian rabbinic culture, Haskalah, the Mussar controversies of the 1890s, and the emergence of Jewish ethical radicalism and Zionist nationalism in response to the massive crises of Jewish religion, politics, and society in the late nineteenth century. The book traces how, ultimately, in the mind of this one thinker, these points converged.

We will, in the first, second, and third chapters, view his thinking well within the frames of Lithuanian Talmudism and moderate Haskalah, placing particular focus on medieval philosophy and Lithuanian Kabbalah—and in the primacy which those currents accord to Mind as the defining principle of humanity and the world. In response to events in his own life, most notably the death of his first wife, as well as external events, in particular the debates over the Mussar movement and its emphasis on self-cultivation within a non-Hasidic framework, we will see Rav Kook using those traditions as maps to the inner life, especially in his journals. We will also see his burgeoning interest in the relationship between Judaism and ethical universalism and between body and soul.

The midpoint, the fourth chapter of the book, and in some ways its fulcrum, is an extended discussion of his aggadic commentary, noteworthy for his choice of subject, and for the ways in which a close reading of that commentary demonstrates subtle but deeply consequential shifts in his understanding of the conceptual vocabulary of the tradition. We will watch him broadening his horizons towards a richer palette of human consciousness and metaphysics, encompassing imagination and feeling, and observe how his exploration of the relationships between these dimensions of human experience led him to develop a dialectical view of the inner life, in which the tension of seeming opposites yields a greater, richer whole. This recourse to dialectical thinking as the way to engage contradictions assumed increasing significance in his thought, as he came to extend it beyond the individual's life, and towards the highly conflicted social, political, and ideological struggles of his times.

The fifth chapter looks at his early reflections on Zionism and first published writings on Jewish nationalism. In them, we see him fashioning nationalism and ethics into a mutually supportive structure that might speak to the youth culture of the time, as well as a robust affirmation of tradition. The final, sixth, chapter discusses at length his attempt to present youthful radicals with a perspective on ethics and comparative religion that would integrate traditional Judaism and ethical universalism—and how that exoteric view was rooted in the esoteric refections in his private journals and their far-reaching explorations of the Kabbalah.

The conclusion starts by examining how this story set the stage for deeply consequential shifts in his thought after his arrival in Palestine, and closes with reflections on this story—of a man who developed an extraordinary theology in an effort to understand not only his times, but himself—for the study of Jewish thought and religion and the meaning of religious experience.

***

The present volume revises and expands my doctoral dissertation, *An Intellectual and Spiritual Biography of Rabbi Avraham Yitzhaq Ha-Cohen Kook from 1865 to 1904*, submitted to Harvard University's Committee on the Study of Religion in the Spring of 2007.

More than a dozen years have passed. Since then, I have published a number of studies of Rav Kook and, in 2014, a volume surveying Rav Kook's life, times, and legacy as a whole—*Rav Kook: Mystic in a Time of Revolution*. I chose for a number of reasons to publish that work first, and only then return to this much more detailed monograph on his formative years. Those intervening years also saw my moving from Jerusalem to Boston's Brandeis University and, while completing this book, a move back to Jerusalem, and a shift in my scholarly interests to questions of religion and nationalism and the theological foundations of liberalism and human rights. Yet time has not diminished my sense of the stakes, urgency, and deep intellectual, spiritual, and moral rewards of the careful study of Rav Kook's life and thought.

Research into Rav Kook's corpus has, to put it mildly, continued apace in the intervening years, including, in some part due to my dissertation, intensified interest in his Eastern European decades and in tracing the development of his thought over time. Most significantly, more and more hitherto unavailable and even unknown writings of his have been published from manuscript, in various editions, including some written during the period we will be learning about here. I have done my best to incorporate these new researches and primary sources into this revision, which, if nothing else, provides a survey of these voluminous writings and leaves road markers for others to follow. Similarly, I have decided to leave much material in the footnotes, along with citations of my innmumerable scholarly debts, in the hopes that students and scholars will find, pick up, and carry forward all that I have not had time to do. In general, because there are few full-length studies of Rav Kook in English, I have chosen to err on the side of inclusion. While this is in many ways an academic volume, I hope it will find readers outside the precincts of universities, as would befit its subject, who himself tried greatly to expand communities of learning and understanding.

How well I have achieved this I leave the reader to judge; I hope that I have at least provided an introduction to, and initial framing of, these additions to the corpus of his Rav Kook's writings, still expanding some eighty-five years after his death. I have, in light of the new publications, somewhat revised and amplified earlier findings, but the basic outlines that I traced a dozen years ago still, I think, endure.

Doing full justice to even these few decades in the life of as colossal a figure as Rav Kook would have taken even more years; I have chosen to publish now, heeding Winston Churchill's legendary maxim that we must not let the best be the enemy of the good or, at least, the good enough.

Abbreviations and Acronyms

Aderet—Eliyahu David Rabinowitz-Teomim
DC—*Da'at Cohen*
EAB—*'Eyn Ayah* to BT Berakhot
EC—*'Ezrat Cohen*
EJ—*Encyclopedia Judaica*
HP—*Hevesh Pe'er*
IS—*'Ittur Sofrim*
Igrot—*Igrot Ha-Re'ayah*
NLI—National Library of Israel, Givat Ram, Jerusalem
LNH—*Li-Nevukhei Ha-Dor*
Maimon, *Azkarah*—J. L. Fishman (Maimon), *Toldot Ha-Rav*
MA—*Mussar Avikha*
MH—*Ma'amarei Ha-Re'ayah*
MQ—*Metziot Qatan*
MQB—*Mahberot Qetanot Boisk*
MS—*Midbar Shur*
Neriah, *Sihot*—Moshe Zvi Neriah, *Sihot Ha-Re'ayah*
Neriah, *Tal*—Moshe Zvi Neriah, *Tal Ha-Re'ayah*
Netziv—Naftali Zvi Yehudah Berlin
OM—*Orah Mishpat*
Otzarot—Moshe Zuriel, ed., *Otzarot Ha-Re'ayah*, 2nd ed.
PAB—*Pinqas Aharon be-Boisk*

Note on Translation and Transliteration

Unless otherwise stated, all translations from Rav Kook and from most other texts are my own. For translations of Hebrew Bible, I have consulted the Jewish Publication Society translation of 1985, as well as the translations of Robert Alter, Ariel and Chana Bloch, Harold Fisch, Everett Fox, and the King James Version, and in each instance have chosen the translation best suited to the text and context in which that Biblical verse appears. Translations from the Talmud are largely my own, though I have occasionally made use of the Artscroll, Soncino, and Steinsaltz translations of the Babylonian Talmud.

My transliteration essentially follows the style of the Society for Biblical Literature, while adopting as necessary other transliterations that either have become widely accepted (Kabbalah, Kook, Yitzhak) or have been chosen as such by the subjects themselves (e.g., Chayim Pearl).

Inevitable errors and infelicities of translation and transliteration, as well as fact and interpretation, are mine.

I knew what a large role a rabbi like this would play in the development of the Yishuv [the Jewish community of Palestine], but I was not terribly interested in this rabbi. He had taken no part in Hibat Tzion, or, later, Zionism. He hadn't written important books, so what would I have had to do with him? So I decided to be in the new rabbi's home and get a proper sense of him. I spent three days in the city of Boisk, and spent several hours each day in the rabbi's home and we discussed various matters in halakhah, aggadah, and life questions. I saw before me no ordinary rabbi, following well-worn paths, but a man of the spirit, paving his own way. He hadn't found it yet, but was searching for it, in all the length and breadth of Judaism. He was diving into the seas of the Talmuds, Midrashim, Philosophy, Kabbalah, Hasidism, and the new Hebrew literature, and bringing up precious stones with which to pave his way.

—Yitzhaq Nissenbaum (1868–1942),
'Alei Heldi (Warsaw: Halter,
1929), 188[1]

---

1 Nissenbaum, rabbi, writer, and activist, was, from the 1890s on, until his death in the Warsaw Ghetto, a leading figure in Religious Zionism.

Introduction

Precis

In dealing with a character of Rav Kook's stature one cannot make do with dry facts. We need a biography describing the man's path, his spiritual development, and his personal and public struggles. . . . Dynamic unity was the goal of his thought in all its dimensions, and one can nearly say that an astounding unitive instinct came to expression in an equally astounding range of issues. How can one convey that intuition? By a reflective reconstruction of the process of his thought. The scholar must construct Rav Kook's view in all its scope by attending to the process through which it took shape.[1]

If one has, as I do, theological mentors from across the ages, then it is valuable to realize that their insights on spiritual matters come framed by their particular personal and cultural circumstances. . . . Everything is, of course, time-bound and there is a danger for us who are so shaped by historical consciousness to dismiss every authority from the past once we have understood the peculiarities of the historical, personal, or theoretical factors that shaped its outlook. A far more profitable approach is to employ historical consciousness for developing more *discriminating* assessments of the wisdom of the past. The point of historical scholarship should not be, as it so often is today, simply to take things apart, to destroy myths, or to say that what looks simple is really quite complex. It should also be to help people see how to put things back together again. We need to use history for the guidance it offers, learning from great figures in the past—both in their brilliance and in their shortcomings. Otherwise we are stuck with only the wisdom of the present.[2]

Trying fully to grasp how anyone came to be, is as futile as it is essential. All the more so when approaching one of those colossal spiritual figures, whose ideas fundamentally recast the worlds of actions and ideas.

The coming to be of Rabbi (Rav) Avraham Yitzhak Ha-Cohen Kook (1865–1935) is no exception. How did a Lithuanian Talmudist with a Hasidic strain become a profound theologian, jurist, lyric poet, major communal leader, and astounding mystic, who

---

1 Eliezer Schweid, "Sefer Hadash 'al Mishnat Ha-Re'ayah Kook," *Petahim* 28, no. 2 (1974): 36–37. Schweid was reviewing Zvi Yaron's pioneering book-length exposition of Rav Kook's teachings *Mishnato shel Ha-Rav Kook* (Jerusalem: Jewish Agency, 1974).
2 George M. Marsden, *Jonathan Edwards: A Life* (New Haven: Yale University Press, 2003), 502.

reconceived modernity's revolt against tradition as the advent of redemption and its celebration of personal experience as "holiness"'s own rebirth? The question takes on more urgency due to his deep influence on society and politics, down to the present, perhaps more than any other rabbinic thinker in modern times.

"Of the making of books there is no end" (Eccles. 12:12); that is certainly the case with Rav Kook as volumes by and about him continue to appear[3] and the interpretation of his teachings, especially their political dimensions, still makes for daily editorial and ideological fare.[4] Yet, there are still many holes to fill, thematic and methodological both, and this work seeks to start on one of them: Rav Kook's first thirty-eight years, before his immigration to Palestine.[5]

---

3   The most significant of Rav Kook's own writings to emerge from manuscript in recent years are: the eight volumes of spiritual diaries which formed the basis of *Orot* and *Orot Ha-Qodesh*, published as *Shemonah Qevatzim* [Eight Compilations], 3 vols., rev. ed. (Jerusalem: n.p., 2004); his commentary to the aggadic passages of BT Berakhot and Shabbat, *'Eyn Ayah*, 4 vols. (Jerusalem: Makhon Ha-Ratzyah Kook ztz"l, 5755–5760/1995–2000), his early collection of sermons *Midbar Shur* (Jerusalem: Makhon Ha-Ratzyah Kook ztz"l, 1999); a collection of deeply personal reflections entitled *Hadarav*, 2nd ed. (Mevaseret Tzion: Re'ut, 2002); and several other spiritual diaries, including five which we will discuss here at greater length: *Pinqasim* 15 and 16, *Metziot Qatan*, *Mahberot Qetanot Boisk* and *Pinqas Aharon be-Boisk*, and the long-unpublished treatise *Li-Nevukhei Ha-Dor*. Many of those appear in a series of journals which have been published in three volumes—see *Qevatzim mi-Ketav Yad Qodsho*, 3 vols., ed. Boaz Ofan (Jerusalem: n.p., 2006-2008). They have also been published under the imprint of Ha-Makhon Ha-Ratzyah Kook ztz"l, whose editorial practices regularly cross the line between editing and censorship. To take one example: one of the diaries in this collection, and the first written by Rav Kook after his immigration to Palestine in 1904, was published as *Pinqas Yud-Gimel* (Jerusalem: Makhon Ha-Ratzyah Kook ztz"l, 2004). Comparing it with the version printed by Ofan, the manuscript photocopy of which is in the Schatz collection of Hebrew University, we see that roughly one-quarter was excised from the printed edition, with scarcely any notice to the reader. The excisions are notes and restored in Boaz Ofan's edition.

    Other crucial tools are Boaz Ofan's invaluable topical index of Rav Kook's writings, *Maftehot le-Khitvei Ha-Re'ayah* (Ramat Gan: Re'ut, 2002) and the multiple indices to be found in Moshe Zuriel's series *Otzarot*.

4   The literature on the political uses of Rav Kook's teachings is vast and of varying quality; for three, excellent studies of different aspect of Rav Kook's contemporary political legacy in Israel, see Yosef (Yoske) Ahituv, "Erkei Mussar u-Le'umiyut be-Hugei Merkaz Ha-Rav," in *Sefer Zikaron le-Professor Zev Falk zl: Ma'amarim be-Mada'ei Ha-Yahadut u-vi-She'elot Ha-Sha'ah*, ed. Rivka Horvitz, Moshe David Herr, Yohanan David Silman, and Michael Cordinali (Jerusalem: Hebrew University/Magnes, 2005), 279–306; Shlomo Fischer, "Self-Expression and Democracy in Radical Religious Zionist Ideology" (PhD diss., Hebrew University, 2007); idem, "Radical Religious Zionism: From the Collective to the Individual," in *Kabbalah and Contemporary Spiritual Revival*, ed. Boaz Huss (Beer-Sheva: Ben-Gurion University of the Negev Press), 2011, 285–310; Idem. "Fundamentalist or Religious Nationalist?: Israeli Modern Orthodoxy," in *Dynamic Belonging: Contemporary Jewish Collective Identities*, ed. Harvey E. Goldberg et al. (New York: Berghahn, 2012), 91–111; and Gershom Gorenberg, *The Accidental Empire: Israel and the Birth of the Settlements, 1967–1977* (New York: Times Books, 2006).

5   While he is conventionally said to have emigrated at age thirty-nine, he in fact was born September 7, 1865/16 Elul 5625, and arrived in Palestine May 13, 1904/28 Iyar 5664, making him thirty-eight at the time.

the voluminous scholarship about him has long scanted those years. Yet in those decades he wrote numerous volumes of textual commentary, sermons, essays, polemic, theology, morals, poetry, responsa, and halakhic discourse, all while serving as a rabbi and communal leader. We still have an insufficient scholarly biography (or bibliography) of him, and no full-scale intellectual biography, about which more below. This work aims to fill, in part, those lacunae.

Along with its biographical and bibliographical excavation, this work argues that these early, largely neglected works repay study in their own right.[6] In contrast to his later, celebrated writings, grounded in mystical experience and centered on the interlocking relationships between subjective selfhood, national identity, universalist ethics and an overarching metaphysic, these earlier works are concerned chiefly with the moral and spiritual self-cultivation of the individual person. They are richly insightful and lay bare the groundwork for his eventual turns towards nationalism and ecstatic mysticism.

As we will see, Rav Kook's writings in the first decade of his rabbinical life, from the mid–1880s to the mid–1890s, are chiefly preoccupied with the lone sage's cultivation of perfection—through the body's alignment with the mind. In these writings, he reworks ideas of self-cultivation taken from the medieval philosophical tradition into the terms set by Lithuanian Kabbalah. This concern with self-cultivation on the medieval model stands in marked contrast to—yet constructs much of the scaffolding for—his later canonical writings, which are marked by mystic ecstasy and deeply concerned with nationalism, Messianism, and the depiction and exploration of the expressive subject, individual and national, as the locus of the divine.

In the mid–1890s these explorations become linked to his mounting reflection on the meaning of Jewish nationhood, and the relationship of Jewish morality to the moral lives of non-Jews, who, as well, are God's creatures and part of His plan for the world. In the first years of the twentieth century, Rav Kook begins actively to bring these reflections to bear on interpreting the broader political, intellectual, and social currents of his times.

While, as we shall see, Rav Kook did indeed study Kabbalah from early on, his internalizing Kabbalistic ideas as maps to his own dynamic inner world, society, the nation, and the world, grew over time. This shift in his thinking, from what one may call a top-down image of the religious life, in which the sovereign mind disciplines the emotions and the body, to a bottom-up image, in which the body and the emotions reach upwards towards reunion with the dynamic divine subject, all within the highly structured forms of tradition, is a chief focus of our study. A related shift is his move from the individual to the collective, deploying the thought structures he developed to map his inner world and those of the people around him to map the inner life of the collective, and, eventually, the cosmos.

---

6   This assertion has become more widely accepted since the dissertation on which this work is based was completed in 2007, but is still worth repeating.

Mapping Rav Kook

The mapping doesn't stop there. Disciples and students of Rav Kook, in the *beit mid-rash* and in the academy, in his lifetime and afterwards, have found, and still find themselves, confronted by a colossal figure, controversial in his time and today, defying easy characterization. He was first and foremost a halakhist reared and educated in the high scholastic traditions of Lithuanian Talmudism, and throughout his life his communal responsibilities as rabbi and halakhic decision maker took up most of his time. Rav Kook's stature as a Talmudist was the backbone of his personal and public identity (much of which was devoted not to theology but to hands-on communal leadership), lent force to his distinctive endorsements of modernity and made him so challenging and provocative a figure within the Orthodox rabbinic fraternity, many if not most of whose members regarded his *sui generis* worldview as misguided if not downright heretical.

At the same time he exhibited deep knowledge of, and engagement with, non-halakhic literature, including such medieval and early modern philosophical classics as Bahya's *Hovot Ha-Levavot*, Yehudah Ha-Levi's *Kuzari*, Maimonides's *Guide*, and Isaac Arama's *'Aqedat Yitzhaq*. He was, as we will see, in love with the study of aggadah, the non-halakhic texts of rabbinic literature. The then-less-well-known works of Maharal of Prague were also of great importance to him for their ideas and, more importantly, for their hermeneutic method.[7] He was, crucially, steeped in Kabbalah; in his youth he studied and imbibed the the classics of Kabbalah from antiquity through early modernity; the works of Moshe Hayim Luzzatto, and the traditions of Lithuanian Kabbalah; with time he engaged deeply with Hasidic thought, and even had some experience of practical and magical Kabbalah. Further, elements of Haskalah literature and of general literature and philosophy played a substantial role in his thought-world.

He lived an unimpeachable if at times unconventional ultra-Orthodox life (his practice of wearing phylacteries all day, though not unheard of, was by no means common) and was a decidedly conservative halakhist; yet in his theological writings he affirms key elements of modernity, explicitly refers to Kant, Schopenhauer, Nietzsche, Soloviev, and Bergson, and regularly engages in explicit dialogue with Spinoza and implicit though unmistakable dialogue with Schelling, Moses Hess, Herder, and Hegel. We know he read William James and Hermann Cohen, as well as, later on, Charles Dickens. Much of his acquaintance with these writings was derived second hand from the rich Hebrew periodical literature of the time, and the writings of modern Jewish thinkers such as Krochmal and lesser-known cultural intermediaries such as Shimon Bernfeld and David Neumark. The striking thing is the way in which he tried to incorporate as much as he could of these ideas into his own evolving worldview. The stakes of this engagement with modern thought went far deeper than intellectual exploration. While most of his rabbinic colleagues saw modernity as a catastrophe, he came to see it for all its vicissitudes as perhaps

---

7   See Adin Steinsaltz, "Ha-Ba'ayatiyut be'-Orot Ha-Qodesh," in *Ha-Re'ayah*, ed. Yizhak Refael (Jerusalem: Mossad Ha-Rav Kook, 1966), 102–105. I will have more to say about his relationship to the works of Maharal in chapter four.

the most deeply promising and even redemptive chapter in Jewish and world history. And he actively worked to put that vision into action.

After his move to Palestine in 1904, and especially after about 1910, Rav Kook developed and expressed his theological views in an avowedly unsystematic, lyrical idiom, drawing on the full range of his reading. The interpretive challenge here was well captured by Jacob Agus in a pioneering essay in 1948, in which he characterized Rav Kook as "perhaps the first mystical literary philosopher in the history of Jewish religion."[8]

His personal charisma, enhanced by his vivid personal appearance, and the great gentleness and saintliness with which he tried to conduct himself, left a deep impression on many of those who met him[9]—with significant exceptions, of course[10]—and indeed much of that charisma courses through his writings and accounts for their electrifying effect on many of his readers.[11]

It is small wonder, then, that students and scholars, confronted with this compelling and complex persona, have tried to gain some footing by way of numerous points of view. One complicating feature of Rav Kook studies is the Byzantine state of his corpus.[12]

---

8   Jacob Agus, "Ish Ha-Mistorin," *Talpiot* 3, nos. 3–4 (1948): 528–578, 528. Indeed, he very much wished to be thought of as a member of the Hebrew literary fraternity, see the striking comments of his recorded by one of his disciples during the 1920s, Samuel K. Mirsky, "Ha-Dor bi-Reiy Ha-Re'ayah," *Or Ha-Mizrah*, December 1965, 101–105, 104–105:

יודע אני מתוך שיחות אינטימיות שהיו לי עם הרב זצ״ל, שהיה מאוכזב ממאמריו שלו שכתב בצורה ספרותית נאה ובבהירות רבה, ולא היתה להן התגובה המקווה. בהרבה מהם קלע כנגד אחד העם אם כי לא בהזכרת שמו, ופעם אמר לי: אחד העם היה בעל מוח אך חסר לב, כלומר חסר רגש, והתפלא על השפעתו על הדור. ומה תועלת, אמר, בכתיבת דברים ברורים בשאלות שהדור מתחבט בהן אם אין להם הד. דברי תורה בהלכה ובאגדה סופם שילמדו בבית המדרש ויעשו להם אזנים מה שאין כן במאמרים פובליציסטיים.

9   The testimonies to his personal charisma are legion. One very powerful testament of the deep impression Rav Kook regularly left on his interlocutors is the memoir of S. Y. Agnon written in 1967 and reprinted in his collection *Me-'Atzmi el 'Atzmi* (Jerusalem and Tel Aviv: Schocken, 2000), noteworthy in its own right and for his recording the deep impression Rav Kook's penetrating eyes left on none other than Marc Chagall. Agnon's story "Ha-Taba'at," reprinted in his posthumous collection *Takhrikh shel Sippurim* (Jerusalem and Tel Aviv: Schocken, 1984), 218–220, was, he said to Dov Sadan, about Rav Kook (this was related to me by Professor Menachem Friedman in the summer of 1998). See also the passage in Agnon's novel *Temol Shilshom* (Jerusalem and Tel Aviv: Schocken, 1967), 482, wherein Rav Kook appears as the unnamed "Rabbi from Jaffa." See also the powerful sketch by Rebbe Binyomin (Joshua Radler-Feldman) in his *Partzufim*, vol. 2 (Tel Aviv: Mitzpeh, 1936), 125–133.

10   The opposition which Rav Kook met among his more conservative-minded rabbinic peers is the stuff of legend; more interesting are the mixed reactions he garnered among the secular Zionists who played such a large role in his historiosophy; for more on this, see at length, Yehudah Mirsky, *Rav Kook: Mystic in a Time of Revolution* (New Haven: Yale University Press, 2014). A revised Hebrew edition is idem, *Rav Kook: Mabat Hadash* (Tel Aviv: Devir, 2021).

11   His saintliness and charisma are the thrust of much of the hagiographic writing about him; for one of the better-known, and least floridly done, hagiographies of him, see Hayim Lifshitz, *Shivhei Ha-Re'ayah* (Jerusalem: Makhon Harry Fischel, 1979).

12   A selective scholarly bibliography published in 1995 listed (after the then-standing list of thirty-two primary works by him) some 254 books, chapters, essays, articles, and monographs

Manuscripts, not least his spiritual diaries, from which most of his canon was culled, have emerged in printed editions of varying integrity; readers have had to wade through the great masses of materials gathered in the sprawling (and often hard-to-find) volumes of Moshe Zvi Neriah, Yehoshua Be'eri, and Moshe Zuriel.[13]

Consequently, it is worth taking a moment to say something about this cataloguing itself, which, in the multifaceted and very complicated case of Rav Kook, is better thought of as "mapping."[14]

The process of "mapping" Rav Kook began even in his lifetime. Yossi Avneri has traced some of the formation of his public image, among the elites and the public, his supporters and opponents, those (both within and without the Zionist camp) who saw him as a rubber stamp for the Zionist enterprise, and those who saw him as yet another rabbinic obscurantist; those who admired his freedom and courage, and those who unfavorably contrasted the comparative boldness he exhibited during his years in the frontier region of Jaffa with the more cautious posture with which he threaded his way among the legendary fanatics of Jerusalem; and, finally, those, both religious and secular, who saw him as spiritual giant, as well as people for whom he was a *faux* modernist and essentially reactionary. Avneri wisely suggests that none of the one-dimensional views of Rav Kook, from any camp, do justice to the complexity of his personality.[15]

---

devoted to him, along with sixteen annotated translations of various texts into English. The bibliography appears as an appendix to Lawrence Kaplan and David Shatz, *Rabbi Abraham Isaac Kook and Jewish Spirituality* (New York: New York University Press, 1995), 309–324. Among the more significant omissions from that list are: Martin Buber's essay on Rav Kook in *On Zion*, trans. Stanley Goodman (New York: Schocken, 1973), 147–154; Agnon's various writings on Rav Kook in his *Me-'Atzmi el 'Atzmi* and elsewhere (about which more below); Gershom Scholem's brief but significant remarks in his essay of 1963 "Hirhurim 'al Efsharutah shel Mistikah Yehudit be-Yameinu," reprinted in his *Devarim be-Go: Pirqei Morasha u-Tehiya*, vol. 1 (Tel Aviv: 'Am 'Oved, 1982), 71–83. The academic corpus continues to grow as will be seen by the many scholarly studies cited in this work.

13　Moshe Zuriel, *Otzarot Ha-Re'ayah*, 7 vols., 2nd ed. (Rishon le-Zion: Yeshivat Ha-Hesder Rishon Le-Zion, 2002–2016) (from here on, *Otzarot*); Yehoshua Be'eri, *'Oved Yisrael bi-Qedushah*, 5 vols. (Tel Aviv: H. Y. KH., 1989). Zuriel's volumes are a fantastic resource, as will become clear in the course of this work. Be'eri also has much valuable information to offer. Neriah's works, which are invaluable but must, as will become clear, be read with some caution, are too numerous to list here, but will appear throughout.

14　I am here taking a leaf from the title essay of J. Z. Smith's extraordinary collection *Map Is Not Territory*. He writes: "Such are three maps of the worlds of other men [which he designates as the 'locative,' 'utopian,' and 'incongruous']. . . . They remain coeval possibilities which may be appropriated whenever and wherever they correspond to man's experience of the world. Other maps will be drawn as the scholar of religions continues his task. . . . We need to reflect on and play with the necessary incongruity of our maps before we set out on a voyage of discovery to chart the worlds of other men. For the dictum of Alfred Korzybski is inescapable: 'Map is not territory'—but maps are all we possess." Jonathan Z. Smith, *Map Is Not Territory: Studies in the History of Religions* (Leiden: E. J. Brill, 1978), 289–309, 309.

15　Yossi Avneri, "Ha-Re'ayah Kook—Tadmit be-Tahalikhei Hitgabshut," *Sefer Bar-Ilan* 23–24 (2001): 161–187.

In some ways this "mapping" began with Rav Kook's own attempts to understand himself, as in his spiritual diaries he again and again tries to order the categories of his own thinking, categories he then abandons, until his next try.[16] In the early decades that are our subject he tried writing in a variety of genres; all, I believe, were part of his attempt to find a proper voice for himself, and his increasingly far-reaching visions. In the end, as we will see, he settled more or less on the spiritual diary as the most fitting vehicle of his explorations, a genre that fit the highly eclectic nature of his thinking, as well as the very personal subjective directions in which he and his thinking were headed.

Many Editorial Hands

It cannot be emphasized strongly enough that most of the volumes bearing Rav Kook's name, and virtually all those that became canonical in the first sixty years after his death, were compiled and edited by his disciples and successors.[17] The most renowned of these are the volumes edited by his son Zvi Yehudah, *Orot* and *Orot Ha-Teshuvah*, on, respectively, the religious meaning of modern Jewish nationalism and the metaphysics (if you will, metahistorics) of repentance; and the theological magnum opus edited by David Cohen (also called *Ha-Nazir*, the Nazirite), *Orot Ha-Qodesh*.[18] In terms of editing style,

---

16 See for instance the three opening chapters of *Orot Ha-Teshuvah*, published in his lifetime in 1925, where he begins a systematic classification of forms of repentance, only to abandon it, leaving his son to cull from the spiritual diaries the remaining fourteen chapters, which are unquestionably more riveting and dynamic than the first three; for another example, see the passage with which Nazir editorially chose to open volume three of *Orot Ha-Qodesh*, entitled *Mussar Ha-Qodesh*, wherein Rav Kook says that an introduction to the study of Mussar/ morality-cum-ethics needs to distinguish between eighteen different kinds of Mussar (*Orot Ha-Qodesh*, 3:19; the original is found in *Qevatzim*, 1:683 and was written in about 1910). While Nazir places this passage at the outset of his discussion of ethics, the thrust of this dissertation will read it after decades of writing by Rav Kook, chiefly in Eastern Europe, about the meaning of Mussar, that is, this passage reflects his own recogntion of the extraordainrily broad range of meanings he had hitherto been assigning the term.

17 Meir Munitz treats this at length in his dissertation. Some key findings are discussed in his article, "'Arikhat Ha-Sefer Orot, le-Re'ayah Kook," *'Alei Sefer* 20 (2008): 125–170. See also Udi Abramovich, "Ha-Shelihut, Ha-Monopol ve-Ha-Tzensurah—Ha-Ratzyah Kook ve-'Arikhat Kitvei Ha-Re'ayah," *Da'at* 60 (2007): 121–152. Jonatan Meir, "Orot ve-Kelim: Behinah Mehudeshet shel 'Hug' Ha-Re'ayah Kook ve-'Orkhei Ketavav," *Qabbalah* 13 (2005): 163–247 is a truly indispensable guide to this crucial and complicated question and a treasure of cultural history in its own right. The protocols of the society formed after Rav Kook's passing in 1935 for the purpose of editing and publishing his works is to be found in Gutel, "Protocol Ha-Agudah le-Hotza'at Kitvei Ha-Rav Kook," 340–353. The society's prospectus was published in the fall of 1937 as *Prospekt le-Hotza'at Kitvei Rabeinu Ha-Gadol, Sar Ha-Torah ve-Abir Ha-Umah, Tzadiq Yesod 'Olam Maran Avraham Yitzhak Ha-Cohen Kook zl* (Jerusalem: n.p., 1937). The text of the prospectus was written by the society's chair, Meir Berlin (Bar-Ilan).

18 For the genesis of Nazir's editorial project, begun in 1922, see his memoir reprinted in the memorial volume edited by his son Shear-Yashuv Cohen et al., *Nezir Ehav*, vol. 1 (Jerusalem: Nezer David, 1977), 297–302. The very last passage of *Orot Ha-Qodesh* in galleys that Rav

while Zvi Yehudah Kook kept lengthy passages intact even as he wove them into essays, Ha-Nazir imposed order and system, embedding discrete passages into a vast latticework of his own devising.[19] Zvi Yehudah Kook was also responsible for editing, *inter alia*, most of Rav Kook's commentary to the prayer book *'Olat Re'ayah*,[20] a slim but powerful volume on Torah study, *Orot Ha-Torah*, the Mussar treatise we will explore at length entitled *Mussar Avikha*, and a number of his halakhic works. Several compilations were made by others with Rav Kook's cooperation in his lifetime.[21] Indeed, the more Rav Kook's journals have been published in their original form the more we see how much editing they needed before publication, and how hard his editors had to work.

It is instructive to compare the 1920 edition of *Orot* prepared by Zvi Yehudah Kook with another, much smaller, anthology of Rav Kook's writings, *Ha-Mahshavah Ha-Yisraelit*, compiled by Elhanan Kalmanson in the same year.[22] Kalmanson was a journalist and socialist; he, unlike Zvi Yehudah Kook, had no access to Rav Kook's spiritual diaries but was in contact with the literary circle gathered around Rav Kook in Jaffa, notably Alexander Ziskind Rabinowitz (Azar);[23] the Rav Kook who emerges in those pages is far more conflicted and, you might say, contemporary than one would gather from the ex cathedra pronouncements of *Orot*.[24]

The differing ideational emphases of Zvi Yehudah Kook and Ha-Nazir are unmistakable: whereas Zvi Yehudah Kook's editorial work proceeded with a decidedly nationalist

---

Kook saw in his lifetime was the passage entitled "binyan ha-qodesh" [2:310] (section 16 of "Ha-Qodesh Ha-Kelali"). This is according to Shmuel Barukh Shulman's *Esh Dat* (Jerusalem: Eretz Yizrael Press, 1936), 10, in which he says that the Nazir brought it to Rav Kook on Friday, Rosh Hodesh Elul, just three days before his death, and that when Rav Kook looked at it "he laughed and cried."

19 See Bezalel Naor's comments in the preface to his translation of the 1920 edition of *Orot* (Northvale: Aronson, 1993), 3. Neriah Gutel has argued that Zvi Yehudah Kook's editing greatly improved his father's work; see his "Omanut ve-Aminut be-'Arikhat Ha-Ratzyah Kook et Kitvei Ha-Re'ayah Kook: 'Arikhat Ha-Mavo' le-'Shabbat Ha-Aretz'—Miqreh Mivhan," *Tarbitz* 70 (2001): 601–625. However, in that essay he does not present us with the full original of the particular text he uses to buttress his claim (the introduction to *Shabbat Ha-Aretz*, Rav Kook's controversial 1910 treatise on the laws of the Sabbatical year), presumably because his receipt of the manuscript was contingent on his not publishing it, so we have to take his word for it.

20 Much of *'Olat Re'ayah* was taken from the aggadic commentary *'Eyn Ayah*, which is the subject of this book's fourth chapter.

21 These are *Orot Ha-Emunah* edited by Moshe Gurvitz and published only in Jerusalem: n.p., 1985; *Eretz Hefetz*, edited by Yeshayahu Shapira (Jerusalem: Darom, 1930). Shapira, known as the Admor He-Halutz, was a rarity, a dynastic Hasidic rabbi who embraced Zionism; his brother was the celebrated Kalonymous Shapiro, best known for the sermons he preached in the Warsaw Ghetto, published posthumously as *Esh Qodesh* (Jerusalem, n.p., 1960). For more on them, see Meir, "Orot ve-Kelim": 202–208, 214–216.

22 Rav Kook, *Ha-Mahshavah Ha-Yisraelit*, comp. Elhanan Kalmanson (Jerusalem: Levi, 1920).

23 For more on Kalmanson, see Meir, "Orot ve-Kelim": 199–202.

24 For instance it is in Kalmanson's volume that we find Rav Kook's comment, apropos Yosef Hayim Brenner, "He who says my soul is torn, is right." On this see my *Rav Kook*, 90-91.

slant, Ha-Nazir tried to construct out of Rav Kook's diaries a universal metaphysics.[25] This emphasis is evident among Zvi Yehudah's disciples—most notably Shlomo Aviner, Zvi Tau, Uzi Kalcheim, Ya'aqov Filber—for whom Rav Kook's teachings on nationalism are the central organizing principle of the corpus (Yoel Bin-Nun is an interesting exception here).[26] Nazir, for his part, himself very much imbued with the Messianic consciousness of Rav Kook's immediate and mystically oriented Jerusalem circle, and the one member thereof with a broad philosophical education, nonetheless saw in his master's teachings a sacred epistemology and ethics that would take their own (albeit crowning) place in universal philosophy and theology.[27] Crucially, they both took pains to present the work as a new canon, speaking to the present yet ultimately above the passage of time.

Even before the notebooks' publication, sensitive scholars noted that Rav Kook's ideas could be presented through other frames. An extraordinary reckoning with, and remapping of, the Nazir's own map was provided by Yonina Dison in a 1990 monograph, in which she took apart the hundreds of passages comprising the first three volumes of *Orot Ha-Qodesh* edited by the Nazir, and reconstructed them into four projected volumes of her own, organized around four clusters of images: restoration and light emerging from destruction and darkness; the upward movement of all things; the spark of holiness hidden in every aspect of creation; and the complementarity of seeming opposites. All, she argued, reflect a wedding of intellect to imagination, and aim towards *hishtavut*, a moral-metaphysical equanimity in which all of existence is joined.[28] Smadar Sherlo, on the publication of the notebooks from which the Nazir was working, drew attention to the profoundly experiential dimensions of Rav Kook's thought, and suggested her own set

---

25 For a remarkable and deeply consequential study of Zvi Yehudah's editorial craft on the crucial subject of war, see Hanoch Ben-Pazi, "R. Abraham Isaac Kook and the Opening Passage of 'The War,'" *Journal of Jewish Thought and Philosophy* 25, no. 2 (2017): 256–278.

26 An important discussion of these latter figures and the ideological differences among them is Dov Schwartz, *Etgar u-Mashber be-Hug Ha-Rav Kook* (Tel Aviv: 'Am 'Oved, 2001). Tau's oral lectures are periodically published in a multivolume series entitled *Le-Emunat 'Itenu*. Aviner has published, inter alia, a four-volume encyclopedia of Rav Kook's writings and utterances, culled from the printed corpus, organized under three rubrics: "Torah," "the Jewish People," and "the Land of Israel"; Shlomo Aviner, *Halikhot Ha-Re'ayah*, 4 vols. (Jerusalem/Beit El: Sifriyat Beit El, 2005). "Torah" takes up the first two volumes, and is divided into: vol. 1—Torah Study, character, *Orakh Hayim*, army and war (!), *Yoreh De'ah*, and *Even Ha-'Ezer* (the third, fifth, and sixth being the names of the sections of *Shulhan 'Arukh* dealing with, respectively, daily ritual life, prayer, and festivals; ritual laws; domestic relations); vol. 2—education, rabbinate, literature, journalism, the revivial of spoken Hebrew, culture. Aviner's prolific writings are, like Tau's, crucial for understanding religious Zionism's recent decades.

27 Ha-Nazir's own deep engagement with a broad range of philosophical and religious literature, Jewish and non-Jewish alike, is made abundantly clear in his own work *Qol Ha-Nevu'ah* (Jerusalem: Mossad Ha-Rav Kook, 1970) as well as in the two volumes of his lectures on Rav Kook's thought, published in recent years as *Hug Ha-Re'ayah* (Jerusalem: Makhon Nezer David, 2015-18), though in the source notes he supplied to *Orot Ha-Qodesh* he cites only Jewish sources.

28 Yonina Dison, "Arba'ah Motivim be-Orot Ha-Qodesh," *Da'at* 24 (1990): 41–86.

of categories: *devequt*, prophecy, poetic creativity, and Messianic awareness.[29] In a deep sense, most every scholar working the ranges, meadows, and rivers of Rav Kook's corpus must draw a map of their own.

Rav Kook beyond the Academy

Unlike many of the figures regularly studied in philosophy or even theology departments, Rav Kook is the subject of intense interest well beyond the academy. It is hard to think of a comparable figure who has so deeply influenced contemporary politics and society not only through his institutional presence but his theology.[30] The only comparable figures would seem to be Ovadia Yosef, the seventh Lubavitcher Rebbe, Menachem Mendel Schneersohn, and Abraham Joshua Heschel. The contrasts are instructive: Rav Ovadia's influence qua thinker was not through theology but through halakhah; the Rebbe's influence on the "hard" politics of statecraft, though genuine, was limited, and never the program of a leading Israeli political movement or party; and profound as Abraham Joshua Heschel's influence on American Jewish liberalism has been and remains, that particular ethos emerged without him and his thought has not seemed to shape its own political choices.

Rav Kook's thought is itself the subject of rich and consequential discussion beyond the academy and in traditionalist Religious Zionism—one need only invoke the names of contemporary figures such as Shlomo Aviner, Zvi Tau, Yair Cherqi, to name a few—yet only some of that work will be reflected here, even as this work is meant to be, among other things, an intervention in conversations on Rav Kook among his more traditionalist readers who engage with academic research.[31] These dichotomies are not hard and fast, and there are marvelous examples of more traditionalist readings of Rav Kook that are deeply informed by historical context—such as the works of Yoel Bin-Nun and the remarkable writings of Bezalel Naor.

While traditionalist figures tend not to account for the absence of academic works in their repertoires, I think it appropriate and only fair to lay out those figures' absence here. I will discuss my own reasons for my choosing to work here in a vein different from theirs at the close of this Introduction.

Academic Approaches

Surveying academic research on Rav Kook means looking at two distinct but related questions: first, the methods adopted, texts surveyed, and questions being asked of the

---

29 Smadar Sherlo (Cherlow), *Tzadiq Yesod 'Olam: Ha-Shelihut Ha-Sodit ve-Ha-Havayah Ha-Mistit shel Ha-Rav Kook* (Ramat Gan: Bar-Ilan University Press, 2012). See also her article, "Tzadiq Yesod 'Olam—Shelihuto Ha-Mistit shel Ha-Rav Kook," *Da'at* 49 (2002): 99–135.

30 My thanks for that observation to Prof. Noah Feldman.

31 Readers looking for immersion in this other world of Rav Kook scholarship will find riches online in the RAMBISH Index at www.rambish.org.il and at asif.co.il.

materials; second, the categories, or characterization, that best capture his place on the horizon of Jewish thought.

Turning to the first: in an important article, Naamah Bindiger carefully presents the state of research into Rav Kook's writings and of the bibliographic record of his works.[32] She observes that while most twentieth-century scholarly studies of Rav Kook focused on the philosophical dimensions of his corpus, and large thematic questions such as his Messianism, theosophy, relationship to Zionism and secular culture, the century also saw much discussion of the textual sources of his thought, and principally, the relative weights to be assigned to philosophy and Kabbalah. The past twenty years or so have seen a shift in inquiry towards other questions—such as his relationship to feminism and his significance for contemporary political sociology. These years have also seen, with the publication of many of his works in their original form, concentrated study of the editing and composition of his work, and of the development of his thought over time.

I have contended for some while that we still have no comprehensive bibliography even of Rav Kook's published works, let alone of the many unpublished works still in manuscript: most in avowedly sectarian and secretive hands.[33] (Bindiger differs with my bibliographical assessment in some respects, but concurs that the bibliographies we currently have are not well coordinated in terms of dates or different versions of items.) Recent years have seen some major developments here—the publication of hitherto unavailable manuscripts (a number of which figure prominently in this work) and the very significant scholarly discussions of the state of Rav Kook's corpus and the history of its many editorial layers.[34] This volume, inter alia, hopes to add to the basic bibliographic spadework still necessary to put Rav Kook studies onto a firmer footing.

Turning to the important question of the development of Rav Kook's thought, Bindiger discusses how several writers, this one included, have tried to differentiate

---

32 Naamah Bindiger, "Heqer Hitpathut Hagut Ha-Rav Kook—Tashtit Bibliografit ve-Temunah Mehqar 'Adqanit,'" forthcoming in *'Alei Sefer* 30. My thanks to Dr. Bindiger for sharing her article with me prior to its publication. Her article is a trove of references and will be helpful to all researchers in the field.

33 The first, and, for many years, only full bibliography of materials then appearing in print was published in 1938 by Yizhak Werfel (Refael) in volume one of the Rav Kook memorial volume, *Azkarah le-Nishmat Ha-Ga'on Rabbi Avraham Yitzhak Ha-Cohen Kook: Qovetz Torani Mada'i*, ed. J. L. Fishman (Maimon) (Jerusalem: Mossad Ha-Rav Kook, 1937–1938); it was supplemented by Moshe Zvi Manekin (Neriah) in *Be-Mishor* 1, no. 33 (1940): 10–11 with Werfel (Refael)'s comments therein on p. 11. One small item Refael misses from the period under discussion here is Rav Kook's comments to Aderet's discussion of halakhic aspects of circumcision appearing in *Knesset Ha-Gedolah* 2 (1890): 33–34. The bibliography in Frankel's encyclopedia article is very helpful. For discussion of the pitfalls that this state of affairs has put in the way even of excellent scholars, see Jonatan Meir, "'Al Shir Ganuz shel Ha-Rav Kook ve-Naftulei Pirsumo," *Da'at* 55 (2005): 165–168.

34 On some of the political stakes involved here, see Avinoam Rosenak, "Mi Mefahed me-Qevatzim Genuzim shel Ha-Rav Kook?," *Tarbitz* 69, no. 2 (2000): 257–291. See also Uriel Eytam, "Sqirat Kitvei He-Hagut shel Ha-Re'ayah," *Tzohar* 18 (2004): 19–38, who persuasively argues that the *Shemonah Qevatzim* date only from 1910 onwards.

between periods, and in particular, the difference between his decades before and after his move to Palestine. She notes, correctly in my view, that each feature of Rav Kook's thought deserves to be studied as its own developmental phase, an approach helpful for understanding any number of movements and thinkers.

Turning to the second question, of how best to characterize Rav Kook's place in the landscape of Jewish thought, Mordechai Pachter in a very helpful 2001 article discerned three sets of studies: on Rav Kook qua philosopher, qua mystic, and as a figure in between.[35] In the first camp he placed above all Benjamin Ish-Shalom, along with Eliezer Goldman, Nathan Rotenstreich, and Hugo Bergmann.[36] The leading exemplar of the second in Pachter's scheme is Yosef Avivi,[37] along with Scholem,[38] Hillel Zeitlin, and

---

35 Mordechai Pachter, "Ha-Tashtit Ha-Qabbalit shel Tefisat Ha-Emunah ve-Ha-Kefirah be-Mishnat Ha-Rav Kook," *Da'at* 47 (2001): 69–100,

36 My own sense is that this is something of a misreading of Bergmann (1883–1975), who, though very much a philosopher was also much more, such that his engagement with Rav Kook was part of a broader spiritual quest, of which philosophy was just a part. I hope to return to Bergmann's relationship to Rav Kook someday; see for now his excellent essay on Rav Kook from his *Faith and Reason in Modern Jewish Thought*, trans. Alfred Jospe (New York: Schocken, 1961), 121–141. He was, I believe, the first to characterize Rav Kook's thought as panentheist, in an article on Rav Kook's views on death and immortality, in *Haaretz*, December 12, 1948, later republished in his volume *Hogim u-Ma'aminim* (Tel Aviv: Devir, 1959), 103–111. It is worth noting that Bergmann's final, deathbed writings were on Rav Kook's understanding of immortality, see his posthumous *Toldot Ha-Filosofiyah He-Hadashah: Jacobi, Fichte, Schelling* (Jerusalem: Mossad Bialik, 1977), 239–240 and Moshe Barash's prefatory comments to that volume.

37 Yosef Avivi, starting with his "Meqor Ha-Orot," *Tzohar* 1 (Fall 2000): 93–111, argued that the new publications proved his long-held thesis that Rav Kook is essentially, and indeed almost exclusively, an interpreter of Lurianism. He has most recently published the monumental *Qabbalat Ha-Re'ayah*, 4 vols. (Jerusalem: Yad Ben-Tzvi, 2018), in which he walks through the vast corpus of Rav Kook's writings to mine a consistent teaching on core Kabbalistic concepts such as emanation. This work appeared after the present work was largely completed, but I have tried to take as much notice of it as I can. Suffice it to say that his stunning erudition and astonishing acuity do indeed establish the overwhelmingly Kabbalistic provenance of Rav Kook's thought; at the same time, a richer conceptualization of what mysticism and philosophy respectively are trying to do, and the different kinds of knowledge and experience they offer, is needed to assess Rav Kook's thought, along with a nuanced appreciation of his historical as well as textual contexts. For a summary of Avivi's views, see his "Aqdamot le-Qabbalat Ha-Re'ayah," in *Mah Ahavti Toratekhah*, ed. Yitzhak Recanati and Shaul Barth (Jerusalem: Alon Shvut: 2014), 153–181, available online along with many of his other writings on a range of Kabbalistic subjects at http://yosefavivi.blogspot.com/.

38 See Scholem's brief but significant remarks in "Hirhurim 'al Efsharutah shel Mistikah Yehudit be-Yameinu," 71–83. Scholem writes half-jokingly in a letter of 1961 that he is teaching a course in Jewish mysticism from Adam onwards and doesn't know if the end point is Buber, Rav Kook, or the Lubavitcher rebbe—see Gershom Scholem, *Briefe*, vol. 2, *1948-1970*, ed. Thomas Sparr (Munich: C. H. Beck, 1995), 81. More broadly, for several important studies, see Uriel Barak, "Kabbalah versus Philosophy: Rabbi Avraham Itzhak Kook's Critique of the Spiritual World of Franz Rosenzweig," *Journal of Jewish Thought and Philosophy* 23, no. 1

Jacob Agus (to whom we would today add Jonathan Garb, Haviva Pedaya, and Smadar Sherlo, to name just a few).[39] And in the third category he put the majority of academic students of Rav Kook, such as Tamar Ross, Yosef Ben-Shlomo, Avinoam Rosenak, Shalom Rosenberg, and Yoel Bin-Nun who see him as a mix of philosopher and mystic.[40] (One category Pachter did not mention was the study of halakhah.)[41]

As will become clear, I would place myself in this last camp.[42] I hope to show through this work that much of the internal scaffolding of Rav Kook's mystical teaching derived

---

(2015): 27–59, and Moshe Idel, "Abraham Abulafia, Gershom Scholem ve-Rabbi David Cohen ('Ha-Nazir')," in "The Eliezer Schweid Jubilee Volume," *Jerusalem Studies in Jewish Thought* 19 (2005): 819–834.

39   See Sherlo, *Tzadiq Yesod 'Olam*; for a summary, see her article, "Tzadiq Yesod 'Olam," 99–135. Haviva Pedaya, "Eretz Zeman u-Maqom—Apocalypsot shel Sof ve-Apokalypsah shel Hathalah," in *Eretz Yisrael be-Hagut Yehudit be-Me'ah Ha-'Esrim*, ed. Aviezer Ravitzky (Jerusalem: Yad Ben-Tzvi, 2004), 560–624, 585–602. Jonathan Garb, "Ha-Re'ayah Kook— Hogeh Le'umi o Meshorer Misti?," *Da'at* 54 (2004): 69–96; idem, "Rabbi Kook and His Sources: From Kabbalistic Historiosophy to National Mysticism," in *Studies in Modern Religions, Religious Movements and the Babi-Baha'i Faiths*, ed. Moshe Sharon (Leiden: E. J. Brill, 2004), 77–96, idem, *The Chosen Will Become Herds: Studies in Twentieth-Century Kabbalah* (New Haven: Yale University Press, 2009) and other works of his referenced throughout this volume. See also Elliot Wolfson, "Secrecy, Apophasis and Atheistic Faith in the Teachings of Rav Kook," in *Negative Theology as Jewish Modernity*, ed. Michael Fagenblatt (Bloomington: Indiana University Press, 2017), 131-160.

40   Yoel Bin-Nun, *Ha-Maqor Ha-Kaful: Hashra'ah ve-Samkhut be-Mishnat Ha-Rav Kook* (Tel Aviv: Ha-Kibbutz Ha-Meuhad, 2014). In addition to the works referred to in the course of this work, see Yosef Ben-Shlomo, *Shirat Ha-Hayim: Peraqim be-Mishnato shel Ha-Rav Kook* (Tel Aviv: Misrad Ha-Bitahon/Broadcast University, 1989). See Rosenberg's "Mavo' le-Haguto shel Ha-Re'ayah" and his "Haguto shel Ha-Re'ayah Kook beyn Yahadut le-Tarbut Kelalit," in *Yovel Orot: Haguto shel Ha-Rav Avraham Yitzhak Ha-Cohen Kook*, ed. Benjamin Ish-Shalom and Shalom Rosenberg (Jerusalem: Sifiyat Eliner, 1988).

41   See Neriah Gutel, *Hadashim gam Yeshanim: Bi-Netivei Mishnato Ha-Hilkhatit-Hagutit shel Ha-Rav Kook* (Jerusalem: Hebrew University/Magnes, 2005) and Avinoam Rosenak, *Ha-Halakhah Ha-Nevi'ut* (Jerusalem: Hebrew University/Magnes, 2007); and, more briefly, his "'Torat Eretz Yisrael' Ha-Nevu'it be-Mishnat Ha-Re'ayah Kook," in Ravitzky, *Eretz Yisrael be-Hagut Ha-Yehudit be-Me'ah Ha-'Esrim*, 26–70. An interesting attempt at a "multi-layered" approach to Rav Kook, integrating theology, halakhah, and some historical context on specific issues, is Moshe Falukh, "Nitzotzot she-Eyn ba-Hem Mamash: Yahaso Ha-Haguti ve-Ha-Hilkhati shel Ha-Re'ayah Kook le-Hiloni ve-la-Hilun: Keriy'ah Rav-Shikhvatit," in Horvitz, Herr, Silman, and Cordinali, eds., *Sefer Zikaron le-Professor Zev Falk zl*, 89–122.

42   Pachter also notes that there are some who see him as primarily a poet, such as Marvin Fox and Avraham Regelson. There is very little work that looks at Rav Kook in terms of psychology and psychoanalysis, though Hanokh Ben-Pazi has begun to discuss Rav Kook as part of a larger project on psychoanalysis and modern Jewish thought. See his "Ha-Yitzriyut eitzel Ha-Rav Kook," in *Sihot 'im Ha-Yetzer Ha-Ra'*, ed. Asa Qeidar (Tel Aviv: Yedi'ot/Hemed, 2007), 155–163. It also bears noting that there are few genuinely comparative studies of Rav Kook, for a brief exception, see Margaret Chatterjee, "Rabbi Abraham Isaac Kook and Sri Aurobindo: Towards a Comparison," in *Between Jerusalem and Benares: Comparative Studies in Judaism and Hinduism*, ed. Hananya Goodman (Albany: State University of New York Press, 1994),

from the philosophical tradition. And like some others I am trying to place Rav Kook in historical context, of modern Jewish history and the larger intellectual history of modernity.[43] He was by no means the first Kabbalist whose ideas emerged out of deep engagement with philosophy.[44] But the ways in which he did so, in both style and substance were in many ways unprecedented, both in his ideas and in his intense dialectical engagement with the social and political currents of his time.

Biographical Research

A long-standing feature of much scholarly study of Rav Kook has been its pronounced ahistorical character. This is due not only to the traditionalist leanings of many of his interpreters, but perhaps more importantly, to the fact that his theological writings were edited and published by his disciples precisely in order to blur their historicity—chiefly as a way to present readers with a coherent worldview and, invariably, blunt the edges of his theological radicalism. Biographical volumes by his traditionalist disciples have tended towards hagiography, even if not nearly as much as in works about comparable figures in ultra-Orthodoxy.[45]

243–266, though all of her quotes from Rav Kook are from sources in translation. Another is Jack Cohen's book-length comparison of Rav Kook with Mordecai Kaplan, *Guides for an Age of Confusion* (New York: Fordham University Press, 1999).

43 Briefly to anticipate some of what I will have to say later on: the respective proportions of philosophy and Kabbalah in Rav Kook's writings are, of course, a major bone of contention among scholarly interpreters; this was most clearly exemplified in the significant disagreements between Yosef Avivi and Benjamin Ish-Shalom, with the former arguing for the primacy of Kabbalah in general, and Moshe Hayim Luzzatto's writings in particular, as the chief framework of Rav Kook's thought, and the latter arguing for the significance of philosophy, which I will discuss at greater length in coming chapters. See Avivi's "Historiyah Tzorekh Gevohah," in *Sefer Ha-Yovel li-Khvod Mordechai Breuer*, ed. Moshe Bar-Asher (Jerusalem: Aqademon, 1992), 709–771 and Ish-Shalom's response "Beyn Rav Kook li-Spinoza ve-Goethe," in *Qolot Rabim: Sefer Ha-Ziqaron le-Rivka Schatz-Uffenheimer*, vol. 13 of *Jerusalem Studies in Jewish Thought*, ed. Rachel Elior and Joseph Dan (Jerusalem: Hebrew University Press, 1996), 525–556. Suffice it to say for now, that our reading, or unearthing, of these early writings, will show both that Luzzatto is indeed indispensable for a proper understanding of Rav Kook's major writings, and that the philosophical tradition provides the infrastructure for many of his ideas. Avivi's crucial contention that Rav Kook systematically offers his own reading and terminological reworking of the Lurianic structure of emanations (*derekh ha-atzilut*) seems accurate to this reader; yet that too seems but one facet of Rav Kook's thought, not least since the publication of the *Qevatzim*.

44 For a very helpful discussion, see Sandra Valabregue, "Philosophy, Heresy and Kabbalah's Counter-Theology," *Harvard Theological Review* 109, no. 2 (2016): 233-256.

45 A lengthy and extremely nuanced exploration of the historiographical and ethical issues involved in the editing and publication of modern rabbinic writings by historians on the one hand and hagiographers on the other, is presented by Jacob J. Schacter, "Facing the Truths of History," *Torah u-Madda Journal* 8 (1998–1999): 200–276, and letters to the editor in subsequent issues of that journal.

To this day we lack a full-fledged scholarly biography of Rav Kook, though recent years have seen a scholarly "thickening" of some of the context in which he lived, thought, and wrote.[46] An invaluable starting point, though not as well known as it should be, is the lengthy entry by Aryeh Frankel in the *Encyclopedia of Religious Zionism*, which offers a

---

46 One significant development in Rav Kook studies has been Dov Schwartz's intense and illuminating focus in a series of books and articles on Rav Kook's "circle," that is, his son, Zvi Yehudah, his apostle and editor David Cohen (aka "The Nazir"), and his mystical soul-mate Ya'aqov Moshe Harlap. See his *Ha-Tzionut Ha-Datit beyn Higayon li-Meshihiyut* (Tel Aviv: 'Am 'Oved, 1999), which forcefully argues for the centrality not only of Nazir's editorial hand but his philosophical perspectives as well. Benjamin Ish-Shalom forcefully, and, to this writer, compellingly, criticized Schwartz's contention that Rav Kook's writings are best, and perhaps only to be, understood via the readings of his disciples. See his review of Schwartz, "Tzionut Datit beyn Apologiyah le-Hitmodedut," *Cathedra* 90 (1999): 145–149. Moreover, Schwartz's definition of the "circle" excludes all of the figures discussed in the pages of this dissertation, who were children during this period; in other words, he defines Rav Kook's first four decades out of the discussion a priori. Another, important work of Schwartz's, especially valuable for its availability in English, is his *The Religious Genius in Rabbi Kook's Thought: National "Saint"?* (Boston: Academic Studies Press, 2014); we will have more to say on this work later on.

Smadar Sherlo (Cherlow) has integrated two trends in Rav Kook studies of recent years, that of looking at his circle and of reading him as primarily a mystic: see in brief her "Hug Ha-Re'ayah ke-Havurah Mistit," *Tarbitz* 74, no. 2 (2005): 261–303.

An attempt at mapping Rav Kook's circle is the volume by Neriah Gutel, *Mekhutavei Re'ayah* (Jerusalem: Makhon Ha-Ratzyah Kook ztz"l, 2000), a listing of Rav Kook's correspondents, along with some biographical and other materials. Gutel offers a wealth of information; at the same time, because he lists only those correspondents who appear in Rav Kook's published correspondence, this work does not provide as full a picture as one would hope for. Indeed, Jonatan Meir has argued in several richly documented studies that the notion of Rav Kook's "circle," if it is to be meaningful at all, must be expanded to include such figures as Yosef Hayim Brenner, S. Y. Agnon, Hillel Zeitlin, Yosef Zvi Rimon, A. Z. Rabinowitz, Hugo Bergmann, and others outside the rabbinic ambit as such.

Letters to Rav Kook by leading rabbinic figures have been gathered in Ben-Zion Shapira, ed., *Igrot La-Re'ayah*, 2nd ed. (Jerusalem: Makhon Ha-Ratzyah Kook ztz"l, 1990). This collection explicitly aims to show that Rav Kook was an honored member of the Orthodox and ultra-Orthodox rabbinic fraternity. It succeeds at that, but one cannot help noting that many, many of the letters therein are addressed to him in his capacity as chief rabbi, asking for help with such matters as charitable allocations and immigration certificates. (An interesting and important exception is Hayim Ozer Grodzinski, whose correspondence with Rav Kook is marked by unmistakable regard and respect.)

Rav Kook's letters of approbation to various volumes of rabbinic literature are listed and in some cases are to be found in Ari Shvat and Zuriel Halamish, eds., *Haskamot Ha-Re'ayah* (Jerusalem: Beit Ha-Rav, 2017). I will have more to say about his haskamot in this period in chapter three. Marc B. Shapiro has detailed the omissions of Rav Kook's haskamot from many reprinted editions of various works in his *Changing the Immutable: How Orthodox Judaism Rewrites its History* (Oxford: Littman, 2015). For a brief but fascinating excursus on haskamot as a genre, and discussion of how and why things get left out of different editions for different reasons, including some discussion of Rav Kook, see Avishai Elbaum, "Shinuyim be-Haskamot," *Ha-Ma'ayan* 38, no. 1 (Tishrei 5758): 34–38.

nearly month-by-month account of Rav Kook's public career from his arrival in Palestine onwards, and devotes proportionally more space than most to his pre-Palestine life.[47] Yet even there, his first thirty-eight years are dispensed with in some ten pages. Other essential works are Yossi Avneri's invaluable, unpublished dissertation, as well as his published articles, and the work of Menahem Friedman.[48]

We are dependent for biographic information above all on the works of J. L. (Fishman) Maimon and Moshe Zvi Neriah, especially the latter's many volumes. Maimon (1875–1962), aside from his formidable public and political achievements as a leader of Religious Zionism and a high government official, was a richly productive writer, researcher, and editor in his own right and knew, worked (and occasionally locked horns) with Rav Kook for decades, since their first meeting in 1908.[49] Neriah (1913–1996), a disciple of Rav Kook from 1930 on and the founder of the Bnei Aqiva network of yeshivot, devoted much of his long career to anthologizing Rav Kook and gathering much primary material in a series of volumes about which we will have more to say as we proceed.[50] Briefly, Neriah's works, a decades-long labor of love, are undoubtedly hagiographic, and yet they gather so much material that they transcend their own flaws; moreover, his instincts about how to understand his master seem to this writer often on the mark. Like many hagiographers, Neriah had the defects of his virtues, that is, his intense reverence for his subject led him to dig up most every scrap of information he could, which he then assembled in volumes sorely lacking in historical, and certainly critical, perspective. Still, Neriah's volumes are

---

47 *Entziklopedia shel Ha-Tzionut Ha-Datit* (1983), s.v. "Kook, Avraham Yitzhak."

48 Yosef Avneri, "Ha-Re'ayah Kook ke-Rabbah shel Eretz Yisrael" (PhD diss., Bar-Ilan University, 1989); Menahem Friedman, *Hevrah va-Dat: Ha-Ortodoksiyah Ha-Lo-Tzionit be-Eretz Yisrael, 1918–1936* (Jerusalem: Yad Ben Tzvi, 1988). Two helpful steps towards providing academically informed biography are Avinoam Rosenak, *Ha-Rav Kook* (Jerusalem: Merkaz Shazar, 2006) and the present writer's *Rav Kook*, and the revised, Hebrew, edition, *Rav Kook: Mabat Hadash* (Tel Aviv: Devir, 2021). For a synopsis of that volume, see my "Revelation and Redemption: Avraham Yitzhak Ha-Cohen Kook, 1865–1935," in *Makers of Jewish Modernity*, ed. J. Picard et al. (Princeton: Princeton University Press, 2016), 92–107. For an early but still significant treatment of the scholarly and political dimensions of this willful hiding of Rav Kook's manuscripts, see Rosenak, "Mi Mefahed me-Qevatzim Genuzim shel Ha-Rav Kook." A recent journalistic treatment of the controversies surrounding Rav Kook's manuscripts is Yehudah Yifrah, "Ke-Domen 'al Pnei Ha-Sadeh," *Makor Rishon*, Shabbat Supplement, July 25, 2017, 10–15.

49 Maimon's chief biographical work on Rav Kook was the lengthy essay he published in 1937 in the Rav Kook memorial volume, which set the outlines for most every Rav Kook biography or hagiography to follow. A full-length biography of Maimon was written by his daughter—see Geula Bat-Yehudah (Refael), *Ha-Rav Maimon be-Dorotav* (Jerusalem: Mossad Ha-Rav Kook, 1979). Maimon founded Mossad Ha-Rav Kook in 1937.

50 A biography of Neriah, including his years with Rav Kook and up to his founding of the first, and flagship, Bnei Aqiva yeshiva in Kefar Ha-Ro'e (the latter named for Rav Kook) is Tzila Bar-Eli, *Shahar Oro: Ha-Rav Moshe Zvi Neriah ztz"l* (Jerusalem/Psagot: n.p., 2002). See also a collection of interviews and reminiscences, *Ner le-Neriah* (Haifa: Yeshivat Pirhei Aharon of Kiryat Shmuel, 1996).

an invaluable resource, and in the coming chapters we will try to sift through their qua-si-hagiographic elements to draw a reasonably credible and critical picture. Briefly, while Maimon and Neriah see Rav Kook as riding above the turbulences of his times, I see him amid them.[51]

There has been some, but not too much, scholarly biography. Jacob Agus devoted the first half of his 1946 volume to Rav Kook's Eastern European life, but only as it touched upon nationalism.[52] In addition to his dissertation, Yossi Avneri has written a number of remarkably important, detailed studies to Rav Kook's public career in Jaffa and later as chief rabbi; focusing less on the thought and more on the life (above all on Rav Kook's Jerusalem years)—work which is yet (tragically) unpublished.[53] Some other scholars, while not writing biographies as such, have taken a more developmental approach to Rav Kook's thought itself, such as Hagi ben Artzi in his study of key episodes in the juristic elements of Rav Kook's career, though his study devotes almost no attention to Rav Kook's years as an active jurist in Eastern Europe.[54] Reuven Gerber also took a developmental approach, tracing one dimension of Rav Kook's thought, what he terms "the revolution of illumi-nation" towards a progressively spiritual (as opposed to narrowly national) perspective.[55] He devotes only a few pages to Rav Kook's pre-Palestine years. Michal Lanir has devoted considerably more space to those years, but almost entirely in terms of Rav Kook's writings

---

51 The various biographies by Efraim Zoref, Ya'aqov Even-Hen (Edelstein), Simha Raz, and Shmuel Avidor are, sadly, unsourced, and all largely structured along the lines laid down by Maimon in his pioneering essay, though some, particularly Even-Hen's and Avidor's, offer richer detail derived from their own researches. Even-Hen (1928–1997) was longtime editor of *Mabu'a*, a task he took up at the urging of Rebbe Binyomin (Joshua Radler-Feldman)—this was recounted to me in a telephone conversation with his widow, Nehama Edelstein, September 26, 2006; it may be that Rebbe Binyomin was one of his sources for more intimate details of Rav Kook's life. He does not source his book (which was posthumously completed by Yehudah Azrieli), yet he regularly offers prosaic details bearing verisimilitude, and there is, at least to this reader, a lucid and at times faintly ironic sensibility lurking just below the surface of his seemingly hagiographic prose.

52 Jacob B. Agus, *Banner of Jerusalem* (New York: Bloch, 1946). Agus's work on Rav Kook has long been neglected, though his Hebrew essays have recently been made good use of by Smadar Sherlo (Cherlow).

53 See inter alia Avneri's "Ha-Re'ayah Kook ke-Rabbah Ha-Rashi shel Eretz Yisrael." See also Yossi Avneri, "Ha-Rav Avraham Yitzhak Ha-Cohen Kook, Rabbah shel Yafo (1904–1914)," *Cathedra* 37 (1985): 49–82; idem, "Ha-Rav Avraham Yitzhak Ha-Cohen Kook ve-She'elat Yahasei Yehudim-'Aravim be-Eretz Yisrael, 1904–1935," *Proceedings of the Tenth World Congress of Jewish Studies* 2, no. 1 (1990): 331–338.

54 Hagi Ben-Artzi, "Ha-Re'ayah Kook ke-Posek—Yesodot Hadshaniyyim be-Pesikato shel Ha-Rav Kook" (PhD diss., Hebrew University, 2004). On the other hand, his master's thesis, which I discuss in chapter five, is devoted precisely to this period and in particular to Rav Kook's writings on nationalism.

55 Reuven Gerber, *Mahapekhat Ha-Hearah: Darko Ha-Ruhanit shel Ha-Re'ayah Kook* (Jerusalem: Mossad Bialik/Ha-Sifriyah Ha-Tzionit, 2005).

on nationalism from the turn of the century;[56] the same is true for Eliezer Goldman's pioneering study of some of those writings, Rav Kook's essays in *Ha-Peles*.[57] I hope to show that those writings are themselves the result of a long process which involved much more than nationalism—and indeed until 1901 hardly involved it at all—the recognition of which demands that they, and the works which came after, be read in a different light.[58] Yoel Bin-Nun in his brilliant, penetrating study of Rav Kook's thought has also reckoned with shifts in his thinking over time.[59]

Avinoam Rosenak published a brief, yet significant, biography which makes a genuine contribution to the field, not least for studying Rav Kook in a chronological framework and making ample use of the materials published in recent years.[60] And this writer has tried his hand at that as well, in a brief book encompassing Rav Kook's life, thought, and legacy.[61]

The Long-Missing Early Decades in Rav Kook's Corpus

Virtually all of Rav Kook's best-known and canonical writings date from 1904 onward, and the range of ideas therein are taken as the expression of his thought.[62] Yet throughout the years preceding his move to Palestine at age thirty-eight he was writing

---

56 Michal Lanir, *Ha-Re'ayah Kook ve-Ha-Tzionut—Gilgulah shel Tiqvah* (Tel Aviv: Safra, 2015). Chapter two is devoted to the Eastern European years.

57 Eliezer Goldman's essay "Tzionut Hilonit, Te'udat Yisrael ve-Takhlit Ha-Torah—Ma'amarei Rav Kook be-'Ha-Peles': 5661–5664" first appeared in *Da'at* 11 (1983): 103–126, and is reprinted in his collection *Mehqarim ve-'Iyunim* (Jerusalem: Hebrew University/Magnes, 2000), 159–182. Our pagination in citations follows the latter.

58 Indeed, Goldman intuited some of this, and without the benefit of most of the most significant early writings, which were yet unpublished while he was writing.

59 Bin-Nun, *Ha-Maqor Ha-Kaful*.

60 Rosenak, *Ha-Rav Kook*. As part of a series aimed at the general reader the book dispenses with detailed scholarly apparatus as it covers a great deal of ground in, given the magnitude of the subject, a mere 275 pages. Nonetheless, Rosenak manages to offer an important interpretation of Rav Kook's life and career, particularly in his calling attention to the ups and downs of Rav Kook's attitudes towards halakhah over time. The period covered by this dissertation is covered by Rosenak in a few, albeit perceptive, pages (11–31), and, perhaps understandably given the compass of his volume, he does not discuss the many works that are my subject here.

61 Mirsky, *Rav Kook*. Readers looking for a summary of that volume can turn to my essay, "Revelation and Redemption: Avraham Yitzhak Ha-Cohen Kook, 1865–1935," in *Makers of Jewish Modernity*, ed. J. Picard et al. (Princeton: Princeton University Press, 2016), 92–107.

62 I am, of course, referring to the series of volumes published by Mossad Ha-Rav Kook, *Orot*, *Orot Ha-Qodesh*, and *Orot Ha-Teshuvah*, which, by virtue of their distinctive white bindings, have come colloquially to be known as "Ha-Shas Ha-Lavan" (The White Talmud). Two significant works in that series, the commentaries to the prayer book *'Olat Re'ayah* and *Mussar Avikha*, as well as much of his halakhic writing, all of which we will discuss below, were in fact largely composed during his time in Eastern Europe. However, the manner in which they were published deliberately deflects attention from the time of their composition, as we will see. Rav Kook's halakhic writings of this period are published with his other responsa, and

continuously, in various genres: halakhic responsa and Talmudic novellae, commentaries, essays, poetry, and spiritual diaries. Most of these efforts were not published until well after his death in 1935, and many only in the last few decades; some yet remain in manuscript. For a long while his early writings generated little scholarly attention, in part because they do not reflect his mature thought in all its theological audacity, historiosophical sweep, psychological insight, and lyric power (and indeed at times make for plodding reading), and because a kind of (what we may call) Palestinocentrism has colored scholarship on Rav Kook both in and out of the academy. Indeed, Zvi Yehudah Kook gave explicit instruction to his disciples not to publish his father's pre-Palestine writings.[63] One likely explanation for this will be provided by one of this work's findings—that for most of his years in Eastern Europe, the Land of Israel simply was not a significant category in his father's thought. Within the academy, Rav Kook's place in the history of Zionism has largely overshadowed his work of this period; indeed even those scholars who paid attention to these writings focused almost exclusively on those concerning nationalism. The 2007 dissertation on which this book is based helped foster some change there.

Rav Kook and the Medieval Philosophical Tradition

While countless studies have investigated Rav Kook's relationship to the Kabbalah and various currents of modern philosophy, much less has been written about his relationship to the medieval philosophical tradition, aside from his relationship to Ha-Levi's *Kuzari*.[64]

---

with their dates, but they are in a different category from his theological writings, which are the very heart of the discourse around him.

63 See the introduction to Elisha Aviner [Langauer] and David Landau, eds., *Ma'amarei Ha-Re'ayah* (Jerusalem: n.p., 1984). The lengths to which Zvi Yehudah went here are shown in his preface to his edition of his father's commentary to the Siddur (Prayer book) *'Olat Re'ayah*, first published in 1939, only a portion of which was written by his father as straightforward commentary. The vast majority of the printed volumes is composed of excerpts from *'Eyn Ayah*, the aggadic commentary, three-quarters of which was written in Eastern Europe, yet Zvi Yehudah notes in the introduction only that he "gathered and combined gleanings from scattered places in his (father's) manuscripts" (Zvi Yehudah Kook, ed., *'Olat Reiyah* [Jerusalem: Agudah le-Hotza'at Sifrei Ha-Re'ayah Kook zl, 1939–1949], 13. Repr. ed. 2015).

64 An early, significant exception was Lawrence Kaplan, "Rav Kook and the Jewish Philosophical Tradition," in *Rabbi Abraham Isaac Kook and Jewish Spirituality*, ed. Lawrence Kaplan and David Shatz (New York: New York University Press, 1995), 41–77 and his "The Love of God in Maimonides and Rav Kook," *Judaism* 43, no. 3 (1994): 227–239. Rav Kook's affinities with, and divergences from, the harmonizing thrust of the medieval philosophical tradition is taken up by David Shatz, "The Integration of Torah and Culture: Its Scope and Limits in the Thought of Rav Kook," in *Hazon Nahum*, ed. Yaakov Elman and Jeffrey S. Gurock (New York: Yeshiva University Press, 1997), 529–556. See also Yehudah Mirsky, "Ha-Rambam ve-Ha-Re'ayah Kook: Behinah Mehudeshet," *Iggud* 1 (2008): 397–405 and Uriel Barak, "Ha-Hashpa'ah Ha-Me'atzevet shel Tiur Madregat Ha-Nevu'ah Ha-Rishonah be-Moreh Nevukhim 'al Tefisat Athalta de-Ge'ulah be-Hug Ha-Re'ayah," *Da'at* 64–66 (2009): 361–415. See also James A. Diamond, *Maimonides and the Shaping of the Jewish Canon* (Cambridge: Cambridge University

We will argue that this philosophical infrastructure affords helpful insight into the later ecstatic, mystical writings for which Rav Kook is most known and celebrated; a vivid example we will trace is the interplay between intellect, imagination, and feeling. His preoccupation with this theme, it seems, grows out of his interest in the revival of prophecy. That prophecy was of great interest to him is well known; what we will show is that this began at a very early stage, in his early twenties, and that his attempted ascent to prophecy began along the rungs laid out by Maimonidean philosophy.[65] This concern with Maimonides's doctrine of prophecy grew over time into far-reaching explorations of human personhood. We will see in particular how working out the respective relations of intellect and imagination, as laid out in Maimonidean doctrine, led him to substitute feeling for imagination in his understanding of the structure of the soul, and how this gave rise to the emergence of his thinking in terms of subjectivity, his own and that of others, as a point of access to God.

While, as we will see, he became engrossed in Kabbalah in his early twenties, in his early writings he is very much a latter-day inheritor of the medieval philosophical tradition as transmitted via Maimonides, Isaac Arama, and, in modified form, by the Jewish Enlightenment, or Haskalah. These writings also shed light on the intellectual climate of his times, including the abiding presence of the medieval philosophical tradition amid traditional circles in Eastern Europe, a feature of that cultural climate which has not received its due in treatments of the period.[66] This perspective on Rav Kook lends its own bit of weight to Moshe Idel's argument that Jewish intellectual history is best served by what he dubs a "panoramic perspective," which recognizes that thinkers have at their disposal a range of literary and other traditions on which to draw as they work out their spiritual preoccupations, some of them perennials of Jewish thought, others peculiar to

---

Press, 2014), who devotes an entire chapter to Rav Kook's relationship to Maimonides, which we will discuss in chapter 5.

For an early bibliography of secondary writings on Rav Kook and Maimonides, see Yisrael Ya'aqov Dienstag, "Ha-Rambam be-Mishnato shel Ha-Rav Kook ztz"l: Bibliografiyah," in *Sefer Refa'el*, ed. Yosef Mowshowitz (Jerusalem: Mossad Ha-Rav Kook, 2000), 135–138.

65   On the restoration of prophecy as a significant theme in Rav Kook's mature writings, see Eliezer Schweid, *Nevi'im le-'Amam u-le-Enoshut: Nevu'ah u-Neviim be-Hagut Ha-Yehudit shel Ha-Me'ah Ha-'Esrim* (Jerusalem: Hebrew University/Magnes Press, 1999), 190–214; Schweid traces this theme in the works of a number of thinkers, including Hermann Cohen, Ahad Ha-Am, M.Y. Berdyczewsky, H. N. Bialik, A. D. Gordon, Martin Buber, Franz Rosenzweig, Rabbi Leo Baeck, and Rabbi Abraham Joshua Heschel.

The place of prophecy in Rav Kook's halakhic writings is the subject of Avinoam Rosenak's dissertation, "Ha-Filosofiyah shel Ha-Halakhah be-Mishnato shel Ha-Rav Avraham Yitzhak Ha-Cohen Kook" (PhD diss., Hebrew University, 1997); see, in brief, his "'Torat Eretz Yisrael' Ha-Nevu'it," 26–70; for a different treatment, see Gutel, *Hadashim gam Yeshanim*.

66   A happy exception is Adam B. Shear, "Jewish Enlightenment beyond Western Europe," in *The Cambridge History of Jewish Philosophy*, ed. Martin Kavka, Zachary Braiterman, and David Novak (Cambridge: Cambridge University Press, 2012), 252–279.

their times or personalities.[67] I will show Rav Kook drawing, at times self-consciously, on this range of traditions in counterpoint to developments in his own time and place, as well as out of what we can think of as the immanent transmission and interpretation of texts and ideas within the traditions themselves.

The Eastern European Writings: Towards Expressivism and the Subject

In later years Rav Kook found himself, by his own admission, unable to write systematic theology, even if, as Avivi argues, a genuine sytem of Lurianic Kabbalah appears from within the great lattices of his ideas.[68] By contrast, in many of these early writings he regularly works at developing well-ordered structures of ideas. It may well be that his later difficulties with constructing a system were a reflection of the nature of the ideas with which he was contending—namely, that that inability is correlative to the expansive, expressive subjectivity towards which he moved.[69] Moreover, in his case, discovering his subjectivity also meant acknowledging the splits and fissures of his own soul, the dialecti-cal resolution of which became a defining preoccupation of his for decades to come.

---

67 Moshe Idel, *Hasidism: Between Ecstasy and Magic* (Albany: State University of New York Press, 1995), 9–15. Much of Idel's argument here is with Gershom Scholem's depiction of most every development in the history of Kabbalah as a dialectical reaction to that which immediately preceded it.

68 See the well-known introductory comments of David Cohen (*Ha-Nazir*) to Rav Kook's magnum opus, *Orot Ha-Qodesh*, which Cohen compiled and edited from a number of Rav Kook's spiritual diaries. A fuller version of the conversations between the two in 1922 regarding the project and the forging of a system out of Rav Kook's thought, is presented in Cohen's own diaries, reprinted in his memorial volume *Nezir Ehav*, vol. 1, 286–288. Interestingly, therein at 301, describing his posthumous editing of the diaries, he notes it was Ya'aqov Moshe Harlap who most pressed for editorial censorship of Rav Kook's more audacious theological ideas, perhaps reflecting his own difficult experience around the publication of *Orot* in 1920, about which I wrote in *Rav Kook*, 167–169.

In a 1909 letter, Rav Kook, by way of explaining to his brother Dov the reason for the delay in the establishment of his yeshiva in Jaffa, says that on the material side, he is "no expert at all at financial matters. And on the spiritual side—the necessity for order, which also runs counter to my nature, as I love to influence and pour myself *onto every babe in the market and young man in the street* (Jer. 6:11, 9:20), if it were possible." See *Igrot*, 1:261.

Notwithstanding the force of Yosef Avivi's detailed argumentation that virtually all of Rav Kook's later theological writings are to be understood in terms of the highly structured framework of Lurianic mysticism as taught in the Lithuanian tradition, the aphoristic, experiential character of these writings cannot be denied.

69 At the same time, the extraordinary time and other pressures of his multifaceted rabbinical roles certainly afforded little time for more systematic writing. See, for instance, his 1907 letter to Yehiel Mikhel Tukoczinsky, expressing a wish that he might succeed Isaac Blazer as head of the Jerusalem *kollel*, and thus relieve "the public burden of (halakhic) ruling . . . and without the yoke of matters of rabbinate and ruling." See *Igrot*, 1:84. Apologizing for being busy is a staple of rabbinic correspondence; still this is striking for his seeking to leave his susbtantial position for the academic cloister.

An interesting parallel here—one that I will pursue throughout—is the trajectory of his exact contemporary and Volozhin classmate Micah Yosef Berdyczewski, *enfant terrible* of Hebrew letters, who in these years also progressed to a recognition of deep subjectivity, which he experienced as an unreconcilable break with tradition; we will see the two moving at times on parallel tracks, responding to similar *problematiques*, Berdyczewski accepting and even embracing rupture, and Rav Kook working to contain similar conflicts within the framework of a reinterpreted though still normative tradition.[70]

In Rav Kook's Eastern European writings, we see his passage towards Romantic nationalism, a movement across the arc described by Charles Taylor as the passage from the rational self towards the expressive subject; a detailed reconstruction of this arc is a major theme of the coming chapters.[71] In Taylor's account, key to the development of the cluster of events and ideas that we call modernity was the emergence of alternative moral sources to the premodern dispensation, and in particular, the dignity of rationality and the subjective self. Though the two differ, they are related as reflections of the essential goodness of nature, as realized in natural form and embedded in the human person. In what Taylor calls the "expressivist turn," most obviously associated with Rousseau, we open ourselves to nature within as once we opened ourselves to grace. This expressivism, a key facet, first of Romanticism and later of Modernism, is a kind of neo-Augustinianism, in which the truth is to be found deep within the inner self; yet if for the Bishop of Hippo God lay at the foundation, for modern philosophers of nature, at the base is the human person itself, as created by nature.[72] Even so, this expressivism certainly bears enough of the traces of its religious origin to serve as the basis for a reimagining of the religious life from, as it were, the bottom-up, in contrast to what one may call the top-down vector of the medieval philosophical tradition. Indeed, Neoplatonic philosophical and spiritual

---

70 This account of Berdyczewski draws on Avner Holzman, *El Ha-Qer'a she-ba-Lev: Micha Yosef Berdyczewsky, Shenot Ha-Tzemihah: 1887–1902* (Jerusalem/Tel Aviv: Mossad Bialik/Tel Aviv University, 1995).

71 I am of course referring to Charles Taylor's landmark volume, *Sources of the Self: The Making of the Modern Identity* (Cambridge, MA: Harvard University Press, 1989), as well to the discussion of expressivism in the first chapter of his *Hegel and Modern Society* (Cambridge: Cambridge University Press, 1979). My thinking here also reflects Alain Touraine's discussion of what he characterizes as a "tension between reason and the subject" lying at the heart of modernity. See his *Critique of Modernity*, trans. David Macey (Oxford: Blackwell, 1995). I will have more to say on this later, particularly in chapter four, which discusses the interplay of intellect, imagination and feeling in Rav Kook's aggadah commentary *'Eyn Ayah*. Taylor's work has been criticized in Jerrold Seigel, *The Idea of the Self: Thought and Experience in Western Europe Since the Seventeenth Century* (Cambridge: Cambridge University Press, 2005), 41–43, 299. He particularly disagrees with Taylor's seeing Locke as an exemplar of "the punctilious self," and more broadly sees in modernity a richer harvest of forms of selfhood than Taylor allows. These points do not, though, detract from Taylor's helpfulness for our purposes here.

72 One of the virtues of Taylor's formulation is its clarifying just which of the many meanings of Romanticism we are talking about; on this, see Arthur O. Lovejoy's classic 1924 essay "On the Discrimination of Romanticisms," in his *Essays in the History of Ideas* (Baltimore: Johns Hopkins University Press, 1948), 228, 253.

traditions played no small role in the development of Romanticism, as well as in German Idealism, mediated in part by Christian Kabbalah.[73] Leszek Kolakowski has shown just how deeply rooted what he characterizes as Hegel's philosophical eschatology is in the Neoplatonic tradition, the tradition which itself is so central to the history of Kabbalah.[74]

In turn, we see in Rav Kook an exemplar of the phenomenon that Shmuel Noah Eisenstadt called "multiple modernities"—the ways in which modern thinkers and movements radicalize extant tensions within premodern civilization in regularly surprising ways.[75] I will have more to say on this presently.

These same dynamics limned by Taylor are at work in Rav Kook's own development. In his youth he was, within the framework of traditional rabbinic culture, a rationalist; steeped in Lithuanian Talmudism, his Kabbalistic studies were in the Lithuanian tradition, that is, scholastic and well removed from the internalization that characterized Hasidism; he was, we shall see, versed in Haskalah writings; his aggadah commentary was, at least at the outset, I hope to show, an attempt to synthesize several rationalist moments—the medieval philosophical tradition of Maimonides and Isaac Arama on the one hand, and the rationalist self-improvement of Israel Salanter's Mussar movement on the other—in an enterprise of self-cultivation.[76] And I also hope to show that all this eventually gave way to an expressivist turn of his own, as the vectors of his religious life shifted from the top-down to the bottom-up.

---

73 The influence of Neoplatonism on Romanticism is a major theme of M. H. Abrams's classic *Natural Supernaturalism: Tradition and Revolution in Romantic Literature* (New York: Norton, 1971); for the indirect influence of Kabbalah on Schelling via Jakob Boehme, see therein at 170.

 On Kabbalah and Romanticism, see Eveline Goodman-Thau, Gerd Mattenklott, and Christoph Schulte, eds., *Kabbala und Romantik* (Tubingen: Max Niemeyer, 1994) and idem, *Kabbala und die Literatur der Romantik* (Tubingen: Max Niemeyer, 1999). See also, Christoph Schulte, "Kabbala-Rezeption in der Deutschen Romantik," in *Mysticism, Magic and Kabbalah in Ashkenazi Judaism*, ed. Karl Erich Grozinger and Joseph Dan (Berlin: Walter de Gruyter, 1995), 295-313, as well as Wilhelm Schmidt Biggemann, ed., *Christliche Kabbala* (Ostfildern: Jan Thorbecke Verlag, 2003), and his essay therein, "Jakob Boehme und die Kabbala," 157–181. See also Wilhelm August Schulze, "Schelling und die Kabbala," *Judaica* 13, nos. 2–4 (1957): 65–99, 143–170, 210–232. This is a rich and important subject with many implications for modern intellectual and religious history, deserving further study. For an especially interesting demonstration of the possibilities here, see Paul Franks, "Inner Antisemitism or Kabbalistic Legacy? German Idealism's Relationship to Judaism," in *Faith and Reason*, ed. Fred Rush, Jürgen Stolzenberg, and Paul Franks, special issue, *Yearbook of German Idealism* 7 (2010): 254–279.

74 Leszek Kolakowski, *The Main Currents of Marxism*, vol. 1, *The Founders*, trans. P. S. Falla (New York: Oxford University Press, 1978), 1–80. On Neoplatonism and Jewish philosophy and mysticism in general, see Lenn E. Goodman, ed., *Neoplatonism in Jewish Thought* (Albany: State University of New York Press, 1992).

75 Eisenstadt developed this idea in a number of writings. For his best-known statement, see "Multiple Modernities," *Daedalus* 129, no. 1 (2000): 1–29.

76 We will see that the young Rav Kook was familiar with the less well known, and more rationalistic, of Salanter's writings—his essays from 1861–1862.

And yet, for all its modernity, Rav Kook's ultimate subjectivism is still deeply neo-Augustinian, that is, the inner self is ultimately grounded in the divine, albeit a rich, multifaceted divinity.[77] Kabbalah plays a key role here in that the inner motions of the subjective self come to be taken as manifestations of divine forces coursing through both the material and spiritual universes, and in distinctively modern ways, not least in his emphasis on the individual sense of inner freedom. Yet the highly structured tradition out of which this expressivism grew does not vanish; it abides and creates a tension in Rav Kook's mature thought between structure and antistructure, reason and the subject, between the ways in which his theology functions less as doctrine and more as the interpretation of the religious life, his and that of his times. It is this tension that makes his thought so dynamic and at times seemingly self-contradictory.[78] We hope this work will deepen our understanding of those defining tensions, which he exhibits so vividly, and which course through the history of Jewish thought, and indeed of religion, as a whole.

This subjective turn is intimately connected to Rav Kook's eventual turn towards nationalism, which itself represents a transferral of the individualism of the human subject to the life of peoples. As Louis Dumont has written: "The nation is precisely the type of global society which corresponds to the paramountcy (*sic*) of the individual as value. Not only does the one historically accompany the other, but the interdependence between them is clear, so that we may say that the nation is a global society composed of people who think of themselves as individuals."[79] And a key contention of the architect of the Genocide Convention, Raphael Lemkin, was that the murder of a nation and an individual are in many ways deeply the same.[80]

Stylistically, this subjective turn is reflected in Rav Kook's mounting recourse to the genre of spiritual diary, a comparative rarity in Jewish religious history. Moshe Idel

---

77 Lest this sound wildly anachronistic, it is worth noting Peter Brown's observations regarding St. Augustine's *Confessions*: "If to be a 'Romantic' means to be a man acutely aware of being caught in an existence that denies him the fullness for which he craves, to feel that he is defined by his tension towards something else, by his capacity for faith, for hope, for longing, to think of himself as a wanderer seeking a country that is always distant, but made ever-present to him by the quality of the love that 'groans' for it, then Augustine has imperceptibly become a 'Romantic.'" Peter Brown, *Augustine of Hippo: A Biography*, 2nd ed. (Berkeley: University of California Press, 2000), 150.

78 I am here deliberately alluding to a cluster of writings in anthropology, sociology, and theology, which develop these broader themes largely in isolation from each other: Victor Turner, *The Ritual Process: Structure and Anti-Structure* (Chicago: Aldine, 1969); Touraine, *Critique of Modernity*; and George A. Lindbeck, *The Nature of Doctrine: Religion and Theology in a Postliberal Age* (Philadelphia: Westminster, 1984).

79 Louis Dumont, *Essays on Individualism* (Chicago: University of Chicago Press, 1986), 10. In his *German Ideology: From France to Germany and Back* (Chicago: University of Chicago Press, 1994), Dumont discusses at length the difference between nationalist and liberal forms of individualism.

80 Much has been written on this, of course; I am especially indebted to Douglas Irvin-Erickson, *Raphael Lemkin and the Concept of Genocide* (Philadelphia: University of Pennsylvania Press, 2017).

has written of such Jewish mystical diaries as have been written, particularly those of the sixteenth century, that "their emergence is part of a larger phenomenon that may be described as the turn from an objective form of Kabbalah to a much more subjective one," and that they are regularly accompanied by Messianic awareness.[81] We will, in the final chapter, see the salience of that observation with regard to Rav Kook. This is not to say that his journal began as part of a Messianic project, but rather that his journal work, and in particular, his exploration of subjectivity—first his own, and then that of others, was crucial to the process through which his eschatology emerged.

Journal Writing as Spiritual Practice

In the coming chapters we will see Rav Kook writing in a variety of traditional genres: textual commentary, sermonics, responsa, poetry, essays, moralizing tracts, and never entirely finding himself in any of them. In *Midbar Shur* and *'Eyn Ayah* his prolixity and the mounting rush of his ideas overwhelm the respective genres of sermon and commentary, making them rough going for the average student (and likely unhearable for the intended listeners of *Midbar Shur*). We will see him begin and set aside a number of commentarial projects, and one senses a kind of restlessness as he moves through these genres. We will find a genre in which he most truly seems to have found himself qua thinker, the spiritual diary.

It has long been noted that the vast body of Jewish literature contains few if any mystical autobiographies; Moshe Idel has attributed this to the tradition's overwhelming emphasis on the collective personality of Israel, with a concomitantly "objectivistic type of discourse," reflecting a cultural decision that the community is to be shaped by "common denominators that are religiously oriented, synchronized performances."[82] Only in sixteenth-century Safedian Kabalah, Idel writes, do we first find full-fledged autobiography—from the hands of Yoseph Karo, Hayim Vital, and Elazar Azikri—"their emergence is part of a larger phenomenon that may be described as the turn from an objective form of Kabbalah to a much more subjective one" and is of a piece with the Messianic self-perception of the writers.[83]

Jeffrey (Yossi) Chajes has probed the *problematiques* of early modern Jewish spiritual diaries and their evasion of the neat genre divisions of "autobiography" and "diarykeeping."[84] He notes that the term *pinqas* first appears as designating some sort of spiritual diary—the sense in which Rav Kook used the term—in reference to a dream journal kept by the Sabbatian prophet Mordechai Ashkenazi (1650–1729). During the Middle Ages it meant "ledger book" and thus later lent itself to the notion of keeping a ledger for the soul.

---

81 Moshe Idel, preface to *Jewish Mystical Autobiographies*, by Morris M. Faierstein (New York: Paulist Press, 1999), xv–xxii, xviii.

82 Ibid., xv–xxii.

83 Ibid., xviii.

84 J. H. Chajes, "Accounting for the Self: Preliminary Generic Historical Reflections on Early Modern Jewish Egodocuments," *Jewish Quarterly Review* 95, no. 1 (Winter 2005): 1–15.

We find mention of it as a spiritual practice in a major seventeenth-century work with which Rav Kook was familiar, Isaiah Horowitz's *Shnei Luhot Ha-Berit*.[85] Chajes observes that this development seems of a piece with the practice of Puritan diarykeeping, both reflecting a broader cultural process of disciplining the religious life. There is great truth in that, but even so, I believe, attending to the differences between Puritan diaries and the ones we will examine here is instructive.[86]

Tom Webster, in a very enlightening study of Puritan diaries, has described them under the Foucauldian rubric of "technology of the self." The Puritan diary was, he writes, "a means by which the godly self was maintained, indeed constructed, through the action of writing." Further, the "act of writing, then, seems to have power in itself, writing becomes a way of validating experience." Puritan diaries offer an ordering of experience, both internal and external, discerning patterns of the divine in one's daily life, hopefully patterns that reveal salvation; and the patterns, as the diarists read their own lives, range from the "closed," secure in their salvation, to the "open," in which salvation is not yet assured.[87] He points out the relationship between Puritan diarykeeping and the ledgering practices of early modern capitalism, which reflected what Charles Taylor has called "the punctual self."[88] This process also played out in traditional Judaism; indeed, scholars have noted that none other than Benjamin Franklin contributed to the diary keeping of the Mussar movement, which was its own translation of the "punctual self" into the idiom of traditional Judaism.[89]

Here too, Taylor's picture of the modern trajectory is illuminating; just as the "punctual self" eventually transformed into the "expressive self," finding meaning in its own recesses, so too the diarykeeping of Mussar and the rationally ordered sense of self it bespoke, gives way in Rav Kook's journal entries to a more expressive self. And yet unlike

---

85 See therein, *Yoma Derekh Hayim*, §1660, 2:444; see also Meir Poppers, *Hanhagot Ha-Tzadiqim* §31—both cited in Chajes, "Accounting for the Self," 12

86 It also seems to me that the emergence of the spiritual diary seems of a piece with the emergence of the *hanhagot*, or conduct literature, and shares with that genre a latent potential for antinomianism. See Zev Gries, *Sifrut Ha-Hanhagot* (Jerusalem: Mossad Bialik, 1989), 22–28. At the same time, Gries points out, at 102, that the conservative tenor of the *hanhagot* literature shows the limitations of the antinomian impulse even within Kabbalistic circles, and even in some touched by Sabbatianism. Both genres, though, do seem to represent some more pressing personalization of religious life.

87 Tom Webster, "Writing to Redundancy: Approaches to Spiritual Journals and Early Modern Spirituality," *The Historical Journal* 39, no. 1 (1996): 33–56; 40, 47, 55–56. Another helpful discussion of Puritan diaries is chapter five of David D. Hall, *Worlds of Wonder, Days of Judgment: Popular Religious Belief in Early New England* (Cambridge, MA: Harvard University Press, 1990).

88 On the underlying foundations of modern bookkeeping, see Michael Zakim, "Bookkeeping as Ideology: Capitalist Knowledge in Nineteenth Century America," *Commonplace* 6, no. 3 (April 2006), www.common-place.org/vol-06/no-03/zakim.

89 See Nancy Sinkoff, "Strategy and Ruse in the Haskalah of Mendel Lefin of Satanow," in *New Perspectives on the Haskalah*, ed. Shmuel Feiner and David Sorkin (London: Littman, 2001), 86–102.

the Kabbalistic diaries of Vital and others, Rav Kook is not recording specific experiences in narrative form. Rather, his writing *is* the experience: the focal point of his own consciousness is created by the focusing act of his writing, and the comparatively disjointed nature of his diary entries is itself reflective of the divergent, indeed fragmented, range of ideas and experiences he is trying to understand, both within himself and without, in the fragmented Jewish society of early twentieth-century Russia.

Rav Kook's diarykeeping, instead of ordering his experiences as such, as in the writings of Puritan or Kabbalistic diarists, enabled him to register contradictory views and experiences, to try and square the circles of his commitment to tradition, and his openness to the mutually antagonistic dimensions of his personality and his times. (Indeed, it was in these years that Berdyczewsky urged Hebrew writers to take up autobiography as the genre that makes for the greatest authenticity, precisely by registering the individual author in all his contradictions.)[90] Rav Kook's journal was thus an alternative forum to the highly structured genres of rabbinic literature that were his daily fare, a space for what Lewis White Beck has called "philosophical exhibition," an embodiment of ideas as they register on the thinker.[91] I might add that what the reader experiences as "exhibition," Rav Kook seems to have experienced as illumination, and, eventually, revelation. Nevertheless, there is a strong common denominator between Rav Kook's diarykeeping that of the Kabbalists and Puritans—all have a strong soteriological thrust, that is, all seek to discern patterns of redemption. In Rav Kook's distinctively modern idiom, that pattern is to be found precisely in the midst of seeming chaos.

The Early Writings: Esoteric and Exoteric

The works we will chiefly look at here are: his short-lived journal *'Ittur Sofrim*; commentaries to Talmudic passages and other works, including to the *Shulhan 'Arukh*; his polemical work on tefillin *Hevesh Pe'er*; his first spiritual diary, *Metziot Qatan*; the spiritual diaries of his Boisk years, *Pinqasim* 15 and 16, some of which his son wove in to the small gem of a Mussar treatise *Mussar Avikha*; his smaller *Mahberot Qetanot Boisk*; his collection

---

90 See Berdyczewsky's 1889 essay, "Devarim Ahadim 'al Devar Ha-Toladah ve-Ha-Autobiografiyot," reprinted in Holzman's full edition of his collected works, *Kitvei Micha Josef Berdyczewski*, vol. 2 (Tel Aviv: Ha-Kibbutz Ha-Meuhad, 1996–2002), 177–180, and the discussion thereof in Marcus Moseley, *Being for Myself Alone: Origins of Jewish Autobiography* (Stanford: Stanford University Press, 2006), 221ff. Moseley notes, inter alia, that during this period Berdyczewsky was deeply under the sway of Rousseau, whose influence I will argue is also present in Rav Kook's writings of this period.

91 Lewis White Beck, "Philosophy as Literature," in *Philosophical Style*, ed. Berel Lang (Chicago: Nelson Hall, 1980), 234–255. He writes therein at 244: "[T]he great philosophical poets who did not just quote—Dante, Milton, Goethe, Wordsworth, Hardy—their mode of poetically philosophizing is not quoting but exhibiting. They embody philosophical stances in situations and character so that the reader can *see* (emphasis in the original) philosophical models instead of having to think about abstract philosophical concepts. Theirs is a logic of images, not of concepts."

of sermons from the mid–1890s *Midbar Shur*; some essays of his published only posthumously; his massive aggadah commentary *'Eyn Ayah*; his essays from 1901-1904 on Jewish nationalism; the hitherto unpublished treatise recently issued as *Li-Nevukhei Ha-Dor*; and the last of the spiritual diaries he kept in Eastern Europe.[92] We will also briefly look at some other writings of his—poems, halakhic responsa, commentaries, and brief essays.[93]

We will observe that his private notebooks regularly work in an explicitly Kabbalistic vein, more so than his writings intended for public consumption. This in turn raises the question of esoteric versus exoteric writings. As Elliot Wolfson has observed, there are two kinds of esotericism: one is the political, associated with Leo Strauss's influential understanding of Maimonides, in which a discrete truth is shielded from view for its potentially destabilizing, subversive effects; another is what Wolfson calls "essential esotericism," in which the truth being concealed is esoteric in its essence, such that it cannot but be revealed except by concealment, and vice versa—a mind-bending paradox which arises from Kabbalah and philosophy's attempts to grapple with the most basic issues of metaphysics at the farthest limits of understanding.[94] We will explore the ways in which Rav Kook at times translates esoteric concepts in his exoteric writings, while at others, the exoteric—and explicitly philosophical—abides on its own terms.

Self-Cultivation, Philosophical Ethics, Mussar

The theme of self-cultivation animates much of these writings in two ways: first, as an ideational theme with which he seeks to channel the positive energies of the Mussar movement into what he sees as a more positive and richer direction; and second, as a reflection of his own efforts to develop his own identity as a *talmid hakham* who sees himself as standing at the crossroads of several traditions—halakhah, Lithuanian Kabbalah, and medieval Jewish philosophy.[95] I will argue in the conclusion that only later did Hasidism become a genuinely live option for him.

---

92 I discuss the full provenance of this and other diaries in the course of the work.

93 The other available works of his from this period not much discussed in the present work are the sermons printed in Otzarot, 2:148–172; as well as the materials gathered in Menahem Arieli, ed., *Neshamah shel Shabbat: Osef Ma'amarim Toraniyyim le-Zikhro shel Ha-Rav Eliyahu Shlomo Ra'anan ztql* (Hevron: Shalmei Ari'eli, 1999), 52–82, and various sermons in the anthologies on festivals edited by Ben-Zion Shapira and published under the title *Meorot Ha-Re'ayah*. Those volumes have been published in Jerusalem by Ha-Makhon 'al-Shem Ha-Ratzyah on Shavuot (1994), Hanukah and Purim (1995), the festivals of Tishrei (1995), Shabbat (2013) and prayer (2016).

94 See Elliot R. Wolfson, *Abraham Abulafia—Kabbalist and Prophet: Hermeneutics, Theosophy and Theurgy* (Los Angeles: Cherub Press, 2000), 9–93. For a far more succinct presentation, see Wolfson's comments in his untitled book note *Journal of Religion in Europe* 2 (2009): 314–318, reviewing Moshe Halbertal's *Concealment and Revelation*. My thanks to Daniel Abrams for that latter reference.

95 On nineteenth-century Lithuanian Kabbalah as a constituting a distinctive tradition, see Raphael Shuchat, "Qabbalat Lita ke-Zerem 'Atzmai be-Sifrut Ha-Qabbalah," *Qabbalah* 10

A number of moral philosophers writing from very different perspectives have, in recent decades and for reasons of their own—besides a shared sense of the limits of Kantian, and especially Rawlsian, ethics—drawn renewed attention to the role of self-cultivation in the history of Western ethics.[96] Thus, Alasdair MacIntyre in his landmark 1984 volume *After Virtue* sought to shift the emphasis of ethical discussion away from Kantian deontological ethics in favor of a reengagement with an Aristotelian ethics of virtue, whose practices take their shape from their embeddedness within tradition.[97] Martha Nussbaum, to take another prominent example, has written major studies of Hellenistic ethics as a form of self-cultivation and has applied this focus on human flourishing in her writings on contemporary issues.[98] For his part, Michel Foucault also sought to shift the ground of ethical discussion away from Kant and towards Aristotle, not, as did MacIntyre, to recapture the Aristotelian ethos as such, but to draw attention to ethics as a set of actions in and through which one creates the self; or, to be more precisely Foucauldian, view the creation of the self as as a negotiation with the dominant discourses of a time and place.[99] While many Foucauldian analyses seem to spell the death of agency, they do helpfully draw attention to the cultivation of the self as a central feature of ethics in Western

---

(2004): 181–206. We will have much more to say on this in coming chapters. On philosophy as more than the technical exercise of unaided reason, but rather a tradition of its own, see Wilfred Cantwell Smith, "Philosophia as One of the Religious Traditions of Mankind," in his *Modern Culture from a Comparative Perspective* (Albany: State University of New York Press, 1997), 19–50.

96   The convergence I am discussing here is akin to the convergence between virtue ethics and continental philosophy discussed by Sabina Lovibond in her very interesting (but too often opaque) *Ethical Formation* (Cambridge, MA: Harvard University Press, 2002); her attempt to synthesize the two, despite what she calls the "counter-teleology" of Foucauldian ethics, is to be found at 169–174.

The argument that Kant's own ethical oeuvre is itself richer and more directed towards self-cultivation than is generally thought is made at length in Robert B. Louden, *Kant's Impure Ethics: From Rational Beings to Human Beings* (New York: Oxford University Press, 2000).

97   Alasdair MacIntyre, *After Virtue: A Study in Moral Theory* (Notre Dame: University of Notre Dame Press, 1984).

98   Thus see, for example, Nussbaum's exhaustive study *The Therapy of Desire: Theory and Practice in Hellenistic Ethics* (Princeton: Princeton University Press, 1994) and her many other works in this vein on contemporary issues, such as her *Women and Human Development: The Capabilities Approach* (Cambridge: Cambridge University Press, 2000).

99   See generally, Paul Rabinow, ed., *Essential Works of Foucault 1954–1984*, vol. 1, *Ethics: Subjectivity and Truth*, trans. R. Hurley et al. (New York: New Press, 1997), esp. 253–301. Very, very briefly, Foucault called attention to what he characterized as the four elements of ethics: The "substance of ethics," that is, the domain of the self that is the subject of ethical thought and action (in the premodern period, flesh and desire, in the modern, feeling); the "mode of subjectivation," or the nature and means of the authority imposed on the individual; the "techniques of the self," through which one creates oneself under the impress of ethical ideals; and the *telos*, the mode of being which one finally seeks to achieve.

history.[100] Most pertinent for us is Foucault's recognition of the key role of self-cultivation in ancient and medieval philosophy, and his and our indebtedness to the works of the late Pierre Hadot. A historian of philosophy, Hadot, in a series of significant historical studies, called attention to the ways in which much ancient and medieval philosophy, far from being the disembodied analytic discourse so characteristic of contemporary philosophy departments, was a rigorous practice aimed at self-cultivation towards a life lived in wisdom.[101]

These turns in ethical theory have left their mark on the historical study of Jewish ethics. Amram Tropper has demonstrated the deep indebtedness of *Pirqei Avot* to Hellenistic ethics, Jonathan Schofer has written on spiritual exercises in rabbinic culture, and Shmuel (Richie) Lewis has written a remarkably penetrating comparative study of humility in Greco-Roman and rabbinic thought.[102] Josef Stern has made deft use of Hadot in his powerful readings of Maimonides.[103] At much greater length and with vast historical sweep, Hava Tirosh-Samuelson has demonstrated that the cultivation of human flourishing was central to the rabbis of the Talmud, to the medieval philosophers, and to the Kabbalists as well. This long-standing concern with, and discourse on, *eudaemonia*, she writes, underwent a crucial transformation in the fifteenth to sixteenth centuries, as Maimonidean naturalistic ethics and the depersonalized theology in which it was grounded gave way to more rabbinic, personalistic conceptions of God, of the affective dimensions of personality, the essential holiness of Israel, the centrality of obedience and keeping mitzvot and,

---

100 A deft analysis that draws on Foucault while moving beyond him to recapture the idea of agency in a seemingly hidebound traditionalism, even as I differ with some of her approach, is provided by Saba Mahmood, *Politics of Piety: The Islamic Revival and the Feminist Subject* (Princeton: Princeton University Press, 2004), esp. 27–34.

For the argument that in his last years Foucault returned to the idea of the subject, and revised his dissection of power/knowledge as a step towards self-creation, see Eric Paras, *Foucault 2.0: Beyond Power and Knowledge* (New York: Other Press, 2006), esp. chaps. 4 and 5.

101 See Pierre Hadot, *Philosophy as a Way of Life*, trans. Michael Chase (Oxford: Blackwell, 1995); for Hadot's own comments and criticism of Foucault's use of his work, see therein at 206–213. I will return to Hadot in chapter three.

102 Amram Tropper, *Wisdom, Politics and Historiography: Tractate Avot in the Context of the Graeco-Roman Near East* (Oxford: Oxford University Press, 2004), 51–87; Jonathan Schofer, *The Making of a Sage: A Study in Rabbinic Ethics* (Madison: University of Wisconsin Press, 2005); Shmuel (Richie) Lewis, *Ve-Lifnei Kavod 'Anavah: Idiyal Ha-'Anavah ki-Yesod bi-Sefatam Ha-Mussarit shel Hazal* (Jerusalem: Magnes Press, 2013). And, more recently, Yair Furstenberg, "Rabbinic Responses to Greco-Roman Ethics of Self-Formation in Tractate *Avot*," in *Self, Self-Fashioning and Individuality in Late Antiquity: New Perspectives*, ed. Maren R. Niehoff and Joshua Levinson (Tubingen: Mohr Siebeck, 2019), 125–148, surveys recent scholarship and traces further directions for understanding this question's literary horizon.

103 See Josef Stern, "Maimonides on the Growth of Knowledge and the Limitations of the Intellect," in *Maîmonide: Philosophe et Savant*, ed. T. Levy and R. Rashed (Louvain: Peeters, 2004), 143–191, in particular part 4; T. Levy and R. Rashed, "Maimonides' Epistemology," in *The Cambridge Companion to Maimonides*, ed. Kenneth Seeskin (Cambridge: Cambridge University Press, 2005), 105–133, 127–129; and, in general, Alan L. Mittleman, *A Short History of Jewish Ethics* (Oxford: Wiley Blackwell, 2012).

under the influence of Kabbalah, an emphasis on mystical union, *devequt*, with God.[104] In parsing these terms, a genuine difference between the self-cultivation of the philosophic tradition and that of the Kabbalah is that the former does not partake of the theurgic dimensions of the latter—that is, the philosopher does not aim to effect changes in the inner workings of the divine. Indeed, in philosophy's own terms, such a project is literally inconceivable and blasphemous too. Rather, the philosophers seek to bring themselves into alignment with the divine intelligence animating the universe. The Kabbalist by contrast seeks to work restorative changes within the Godhead itself, which is conceived in explicitly mythical terms.

Notwithstanding the accuracy of Tirosh-Samuelson's major conclusions regarding the relative displacement of philosophical ethics by Kabbalah in early modern Jewry and beyond, elements of the philosophical tradition did persist in rabbinical culture in Eastern Europe well into modernity. Thus, for instance, Harris Bor has shown how elements of the medieval philosophical tradition shaped the moral views of the Haskalah, and through its more traditionalist proponents, some of the early teachings of Mussar.[105] Alan Brill has called attention to serious engagement with elements of the philosophical tradition, in particular the writings of Maimonides, on the part of the Gaon of Vilna and some (though by no means all) of his disciples.[106]

For my part I would argue that a century later, the early writings of Rav Kook, and an investigation of his Eastern European milieu, offer important evidence of the persistence of the philosophical tradition, not as a vestigial phenomenon, but as a source on which he actively drew in seeking to meet what he saw as the theological and societal challenges of his day.

Kabbalah, Modernity, and Experience

This work is very much about modernity and the deep modernization of Jewish thought, including the Kabbalah.

What do we mean by that? In an important 2016 monograph, Jonathan Garb argues for what he characterizes as the "autonomy" of modern Kabbalah relative to earlier periods. Modernity's salient feature here "is accelerating and conscious change. Consciousness contributes to acceleration and acceleration of consciousness. And hence the attendant

---

104 Hava Tirosh-Samuelson, *Happiness in Premodern Judaism: Virtue, Knowledge and Well-Being* (Cincinnati: Hebrew Union College Press, 2003); her conclusions as to the change of the fifteenth to sixteenth centuries are to be found therein at 394–498. It bears noting that a good bit of Tirosh's rethinking of conventional discourse on Jewish ethics was prefigured some forty years ago in Jacob B. Agus, *The Vision and the Way: An Interpretation of Jewish Ethics* (New York: Frederick Ungar, 1966); this volume, like much of Agus's work, has yet to receive its due.

105 Harris Bor, "Moral Education in the Age of Jewish Enlightenment" (PhD diss., Cambridge University, 1996). My thanks to Dr. Bor for making a copy of his work available to me.

106 Alan Brill, "Auxiliary to *Hokhmah*: The Writings of the Vilna Gaon and Philosophical Terminology," in *The Vilna Gaon and His Disciples*, ed. Moshe Hallamish, Yosef Rivlin, and Rafael Shuchat (Ramat Gan: Bar-Ilan University Press, 2003), 9–38.

psychological changes, such as individual self-awareness. Therefore, modernity is not, as some still have it, a discrete content, related perhaps to secularization, liberalization or progressive thinking . . . [it] is entirely a process in which we ourselves are embedded."[107]

Garb's observation deeply resonates with my own thoughts and foregrounds two elements crucial to this work: modernity as a set of processes, and its new attention to, and ways of looking at, the inner life.

First, modernity as processes. As noted earlier, in a major essay of 2000, Shmuel Noah Eisenstadt, dean of Israeli sociology and a major figure in social theory, put forth his conception of "multiple modernities," and developed it in a number of influential studies in the ensuing years.[108] For Eisenstadt, the welter of forces and movements we call modernity is best understood as a collection of open-ended processes, which, amid genuinely new sociopolitical conditions, radicalize tensions within premodern civilization, among them universalism and particularity, pragmatism and utopia, discipline and freedom. "The idea of multiple modernities," he writes, "presumes that the best way to understand the contemporary world—indeed to explain the history of modernity—is to see it as a story of continual constitution and reconstitution of a multiplicity of cultural programs." Thus, crucially, "modernity and Westernization are not identical," even if the West, so to speak, came first and still serves as "a basic reference point for others."[109]

What then do we mean by modernity? "[S]hifts in the conception of human agency, and of its place in the flow of time . . . a conception of the future characterized by a number of possibilities realizable through autonomous human agency."[110] In modernity, "the premises on which the social, ontological and political order were based, and the legitimation of that order, were no longer taken for granted."[111] This destabilization of hitherto immutable fixities, accompanied by new forms of self-awareness or self-consciousness and a steady broadening of local horizons, led to "a belief in the possibility that society could be actively formed by conscious human activity." This mix of destabilization and new agency yielded within modernity two alternative visions of social construction. One, which believed in

> the possibility of bridging the gap between the transcendental and the mundane orders—of realizing through conscious human agency, exercised in social life, major utopian and eschatological visions. The second emphasi(zing) a growing recognition of the legitimacy of

---

107 Jonathan Garb, *Ha-Qabbalah be-'Et Ha-Hadashah ki-Tehum Mehqar Autonomi* (Los Angeles: Cherub Press, 2016), ii.

108 Shmuel Noah Eisenstadt, "Multiple Modernities," *Daedalus* 129 (Winter 2000): 1–29. I have discussed some of these themes in relation to Rav Kook in a 2013 paper "Multiple Modernity as Theory and Theology: Shmuel Noah Eisenstadt and Rav Kook," available online at www.academia.edu/41236006/Multiple_Modernity_as_Theory_and_Theology_Shmuel_Noah_Eisenstadt_and_Rav_Kook.

109 Eisenstadt, "Multiple Modernities," 2–3.

110 Ibid., 3.

111 Ibid.

multiple individual and group goals and interests, as a consequence allow(ing) for multiple interpretations of the common good.[112]

Both moments—the pluralist and the monist—attempt to deal with the profound dislocations generated by new science and philosophy that led to, in the words of Claude Lefort so often quoted by Eisenstadt, "the loss of markers of certainty."[113]

Rav Kook, in his life and thought, squarely exemplified both moments, of pluralism and monism. On the one hand, he, like other modern Jewish mystics, was drawn to the meeting, and interpenetration, of transcendence with immanence. At the same time, he worked hard to take full cognizance of as wide a range of views and perspectives as he could—and it was here that we see his most creative uses of Kabbalah, to make sense both of the multiplicity of contradictory lifeworlds in an overarching monotheistic framework, and of their creative interactions in and through massive historical change.

The usefulness of Eisenstadt's framework for understanding Rav Kook becomes clear from Danielle Hervieu-Leger's characterization. This conception, she says:

> stresses plurality while remaining anchored in a conceptual framework of modernity as a specific type of civilization, even though it refuses to determine any specific description of modernity . . . it offers an invitation to grasp the historical configurations of the contradictions inherent in the program of modernity . . . autonomy of individual subjects (vs.) the imperatives of social control . . . the necessity of change (vs.) the need to ensure continuity of the collective bond . . . the pragmatic vision of a world to be constructed here and now (vs.) the utopian call to the advent of a completely different world . . . a realist acceptance of the world as it functions (vs.) transcendence . . . pluralist self-assertion of communities (vs.) the universalist goal of a united, common world . . . (all) take their place as elements in a variety of cultural programs perpetually reworked.[114]

That Rav Kook was able to speak about modernity as an arena of transcendence from within the recesses of tradition may seem puzzling. Yet these dynamics of modernity had, for Eisenstadt and those who share his perspective, deep historical roots in premodernity and in particular the so-called Axial Age civilizations (as first identified by Karl Jaspers): ancient Greece and Israel, Imperial China, Hindu and Buddhist civilization, ancient Persia—further articulated in their inheritors in Judaism, Christianity, and Islam. At their core, these civilizations shared a distinction between mundane and ultimate, or transcendent, reality, and disembeddedness from closed kinship and territorial units, which together gave rise to the idea of reorganizing society along transcendental lines. This in turn generated ongoing tensions within societies about the extent to which

---

112 Ibid., 5.

113 Lefort's comment appears in his *Democracy and Political Theory* (Minneapolis: University of Minnesota Press, 1988), 215.

114 Daniele Hervieu-Leger, "Multiple Religious Modernities: A New Approach to Contemporary Religiosity," in *Comparing Modernities: Pluralism versus Homogeneity; Essays in Honor of Shmuel N. Eisenstadt*, ed. Eliezer Ben-Refael and Yitzhak Sternberg (Leiden: E. J. Brill, 2005), 327–338, 332–333.

they were or were not realizing their transcendent goals, while also generating new social classes tasked with conceptualizing those ideals and managing the inevitable tensions.[115]

Of a piece with modernity's distinctive sense of human agency was what Eisenstadt calls "reflexivity," a new form of self-awareness, opening onto not only dramatically different understandings of the human condition, but "question(ing) the very givenness of such visions and the institutional patterns related to them . . . an awareness of the possibility of multiple visions, that could, in fact, be contested."[116]

A crucial feature of modern thought, then, much of modern Kabbalah included, is its self-awareness as being situated in time. Simply put, medievals didn't think of themselves as medieval, while moderns think of themselves as modern. Se'adyah and Maimonides were perfectly well aware that they were writing in what we call an Islamicate context—but they did not think that that Islamicate context, and certainly not its sociopolitical dimensions, was itself intimately connected to, or mattered for, the abiding truth and persuasive power of their ideas.[117] The same can largely be said for the Iberian and Franco-German figures at the emergence of the Kabbalah. By contrast, as Garb puts it, in modern Kabbalah textual interpretation is regularly refracted through self-perception and sacred biography, reflection on differing forms of Jewish practice and study (of a piece, I would suggest, with the general splintering that so defines modern Jewish experience), a lessening of esotericism, and a regularly explicit distancing from non-Jewish ideas (similarly of a piece with the modern blurring of boundaries between Jews and non-Jews).[118] These too, are features of Rav Kook's oeuvre, even as his exploration of the relationships of Jews to non-Jews synthesizes profound distancing with profound identification.

Another facet of this situatedness in time, and the significance of situatedness in time, is the melding of immanence and transcendence, the fusion of higher meanings with the mundane. This process is best seen in Luther's translation of the Bible into the

---

115 For a very helpful survey of this idea, including critical discussion, see Robert N. Bellah and Hans Joas, eds, *The Axial Age and its Consequences* (Cambridge, MA: Harvard University Press, 2012). For a brief, but very helpful, discussion of the Axial Age idea in the context of Biblical religion, see Alan L. Mittleman, *A Short History of Jewish Ethics* (Oxford: Wiley Blackwell, 2012), 16–52. For a brief, helpful illumination of how these themes structured secular modernity, see Charles Taylor, "Western Secularity," in *Rethinking Secularism*, ed. Craig Calhoun, Mark Juergensmeyer, and Jonathan van Antwerpen (Oxford: Oxford University Press, 2011), 31–53.

116 Eisenstadt, "Multiple Modernities," 4.

117 I am talking here about the broader Islamic cultural and intellectual context, and not about immediate political contexts, of which, as Leo Strauss has shown, medieval and early modern thinkers were acutely aware. But their conception of truth was one that transcended the circumstances of their works' time and place, unlike Strauss's *bête noire* of modern historicism.

118 Garb, *Ha-Qabbalah be-'Et Ha-Hadashah ki-Tehum Mehqar Autonomi*, 82. In a related vein, Adam Shear has demonstrated that the work regularly taken as the fountainhead of Jewish essentialist nationhood, Yehudah Ha-Levi's *Kuzari*, was not seen as such until the turn of the twentieth century, and was a staple of Jewish humanistic writing. See his *The Kuzari and the Shaping of Jewish Identity, 1167–1900* (Cambridge: Cambridge University Press, 2008), which I have briefly discussed in *Makor Rishon*, Shabbat supplement, February 19, 2010.

vernacular, as well as further developments, such as the Protestant ethic as understood by Weber, yielding what Taylor has called "the affirmation of ordinary life," the celebration of the body and its situatedness in time and space—something which we will see preoccupied Rav Kook a great deal. Not to mention one of the most volatile unions of trascendence and immanence: nationalism.

Moderns inescapably see themselves as caught up in historical processes, whether they choose to swim with them or revolt against them.[119] As we shall see, Rav Kook, following and greatly elaborating on the ideas of Moshe Hayim Luzzatto, came to see the acceptance of historical change as crucial, not merely to his own thinking, but more consequentially, to God's own self-fulfillment in and through humanity and the world. We will see this process starting to take shape before his move to Palestine in 1904.

Second, modernity's new attention to *the inner life.* For Garb, the key figure in the sixteenth-century inauguration of this process of Kabbalah's inward turn is Hayim Vital, who canonized his prematurely departed master Luria, and concomitantly elevated the Zohar's stature as the axis joining the historical figure of Bar Yohai to Luria. Indeed, Garb notes, Luria's interpretations of the Zohar became for many the exclusive interpretive grid for the study of Zohar—to the point where the vast portions of the Zohar that fell outside Luria's interests became less studied—precisely because, for so many, Luria's own experience was itself the revelation. His readings, in effect, became a template (or what I call "second scripture") through which the sacred text (i.e., Zohar) is to be understood. In the eighteenth and nineteenth centuries, Garb writes, this modernization of Kabbalah engendered an inward, individualizing turn, with the emergence of Beshtian Hasidism, the schools of Ramhal, of Shalom Sharabi, and of the Gaon of Vilna, each of which took Luria's heritage in new directions. Three of these four figure prominently in our study. Significantly, for each school, a unique, charismatic figure became not only an authority and teacher, but an exemplar whose own life and practice was itself a form of revelation.

Which brings us to the very modern terms—"mysticism" and "experience."

Let's start with "experience." The term was itself most famously introduced into the study of religion in William James's monumental *The Varieties of Religious Experience,* as, in his words, "the feelings, acts, and experiences of individual men in their solitude, so far as they apprehend themselves to stand in relation to whatever they may consider divine."[120] James can helpfully be contrasted here with two other foundational works of the period, Rudolf Otto's *The Idea of the Holy* and Emile Durkheim's *The Elementary Forms of the Religious Life.* Otto, shying away from the seeming open-endedness and implicit naturalism of James's formulation, foregrounds the encounter with the "Wholly Other," as the defining feature of religion; Durkheim, while sharing James's naturalism, argues

---

119 I've discussed some of these issues at greater length, with slightly different framing, in Yehudah Mirsky, "Modernizing Orthodoxies: The Case of Feminism," in *To Be a Jewish Woman / Lihiyot Ishah Yehudiyah,* vol. 4 of *Kolech Proceedings,* ed. Tova Cohen (Jerusalem: Kolech–Religious Women's Forum, 2007), English section, 37–51.

120 William James, *The Varieties of Religious Experience: A Study in Human Nature* (New York: Longmans, Green & Co., 1902).

for the inescapably social and collective nature of religion, as "a unified system of beliefs and practices relative to sacred things . . . that unite its adherents in a single moral community."[121] The idea of religious experience has of course generated intense and heated discussion for over a century. Critics of the concept highlight its essentialism, individualism, and inherent resistance to anything like objective scientific or critical analysis. It also pays scant attention to the legal-ethical dimensions of religion. Others, though, highlight its usefulness for trying to do justice to religious adherents' self-understandings, while inviting conversation among others, including adherents of other traditions.

Ann Taves has, after exhaustively surveying these debates, suggested, following Durkheim, a reframing of religious experience through what she terms an "attributive" approach, namely, turning

> our attention to the processes whereby people sometimes ascribe . . . special characteristics to things that we (as scholars) associate with terms such as "religious," "magical," "mystical," "spiritual," et cetera . . . how humans have used things deemed religious (simple ascriptions—parentheses in original) as building blocks to create the more complex formations (composite ascriptions—parentheses in original) we typically refer to as "religions," or "spiritualities."[122]

This, she suggests, is a way of honoring people's understandings of their worlds, making room for contextualization and analysis, and avoiding reductionism and the shoehorning of any manner of things into rigid categories.

Taves's literally demystifying approach to the question of religious experience is congenial to the present study, concerned as it is with a figure whose mature thought was precisely not only seeing but living divine meaning in the seemingly mundane, and seeing experience, individual and collective, as itself the site of God's revelation in the world. What's more, her approach makes possible the discussion, qua religious experience, of religious phenomena with which conventional analytic categories have a very hard time, such as the text-soaked praxis of rabbinic Judaism.

Turning to "mysticism": In an important recent study, Boaz Huss has raised serious questions about the very term, as used regarding Judaism and other religious traditions. He forcefully argues that not all the texts, figures, movements, and practices brought under that term are best thought of as part of one large category; and that the very category of mysticism is shot through with theological and metaphysical assumptions about whether divinity is personal or abstract, how humans alone or together connect with the divine, assumptions deeply reflecting distinctive features of Western modernity, not least

---

121 Rudolf Otto, *The Idea of the Holy*, trans. John Harvely (Oxford: Oxford University Press, 1923), Emile Durkheim, *Elementary Forms of the Religious Life*, trans. Joseph Ward Swain (New York: Free Press, 1954); Otto's work was first published in 1917, Durkheim's in 1912.

122 Ann Taves, *Religious Experience Reconsidered: A Building-Block Approach to the Study of Religion and Other Special Things* (Princeton: Princeton University Press, 2009), 8–9. In her book, Taves discusses at length how the kind of cross-cultural methods routinely employed in anthropology and ethnography can be employed for the study of religious experience on its own terms.

the focus on individual experience and relative devaluation of ritual practice so characteristic of liberal theology. The study of Jewish mysticism was, relatedly, stamped from the outset (by Buber and Scholem, each in their own way) by a neo-Romantic search for a Judaism that would speak to a modern concern for authenticity, loosed from the bonds of traditional community and authority. Placing further study on a more solid foundation, Huss says, does not require substituting mysticism with some other more successful overarching category, but fundamentally rethinking the history of the phenomena studied under that rubric up to now, paying even more careful attention to the internal dynamics of religious traditions, and studying figures, texts, events, and practices in their distinctive historical contexts.[123]

In looking at such contexts, one very helpful distinction is Moshe Idel's differentiation between theosophy and ecstasy.[124] And it seems to me one way of characterizing Jewish mysticism is that it deliberately seeks to shape religious ecstasy and experience via theosophy and vice versa — through the matrix of Jewish practice and ritual. One way of thinking about Rav Kook, then, is that in his hands Jewish society, and history as such, undergo a kind of theosophical ritualization.[125]

I will in this volume's conclusion discuss the ways in which mysticism, even if understood as carefully as Huss suggests, and religious experience and even philosophy too are perhaps joined at the root.

This Writer's Premises and Commitments

A further corollary to this self-reflective scholarly approach, it seems to me, is greater explicitness about the theological and other assumptions of one's own research, not in order to hermetically seal off discussion, but rather to try and make as clear as possible what it is that we are trying to say.

Taking up the spirit of Huss's exhortations, I will make plain at the outset that this study is historicist: it tries to make sense of one figure's development in his time and place, as he inherited multiple traditions of textual study and religious practice, and worked, as both communal rabbi and burgeoning thinker, to make sense of himself, his time, and his own place within it.[126]

---

123 Huss lays this out at length in his *She'elat Qiyumah shel Mistiqah Yehudit* (Jerusalem/Tel Aviv: Van Leer/Ha-Kibbutz Ha-Meuhad, 2016).

124 Moshe Idel, "Yofyah shel Ishah: Le-Toldotehah shel Ha-Mistiqah Ha-Yehudit," in *Be-Ma'agalei Hasidim: Kovetz Mehqarim le-Zikhro shel Mordechai Wilensky*, ed. Immanuel Etkes et al. (Jerusalem: Mossad Bialik, 2000), 317–334.

125 On the centrality of ritual to Jewish theology, see Moshe Idel, *Enchanted Chains: Techniques and Rituals in Jewish Mysticism* (Los Angeles: Cherub Press, 2005).

126 In my thinking of religion very much in terms of cumulative traditions, I am deeply indebted to Wilfred Cantwell Smith's classic study *The Meaning and End of Religion* (New York: MacMillan, 1961).

All readers and interpreters work with assumptions; the question is which assumptions, and how they are understood. This work is written for readers for whom historical context is key to a work's meaning—the writer's longitudinal positioning within their own and sundry other traditions, as well as the histories of human culture. To the extent that any thinker saw him or herself as interpreting a timeless text in a timeless context, that self-undertstanding must of course be accounted for in a careful, historically minded reading—but also one that does not constrain or delimit the range of interpretation.[127] Religious thinkers, creative and inventive as they may be, work, as do we all, within certain limits and assumptions. Those parameters not only set the terms of their reading and interpretation, but also of the authority they themselves have or do not have, and that the texts and tradition wield over them. Similarly, their readers bring to bear their own limits and assumptions. They see the thinkers and themselves as links in a shared chain or tradition of understanding and authority (and perhaps of revelation). Or they may see the thinkers and themselves as working in different traditions of understanding and authority, even as they work to understand those thinkers not only on their own, the readers', terms, as all share, if not necessarily forms of authority, the fundamentals of the human condition.

James Gordley has nicely captured this distinction between 1.) scholastics, whose commitment to a text from within a normative tradition obligates them to harmonize seeming contradictions and 2.) humanists, for whom the text is not normatively binding in the same way, or who bracket those commitments, and work to understand the text as much as possible in the contexts of how it came to be.[128] One feature of historically minded study, at least to my mind, is that it offers greater promise for imaginatively entering into the thought-worlds of traditionalists and nontraditionalists alike. This meeting point of human recognition and potential for dialogue is where ethics meets epistemology.

And so, I choose in this study not to read Rav Kook's works as a unified canon whose inconsistencies must be resolved in order for him to be authoritative. Rather, I choose to read them, and try to understand him, in terms of his time and place. My preference for this kind of reading is twofold—one epistemological, the other, moral: First, I do, in admittedly modern fashion, think that this reading brings us closer to the truth as we can understand it, which is to say, as lived by human beings like ourselves; second, I believe

---

127 The kind of reading I have in mind here has been nicely characterized as "moderate hermeneutics," in the spirit of Gadamer's "fusion of horizons"; see, in general, Shaun Gallagher, *Hermeneutics and Interpretation* (Albany: State University of New York Press, 1992). One piece of it is suggested by Arnaldo Momigliano's comment that "[m]odern methods of historical research are completely founded on the distinction between original and secondary sources," cited in Paul Veyne, *Did the Greeks Believe Their Own Myths?*, trans. Paula Wissing (Chicago: University of Chicago Press, 1988), 2. While I deeply appreciate much of what Veyne has to say, I differ with his ultimately Nietzschean reading of all knowledge as arbitrary, because that reading leaves us unable to make sense, as readers, of our moral lives.

128 James Gordley, "Humanists and Scholastics," in *Essays on Law and Religion: The Berkeley and Oxford Symposia in Honor of David Daube*, ed. Calum M. Carmichael (Berkeley: University of California at Berkeley, 1993), 13–28.

that historical study, and its interposition of time between past and present, affords a critical distance from which to assess authority claims and their implications for the infliction, or diminution, of human cruelty.[129]

As for my own theological commitments and assumptions, suffice it to say that I am committed to what I think of as the "second-person God" of Abrahamic traditions, such that we and the universe can turn to one another and say, "You"; that at the end of the day, our experience of people, things, and being has a human face, one which summons us to kindness.[130] That You is the ground of our moral obligations and our personhood, and we are the ground of His presence. That You is so all-encompassing, the moral obligations He issues so far-reaching, that utterly identifying Him with any ideology or system is the essence of idolatry; and that eschewal of idolatry is what frees us to be our best selves.[131] I am similarly committed to the Jewish people; to our having a shared, if deeply complicated, history, and our claim to a shared, if sure to be complicated, future. This commitment shapes my angles of vision, areas of concern, and aspiration that studies like this, historicist as they may be, can contribute to Jewish thought and practice in our time.[132]

At the same time, I do not think these commitments preclude dialogue and shared understanding with those who do not also share them, surely not for purposes of an historical study such as the one you are reading now. We can, with inquisitiveness, self-awareness, and humility, imaginatively enter with scholarly tools to a greater or lesser extent into the minds of those living in other times and places, even as we never claim fully to grasp them. On that basis we can arrive at our own judgements—celebratory, critical, and everything in between—aware of our own limitations.

There is perhaps an analogy here to the traditional rabbinic fourfold scheme of reading—*peshat, remez, derash, sod*; which I translate as plain sense, implicit sense, searching, and the unknown: figuring out what the words mean and what the author most likely was trying to say, understanding the historical circumstances and trajectories of ideas of which the writer and text are part, bringing these understandings to bear on our understandings of our own historical trajectories, commitments, and moral existential, questions; and, finally, recognizing the ultimate boundaries of our understandings and the human condition, and how those boundaries shape all we know and do, as we have no choice but to continue to do our best to try, to know, and act.

---

129 For further discussion, see my "Three Questions: Orthodoxy's Power and After" (unpublished paper, 2008), available online at Berman Jewish Policy Archive, bjpa.org/search-results/publication/5241 and at academia.edu.

130 The reader who hears here echoes of Martin Buber, Aharon David Gordon, and Emmanuel Levinas, along with echoes of Rav Kook himself, will not be wrong.

131 The reader who hears here echoes of Reinhold Niebuhr will not be wrong.

132 Much of my own orientation is resonant with that described by Ehud Luz, "Beyn Hagut le-Mehqar be-Mif'alo shel Eliezer Schweid," in *Jerusalem Studies in Jewish Thought: The Eliezer Schweid Jubilee Volume* 19 (2005): 39-62.

1

Childhood and Early Years: Between Mitnagdism, Hasidism, and Haskalah

This chapter outlines Avraham Yitzhak Kook's life and development, from his birth in 1865 to the death of his first wife in 1889, when he was in his first rabbinical post and already embarked on an ambitious program of writing. By early adulthood he had been educated by a range of figures who collectively introduced him to Lithuanian Talmudism, some secular knowledge, currents in medieval and modern Jewish philosophy, some Hasidism, and who gave him entrée into the higher reaches of the rabbinic aristocracy. His earliest writings—and in particular the journal he founded and edited in his early twenties—reveal a deep interest in the thought of Maimonides, and a general orientation that may best be described as a kind of rabbinic Rationalism. He displayed in his youth a striking self-confidence; this was tempered by experiences with which this chapter will close, in particular his having to abandon a promising scholarly career for a rabbinical post in an obscure shtetl out of economic necessity, and the death of his first wife.

The sociocultural milieu of his youth stood at the confluence of several intellectual and cultural traditions, chiefly Lithuanian Talmudism, but also Habad Hasidism, the moderate humanism that was part of the traditional rabbinic literary heritage, and some elements of Haskalah; that latter term is an inescapable if somewhat ambiguous part of the story; the word "Haskalah" is too static and polemically charged to capture the realities of the rabbinic class, as we will see from a close look at one particular example, the *Bildung* of Avraham Yitzhak Kook.

Rabbinic Humanism and Haskalah

Just what "Haskalah" meant across the geographic, temporal, and sociocultural range of Eastern Europe is still open to question and less well understood than the comparatively well-defined contours of German Haskalah.[1] Indeed, one senses that the clichés of both Zionist and Orthodox historiography, and the polemics of which they were a part, have unwittingly conspired to rob the rabbinic classes of Eastern Europe of much of their suppleness and vitality.[2] Benjamin Nathans has called into question the generally accepted picture of Russian Jewish social and political history as driven solely by political and cultural crises, and the same may well be said for intellectual, cultural, and religious history as well. [3] Glenn Dynner has persuasively called attention to the suppleness with which Jewish traditionalists navigated their encounters with modernity, engagements which regularly evade well-worn categories of Orthodoxy, secularization, and Englightenment.[4]

The assumption that tradition and Haskalah were necessarily and always in conflict is, in other words, well past due for revision. Adam Shear has observed that many Eastern European Maskilim saw their engagements as of a piece with tradition; in particular he calls attention to the salience of medieval philosophy as a living intellectual tradition in Eastern Europe well after its passing in the West.[5] What's more, Olga Litvak has spiritedly contested the very characterization of Haskalah as "Enlightenment," as well as the familiar, strong division between Haskalah East and West (inasmuch as a great part of eighteenth-century Germany was for all intents and purposes of a piece with Eastern Europe until the Polish partitions of 1772–1795). Rather, she urges a view of Haskalah as Romanticism, which itself, to her mind, was of a piece with the critical projects of Kant and Rousseau, themselves already moving beyond a narrowly empiricist rationalism.[6] In a different vein, Eliyahu Stern has recently suggested that influential streams of

---

1   See Mordechai Zalkin, "Mehqar Ha-Haskalah be-Mizrah Europa: Hash'arah be-Hash'arah ve-Dimyon be-Dimyon," in *Ha-Haskalah li-Gevanehah: 'Iyunim Hadashim be-Toldot Ha-Haskalah u-ve-Sifrutah*, ed. Israel Bartal and Shmuel Feiner (Jerusalem: Hebrew University/Magnes, 2005), 165–182. More broadly, many conventional and regularly one-dimensional understandings of the term "Enlightenment" in its broader European contexts may themselves be due for some revision. See Jonathan I. Israel's review essay "Enlightenment! Which Enlightenment?," *Journal of the History of Ideas* 67, no. 1 (2006): 523–545. Israel calls particular attention to the comparative neglect of the Radical Enlightenment represented by Spinoza, and of the recognition of national diversity among many Enlightenment thinkers, by historians across the ideological spectrum from conservatives through liberals to postmodernists. Israel's position has been subjected to searching criticism, but is worth noting, if nothing else, for his drawing attention to the semantic range of the word "Enlightenment."

2   See Israel Bartal, "'True Knowledge and Wisdom': On Orthodox Historiography," in "Reshaping the Past: Jewish History and Historians," ed. Jonathan Frankel, special issue, "*Studies in Contemporary Jewry* X (1994): 178–192.

3   Benjamin Nathans, *Beyond the Pale: The Jewish Encounter with Late Imperial Russia* (Berkeley: University of California Press, 2002), 1–15.

4   Glenn Dynner, "Jewish Traditionalism in Eastern Europe: The Historiorgraphical Gadfly," *Polin: Studies in Polish Jewry* 29 (2017): 285–299. While Dynner's primary focus is on Polish Jewry, his observations similarly hold for Jewish traditionalism in the Russian Empire.

5   Shear, "Jewish Enlightenment beyond Western Europe," 252–279.

6   Olga Litvak, *Haskalah: The Romantic Movement in Judaism* (New Brunswick: Rutgers University Press, 2012).

nineteenth-century Eastern European Jewish thought usually labeled Maskilic are better understood asHaskalah are better understood as "Jewish Materialism," a rethinking of Jewish life and history in terms of concrete realities of physical and socioeconomic well-being.[7]

These efforts at rethinking can deepen our understanding of the modern Eastern European rabbinate of late imperial Russia. This group was, certainly, in ideological combat with modernity, but in dialogue with it too, alongside enduring sensibilities bequeathed by a rich premodern rabbinic literature, which made for a more varied range of responses to the genuine intellectual and social dislocations of modernity than is usually assumed.[8]

Thus, Elhanan Reiner has argued that Jewish cultural developments in early modern Central and Eastern Europe, generally regarded as products of the ideological conflicts of modernity, may in truth have resulted as much, and perhaps more so, from internal cultural processes unconnected to those polemics; he points to the advent of printing, which facilitated the republication of medieval philosophical and legal texts, and the flowering of textual and theoretical study in rabbinic culture.[9] Similarly, the eighteenth and nineteenth centuries saw a revival of interest in Maimonides qua philosopher and culture hero among Maskilim, Mitnagdim, and the scholastically oriented Habad school of Hasidism.[10] In other words, rabbinic culture contained components that one may broadly

---

7 Eliyahu Stern, *Jewish Materialism: The Intellectual Revolution of the 1870s* (New Haven: Yale University Press, 2018). Stern's volume appeared after this book was largely completed and a fuller treatment of its relationship to the present work will have to wait for another day.

8 Thus, for instance, Jacob Katz has demonstrated the varied educational experiences of none other than Moses Sofer (aka Hatam Sofer), the founder of Orthodox antimodernity, and Moshe Samet has drawn attention to the nuanced differences between Hatam Sofer's and his disciples' respective attitudes towards Mendelssohn and Wessely; for the English language version of Katz's 1967 study see "Towards a Biography of the Hatam Sofer," in his *Divine Law in Human Hands: Case Studies in Halakhic Flexibility* (Jerusalem: Hebrew University/Magnes, 1998), 403–443. See also Moshe Samet, "M. Mendelssohn, N. H. Wessely ve-Rabbanei Doram," in *Mehqarim be-Toldot 'Am Yisrael ve-Eretz Yisrael le-Zekher Zvi Avneri*, ed. A. Gilboa et al. (Haifa: University of Haifa Press, 1970), 233–257. An interesting volume illustrating Sofer's continuities with traditional philosophical literature is Elimelekh Ozer Bodek, *Bo'u She'arav: Divrei Hatam Sofer 'al Sefer Hovot Ha-Levavot* (Brooklyn: n.p., 1999). The complexity of Sofer's thought, beyond that limned by Katz, and in particular his complex legal and theological dialogue with both rationalism and Romanticism, is richly illuminated in Maoz Kahana's remarkable work *Me-Ha-Noda'-bi-Yehudah le-Hatam Sofer: Halakhah ve-Hagut le-Nokhah Etgarei Ha-Zman* (Jerusalem: Merkaz Shazar, 2015).

9 Elhanan Reiner, "Beyond the Realm of the *Haskalah*: Changing Learning Patterns in the Jewish Traditional Society," *Simon Dubnow Institute Yearbook* 6 (2007): 123-133. My thanks to Prof. Reiner for sharing with me a prepublication version of his work.

10 Allan Nadler, "The 'Rambam Revival' in Early Modern Jewish thought: Maskilim, Mitnagdim and Hasidim on Maimonides' *Guide of the Perplexed*," in *Moses Maimonides: Communal Impact, Historic Legacy*, ed. Benny Kraut (Flushing: Center for Jewish Studies, Queens College, 2005), 36–61. On the uses of medieval philosophical terminology in the circle of the Vilna Gaon, see Allan Brill, "Auxiliary to *Hokhmah*: The Writings of the Vilna Gaon and Philosophical Terminology," 9–37. See also Jay M. Harris, "The Image of Maimonides in

characterize as humanist, which in turn yielded a diverse range of rabbinic responses to modernity, even in Eastern Europe.[11]

Where, then, does premodern rabbinic humanism shade off into Haskalah? At the point where an interest in philosophy, natural sciences, belles-lettres, Bible and Hebrew grammar becomes a self-conscious and critical ideology, explicitly sharing with broader currents in non-Jewish European culture, seeing traditional Jewish society as a mundane structure rather than as a sacred community, a structure that can and should consciously be changed.[12] In this respect, Haskalah partook of what Charles Taylor, reconceptualizing Weber's notion of modernity as "the disenchantment of the world," called "the affirmation of ordinary life," the endowing of nonsacral forms of living with a new significance; and Haskalah's embrace of change was made thinkable by the new understanding of human agency which Eisenstadt identified as a key marker of modernity. Indeed, just as ideological self-consciousness marks the divide between tradition and traditionalism, so too for the divide between premodern rabbinic humanism and Haskalah.[13]

In other words, between the archetypal Russian Maskil, à la J. L. Gordon, and the archetypal antimodern, such as Ya'aqov Lifshitz, lay much middle ground.[14] It was in that middle ground that Rav Kook grew up, and its denizens were his teachers.

No man is merely the sum of his parts, and Rav Kook did eventually create his own syntheses, which we might put in terms of his relationship to a thinker of great consequence, Moshe Hayim Luzzatto, about whom we will have much more to say later on.[15]

Nineteenth-Century Historiography," *Proceedings of the American Academy of Jewish Research* 54 (1987): 116–139 and James H. Lehman, "Maimonides, Mendelssohn and the Me'asfim: Philosophy and the Biographical Imagination in the Early Haskalah," *Leo Baeck Institute Yearbook* 20 (1975): 87–108.

11　My use of "humanism" here follows Eliezer Schweid, *Beyn Ortodoksiyah le-Humanism Dati*, rev. ed. (Jerusalem: Van Leer Institute, 2003).

12　This formulation is suggested to me by the comments of Israel Bartal, "Mordechai Aaron Gunzburg: A Lituanian Maskil Faces Modernity," in *From East and West: Jews in a Changing Europe, 1750–1850*, ed. Frances Malino and David Sorkin (Oxford: Basil Blackwell, 1990), 126–147, and in particular 131–132. My thanks to Dr. Kimmy Caplan for directing me to that essay.

13　I am, of course, in seeing Orthodoxy as a new, ideologically charged response to modernity, following in the large footsteps of Jacob Katz; the distinction between "tradition" and "traditionalism" is taken from Joseph Levenson's work on modern Confucianism; I offer my own understanding and elaboration of these categories in "Modernizing Orthodoxies: The Case of Feminism," in *To Be a Jewish Woman/Lihiyot Ishah Yehudiyah*, Kolech Proceedings, vol. 4, ed. Tova Cohen (Jerusalem: Kolech—Religious Women's Forum, 2007), English section, 37-51.

14　Michael Stanislawski, *For Whom Do I Toil? Judah Leib Gordon and the Crisis of Russian Jewry* (New York: Oxford, 1988). There is as yet no biography of Lifshitz (himself no stranger to modern techniques of publicity and organization), about whom I have more to say in a later chapter.

15　The literature on Luzzatto is steadily growing. For a marvelous discussion of his life and work overall, see Jonathan Garb, *Mequbal be-Lev Ha-Se'arah: Rabbi Moshe Hayim Luzzatto* (Tel

There were, so to speak, three disparate communities of readers of Luzzatto floating around Eastern Europe: the Maskilim who adored his didactic play *La-Yesharim Tehillah*; the Mussar adherents who took his moral-spiritual handbook *Mesillat Yesharim* as their bible; and the Lithuanian Kabbalists for whom the mystical teachings of Luzzato recorded in texts like *Qalah Pithei Hokhmah* were the touchstone. Rav Kook, perhaps uniquely, identified with all three.

Geographic and Cultural Background

The eldest child and firstborn son of Shlomo Zalman and Perel Zlota Kook was born on Thursday, September 7, 1865/16 Elul 5625, in Griva, in the Courland Province of Latvia. He was named Avraham for his maternal grandfather and Yitzhak after a paternal ancestor who was an early follower of Hasidism.[16]

Courland, in southwest Latvia between the Baltic and Western Dvina River, became part of the Russian Empire in 1795. The 1897 census listed some 60,000 Jews.[17] At the time of Avraham Yitzhak's birth in 1865, the total population of Griva numbered some 2,600, with no exact figures for Jews. A suburb of Daugavpils (in German, Dünaburg; in Yiddish, Dvinsk), Griva, which stood on the other side of the Daugava River, essentially consisted of one avenue, roughly two kilometers in length, and several alleyways leading therefrom.[18]

Griva's proximity to Dvinsk gave it a different character from predominantly rural Courland. In the mid–nineteenth century, Jews numbered half of Dvinsk's population of near 23,000, roughly a third of which lived in poverty.[19] Jewish communal leadership was in the hands of several philanthropic, quasi-Maskilic families who endowed the chief charitable institutions. Hasidic-Mitnagdic tensions were also felt at times, to the unusual point, in 1871, of the two groups boycotting each other's hospitals.[20] The Jews of Courland, known as "Courlander Litvaks," were considered a hybrid; many were unlettered, the

---

Aviv: Tel Aviv University Press, 2014) and works to be discussed in further chapters.

16 The couple had a total of seven children, five sons and two daughters.

17 These details are to be found in: Levi Avchinski, *Tolodot Yeshivat Ha-Yehudim be-Kurland*, 2nd ed. (Vilna: Garber, 1912). This edition bears letters of greeting from Rav Kook, as well as from Rav Reines, Baron David Gunzburg, and Rabbi Professor David Simonsen (of Denmark). See also, *EJ*, 5:1003–1006 (all references to *EJ* are to the first edition of 1971). I cannot help noting that Griva's other famous Jewish son was the celebrated abstract expressionist Mark Rothko (1903–1970), who was in his own way, like Rav Kook, a great mystic of light. A similar intuition is at work in Josh Rosenfeld's tender, learned essay "Seeing Silence: Jewish Mystical Experience Refracted through the Art of Mark Rothko," *Hakirah* 21 (Summer 2016): 155–168.

18 Dov Levin, ed. *Pinqas Ha-Qehillot: Latvia ve-Estonia* (Jerusalem: Yad va-Shem, 1988), 80.

19 Ibid., 83–90. See Mordechai Zalkin's "Mehqar Ha-Haskalah," in Levin, *Pinqas Ha-Qehillot*, 181, n. 97, for reference to recent Russian-language studies of the history of Dvinsk Jewry.

20 For the persistence of these tensions over the years, see Zev Aryeh Rabbiner, "Shalosh Qehillot Qodesh," in *Yahadut Latvia: Sefer Zikaron*, ed. A. Ettingen, S. Lifshitz, M. Abramson, and M. Lavi (Tel Aviv: 'Igud Yotzei Latvia ve-Estonia be-Yisrael, 1953), 305–309

synagogues commonly followed the Hasidic rite, people spoke more German than Russian and even more of those languages than Yiddish. At the same time, and certainly among the rabbinic classes, high Lithuanian Talmudism exerted a powerful pull, above all through the educational influence and moral authority of the yeshiva at Volozhin.[21]

Founded in 1803 by Hayim of Volozhin (1749–1821), an outstanding disciple of Elijah ben Solomon, the Gaon of Vilna (1720–1797) (about whom more in a moment), the yeshiva, unlike traditional *batei midrash*, had no formal ties to the local community and fostered an intense youth culture of full-time Talmudic study.[22] A pioneering, vastly influential institution and exemplar to the many Lithuanian yeshivot that were to come, it reflected the interests, passions, and contradictions of its time; through its doors passed many young men who would leave their marks on all sides of the Jewish ideological barricades of the time.

Hayim of Volozhin's master, Elijah ben Solomon, known as the Gaon (roughly, "the great master" or "the genius") of Vilna, had occupied no formal rabbinic post, and indeed his brand of fierce Talmudism was implicitly oppositional to, and at the least distinct from, traditional modes of study and religious practice.[23] Of course, the ideal of *Torah*

---

21 B. Rivkin, "Courlander Litvaks," in *Lite*, ed. Mendel Sudarsky and Uriah Katzenellenbogen (New York: Kulturgeselshaft fun Litvishe Yidn, 1951), 408–416.

22 On the history of Volozhin, see Shaul Stampfer, *Ha-Yeshiva Ha-Litait be-Hithavutah* (Jerusalem: Merkaz Shazar, 1995). References herafter are to this first edition of Stampfer's work, unless otherwise noted.

23 A full-length, comprehensive study of the Gaon remains a desideratum, though given the titanic nature of its subject it may be nearly unattainable. Immanuel Etkes, *Yahid be-Doro: Ha-Gaon mi-Vilna—Demut ve-Dimuy* (Jerusalem: Merkaz Shazar, 1998), presents an essential collection of studies on the Gaon, his circle, influence, relationship to both Hasidism and Haskalah and the perception of him by his contemporaries. A collection of excellent studies covering nearly all his facets, is Hallamish, Rivlin, and Schuchat, *The Vilna Gaon and His Disciples*. For a brief, powerfully argued survey of his Kabbalistic teachings, see Yosef Avivi, *Qabbalat Ha-Gra* (Jerusalem: Kerem Eliyahu, 1993), which will be further discussed below.

Eliyahu Stern's *The Genius: Elijah of Vilna and the Making of Modern Judaism* (New Haven: Yale University Press, 2013) is a noteworthy effort at situating the Gaon's project in broader intellectual horizons, even bearing in mind the issues pointed out by Eliyahu Krakowski in "Between the Genius and the Gaon: Lost in Translation," *Hakirah* 16 (Winter 2013): 153–175. I agree with Stern that the Gaon is in many ways a modern figure, but differ on the specifics, and think the Gaon's distinctive sort of modernizing traditionalism is better understood in terms of Eisenstadt's framework of "multiple modernities." On the Gaon's modernistic approach to textual study, see the incisive discussion in Kahana, *Me-Ha-Noda'-bi-Yehudah le-Hatam Sofer*, 153-161.

The role attributed to the Gaon by his disciples in fostering proto-Zionism has been the subject of lively discussion on both sides; the champion of the traditional view is Arie Morgenstern, whose studies have been collected in his *Meshihiyut ve-Yishuv Eretz Yisrael be-Mahatzit Ha-Rishonah shel Ha-Me'ah Ha–19* (Jerusalem: Yad Ben-Tzvi, 1985) and *Mistiqah u-Meshihiyut* (Jerusalem: Ma'or, 1998). Israel Bartal's spirited responses are to be found in his collection *Galut ba-Aretz* (Jerusalem: Ha-Sifriya Ha-Tzionit, 1994), 236–295. After this book was done there appeared Immanuel Etkes, *Ha-Tzionut Ha-Meshihit shel Ha-Gaon mi-Vilna:*

li-shmah, of Torah study for its own sake, had been a staple of rabbinic Judaism since antiquity, yet through the Gaon's teachings, and perhaps more importantly his personal example, fierce devotion to Torah study as the supreme religious act burned itself into the minds of his followers. Institutionally, the late seventeenth and early nineteenth centuries had seen the development in Central Europe of the *kloyz*, a study house unattached to the local synagogue. This development in some ways prefigured the Gaon, both in terms of the differentiation of Torah study from the range of religious communal activities, and for the comparatively critical and independent inquiry into the texts that was fostered by this new arrangement.[24] The Gaon inspired his disciples to take this model a step forward.

Though as versed in Kabbalah as in Talmud, the Gaon was central to catalyzing Mitnagdism, literally "oppositionalism," a principled resistance to the spread of Hasidism, for what he saw as its reckless dissemination of esotericism, careless denigration of study and detailed halakhic practice, and overly optimistic faith in human nature's resistance to sin.[25] It was through the yeshiva in Volozhin, and Hayim of Volozhin's vision, administrative acumen, and conciliatory personality that the reigning ideal of Mitnagdism— of Torah study as the supreme religious act—received its institutional articulation and much of its hold over Lithuanian Jewry.[26] His treatise *Nefesh Ha-Hayim,* which provided a Kabbalistic argument for the study of exoteric, and strictly legal, rabbinic texts as the

---

Hamtza'atah shel Masoret (Jerusalem: Carmel, 2019); especially pertinent for our work are his exchanges there with Raphael Schuchat.

24 This point emerges from Yisrael Ta-Shma's essay "Ha-Gra u-Ba'al 'Sha'agat Aryeh,' 'Ha-Pnei Yehoshu'a' ve-Sefer 'Tzion le-Nefesh Hayah': Le-Toldoteyhem shel Ha-Zeramim Ha-Hadashim be-Sifrut Ha-Rabbanit 'Erev Tenu'at Ha-Haskalah," *Sidra* 15 (1999): 181–191. See also Elhanan Reiner, "Hon, Ma'amad Hevrati ve-Talmud Torah: Ha-Kloyz ba-Hevrah Ha-Yehudit be-Mizrah Europa ba-Me'ot Ha-17 ve-Ha-18," *Tzion* 58, no. 3 (1993): 287–328, and Maoz Kahana, *op. cit* 11–118, 124–133, 138–141, and 147–148.

25 On the phenomenon of Mitnagdism in general, see Allan Nadler, *The Faith of the Mithnagdim: Rabbinic Responses to Hasidic Rapture* (Baltimore: Johns Hopkins University Press, 1997); I have discussed this work and the possible place of Mitnagidsm in the study of religious experience in "A Severe Ecstasy," *The New Republic*, April 27, 1998, 38–41. It should be remembered that early Hasidism also had a concept of *Torah li-Shmah*, but it was more clearly theurgic, aiming less at the intellectual substance of the text than taking study as a vehicle for *devequt*. See, for instance, Roland Goetschel, "*Torah Lishma* as a Central Concept in the *Degel Mahaneh Efrayim* of Moses Hayyim Ephraim of Sudylkow," in *Hasidism Reappraised*, ed. Ada Rapoport-Albert (London: Littman, 1997), 258–267.

26 See Immanuel Etkes's essay on Hayim of Volozhin in his *Yahid be-Doro*, 162–222. Stampfer, *Ha-Yeshiva Ha-Litait*, 38, correctly points out that opposition to Hasidism per se does not appear in any of the surviving writings of Hayim or his circle regarding the founding of the yeshiva. Yet Etkes seems correct in observing nonetheless that the sense of a crisis of Torah study pervading his writings, and his thoroughgoing attempt in his theological treatise *Nefesh Ha-Hayim* to present Torah study as precisely the spiritual vehicle that Hasidim sought, cannot be detached from his effort at establishing the yeshiva; Etkes, *Yahid be-Doro*, 215–266, n. 14. It may well be that Hayim of Volozhin's generally conciliatory personality and perhaps his desire to put a positive face on his endeavor and entice Hasidim to his institution accounts for the absence of overt reference to Hasidism in the texts Stampfer describes.

preferred form of *devequt*, or *unio mystica* (though in this case the better term is perhaps *unio scholastica*), laid a theological foundation for the comparatively academic structure and non-Kabbalistic curriculum of this new form of yeshiva.

Nonetheless, by the mid- to late nineteenth century, there were in fact significant numbers of Hasidim throughout the Mitnagdic heartland of Northeastern Lithuania, which bordered on Kook's native Courland, including, as we have seen, Dvinsk, Courland's major city and just across the river from Griva. These were largely, though not entirely, the scholastically minded Lubavitch, or Habad, Hasidim, who drew their strength from their proximity to the Habad centers in White Russia.[27]

Family Background

Avraham Kook's father, Shlomo Zalman Kook, born in 1844, was orphaned at a young age and raised in the home of his stepfather, the rabbi of Razhiche.[28] His father, Nahum, a wheat merchant, was an alumnus of Volozhin, and Shlomo Zalman studied there in his turn. Shlomo's mother, Frayde Batya, was the daughter of Rabbi Dov Ber Jaffe, an early disciple of Hayim of Volozhin and staunch opponent of Hasidism, who nonetheless tended toward the Hasidic custom of long, devotional prayer.[29] The Jaffes descended from the great sixteenth-century halakhist Mordechai Jaffe, author of the *Levushim*, an important halakhic compendium, which in some ways presented itself as a somewhat philosophically minded alternative to the *Shulhan 'Arukh*. His descendants took great pride in this ancestry, which at times seems to have given them some sense of aristocracy and may indeed explain some of the striking self-confidence which Kook displayed from early on.[30] Frayde's brother and Shlomo Zalman's uncle, Mordechai Gimpel Jaffe (1820–1891), rabbi

27 See Mordechai Zalkin, "Between Dvinsk and Vilna: The Spread of Hasidism in Nineteenth-Century Lithuania," in *Within Hasidic Circles: Studies in Hasidism in Memory of Mordechai Wilensky*, ed. Immanuel Etkes, D. Asaf, Israel Bartal, and Elchanan Reiner (Jerusalem/Tel Aviv: Mossad Bialik/Hebrew University/Tel Aviv University, 1999), 21–50.

28 It's unclear what the family name originally was; on the title page to his collection of sermons from the mid–1890s *Midbar Shur*, Rav Kook refers to his father's last name as Schorr; if this were the case, then Kook was a Yiddish pun on the Hebrew meaning of the German "Schorr," that is, "seeing."

29 See J. L. Maimon, ed., *Azkarah le-Nishmat Ha-Ga'on Ha-Tzadiq Ha-Re'ayah*, vol. 1 (Jerusalem: Mossad Ha-Rav Kook, 1937–1938), 7–167, 11.

30 See Moshe Zvi Neriah, *Sihot Ha-Re'ayah ve-Orot Mishnato* (Jerusalem: Moreshet, 1979), 99, 134. It bears noting that Rav Kook's 1907 treatise *'Etz Hadar*, his entry into the lists of the long-standing controversies over the *etrogim*, ritual citrons, of Palestine and Corfu, revolves entirely around the Levush's halakhic positions. The sense of halakhic aristocracy among the descendants of Levush was made explicit by another descendant of Levush, Eliyahu Aqiva Rabinowitz (1861–1917), eventually the editor of *Ha-Peles*, the venue of the essays of Rav Kook's that are discussed in chapter five, see Rivkah Blau, *Learn Torah, Live Torah, Love Torah: Ha-Rav Mordechai Pinchas Teitz, the Quintessential Rabbi* (Hoboken: Ktav, 2001), 3–8. On the *Levushim*, see Lawrence Kaplan, "Rabbi Mordechai Jaffe and the Evolution of Jewish Culture in Poland in the Sixteenth Century," in *Jewish Thought in the Sixteenth Century*, ed. Benard

of Otyan and later Ruzhinai, was also an alumnus of Volozhin, a distinguished scholar, communal leader, a moderate rabbinic Maskil, and later a significant figure in proto-Zionist circles.[31] Jaffe was also an in-law of Yosef Zekharia Stern (1831–1904), the rabbi of Shavil, a leading halakhist who combined traditionalist conservatism with wide learning and interests, and whom we will meet as our story unfolds.[32]

Cooperman (Cambridge, MA: Harvard University Press, 1983), 266–282, a condensation of his PhD dissertation.

31 At Volozhin, Jaffe was a contemporary of Mordechai Eliasberg, Shmuel Salant, and the young Naftali Zvi Yehudah Berlin. He was a moderate Maskil, who read history and philosophy and wrote in a fine Hebrew prose style. In his rabbinical posts he reportedly imposed taxes on wealthy merchants for the benefit of the poor and made a point of getting on well with local non-Jews. At the same time, he vigorously polemicized during the Lilienblum controversy of 1869–1870, to be discussed below, and publicly opposed the opening of Reform-minded seminaries. Like other rabbinic Maskilim, he began to see settlement in Palestine as a means of physical and spiritual rejuvenation of the Jewish people that skirted the threats of reform. He eventually moved there and was the rabbi of early Jewish settlements. For a brief biography, see Benjamin Jaffe, *Ha-Rav mi-Yehud* (Jerusalem: Ha-Histadrut Ha-Tzionit, 1958). Brief memoirs and other topical writings are gathered in Jaffe's *Mivhar Ketavim* (Jerusalem: n.p., 1978). See also the entry on him by Meir Geshuri, *Entziklopedia shel Ha-Tzionut Ha-Datit*, s.v. "Rabbi Mordechai Jaffe."

32 On him, see the brief biographical volume by Zev Rabbiner, *Ha-Rav Yosef Zekharia Stern* (Jerusalem: WZO and Mossad Ha-Rav Kook, 1943), A. Yerushalmi, "Yosef Zekharia Shtern," in Sudarsky and Katzenellenbogen, *Lite, 1366–1370*, and the introduction to the critical edition of his responsa to *Even Ha-'Ezer, Zekher Yehosef* (Jerusalem: Makhon Yerushalayim, 1994). There is also lengthy discussion of the ups and downs of his rabbinic career in Mordechai Zalkin, "Social Status and Authority in Nineteenth-Century Lithuanian Jewish Communities," in *Central and East European Jews at the Crossroads of Tradition and Modernity*, ed. J. Verbickiene et al. (Vilnius: The Center for Studies of the Culture and History of East European Jews, 2006), 174–187. My thanks to Prof. Zalkin for sharing this essay with me.

Stern read the works of Mapu, Micha Yosef Levenson, and J. L. Gordon and subscribed to *Ha-Tzefirah*. He published a book on aggadah, which I will discuss in chapter four. By all accounts, he did not suffer fools gladly, but was thought of as a man of the people, kind to the masses, and regularly withering to his colleagues. In his Bible commentaries published in 1874–1875 he defends rabbinic tradition while adopting Maskilic categories of plain sense of the text, reading texts in terms of their political meanings, and explicitly doing so in order to write things "that will win the hearts of all the parties." See Yehuda Galinsky, "Darko be-Parshanut shel Yosef Zekharia Stern" (unpublished paper, 1988). He was a good friend of Hayim Hezekiah Medini (see introduction to Medini's *Sdei Hemed*, vol. 10 (Warsaw: n.p., 1901), 4. On his far-flung correspondence with his rabbinic peers, see Hayim Hamiel, "Yahasei RY"Z Stern ve-Rabbanei Doro be-Shut," in *Sefer Shragai*, vol. 4, ed. Yitzhak Refael (Jerusalem: Mossad Ha-Rav Kook, 1983), 133–167. My thanks to Dr. Galinsky for directing me to this article, as well as for sharing his paper with me. Among his regular correspondents was Rav Kook's future father-in-law, Aderet—see Shlomo Albert, *Aderet Eliyahu* (Jerusalem: n.p., 2003), 45–47.

A brief, interesting article by Shraga Abramson argues that Stern wrote much of his work without recourse to books, working largely from memory, and proves this by showing his

After his studies at Volozhin and his marriage, Shlomo Zalman Kook studied for three years with Rabbi Eliyahu Hayim Meisel (1821–1912), who at the time was rabbi of Drohytshyn (Turets) in the Grodno region.[33] Eventually, Shlomo Zalman moved to his wife's hometown, Griva; he taught the local boys and worked as a mendicant fundraiser for various institutions.[34]

One can gather only a limited impression of Shlomo Zalman from the few mentions of him in the writings of his illustrious son and others; he seems to have been a gentle soul. In one obituary profile he is remembered as a learned Talmudist, a great lover of traditional scholarship and scholars, a man of strong character, characterized by "love of truth and strong hatred of anything with a trace of lying or fakery," as well as being of "gentle disposition and beaming countenance . . . it was truly a pleasure to converse with this man on different matters, and in every subject he showed cleverness and deep understanding."[35] One of the few distinctive halakhic practices attributed to him indicates a mix of piety and humor;[36] his few pages of halakhic writing are glosses to the *Shulhan 'Arukh* and, interestingly, to Israel Meir Ha-Cohen's celebrated moralizing treatise on the evils of gossip *Hafetz Hayim*; the latter would seem to bear out the pietistic personality attested to by his contemporaries.[37]

The one surviving piece of Kook's writing amounting to any sort of personal testament is a brief *cri de couer* entitled "Remove the Stumbling Block" (see Isa. 57:14) in the premier issue of *Ha-Peles* (1901), the same issue in which his son published the first part

---

various mistakes—see "Tiqqunim be-Teshuvah Ahat shel Ha-RY'Z Stern," *Ha-Ma'ayan* 32, no. 1 (Fall 1991): 49–52.

33 Rabbi Meisel, an alumnus of Volozhin, served in a number of rabbinic posts and in 1873 became rabbi of Lodz, a position he held until his death, at age ninety-one in 1912. In this major post, Rabbi Meisel developed a reputation for piety, a gentle disposition, charitable activities, relative ecumenism within the Jewish community, concern for 'agunot (grass widows), and his ability to deal effectively with the local authorities. He was reportedly an intimate of Isaac Elhanan Spektor and Joseph Soloveitchik. See brief biographical information in Raphael Halperin, *Atlas 'Etz Hayim: Aharonim* (Tel Aviv: Heqdesh Ruah Ya'aqov: 1978), 2:197; and Avraham Yehudah Barzhazhinsky, *Rabbi Eliyahu Hayim Meisel, zl* (Tel Aviv: n.p., 1956). There is also a two-volume hagiography in Yiddish, published under the auspices of Jerusalem's 'Edah Haredit—Menahem Mandel, *Dos Leben un Shafn fun dem Gaon un Tzadik, Rabbi Eliyahu Hayim Meisel* (Jerusalem, n.p., 1985). An appreciation of him by Yehi'el Ya'aqov Weinberg, written in 1913, appears in his *Li-Feraqim* (Jerusalem, n.p., 2004), 126–139. My thanks for this reference to Prof. Marc B. Shapiro.

34 This work entailed much travel and Rav Kook reminisced in later years of crossing the river to Dvinsk to meet his father on his return; Neriah, *Sihot*, 41.

35 Shabtai Daniel, *Ha-Hed*, March 1930, 12. See also the comments in Moshe Zvi Neriah, *Tal Ha-Re'ayah* (Bnei Braq: Hai Fisher, 1993), 15.

36 When he would drink some tea with milk before morning prayers, he would first recite Ps. 30, inasmuch as verse 10, "What is to be gained from my death [literally, my blood]? Can dust praise You?," fulfills the Talmudic requirement (BT Berakhot 10b) that one may not eat "before praying for one's blood." This is cited in *'Olat Re'ayah*, 1:186.

37 They appear as an appendix to his son's posthumously published *Mitzvat Re'ayah*, 99–103.

of his major essay on nationalism. In it he comes across as a pious man, anguishing at the religious laxity-cum-financial success of many of the rabbis—far more successful than he—whom he encountered in years of wearying travels as an itinerant fundraiser.[38]

Shlomo Zalman's wife and Rav Kook's mother, Perel Zlota (I have been unable to ascertain her maiden name) was the granddaughter of one Avraham, rabbi of Preil (in Latvian, Preili), near Dvinsk, who composed his own glosses to Zohar and was, in family legend, a saint.[39] His son, her father Refael, studied at Volozhin but nonetheless became a disciple of the third Lubavitcher rebbe, Menahem Mendel Schneerson, known as *Tzemah Tzedeq* (1790–1866), and remained attached to the latter's grandson, Shlomo Zalman of Kapust (Kopst) (1830–1900), protégé of his grandfather, author of *Magen Avot*, and a leading figure of Habad in his time.[40] Shlomo Zalman of Kapust's father, Yehudah Leib, a more ethereal figure than his brother (the fourth Habad Rebbe, Shmuel of Lubavich, aka Maharash [1834–1882]), operated at a remove from the movement as a whole, out of a mix of dynastic politics and subtle, but genuine, theological debates.[41]

There was a Hasidic preacher in Griva, Yehezqel Yanover; according to family tradition, it was Perel Zlota's father Refael who brought him there; according to other sources he had been a roving fundraiser and emissary for Shlomo Zalman of Kapust and after a foot ailment ended his career he was sent by the latter to Griva to spread the teachings of Habad.[42] Rav Kook recalled regularly being taken to Yanover for the third Sabbath meal, done in Hasidic manner, with singing and quasi-mystical discourses, and Habad youngsters were among his childhood friends.[43]

---

38 *Ha-Peles* 1 (1901): 33–34; Neriah incorrectly lists the date as 1900 and offers a brief snippet of quote, omitting the essay's rhetorical heat and pointed critique of contemporary rabbis. The main subject of the essay is laxity as regards tefillin and one cannot help but wonder, the discrepancy in dates notwithstanding, if these experiences of his fueled his son's heated rhetoric on the subject, to be discussed in the next chapter.

39 *Igrot*, 1:129, discusses Rav Kook's unsuccessful attempts to have the glosses published.

40 On him, see briefly H. Heilman, *Beis Rebbe*, vol. 3 (Vilna: Rosenkranz, 1904), 62–64.

41 See Ariel Roth, "Reshimu—Mahloqet Hasidut Lubavitch ve-Kapust," *Da'at* 30 (2013): 221-252 and Eli Rubin, "Rabbi Shmuel Schneersohn of Lubavitch ('Maharash,' 1834-1882) and the False Twilight of Habad Hasidism" (unpublished paper, 2020); my thanks to Rabbi Rubin for sharing his and Roth's article with me.

42 Berel Kagan, *Yiddishe Stodt, Shtetlakh un Dorfishe Yishuvin in Lite* (New York: n.p., 1991), 223.

43 One of them, Yehoshua Herschler, who lived nearby, recounted that when Avraham Yitzhak would come to his house to sip a cup of tea, he would recite texts by heart as he drank—see Zev Rabbiner, *Or Mufla': Maran Ha-Rav Kook ztz"l* (Tel Aviv: n.p., 1972), 68. I don't know of any works by Yanover. However, Avraham Zvi Brodna, in the preface to his *Quntres Liqutim u-Ve'urim* on *Tanya* (Jerusalem: n.p., 1921), writes that Yanover was his teacher in Tanya, and interested readers may want to consult that volume, though so far as I can tell, he does not quote any of Yanover's teachings directly. (My thanks for this reference to the late, lamented, Rabbi Yehoshua Mondschein.)

Social Changes: Haskalah's Shift from Enlightenment to Radicalism

As Avraham Kook grew during the 1870s and early 1880s large changes were affecting Jewish life in the Russian Empire, culminating in dramatic political, cultural, and economic shifts in the 1880s.[44] Earlier, I noted Benjamin Nathans's well-taken caution against the excesses of the "crisis-driven" historiography of Russian Jewry as a whole.[45] That being said, the metamorphosis of tradition into traditionalism that yielded Orthodoxy was clearly a sign of ferment, which the traditionalists experienced as deeply threatening, and Orthodoxy's emergence was dialectically tied to the uncertain fortunes of Russian liberalism.[46] Through the 1870s, Russian liberalism, such as it was, fell on hard times, and socialism and nationalism in their various permutations sought to offer their own alternative solutions for the economic, political, and sociocultural difficulties of the Jews. Among the Jewish intelligentsia this gave a new complexion to the decades-long debates surrounding Haskalah.

Haskalah had been a leading, highly contested edge of cultural change as it moved eastward through the nineteenth century. It projected an optimistic faith in education and progress, and internalized non-Jewish critiques of Jewish society's insularity and economic insufficiency while asserting its own continuity with elements of tradition (for instance, Hebrew and medieval philosophy). At the same time, the mid-century circles of Vilna Haskalah, exemplified by Shmuel Yosef Fuenn (1818–1890), for instance, forcefully asserted Jewish distinctiveness and continuity with the textual heritage of rabbinic Judaism.

One feature of Russian Haskalah had been the way it saw itself not as overthrowing traditional Judaism but as reinterpreting the tradition—in particular, its adaptation of varied intellectual legacies for the sake of a forward-looking engagement with dramatically changing times.[47] Thus, Maskilic ethics emphasized moral education as a synthesis of Enlightenment notions of *Bildung* with traditional Jewish morality, conjoining the themes

---

44 The depiction of the 1880s as a time of crisis is well captured by Jonathan Frankel, who expostulates at length on the traumatic effects of the pogroms of 1880–1881. See his *Prophecy and Politics: Socialism, Nationalism and the Russian Jews, 1862–1917* (Cambridge: Cambridge University Press, 1981), 49–132; for a somewhat different view that lays greater emphasis on the developments of the 1870s, see Stanislawski, *For Whom Do I Toil?*, 146ff.

45 A further, provocative reframing of Russian Jewish history is a major theme of Yuri Slezkine's extraordinary study *The Jewish Century* (Princeton: Princeton University Press, 2004). Slezkine's book is not without its problems, not least his thoroughly ignoring traditional and rabbinic Judaism in, of all settings, Eastern Europe.

46 On the first stirrings of Orthodoxy qua ideology in Russia, see Michael Stanislawski, *Tsar Nicholas I and the Jews: The Transformation of Jewish Society in Russia, 1825–1855* (Philadelphia: Jewish Publication Society, 1983), 148–154.

47 My account here follows Immanuel Etkes, "Immanent Factors and External Influences in the Development of the Haskalah Movement in Russia," in *Toward Modernity: The European Jewish Model*, ed. Jacob Katz (New Brunswick: Transaction Books, 1987), 13–32. On Fuenn, see Shmuel Feiner, ed., *Mi-Haskalah Lohemet le-Haskalah Meshameret: Mivhar mi-Kitvei Rashi Fuenn* (Jerusalem: Merkaz Dinur, 1993).

of self-cultivation found in medieval Jewish philosophical ethics with characteristically modern conceptions of religion as social morality and the subjective self as the locus of reason and meaning.[48] Given the general absence in Russia of widespread, meaningful emancipation, Haskalah "offered a haven for Jews caught between an inaccessible larger cultural world and an unacceptable Jewish one."[49]

The Maskilim overall were never more than a small percentage of Russian-Jewish society, which remained overwhelmingly traditional through the nineteenth century; yet, through their interactions with leading financial and political figures, the new medium of the periodical press, and their reputation for influence among ruling circles, imagined or real, they emerged as a force in Jewish society disproportionate to their numbers. By the 1870s, the Maskilim had their own publications and introduced a new point of orientation—"the voice of the people"—and a new form of competition with the rabbis, namely, means of mass persuasion. As Maskilim became progressively disenchanted with the government, they were, at times, even able to join forces with some rabbis inasmuch as they could see them as representatives of the people.[50] Many younger Maskilim, such as Moshe Leib Lilienblum, largely autodidacts from Lithuania and White Russia, became increasingly distanced from both the hitherto admired Russian intelligentsia and traditional religious society and began to think of both in terms of structural reforms and of national identity.[51]

It was in nationalism that disenchantment with liberalism could meet the continued need to answer the pressing problems facing Russian Jewry from within a framework that respected at least some internal Jewish social and cultural values. It is worth recalling that nationalism and liberalism were not always seen as at odds with one another, certainly not in the nineteenth century when nationalism as a moral claim for both autonomy and the expression of identities of one's own choosing challenged the multinational Russian, Austro-Hungarian, and Ottoman Empires (later swept away in

---

48   See Harris Bor, "Moral Education in the Age of Jewish Enlightenment" (PhD diss., Cambridge University, 1996). For a brief presentation, see his "Enlightenment Values, Jewish Ethics: The Haskalah's Transformation of the Traditional *Musar* Genre," in Feiner and Sorkin, *New Perspectives on the Haskalah*, 48–63. For a characteristic text from the period we are discussing, see the 1841 text of Fuenn's in Feiner, *Mi-Haskalah Lohemet le-Haskalah Meshameret*, 100–102.

49   Steven J. Zipperstein, *The Jews of Odessa: A Cultural History, 1794–1881* (Stanford: Stanford University Press, 1985), 12. My use of the term "semi-neutral society" is taken from Jacob Katz, *Out of the Ghetto: The Social Background of Jewish Emancipation, 1770–1870* (New York: Schocken Books, 1978).

50   Eli Lederhendler, *The Road to Modern Jewish Politics: Political Tradition and Political Reconstruction in the Jewish Community of Tsarist Russia* (New York: Oxford University Press, 1989), 133. Lederhendler, "Modernity without Emancipation or Assimilation? The Case of Russian Jewry," in *Assimilation and Community: The Jews in Nineteenth-Century Europe*, ed. Jonthan Frankel and Steven J. Zipperstein (Cambridge: Cambridge University Press, 1992), 324–343.

51   See Israel Bartal, "Beyn Haskalah Radiqalit le-Sotzialism Yehudi," in *Ha-Dat ve-Ha-Hayim*, ed. Immanuel Etkes (Jerusalem: Merkaz Shazar, 1993), 328–335.

World War I) from below.[52] It is no accident that liberal nationalism had an easier time and more lasting legacy under the broadly tolerant Hapsburgs than under the autocratic tsars. As Haskalah metamorphosed into radicalism and nationalism it partook of currents coursing through Russian society as a whole, such as the return to the people, the call for apocalyptic change, and the self-perception of some Romantic radicals as inspired prophetic leaders.[53]

Rabbinic Maskilim

The last third of the nineteenth century was also a time of great turmoil within the rabbinic fraternity. The early decades of the century had seen some, though not many, Eastern European rabbinic Maskilim, such as the singular Menashe of Ilya (1767–1831), a disciple of the Gaon, and Menahem Mendel Lefin (1749–1826), respected figures who, while not representing a broadly based social movement, nonetheless drew on Enlightenment ideas, as well as medieval and Renaissance Jewish philosophy, in formulating their various programs of intellectual and educational reform.[54]

In mid-century, the Mussar movement inaugurated by Israel Lipkin, known as Israel Salanter (1810–1883), another alumnus of Volozhin, arose within Mitnagdism as a limited if probing critique of the single-mindedness of Torah study relative to the challenges of modernity, and sought to place greater emphasis on moral and religious self-cultivation.[55] The Mussar writings of Israel Salanter—drawing in part on Maskilic writings—also confronted the notion of the internal, subjective self that was accepted by Haskalah, even if only to defeat, or at best transform it; like Mitnagdism, it also proceeded without

---

52 Recent years have seen a resurgence of interest in late ninteteenth century liberal nationalism. Among the works I have found most helpful are the discussion of Austro-Marxism in Douglas Irvin-Erickson, *Raphael Lemkin and the Concept of Genocide* (Philadelphia: University of Pennsylvania Press, 2017), Yael Tamir, *Liberal Nationalism* (Princeton: Princeton University Press, 1995), and Eric D. Weitz, "Self-Determination: How a German Enlightenment Idea Became the Slogan of National Liberation and a Human Right," *The American Historical Review* 120, no. 2 (April 2015): 462–496.

53 A very helpful formulation of this cluster of phenomena is Hamutal Bar-Yosef, "Mah le-Tzionut u-le-Geulah Meshihit? Ha-Reqa' Ha-Russi ve-Hidhudav ba-Sifrut Ha-Ivrit," in *Mehuyavut Yehudit Mithadeshet*, vol. 2, ed. Avi Sagi and Zvi Zohar (Jerusalem/Tel Aviv: Hartman Institute, Ha-Kibbutz Ha-Meuhad, 2001), 773–799.

54 On Menashe, see Yizhak Barzilay, *Manasseh of Ilya: Precursor of Modernity Among the Jews of Eastern Europe* (Jerusalem: Magnes Press/Hebrew University, 1999), as well as David Kamenetzky, "Ha-Ga'on Rabbi Menashe me-Ilya ztz"l," *Yeshurun* 20 (2008): 729–781, who forcefully argues for Menashe's committed traditionalism. On Lefin, see Nancy Sinkoff, "Strategy and Ruse in the Haskalah of Mendel Lefin of Satanow," in Feiner, *New Perspectives*, 86–102; Lefin's *Heshbon Ha-Nefesh*, which made a deep impression on Salanter, draws heavily on the self-improvement regimens of Benjamin Franklin, whose French memoirs Lefin read.

55 See generally, Immanuel Etkes, *Rabbi Yisrael Salanter ve-Rei'shitah shel Tenu'at Ha-Mussar* (Jerusalem: Magnes/Hebrew University Press, 1982). Lefin's influence on Salanter is discussed therein on 143–146.

reference to the spiritual vocabulary once associated with Kabbalah, and with no connection to Hasidism, which had little traction in Lithuanian Jewry.[56] I will have much more to say on this later on.

Mid-century figures of the Vilna Haskalah took an active part in public and religious life, trying to integrate tradition and reform. The following generation of the 1860s-1870s saw the emergence of a new subgroup within the heart of the rabbinical community, figures who despite their resolute commitment to traditional halakhah and Torah study, were willing to approach social problems with new intellectual tools and categories, and sought to create a middle ground between radical Maskilim and traditionalist rabbis. Among them we find Rav Kook's great uncle Mordechai Gimpel Jaffe and his in-law Yosef Zekharia Stern, Mordechai Eliasberg (who would be Rav Kook's near, though not immediate, predecessor in his second rabbinical post), along with Yehiel Mikhel Pines, Yitzhak Reines, Shmuel Mohilever, and others.[57] These men, born between 1820–1840, had been educated and socialized into the traditional rabbinic elite, often at Volozhin, regularly had some knowledge of languages (usually German) along with natural sciences and grammar, and wrote mainly in the Hebrew periodical press of the time. One can trace among them a shared path of intellectual development, beginning with criticism of the economics of Jewish life, moving towards calls for educational reform, then some halakhic reform and, finally, in the 1880s, association with the nascent Hibat Tzion, whose nationalist agenda was seen as the rational follow-on to their earlier concerns.

It also bears noting that these men were not Hasidic, as Hasidic elites seemed largely immune both to moderate Haskalah and, later, nationalism.[58] This perhaps resulted from Hasidism's strong internal organization, as well as from the political quietism engendered by its mystical religiosity.[59]

---

56 The point is made in ibid., 132–134; it bears noting that throughout Hayim of Volozhin's commentary on Tractate *Avot*, *Ruah Hayim*, a compilation of lecture notes by his students and published in Vilna in 1859 by the legendary Romm printing house, humility is featured as a, and perhaps the, paramount religious virtue inasmuch as it is the necessary prerequisite to Torah study.

57 For the generational understanding of this phenomenon, see Yosef Salmon, "Masoret, Modernizatziyah u-Le'umiyut: Ha-Rav Ha-Maskil ke-Reformator ba-Hevrah Ha-Yehudit be-Russia," *Sefer Bar-Ilan* 28–29 (2001): 23–39. An English version of this essay is: "Enlightened Rabbis as Reformers in Russian Jewish Society," in Feiner and Sorkin, *New Perspectives on the Haskalah*, 166–183.

58 For instance, Mordechai Jaffe's rabbinical seat, Ruzhinai, was known—along with Kosoveh (home of the Hazon Ish), Pruzhin (seat of Hayim Soloveitchik's in-law Eliyahu Feinstein), and Slutzk—as one of the four Lithuanian *karpas* towns where Hasidism never had any adherents at all. *Pinqas Slutzk*, 101, cited in Nathan Kamenetsky, *Making of a Godol* (Jerusalem: Ha-Mesorah, 2002), 136.

59 This is the analysis of Ehud Luz, *Maqbilim Nifgashim: Dat u-Le'umiyut bi-Tenu'ah Ha-Tzionit be-Mizrah Europa be-Rei'shitah, 1882–1904* (Tel Aviv: 'Am 'Oved, 1985), 159. See also Joseph Dan, "Kefel Ha-Panim shel Ha-Meshihiyut be-Hasidut," in Etkes et al., *Be-Ma'agalei Hasidim*, 299–315, and, on early Habad anti-Zionism, Aviezer Ravitzky, *Ha-Qetz Ha-Meguleh u-Medinat Ha-Yehudim: Meshihiyut, Tzionut ve-Radikalism Dati be-Yisrael* (Tel Aviv: 'Am 'Oved, 1993).

Of particular interest are the polemics of the late 1860s around religious change.[60] In the mid–1860s, moderate Maskilim sought some rapprochement with moderate rabbis and the Maskilic journal *Ha-Melitz* opened its pages to, among others, Y. M. Pines, who, beginning in 1867, penned a series of articles arguing for limited but genuine halakhic change in the light of changing times, particularly as regards commerce with non-Jews. In response to these discussions Moshe Leib Lilienblum wrote a series of progressively radical articles on halakhic change, with increasingly stringent criticisms of halakhic method and the notion of a divine Oral Torah, and he called on rabbis to support his program of reform. Lilienblum's essays drove a wedge between radicals and the Maskilic rabbis and provided a powerful stimulus to the crystallization of a separatist Orthodoxy more self-conscious and ideologically mobilized than the Orthodoxy that had first taken shape in the 1840s.[61] At that point, possible rabbinic involvement in religious reforms went by the boards.

In this episode, the discourse surrounding halakhic change that had animated and agitated Western European Jewish thinkers since the earlier part of the nineteenth century attempted to migrate eastward. There it encountered a rabbinic culture that had, as it were, been fortified by the culture of Talmudism championed by Volozhin, or put a bit differently, whose members had been profoundly socialized into an identity that left them able and prone to resist. In other words, tradition had by then become traditionalism, or Orthodoxy. Moreover, the generally uncertain fortunes of liberalism in the East effectively gave the notion of reform little traction in a social setting where what was required was a large-scale solution for the suffering of the masses rather than, as in the West, facilitating the adaptation of individual Jews to a surrounding society that offered some welcome, however limited.

By the 1880s, the cohort of traditionalist Maskilic rabbis had effectively shifted their interests and thinking from moderate reform within Russia towards the nascent idea of rejuvenating Jewish life by the development of Palestine, under the rubric of Hibat Tzion, about which I will have more to say in chapter five.[62] Olga Litvak has argued that the turn to Jewish nationalism starting in the 1880s, rather than being a turn away from Enlightenment, is better seen less as a rejection of Haskalah, than as a continuation by other means of the overall project of "Jewish regeneration sponsored through a reforming state," albeit rather a different state than the one earlier Maskilim had in mind.[63] While

---

60 On this episode, see Gideon Katznelson, *Ha-Milhamah Ha-Sifrutit beyn Ha-Haredim ve-Ha-Maskilim* (Tel Aviv: Devir, 1954). The Lilienblum controversy is discussed at length in Stern, *Jewish Materialism*.

61 Around this time Spektor's secretary Ya'aqov Lifshitz bought *Ha-Levanon* so as to provide a mouthpiece for staunchly traditional rabbis.

62 See Yosef Salmon, *Religion and Zionism: First Encounters* (Jerusalem: Magnes/Hebrew University Press, 2002), 96–140.

63 That the notion of sovereign statehood was likely not as utterly central to nascent Zionist thought as is regularly thought is forcefully argued by Dmitry Shumsky in *Beyond the Nation-State: The Zionist Political Imagination from Pinsker to Ben-Gurion* (New Haven: Yale University Press, 2018).

Litvak may be overstating the role of the state as such, certainly when it comes to Maskilic-minded traditionalist rabbis, she is right to note the more subtle gradations of responses to modernity those figures lived and thought.

This was the setting in which Avraham Yitzhak Kook grew up and these men were among his relatives and teachers.

Childhood and Early Education

Avraham Yitzhak Kook's early education was supervised by his father and by his maternal grandfather. Reports of his childhood in many ways match the familiar narrative of the young Talmudic prodigy, or *iluy*, known to us from elsewhere in Eastern Europe: photographic memory, prodigious capacities for long hours of study, powerful concentration, and an agile mind, all receiving much encouragement and positive reinforcement from parents and teachers.[64] At the same time, the anecdotes about him also bespeak a highly emotional sensibility, a love of nature, fervent prayer, and rich verbal gifts. He tellingly reminisced in later years that his parents had a playful running disagreement as to whether he would in the end be a Mitnagdic Talmudist or a Hasidic rebbe.[65]

At the age of nine, Avraham Yitzhak Kook was sent across the river by his father to study with Reuven Levin (1810–1887), the Mitnagdic rabbi of Dvinsk, a rabbinic apprenticeship which lasted until he was fifteen.[66] A native of Smorgon, known by the nickname "Rav Ruvele,"[67] he was in his youth a student of Yehudah Leib Shapira, rabbi of Smorgon (1787–1853), disciple of Hayim of Volozhin, and of Menashe of Ilya (1767–1831).[68]

Levin was a much revered and somewhat individualistic figure in Lithuanian rabbinic circles, a kind of "Talmudist's Talmudist" despite his never achieving the fame or communal authority of some of his contemporaries.[69] While Neriah recounts Rav Kook's saying

---

64 I have long thought that a sociohistorical study of the *iluy* as cultural type in Eastern Europe with comparison to Jewish communities in the Middle East, the Ottoman Empire, and North Africa would be very worthwhile.

65 He related this in the early 1930s to his disciple Shmuel Kalmanson, who recorded it in his collection of Rav Kook's Shabbat afternoon homilies, *Shemu'ot Ha-Re'ayah* (Jerusalem: Agudat Ha-Sneh, 1939), 6.

66 J. L. Maimon recounts a conversation with Rav Kook in which Rav Kook said that he had been interested in going to study with Levin and so his father sent him— Maimon, *Azkarah*, 21–22.

67 Before going to Dvinsk he was rabbi in the communities of Lavdova, Ayonya, Ilya, Nasvizh, and Amchislav. A brief biographical sketch of him appears as an appendix to Zev Rabbiner's biography of his celebrated successor Meir Katz, known for his commentaries on, respectively, the Bible and Maimonides' Code, *Meshekh Hokhmah* and *Or Sameah*; see his *Maran Rabbeinu Meir Simha Kohen ztz"l* (Tel Aviv: n.p., 1967), 265–287.

68 Menashe was himself a native of Smorgon, where the young Kook would study, regularly spent time there in his later years and served as rabbi in 1827–1828. Levin's having studied with Menashe of Ilya in his youth was conveyed to me in an interview (Jerusalem, April 28, 2003) with Rabbi Elhanan Shapira, a direct descendant of Yehudah Leib Shapira.

69 This emerges from the comments about him by none other than Eleazar Shakh in his *Shimushah shel Torah* (Bnei Braq: Bergman, 1998), 65–75. Levin's one volume of forty-three responsa and

in later years that Levin rarely consulted *Shulhan 'Arukh* in his responsa and preferred to work directly from the medievals, in truth, his responsa themselves, notwithstanding their lengthy theoretical flavor, display more than ample discussion of the views of *Shulhan 'Arukh* and its latter-day commentators.[70] It stands to reason that his reported comments to various students seemingly scanting *Shulhan 'Arukh* were meant partially as pedagogy, partially in jest even as, like other halakhists of his time and place, Levin would cite and relate, but not defer, to it.[71] In later years, Rav Kook recounted Levin's emphasis on the works of the Geonim and medieval Talmudists as more faithful guides to the Talmud than later commentators, inasmuch as those authors worked first and foremost to understand the texts and arrive at proper halakhic decisions, and his downplaying innovating brilliant novellae.[72] One of Levin's specialties was finding novel halakhic arguments that would enable *'agunot* (grass widows) to remarry.[73] When, in one such case, young Kook tried to outdo his master in argumentation and thus undo his permissive ruling, Levin cited to him the Talmudic passage (BT 'Eruvin 48a) "If we are so exacting we will not be able to study."[74]

---

sermons *Rosh la-Re'uveni* (Daugavpils and Riga: Bilike, 1936), appearing nearly half a century after his death, was published by his grandson, Yitzchak Levin, with the financial support of his brothers who had migrated to Los Angeles and the Bronx.

70 In his preface, the publisher, Levin's grandson, cites three passages in the responsa, nos. 4, 10, and 11, which seem to illustrate a Talmudic methodology which eschews casuistry and the writings of later authorities; these comments are cited by Neriah and others by way of explaining the fascination and suasion exercised by Levin on the young Avraham Kook— Neriah, *Sihot*, 72. On closer inspection, they are less illuminating than they seem. The first is directed to a rabbi who tried to use what at best would be a minority opinion among medieval commentators to allow the innovation of using a telegraph pole as a marker for the Sabbath boundary (Hebrew: *'eruv*), while the latter two of those three comments are directed to one particular correspondent, whom Levin took to task in two separate responsa for his systematic misunderstanding of the plain sense of rabbinic texts.

For some evidence of a theoretical cast of mind in Levin's work, see for instance his responsum no. 19, 58–73, in which a question about illicit cohabitation becomes the springboard for a small treatise on Maimonides's understanding of legal doubt and probabilities. The second part of the book (208–254) consists of his sermons. They tend to be long pilpulistic sermons for Shabbat Ha-Gadol and Shabbat Shuvah.

71 My thanks to Prof. Jay Harris for this formulation.

72 Neriah, *Sihot* 69. Rav Kook quotes Levin several times in later halakhic works; see his *'Etz Hadar* (Jerusalem: n.p. 1907), 26b (section 18); more strikingly, for the long memory displayed therein, see his reponsum in *Da'at Cohen* (1933), no. 30, 82. For several anecdotes regarding his memories of Levin, see Neriah, *Sihot*, 66–74.

73 This is noted in Rabbiner, *Maran Rabbeinu Meir Simha Kohen ztz"l*, 267. For a discussion of how and why this was a major problem of the time and the broader social, economic, and legal trends involved, see ChaeRan Y. Freeze, *Jewish Marriage and Divorce in Imperial Russia* (Hanover: Brandeis University Press/University Press of New England, 2002).

74 This, according to Maimon. In Neriah's version, the the question was regarding a dispensation from levirate marriage to a freethinker—*Sihot*, 70

Studies in Lyutsin and Smorgon and Engagement with Haskalah

In the custom of peripatetic young Talmudists, Kook, at the age of fifteen, in 1880, left home for Lyutsin (Ludza), a Latvian town whose Jews, a number of them Maskilim, comprised one half of the population of some four thousand,.[75] The rabbi there was Eliezer Don-Yehiya (1838–1924), whose family was associated with the Lubavitch offshoot favored by Rav Kook's grandfather.[76] Rav Kook later recalled "his shining face, greatness of soul, treasure of good and grace, straightforward reasoning and broad knowledge . . . and all residing in a well-sculpted physical form, amazingly fit and healthy."[77] The rabbi had no yeshiva, and instead sat with his students in a traditional *beit midrash*.[78] Don-Yehiya's biographer tells us that he made a point of teaching regular classes to laypeople, including classes in the aggadic compilation *'Eyn Ya'aqov* as well as *Menorat Ha-Maor*, a precedent which Kook would later follow.[79] He also studied the works of Albo and Maharal;[80] the latter was not standard fare among Lithuanian rabbis but more common among Hasidim

---

75 Levin, *Pinqas Ha-Kehillot*, 160–167. According to the available information listed in the table on 160, the total population of Lyutsin was 3,578 in 1868 and 5,140 in 1897. A school of general education for Jewish boys was established in 1865, the same year as the local Talmud Torah's founding. In 1887, five years after Kook left, the local merchants founded a Talmud Torah that incorporated Russian and mathematics as well, with some forty students.

76 His father Shabtai, was, like Kook's maternal grandfather, a disciple of the *Tzemah Tzedeq*, and one of Don-Yehiya's brothers was the rabbi in Kapust; see Shabtai Daniel, *Eliezer Don-Yehiya* (Jerusalem: Urim, 1932), 10–11, 37n10. Though the name was in all likelihood originally pronounced as "Don-Yahya," I am following the pronunciation adopted by the rabbi's descendants.

77 This vigorous appearance, he continues, "recalled to us the physical heroism of the primal forefathers, the heroes of Israel, David and Solomon and the prowess of individual Talmudic sages, fathers of Torah, whose physical heroism, bequeathed to us by the sacred tradition, adorned their great, holy, soul, rich in supernal beauty." This is in his preface to Daniel, *Rabbi Eliezer Don-Yehiya*, 4-5 and is to be found as well in Neriah, *Sihot*, 58.

78 As noted earlier, Volozhin was the first yeshiva to function as a stand-alone institution unconnected to the local community.

79 Daniel, *Rabbi Eliezer Don-Yehiya*, 21.

80 During those years, Rabbi Don-Yehiya was compiling the responsa he would complete in 1891 and eventually publish in 1893, with letters of approbation from Rabbis Isaac Elhanan Spektor and Shlomo Ha-Cohen of Vilna, under the title *Even Shtiyah*; in the preface, he cites Maharal and Albo; Eliezer Don-Yehiya, *Even Shtiyah* (Vilna: Katzenellenbogen, 1893). Contemporary issues figure in the book in some interesting ways; in his introduction he discusses at length the Talmudic narrative of the tensions between Rabbi Meir and Rabbi Shimon ben Gamliel (BT Horayot 13b–14a) which he reads in terms of two tensions: the time-honored Talmudic distinction between textual erudition and analytic acuity (*Sinai ve-'oqer harim*) and that between rabbis who have acquired their posts by inheritance or governmental appointment rather than by dint of their own accomplishments. In responsum no. 5 he polemicizes with those who would read Talmudic passages to say that some sages would forego the mitzvah of Sukkah on account of economic necessity. The volume also includes an exchange between himself and Rabbi Levin of Dvinsk (165–168, responsa nos. 70–71).

and it may have been Don-Yehiya who first introduced Kook to the works of Maharal, which would later serve him as a model of aggadic exegesis.[81]

Also resident in Lyutsin at the time was a former student of Levin's and a relative of the Kooks, Ya'aqov Rabinowitz, Shlomo Zalman Kook's first cousin.[82] Rabinowitz worked as a banker and taught Talmud to a small circle of half a dozen or so students, which his young cousin now joined. In later years, Rav Kook recalled that his two teachers exemplified the two faces of Talmud study: Don-Yehiya emphasized encyclopedic knowledge of many texts, while Ya'aqov Rabinowitz emphasized in-depth study of specific passages.

Rabinowitz was a self-professed Maskil, a Bible enthusiast with a fine Hebrew prose style, who maintained a large personal library, including works of philosophy and *Wissenschaft,* in which his young cousin spent many hours; in later years Rav Kook recalled him as "great scholar and a man of broad knowledge."[83] It seems likely that Rabinowitz served as what Iris Porush has characterized as a "Maskilic tutor," the older friend or relative who would introduce a young protégé to the unfamiliar precincts of Haskalah.[84] Indeed, during his hours in Ya'aqov Rabinowitz's library Avraham Yitzhak Kook began to craft verse, including parodies of Maskilic poetry; when on his return to Griva for the High Holidays he brought his father his notebook of poems the latter did not hide his disappointment; the next year he brought home a notebook full of Talmudic studies.[85]

---

81 See the introduction to Moshe S. Kasher and Yaacov Belkhrovitz, eds., *Perushei Ha-Maharal Mi-Prag Le-Aggadot Ha-Shas* (Jerusalem: Torah Shlemah, 1968), particularly 26–35. See also Bezalel Safran, "Maharal and Early Hasidism," in *Hasidism: Continuity or Innovation?,* ed. Bezalel Safran (Cambridge, MA: Harvard University Center for Jewish Studies/Harvard University Press, 1988), 47–144. We will have much more to say on this in chapter four.

82 Basic biographical details are to be found in Neriah, *Tal,* 46-47, n. 1. It was at Rabinowitz's wedding to the daughter of a wealthy townsman that the young Kook first met his famous great-uncle Mordechai Gimpel Jaffe. According to familial legend, when, as was customary at weddings, the male guests engaged in learned discussion, Jaffe was struck by the intelligence and knowledge of "the boy from Griva" and asked as to who he was, he discovered that this was none other than his grand-nephew. Either he hadn't known him beforehand, or was perhaps being coy.

83 *Talmid Hakham gadol ve-ba'al de'ah rehavah,* cited in Neriah, *Tal,* 47.

84 On the formative experiences of reading for Eastern European Maskilim and their tutelage at the hands of their tutors, see Iris Parush, *Nashim Qor'ot: Yitronah shel Shuliyut* (Tel Aviv: 'Am 'Oved, 2001), 101–135. Another student of Rabinowitz's who gained exposure to Maskilic writing in his circle, a few years after Avraham Kook, was none other than Hayim Tchernowitz (Rav Tzair)—see his memoir *Pirqei Hayim* (New York: Bitzaron, 1954), 79–81.

85 This is taken from part 4 of Neriah's serialized life of Rav Kook, which appeared in *Zera'im* 6 (Nisan 5636/Spring 1936): 3–4. The stories about young Rav Kook's attraction to Maskilic literature and to poetry and the minor conflict with his father do not appear in Neriah's later volumes.

A written version of a sermon he delivered in his home town on that visit home in the fall of 1881 is Kook's earliest extant writing; he plays on Ps. 11:2–3 ("For see the wicked bend the bow. . . . When the foundations are destroyed, what can the righteous do?"), reading it as saying that the evildoer who seeks to lure others away from divine service will begin by

The detailed reminiscences of his study partner, *havruta*, in Lyutsin, the journalist and educator Avraham Schower (1960–1930), written in the 1920s and '30s, add to our store of anecdotes about the young Kook's piety, prodigious capacity for study, and heightened emotional sensibility.[86] More interestingly we learn that he dressed in the style of Maskilic boys, took care to pronounce Hebrew grammatically, wrote verse, read the works of Malbim and Moshe Hayim Luzzatto's didactic play *La-Yesharim Tehillah*, a favorite of East European Maskilim,[87] and exhibited other characteristically Maskilic behaviors. He also regularly expressed Orthodox attitudes severely critical of modernization and secular university education; his priestly lineage as a Cohen meant a great deal to him; and he did not know Russian.

A lengthy (seemingly unfinished) essay by Kook, quite possibly written during his time in Lyutsin, in which he attempts to thrash out the claims and merits of natural science, affords a glimpse into some of his theological preoccupations during this time.[88] The tone throughout is one of guarded appreciation of scientific knowledge along with resistance to its claims to larger meaning. With explicit citations to a range of texts and thinkers,[89] he defends the superiority of Torah and tradition over and against the pre-

---

chipping away at rabbinic enactments and ordinances. It is reproduced in Maimon, *Azkarah*, 26.

86 Schower's reminiscences first appeared in New York's *Yiddishe Tageblat*, March 11, 1924, were translated into Hebrew in *Zer'aim* (Kislev 5696/Winter 1935), and are reprinted in Neriah, *Tal*, 21–27. His correspondence regarding Rav Kook and the latter's visit to the US in 1924 are therein at 27–33, and further recollections are on pp. 194–209. A longer version of Schower's reminiscences was published in Hebrew under the title "Mi-Zikhronotai 'al Ha-Rav Avraham Yitzhak Ha-Cohen Kook," in *Hedenu: Jubilee Publication* [*of the Students' Organization of the Rabbi Isaac Elchanan Theological Seminary and Yeshiva College*], ed. Hyman E. Bloom (Bernard Revel festschrift) (New York: Talmidei Yeshivat Rav Yitzḥaḳ Elḥanan, 1936), 184–191. A further reminiscence of Schower's is recorded by Samuel K. Mirsky, *Beyn Sheqiyah li-Zerihah* (New York and Jerusalem: Sura, 1951), 211. A brief sketch and necrology of Schower appears in Mirsky's *Eretz ve-Yamim* (New York/Jerusalem: Sura, 1953), 94–96. Schower was the father of the well-known artist Raphael Soyer and grandfather of the late distinguished historian Ezra Mendelsohn.

87 See Shmuel Verses's monograph, "Dimuyo shel Rabbi Moshe Hayim Luzzatto be-Sifrut Ha-Haskalah," in his *Haqitzah 'Ami: Sifrut Ha-Haskalah be-'Idan Ha-Modernizatziyah* (Jerusalem: Hebrew University/Magnes Press, 2004), 3–24, esp. 4.

88 It is reprinted in *Otzarot*, 2:269–286; the editor suggests that it was written sometime before 1883. Indeed, given his Maskilic turn during his time in Lyutsin, it seems the likely venue for this youthful composition.

89 In the course of the essay he makes reference to Maimonides, ibn Ezra, Bahya ibn Paquda, Yedaya Bedershi (not an obvious choice), *Sefer Yetzirah*, and *Tiqqunei Zohar*; he also speaks in terms reminiscent of Maharal (specifically, repeated invocations of the *sikhli* as the defining characteristic of both humanity and Torah), and perhaps reminiscent as well of the *Binah le-'Ittim* of Azariah Figo (Picho) (1579–1647) which was reprinted numerous times in Eastern Europe and which, we will later see, he explicitly quotes in one of his first published essays. On Figo and, in particular, his discussion of science, see David B. Ruderman, "Jewish Preaching and the Language of Science: The Sermons of Azariah Figo," in *Preachers of the Italian*

tensions of modern science which, its obvious accomplishments notwithstanding, is no match for rabbinic tradition in the depth of its understanding, its grasp of the underlying ideational structure of the universe or its contribution to human perfection—the first appearance of a concept which we will see emerge as a major theme in Kook's early writings.

After his two years in Lyutsin, at age eighteen, in 1883, Kook spent a year in Smorgon (Smorgonie) in Grodno.[90] He studied with the local rabbi Hayim Avraham Shapira (1821–1887), who provided him with room and board and offered as his study partner his own young son-in-law, Tanhum-Gershon Belinski. A successful merchant who never took a salary, Hayim Avraham is referred to in an obituary notice in *Ha-Levanon* as "a man wise in the ways of the world," and was a member of the Lithuanian rabbinic aristocracy.[91] It was in all likelihood Shapira's connections that had led Levin to steer Kook there, notwithstanding his initial plans to study elsewhere, which in turn tells us something about Levin's estimate of his student's future potential in the Lithuanian rabbinic aristocracy.[92]

Ghetto, ed. David B. Ruderman (Berkeley: University of California Press, 1992), 89–104. He may have been influenced as well here by Pinhas Horowitz's *Sefer Ha-Berit*, which we will discuss in Chapter Four.

90   Smorgon was an industrial town filled with tanneries, along with other light industry and bakeries (the town's bagels achieved special notoriety). Jews comprised roughly two-thirds to three-quarters of the town's population of 8,000–9,000—see *EJ* 15:12–13.

91   His brother Raphael Shapira of Volozhin was the son-in-law of Naftali Berlin and father-in-law of Hayim Soloveitchik. Hayim Shapira had inherited the post from his father, the famous Yehudah Aryeh Leib, a disciple of Hayim of Volozhin and, as we have seen, a teacher of Reuven Levin of Dvinsk; Abba Gordon et al., eds., *Smorgon: Mehoz Vilna: Sefer, 'Edut ve-Zikaron* (Tel Aviv: Irgun Yotz'ei Smorgon be-Yisrael, 1965), 88, 90–91. Among Hayim Avraham Shapira's better-remembered actions as rabbi was the levying of a tax on local merchants to provide for the poor and for soldiers being taken to the tsar's army. In the entry on Rav Kook in Samuel Noah Gottlieb's rabbinic directory *'Ohalei Shem* (Pinsk: Gluberman, 1912), 492–493, Shapira is described as *ha-gevir*, or "the man of means." The entry also makes a point of mentioning the shaping influence of Levin on Rav Kook. See also the reminiscences of his great-grandson Hayim Karlinsky in *Ha-Darom* 40 (Tishrei 5735/Fall 1974): 186–187.

92   In 1924 Rav Kook related to Rabbi Belinski's grandson Hayim Karlinsky the circumstances of his arrival in Smorgon. En route to study in Kreve (Krewo) for that year, he stopped at Smorgon after a wheel on the carriage broke and needed repair. Visiting Shapira as the wagon was being fixed, he presented the rabbi with an impromptu discourse on the Talmudic laws of ritual purity regarding unhitched carriages (Mishnah Kelim 18:1–2, cited in BT Shabbat 42b, 46a), and it was that which led the rabbi to ask his young visitor to stay. Rav Kook's younger brother Dov later told Karlinsky that, in fact, while going to Kreva had been Don-Yehiya's idea, Levin had not been in favor and so urged Kook to visit Shapira en route in Smorgon, his hometown, and give his regards. The broken axle afforded him the time to go pay the call, during which he was won over by Shapira's warmth and generosity; Hayim Karlinsky, "'Al Tekufat Limudo shel Maran Ha-Grayah Kook be-Smorgon," *Shanah be-Shanah* (Jerusalem: Heikhal Shlomo, 1982): 389–398. Information on Kreva is scarce; see Kagan, *Yiddishe Stodt*, 695. One can only guess as to Levin's thinking here; in all likelihood he thought that Kreva

Both Maimon and Neriah assert that it was during his year in Smorgon that Kook took to heart the teachings of Israel Salanter; neither provides evidence for that claim other than an anecdote reported by the mature Rav Kook's intimate disciple Ya'aqov Moshe Harlap—no doubt striking in its own right—that on hearing of Salanter's passing, on 25 Shevat 5643/February 2, 1883, he rent his clothes and performed other rites of mourning.[93] Interestingly, Rav Kook also reminisced in later years that traces of Menashe of Ilya still lingered in Smorgon, and that the town elders regularly recalled his tenure and in particular the empathic moralizing of his sermons.[94]

Taken together, by age eighteen, Avraham Yizhak Kook had been exposed via a variety of teachers and personalities not only to Talmudism but to the classics of medieval philosophy, to more explicitly Maskilic ideas and to some Hasidic and Mussar ideas as well. He had received much encouragement and seemed on his way to a promising rabbinic career.

Betrothal and Aderet

On his return from Smorgon in the spring of 1884 he met with Rabbi Eliyahu David Rabinowitz-Teomim, renowned Talmudist, rabbi of Ponevezh and later of Mir (1842/3?–1905), who sought a husband for his eldest daughter Bat-Sheva Sarah Rivka, who was born in 1867.[95] He was to leave an extraordinary impression on his son-in-law, who published

---

was a rural hamlet beneath his protégé's talents; the rabbi there at the time, Nisan Broyde, a student of Mordechai Gimpel Jaffe and supporter of Hibat Tzion, was a young man, only eight years senior to Kook; he died an untimely death in 1904 at age forty-seven, see *Entziklopedia shel Ha-Tzionut Ha-Datit*, s.v. Broyde, Nisan.

93 Maimon, *Azkarah*, 32, 35; Neirah, *Sihot*, 85.

94 Ibid., 78. Years later, in a letter to his brother, then studying in Smorgon in a study circle known as the *kibbutz*, in the winter of 1897, he recalls the place "whose name and memory is engraved for love on the tablet of my heart . . . the city in which [I] found at the beginning of my way a holy grouping full of sages and scribes, acute and erudite, pious and God-fearing, whose company broadened my heart and led me to cultivate the talents of my youth." *Igrot*, 1:7. On the history of his brother's study circle, organized along more formal lines and among whose other members included Eliezer Silver, Meir Karelitz (brother of the Hazon Ish, and son-in-law of Shlomo Ha-Cohen of Vilna), Mordechai Rozenson, father of Esther Raziel, and a number of eventual Socialists, see Gordon et al., *Smorgon*, 95–97. Some early halakhic novellae written by Kook during his time in Smorgon are to be found at Maimon, *Azkarah*, 27–37.

95 For a brief biographical sketch of Aderet, see *EJ* 13:1479–1480. In his lifetime, Aderet published only a small measure of his many novellae and responsa; a number of his works, displaying his great erudition and regularly ingenious interpretive abilities, have been published in recent years, see in particular the responsa collection *Ma'aneh Eliyahu* (Merkaz Shapira: Or Etzion, 2003). Interestingly, he also authored a commentary on the *Sefer Ha-Hinukh*, and a supercommentary on the *Minhat Hinukh* of Joseph Babad, entitled *Heshbonot shel Mitzvah*, which has recently been published from manuscript (Jerusalem: Makhon Yerushalayim, 2005). See also his novellae published as *Hidushei Ha-Ga'on Ha-Aderet* (Brooklyn: Makhon Kitvei Ha-Aderet be-Artzot Ha-Berit, 2003). That edition contains a lengthy biographical

a book-length appreciation of him on his death.[96] Rabinowitz-Teomim, known by his acronym Aderet, was phenomenally learned and gifted; shortly after turning bar-mitzvah, he composed *Shevet Ahim* with his twin brother Zvi Yehudah, a treatise surveying the implicit editorial and juridical rules of the Talmud, displaying vast knowledge of the entirety of rabbinic literature, all the more remarkable for the authors' tender ages. On the manuscript's publication in 2003, the editor's introduction lists no fewer than eighty-eight works by him, most still in manuscript, not to mention twenty sets of glosses to other works and articles of his in rabbinic periodicals.[97]

Aderet left a memoir, *Seder Eliyahu,* begun in 1900, a strikingly, at times embarrassingly, candid depiction of his life and experiences.[98] Appended to it is his ethical will, *Nefesh David,* a moving and powerful document in the light of which one understands why he was such a powerful role model of piety for his son-in-law and many others.[99]

In the memoir's pages, Aderet comes across as an erudite, gentle, harried soul, longing for the peace of the study hall, burdened by much wounded pride, recounting again and again how, though his erudition and acuity had always amazed his interlocutors over the years, he never quite proved able to reap the rewards of his intellectual talents. His life story, an unrelenting chronicle of bereavement, poor health, premature mortalities, bitter squabbles among rival rabbis for decently paying pulpits, and promises broken by capricious in-laws and rapacious congregants, sheds a harsh light on the dire socioeconomic circumstances of many Lithuanian rabbis of the time.[100]

---

introduction by Eliezer Katzman, which in keeping with the norms of Haredi censorship, does not mention Rav Kook by name but only as "his son-in-law the rabbi."

96 *Eder Ha-Yaqar,* (Jerusalem: n.p., 1906) Admittedly, the volume is more a forum for Rav Kook's ideas, many of them we will see him developing in this work, than a full-length study of Aderet, but his reverence for his father-in-law is unmistakable. On the circumstances surrounding that volume's appearance, see A. R. Malachi, "Ha-Pulmus 'al Ha-Rav Kook ve-Sifro 'Eder Ha-Yaqar,'" *Or Ha-Mizrah* 15, no. 3 (1965): 136–144.

97 *Sefer Shevet Ahim,* ed. Ya'aqov Moshe Hillel (Jerusalem: Ahavat Shalom and Yad Shmuel Franco, 2003). My thanks to Eliezer Brodt for this very valuable reference.

98 *Seder Eliyahu: Toldot Ha-Ga'on Rabbi Eliyahu David Rabinowitz-Teomim (Ha-Aderet), Ketuvot bi-Yedei 'Atzmo* (Jerusalem: Mossad Ha-Rav Kook, 1983). Rabbinic autobiography was not a common genre, but not entirely unknown. For a listing of rabbinic memoirs and discussion of some of the historiographical issues involved, see Jacob J. Schacter, "History and Memory of Self: The Autobiography of Rabbi Jacob Emden," in *Jewish History and Jewish Memory: Essays in Honor of Yosef Hayim Yerushalmi,* ed. Elisheva Carlebach, John M. Efron, and David N. Myers (Hanover: Brandeis University Press, 1998), 428–452, esp. 442–446.

99 It is also published as an appendix to *Eder Ha-Yaqar.* He seems also to have kept a journal of his dreams and of halakhic novellae revealed to him in dreams. See Neriah, *Tal,* 88; Katzman says it was titled *Ba-Halom Adaber.*

100 On the economic travails of the Lithuanian rabbinate, see Mordechai Zalkin, "Issachar and Zebulun—A Profile of a Lithuanian Scholar of the 19th Century," *Gal-Ed* 18 (2002): 125–154; my thanks to Prof. Jay Harris for directing me to this article. Another discussion, which draws heavily on Aderet's memoir, is Immanuel Etkes's "Beyn Lamdanut Le-Rabbanut be-Yahadut Lita ba-Me'ah Ha–19" in his *Yahid Be-Doro,* 223–246. An English version is "The Relationship

Over the years, nine of his thirteen children died at young ages, calamities that he took to be divine punishment for his own sins; heart, eyesight, and respiratory problems began to afflict him. As his wife slipped into serious, if understandable, depressions he undertook years of wanderings around the cities of Europe in search of physicians and Torah scholars. His travels took him to Vilna, Warsaw, Bialystok, and farther west to Vienna and Pressburg, all along the way picking up letters of recommendation from rabbis and scholars, presumably in the hope that these would help him secure some sort of position down the road. In 1874 he finally became rabbi of Ponevezh, where he had been lecturing for some years. His weekly salary of nine rubles was paid intermittently, and the townspeople were not above taking advantage of his naiveté in business matters. At some points he was forced to take the extraordinary expedient of going on strike, which consisted of refusing to answer halakhic questions. In this respect at least the nascent socialist stirrings of the time seem not to have passed Aderet by.

When it came time to find his eldest daughter a husband he began to ask around and heard about young Kook, who, aside from being an upstanding young man and pious scholar from a fine family, had saintly parents to whom Aderet's poverty didn't matter.[101] He suggested they meet in Riga in the summer, and his reaction to his prospective son-in-law was immediate and moving: "And when I laid eyes on him and spoke to him for several hours, my soul cleaved to him, I loved him profoundly, as I got my first glimpse of him and his extraordinary talents and piety and [saw] that he would become a mighty cedar." After a meeting between the prospective couple in Dobvelen (Dubulti), where Aderet would sometimes go to take the waters, the betrothal agreement was signed back in Dvinsk in the fall, and Avraham Yizhak Kook set off for a year's study in Volozhin.[102] His prospective father-in-law promised him several years of room and board after the wedding so he could further his studies.[103]

---

between Talmudic Scholarship and the Institution of the Rabbinate in Nineteenth-Century Lithuanian Jewry," in *Scholars and Scholarship*, ed. Leo Landman (New York: Yeshiva University Press, 1990), 107–132.

101 This clearly emerges from the relevant pages in his memoir.

102 By the terms of their agreement, Aderet sent him a ruble a week, and clothing for his year in Volozhin, and promised him a total of 800 rubles and three years of room and board upon the marriage.

103 In 2012, the Kedem Auction House sold a letter by an unidentified author to Ya'aqov Rabinowitz (Auction 27, Lot no. 466), dated two months after Avraham Yitzhak Kook's betrothal to Bat-Sheva Rabinowitz-Teomim, which mentions a prior, broken engagement. In the portion available online at the time of the auction, one can read in the margins: "I was informed that our relative Reb Avraham Yitzhak Ha-Cohen became engaged to daughter of Av Bet Din of Ponevezh; I would like to know whether this is true as well as additional details since I was very happy to hear that he was miraculously saved from Av Bet Din of Turetz" (Eli Stern and Shay Mendelovich, *Auction 27 Catalogue—Books, Manuscripts, Rabbinical Letters*, June 11, 2012, Kedem Auction House, Jerusalem (Jerusalem: Keter Press Enterprises, 2012), 258. While this seems to be referring to Eliyahu CHayim of Turetz, whose *Aderet Eliyahu* was published in Vilna in 1894 by Rosenkranz and Schriftzetser (the latter is, presumably, not a proper name but a reference to the typesetters). in his introduction to that volume, the

Avraham Kook Goes to Volozhin

On his arrival in Volozhin, Avraham Yitzhak Kook was thrust into a more dynamic yeshiva environment than he had known before, as indeed, it hardly existed anywhere else. Talented young men came to Volozhin from all over Eastern Europe for intensive study, 365 days a year.[104]

There he studied with, and became a disciple of, a world-class Talmudist, the head of the yeshiva. Naftali Zvi Yehudah Berlin (1816–1893), whom he regularly and reverently referred to as his master and teacher for the rest of his life.[105] Known by his acronym,

---

author laments at length his childlessness, such that he could not have been the prospective father-in-law.

My efforts to see the letter have been unsuccessful and I know nothing more about this episode.

104 As another student later recalled: "When I first entered the yeshiva and looked around I was astonished by what I saw. In all my life, never had I seen a yeshiva of comparable grandeur and beauty, a broad, long study hall, tables arrayed along its length and width from end to end with only a narrow aisle between them, the tables tapered along the sides so that the Talmud folio of one not touch that of the other standing in front of him." Joshua Leib Rados, *Zikhronot* (Johannesburg: n.p., 1936), 64.

105 There are not enough full-scale scholarly treatments of Netziv as befits his stature, though the number of monographs is growing. Much biographical information is to be found in the memoir of his son, Meir Berlin (Bar-Ilan), *Mi-Volozhin 'ad Yerushalayim* (Tel Aviv: Kohen Yalqut, 1939–1940), who also wrote a reverential biography of his father called *Rabban shel Yisrael* (New York: Histadrut Ha-Mizrahi, 1943); and of his nephew, Barukh Epstein, *Meqor Barukh* (Vilna: Romm, 1928). Epstein's work, valuable as it is, has been the subject of lively critical discussion, not least for his depiction of Berlin's first wife, Rayna Batya, and her aspirations towards Torah study; for a helpful discussion, see Eliyana Adler, "Reading Rayna Batya: The Rebellious Rebbetzin as Self-Reflection," *Nashim: A Journal of Women's Studies and Gender Issues* 16, no. 2 (Fall 2018): 130-152. Epstein's controversial renderings of aspects of Habad's history are thoroughly discussed in Eitam Henkin, *Ta'arokh le-Fanai Shulhan: Hayav, Zemano u-Mif'alo shel HRY"M Epstein, Ba'al 'Arukh Ha-Shulhan*, ed. Eliezer Brodt (Jerusalem: Maggid/Koren, 2018), 321-348. Among the more helpful and significant studies are: Gil S. Perl, *The Pillar of Volozhin: Rabbi Naftali Zvi Yehuda Berlin and the World of Nineteenth-Century Lithuanian Torah Scholarship* (Boston: Academic Studies Press, 2013); and idem, "'No Two Minds are Alike': Tolerance and Pluralism in the Work of Netziv," *Torah u-Madda Journal* 12 (2004): 74–98. The chapter on him in Shlomo Yosef Zevin, *Ishim ve-Shittot* (Jerusalem: Beit Hillel, 1956), 13–37 is essential for understanding his Talmudic methodology; Hannah Katz (Kehat), *Mishnat Ha-Netziv* (Jerusalem: n.p., 1990), though far from comprehensive, is nonetheless a serviceable sketch of the man and his ideas with some attention to the cultural climate of his times; Nissim Elyakim's *Ha-'ameq Davar La-Netziv* (Rechovot: Moreshet Ya'aqov, 2002) is a book-length treatment of his Biblical exegetical techniques; his attitude towards *midrash halakhah* is explored in Jay M. Harris, *How Do We Know This?: Midrash and the Fragmentation of Modern Judaism* (Albany: SUNY, 1995), 239–244; on the best-known, and ultimately tragic, public episode of his career, the decision to close the yeshiva rather than allow secular studies by non-Jewish teachers in the yeshiva, see Jacob J. Schacter, "Haskalah, Secular Studies and the Close of the Yeshiva in Volozhin in 1892," *Torah u-Madda Journal* 2 (1990): 76–133; and the extraordinary materials unearthed in the second, 2005, edition of

Netziv, Berlin had come to Volozhin at age eleven and at thirteen married Rayna Batya, the second daughter of Yitzhak of Volozhin, the son and successor of the yeshiva's founder Hayim, and a woman of serious intellectual achievement in her own right.[106] His staggering erudition in the whole of rabbinic literature, coupled with keen analytic powers, felicitous style, and charismatic personality, enabled him eventually to succeed to the deanship of the yeshiva.[107] He was perhaps the truest inheritor of the Gaon of Vilna's textual revolution, incorporating rabbinic works outside the Babylonian Talmud into the curriculum and bringing text criticism to bear on their contents alongside conceptual analyses, though unlike the Gaon he did not, especially in his early writings, try to harmonize the various texts, but allowed each its own distinctive voice.[108] Moreover, again unlike the Gaon, he seems to have had little truck with Kabbalah, aside from the passages of Zohar and *Nefesh Ha-Hayim* that were de rigueur for someone of his education and station.

This major figure is not easily summarized. Netziv appears to have had a complex attitude towards modernity and Haskalah. He was of course a staunch traditionalist and classical Talmudist; yet he taught a daily Bible class, which formed the basis of the major work of his later period, a nonsermonic and textually oriented Torah commentary *Ha'ameq Davar*; he also authored a commentary on the Song of Songs and encouraged his students to develop a Hebrew prose style; he allowed the reading of newspapers on limited occasions; was a participant, albeit with serious reservations, in the proto-Zionist movement Hibat Tzion; in a significant departure from rabbinic conventions, his magnum opus *Ha'ameq She'elah* was a massive commentary on a Geonic work, based in part on manuscript research. To it he appended a lengthy introductory essay entitled "Qidmat Ha-'Emeq," the first section of which, seemingly (though implicitly) a response to the Lilienblum controversy, lays out an understanding of the history of halakhah as entirely generated from within scholarly give-and-take, an historical process nonetheless

---

Stampfer's *Ha-Yeshiva*; Hannah Kehat has authored a brief essay on Netziv's influece on Rav Kook's understanding of Torah study "Talmud Torah be-Mishnat Ha-Re"ayah Kook: Bein Ha-Mizrahi le-'Olam Ha-Lamdani," *Qovetz Ha-Tzionut Ha-Datit* 5 (2002): 38–55; see, as well, Gerald Blidstein, "Torat Eretz Yisrael ve-Torat Bavel be-Mishnat Ha-Netziv Mi-Volozhin," in *Eretz Yisrael be-Hagut Yehudit be-'Et Ha-Hadasha*, ed. Aviezer Ravitzky (Jerusalem: Yad Ben-Tzvi, 1998), 466–479.

Finally, see the deft literary portrait of him in Yehoshua Fischel Schneersohn's remarkable novel *Hayim Gravitzer: Sippuro shel Nofel*, ed. Netanel Lederberg (Tel Aviv: Yedi'ot Aharonot, 2013). This extraordinary *tour d'horizon* of mid-nineteenth-century Eastern European Judaism was first written and serialized in Yiddish in the 1920s and '30s and translated into Hebrew by Avraham Shlonsky in the 1940s.

106 See the article by Eliyana Adler, noted above. Rayna Batya passed away in 1878, well before Kook's arrival in Volozhin.

107 It bears noting that one of his competitors, Yehoshua Heschel Levin, had lost out in no small measure due to his perceived Maskilic tendencies; see Stampfer, *Ha-Yeshiva*, 75.

108 Jay M. Harris, "Rabbinic Literature in Lithuania after the Death of the Gaon," in *The Gaon of Vilnius and the Annals of Jewish Culture: Materials of the International Scientific Conference, Vilnius, September 10–12, 1997*, ed. Izraelis Lempertas (Vilnius: UNESCO/Community of Lithuanian Jews/Vilnius University Publishing House, 1998), 88–95.

vouchsafed by divine sanction. At the same time, he straightforwardly dismissed Yitzhak Reines's attempt to remake halakhic reasoning along the lines of a thoroughgoing systematic conceptualization that would at the least supplement and perhaps deemphasize textual exegesis, as an assault on the very practice of Torah study.[109] He polemicized with ultra-Orthodox separatists, and yet ruled that one may not pray with avowedly secular Jewish nationalists.[110] He was a gifted administrator, who yet wore tefillin all day.[111] In an important study, Gil S. Perl has demonstrated that Berlin's earlier works were in deep dialogue with Maskillic currents in Eastern Europe, while his later writings have a more traditionalist cast.[112] In short, a remarkable man of many parts.

In 1885 the yeshiva supported some 260 students; each received about thirty-one rubles a year.[113] Class considerations played no small role in the life of the students; stipends were tied to the amount of financial support provided by the student's hometown, as well as to behavior (among the offenses leading to a reduction in support were the reading of books deemed heretical). One incentive for studying there was enhancing one's own marital prospects vis-à-vis the daughters of the wealthy, though by the 1880s the demand for yeshiva alumni as sons-in-law had waned.[114]

Though the overwhelming majority of the students were of Mitnagdic background, there were a few Hasidim, including Kook's study partner, a contemplative Habad Hasid from Poltava named Yoel Shurin (1871–1927).[115] Another student of Hasidic background was none other than Micah Yosef Berdyczewsky, who in the coming years would emerge as the *enfant terrible* of Hebrew literary culture. Far from being a "Litvak," Berdyczewsky was the son of a Hasidic rabbi; he arrived in Volozhin after being driven from the home of his father-in-law upon the discovery of his burgeoning interest in Haskalah literature. His leading biographer suggests that he was drawn to Volozhin because of its seeming poised on the cusp between tradition and Haskalah, which latter the yeshiva administration neither encouraged nor condemned.[116] A fellow student recalled years later that Berdyczewsky sat all day in tallit and tefillin (and yet, he said, Netziv recognized that Berdyczewsky was "of a different world").[117] We will, in the course of this work, meet him time and again.

---

109 See his responsa *Meshiv Davar*, 5:44.

110 See ibid., 1:44 and 1:9.

111 We will have much more to say later on about this practice of his and others.

112 Perl, *The Pillar of Volozhin*.

113 The following pages draw heavily on Stampfer, *Ha-Yeshiva*, 115–168.

114 Ibid., 115–122; interestingly, the students from Rav Kook's area were considered among the poorer; ibid., 129.

115 Neriah, *Tal*, 70, 239–245

116 Avner Holtzman, *El Ha-Kera' she-ba-Lev: Micah Yosef Berdyczewsky: Shnot Ha-Zmiha, 1887–1902* (Jerusalem: Mossad Bialik, 1995), 64–65.

117 Alter Druyanov, cited in Samuel K. Mirsky, "Yeshivat Volozhin," in *Mosdot Torah be-Europa be-Vinyanam u-ve-Hurbanam*, ed. Samuel Mirsky (New York: 'Ogen/Histadrut 'Ivrit, 1956), 61n6.

The extent of Maskilic culture at Volozhin is unclear.[118] Haskalah and other literature was certainly in circulation (as we shall see, Kook was suspected by some of indulging in it himself) and the yeshiva was pervaded by a strong youth culture, one in which the students often chose to challenge their rabbis on matters of finance and administration.[119] A nuanced approach to this question is offered by one alumnus, who wrote that "while Haskalah itself wasn't found there, its aroma and spirit were present in small doses . . . it was the sort of thing one didn't read in public but was acceptable in private."[120]

One doesn't know for sure Kook's reaction to the atmosphere in Volozhin at the time. Neriah reports that Netziv urged students undergoing crises of faith to go and talk with him, which would indicate that he was deemed both safely secured from such crises and able to sympathetically discuss them with his peers.[121] Nevertheless, according to several anecdotes, he directed biting sarcasm towards freethinkers, a form of conduct far removed from the deep and principled tolerance of his later years.[122]

---

118 While Berdyczewsky memorably painted a picture of acute Modernist ferment within the walls of the yeshiva in his "Yeshivat 'Etz Hayyim," *He-'Asif* 3 (1886): 238–237, Hayim Nahman Bialik, in a letter dated late summer 1890, wrote: "Aside from sacred studies nobody here studies anything, and all the stuff that Berdyczewsky wrote in *He-'Asif*—not at all. God grant that I add diligence to my studies for good all my days," Bialik, *Igrot* [Tel Aviv: Devir, 1938], 15–16.

119 Kook's year at Volozhin saw the founding of a proto-Zionist society named Nes Tzionah, whose fifty-odd members were sworn to an oath of secrecy, and whose chief activity was collecting and disseminating nationalist literature. By all accounts, Netziv was not fundamentally opposed, but thought it was a waste of time and source of potential trouble with the authorities. That latter point became abundantly clear in 1889 when the tsarist police cracked down on the society. Avraham Yitzhak may indeed have been a member but there is no conclusive evidence that he was. A brief history of the society based on its few surviving original protocols and other documents is Yisrael Klausner, *Toldot Ha-Agudah Nes Tzionah bi-Volozhin* (Jerusalem: Mossad Ha-Rav Kook, 1954). There is no mention of Rav Kook anywhere in this volume (nor of Berdyczewsky either, for that matter). Yet Yitzhak Rivkind, in a very critical review of the volume in "Nes Tzionah bi-Yeshivat Volozhin," *Ha-Do'ar* 34, no. 24 (Av 5715/August 12, 1955): 673–674, argues that given the fact that all the members were sworn to secrecy and indeed kept this confidentiality all their lives, the fact that Rav Kook answered all of J. L. Maimon's queries as to his membership with silence indicates that he was in fact a member. This is, of course, quite literally an argument from silence and thus inconclusive. Moreover, Rav Kook was not at all active in Hibat Tzion through the 1880s or 1890s. Among younger contemporaries of Rav Kook's known to be members were the future luminaries Isser Zalman Meltzer and Moshe Mordechai Epstein. My thanks to Menachem Butler for providing a copy of Rivkind's article.

120 Abba Balosher, "Bialik be-Volozhin," reprinted in *Yeshivot Lita: Pirqei Zikhronot*, ed. Immanuel Etkes and Shlomo Tyckochinski (Jerusalem: Merkaz Shazar, 2004), 172.

121 Neriah, *Tal*, 71.

122 Maimon records that a question circulated in the *beit midrash*: according to the Mishnah Hullin 3:5, an animal that has been poisoned or bitten by a snake is permitted qua kashrut as such but forbidden as a health hazard. What practical difference, the students asked, does it make for it to be permitted at all if it is ultimately forbidden? Avraham Yitzhak answered that the Mishnah was directed against a heretic (and reportedly all knew the individual he had in

Among Volozhin's students at the time, the serious Talmudists divided into adherents of Netziv on the one hand and, on the other, Hayim Soloveitchik. The latter's method of elegant, abstract conceptualization contrasted with the dogged textuality of Netziv, he was far more critical of Hibat Tzion and Haskalah, and he seems unwittingly to have reaped the benefits of some students' inevitable resentments of the powers that be.[123] Soloveitchik's relations with Kook were cool; indeed, according to a Soloveitchik family tradition, the latter told his disciples to "beware of the pious young man from Griva."[124] For his part, Rav Kook said in later years that the reason he didn't fall under the spell of Hayim Soloveitchik was that he had already been taught by Levin of Dvinsk to mistrust every argument that was not clearly stated, or nearly so, in the Talmudic or medieval text.[125]

Kook distinguished himself by his piety; he prayed with an intensity at variance with the cool intellectualism of most of the students; unlike his mostly clean-shaven peers, he had a beard; he had a sign citing the famous passage of Ps. 16:8 "I will always set God before me" attached to the lamp facing his seat—something that engendered the disapproval of some of the other students;[126] he spoke Hebrew.[127] His otherworldly fervor sometimes frustrated his peers.[128] He was also was known there as "the prodigy from Dvinsk" (*der iluy fun Dvinsk*) and was highly regarded for his wide ranging knowledge of responsa literature in general and those of Rabbi Aqiva Eger in particular.[129]

---

mind), against whom the Talmud (BT ʿAvodah Zarah 16b), at least according to some of the commentators, gives license to do violence. This is found in Maimon, *Azkarah*, 38.

123 For an excellent discussion of Soloveitchik's innovations in Talmudic methodology, see CHayim Saiman, "Legal Theology: The Turn to Conceptualism in Nineteenth Century Jewish Law," *Journal of Law and Religion* 21 (2005–2006): 39–100. Soloveitchik's method and that of Netziv are contrasted in detail in Shlomo Tyckochinski, "Darkhei Ha-Limmud bi-Yeshivot Lita ba-Meʾah Ha–19" (master's thesis, Hebrew University, 2004). Paul E. Nahme has limned a fascinating comparison of the affinities of Soloveitchik's Idealism with that of Hermann Cohen, suggesting that both sought to secure an essentialized tradition in the face of modern historicism; see his "Wissen und Lomdus: Idealism, Modernity, and History in some Nineteenth-Century Rabbinic and Philosophical Responses to the Wissenschaft des Judentums," *Harvard Theological Review* 110, no. 3 (2017): 393-420.

124 *Der frumer bucher fun Grive*, cited in Kamenetsky, *Making of a Godol*, 1087.

125 Neriah, *Sihot*, 71.

126 Hayim Levin, son of Rav Kook's celebrated disciple Aryeh Levin, and an important scholar in his own right, reported that Kook's peers resented his overweening piety and his habit of informing on freethinkers to the authorities; this is recorded in the biography of Isser Zalman Meltzer by the latter's grandson, Yedaʾel Meltzer, *Be-Derekh ʿEtz Ha-Hayim*, vol. 1 (n.p.: Artzei Ha-Hen, 1986), 47.

127 Neriah, in his *Pirqei Volozhin* (Jerusalem: n.p., 1964), 38–39, says that this was a practice of none other than Hayim of Volozhin; at the same time, one wonders if he is trying to diminish the seemingly Maskilic nature of this particular idiosyncrasy.

128 See the reminiscences of his roommate Ephraim Teitelbaum in Neriah, *Tal*, 65.

129 Rabbiner, *Or Mufla'*, 16.

We learn other details from a memoir of Kook in his Volozhin days by Mordechai Rabbiner of Boisk.[130] He writes that Kook studied from seven in the morning until midnight; that Netziv affectionately referred to him as *mayn Avraham Izci*, and said he was the equal of all his peers put together (*hu shaqul ke-neged kulam*). He was designated "Purim Rabbi," a sign of the esteem of his peers (and perhaps of their confidence that, unlike other "Purim rabbis," he would not take liberties with Netziv's status and dignity).[131] When a glass broke one Passover at the home of Netziv, Kook extemporized a rhymed medieval-style ode to the shattered vessel.[132]

A fascinating anecdote, reportedly transmitted by a contemporary of his there, Zelig Reuven Bengis (1864–1953), a Talmudic prodigy who went on to become an important scholar and rabbinic judge in Jerusalem, captures the decidedly mixed responses of Kook's peers to his idiosyncratic devotion, as well as the esteem in which he was held by Netziv. Bengis noticed that young Kook would, during his Talmud study, repeatedly glance down at some papers on a shelf of his study stand. This was generally a sign that a student was stealing glances at Maskilic literature or newspapers, and Bengis reported his fears to Netziv who told him to leave Kook alone, saying, "he's a *tzadiq*." Unable to restrain himself, Bengis eventually peeked a glance at Kook's mysterious papers, "and what did I find? Pieces of paper, handwritten with the Name of God." Duly humbled, Bengis reported his find back to Netziv.[133]

During his time in Volozhin, Kook corresponded with his parents (though not as often as he might have liked)[134] and with his future father-in-law on Talmudic matters. Particularly with the latter, he discussed the laws of Temple sacrifices, a subject which was prized by Lithuanian Talmudists precisely not only for its technical difficulty but for the extreme devotion to pure Torah study demonstrated by a commitment to mastering such legal esotericism.[135]

---

130 A letter written by him in 1935 to his brother Zev is reprinted in ibid., 178–185. Mordechai was eventually murdered in the Holocaust.

131 Mordechai Rabbiner also writes that by the time of Kook's arrival he had already mastered *Tur Yoreh De'ah* and *Hoshen Mishpat* and that while at Volozhin he studied *Orakh Hayim* with the commentary of his ancestor the Levush, ibid., 179.

132 Ibid., 180.

133 Shalom Grey, "Toldot Ha-Ga'on Rabbi Zelig Reuven Bengis," *Yeshurun* 12 (Nissan 5763/Spring 2003): 150–192, 156. My thanks to Dr. Yehuda Galinsky for directing me to this source.

134 In a letter dated 13 Adar 5645/February 28, 1885, he tells his parents that he is breaking protocol to write them though he has not heard from them, adding that it is perhaps the fault of the post office. That portion of the letter, along with a halakhic discourse sent to his father is deleted from the excerpt in Neriah, *Tal*, 63–65; a typescript of the original is in the archive of Beit Ha-Rav Kook in Jerusalem, א, ב, 3.

135 The correspondence appears in *Mishpat Cohen*, 232–244.

Marriage, Poverty, and First Rabbinic Post

His wedding to Bat-Sheva Rabinowitz-Teomim took place in Ponevezh in the spring of 1886 and there he resumed his studies, largely with his father-in-law. In Ponevezh, he also studied Kabbalah with one of the local rabbinic judges, Moshe Yitzhak Rabin, about whom we know little.[136] He also enjoyed a warm relationship with Rabin's son Nisan, a man of broad learning.[137] Nisan writes in the introduction to his father's one, posthumous, volume, that besides his Talmudic studies his father, a retiring and somewhat reclusive scholar, studied philosophical works—*Kuzari*, Maimonides's *Guide*, Albo's *'Iqarim*, and Isaac Arama's *'Aqedat Yitzhaq*—as well as Kabbalah, on which he composed a treatise.[138]

This brief listing illustrates what seems to have been a standard curriculum for East Europeans interested in theology: works written in, or derived from the Jewish philosophical tradition of medieval Spain, and especially Maimonides, Albo, and Arama, who show up repeatedly in literary memoirs and booklists, and give us an important clue as to what Avraham Yitzhak Kook was reading.[139]

The idyll was short-lived. Financial troubles descended on Aderet and his family almost immediately after the wedding, as the gifts from townspeople and friends turned out to be far less than expected.[140] His salary of nine rubles a week was, once again, only intermittently paid, and so, once again, he went on strike, this time after "the elder sage of the generation from Kovno," that is, Yitzhak Elhanan Spektor, told him he could and that

---

136 Neriah, *Tal*, 74. In later years, Rav Kook recalled him warmly for "his clear thinking and deep intellect, combined with strenuous devotion to study, and a pure piety that lit up his heart, conjoined to the love of truth in an elevated manner, that added to his acuity, broad knowledge and humble righteousness." *Igrot*, 1:268–269; the letter from the summer of 1919, is to Nisan Rabin, thanking him for a copy of his father's posthumous work.

137 In the same letter he says: "I would very much like to converse freely (*lehishtashe'a*) with his honor. He was very dear to me, and is precious to me even now, in particular for the soul-connection and deep love of truth that were between him and his honored departed father."

138 These comments are found in the unpaginated introduction to Moshe Yitzhak bar Shlomo Rabin, *Sefer Milu'im le-Moshe* (Vilna: Pirashnikov, 1909):

ולבד שקידתו בתלמוד ומפרשיו, שקד גם בספרי המחקר אשר עומדים לנס בישראל ה"ה: הכוזרי, המו"ח, העיקרים והעקידה, הרבה מעתותיו אצל גם עליהם. בעברו עליו ימי הבינה החל לשקוד גם על ספרי הקבלה בידיעת הנסתר וגם בשדי החכמה הזאת הגדיל לעשות בחידושיו. הוא השאיר אחריו ספר שלם בעניני הקבלה.

The volume is a supercommentary addressing a particularly thorny and detailed area in the laws of kashrut.

The son Nisan is referred to as "הרב המשכיל המופלג" (the distinguished enlightened/Maskilic rabbi) by none other than Rabbi Eliezer Gordon of Telz in his approbation to the elder Rabin's volume, though the exact meaning of the phrase here is unclear. Nisan went on to write Yiddish volumes in economics and a novel about intergenerational conflicts over Zionism, socialism, etc. See his *Der Yeshiva Bukher, oder di Yiddishe Shtimme* (Vilna: n.p., 1910).

He was also the father-in-law of Ben-Zion Alfes, to whose lengthily serialized novels he occasionally contributed comments of a decidedly universalist cast; see for instance Alfes's *Eretz Hemdah* (Tel Aviv: Moses, 1940).

139 See Parush, *Nashim Qor'ot*, 107, 113–114.

140 The following account is drawn from Aderet's *Seder Eliyahu*, 64–67.

he himself had resorted to it at times.[141] Even when restored, Aderet's meager salary was insufficient for the rent, and 1887 found Aderet, his wife, children, and son-in-law living for free in cramped quarters in the courtyard of a local hospital; members of the family regularly slept on several of the six chairs and hard benches that were nearly the sum of their furniture.

Rav Kook's turn to the rabbinate at a comparatively early stage in his career has been largely attributed to the exhortation of the saintly, renowned Israel Meir Kagan that he do so for the good of the Jewish people. While that encouragement did play a role, it seems, the immediate stimulus was the dire economic straits in which he found himself, as Aderet's memoir makes clear.[142] Indeed, the communal rabbinate was, in late nineteenth-century Lithuania, a regularly grueling, thankless and unenviable situation, and it is unlikely that as promising a young Talmudist and rabbinic writer as Rav Kook would have gone looking for it if he hadn't had to.[143]

Realizing that the situation was untenable, Avraham Yitzhak Kook went looking for a rabbinical position and made inquiries as to the possibility of a job in Zeimel (Zeimelis), a town of some 1000–1200 inhabitants, a little more than half of them Jews, four kilometers from the border with Latvia. Most of the town's families engaged in some sort of agriculture and the Jews were tradesmen as well.[144] One member of the town subscribed to *Ha-Maggid* and three to *Ha-Melitz*.[145]

A Sabbath visit to the town in the winter of 1888 proved successful and the townspeople elected him as their rabbi. This was, for Aderet, a bittersweet moment:

---

141 Spektor may have been trying to compensate Aderet here for an earlier wrongdoing. In 1883 he was candidate for a major rabbinical post, the rabbinate of Riga, and was, in his telling, the people's choice. Yet Spektor decided it should go to his rival, a member of the Shapira family, who, Spektor admitted, was a lesser scholar than Aderet, but further on in his career and more in need of the job. This was a particularly humiliating disappointment and Aderet fired off an angry letter of protest to Kovno. Spektor's secretary Ya'aqov Lifshitz later told a friend of Aderet's that had anyone other than Aderet written him a comparable letter, the complainant's rabbinic career would have been over for good; ibid., 61.

142 The conventional view emphasizing Kagan's role is found in Neriah, *Sihot*, 122; Neriah, *Tal*, 92–94 alludes to the more complicated truth, but only just.

143 See Zalkin, "Social Status," whose conclusion at 182-183 is worth quoting: "Both poverty and instability of nineteenth-century communal rabbis were not inevitable . . . (but rather) an intentional, constant and widespread policy of the local economic and policy elites, aiming at preserving their total and unchallenged control over all aspects of Jewish life," which in turn resulted from their own struggles to maintain status in the face of convulsive social, political and economic change. The rabbi who supplies Zalkin's case study is none other than Yosef Zekharia Stern.

144 This was one of Lithuania's oldest Jewish communities, dating back several centuries; among its better-known sons was Shlomo Zalkind Horowitz, student of Mendelssohn, noted Orientalist and member of the Napoleonic Sanhedrin. See Dov Levin, ed., *Pinqas Ha-Kehillot: Lita* (Jerusalem: Yad va-Shem, 1996), 291–292.

145 Kagan, *Yiddishe Shtodt*, 174.

And in my heart I chuckled at their dreams, and told them that they could be sure that in a few years they would be boasting of his fame—and then and there they gave him the rabbinic crown with beauty and dignity and escorted him under a festive canopy to the *beit midrash* and he continued to discourse. And I wept with a bitter heart that because of my sins he had been forced to accept a rabbinic post in the springtime of his days on account of my stress and scarcity, that I could not support him in my home.[146]

There is yet a further piece of the story here, unmentioned by Aderet. The town had been divided over class issues, as its two rabbis had been regarded as the respective patrons of the merchants and Talmudists, on the one hand, and of the tradespeople, on the other. Aderet had served on an ad hoc court that had decided that both rabbis should leave (one left for Riga and the other for America).[147] This created an opportune possibility for his son-in-law, and not a moment too soon.

En route to his new post, Avraham Yitzhak visited Navaredok, where he received rabbinic ordination from Netziv's brother-in-law, the eminent scholar and author of *'Arukh Ha-Shulhan*, Yehiel Mikhel Epstein. His doing so only when he needed it for employment reflects Lithuanian Talmudism's general reluctance and embarrassment around the practical rabbinate.[148]

Rav Kook served as rabbi there until 1896. Before his move he had taken his first steps towards establishing his literary persona.

Literary Debut

Before moving to Zeimel, Rav Kook wrote his first published articles, both centered on his master Netziv, defending Berlin's piety in the face of zealous Orthodox criticism and praising his modernity to general readers.

His first published article appeared in January 1886, shortly before his marriage, in the Orthodox journal *Mahaziqei Ha-Dat,* the first Orthodox weekly and a staunch

---

146 Aderet, *Seder Eliyahu*, 67.
147 Rabbiner doesn't give the background to this. This is reported by Ya'aqov Even-Hen (Edelstein), *Rav u-Manhig: Hayav u-Demuto shel Ha-Rav Avraham Yitzhak Ha-Cohen Kook* (Jerusalem: Sifriyat Eliner, 1998), 52, though he for his part does not mention Aderet's poverty.

   Zev Rabbiner, "Boisk ve-Rabbanehah," *Sinai* 17 (1945): 76, writes that the town was riven by controversy at the time, but offers no details. Some background on the succession battle in Zeimel that preceded him can be found *Ha-Melitz*, 3 Kislev 5645/November 21, 1884, where correspondent Benjamin Zimmerman reported that an earlier choice, Shalom Elhanan Ha-Levi, was denounced by his foes to the authorities as a draft-dodger.
148 For details of the ordination, see Eitam Henkin, *Ta'arokh le-Fanai Shulhan: Hayav, Zemano u-Mif'alo shel HRY"M Epstein, Ba'al 'Arukh Ha-Shulhan*, ed. Eliezer Brodt (Jerusalem: Maggid/Koren, 2018), 371–375. Henkin, drawing on Rav Kook's own testimony, gently dispels the legend that the ordination was unsolicited and that Rav Kook hid it from his father-in-law.

mouthpiece of antimodernity. [149] In an essay entitled "Tzvi Le-Tzadiq" (based on Isa. 24:16, "glory to the righteous," and a pun on Berlin's middle name), signed as Avraham Yitzhak Ha-Cohen, he came to Berlin's defense after his Pentateuch commentary *Ha'ameq Davar* had been criticized in the journal's pages by an anonymous author for a passage which seemed insufficiently respectful of the rabbis (and likely reflected a not inaccurate sense that Berlin was far more receptive to Maskilic currents than were the paper's readers).[150] In these essays the young Rav Kook first flexes his literary and rhetorical muscles, displays great reverence for his injured teacher, and maintains the latter's honor amid the polemics of the time regarding the critical study of sacred texts.[151]

This essay is of interest for both substance and style. Substantively, he uses Maimonidean categories as a fundamental reference point, as he will repeatedly in his writings of this period. Stylistically, we find here early evidence of what we know as the later Rav Kook's famously loquacious literary style, but also slash-and-burn polemics that are markedly different from his mature writings. Indeed, so withering is his tone that a publisher's note appended to the article assures the reader that the offending articles of course meant no disrespect to Netziv, whose student ("the sharp-witted and learned young man") makes clear his master's intentions ("to thwart those who disparage the Godly emissaries, the words of Hazal").[152]

The essay begins with a lengthy elaboration on the need to take special care before criticizing rabbinic authorities. Rav Kook then turns to the issue at hand. Berlin, in his commentary to Deut. 10:12 ("And now Israel what does the Lord your God want from you but to revere the Lord your God, to walk only in His paths, to love Him and to serve the Lord your God with all your heart and soul") had paraphrased the comment of the

---

149 A brief history of the journal is given by Yitzhak Alfasi, "Mahaziqei Ha-Dat—Ha-Shevu'on Ha-Dati Ha-Rishon," in idem, *Sefer Ha-Shanah shel Ha-'Orkhim ve-Ha-'Itonaim bi-Kitvei Ha-'Et be-Yisrael* (1990–1991): 193–203. Founded in 1879 as the organ of the society of the same name, established by the Belzer Rebbe and publicly fronted by Rabbi Shimon Sofer, son of none other than Hatam Sofer, it combined passionate polemic against Haskalah with measured approval and qualified endorsement for settlement activity in Palestine and even, later, some aspects of Zionist activity. This mix, it seems to me, was not uncommon in Hungarian circles, as seen most clearly in the case of Aqiva Yosef Schlesinger; see Michael K. Silber, "The Emergence of Ultra-Orthodoxy: The Invention of a Tradition," in *The Uses of Tradition: Jewish Continuity since Emancipation*, ed. Jack Wertheimer (New York/Jerusalem: Jewish Theological Seminary/Harvard University Press, 1992), 23–84.

150 Berlin's deep dialogue with Haskalah is discussed at length in Perl, *The Pillar of Volozhin*.

151 Avraham Yitzhak Ha-Cohen (Kook), "Tzvi le-Tzadiq," *Mahaziqei Ha-Dat* 8, no. 15 (7 Shevat 5646/January 15, 1886): 6–7, and idem, *Mahaziqei Ha-Dat* 8, no. 16 (Adar I 5646/February 12, 1886): 6–7. This contra Neriah, who has Rav Kook's *Knesset Yisrael* article of 1888 as his first publication. One surmises that Neriah chose not to mention this due to the harsh polemic tone taken by the young author. I have been unable to locate a copy of the original articles attacking Berlin, which appeared in the previous year's volume 7, nos. 16, 17, and 18, as they do not appear on the relevant microfilm rolls at NLI, nor on its website. Kook's essays are reprinted in *Otzarot*, 2:139–147.

152 The publisher's note appears in the original and is omitted in the reproduction in ibid.

Midrash Shoher Tov to Ps. 27:4—God said to David, you ask "for but one thing" and in truth it is quite a lot, to which David replied, "you have asked for but one thing, and it is quite a lot"—and characterized it as *lashon haltziyi*, that is, "figurative," also possibly translatable as "facetious."[153] To this the anonymous author responded with a series of citations from authorities about the need to accept the words of the rabbis without criticism.

To begin with, Kook writes, even if the anonymous critic had understood the master's commentary, mustering a defense of the midrash drawn entirely from quotes from later rabbinic authorities is perforce convincing only to those already safely within the fold. The critic, he says, could have spared us all the trouble had he taken a moment to ponder the Talmudic statement: "The Torah sometimes spoke an exaggerated tongue, the Prophets spoke an exaggerated tongue, the Sages spoke an exaggerated tongue" (BT Hullin 90b, Tamid 29a).[154] Indeed, he writes, had he taken the trouble to read Maimonides's introduction to his commentary on the Mishnah, he would have seen the careful and authoritative parsing of distinctions between *levush* (garment), *qelippah* (shell), *penim* (interior), and *tokh* (inside), as well as the fact that the rabbis adopted various rhetorical and literary strategies to make their many profound and sometimes esoteric points.

Oddly, these specific terms do not appear there in the translation of Maimonides's work available to Kook;[155] nor do they appear in Maimonides's introduction to Sanhedrin Pereq Heleq where he explicitly addresses the status of aggadot. Maimonides's Hebrew translator does however use the term *qelippot* in *Guide*, 1:71 (107b [Warsaw, 1872]), to denote the exoteric meanings of midrashic traditions, which divert the untutored from their real meanings; and Crescas in his commentary there characterizes those midrashim properly understood as a matter of *she-yesh lo tokh* (something that has an interior).[156]

In the second installment of his essay, Kook turns directly to the anonymous critic and rhetorically asks what he possibly meant to achieve by his sally against Berlin, whose

---

153 See *Midrash Shoher Tov—Tehillim*, 226 (Warsaw: Kalter-Goldman, 1865, first edition Vilna: Romm, 1850),166 54 (as well as *Yalqut Shimoni*, ibid.). A typographical error in *Ha'ameq Davar* attributes this comment to Ps. 36 when it is clearly to Ps. 27. That error is corrected in the 1999 edition published by Berlin's descendants; moreover, in that edition *lashon haltziyi* is changed to the far more respectable *lashon melitzi* (figurative speech), thus obviating the question of the critic in *Mahaziqei Ha-Dat*.

154 On the word *havay*, see Eliezer Ben Yehuda, *Milon Ha-Lashon Ha-'Ivrit*, vol. 2 (Tel Aviv: La-'Am, 1948), 1026. The medieval understandings of the word are summarized by Yom Tov Lipman Heller in his commentary to Mishnah Nedarim 3:2. I have not as yet found many discussions of this particular statement. Abraham Joshua Heschel understands this passage as of a piece with the more celebrated "Scripture speaks a human tongue" (BT Bava Metzia 31b *et seq.*) and both as regulative principles meant to set limits of rationality in the interpretation of scripture, per his general theory of Biblical interpretation among the rabbis—see his *Torah min Ha-Shamayim*, vol. 1 (London: Soncino, 1962), 206–208.

155 See Maimonides's introduction to the Mishnah as printed in the Vilna: Romm, 1886 edition, 55, col. a, where Maimonides does discuss the rationale for esotericism in Talmudic aggadah and metaphor.

156 In a 1908 letter, Rav Kook returned to the distinction between *tokh* and interior as a way of dealing with the issues posed by academic Bible study (*Igrot*, 1:134, 163).

works he seems not to have understood, and by taking up the cudgels on behalf of the most commonplace and basic beliefs of rabbinic Judaism, to which none subscribe more completely than Berlin himself! Moreover, he says, have you not considered that the ostensibly offending word used by Berlin, *haltziyiy* is related to *melitzah*, "figurative," a term of Biblical origin (Prov. 1:6) understood to mean "an idea whose interior is lovelier than its exterior" (*ra'ayon she-tokho yafeh mi-bar'o*). Indeed, the central idea being put forth by Berlin here, he says, is precisely that one must delve deeply into the words of the rabbis in order to grasp their meaning, and not content oneself with superficial understanding.[157]

In closing, he calls on the readers of *Mahaziqei Ha-Dat* to study Berlin's works and judge for themselves as to the stirring power and textual sensitivity of his analyses and the piety evident on every page. He closes with "To be continued," though no further part of this essay has ever come to light. It may well be that the editors of *Mahaziqei Ha-Dat* concluded that the young author had conclusively made his point.

His second appearance in print, in the fall of 1887, was a three-page essay on, again, Netziv, this time not in polemic but encomium.[158] This appeared in the second issue of *Knesset Yisrael*, edited by Shaul Pinhas Rabinowitz, as part of a series of profiles of contemporary rabbinic figures, including some with a decidedly Maskilic bent.[159] How he came to write this is unclear; Netziv himself may have suggested him to the editor.[160] Be that as it may, it further demonstrates both his identification with Netziv, and a burgeoning literary ambition, well beyond the confines of Orthodox journals.

While in the pages of *Mahaziqei Ha-Dat* he praised Netziv as a staunch traditionalist, here he highlights his responsiveness to changing times; more striking is his emphasizing what he characterizes as the "critical" bent of Netziv's scholarly enterprises. The words

---

157 He goes on to cite the *Binah le-'Ittim* of Azariah Figo (Picho) (1579–1647), no. 52, who similarly uses the phrase *hamtza'ah haltziyit* (figurative conceit) in describing a midrash cited by the fourteenth-century commentator David Abudarham as proof of the term's utter respectability

158 He also was one of several contestants to answer a halakhic quiz in *Ha-Tzefirah*; the answers appeared therein on May 4, 1887. He is listed as "Rabbi Avraham Yitzhak Ha-Cohen, son-in-law of the Gaon, judge of the rabbinical court in Ponevezh."

159 Avraham Yitzhak Kook, "Rosh Yeshivat Etz Hayim," *Knesset Yisrael* 2 (1887): 138–142, reprinted in *Ma'amrei Ha-Re'ayah* (Jerusalem: n.p., 1984), 123–126. Among those profiled in the issue were Heinrich Graetz, Zekharia Fraenkel, and Nathan Adler (of London). Netziv's son writes that this was the first time Netziv was ever profiled in print, see Bar-Ilan, *Rabban shel Yisrael*, 11.

160 According to Zvi Yehudah Kook, Avraham Yitzhak had entered Netziv's room, found him upset, and asked why. When Netziv answered that he had been asked by the editor to provide a profile of himself, and yet he was reluctant to do so, saying that such profiles ought to be reserved for the dead, or those who are dead in life (a rabbinic euphemism for reprobates), his protégé Avraham Yitzhak volunteered. This story appeared in a newspaper article in *Ha-Tzofeh* 27 Av 5703/August 28, 1943 and was repeated by, inter alia, Zev Rabbiner, *Maran Ha-Rav Kook ztz"l* (Tel Aviv: n.p., 1972), 235. The story itself seems unlikely, not least because the profile appeared well after he left the yeshiva; moreover none of the other profiles in that issue were authored by their subjects.

biqoret and *biqorti* appear repeatedly in the essay and as a mark of praise.[161] Much of the essay discusses Netziv's intellectual biography and the evolution of his scholarly method, followed by a discussion of his leadership role in Volozhin, closing with mention of his support for settlement in Palestine and expressing the desire that more leaders like him arise in Israel. The vehemence of Rav Kook's hero-worship, and the ambition implicit in it, was not lost on, and was noted with some irony by, his contemporary Berdyczewsky.[162]

'Ittur Sofrim

In 1888, at age twenty-three, Rav Kook launched a projected monthly periodical entitled *'Ittur Sofrim* (literally, *Scribal Ornamentation*, after BT Nedarim 37b).[163] The journal, which has received scant scholarly notice, offers a first schematic view of several of the mature Rav Kook's large concerns, such as prophecy, the relationship between Jewish and non-Jewish ethics, and the primacy of literary expression. It also strongly reflects a nascent program for the streamlining and updating of contemporary rabbinic literature, including a call to institutional and legal systematization of halakhah and legal theory. We see in embryo some of his later thoughts on Zionism's halakhic possibilities, but here directed solely as a coherent response to the social problems facing the Jews of Eastern Europe.[164]

---

161 Shlomo Tyckochinski reasons that by "critical," he seems to mean both non-pilpulistic, and drawing on a broad range of rabbinic literature; see his "Darkhei Ha-Limmud bi-Yeshivot Lita ba-Me'ah Ha–19," 30.

162 Berdyczewsky wrote in *Ha-Melitz* in the early spring of 1888: "The one who aspired to be an editor (*radiktor*), Yitzhak Ha-Cohen Kook, in his article simply weaves garlands (*kosher ketarim*) for our Master Netziv Shl'ita; and if I so much as touch his words in the slightest, he will cry out against us: They have stabbed their own Master!! (*rabbam daqar*)." Reprinted in M. Y. Berdichevsky, *Pirqei Volozhin* (Holon/Tel Aviv: Beit David ve-Emanuel/Reshafim, 1984), 46.

163 Hereinafter IS 1 for *'Ittur Sofrim* 1 and IS 2 for *'Ittur Sofrim* 2. Page numbers refer to the photo-offset edition with some notes identifying anonymous authors, published in Jerusalem in 1974. The journal's printing was supervised in Vilna by his father and it occasioned halakhic give and take between them as to the proper disposal of printing plates with sacred writing on them, see Responsa in DC, no. 161. Rav Kook's various essays, though not those of other contributors, are printed in *Otzarot*, 3:91–136. A photo offset of the orginal appeared in 1974 and an annotated, reformatted edition was published under the imprint of Hosen Yeshuot/ Yeshivat Har Ha-Mor in Jerusalem in 2011.

164 We will later see that his most immediate response to Theodore Herzl's call for a Jewish State at the fin-de-siècle was indeed legal. His program for rabbinic literature in his later period is laid out in a lecture on December 31, 1920, reprinted as *Hartza'at Ha-Rav* (Jerusalem: Merkaz Ha-Rav/Degel Yerushalayim, 1921), and many times since. There too he argues for a systematization of rabbinic literature, though less in terms of conceptual analysis as such and more in terms of organization and presentation, for example, through introductions, encyclopedias, and indices.

In the 1860s and 1870s several Orthodox figures began to take their own place in the thriving journalistic and periodical culture of the time.[165] This trend continued and intensified in the 1880s and 1890s as an Orthodox intelligentsia further asserted itself and began to find its voice.[166]

The first issue bore letters of approval (*haskamot*) from some of the most distinguished rabbis of the day, presumably thanks in no small part to Aderet.[167] The endors-

---

165 For a listing and brief description of the Orthodox press of the mid-nineteenth century, see Tsemach M. Tsamriyon, *Die Hebraische Presse in Europa* (Haifa: n.p., 1976), 255–264.

166 Thus for instance Yehoshua Yosef Preil (1858–1896), rabbi of Krak and a talented writer, polemicized with Maskilim, first out of some sympathy with Hibat Tzion, later shifting towards a rejection of nationalism as a principle of identity in favor of the centrality of Torah and mitzvot, but all in good modern Hebrew and in the Maskilic press. In the process he left a great impression on many, including his younger contemporary Rav Kook. In a prefatory approbation to Preil's *Ketavim Nivharim* (New York: n.p., 1924), published posthumously by Preil's brother Elazar Meir, then-rabbi in Elizabeth, New Jersey, Rav Kook writes: "These articles made a deep impression and great noise in their time in the various circles of our brethren's camps . . . with an intrepid spirit and clear logic and compelling reasoning to which even the opposing side, like it or not, would have to listen as true and fitting words, and this was practically the first trumpet that sounded to gather all the camps, every man with a spirit of God and literary talent, to begin emerging from hiding and proudly answer the enemies of Torah." The other approbations are by Moshe Mordechai Epstein and Avraham Duber Kahane Shapira. Bezalel Naor has pointed out some similarities between Rav Kook's differentiation of Jewish from other nationalisms and that of Preil's (in his own 1902 essays in *Ha-Peles)* in a brief essay note "Leumiyut: Sibuv Sheni," *Ha-Tzofeh* (26 Kislev 5744/December 12, 1983), 7; for Preil's influence on another young thinker see Hayim Tchernowitz, *Pirkei Hayim* (New York: Bitzaron, 1954), 142–143.

According to his brother's biographical preface, Preil, a Talmudic prodigy, enjoyed friendly relations with both Yizhak Elhanan Spektor and Yizhak Ya'aqov Reines, and edited the latter's *Hotem Tokhnit*. Aside from his Talmudic studies he also learned Russian, German and some French.

Preil, more than most of his colleagues, recognized the complexity of the motives of secular Jewish nationalists, and in the last years before his death polemicized against cultural Zionism as a dangerously seductive turn away from Jewish religion, even as he supported political Zionism's goals. On Preil's polemics in the mid–1890s, see Luz, *Maqbilim Nifgashim*, 79–80, and at greater length, Salmon, *Dat ve-Tzionut*, 215–221, and in English, "Rabbi Joshua Joseph Preil, 'Protesting at the Gate'," *Modern Judaism* 35, no. 1 (February 2015): 66–82. Some of Preil's essays were published posthumously in *Ha-Peles*. His posthumous philosophic work is *Eglei Tal* (Warsaw: Schuldberg, 1891–1901). His halakhic work was published posthumously as *Mo'atzot ve-Da'at* (Odessa: n.p., 1899). His youthful glosses to the *Iggeret Ha-Mussar* of Shlomo El-'Ami, chiefly consisting of citations to Talmudic sources, were published in Vilna by Lipman Metz in 1878.

167 Among the endorsers were Isaac Elhanan Spektor, who effusively refers to young Rav Kook as "ha-gaon ha-mefursam" (the famed genius), and Netziv, who, notwithstanding his enthusiasm for the project as a whole, details his misgivings about its diverting the young editor's energies, but says that since his father-in-law (i.e., Aderet) has pledged to be involved and help, and that a subscription agent has been hired and the project is gathering support, wishes him every success. Indeed several others endorsers, including Kook's great-uncle Mordechai Jaffe, say

ers clearly convey that they see this as a journal of responsa and such, and so it is also described in the government censor's approval.

Rav Kook makes clear at the outset that his ambitions for the journal are considerably larger than Talmudic give-and-take. In a twelve-page essay entitled "Sha'ar Ha-Sofer,"[168] by way of delivering the conventional apologia preceding any rabbinic work, especially one adopting the modern periodical form, he discourses at length on *sifrut*, best translated here as "the art of writing." Though the subjects of human inquiry that have progressed over time are those built around writing, he says, the Oral Torah flowered in antiquity precisely because it was not committed to writing, necessitating face-to-face communities of scholarship.[169] In "the last two generations," he says, "matter has overpowered mind" and people are willing to undertake Torah study only if they need not leave their homes; the rabbis, having in their wisdom foreseen these eventualities, committed the Oral Torah to writing.[170] His journal, he writes, seeks to restore the social dimension of Torah study within the comparatively new medium of the periodical. It will be a kind of gathering place in print, a forum both for halakhic discussions and for Talmudic novellae, and will advocate for matters regarding Judaism and the Jewish people. "[S]tarting the project is a large step on the road to the great restoration [*tiqqun*] to come" and part of that project is "to join with bonds of love all the parties of the disjointed nation."[171]

He then unravels a skein of large ambitions: half the profits will go to a substantial project to strengthen Torah scholars; he also asks for hitherto unpublished manuscripts and will gladly provide a share of the profits to the heirs of deceased authors. He asks his readers not to spare him the rod of criticism, but to wield it justly and substantively; those whose criticisms "are composed of criticism and counsel, who join the attribute of mercy to that of judgment, I will devour their scrolls" (after Ezek. 3:1–3).[172]

In setting forth the halakhic program of the journal, he reports the suggestions of a correspondent who chooses anonymity—identified in the 1974 reprint edition as the young Hasidic scholar Zev Twersky of Rahmistrivka[173]—who argues for bringing what

---

they approve of the project because they know it will be under the trustworthy guidance of Aderet. In his own introductory letter, Aderet says that half of the profits will be going to some large and unspecified project and that the learned discussions in this journal will undoubtedly aid in restoring the Torah to its glory out of the "fantastic depths to which it has fallen in our day, with its seekers pained and dwindling, to the disastrous effect of our people" (Isa. 1:3).

My thanks to Ms. Shelly Benvenisti, formerly of NLI, for her help in translating the censor's note from Russian.

168 IS 1:6–18. He appends a running commentary to his introduction, about which I will have a little more to say later on.

169 Ibid. 1:8.

170 Ibid., 9.

171 Ibid., 15–16.

172 Ibid., 16–17.

173 In the few notes he supplied to the 1974 reprint, Zvi Yehudah Kook identifies him as "Zev the son of Yohanan of Rahmystryvka." Yohanan Twersky of Rahmystryvka/Rotmistrovka (1816–1895) was a well-known Hasidic rebbe, a fifth-generation descendant of Nahum

Max Weber would later characterize as "formal-rational" order to the institutionally and intellectually decentralized framework of halakhah.[174] This includes a more systematic approach to the classification and treatment of laws and responsa, gathering bodies of decisions so they can be conceptually analyzed, initiating critical editions of texts, treating the journal as a forum for queries to rabbinic colleagues, and identifying rabbis with particular specializations who can write for the journal on their areas of halakhic expertise.

The remaining eighteen pages of the issue are devoted to strictly halakhic matters, discussed in conventional fashion, the most noteworthy being Netziv's permissive ruling regarding the reading of newspapers and journals on the Sabbath.[175]

The journal closes with two sets of Rav Kook's own glosses on some of the journal's contents. Regarding Zev Twersky's halakhic program, and specifically the latter's call for a large project of ascertaining the reasonings behind the various laws and customs scattered through the halakhic compendia, he presents his understanding of Maimonides's own view of the matter, namely, that while in-depth halakhic analysis is no prerequisite to fulfillment of the law by the individual—hence the utility of Maimonides's own *Code*—it *is* a prerequisite to rendering halakhic decisions on a question of first impression for which there is no black-letter precedent. Regarding Netziv's discussion of reading periodicals on the Sabbath, which was based on a distinction between passive reading and reading out loud, he suggests that because one's thoughts are not entirely under one's own control, they have no halakhic significance in the absence of an external act, such as speaking aloud or writing.

The relation between interiority and speech figures in his closing essay, written under the pen name *AY"H Sofer* (taken from Isa. 33:18), that is, Avraham Yitzhak Ha-Cohen, Author, itself noteworthy for its self-consciously literary associations, about which more

---

of Chernobyl; see Halperin, *Atlas 'Etz Hayim: Aharonim*, 2:142. His son Zev (1850–1936) was, according to Yitzhak Alfasi, "famous for his learning, and several of his responsa were published anonymously. He had broad knowledge of Jewish philosophy and left behind him numerous writings in halakhah and Hasidism." He moved to Palestine in 1934—and passed away in 1937, Yitzhaq Alfasi, vol. 1, 120. Alfasi further identifies him as Rav Kook's anonymous contributor in his *Entziklopedia le-Hasidut*, 513.

174 IS 1:18–22. Weber's formulation appears in his classic essay of 1919, "Politics as a Vocation."
175 The issue of Netziv's reading newspapers on Shabbat has occasioned lively discussion and polemics in contemporary Haredi circles, see Eliezer Brodt, "The Netziv, Reading Newspapers on Shabbos and Censorship," *The Seforim Blog* (Blog), last modified March 5, 2014, http:// seforim.blogspot.com/2014/03/the-netziv-reading-newspapers-on.html.

Also appearing are assorted Talmudic novellae by two rabbis of Vilna, including Shlomo Ha-Cohen and one Meir Michel; hitherto unpublished novellae by the late Shlomo Kluger; and, interestingly in light of Rav Kook's writings on tefillin just a few years down the road, a call by Aderet for better supervision of scribes, arguing that all scribes should be licensed by appropriate local rabbinic authorities, as many are "of loose morals, devoid of all proper understanding of Torah and piety, and entered the scribal profession as mere job-seekers," asking that major rabbinic figures band together to this task. Appended to this is a footnote by another Vilna rabbi (Pesah Ha-Kohen).

shortly, undertaking an initial exploration of the nature of prophecy.[176] Before getting to the substance of the essay, the very choice of subject matter piques our interest.

Of course, prophecy is a much-discussed subject throughout Jewish history, and early modern Jewish history saw a revival of interest in prophecy, especially around Sabbatianism, and the possibly prophetic status of Isaac Luria.[177] Yet it bears noting that a revival of interest in prophecy and a reconception of the prophet as artist seer-cum-revolutionary was precisely at this time beginning to appear in Russian radical circles, not least in the work of Vladimir Soloviev, whose writings reverberated in the Jewish press of the time.[178] In this discourse the prophet is moralist, political liberator, national oracle, and artist par excellence, synthesizing collective and national expression in their highest forms. Prophecy offered an immediacy that might recapture the vital energies of tradition after the ruptures and critiques of modernity.[179] His signing this essay with a self-consciously literary pseudonym perhaps bespeaks his own coming to see the literary artist as a latter-day prophet. Prophecy and its renewal came to engage Rav Kook more and more throughout his life, and I will have much more to say on this in our discussion

---

176 IS 1:36–38; the springboard of the essay is an exegetical problem, that is, how to square Moses's being "of heavy mouth and heavy tongue" with the Maimonidean requirement that the prophet be physically without blemish (*Guide*, 2:32).

177 See the wonderful survey by Matt Goldish, *The Sabbatean Prophets* (Cambridge, MA: Harvard University Press, 2004).

178 See Hamutal Bar-Yosef, "The Jewish Reception of Vladimir Solov'ev," in *Vladimir Solov'ev: Reconciler and Polemicist, Eastern Christian Studies*, vol. 2, ed. Wil ven den Bercken, Manon de Courten, and Evertvan der Zweerde (Peeters: Leuven, 2000), 363–392 and esp. 781–784, and Pamela Davidson, "Vladimir Soloviev and the Ideal of Prophecy," *Slavonic and East European Review* 78, no. 4 (October 2000): 643–670. Brian Horowitz puts forward a more critical view of his philosemitism, seeing it in terms of a Christian theology looking forward to Jews' eventual conversion into a Christian Kingdom of Heaven purged of Judeophobia. See his "Vladimir Solov'ev and the Jews: A View from Today," in his *The Russian Jewish Tradition: Intellectuals, Historians, Revolutionaries* (Boston: Academic Studies Press, 2017), 198–214. We will further see the relevance of Soloviev's thought for Rav Kook later on.

179 Eliezer Schweid argues that a preoccupation with prophecy and its possible renewal is a major theme for the most significant modern Jewish thinkers—see his *Neviim Le-'Amam ve-la-Enoshut*.

of his aggadic commentary '*Eyn Ayah*.[180] At this early stage, as with other elements of his religious life, his touchstone was Maimonides.[181]

For centuries, Jewish philosophers had struggled to reconcile the tension—felt above all in and around the writings of Maimonides—between prophecy as a naturalistic phenomenon arising out of the exertions of the philosopher towards moral and intellectual perfection, and prophecy as something bestowed through God's own free will.[182] The young Rav Kook attempts his own solution to this problem and, extending the metaphors of inner and outer meanings he first attributed to Maimonides in the *Mahaziqei Ha-Dat* essay, draws a distinction between the interiority of prophecy and its external, verbal expression; the former is the summit of naturalistic human exertion, the latter is given, or not, by the untrammeled will of God.

God, he writes, has established eternal laws of nature both for corporeal matters and for "many other things hidden in the recesses of creation and hiding places (*matmonim*) of the soul," and He is unwilling to change them in the absence of exigent circumstance.[183] Prophecy too is governed by those immutable laws as regards the inner life of the prophet, while the public expression of prophecy results from God's free will:

---

180 It is worth noting that the opening words of his first sermon at Zeimel were from Isa. 6:6: "And one of the seraphs flew over to me with a live coal, which he had taken from the altar." See the memoir of Aharon Chajes, son of a leading member of the town and patron of Rav Kook, *Shishim ve-Shalosh Shanah bi-Yerushalayim* (Jerusalem: Salomon Press, 1953), 30. Aderet says in *Seder Eliyahu*, 67, that the Pentateuchal lection for the Sabbath on which he and Rav Kook first visited the town together was *Parshat Yitro* (Ex. 18:1–20:26), the *haftarah* (prophetic lection) for which is none other than Isa. 6. Yet, given the richness of that week's Pentateuchal reading, which includes the Sinai revelation itself, his choice of Isaiah's prophetic vision as his point of departure is telling.

181 Maimonides's chief exposition of his doctrine of prophecy is at the *Guide*, 2:35–47 and in the seventh chapter of his *Code's Hilkhot Yesodei Ha-Torah*. The latter is the basis of Kook's discussion here. The *Guide* passages figure prominently in his aggadah commentary *'Eyn Ayah*, as we will see.

182 This tension was formulated by Harry Wolfson in a classic essay, first written in 1942, in terms of the divergent views of Yehudah Ha-Levi and Maimonides: "Both Hallevi [*sic*] and Maimonides agree that [prophecy] is a process dependent upon the will of God. But in conformity with their respective views as to the operation of the divine Will in nature, they differ also as to the operation of the divine Will in prophecy. To Hallevi it is a direct act of God's will; to Maimonides, it is an act of God's will through the intermediacy of the Active Intellect . . . they differ also as to the prerequisite qualifications for prophecy. To Hallevi, right action as prescribed by the Law is sufficient; to Maimonides, intellectual perfection is an additional essential condition." Harry A. Wolfson, "Maimonides and Hallevi on Prophecy," in his *Studies in the History and Philosophy of Religion* (Cambridge, MA: Harvard University Press, 1973–1979), 60–119, 116; the essay was first published in *Jewish Quarterly Review* [n.s.] 32, no. 4 (April 1942): 345–370 and *Jewish Quarterly Review* [n.s.] 33, no. 1 (July 1942): 49–82.

The issue reverberates elsewhere as well; see, for instance, Isaac Arama's criticisms and attempted synthesis of Maimonides and Ha-Levi, in Sara Heller-Wilensky, *Rabbi Yitzhaq Arama u-Mishnato* (Jerusalem/Tel Aviv: Mossad Bialik/Devir, 1956), 166–182.

183 IS 1:36.

In truth, the interiority of prophecy, which is the superior knowledge deriving from greatness of soul and its clinging to the heavens, is a natural law established by God within the soul at the beginning of its emanation, but the outpouring of prophetic words cannot be an abiding nature from the outset of creation, for the prophet has attained his station by a series of intellectual causalities from the sacrality of his thought, and the clothing of prophecy in speech as conjoining the spiritual and corporeal is utterly a wonder.[184]

This, he says, is why Maimonides, in the naturalistic presentation of prophecy in his Code, speaks of the "holy spirit" and not of "prophecy," since the former is a function of the individual's own preparedness, while the latter is entirely dependent on God's free will.[185]

We hear in this passage echoes of the terms Rav Took attributed to Maimonides in his essay in *Mahaziqei Ha-Dat* and 'Azariah de Figo's *Binah le-'Ittim* (the latter of which he explicitly cited in his essay and as we have seen seems to have influenced the essay on science he wrote in his teens),[186] and echoes also perhaps of Isaac Arama—who, we have also seen, was a likely part of his curriculum and, as we will see before long, he regularly quotes in this period. For all these writers, the word "interiority" (*tokhiyut*) has a usage almost entirely peculiar to them.[187]

The second issue of *'Ittur Sofrim* appeared later that same year, 1888. Most of the issue was again taken up with Rav Kook's own writings, and he once again explored the systematizing of halakhah under the aegis of the Maimonidean corpus, and the meaning of prophecy.[188] The most interesting of the other contributions was an explicitly *wissenschaftliche* essay on the authorship of the Mishnah by Nathan Hayim David Stern of

---

184 Ibid. 1:37:

והנה תוכיות הנבואה שהיא הידיעה המעולה הבאה מגדולת הנפש והדבקה בעליונים זהו חק טבעי כנן השם ית'

בנפש בתחלת אצילותה, אבל השפעת הדברים הנבואיים אי אפשר לומר שיהי' טבע קיים מראשית היצירה שהסיבות

שהביאו הנביא למדרגתו הרמה המה סיבות שכליות מקדושת מחשבתו והתלבשות הנבואה בדברים אינה רק כולה

פלא על קישור רוחני בגשמי.

185 Ibid. He is here answering the question of *Lehem Mishnah* to Maimonides, *Mishneh Torah*, *Hilkhot Yesodei Ha-Torah* 7:1, who expressed astonishment at the seeming naturalism of his position.

186 The citation of Figo in *Mahaziqei Ha-Dat* is to be found in *Otzarot*, 2:146.

187 A search of the DBS CD-Rom *Taqlitor Torani Jerusalem: Disc Book Systems,* 1974 shows a total of ten appearances of the word in medieval and early modern Jewish philosophical literature, two each in *'Aqedat Yitzhaq* and *Reishit Hokhmah*, and six times in *Binah le-'Ittim*. (Rav Kook had read *Rei'shit Hokhmah* as well, as we will see in chapter three.) Indeed, in *Binah le-'Ittim* (pt. 2, *Derush le-Shabbat Ha-Gadol*) we see the word used in reference to Balaam, the mere mouthpiece of God, admitting to not understanding the *tokhiyut* of his own prophecy. Moreover, Arama characterizes a prophet as "a living creature speaking divine utterance" (*hay medabber dibbur Elohi*), *'Aqedat Yitzhaq* 44:95a; Heller-Wilensky, *Rabbi Yitzhaq Arama u-Mishnato*, 175.

188 Aside from Rav Kook's own essays, it consisted of, again, novellae from Meir Mikhel of Vilna, one from one Eliyahu Brill Bachrach, another paragraph of unpublished posthumous novellae from Shlomo Kluger, and a eulogy delivered by Alexander Moshe of Raisin for Eliyahu Levinson Kratinger.

Shavil, son of Yosef Zekhariah Stern (who, not long after publishing this essay, died an untimely death).[189]

In one of the essays Kook offers an interesting rendering of how he sees his project, which demonstrates some ambivalence about his self-appointed role:[190]

> The path I have laid down for myself in editing 'Ittur Sofrim is to tie together, with God's help, Torah and praxis per the will of the great and wise men of our generation who understand what the situation of Torah in these our times requires of us; this precious and effective path—which was taught and thought out not by my spirit, I am not its father, but rather the whispered spirit of life that blows slowly through God's grace in the houses of Holy Torah and chambers of piety—will keep 'Ittur Sofrim from uttering not a word outside its fitting time, when there is some hope that those who bear the seeds of the words and halakhot will return rejoicing with the fruit of deeds in the world of action [after Ps. 126:5].[191]

A responsum on whether a bar-mitzvah boy on the eve of his thirteenth birthday must say the blessing for Torah study serves as a springboard for a much broader jurisprudential discussion as to the meaning of the distinction between Biblically and rabbinically based laws, and to a discussion, again, of the difference between "holy spirit" and "prophecy." Building on his discussion of this distinction in the previous issue and taking up the question of the legal status of prophecy, which had exercised other nineteenth-century rabbinic thinkers, he argues that "prophecy" is normatively authoritative while "holy spirit" is not.[192] He further takes up the systematics of Maimonidean halakhah and the role of scripture therein in some lengthy glosses to some of his father-in-law Aderet's novellae to Talmudic discussion of the Paschal sacrifice.[193]

In an essay on ethics, again using the pen name *AY"H Sofer*, and perhaps reflecting his financial travails and his first impression of his new flock in Zeimel, he offers an appreciation of the religious merit of ordinary people vis-à-vis that of professional Torah scholars, as the latter are spared the trials of daily survival in the unforgiving world of the marketplace.[194] Here too his choosing to use his nom de plume indicates an attempt to identify with a larger spirit of the times, in this case, social and economic criticism.

---

189 This essay is noteworthy for citing the *Darkhei Ha-Mishnah* of Zecharia Frankel (albeit by his initials Rzf), along with Sherira Gaon, Maimonides's *Guide*, Zvi Hirsch Chajes, and Moshe Hayim Luzzatto, taken together, reflecting a traditionalist Maskilic bent. In the issue he used only his initials, Nhds, and was identified in the 1974 edition.

190 The essay, entitled "Hilulei Peri Qodesh," IS 2:24–27, discusses the question of etrogim of the Land of Israel versus those of Corfu, an issue which, throughout the nineteenth century served as a nodal point of discussion around the need to encourage Jewish settlement and agricultural development in Palestine; see Yosef Salmon, "Ha-Pulmus 'al Etrogei Corfu ve-Etrogei Eretz Yisrael—1875–1891," *Tzion* 65, no. 1 (2000): 106–175.

191 IS 2:24.

192 IS 2:17–19. Zevi Hirsch Chajes authored an 1836 treatise, *Torat Neviim*, on this subject.

193 Ibid., 23ff.

194 Ibid., 33–35.

A lengthy essay continues his discussion in the previous issue as to whether the reasons behind laws need to be a part of discussion and adjudication as part of a broader systematization of law.[195] His fundamental reference point is the classic Mitnagdic position that Torah study is the supreme religious command; indeed, in his presentation the significant difference between precept and practice resides chiefly in the distinctive sorts of study they evoke. He discerns a disagreement here between Maimonides's view that one may render halakhic decisions without knowing the reason as such, and Rashi's, for whom one cannot adjudicate without knowing the reason.[196] For the former, the imperative of adjudication by Torah can be fulfilled by a straightforward reference to black-letter law, while for the latter the exploration of reasons and rationales across the board is the very essence of study.

He then proceeds to ask if a halakhist must survey every opinion and precedent before arriving at a decision and concludes that one can rely on an individual respected decisor if need be; he reaches this by an ingenious understanding of the well-settled halakhic principle of *rov*, or majority rule, namely, we can presume that a solid majority of any given decisor's opinions are more or less correct, and that enables us to follow his views.[197] This unconventional reading seems to tell us something about his sense of himself as he stakes out a place for the role of lone authority.

This second issue of *'Ittur Sofrim* opened with a lengthy "letter to the publisher" by the writer, editor, and journalistic entrepreneur Yitzhak Suvalski criticizing the first issue for not living up to its promise; in a time of unprecedented historical, social, and cultural challenges, he wrote, publishing energies and resources ought not to be wasted on the same old Talmudic novellae and run-of-the-mill responsa, but rather on: questions about Europe and Palestine; contemporary halakhic issues; pithy analyses of Talmudic problems; brief discussion of halakhic novellae; book reviews; necrologies; listings of newly ordained rabbis; and *tiqqun 'agunot*. Much of the issue failed to satisfy theses criteria, and so a year later Suvalski put his own program into action by founding his own periodical *Knesset Ha-Gedolah*.[198]

---

195 Ibid., 35–40.

196 The statements of Rashi's on which he bases himself here are listed in IS 1:21, and therein at 38 he suggests that a similar view of Rashi's position was held by Shneur Zalman of Liady. His assertion of what he takes to be Maimonides's view is at IS 2:35.

197 The principle of majority rule generally refers to the majority of opinions by a group of decisors centered on one specific matter, and is not a presumption as to the reliability of any one decisor deriving from the majority of opinions within his own corpus, dealing with a range of matters; see *Entziklopedia Talmudit*, s.v. "halakhah." By contrast, the latter-day authority Moshe Feinstein offers a defense of an individual decisor's freedom without recourse to arguments of *rov* and simply by virtue of one's own study and rectitude, see his *Igrot Moshe*, *Yoreh De'ah* 1, no. 101, s.v. *U-Mah*.

198 On Suvalski, see briefly *EJ* 15:540. Born in 1863, an alumnus of Volozhin, and regular contributor to *Ha-Levanon*, *Ha-Tzefirah*, *Ha-Melitz*, and *He-'Asif*, and the founding editor of *Knesset Ha-Gedolah*, he identified with the religious Zionist movement and eventually moved to London where he single-handedly (serving as editor, typesetter, proofreader,

It is, in light of these criticisms, interesting and instructive to note that in the very same year in which 'Ittur Sofrim first appeared Berdyczewsky published a similar journal of his own, *Beit Ha-Midrash*.[199] This journal, too, largely consists of essays written by its editor, who also, in an introductory essay, calls on men of letters to illuminate the Torah and enlighten the age. Unlike 'Ittur Sofrim, this journal does not offer letters of approbation from leading rabbinic authorities or writings by significant rabbis, with the telling exception of Yitzhak Ya'aqov Reines, who was conspicuously absent from Rav Kook's 'Ittur Sofrim. In his own essays, Berdyczewsky directly addresses problems of the day;[200] forthrightly tries to negotiate between the Talmud methodologies of the yeshivot and the nascent academic study of Talmud;[201] offers his own understanding of the relationship between halakhah and aggadah;[202] presents an essay on the political structure of ancient Israel;[203] and offers a series of book reviews, covering history, philosophy, and halakhah.[204] He closes with a series of playful, satiric sallies against the mediocrity of Hebrew authors, ostensibly copied from "an ancient manuscript."[205]

Placing the two journals side by side, we see the extent to which the young Rav Kook remained far more rooted than his contemporary in the culture of Lithuanian Talmudism, even as he allowed himself to experience and experiment with other currents of his day: journalism, legal theorizing, and perhaps even the renewal of prophecy. He did so while rooted in a pietistic outlook that would never have allowed for Berdyczewsky's satires, or his more freely critical spirit. The two alumni of Volozhin would go on paralleling each other in the coming years, Berdyczewsky following the tumultuous spirits of modernity while Rav Kook doing his best to remain squarely within the rabbinic camp and the canons of the tradition, even as he came to experience some of those spirits themselves.

Assessing 'Ittur Sofrim as a whole, we see the youthful Rav Kook trying to integrate a firm anchoring in Mitnagdic Talmudism with quasi-Maskilic interests in the

---

and administrator) published a Hebrew weekly for an unprecedented seventeen years until his death in 1913; see Risa Domb, "A Hebrew Island in the British Isles: *Hayehoody* and Its Editor I. Suwalski (1897–1913)," in *Jewish History: Essays in Honour of Chimen Abramsky*, ed. Ada Rapoport-Albert and Steven J. Zipperstein (London: Peter Halban, 1988), 127–137; a condensed Hebrew version of this essay appears in *Proceedings of the Ninth World Congress of Jewish Studies* 3 (1985): Hebrew Section, 251–256.

199 *Beit Ha-Midrash: Miqdash Le-Torah u-le-Hokhmat Yisrael*, edited by Berdyczewsky, was published by Shelatiel Gruber as a supplement to his annual *Otzar Ha-Sefarim*, in Cracow, 1888. Aside from Reines, the other contributors are young men, one of them Shmuel Alexandrov, who was later to become one of Rav Kook's more fascinating correspondents, as we will see.

200 *Beit Ha-Midrash*, 1–12.

201 Ibid., 13–16, 19–21, 24–25.

202 Ibid., 25–26.

203 Ibid., 43–48.

204 Ibid., 86–109; among the authors he reviews are Eliezer Zweifel, Hayim Hirschensohn, and Yitzhak Ya'aqov Reines.

205 Ibid., 111–112—*ne'etqu mi-ktav yashan noshan*. Berdyczewsky's essays are reprinted in volume 2 of Avner Holzman's edition of his collected works.

systematization of halakhah and the art of writing. Aside from the essays on etrogim, there is little overt concern with proto-Zionism. In his halakhic essays he recurs over and over to issues of systematic classification of laws and the rationalization of halakhic decision-making. In this respect he seems to have been more than touched by the spirit of the times. As he moved deeper into the practical work of the rabbinate, the comparative luxury and intellectual detachment which facilitated these sorts of reflections became less available (though a decade later his first response to Zionism was an essay on the possibilities it presented for the rationalization and systematization of halakhah).

As we have seen, in essays on prophecy and on social ethics, he uses the pen name *AY"H Sofer*; this seems both a striking assertion of a self-conscious literary identity as well as a provocation, that is, when vocalized, "*ayeh sofer?*"—where is the writer who will rise to the challenges of the time? The pseudonym leaves the question explicitly open and implicitly answered: here I am.

Loss

The second issue of *'Ittur Sofrim* was the last. In the spring of 1889, Bat-Sheva died at age twenty-two of what seems to have been pneumonia.[206] In a letter to Hayim Hezekiah Medini after her death, accompanying a revised version of his final essay on halakhic decision making for publication in Medini's *Sdei Hemed*, he writes: "I was forced to cease the work of *'Ittur Sofrim* due to the illness of my wife . . . and since then I have been very broken and much time has passed with great cares and sadness in my heart, and I have not had the strength to return to the work."[207]

Another publishing ambition was laid aside; the previous fall, he had written to Hayim Berlin, son of Netziv and then-rabbi of Moscow, to suggest publishing a small-format Babylonian Talmud with a brief commentary to be written by a consortium of leading scholars. In the letter he laid out a whole publication schedule with sample pages.[208] This project, too, was derailed by the tragic death of his wife.

By age twenty-three, Avraham Yitzhak Kook, having been driven by economic circumstance to a comparatively insignificant rabbinic post, was now a bereaved widower and father, his ambitious journal undone. At Aderet's urging, he remarried, to his wife's cousin, Raiza Rivka Rabinowitz-Teomim.[209]

---

206 The details of her illness are given by her father in *Seder Eliyahu*, 69–71.

207 This personal note is appended to the 1974 edition; it is omitted from the excerpts reprinted in *Otzarot* and is quoted by Neriah, *Tal*, 114.

208 *Igrot*, 1:3–6, no. 3.

209 Neriah, *Tal*, 114.

   Little has been written about Raiza Rivka Kook; see Neriah, *Liqutei Ha-Re'ayah*, vol. 2 (Kfar Ha-Ro'eh: Hai Roi 1991), 251–260; for a photo and brief profile of her by the well-known early twentieth-century Jerusalem chronicler Pinhas Grayevsky, see *Benot Tzion vi-Yerushalayim* 7 (Jerusalem: Yad Ben-Tzvi, 2000 [1929]), 316–317; see also the brief but poignant mention of her in Shmuel Yosef Agnon, *Me-'Atzmi el 'Atzmi* (Jerusalem: Schocken, 2000), 201. Even-Hen, *Rav u-Manhig*, 87–92, recounts conversations around their wedding indicating that the tragic

He also undertook, with his flock's permission, a pilgrimage to the great Kabbalist Shlomo Elyashiv (1841–1926), author of the multivolume *Leshem Shevo ve-Ahlamah* (*Ligure, Agate, and Jasper* [after Ex. 28:19]).[210] A Lithuanian Kabbalist of a strikingly independent bent, Elyashiv resisted the allegorical reading of Kabbalistic doctrines, which had been put forward by Moshe Hayim Luzzatto, endorsed by the Gaon, and was a defining feature of Lithuanian Kabbalah, about which I will have more to say in the coming chapters.[211] Elyashiv's Kabbalah was deeply theurgical; indeed, one of his chief criticisms of Luzzatto's allegorizations was that they obscure and detract from the most urgent task facing the Kabbalist, that is, the cosmic task of restoration and repair within the Godhead, which is the deepest meaning of the ostensibly this-worldly command to "know God in all your ways" (Prov. 3:6).[212] (Despite his criticisms of Luzzatto, Elyashiv made great efforts to see to the publication of his writings;[213] it is presumably through him that Rav Kook encountered them.) We will have more to say in the coming chapters about Elyashiv and much more about Luzzatto.

This pilgrimage to Elyashiv, in my view, was an early sign of a genuine and crucial shift, as this hitherto very self-confident, indeed brash young man seems more humbled and concomitantly draws inward. In the next dozen years he published next to nothing, though he wrote a great deal, turning from his large project of reforming halakhic practice and redefining prophecy to exploring moral and spiritual self-cultivation. This deepening interiority led over time to far-reaching changes in his religious outlook, from a self-confident rationalism to a subjectivity through which he explains and justifies himself to himself. It is to the beginnings of this new path that we now turn.

---

circumstances of Bat-Sheva's death, to say the least, cast a pall on the occasion. Here too, his account is unsourced but has the ring of truth.

210 The connection between his wife's death and his trip to Elyashiv is made explicitly by Aryeh Frankel in his lengthy entry on Rav Kook in *Entziklopedia Ha-Tzionut Ha-Datit*, vol. 5., at col. 95. Elyashiv lived in Shavil, where Yosef Zekharia Stern was rabbi; Rav Kook presumably deepened his acquaintance with Stern at the time as well.

211 A brief biography of Elyashiv was written by the legendary Jerusalem saint Aryeh Levin, *Toldot Ha-Gaon Ha-Kadosh Mehabber Sifrei Leshem Shevo ve-Ahlamah* (Jerusalem: Verker, 1935). His principal Kabbalistic teachings and their relationship to other currents in Lithuanian Kabalah are the subject of Ron Wachs, "Peraqim be-Mishnato Ha-Kabalit shel Ha-Rav Shlomo Elyashiv" (master's thesis, Hebrew University, 1995). Elyashiv's independence also emerges clearly in Mordechai Pachter, "Kabbalat Ha-Gra be-Aspaqlaryah shel Shtei Mesorot," in Hallamish, Rivlin, and Schuchat, *The Vilna Gaon and His Disciples*, 119–136. For the views of the Gaon to which he was reacting see generally Raphael Shuchat, "Ha-Parshanut Ha-Historiosofit Ha-Kabbalit shel Ha-Gra ve-Hashpa'at Ramhal 'alav ve-'al Beit Midrasho," *Da'at* 40 (1998): 125–152 as well as Eliezer Baumgarten's studeis to be discussed later on.

212 Elyashiv's differences with Luzzatto were not only doctrinal but stylistic, as he wrote in a deeply esoteric idiom entirely inaccessible to any other than deeply learned students of Lurianic Kabbalah, in strong contrast to Luzzatto's lucid prose style.

213 Wachs, "Peraqim be-Mishnato Ha-Kabalit shel Ha-Rav Shlomo Elyashiv," 111.

2

All in the Mind: The Writings of the Zeimel Period

By 1889, at age twenty-three, Rav Kook had assumed his first rabbinic post, become a father, launched and then folded his first signifcant writing project, and with the loss of his wife Bat-Sheva Alta Rabinowitz had remarried to her cousin Raiza Rivka Rabinowitz. Together, they would have several more children, and bury one.[1] In Zeimel, he wrote halakhic responsa and Talmudic novellae, deepened his reading in philosophy, and intensified his Kabbalistic studies. The extent of his writing in that period has recently been made dramatically clear by the publication of his first journal from that time, *Metziot Qatan*, in which we see themes preoccupying him then and in the future.[2] He stayed in Zeimel until 1896, when he left to take up a position in the much larger town of Boisk, and, as we will see, deepened his engagement with the spiritual crises rocking the Lithunian yeshivot, and in broader currents of Jewish nationalist and intellectual life.[3]

Rav Kook was in this period of his life more subdued, humbled by experience. The one volume he published was anonymous. He stayed out of the public eye and, it seems,

---

1   Rav Kook and his first wife Bat-Sheva had one daughter, Frayda Chana, born in 1887. His second wife and Bastsheva's cousin, Raiza Rifka, gave birth in Zeimel to a son, Zvi Yehudah (b. 15 Nisan 5651/April 23, 1891), and in Boisk, to two daughters, Batya Miriam (born on 29 Shvat 5757/February 1, 1897) and Ruhama Toyve, in 1897. She died at age two and a half of pneumonia on 12 Tamuz 5660/July 9, 1900. She was, until recently, entirely unknown, see Harel Kohen, ed., introduction to *Metziot Qatan* (Jerusalem/Beit El: Koren/Me-Avnei Ha-Maqom, 2018), 30. A third daughter, Esther Yael, was borin on 13 Adar 5667/February 27, 1907. My thanks to Rabbi Ari Shvat for clarifying a number of these details. Neriah makes little mention of Rav Kook's daughters. The births of all but Ruhama are briefly mentioned by Lifshitz, *Shivhei Ha-Re'ayah*, 60. Esther Yael's tragic death in 1919 is recounted there at 148. For more on the special relationship she enjoyed with her father, and the sad circumstances of her passing, see Shemarya Gershuni, "'Yaldah Hakhamah ve-Tovat Sekhel' . . . 'Al Esther Kook, Bito shel Ha-Re'ayah," *Ha-Ma'ayan* 224, no. 58:2, (Kislev 5778/2017-2018): 75–92.

2   Hereinafter MQ.

3   1895 is the date given in all his biographies for his transit to Boisk. Yet the note he appends to the end of his collection of sermons *Midbar Shur* is dated "3 Nisan 5656, Zeimel," and that

undertook a kind of inner pilgrimage, nourished by his reading in Kabbalah and medieval Jewish philosophy. At this stage he laid great stress on the primacy of intellect and the mind in his picture of both humanity and the religious life, coupled with an interest in the God-given nature of the material world and the body, which he joins to pietist dimensions most vividly in his writings on phylacteries, *tefillin*. In the volume of sermons he composed at the close of this period, *Midbar Shur*, the emphasis on mind becomes the touchstone of extensive thought on the relationship between Jewish and gentile morality. At this chapter's close we will see how the death of his first wife continued to haunt him during these years, reinforcing our impression that her tragic death was one of the things that drove him inward in his search for the foundations of his own religious life.

The Small-Town Rabbinate

Zeimel was a small community, and aside from the usual rabbinic duties of answering halakhic questions and adjudicating disputes, he was left with much time for the study of Talmud (Babylonian and Palestinian), works of philosophy, and Kabbalah (the latter with a friend), and spent much of the day in study, wrapped in tallit and tefillin. Though he himself studied Maimonides's *Guide*, he was wary of encouraging young people to do so.[4] He devoted roughly an hour and a half each day to the study of aggadah, and began his aggadic commentary, to which I will devote a subsequent chapter.[5] It was there that he

---

date corresponds to March 17, 1896. Moreover, according to a notice in *Ha-Melitz*, August 18, 1896, 4, he took up the position in Boisk in August 13 of that year.

During those years his father Shlomo Zalman became, at his son's suggestion, a roving fundraiser for Volozhin in the Caucasus, where he developed a friendship with Hayim Hezekiah Medini, author of the massive halakhic encyclopedia *Sdei Hemed*, to which Rav Kook contributed, as we saw in the previous chapter. See Neriah, *Sihot*, 154–155. His and his father's correspondence with Netziv regarding this commission has been reprinted in *Sinai* 61 (1967): 67–68. It also emerges there that Rav Kook's mother supplemented her husband's income by producing wines and grape juices. It is, epistolary hyperboles notwithstanding, worth noting the lavish encomia with which Netziv addresses the young Rav Kook, then all of twenty-one:

ידיד נאמן הרב הגדול חו״ב י״א מרבים כש״ת מ׳ אברהם יצחק . . .

In a letter reprinted there from 1888, Netziv's son Hayim Berlin addresses him as

האי גברא רבא יקירא וחביבא הרב הגאון הנאדר ומהולל בתשבחות והוא כהן לאל עליון עין העדה לתורה ולתעודה
מ׳ אברהם יצחק . . .

This is an extraordinary set of encomia for a twenty-three-year-old to receive, even by the generally florid standards of rabbinic epistolary.

An attempt at finding his father similar work as the American fundraiser for the Mir yeshiva proved unsuccessful, see the letter to Rav Kook from Hayim Yehudah Tikoczynsky, founder of the Mir yeshiva, in *Igrot*, 29.

4   More details on Zeimel are to be found in the extensive editor's introduction to *Metziot Qatan*. See also, Neriah, *Sihot*, 148.

5   Ibid., 150.

began his lifelong practice of keeping a spiritual diary.[6] In the course of his reading he also garnered knowledge of broader intellectual and cultural currents from the rich Hebrew periodical press of the time.[7] He developed the community's library and devoted time and energy to local charitable and welfare societies. Maimon and Neriah report that one year during an outbreak of cholera (presumably the epidemic of 1893), he ate on Yom Kippur, following the legendary—and not uncontroversial—precedent of Israel Salanter who had done the same thing during the epidemic of 1868.[8]

---

6   Neriah, *Tal*, 118.

7   In a 1988 essay on the sources of Rav Kook's philosophic knowledge, the late Eliezer Goldman singled out Fabius Mieses's Hebrew popularization *Qorot Ha-Filosofiya Ha-Hadashah* (Leipzig: Mortiz Schafer, 1877) as a decisive influence; the essay was reprinted in his *Mehqarim ve-'Iyunim*, 217–224. Goldman had no external evidence of Rav Kook's having read the volume but called attention to what he saw as striking parallels between Mieses's formulations of Schelling's doctrine of the "unity of opposites" and similar formulations in later works of Rav Kook. Avinoam Rosenak later devoted a stream of articles to an interpretation of Rav Kook in these Schellingian terms. Benjamin Ish-Shalom has argued, correctly in my view, that overreliance on this one source is misplaced, given the range of sources available to Rav Kook at the time; see his "Beyn Rav Kook le-Spinoza ve-Goethe," in *Rivka Schatz-Uffenheimer Memorial Volume 2*, ed. Rachel Elior and Joseph Dan, special issue, *Jerusalem Studies in Jewish Thought* 13 (1996): 525–556.

Goldman's asserted parallels between Rav Kook and Mieses's Schelling are not entirely convincing to this reader. While it is more than reasonable to say that Rav Kook knew of Schelling, he need not necessarily have read much of him in order to be familiar with some of his ideas, not least because of Schelling's own intellectual sources within Kabalistic tradition, as mediated via Jakob Boehme; see M. H. Abrams, *Natural Supernaturalism: Tradition and Revolution in Romantic Literature* (New York: Norton, 1971), 170. For a nuanced discussion of Boehme's dependence on Kabbalah, see Wilhelm Schmidt Biggemann, "Jakob Boehme und die Kabbala," in *Christliche Kabbala*, ed. Wilhelm Schmidt Biggermann (Ostfildern: Jan Thorbecke, 2003), 157–181. The "unity of opposites" has deep antecedents within Kabbalah, not least in Habad, see Rachel Elior, *The Paradoxical Ascent to God*, trans. Jeffrey M. Green (Albany: State University of New York Press, 1993). Moreover, Schelling shows up in the writings of other well-read rabbis of the time, such as Yehoshua Yosef Preil, in the latter's *Eglei Tal*, 2 vols. (Warsaw: Schuldberg, 1899–1901).

Finally, Mieses was not the only Hebrew popularization of philosophy available at the time; see, for example, Shimon Bernfeld's *Da'at Elohim* (Warsaw: Schuldberg, 1899), esp. part 2, dedicated to modern philosophy and Kabbalah; Bernfeld's writings in *Ha-Shiloah* were presumably familiar to Rav Kook, and his volume was published farther East than Leipzig. Moreover, the writings of David Neumark and Hillel Zeitlin in *Ha-Shiloah*, *Luah Ahi'asaf* and other periodicals Rav Kook was reading, as well as his conversations and correspondence with well-read peers, were almost certainly sources of Rav Kook's knowledge of philosophy.

The fact that Schelling, unlike Kant, Spinoza, Schopenhauer, and Bergson, goes unmentioned in Rav Kook's writings is not in itself dispositive, as Rav Kook mentions Nietzsche by name only once, as we will see, though the latter's influence on him is unmistakable.

8   Maimon, *Azkarah*, 58. Following on the famine of the two preceding years, the 1893 epidemic, in addition to its human tragedy, demonstrated the tsarist regime's increasing inability to govern effectively, further alienated many of the educated middle classes, and gave renewed impetus to radical movements. On the famine and epidemics of 1891–1893 and their sociopolitical

Some of the anecdotes that have come down to us from the Zeimel years indicate his wish to retain his moral and spiritual scrupulousness amid the blandishments and dulling routines of the small-town rabbinate. For instance, his salary, like that of other rabbis in poor communities, was paid in part by the proceeds of sales of salt in the local market, and he insisted on the salt being weighed in nonabsorbent, transparent glass pans so that he would be given his exact due and not a grain more, and when merchants balked at this extra cost to them he chose to forego that element of his salary.[9] On the walls of the room in which he adjudicated lawsuits he posted quotes from the Bible and Talmud on the exacting severity of the law.[10] He seems to have been uneasy about the vacations taken by area rabbis at the resort in Dubulti (in Yiddish, Dubbelen), twenty-two kilometers outside Riga on the shores of the Baltic. According to one anecdote, Dov Lifshitz, rabbi of Srednik, once admonished him, while vacationing at the spa, not to study with such intensity, and said: "Rabbi of Zeimel, here one should rest, not study!"[11]

Talmudic Commentary and a Sage's Discontents

His anxieties about the moral and spiritual challenges of the Rabbinate, and the widening scope of his theological reflections, found expression in a commentary he wrote in 1890, at age twenty-five, to the fantastic seafaring tales of the Talmudic sage Rabbah bar bar Hannah, recorded in BT Bava Batra 73a–74a.[12]

---

effects, see John F. Hutchinson, *Later Imperial Russia, 1890–1917* (London: Longman, 2001), 14–16, 24–27. On Salanter's episode and rabbinic disagreements over it at the time, see Eliezer Mermelstein, "Akhilah be-Yom Ha-Kippurim bi-Meqom Holi u-Zman Magefah—Mahalat Ha-Kholera—Hetero shel Ha-Gaʾon Rabbi Yisrael Salanter u-Svarat Ha-Holqim ʿAlav," *Qovetz ʾEtz Hayim—Bobov* 7 (Tishrei 5769/2008): 273–294.

9 Ibid., 146. Neriah, *Tal*, 102.

10 Ibid. Yitzhak Nissenbaum relates a story told about Rav Kook during his time in Zeimel, that when a visitor from elsewhere would depart he would place a piece of bread in his pocket and escort him for a bit outside his home, to fulfill the rabbinic admonition (Mishnah Sotah 9:6) that sending visitors on their way without provisions is akin to murder (Nissenbaum, ʿAlei Heldi, 188).

11 Neriah, *Tal*, 105–107. It was there that he first met Samuel Mohilever, perhaps the leading rabbinic figure of Hibat Tzion, after the latter's return from his first visit to Palestine, in 1890. Rav Kook's later reminiscences of Mohilever as a mold-breaking "rabbi hero" were published in 1923 and are reprinted in MH, 127–130. He also developed a friendship with Mohilever's aide Isaac Ben-Tovim; see his letter to the latter from 1911, *Igrot*, 2:21–22, and Neriah, *Sihot*, 275.

12 The commentaries are printed in *Maʾamarei Ha-Reʾayah* (Jerusalem: n.p., 1984) [hereinafter MH], 419–448. The date of their authorship is given by Neriah, *Tal*, 124. As this present volume was nearing completion, Bezalel Naor pubished an English translation of this text, based on a photocopy of the original manuscript, to which he has added characteristically erudite commentary, and several fascinating appendices; see Bezalel Naor, ed., *The Legends of Rabbah bar bar Hannah with the Commentary of Rabbi Abraham Isaac Hacohen Kook* (New York/Monsey: Kodesh/Orot, 2019). Naor finds the printed and manuscript editions to be

The commentary is striking for the range of Kabalistic texts with which he had become familiar by that time, in particular those associated with Lithuanian Kabbalah.[13] It is also deeply revealing of some of the concerns and perhaps tensions animating him at the time: the temptations of arrogance, the tension between exoteric and esoteric study, the sage's relationship to the community, the relationship between practical and contemplative wisdom, between Jewish and gentile morals, and between wisdom and the ecstasy of *unio mystica*, of *devequt*.

Set-piece commentaries on these tales were popular and widely printed, and at least two precedents were likely known to him. The Gaon of Vilna authored a commentary to six of the eleven tales of Rabbah bar bar Hannah. And the tales comprise the textual backbone of the first eighteen discourses of Nahman of Bratslav's major theological work *Liqutei Moharan*. [14]

The Gaon's commentary depicts the tales as fairly straightforward moralizing allegories; the boat is the body, the sea represents the troubles of this world, and the tales are a "pilgrim's progress" among the snares of earthly existence. Nahman's readings, by contrast, are overtly Kabbalistic and concerned with challenges facing the individual in his inner life, in particular the allure, not of the material, but of the demonic; the dialectical tensions animating the inner life; and the extraordinary powers and licenses of the *tzadiq* as he smelts and purifies the consciousnesses of his adherents.

Rav Kook's basic approach in part reflects both these predecessors—like the Gaon, he reads the tales as moralistic allegories of the challenges facing the pious in the world; and, like Nahman, he draws on explicitly Kabbalistic texts and imagery and the Kabbalistic view of the universe as an arena of contending, often demonic, forces. At the same time he differs from both of them in his steady focus on the sage, rather than on the common man or on the *tzadiq*, and on the particular challenges attending the life of the mind, especially the temptations of arrogance and the tension between action and contemplation. Further,

---

largely the same, with one exception, regarding the possibility of halakhic change; see ibid., 13–14.

13 Among the works cited (along with the page numbers on which they appear in MH) are: Cordovero's *Or Ne'erav* (427); Shneur Zalman of Liady's *Liqutei Torah* (432); Shalom Buzaglo's popular Zohar commentary *Miqdash Melekh* (432); Hayim Vital's *Sefer Ha-Gilgulim* (432, 441); Gra's commentaries on *Tiqqunei Zohar* (439) and on Proverbs (440); Luzzatto's commentary on the *Idra Rabbah, Adir Ba-Marom* (440, 446) as well as his *Qalah Pithei Hokhmah* (445); Hayim of Volozhin's *Nefesh Ha-Hayim* (442); and Issac Haver Wildman's commentary to the *Idrah Rabbah, Beit 'Olamim* (445). And, of course, the Bible. Talmud and Zohar are regularly referred to throughout, as is the Zohar, and there is also reference to Arama's *'Aqedat Yitzhaq* (423) and Bahya ibn Paquda, *Hovot Ha-Levavot*, trans. Yehudah ibn Tibbon (Warsaw: Goldman, 1875), (428).

14 The Gaon's commentaries were first published in his *Peirush 'al Kamah Aggadot* (Vilna: Rotenberg, 1830), 1–4. It is also worth noting that though the Gaon did not generally write approbations to rabbinic works, he did write one for a commentary on these aggadot by Shmuel ben Elieizer of Kalvarija, entitled *Darkhei No'am* (Koenigsberg: Jahn Friedrich Drost, 1764). My thanks to the remarkable CHayim Steinmetz for bringing this to my attention.

he broaches the parallel relationships between secular and sacred learning and between the gentiles and Israel—and projects the former not as demonic, as did many Kabbalists, but as currently unredeemed and en route to redemption.[15]

Throughout, he takes the image of seafaring as a metaphor for navigating the paths to wisdom.[16] The sea, he says, represents esoteric wisdom, the land exoteric.[17] The challenges explored in the seafaring tales are how the sage can navigate the contending seas of knowledge, that is, the mundane halakhah and the esoteric Kabbalah, as well the natural sciences, and actualize both the practical and contemplative intellects, a synthesis which, he says, can only be achieved by Israel.

Thus, commenting on the tale of the wave that seeks to swamp and drown the seafaring vessel, he writes: "[W]isdom is the waters of the sea, but to us has been given to ply the great seas via the vessels, that is, mitzvot, and one who seeks to abrogate the practical mitzvot seeks to drown the vessel in the sea."[18] This polemic against antinomianism also reflects a positive attitude towards the body, which he continues in his reading of the second tale. The seafarers hurled by the waves into the fourfold outer space are read by him as those who pass through demonic and impure realms yet are vouchsafed the possibility of repentance so long as they are within their bodies, "for their souls are thus tied to the dimension of choice and may in a moment return in true repentance."[19]

In the fourth tale, the monstrously destructive ram (as big as Mount Tabor) that pollutes the Jordan is the arrogant and vain student who neglects the humbling and leveling study of the plain sense of texts and laws for the sake of Kabbalistic esoterica that do nothing to improve his character.[20] Giving his own interpretation of the Talmudic concept that was central to the ethos of the Mitnagdim, the concept of "Torah for its own sake," *Torah li-shmah*, he says it means the patient and regular study of all of Torah, including its humbler and less dramatic dimensions.

---

15 The demonization of non-Jews in much Kabbalah, and its roots in a number of earlier rabbinic texts and teachings is of course a large, fraught, and regularly painful subject. For a comprehensive survey and analysis, see Elliot R. Wolfson, *Venturing Beyond: Law and Morality in Kabbalistic Mysticism* (New York and Oxford: Oxford University Press, 2006), and in particular chapters 1 and 2.

16 He was certainly familiar with the Zoharic (III, 223b) identification of the sea in which Rabbah bar bar Hannah traveled as *yama de-orayta*, "the sea of Torah."

17 He says this explicitly at MH, 439.

18 Ibid., 421:

כי החכמה היא המים, אבל לנו נמסר לעשות מלאכה במים רבים ע״י כלים שהם המצוות, והרוצה לבטל את המצוות המעשיות רוצה להטביע בים את הספינה.

He makes clear that "the one who seeks to drown the vessel" is Jesus.

19 Ibid., 424:

זה נודע כי גם הנפשות הנופלות בידם מ״מ כ״ז שהם בתוך הגוף אינם שולטים בהם ממש כי הן קשורות בענין הבחירה ויוכל לשוב בשעה קלה בתשובה אמיתית.

20 Ibid., 427–428. While Mount Tabor itself is four parsangs, representing the fourfold interpretive framework of *peshat, remez, derash,* and *sod*, the beast's neck is three parsangs; thus the unworthy student arrogates to himself the last three.

The gigantic fish whose violent beaching destroys sixty cities and whose carcass later provides sustenance and building materials to all the inhabitants represents the sage "*in whose heart impurity has risen* [after BT Hagigah 15b] via an evil thought that has keened in his intellect." While he himself may be ruined, the benefit of the Torah he has learned, and in particular "the contemplative dimensions of intellectual matters," will continue to generate a beneficial spiritual energy to others, and those benefits will eventually reaccrue to himself once he is reincarnated.[21] Torah, in other words, is larger than, and not the property of, the sage who acquires it, and its saving power for others transcends the limitations of the sage who professes it.

The inviting beach that turns out to be the back of a dangerous leviathan is a great man who has attained such perfection that he is able to engage in earthly matters all day long and yet be in a state of constant *devequt*; attractive as this figure is, danger lies in his inimitability, and he is not to be any source of emulation for his students or inferiors.[22] The immense fish whose two fins could be traversed in three days represents wisdom; the two fins are the contemplative and practical intellect, of Torah and worldly wisdom, respectively, each working esoterically and exoterically, at the three levels of the human person—self, spirit, and soul—*nefesh*, *ruah*, and *neshamah*.[23] At the higher reaches of comprehension, the practical and contemplative are joined, as the latter is the root of the former.

Interestingly, he sees secular knowledge as potentially sacred and itself in need of redemption—as the geese laid up for the righteous at the end of days. Further, suffering from their overabundant fat, the geese represent wisdom and specifically conventional knowledge, *mefursamot*, such as natural science.[24] For now, the sciences have been given over to the gentiles and so, like the geese, "lose their wings," that is, their transcendent possibilities. Israel's engagement with the sciences will thus itself hasten the redemption.[25]

One tale recounts Rabbah's exchanges with an Ishmaelite trader who is able to smell the desert dust that will lead him to water. The trader, Rav Kook says, represents the kind of sage who draws on all that he finds in his travels; he is the Kabbalist who can discern

---

21 Ibid., 431–432.

22 Ibid., 432–433.

23 This tripartite division entered the corpus of Jewish thought with Se'adyah Gaon (882–942); see his *Beliefs and Opinions* 6:3, and was a staple of Zoharic literature, see, for example, Zohar III, 71b, 178b. For a brief survey of how the idea was used by a range of medieval Jewish philosophers, see Chayim Pearl, *The Medieval Jewish Mind: The Religious Philosophy of Isaac Arama* (London: Valentine Mitchell, 1971), 65–66. For a pithy and representative example of how the idea was usually framed, see Abraham ibn Ezra to Ex. 23:26.

24 This is based on the identification of geese with wisdom in the dream divination of Berakhot 57a, and Prov. 1:2: "wisdoms cry out in the open," namely, that these worldly sciences are external while Torah is internal. Ideally, Israel should make those sciences its own in order to sanctify worldly matters and God's name among the nations, and to elevate those sciences themselves. (And it is here that he quotes the famous comment attributed to the Gaon of Vilna as to the need for some secular knowledge.)

25 MH, 438–439.

a man's soul and thus teach him exactly the Torah that he needs by observing his physiognomy and, above all, by his sense of smell, whose immediate relation to the breathing *neshamah* represents a kind of immediate knowledge of the soul, untroubled by the intellect's uncertainties and questions. This sage can thus attain a full knowledge of the perfection of the soul even as it partakes of the immediacy of the senses.[26] He is a kind of mendicant figure "wandering the roads to see God's work and wonders, and he knows the ways of virtue and its paths befitting each man in his own right . . . and shows him the path to his perfection, for the paths are not equal for every man."[27]

The sage's dialogue with the Ishmaelite trader continues; he unfurls a vision of Sinai surrounded by scorpions and haunted by a divine voice calling on anyone who can to undo His vow to exile His people. The mountain, Rav Kook says, is a metonym for Torah, and the scorpions are the nations who have become enemies to Israel during the current, unredeemed phase of history: "[A]nd yet they are ready in their interiority to be enslaved by the yoke of Torah . . . and they too will return to be among the masters of loving-kindness."[28] In other words, in the *eschaton*, the gentiles will become bearers of goodness, even if against their own will.

On the Ishmaelite's showing Rabbah the smoking pits in the desert from which emanate the cries of Korah and his coconspirators, belatedly acknowledging the truth of Moses and his Torah, Rav Kook says that by rejecting the authority of Oral Torah, Korah had turned its sacred flame into a destructive force, and moreover, had attempted "to rouse the forces of *hesed* from too high a place for the world to bear."[29] The truth

---

26 Ibid., 440:

ויש חכמה בזה להכיר בריח ממש, ויש ג״כ בחי׳ בענין הריח שהוא רומז על השגה גדולה אבל היא מבוררת הרבה. . . . והשכל יש בו לפעמים ספיקות אכל השגתו נתלית בנשגבות, אבל הריח הוא מיוחס לנשמה והוא הנאה נעלה מאד ומבוררת, שעכ״פ הוא חוש. ע״כ החכם הזה, ששם דרך מחקרו על שלמות נשמתו של אדם ע״י גופו, היתה בהשגתו ב׳ מעלות, שהיתה השגתו קרובה לחוש ומבוררת, ומכ״מ עלה מתוך השכלת הגוף, שהיא נגלית בערך הנשמה, לענינים גבוהים רבי ערך.

The *locus classicus* of the sense of smell as an immediate source of religious knowledge is Isa. 11:3. Some of the Messianic reverberations of that verse are to be found at BT Sanhedrin 93b (wherein the rabbis test the sense of smell of the Messianic aspirant, Bar-Koziva, i.e. Bar Kokhba) and in Zoharic literature at Zohar II, 78a, 213b; the sense of smell is identified with the *tzadiq* at *Tiqqunei Zohar* § 69.

27 MH, 441:

הוא תר וחופש ונודד לדרכים לראות מעשה ד׳ ונפלאותיו והוא יודע דרכי המדות והמעלות ותהלוכותיהם כראוי לכל אדם לפי ענינו . . . ומראהו איזה דרך יבחר בו לבוא לשלמותו כי אין הדרכים שוים לכל אדם.

28 Ibid., 444:

הנה הר סיני מקור נתינת התורה וע״י נתינת תורה לישראל הם שולטים לע״ל על האוה״ע ומלמדים אותם דרך ד׳, אבל כ״ז שלא נשלם התיקון, כל האומות נעשו מצירים לישראל ע״י שקבלו התורה. נמצא שכעת כל האומות סובבות וכוחות המקטרגים שלהם ומכינים עצמם לעקוק את ישראל, אכל בפנימיות כוחותם הם מוכנים להיות משועבדים לעול התורה . . . ויחזרו להיות גם המה מכלל בעלי חסד.

29 Ibid., 446. This, he adds, is akin to the death of the primeval kings by the overabundance of light in the Lurianic myth.

of Moses's Torah, to which Korah and his coconspirators now confess is, in the classic sefirotic structure, the middle line (*qav ha-emtza'i*) linking the Oral Torah below with the Written Torah above.

Finally, the Ishmaelite offers to show Rabbah "the place where earth and heaven kiss." Rabbah places his bread basket on "the window in the sky"; he turns to pray and it vanishes. The Ishmaelite tells him that they are part of the sphere of the heaven and so in the next cycle will be returned. This Rav Kook interprets along the lines of a distinction between divine Providence directed towards the general and universal (heaven) and the local and particular (earth). The two kinds of Providence are ultimately one; with patience one will see how his own particular good is brought about by the good of the many in the fullness of time, which in turn brings about the return of everything to its source.

At the close of this set-piece commentary, he offers a moving coda thanking God for helping him to complete these fifteen teachings, corresponding to the psalmist's fifteen songs of ascent, and the fifteen teachings drawn from the well in Tractate Sukkah (presumably referring to Mishnah Sukkah 5:2 and BT Sukkah 53a–b). In other words, his work on this commentary represented for him some kind of internal passage towards a self-understanding qua would-be sage himself; on the temptations of arrogance and esoteric study and mystical experience untethered to quotidian reality; on the ultimately positive and complementary relations between religious and secular knowledge and between Israel and the gentiles to the extent to which both are linked in a sacred teleology of the cosmos.[30]

The complementary horizons of broader theological exploration and growing self-consciousness appear and move towards one another in his remarkable journal of these years, *Metziot Qatan*.

Metziot Qatan: Mind, Body, Jew, Gentile, and the Call of Theology

Early 2018 saw the publication, from manuscript, of Rav Kook's first, hitherto nearly unknown, spiritual diary, *Metziot Qatan* (literally, *A Minor's Findings*, loosely based on BT Bava Metzia 12b), written during his years in Zeimel. This lengthy work runs to 459 separate entries, and more than 500 printed pages.[31] This meticulously edited volume contains detailed source notes for Rav Kook's many allusions, cross-references to his later works, and very helpful indices of where in his later (published) oeuvre passages from this work appeared; from them we see that roughly half of this notebook has never been published before.

The notebook makes for a large and complex text—freely mixing halakhah, philosophy, sermonics, and Kabbalah—opens an indispensable window into Rav Kook's

---

30 This latter point reflects his study of the works of Luzzatto which I will discuss at length later on.

31 Hereinafter MQ. It was also published as *Pinqasei Ha-Re'ayah*, vols. 5 and 6 (Jerusalem: Makhon Ha-Ratzyah: 2019). I have not had the time to consult and compare those with the 2018 edition that I follow here.

development in those crucial years, and deserves careful study on its own. It was published after this present work was largely completed, precluding full-length treatment here. We can, though, present an overview of this text and, in particular, of the first appearances of those philosophical and theological themes which, we will see, set the terms of many of Rav Kook's future engagements. This in turn will help us better understand the roots of his thought and its trajectory over time.

Two questions predominate in this journal. The first is the relationship between the body, mind, and soul; and its corollary—the status of nature in God's creation.[32] The second is the relationship between Jewish and gentile morality, especially as regards ethics, which they seem to share. With great creativity, he weaves these two questions together.

The very first paragraphs, bearing the title "Rosh Amanah," seem to be the beginning of a Maimonidean-style exposition on faith, with Kabbalistic undertones: "And this is the telos of the *tiqqun* of the world in His kingdom, blessed be He, that there be nothing intruding between the commonwealth of matter and the commonwealth of mind." [33]

Of course, worship through the corporeal was central to Hasidic teaching; he notes, echoing Hasidic terminology, that Temple sacrifices were "worship through bodily essences," and then adds, weaving Lithuanian priorities with Hasidic ideas, that "Torah study, too, on lowly matters of civil law" is a form of worship through the corporeal, "for thus the material is held by its heavenly root."[34]

While matter is related to nature, it is not identical with it. Thus, he writes, there are three levels of divine service—one who worships God only through his materiality; one who entirely subjugates matter to mind; and greater than those, the one "who worship[s] with the very nature of their matter."[35] "Nature," in other words, is not a synonym for the material world, but connotes the very selfhood of something, what it most truly *is*—the material world we so often call "nature" being just the most vivid example.

The idea of nature, in turn, becomes a conceptual lens for the differences between Jewish and gentile worship. Those latter are, like Jews, created in God's image, but "their character doesn't have the power to rise above the limits of nature, and all that God asks

---

32 Concern with relations between body, mind, and soul were of course a staple of Jewish thought for centuries; see Tsippi Kaufmann, *Be-Khol Derakhekah Da'ehu: Tefisat Ha-Elohut ve-Ha-'Avodah be-Gashmiyut be-Rei'shit Ha-Hasidut* (Ramat Gan: Bar-Ilan University Press, 2009). The particular emphasis Rav Kook places on the body here, though, is striking, and may be related to the currents recently described by Stern in his newly published *Jewish Materialism*. As noted earlier, Stern's book appeared after the present work was largely complete, and fuller treatment of this dimension will have to wait for another day. As this book was going to press, I became aware of Oliver Smith, *Vladimir Soloviev and the Spiritualization of Matter* (Boston: Academic Studies Press, 2011); an examination of that volume may indeed be a fruitful avenue for better understanding some of Rav Kook's concerns.

33 MQ, 10:

וזהו תכלית תיקון העולם במלכותו יתברך, כי לא יהיה דבר חוצץ בין ישוב החומר לישוב השכל.

34 Ibid., 66:

כי גם החומר אחוז בשרשו העליון . . .

35 Ibid., 124.

of them is simply to keep the paths of beneficence, and not despoil their natures, not to follow the lusts of their heart, and violate the just laws of nature that God has created."[36] This, he says, is why fear of God is not included in the seven Noahide commandments. Israel, by contrast, is both within nature and above it at the same time.[37]

Another aspect of his interest in this question becomes clear—his mourning for his wife. In a lengthy passage bearing the title "Mussar Hokhmah" (Reproof of Wisdom) he writes that death vanquishes matter, but not life, "which is the root of will flowing onto motions and feeling."[38] Further on, he refers to the Talmudic sage Abaye's statement that his prayer is joyous rather than somber "because I lay tefillin" (BT Berakhot 30a). Abaye, Rav Kook writes, "saw and understood joy in his mind's eye, and removed the memory of death from his eyes."[39]

Most interestingly, he relates this concern with the relation between the body and the mind to a social and political question—the meaning and significance of disagreement, and of heresy, an inquiry echoing the vivid ideological disagreements of the time, and a question that would preoccupy him for the rest of his life.

"Righteousness and justice and truth—all these we feel, in nature, their necessity and binding force."[40] Thus one who yields to bodily temptation will despoil both their own natural righteousness as well as their mind to the point of being unable "to feel the truth of the taste of truth."[41] Of course, the natural body's potential to corrupt the mind was for centuries a staple of Jewish ethics and moral philosophy. What is striking here, though, is his seeing that failing as the corruption of a fundamentally good, God-given nature—a nature that includes moral sentiments.

This in turn makes for him a possible recasting of principled debate and disagreement as the working out of the various elements of that God-given sense of the good. Thus, he says, peace is the fundamental character of the world, and the multiplicity of contending views of the good all point towards the final telos, the peace, which will emerge precisely from the cauldron of disagreement.[42]

Speaking of those who rebel against the tradition, he singles out for reflection the most consequential of them all, Jesus.

> [A]nd lo, evil is clarified by human choice, which is to say that once evil has been separated
> from the good, and there remains in it a bit of good, this little bit of good, too, can raise itself

---

36 Ibid., 47:

אלא שהם בכללם אין בטיבם כח להתרומם יותר מעל גבולי הטבע, וכל אשר דורש ד' מעמם הוא רק לנצור אורחות
הטבע ושלא יקלקלו מטבעם ושלא ילכו אחרי תאוות לב להפר חוקי הטבע הישרים אשר ברא ד'.

37 Ibid., 74. Later, we will have more to say about Rav Kook's thinking on natural law.
38 Ibid., 279.
39 Ibid., 282.
40 Ibid., 259:

היושר הצדק והאמת—כולם אנו מרגישים בטבע הכרחם וחיובם.

41 Ibid., 260.
42 Ibid., 366.

. . . for in truth, the element of *qelippah* [in Kabbalistic terms, to be discussed later, the hard shell of failed divinity whose negative energy makes for the evil of this world— Y. M.] in the selfhood of the Messiah . . . descended, truly, into the body of that man [the classic rabbinic euphemism for Jesus—Y. M.] and thus inevitably he would have large vessels of his own . . . and he could have transformed himself to be good . . . then his own evil would have been clarified, and the good rise of itself, but he ruined it, *flimsy he made it and rendered it false* [after Ezek. 13:10–11] *and preached disloyalty to God* [after Isa. 32:6] and so ruined much for himself.[43]

"And the good rise of itself." This is no mere figure of speech, but relates to another, striking, idea, that all of existence, not only human, but animal, vegetable, and mineral too, in some way vibrates with divinity and strives to return to its heavenly source: "And so, when the light of God's glorious presence will fill all the earth, just as the great flowing abundance will swell in each one, according to his worth, it can't be that all this increase will not benefit all existents, each according to the worth of their selves."[44]

This journal not only reflects his growing preoccupations with theology and aggadic literature, but also, as it proceeds, his reflections on his preoccupation, a predilection out of step with the norms and expectations of Lithuanian Talmudism: "And if one feels in himself at times that his thoughts are more polished in reflecting on the aggadah for insight into the paths of the soul and ordering one's thoughts, he should at that time, direct himself to that."[45] This bit of pedagogic insight draws on his burgeoning understanding as to the nature of the soul.

There is at times, another dimension, when there is roused in one a spirit of purity, to love God with a boundless love . . . and that certainly comes from a place supreme, and a moment like this certainly he should not forsake. And even if by this longing in love he refrains from studying Torah, at any rate, since he is being roused from Heaven, he should prepare himself in anticipation of God on high, our Father who Has loved us with an eternal love.[46]

---

43 Ibid., 287:

. . . והנה הרע מתברר על ידי בחירת האדם והיינו כשנפרד הרע מהטוב ונותר בו מעט טוב יוכל הטוב המועט גם כן להתעלות. . . . שבאמת בחינת הקליפה מצד [נפשו] של משיח . . . ירדה באמת בגוף אותו האיש וממילא הכרח שיהיה לו כלים גדולים . . . .והיה יכול להפוך עצמו לטוב . . . אז היה הרע שלו מתברר, והטוב מתעלה, אך קלקל בבחינת ותפל שמו וטפל ודיבר על ד' תועה, על כן קלקל הרבה לעצמו.

44 Ibid., 296–297. He uses this idea to explain why Moses sinned in striking rather than hitting the rock, as recounted in Num. 20.

על כן כשיתמלא אור כבוד ד' את כל הארץ, כמו שירבה השפע בהרגש האדם לפי ערכו, אי אפשר כלל שלא יועיל זה הריבוי גם כן לכל הנמצאים לפי ערך נפשותיהם. . . .

45 Ibid., 347.

46 Ibid.:

ואם ירגיש בעצמו בזמן מהזמנים שרעיוניו מלוטשים להבין באגדה בדרכי הנפש ומערכי הלב, ישים לבו בזמן ההוא . . . אמנם יש בחינה אחרת, שלפעמים תעורר על האדם רוח טהרה לאהבה את ד' אהבה בלא מצרים . . . וזה בא ממקום עליון בודאי, הנה שעה כזאת לא יעזוב בודאי. ואף שעל ידי השתוקקות האהבה יתבטל מתלמוד תורה, מכל מקום כיון שמעוררים אותו מהשמים, יכין עצמו לקראת ד' אלקי מרום, אבינו אשר אהבת עולם אהבנו.

The fundamental affirmation of the body and the natural world is of a piece with his affirmation of one's own self, a theme that will grow over time. (In our discussion of his aggadah commentary, we will see that one source of this positive attitude towards the body was his reading, of all people, of Maimonides.)

Alongside his theological and aggadic explorations, this notebook brims with detailed halakhic analyses too, and his burgeoning self-consciousness extends as well to these seemingly disparate pursuits.

> This is the distinction between the practical and the inner Torah. For the practical, by its needing to define material particulars, cannot take in sweeping perspective by itself, but only by the repeated study of every particular . . . but the interiority of Torah all proceed from the principle that God is perfect to the utmost and so one finds that this knowledge expands and proceeds according to the degree of the purity of the soul.[47]

This in turn leads him to an insight into interpersonal relations: "And so it is utterly impossible for one to know the mental state of another even when he explains it to him."[48] Strikingly, he is working here to manage the seeming tensions between Talmudism and spiritual strivings by deeming them complementary rather than antithetical, and speaking to different dimensions of one's relationship to God, and thus of God Himself, who suffuses all particulars even as He is Himself the whole.

Halakhic Writings and a Touch of Philosophy

Some fifty of his published responsa and halakhic correspondences are datable to this period; those and more appear in the recently published *Metziot Qatan*, and a detailed index is to be found there. Not surprisingly, the vast majority take up straightforward matters of halakhah, and most discuss various issues of kashrut, reflecting the daily fare of a small community's rabbi.[49] He shows himself to be a biting controversialist in the responsum published at *Da'at Cohen*, number forty-five, written in 1894, a fierce and lengthy

---

47 Ibid., 553:

זה הוא הפרש בין התורה המעשית לתורה הפנימית. כי המעשית מצד הגדרה בפרטים חומריים, אי אפשר להשקיף מאליו, רק על ידי שנון ולמוד בכל פרט. . .אבל פנימיות התורה המה כולם תולדות מהעיקר שהשי״ת שלם בתכלית ונמצא שידיעה זו מתרחבת והולכת לפי רוב טהרת הנפש. . . .

48 Ibid.:

וזה אי אפשר כלל לאדם לדעת אופן ציורו של חבירו אפילו כשיסביר לו. . . .

49 The following hitherto published responsa date from his time in Zeimel (those which appear in MQ are in bold): *Da'at Cohen*, nos. 8 (pts. 1 and 2), 14, **17, 19**, 21, 22, 23, 25, **26** (pts. 1–4), 32, 34, 37, 39, 41, 42, 44, 45, **47** (except for pt. 2), 49, 62, 63 (pt. 1), 76, 77, 87, 90, **137**, 144, **145**, 151, 156, 161 (this also includes a query from his father regarding the printing of '*Ittur Sofrim*), 168 (whether women can write Torah scrolls), 169 (whether women may sew Torah parchments), 179, 180, 209, 226, 227; '*Ezrat Cohen* 1, 32 (60?), 78 (to Rabbi Eliasberg), 94; *Orah Mishpat, Orakh Hayim*—5, 10, 11, 15, 40, 41, 42 (43?), 44, 49 (to his father), 60 (62; see 10) (139?) (143?) (144?); *Miluim* 1 (including discussion about possible rabbinic posts), 4, 7, 12 (13?) 14; *Hoshen Mishpat*: (5?) (as these abstract studies seem to date from then), 21

polemic regarding the laws of forbidden fats and the regularly contentious halakhic matter of blemishes on lungs; this polemic seems to have been animated by perceived challenges to the authority of rabbinic law as a whole, even from so unlikely a precinct as an
ostensibly Orthodox halakhist.[50] This, taken with the biting polemics in Netziv's defense
which we saw in the previous chapter, drives home the point that Rav Kook's celebrated
tolerance in later years was not simply (or not even) an expression of character, but very
much a principled stance and personal achievement, with genuine limits.

Rav Kook's halakhic writing of this period, deeply impressive for its erudition and
analytic subtlety, was not, he thought, terribly interesting; it is in the realm of theology,
he writes in 1899, that he sees himself as having uniquely innovative things to say.[51] As we
will see, his coming to accept this deep inclination of his towards theology and aggadah

---

(discussion of rabbinic contracts; perhaps reflecting his contemplated move to Boisk); *Mishpat
Cohen*, Introductory essay, 39, 55, 56, 98, 147.

50 See the lengthy responsum at *Da'at Cohen*, nos. 98–119, striking for the seeming
incommensurability between its rhetorical ferocity and its seemingly tame subject: a sixteen-
page booklet entitled *Mei Sasson*, by Ya'aqov Meir Horodensky of Minsk (Warsaw: Halter
and Eisenstadt, 1894), whom he refuses to mention by name; Rav Kook says at the outset
that while he hates controversy he is writing this at the request of an unnamed Torah "giant"
(perhaps his father-in-law Aderet?); Horodensky had cast aspersions on a permissive ruling
of Moses Isserles in Yoreh Deah 64:15. Some of his wrath at Horodensky arises from the
latter's criticizing Isserles on the basis of a seemingly literal reading of the Biblical verse,
which question, Rav Kook says, "resembles a question of the Sadducees," 100. The second
part of this polemic, 116–119, attacks Horodensky's attempt to permit certain kinds of lung
blemishes (*sirkhot*). This, too, Rav Kook sees as an assault, albeit from a different direction, on
the authority of the Oral Law, and the stringencies adopted by the Rabbis on this matter. At
the conclusion of this withering polemic, Rav Kook, then all of twenty-nine, says that he has in
fact heard that Horodensky is a basically pious man, albeit one who has waded in well over his
head, and he prays that God will spare the poor unfortunate from further error. Horodensky
tried to answer his various critics in his *Quntres Hosafah Le-Sefer Mei Sasson* (Warsaw: Halter
& Eisenstadt, 1898).

These were highly charged matters of halakhic dispute at the time in part because of the
leniencies on the matter earlier adopted by the Hasidic master Levi Yitzhak of Berdichev
(1740–1809). For a number of the pertinent sources, see Zvi Hirsch Shapira of Munkacz,
Darkhei Teshuvah [1893] (Brooklyn: Shraga, 1946), preface (where he states his own standing
polemic with Shalom Schwadron's *Daat Torah*), and comments to YD 33:13, 492ff. My thanks
to Prof. Sid Z. Leiman for directing me to this latter work.

51 In his 1899 introduction to his collection of sermons *Midbar Shur*, he writes that while custom
dictates that he should first publish his halakhic works before the ostensibly lesser aggadic,
"My soul well knows that while my halakhic novellae in manuscript contain, with God's help,
accurate comments and straight arguments, I cannot think that I have paved any new path
that will aid the development of halakhic analysis and innovation in any wise more than the
books that have already, with God's help, multiplied":

אבל נפשי יודעת מאד כי החידושים שהנם תחת ידי בעזה"י בכתובים בהלכה אם כי יש בהם בע"ה הערות נכונות
וסברות ישרות אבל לא אוכל לחשב שסלותי איזו דרך חדשה שתועיל להתפתחות חלק הפלפול והחידוש בהלכה
באופן רשום מהספרים שכבר רבו בע"ה.

was a significant element of his acceptance of subjectivity as a key element of human and religious experience.

His own self-deprecation notwithstanding, he does in some of these responsa draw on Kabbalistic sources, and make interesting use of nonlegal value-concepts, something which would emerge in later decades as a feature of his halakhic writing.[52] At the same time, his comments in 1899 mentioned above indicate that he himself may not have recognized his own budding legal innovation in introducing value concepts into his responsa.[53]

Orah Mishpat §§168 and 169, both written in 1895, address the religious lives of women, specifically whether they can, respectively, write Torah scrolls and sew the parchments thereof. It is worth noting that there were learned women in Rav Kook's extended family circle, and, he did, during his years in Boisk, teach a class in *Tze'na u-Re'na* to the male members of the community, indicating pedagogic flexibility, as well as respect for the piety of traditional women. [54]

In §168 Rav Kook simply and strikingly discounts Maimonides's ruling that women are exempted from the mitzvah to write one's own personal Torah scroll and thus from preparing a Torah scroll at all (*Sefer Ha-Mitzvot*, *'Aseh* 18) as a scribal or printer's error, since it is well known, he says, that the published text of *Sefer Ha-Mitzvot* is highly corrupted; moreover there are good reasons for including women in the mitzvah on the grounds laid out by Aryeh Leib Ginzburg of Metz (1695–1785) in his *Sha'agat Aryeh* §34–36, who, though he upheld Maimonides's ruling, did so only after initial hesitation (indeed, *Sha'agat Aryeh*'s tone there suggests to me that he is seeking to exempt women from an otherwise onerous obligation).[55] And, Rav Kook continues, there is

---

52 See *Da'at Cohen*, nos. 168–169, *Orah Mishpat*, Addenda 12:1–2, *'Ezrat Cohen* 32. Oddly, none of them are discussed in Neriah Gutel's otherwise exhaustive and strikingly erudite—if less theoretically oriented than one might hope—study of the value-based elements in Rav Kook's responsa, *Hadashim gam Yeshanim*.

My own working definition of "value-concepts" is a factor in judicial decision making that is not formulated, or formulable, as a distinctive, casuistic legal rule, of the form "if x then y, or "all x are y"." This is of course a large and contentious subject; for now, see Lon Fuller, *The Morality of Law* (New Haven: Yale University Press, 1963), Richard A. Posner, *The Problematics of Moral and Legal Theory* (Cambridge, MA: Harvard University Press, 1990), esp. 107–144, and Aharon Barak's magnum opus *Parshanut Takhlitit be-Mishpat* (Jerusalem: Nevo, 2003), in particular, 259–271. I deliberately use the term "value" rather than the more current "meta-halakhah," as that term, certainly as meant by its originator, Eliezer Goldman, denotes not moral or spiritual values, but rather principles of interpretation reflecting the structure and aims of the halakhah. I am indebted here to the marvelous discussion by Alexander Kaye, "Eliezer Goldman and the Origins of Meta-Halacha," *Modern Judaism* 34, no. 3 (2014): 309-333.

53 My thanks to Prof. Jay Harris for this observation.

54 See the extraordinary memoir of Aderet's sister-in-law Rivka Rabinowitz (?–1875) written by her son Eliyahu Aqiva Rabinowitz, the well-known editor of *Ha-Peles*, in his introduction to his father's posthumous responsa collection *Divrei Emet* (Poltava: Rabinowitz, 1913), 3–8.

55 On this independent-minded halakhist's innovative methodologies, see Israel M. Ta-Shma, "Ha-Gra u-Ba'al Sha'agat Aryeh," 181–191.

an extra-halakhic reason to permit this, of a piece with the Talmud's allowing women limited participation in sacrificial rituals (BT Hagigah 16b) "in order to please their spirits."[56]

Orah Mishpat §169 takes up the issue of women sewing Torah scrolls and he rules that "because the women want this and preventing them would affront human dignity [*kavod ha-beri'yot*], regarding which rabbinic prohibitions are lifted, so too in our case they are not to be prevented."[57] This extralegal value concept, derived from BT Berakhot 19b–20a, generally carries little directive force, but is a broadly subjective license occasionally to suspend rabbinic prohibitions where doing so would deeply wound the dignity of another.[58]

It is tempting to see these responsa in a proto-feminist light—and indeed—they have been cited by perhaps the most distinguished contemporary proponent of women's participation in Torah reading alongside men in Orthodox services.[59] At the same time, one must be very, very careful here—not least for the deeply conservative nature of Rav Kook's rulings on women's issues throughout his career, such as his opposition to women's suffrage—which he publicly expressed less on halakhic reasoning than on larger meta-values of Jewish peoplehood, especially in the eyes of the nations.[60]

In looking at his use of value concepts, it is especially interesting to juxtapose two responsa from the Zeimel period in which he takes up highly charged and intimate matters. Extralegal arguments figure in both, in one case towards a permissive result, in the other towards a restriction, and in the latter case, the extralegal argument is implicitly Kabbalistic.

In *Orah Mishpat*, Addenda 12 (1–2), in an undated letter to his father-in-law identified as having been written in Zeimel, he requests a permissive ruling on the use of a barrier contraceptive (*mokh*) by a tubercular woman whom doctors have advised to avoid pregnancy, and invokes the principle of *shalom bayit* (domestic tranquility). In a subsequent letter to his father-in-law on the matter, in which he mentions having consulted with, and received a permissive ruling from, Yosef Zekharia Stern of Shavil, he asks for

---

56 This passage was regularly cited by Ashkenazic authorities in approval of women voluntarily assuming religious obligations, from the Tosafists on; see the sources referred to in Elisheva Baumgarten, *Practicing Piety in Medieval Ashkenaz: Men, Women, and Everyday Religious Observance* (Philadelphia: University of Pennsylvania Press, 2014), 273, n. 163.

57 *Orah Mishpat*, 313.

58 Interestingly, he devotes a lengthy discussion to its parameters in his commentary to *Shulhan 'Arukh, Mitzvat Re'ayah* §8:1.

59 See Daniel Sperber, "Kavod Ha-Tzibur u-Khevod Ha-Beri'yot: Nashim u-Keri'yat Ha-Torah," *De'ot* 16 (June 2003): 17–20, 44.

60 Much has been written on this; see, for a brief summary, David Ellenson, "Gender, Halakhah and Women's Suffrage," in his *After Emancipation: Jewish Religious Responses to Modernity* (Cincinnati: Hebrew Union College Press, 2004), 344–366.

his father-in-law's approval of his ruling, urging him "to pay heed to the betterment of the miserable" (*na le'ayen be-taqnat ha-'aluvim*) and the dictates of *darkhei no'am*.[61]

In *'Ezrat Cohen* §32, dated 1896, Rav Kook makes extralegal arguments for a more restrictive ruling, forbidding a man who has not fathered children after several years of marriage from taking a sperm test. In a rare halakhic move he invokes the Sin of the Generation of the Flood (Gen. 6:12); indeed, his celebrated ancestor Mordechai Jaffe was distinctive among early modern halakhists in identifying masturbation as the Sin of the Flood.[62]

We have from this time several Talmudic and halakhic commentarial projects—Talmudic novellae to Tractate Hullin, a super-commentary to the Gaon's *Shulhan 'Arukh* commentary, and a commentary of his own to *Shulhan 'Arukh, Mitzvat Re'ayah*—all left unfinished and it is unclear if indeed they were meant for publication. The novellae, eventually published in 1924 under the title *Zivhei Re'ayah*, are straightforward exempla of the genre.[63] The super-commentary is significant for its revealing his self-perception as a

---

61 OM, 255–256. In Stern's responsa collection *Zekher Yehosef: Even Ha-'Ezer* (Jerusalem: Makhon Yerushalayim, 1994) published from manuscript, we find at no. 37, 155–157 a responsum on this very subject, and citing the same arguments as Rav Kook quotes in his name, directed to an unnamed correspondent described "a diligent student" (*me-lomdei lemed*). This consultation with his older colleague and distant relative Stern is a further bit of evidence of the tie between the two, whose greater significance will emerge in our discussions in a further chapter of what we see as Stern's influence on Rav Kook's study of aggadah.

62 See *Levushim* to *Even Ha-'Ezer* 23:1. It is also invoked by the halakhist and Kabbalist Yoseph Hayim ben Eliyahu al-Hakham of Baghdad, better-known as Ben Ish Hai (1835?–1909) in a responsum in which he also forbids a sperm test for medical purposes; *Torah li-Shmah*, no. 481. This was the volume of responsa which Ben Ish Hai claimed to have published from a forgotten manuscript of one Yehezkel Kahali (whose name is the numerical equivalent of his own). For a remarkable account of how Professor S. Z. Havlin of Bar-Ilan University scientifically proved Ben Ish Hai's authorship, see Yemimah Evron, "Mi Kotevet et Ha-Sefarim shel Dick Francis," *Ha-Aretz*, April 1, 2004. By contrast, perhaps the most outstanding Lithuanian halakhist to succeed Isaac Elhanan Spektor, Shalom Mordekhai Shvadron (1835–1911), who had little or no truck with mysticism, argued that to the extent to which the "Sin of the Flood" was indeed masturbation, it was thus of a lesser status than the sin of adultery, and more readily atoned for, via Torah study, see his *She'elot u-Teshuvot Maharsham*, 1:58. Interestingly, other rabbinic authorities of the time did find room for leniency on this very issue; for example, Hayim Ozer Grodzinsky (1863–1940), Rav Kook's contemporary and eventually the leading rabbinic authority in Vilna, ruled permissively on this; *Ahi'ezer*, pt. 3, no. 24:4, as did the Sephardic halakhist later to become Rav Kook's younger colleague in Palestine, in a ruling from 1950; see Ben-Zion Meir Hai Uziel (1880–1953), *Mishpetei Uziel*, vol. 7, *Even Ha-'Ezer* no. 50, 2nd ed. (Jerusalem: Ha-Ve'adah le-Hotza'at Kitvei Ha-Rav Uziel, 2005), 255, 23. A good discussion of *'Ezrat Cohen* no. 32 and Rav Kook's responsa on contraception throughout his career is Zvi Tal, "Shalosh Nashim Meshamshot be-Mokh: 'Iyun be-'Ezrat Cohen," in *Berurim be-Hilkhot Ha-Re'ayah*, ed. Moshe Zvi Neriah, Aryeh Stern, and Neriah Gutel (Jerusalem: Beit Ha-Rav, 1992), 271–280 and no. 32 is in particular, 278–280; Tal does not, though, note the jurisprudential elements I have discussed here.

63 They were published as an appendix to Moshe Goldstein's posthumous *Sefer Yabia' Omer u-Shegiyot Mi Yavin* (Jerusalem: Rohaldt, 1924), the sale proceeds of which went to Rav Kook's

disciple of the Gaon, and his seeking to further elements of the Gaon's halakhic agenda, in particular the tracing of later halakhot back to their earliest Talmudic and ultimately biblical sources.[64] The Gaon's commentarial project was at one and the same time a modernist organization and rationalization of a massively complex corpus of texts and traditions, and a bid for direct experience of revelation; of, so to speak, a disciplined Sinai of one's own.[65] Rav Kook's work on the Gaon's commentary helps bring into clearer focus some of what was driving him in these years—a synthesis of halakhic and spiritual exploration very informed by the legacy of the Gaon of Vilna.

Of particular interest for our purposes is Rav Kook's own *Shulhan 'Arukh* commentary, sections of which were first published in 1924, which shows signs of his interest in, and connection to, some themes of the medieval philosophical tradition, and in particular, the primacy of intellect and the cultivation of virtue.[66]

yeshiva. In a brief prefatory note, Yitzhak Levi, the yeshiva's secretary, writes, with striking and somewhat peculiar exactitude, that "these first fruits of our Rabbi were written thirty-three years ago," that is, sometime before 1891. While he studied Tractate Hullin in Volozhin, he studied the second half there and inasmuch as these novellae are from Hullin's early portions they likely date to Zeimel. Interestingly, the 1994 photocopy edition of Goldstein's volume entirely omits this appendix of Rav Kook's. Novellae of Rav Kook to BT Shabbat 4a–b appear in Menahem Arieli, ed., *Neshamah shel Shabbat: 'Osef Ma'amarim Toraniyyim le-Zikhro shel Ha-Rav Eliyahu Shlomo Ra'anan ztql* (Hevron: Talmei Ariel, 5759), 80–82. It seems reasonable to date them from this period as the other materials of Rav Kook appearing in that volume are early as well.

64 Part 1 of this commentary, entitled *Be'er Eliyahu*, explicating the Gaon's terse glosses to *Hilkhot Dayyanim*, was published by Mossad Ha-Rav Kook in 1985; part 2, on *Hilkhot 'Edut* and some of *Hilkhot Halvaah*, was published by Makhon Ha-Ratzyah Kook ztz"l in 2000, and neither edition affords information as to the time of composition. However, a fragment discussing the Gaon's glosses to *Even Ha-'Ezer* 66 was published in 1988 and on the last page there is a notation telling us that this is from Boisk, and that a variant, also said to be from his time in Boisk, appears at *Mitzvat Re'ayah*, 157, see the 1985 Mossad Ha-Rav Kook edition, 22.

65 My formulation here is based on my understanding of the Gaon as reflected in previous chapters and those to come, and on Elyakim Krumbein's marvelous study, "El Ha-Maqor: Le-Darko shel Ha-GRA bi-Vei'uro La-Shulhan 'Arukh," *Ma'aseh Hoshev* 1 (2015): 209-226.

66 The commentary appears as scattered passages throughout the newly released *Pinqas Metziot Qatan*. An excerpt of this commentary to *Shulhan 'Arukh, Orah Hayim*, up to §7:3, was published as an appendix to Menahem Auerbach's *Oreah Ne'eman* (Jerusalem: Solomon, 1924); in an introduction to the excerpt, Auerbach's son Ben Zion refers to "these novellae and Torah excurses taken from the pouch of his sacred writings! This is the Torah of the Cohen (priest) from his youth" (pt. 1, 128). In a letter accompanying the excerpt, Rav Kook writes: "In sacred affection for our faithful friendship I am giving my dear friend a notebook from my youth, on the first eight chapters of *Shulhan 'Arukh*," and goes on to say that inasmuch as Auerbach refused to let him help defray the publishing costs, he hopes that his modest addition will lead others to purchase the book; ibid., 159. The publication of these three volumes of Auerbach's seems to have entailed considerable expense, judging from the fundraising testimonials from the US as well as Palestine printed in the volumes. In his brief preface to the 1970 edition of *Mitzvat Re'ayah*, Zvi Yehudah Kook says that much of the work was posthumously edited by

Thus the *Shulhan 'Arukh*'s opening words: "One should be brave as a lion on rising in the morning to serve one's Creator and himself rouse the dawn" serve as the basis for a discourse on the need to internalize the virtues of courage and modesty.[67] He regularly recurs to the question of intentionality (*kavvanah*) in mitzvot and at §1:4 he makes a strong argument for the primacy of intentionality, *kavvanah*, as the decisive factor in the performance of mitzvot, taking note of the controversial nature of his position.[68]

The theme of self-cultivation emerges clearly at §2:3, where he says that the Talmudic comment (Shabbat 114a) that one may presumptively be treated as a sage on the basis of his personal grooming is no longer applicable; grooming as such is not an obligation, he says, but rather:

> (a) sign that Torah has worked on all of one's behaviors . . . and so this is pertinent only when undertaken by his own initiative, but now that it has been committed to writing, and thought to be obligatory, or at least a mark of piety, it is no proof of a sage's internal feeling . . . one who does not feel this in himself has not reached the boundary of delicate feeling in all delicate and pleasant acts befitting a sage.

At §4:1, after discussing the details of the handwashing and accompanying blessings required immediately upon awakening, traditionally explained by reference to the malign spirits alighting on the sleeper, he adds a more rationalistic comment that these are meant so as "to do nothing arbitrary in his first action of the day, to know that such action is ill-becoming the virtue of self-mastery, and there are seventy faces to Torah." At §6:1 he cites Maimonides on the importance of bodily health for spiritual health, and discusses the "wisdom" referred to in the blessing of *asher yatzar* recited over the exercise of bodily functions. The "empty cavities" referred to in the blessing serve as the starting point for a discussion of Maimonides's comment in *Guide*, 3:10, that darkness, though a void, is nonetheless created, contra the view of the Gaon of Vilna that darkness is not a void but an existent.[69]

Ya'aqov Moshe Harlap's son Yosef David, and that he himself made many additions "from scattered notebooks and from the margins of volumes of responsa."

67 In addition, at §2:6 he expresses reservations about asceticism when not in the context of performing mitzvot, and even then says it must be done with humility.

68 He recurs to the question at §5 and subscribes to the view of the Gaon that the *kavvanah* required is that of the name of God as pronounced, not as written. At §8:8 he returns to the subject and distinguishes between mitzvot which require *kavanah* only at the outset, and throughout. The question is a hardy perennial of halakhic literature. The *Shulhan 'Arukh*'s own brief discussion on the matter is to be found in *Orah Hayim* 60:14.

69 He limits Maimonides's view to darkness such that other voids are not existents, adding that darkness, as opposed to absence of light, exists in the imagination, which is an existence of its own; Rav Kook's deep interest in the imagination will be discussed at length in chapter four.

Several of his comments reflect some of the broadly jurisprudential concerns we saw at work in his essays in *'Ittur Sofrim*;[70] he registers awareness of—though no identification with—contemporary moral critiques of halakhah;[71] and he has some recourse to some value principles.[72]

Taken together, his glosses to *Shulhan 'Arukh* attempt to integrate the self-cultivation tradition of the medievals into halakhic writing. His interest in medieval philosophy and its complex linkages to other elements of his intellectual and spiritual life—not least the relations of body and soul—vividly appear in his obscure tract on phylacteries *Hevesh Pe'er*—the first public intervention to emerge from this new chapter in his spiritual and intellectual life.

Hevesh Pe'er and a Solitary Journey

In 1891, at age twenty-six, Rav Kook published, under the pseudonym Cohen Da'ato Yafeh, a Priest of Immaculate Mind, a slender book of thirty-six pages entitled *Hevesh Pe'er* (literally, *Turban of Beauty*, a common liturgical trope for phylacteries, after Ezek. 24:17), a rousing polemic for the proper observance of the mitzvah of phylacteries, tefillin, and particularly those worn on the head, *tefillin shel rosh*.[73] After the book was published he embarked on a crusade to distribute and preach on it (claiming to be merely the

---

70 At §2:4 he shows awareness of historical change in his discussion of Maimonides's omission of some halakhot found in *Shulhan 'Arukh*. At §4:13 he introduces a distinction by which the principle of *lo plug* ("no differentiation" regarding the status of Rabbinically based halakhot) only applies to a rabbinic enactment, and not to a halakhah derived from the processes of legal reasoning. At §8:1 he acknowledges that some halakhic views are ex post derivations from already-existing customs.

71 This is in his discussion of Isserles's ruling at §1:5 that the Ten Commandments may liturgically be recited only in private and not in public, reflecting the Talmudic statement at BT Berakhot 12a that they were removed from the service as a response to *minim*, that is, heretics, or early Christians. These latter, Rav Kook says, are "those heretics who say that the practical Torah has been abrogated, God forbid, and only the moral obligations remain."

72 At §6:2 he invokes *kol Yisrael 'areivim* for the extension of the public recitation of *'amidah* to other prayers, and at §8:1 has lengthy discussion of the classic crux of human dignity, *kavod ha-beri'yot*, a concept that, as noted above, he employed in a responsum of the time; see *Da'at Cohen*, nos. 169, 313.

73 The work seems to have been in progress for a while; Aderet writes in his memoir *Seder Eliyahu* that his in-law, Shlomo Zalman Kook, brought the manuscript to him in 1888, shortly after Aderet's daughter, Bat-Sheva Kook, had taken ill. In a fragment dated 1889/90 and published in *Orah Mishpat* no. 5, Rav Kook says that tefillin must be placed a bit higher than the roots of the one's hair such that it is clearly visible that they are being worn properly. In the 1889 letter to his father-in-law mentioned above, he says that as long as the latter writes his approbation, his own name is unnecessary, and he discusses some of the halakhic issues, see *Orah Mishpat*, Addenda §1. He first admitted to its authorship in an essay entitled "Kelil Tiferet," published in 1900 in *Torah mi-Tzion* 5, no. 4 (1900): 3–5, reprinted in the Mossad Ha-Rav Kook edition, 36–48.

representative of the anonymous author). In 1925 at the height of Rav Kook's fame, the volume was reprinted with additional Hebrew texts to be described below.[74]

The burden of the book is that improper placement of tefillin on the forehead, and not on their rightful place above the roots of the hair, utterly undoes the performance of the mitzvah, and furthermore constitutes an open rebellion against Talmudic authority. He vents serious criticism of contemporary rabbis for their countenancing of such behavior and denounces the men of means who purchase expensive tefillin yet fail to wear them properly. In chapter five we also find the extraordinary statement that:

> I have no doubt that the reason for all the ills that have befallen us and our lowly situation and standing among the nations is none other than that we should think deeply on the glory of our Creator and the garland with which He has garlanded us, the tefillin, on which His name is inscribed, and we denigrate it. And we are all guilty.

Why is this? Because of tefillin's integral relation to the mind, and the mind's centrality to the religious life:

> *Tefillin shel rosh* are placed on the brain, to subordinate all thoughts of heart and mind to His service, if we kept this mitzvah properly we would feel a flow of the light of knowledge and intellect . . . for the light of intellect illuminates all darkness and makes peace between adversaries . . . the *tefillin shel rosh* are laid on the vessel of thought, whose special ability is to add to the individual and the nation as a whole the light of knowledge and fear of God, which are the sources of all good and kindness.[75]

---

74 The first edition was Warsaw: Levenson Press, 1891. The 1925 Jerusalem edition, edited by Yitzhak Arieli and Uri Segal Hamburger, was reprinted in 1985 by Mossad Ha-Rav Kook, Jerusalem, and page citations refer to that last edition, hereinafter HP. Arieli (1896–1974), known for his work *'Eynayim le-Mishpat*, was a close disciple of Rav Kook and his regular study partner for many years. On him, see Eitam Henkin, "Ha-Rav Yitzhak Arieli ve-Shikhihato be-Hug Ha-Re'ayah u-Merkaz Ha-Rav," *Assif* 4 (2017): 463–493. (My thanks to Yosef Avivi for this reference.) Hamburger (1886–1964) was a nephew of Ya'aqov Moshe Harlap (whose niece he married, on the strength of Ya'aqov Moshe's recommendation to his brother Yitzhak Eli'ezer for the latter's daughter, Leah, at age thirteen). See on him N. Ben Avraham (Natan Anshin), "Demut 'Atiqah me-Qatamon," in Ben Avraham, *Sipurim Yerushalmiyim*, vol. 3 (Jerusalem: Meimey Ha-Da'at/Mish'an Menahem, 1996), 113–136. The 1925 edition is available online at www.hebrewbooks.org.

The 1925 edition included, besides the sermons to be discussed presently, a new introductory essay; halakhic discourses on the material by several then-leading rabbis of Jerusalem and his responses, and excerpts from his then unpublished aggadic commentary *'Eyn Ayah*. It omitted the one Yiddish sermon, which appeared in the first edition, I surmise, because it is a straightforward bit of moralizing sermonics with no conceptual content. Moreover, its omission may also reflect the tendency of Rav Kook's followers then and since to downplay the diasporic element of his makeup, reflected in Yiddish, in favor of the Hebraist element, more congenial to Zionism; my thanks for the latter observation to Prof. Jay Harris.

75 HP, 17:

אין ספק אצלי כי סבת כל הרעות אשר מצאנו ושפלות מצבנו וערך כבודנו בעמים אינו כ"א למען נתבונן על כבוד יוצרנו והעטרה שעטר אותנו בפאר התפילין ששמו נקרא עליהם ואנו מזלזלים בהם והננו כולנו אשמים . . . התפלה

He proceeds to make a series of far-reaching halakhic arguments: that one who improperly places his tefillin is not just in dereliction of the specific precept, but effectively giving false testimony and in open rebellion against the oral law, and would be better off not wearing tefillin at all;[76] that one who sees someone with improperly placed tefillin must rebuke him immediately, notwithstanding the general prohibition on conversation during times of prayer, and even if the target of rebuke is a notable or sage;[77] that this is a situation akin to those life-or-death matters in which other commandments and prohibitions are abrogated in order to save another's life.[78] He calls on the sages of his time to take upon themselves the responsibility of rectifying the matter and suggests the formation of societies to this end, as indeed contemporary opponents of traditional religion are a divine punishment to the rabbis for their neglect of this mitzvah.[79] This last comment is really striking when we recall that his essays in *'Ittur Sofrim* displayed a much more nuanced understanding of, and response to, contemporary challenges to rabbinic authority.

Hevesh Pe'er is undoubtedly an idiosyncratic and even strange tract. That his halakhic conclusions were highly novel and even startling was made abundantly clear by the critical give and take with his rabbinic peers in the 1925 edition, more than twice the length of the original volume, not to mention the critical glosses by his father-in-law Aderet to the first edition.[80] Indeed, on its publication the work met with genuine and understandable criticism.[81]

Several elements are at work here; one cannot help but wonder if there is here an echo of the humiliations and anger articulated by his father over the laxity with regard to tefillin he saw on his wanderings among the wealthy; Rav Kook's own pilgrimage reflects

---

של ראש שהוא על המוח כדי לשעבד כל מחשבות הלב והשכל לעבודתו ית', אם היינו משמרים מצוה זו כתקונה היינו מרגישים שפע אור דעה והשכל . . . כי אור השכל מאיר כל מחשך ועושה שלום בין יריבי עם . . . מצות תפילין של ראש הנתונה על כלי המחשבה שסגולתה בודאי להוסיף באדם הפרט ובכל האומה בכלל אור דעת ויראת ד' שהמה מקורי כל טוב וחסד. . . .

The 1985 edition makes an extraordinary, ideologically charged change in this passage; while the first and second editions refer to those who are *mashlihim shikuzim al talmidei hahakhamim,* "casting abominations on sages," the 1985 edition has *maskilim shikutzim,* "Maskilic abominators."

76 HP, 20. The source for this is the Mishnah Megillah 4:8, BT Megillah 24b, codified by Maimonides, *Hilkhot Tefillin* 4:3. The printed editions of Maimonides refer to this infraction as "the way of the Sadducees," though other versions preserve the Mishnaic term "heresy," *minut,* see, for example, the Yemenite MSS, edited by Yosef Qafah, *Sefer Ha-Ahavah,* 348. That is the version cited in Yeshayahu Ha-Levi Horowitz (1558–1630), *Shnei Luhot Ha-Berit, Ner Mitzvah, Hullin* no. 34, ed. Meir Katz, (Haifa: Makhon Yad Ramah, 2010), vol. 2, 10.

77 HP, 22–26.

78 Ibid., 31.

79 Ibid., 33–35.

80 These are to be found at 96–169 of the 1985 edition; his rabbinic interlocutors there are Zvi Pesah Frank, Ya'aqov Moshe Harlap, and Yehiel Mikhel Tykoczinsky.

81 Zev Wolf Turbowicz, rabbi of Krak, wrote that "I was asked about a newly published book that has shaken the world regarding the masses who are not careful with *tefillin shel rosh* . . . the author's intentions are pious, but he has defamed God's people and may God forgive him."

a restlessness coupled with pietism. We have already seen his concern with the place of Mind in the religious life in his texts of this time; and we also see here a further sign of his deep identification with the heritage of the Gaon of Vilna.[82]

The Gaon was especially scrupulous about tefillin, and indeed through the nineteenth-century depictions of him in lithographs and paintings almost always have him wearing tefillin, an uncommon detail.[83] The Gaon encouraged his disciples to wear tefillin all day long;[84] moreover, Rav Kook's master in Volozhin, Netziv, is reported to have worn tefillin all day, as did Aderet[85] (and his celebrated ancestor Mordechai Jaffe ruled that this was mandatory).[86] Day-long tefillin wearing seems to have in general been a distinctively Mitnagdic form of spirituality—and we will shortly see why.[87] In the Warsaw 1857 edition of *Ma'aseh Rav*, the compilation of sayings and practices attributed to the Gaon, we find:

Zev Wolf Turbowicz, *Tiferet Ziv* (Warsaw: Unterhendler, 1896), responsum 1 (dating from the summer of 1891), 1:

נשאלתי בדבר אחד חדש שיצא לאור שהרעיש עולם ומלואה על רוב ההמון שאינם נזהרין בתפילין של ראש שיהא מונח כולו במקומו . . . תשובה: המחבר הזה כוונתו לשמים אבל עכ״ז דבר סרה על עם ה' ושארי ליה מאריה.

. . .

Turbowicz was born in 1840 and spent most of his life in the vicinity of Minsk; see on him Ben-Zion Eisenstadt, *Dor Rabbanav ve-Sofrav*, vol. 3 (Vilna: Katzenellenbogen, 1901), 19–20. Turbowicz's lengthy response to the volume became the basis of the rejoinder by Rav Kook, published in 1900 in *Torah mi-Tzion*. In that essay he elaborates on the well-established halakhah regarding the proper placement of the tefillin shel rosh, but does not address the criticisms levelled at the other, far-reaching arguments he had made.

Favorable citations of the work are mentioned at Neriah, *Sihot*, 188, including *Sdei Hemed* (Kelalim, 40:2).

82 See his father's essay in *Ha-Peles*, discussed in chapter 1, the discrepancies in the publication dates notwithstanding.

83 See Rachel Schnold, "Elijah's Face: The Portrait of the Vilna Gaon in Folk Art," in *The Gaon of Vilna: The Man and His Legacy* [Bilingual edition], ed. Rachel Schnold (Tel Aviv: Beth Hatefusoth, the Nahum Goldmann Museum of the Jewish Diaspora, 1998), 35–45 in Hebrew version and 48–58 in English version; my thanks to Prof. Jay Harris for directing me to this essay. See also the late nineteenth-century broadside reproduced in Richard I. Cohen, *Jewish Icons: Art and Society in Modern Europe* (Berkeley: University of California Press, 1998), 146.

84 In the ordinances of the endowed study circle in Vilna that bore his name, *Kloyz Ha-Gra*, established in 1813, all those receiving stipends were enjoined to wear tefillin all day long and up to nightfall; eyewitness accounts of the practice go to the 1890s and it may even have persisted to the interwar period. See Dov Eliah, *Ha-Gaon*, vol. 3 (Jerusalem: Moreshet Ha-Yeshivot, 2002), 800–801.

85 Horovitz, *Zikhrones*, vol. 1, 229; see also Nissenbaum, *'Alei Heldi*, 43.

86 For lengthy discussion of classic halakhic views on the matter, see Menahem Kasher, *Torah Shleimah*, vol. 12 (New York: n.p., 1948), 240–247 (addendum 39); Levush's view is discussed therein at 243–244.

87 See the sources collected by Eliezer Brodt, *Beyn Keseh le-'Asor* (Jerusalem: Brodt, 2008): 229-234, esp. 233 for materials on Netziv and Aderet, and Saraya Devlitzki, *Quntres Sarid me-'Ir*, in his reprint of Ya'aqov Moshe Harlap's 1907 collection of the letters of his teacher, Yehoshua Zvi Mikhel Shapira, *Tzvi le-Tzadiq* (Bnei Braq: Devlitzki, 2007): 118-123. My thanks to Eliezer Brodt for that latter reference. Shneur Zalman of Liady reportedly wearing tefillin

"As for tefillin, the higher on the head, the better,"[88] a comment cited by Rav Kook at the outset of his 1900 rejoinder to his critics.[89] This concern was also shared by latter-day disciples of the Gaon. [90]

The Gaon's legacy also figures in his decision to wander. Hayim of Volozhin reported that the Gaon was greatly disturbed at the neglect of tefillin in his day and said that just as the legendary thirteenth-century Rabbi Moses of Coucy (author of the *Sefer Mitzvot Gadol*) made the rounds in his time to rouse people to this mitzvah, so too would he (i.e., the Gaon) have done so, had his physical health permitted.[91] Rav Kook, of course, cites this

---

all day would presumably be in keeping with the scholastic Lituanian character of his Hasidic practice and teaching.

88   8a, תפילין כל מה שהם בגובה הראש משובח.

89   HP, 36. In that rejoinder, at 44–45, he also cites a responsum by his teacher in Lyutsin, Eliezer Don-Yehiya, who in an undated responsum, *Even Shtiyah*, no. 12, makes the far-reaching argument that even if one's tefillin are only a bit misplaced on the forehead one has not fulfilled the commandment at all. We cannot know if this influenced his early thinking on the subject, and at any rate the Gaon's influence seems far more decisive.

90   In passing he mentions as precedent for his own work a volume entitled *Quntres Tiqqun 'Olam* though he does not give the author's name; HP, 10. The author turns out to be Eliezer Lipman Metz, who had been a contributor to Rav Kook's periodical *'Ittur Sofrim*. Lipman's work of several pages, whose originality resided in its accompanying illustrations, appeared as a preface to a prayer book entitled *Seder Tefilat Yisrael* (Vilna: Yehudah Leib Metz, 1880), the same publishing house that had published Kook's *Ittur Sofrim*. Eliezer prefaces his illustrations and their accompanying explanations in Yiddish, with observations about sloppy tefillin habits all around. The Siddur has an additional preface (iv–vi) by Shlomo Ha-Cohen of Vilna (1831–1906), a rabbinical judge in Vilna and one of the contributors to the first issue of the young Rav Kook's journal *'Ittur Sofrim*, followed by an halakhic discussion by the latter's brother Bezalel (1821–1878), also a rabbinical judge in Vilna, composed shortly before his death (1–2). Bezalel Cohen made glosses to the famous Vilna/Romm edition of the Talmud. He was comparatively tolerant of Maskilim, a supporter of Rabbi Reines's innovations in Talmudic scholarship—see the brief mentions of him in *Yahadut Lita*, vol. 1 (Tel Aviv: 'Am Ha-Sefer, 1959), 220, 242, 271, 297—and the author of a volume of responsa, *Reshit Bikkurim* (Vilna, press 1869). Shlomo authored *Binyan Shlomo* (Vilna: n.p., 1888) and *'Atzei Broshim* (Vilna, n.p., 1903). A halakhic exchange of his with Netziv can be found as an appendix to *Ha'ameq She'elah* to Leviticus.

91   This was reported by Asher Cohen in paragraph 15 of his compilation of Hayim of Volozhin's sayings *Keter Rosh*, written in 1819, cited in Dov Eliah, ed. *Kol He-Katuv le-Hayim* (Jerusalem: n.p., 1988), 118.

The historical background to this comment was the neglect of tefillin in medieval Europe. To be sure, throughout Jewish history, the mitzvah of tefillin was often honored in the breach, see the materials on this gathered by Kasher, *Torah Shleimah*, 259–268; yet Moses of Coucy's episode is the best-known. While some contemporaries offered explanation-cum-rationalizations for this desuetude, along the lines of the difficulties and complexities of the proper observance of the practice, a far more strenuous response issued from Moses of Coucy, who, beginning in 1236, under the impress of a spiritual revelation, undertook rounds of sermons in France, Germany, and also in Spain. He offered no justifications for neglect of the practice but forcefully argued for its fulfillment (and interestingly cautioned against those who might see it as more of a metaphysical or metaphorical concept than a literal requirement).

historical precedent, and one wonders to what extent he was trying to fashion himself as a latter-day Moses of Coucy, enacting a particular paradigm of revival.[92] In this light it is all the more striking that while Moses of Coucy was stirred to action by the neglect of tefillin in toto, Rav Kook was stirred by the neglect of one particular detail.[93] There is a kind of pietism at work here, an impression deepened by his publishing this work anonymously and undertaking a sort of pilgrimage for his itinerant preaching on the matter. He travels took him about 250 kilometers away from Zeimel into the heartlands of Lithuania and Belarus.[94] That he sought anonymity is made clear from the fact that, though this region was the haunt of his youth, there is no record of his returning to Smorgon or Volozhin for a visit.[95] The solitary quality of this journey is reinforced by the report that he did not trust anyone to do ritual slaughtering for him and learned to slaughter chickens on his own.[96] In later years he said that the experience "helped me greatly in matters of serving God."[97]

During the course of his travels he made the acquaintance of two figures who left a deep impression on him—individualists who marched to a different drummer than most other Lithuanian Talmudists. Mordechai Rosenblatt (1837–1915?), known as the "Butener Tzadiq" from his time as rabbi of Butan, served as rabbi in Oshmany (Asmina)

For a brief history of this episode, see Ephraim Kanarfogel, "Rabbinic Attitudes toward Nonobservance in the Medieval Period," in *Jewish Tradition and the Nontraditional Jew*, ed. Jacob J. Schacter (Northvale: Aronson, 1992), 3–35, and esp. 7–14. One of Moses of Coucy's sermons on the subject is to be found in his *Sefer Mitzvot Gadol, Mitzvot 'Aseh* no. 3.

92   HP, 11.

93   In considering Rav Kook's self-fashioning here in light of the precedent of Moses of Coucy, I am drawing on Victor Turner's essay, "Religious Paradigms and Political Action," reprinted in his *Dramas, Fields and Metaphors: Symbolic Action in Human Society* (Ithaca: Cornell University Press, 1974), 60–97. There, Turner develops the idea that Thomas Becket, in his confrontation with Henry II, drew on and reenacted the paradigmatic passage to martyrdom he had absorbed through Church tradition. Here I am suggesting that Rav Kook took the historical precedent and example of Moses of Coucy and used it to fashion a pietistic odyssey of his own.

94   I arrived at this conclusion because the few people whose meetings with him on this trip are recorded were in Birzai, near Zeimel, and in Oshmany and Kossow (in the latter he may have met the father of Hazon Ish; see Neriah, *Sihot*, 193).

95   Presumably he also enjoyed the respite from mundane rabbinical duties though the experience of the book and the journey cannot be reduced to that.

96   Neriah, *Sihot*, 193.

97   Ibid., 194.

from 1891 to his death.[98] Unlike other Lithuanian Talmudists, he was a wonder worker[99] and a mystic given over to decidedly imaginative visions.[100]

Pinhas Ha-Cohen Lintop (1852–1914), rabbi of the Hasidic community of Birzh (Birzai), published a number of writings veering between analysis and polemic, weaving together Kabbalistic and philosophical themes while arguing for tolerance and a spirit of unity in the increasingly fractious Jewish community; Lintop, who did not shy away from controversy, was willing to say that Orthodoxy was, in its combativeness, intellectual elitism, and unresponsiveness to contemporary problems in some ways to blame for its own troubles.[101] He was also a steadfast critic of Elyashiv's understanding of Kabbalah, as we will see.

---

98 For biography of Rosenblatt, see: Hayim Levinsky, *Toldot Ha-Ga'on Rabbi Mordechai Weisel (Rosenblatt)* (Vilna: Garber, 1917); Kalman Lichtenstein and Yehezqel Rabinowitz, eds., *Pinqas Slonim* (Tel Aviv: Defus Ha-Po'el Ha-Tza'ir, 1972), 270–278; and Joseph Levin, ed., *Antopol Yizkor Book* (Tel Aviv, Ha-Po'el Ha-Mizrahi 1967), 127. He authored a volume of responsa and *hadranim*, *Hadrat Mordechai* (Vilna: Romm, 1899). Rav Kook himself, according to his secretary in later years, Shimon Gliczenstein, extemporized at this time a series of hadranim in Zeimel; this is reported in Lifshitz, *Shivhei Ha-Re'ayah*, 58.

99 This dimension of Rosenblatt's personality is the subject of A. Litwin, "Der Letzter 'Guter Yid'" in A. Litwin, *Yiddische Neshomes*, vol. 3 (New York: Folksbildung, 1917). "A. Litwin" was the pseudonym of Shmuel Leib Horvitz, 1862–1943. The volume is an unpaginated collection of sketches and feuilletons, this piece is the penultimate of the volume. My thanks to Rabbi Zalman Alpert for directing me to this source.

100 The story of Rosenblatt's most celebrated vision and its popularity is oddly fascinating. On Simhat Torah 1880, he had a remarkable dream vision, in which he was visited by the sixteenth-century Turkish rabbi and judge, Joseph ben David ibn Lev (1501–1580), who told Rosenblatt that one of his ancestors had been a disgruntled litigant who had struck the rabbi after losing a case before him and that it was up to Rosenblatt to atone for this so that his ancestor could be resurrected at the end of days. This was to be done by his acquiring a volume of Rabbi ibn Lev's responsa and mastering it over the next four years, with the stipulation that the volume be purchased from the rabbi of Antipol. After some months' hesitation he finally wrote to the rabbi of Antipol, begging for the volume at any price. A yeshiva student passing through Antipol and staying at the rabbi's came upon a copy of the letter, copied it, and it was printed by Yitzhak Hirschensohn in Jerusalem and reprinted several times. It was included as an appendix to a Hebrew-Yiddish collection of gothic tales, exorcisms and so forth entitled *Sefer Ha-Mora Ha-Gadol/Shreklikhe Geshikhte* (Warsaw: David Weissman, 1902). It was reprinted in Eliezer Tziegelman's *Nahalei Emunah* (Lublin: Schneidmesser, 1935), a volume which included a brief approbation from Rav Kook, and by Rosenblatt's descendants under the title *Halom Nifla* (Tel Aviv: n.p., 1939), and again in *Otzar Sifrei Mussar* (Jerusalem: n.p., 1972).

101 In 1880, he published *Pithei She'arim*, one of whose three approbations was written by Aderet (Vilna: Katzenellenbogen, 5641/1880). Parenthetically, he says that he has in his possession a manuscript of Luzzatto's commentary to the *Idra Rabbah* and makes several references thereto in the course of the book, such as 18a. For a powerful summary of his ideas, see therein at 18–19. He returned to these themes with a collection of ten tracts entitled *Yalqut Avnei Emunat Yisrael* (Warsaw: Torsz, 1895) which also appeared with a warm letter of approbation from Aderet. Bezalel Naor has gathered much information on Lintop as well as explored his Kabbalistc ideas in his *Qana'utei de-Pinhas* (Spring Valley: Orot, 2013).

The Primacy of the Mind in the Additional Texts of *Ḥevesh Pe'er*

The 1925 edition of *Hevesh Pe'er* contains seven texts, described as sermons, which according to the editors were given by Rav Kook during his travels in the 1890s.[102] It is not clear that these are actual sermons that were given then. One of them appears in a notebook from a later period, and in the others on several occasions we find the words "as we have written elsewhere."[103] Indeed, they appear in the recently published notebook *Metziot Qatan*.[104] These texts may well have been provided by Rav Kook to the editors as representative samples of the thinking behind his project and the themes he had in mind, and it is by no means unlikely that his sermons did indeed reflect these ideas. Here I take them as they were published in 1925, meant as they presumably were to crystallize the underlying themes at work in this text.

We encounter in these texts two topics which will appear with gathering force in the coming pages: the primacy of Mind as the link between God and man—as he depicts tefillin as vessels of *da'at*, understanding or consciousness, an association with roots in Kabbalistic ethical literature[105]—and the relationship between Jewish and gentile morality, itself a function of gradations within the sphere of Mind. (His thinking on this during this period will come to fullest expression in *Midbar Shur*.) We also see here a marriage of Lithuanian halakhic punctiliousness and preoccupation with the cosmic principle of Mind with the heritage of medieval philosophy.

Interestingly, while Rav Kook here reads *tefillin shel rosh* in the terms of the philosophical tradition's concern with Mind and its complicated relationship with the body, the philosophers themselves did not. Maimonides, for instance, makes only cursory mention of tefillin in his *Guide*, and in the *Code* he discusses it in quotidian terms as a helpful tool for keeping one's mind out of the gutter and on "matters of truth and justice" while going about one's day.[106] Isaac Arama treats tefillin at times allegorically and at others as helpful aids to spiritual mindfulness, as did Maimonides, though a bit more passionately.[107] Maharal, though, does cast the practice in somewhat philosophical terms, saying that via tefillin one actualizes the intellectual faculty via the intellectual entity that is Torah.[108]

---

102 HP, 49–69. The sermons were almost certainly delivered in Yiddish, as was the one sermon printed in the first edition, which as I have noted was devoid of the larger themes broached in the sermons reprinted in 1925.

103 One sermon appears in *Pinqas* 16:36, and references to "as we have written elsewhere" appear in four places in the 1925 edition.

104 See therein, paragraphs 237, 238, 404, 405, 410, 417, for sermons 5, 6, 2, 4, 7, 3, respectively, as well as paragraph 149 of MQ.

105 Thus see, for instance, Bahya ben Asher's well-known thirteenth-century treatise Hayim Chavel, ed., *Kad Ha-Qemah* (Jerusalem: Mossad Ha-Rav Kook, 1995), 443–444.

106 *Hilkhot Tefillin* 4:25. The mentions in the *Guide* are at 3:32, 44.

107 See *'Aqedat Yitzhaq* 90:29a; 98:94a.

108 See *Netivot 'Olam, Netiv Ha-'Avodah*, chapter 15 and particularly 2, 300–302 in the 1982 Hayim Pardes edition (Tel Aviv: Makhon Yad Mordechai, 1982).

Rav Kook's first sermon in the 1925 edition takes as its text the Talmudic comment that wearing tefillin is the condition precedent to entering the Land of Israel (BT Bekhorot 5a).[109] Indeed, this is one of the few discussions of the Land of Israel in his pre-Palestine years, which may account for its prominence in the 1925 edition. He sets out the familiar dichotomy between matter and form, as the dichotomy of mind and body; yet, echoing the comments in his commentary to Rabbah bar bar Hannah, and notwithstanding the negative valuation of the body in Maimonides and Bahya, the body, he says, cannot entirely be bad in itself inasmuch as it is destined to be resurrected in the *eschaton*.[110] Rather, the body must be mastered by the mind so that the body and its works may themselves be transformed to good, which is "the telos of all wisdoms, which is none other than to recognize God and know him, and from that knowledge acquire the love of Him, as Maimonides wrote."[111] This of course requires cooperation of Mind and Will; to that end, Torah and faith serve as a boundary between Mind and the Will, which latter is the body's vehicle of expression, and it is through them that the Will becomes a vessel of the Mind.[112] The wearing of Tefillin finds its meaning as part of this process as it works on the vessels of Mind, namely, the heart and brain; "the power of divine mind that is in tefillin shines the rays of the light of the mind onto the body—to the heart and brain—and thus the mind works upon the Will."[113] In language reflecting the influence of Maharal, he says that "when one wears tefillin there flows onto his mind a sacred, separate intellect."[114] As tefillin work to impress the mind onto the body and thus transform it, so the Land of Israel represents the transformation of body into Mind. This theme of Mind's relationship to the corporeal world will resonate throughout.

The second sermon (MQ 490) takes as its text the well-known Talmudic dictum that God is enveloped in Torah and tefillin (BT Berakhot 6a), which he reads as the schemata of a tripartite structure of Mind and its relation to the world: "Mind in its own broad self, in and of itself and at its great height, has nothing to do with particular actions, it does not even cognize particularity. Then comes the intellect which knows particulars

---

109 The printed edition mistakenly gives as the source BT Qiddushin 37.
110 HP, 49:

שאי אפשר לומר כלל שענין הגוף וישוב העולם יהיה בעצמו ענין רע שהרי לעתיד לבא יעמוד הגוף בתחית המתים ואם היו עניני החומר חסרון מוחלט איך זה יהיה תכלית נכבד.

111 Ibid.:

והנה תכלית כל החכמות הוא רק להכיר את השם ית׳ ולדעהו ומן הדעת יקנה אהבה לו ית׳ כמו שכתב הרמב״ם. . . .

112 Ibid. 50–51:

אמנם אם תהיה מחיצה מפסקת בין השכל והרצון אז יפעל השכל על הרצון וכל מה שיתחזק הגוף בכוחותיו כן ירבה השכל בעבודתו כי יהיה לו כלי תשמיש נכונים ומתוקנים. המחיצה היא שיהיו כל מערכי לבבו בעניני הנהגותיו הולכים על פי סדר תורת ד׳ . . . והנה אז תהיה לו האמונה מחיצה מבדלת בין החומר והשכל.

113 Ibid. 52:

והנה התפילין הם כנגד כלי השכל, המוח והלב, שבהם השכל הנשמה (!) מגלה שם את כחותיה. אך הלב הטבעי והמוח הטבעי אחוזים הם בחבלי הרצון . . . ומצד כח השכל שיש בתפילין מאיר אל הגוף בשליחות קוי אור שכל— אל הלב והמוח ונמצא שפועל השכל על הרצון. . . .

114 Ibid.:

המניח תפילין שופעת על שכלו קדושת שכלי נבדל.

as it perceives them. And then it cleaves to a body acting within nature, to the point of transforming the latter's actions into those of the mind."[115] *Tefillin shel rosh* are thus the fountainhead of intellect's emanation, or devolution, through particulars.

Whether the divine mind cognizes particulars was a longstanding problem in medieval Jewish philosophy, with ramifications for the theory of divine Providence, and though Rav Kook does not cite those interlocutors by name here they clearly set the terms of his discussion. Maimonides had argued that divine knowledge is fundamentally different from human knowledge and can cognize the infinite, the nonexistent as well as the contingent, such as the free human will, without thereby undergoing mutability; moreover what we call "Providence" is the congruence of the actualized human mind—in thought and by its handmaiden, action—with the divine mind.[116] Gersonides contended that God's knowledge of human action extends only to the general laws of human nature but not to the particulars of action.[117] Isaac Arama argued, contra Maimonides, that Providence is not a function of a divine intellect which ordains natural laws, but of a moral order, a moral causality within the world, revealed uniquely to Israel.[118]

Rav Kook attempts his own answer to the problem by recourse to the threefold classification of the soul discussed above, *nefesh*, *ruah*, and *neshamah*, which appears in Arama as a continuum from the body, to "Actualized" or "Acquired Intellect" (i.e., one that has been "fortified" or energized by contact with the Active Intellect, sent by God, and thus become an independently existing being) to pure, detached Mind.[119] Arama himself had offered, contra Maimonides, a straightforwardly theistic solution to the problem of the intellect's knowledge of particulars. Rav Kook makes use of Arama's tripartite picture of the continuum of mind-cognition-body, which itself is Arama's translation into philosophical terms of the Zoharic picture of the soul, to provide a quasi-Maimonidean answer to the problem of the cognition of particulars: that the human mind can, to a

---

115 Ibid. 57:

והנה ישנם בכלל השכל וההנהגה הבאה בגלוי שלש חלוקות חיוביות. השכל בעצמו הכללי, שמצד עצמו גבהו ואיננו אומר לפעול פעולות פרטיות וגם אפילו לא להשכיל בפרטיות. ואחר כך יבא השכל המשכיל פרטים לפי ההשקפה בהם. ואחר כך ידבק בגוף הפועל בטבע עד שתהיה עשיתו כעשית השכל. . . .

116 The relevant chapters of the *Guide* are 3:16–21. For discussion of the issue and the range of scholarly views on Maimonides here, see Michael Schwarz, "Remarks Concerning Maimonides' Conception of God's Knowledge of Particulars," in *Torah and Wisdom: Studies in Jewish Philosophy, Kabbalah and Halacha, Essays in Honor of Arthur Hyman*, ed. Ruth Link-Salinger (New York: Shengold, 1992), 189–197.

117 On this, see briefly Seymour Feldman, "Maimonides—A Guide for Posterity," in Seeskin, ed., *Cambridge Companion to Maimonides*, 338–339, and the sources cited therein. For a slightly different presentation, see Charles H. Manekin, "Conservative Tendencies in Gersonides' Religious Philosophy," in *The Cambridge Companion to Medieval Jewish Philosophy*, ed. Daniel H. Frank and Oliver Leaman (Cambridge: Cambridge University Press, 2003), 304–342, 310–315.

118 See Heller-Wilensky, *Rabbi Yitzhaq Arama u-Mishnato*, 132–136.

119 See ibid., 140–141. Unlike other medieval philosophers who adopted the threefold classification of the soul, Arama regards the soul as a unitary being, and not as a concatenation of distinct souls; see Pearl, *The Medieval Jewish Mind*.

point, seamlessly mesh with the divine mind, such that the latter can participate in the particulars of human action with its ontological uniqueness intact. A Kabbalistic accent, though, whispers through the positive valuation of the body—and the tool for that bodily transformation is tefillin.

In the following sermon (MQ 237) he offers an explanation for the Talmudic comment that improper placement of tefillin low on the forehead is "the way of the heretics" (BT Megillah 24). He writes: "(T)ruly the intellect comes from a high place, from God, and its strength is greater than all bodily matters and actions of the practical soul, and its sanctity is great."[120] Thus the improper placement of tefillin confuses the boundary between body and mind, and, interestingly, between the nations and Israel. This is because while the former are bound by the Seven Noahide Laws, rooted in natural law and governed by the practical intellect, Israel's mitzvot are "sacred lights, whose foundations are not in the natural intellect at all," and indeed will be despoiled if regulated by practical intellect and natural law.[121]

This fifth sermon contains early seeds of what will emerge as significant themes later on: the thoroughgoing relativity of human understanding relative to the true, divinely ordered nature of reality, and the critical importance of *yosher*, a sort of given natural law, embedded by God in humanity and the world and a key term in Lurianic Kabbalah (about all of which we will have more to say in coming chapters). The Talmud says that when in response to Moses's request to see God's presence He revealed to him His back but not His face (Ex. 33:17–23), what was revealed was the knot of God's tefillin (BT Berakhot 7a). Rav Kook reads this divine tefillin knot as the nexus of divine disclosure and inaccessibility, and thus of body and mind. The nape of the neck, where one finds the knot of tefillin, both of people and of God, is "the locus of organization by which the intellect orders bodily activities, ordering one's footsteps by the governance of intellect and memory."[122] This locus also marks the boundary of human understanding:

> And lo from all that we know and comprehend by receiving true wisdom [that is, Kabbalah] . . . we know nothing about the reasons for the essence of existence, why it is this or that, which is His entirely incomprehensible wisdom, and all our wisdom and comprehension is of nothing more than the justice (*yosher*) of order and relation.[123]

---

120 HP, 62:
שנדע שכן הוא באמת שהשכל בא ממקום גבוה מאת השי״ת וגדול הוא בעצמותו מכל עניני הגוף ופעולות הנפש המעשיות וקדושתו גדולה.

121 Ibid., 63:
והנה אומות העולם שאינם מוזהרים כ״א על שבע מצות ב״נ שמיוסדים ומושרשים גם בטבעו של אדם, השכל המעשי שהם צריכים לו לא ישתנה מצד טבע החומר כ״כ לפי מקור תולדתו אבל ישראל שנתעלו לתרי״ג מצות, אורות קדושים שאין יסודותם בשכל הטבעי כלל, ממילא השכל הטבעי שבנוי על שרשי החושים מתנגד לאותו השכל המעשי שהם צריכים לו ואיך יקום.

122 Ibid., 66:
הוא מקום הסדור הנותן סדר לפי השכל לפעולות הגוף, הוא יסדר פעמי הרגל לפי הנהגת השכל והזכרון. . . .

123 Ibid.:
והנה מכל מה שאנו יודעים ומשיגים על-ידי קבלת חכמת אמת . . . אין אנו יודעים מאומה מטעמי עיקר המציאות

The essential theme of the sermons of the 1925 edition as a whole is stated succinctly in the seventh, and last:

> The chief action that guides one's powers to act themselves per the Torah-Intellect comes from the sanctity of tefillin, which is unified with the body and causes God's Torah to take hold in the body, and without tefillin, God's Torah cannot be unified with it.[124]

Mind is the link between God and humanity and the ordering principle of lower, natural, bodily realms.

How do his ideas relate to the place of tefillin in the mystical tradition, in which *tefillin shel rosh* are endowed with deep significance? Jacob Katz has pointed out that the mythic and mystic overtones of Talmudic discussions of tefillin stimulated the casting of its halakhot in mystic terms from an early stage in the history of the Kabbalah, as part of what he characterizes as "an impulse to deepen the religious experience."[125] In the Zoharic myth of the divine anthropos *Adam Qadmon*, creative energy flows through three illuminated chambers of consciousness, *mohin*, of which tefillin are the visible manifestation.[126]

In the Gaon's commentary to *Tiqqunei Zohar*, and specifically the central passage *Patah Eliyahu* (Elijah Commenced), commenting on the text's identification of the sefirah *Keter* with the *qarqafta de-tefillei* (the tefillin-wearing head)[127] he identifies *qarqafta* as "the skull on which tefillin rest . . . as tefillin are YHWH which proceeds from the (second sefirah of) *Hokhmah* (Wisdom) and downwards and it rests upon it."[128] In other words, divine tefillin are the divine name YHWH which rests upon the sefirah of *Hokhmah*, the primal, undifferentiated source of all knowledge and understanding. That the Gaon felt

---

למה הוא בדרך זה ואופן זה, שהיא חכמתו הבלתי מושגת כלל, וכל חכמתנו והשגתינו אינה כי"א ביושר הסדור
והיחש. . . . .

124 Ibid., 68.:

עיקר הפעולה שיהו הכחות מתנהגים בעצמם על פי השכל התוריי—בא מקדושת תפלין המתאחדת בגוף וגורמת
לתורת ה' שתהיה לה אחיזה בגוף, ובלא תפלין אין תורת ד' מתאחדת בו.

It is at this point perhaps worth remarking that the fact that in according tefillin so central a place in the religious life, he clearly counts women out. This is not particularly surprising, but a helpful reminder that he was a man of his place and time and, for better or worse, a faithful representative of much rabbinic tradition.

125 See his *Halakhah ve-Kabbalah* (Jerusalem: Magnes/Hebrew University, 1984), 15, 23 (the quote is from the latter).

126 Zohar (*Idra Zuta*), III, 292b:

בחללא דגולגלתא נהירין תלת נהורין, ואי תימא תלת, ארבע אינון, כמה דאמינא, אחסנתיה דאבוי ואמיה ותרין
גניזין דלהון דמתעטרן כלהו ברישיה ואינון תפלין דרישא לבתר מתחברן בסטרוי ונהרין ועאלין בתלת חללי
דגולגלתא, נפקין כל חד בסטרוי ומתפשטין בכל גופא, ואלין מתחברן בתרי מוחי, ומוחא תליתאה כליל לון ואחיד
(נ''א ואינון תפלין דרישא ואלין מתחברן בתרי מוחי ומוחא תליתאה כליל לון ועאלין בתלת חללי דגולגלתא לבתר
נפקין כל חד בסטרוי ומתפשטין בכל גופא והאי מוחא תליתאה אחיד).

127 In a well-known Talmudic passage, BT Rosh Hashanah 17a, "Israelites who sin with their very bodies" are identified as *qarqafta de-lo manah tefillin 'alei* (a skull that did not ever don tefillin).

128 *Tiqqunei Zohar 'im Be'iur Ha-Gra* (Vilna: Shmuel Yosef Fuenn & Avraham Zvi Rosenkranz, 1867), 19a.

the need to identify *qarqafta* specifically as the skull, when any reader of the *Tiqqunim* is presumably already proficient in Aramaic and familiar with the Talmudic passage that is its source, would seem to indicate that tefillin's placement lower on the forehead would vitiate the tefillin-wearer's correlation with the divine tefillin of *Hokhmah*. The Gaon's attitude here is interestingly at variance with Moshe Hayim Luzzatto's correlation of tefillin with the forehead, and not the crown of the head, of *Adam Qadmon*, the divine anthropos.[129]

In the fourth sermon of the 1925 edition the Kabbalistic terminology becomes explicit as *sekhel* is identified with the Kabbalistic *mohin*,[130] and the comparatively static philosophical worldview of the other sermons shifts to a more dynamic universe, in which Mind, rather than simply seeking to align itself with the Divine Intellect, must rouse itself to do battle with the *Sitra Ahra* within a metaphysically variegated universe, i.e., the four worlds, that is an arena of contending forces.[131]

Indeed, the profound theurgic significance which the Kabbalistic tradition, in response to this myth, attributed to the wearing of *tefillin shel rosh* seems a far more satisfactory explanation for the urgency and rhetorical passion of Rav Kook's tefillin crusade than do the at times bloodless excurses on the primacy of the Intellect. He was trying to navigate his way between the several spiritual traditions that he saw as his inheritance—Lithuanian Talmudism, medieval philosophy, and Kabbalah—granting primacy to the mind while linking it to a more dynamic cosmos than the one imagined by the philosophers, and grounded in pieist religious practice, including the abnegations of anonymous pilgrimage.[132]

The question of how the primacy of mind relates to the project of self-perfection, divine and human, and Israel's place in the world preoccupied him further, resulting in his volume several years later, *Midbar Shur*.

---

129 See Ramhal, *Qalah Pithei Hokhmah*, ed. Hayim Friedlander (Bnei Braq: Sifriyati/Gitler, 1992), §32, 121:

וגם מן המצח יוצא הארתו . . . וה״ס התפלין העומדים במצח. . . .

130 HP, 64, MQ 405:

והנה נודע דתפילין של יד לית לה מגרמה כלום (זוהר פ׳ בא) וכשהמוחין מסולקים אז אדרבא כל חסרון וקלקול בא.

The Zohar passage he is referring to is at II, 43a.

131 Ibid.:

והנה השל-ראש מפאר ומוציא לאור יתרון קדושת ישראל . . . וכשהיצר הרע מתגדל עד שבועט ח״ו בתפילין ש״ר אז אדרבה מצד השפע המעשה נתהפך לרועץ ונתקלקל יותר שמשתמש בכוחותיו הרמים לנאצה וחבל נמרץ ח״ו א״כ נעשה אפר מפאר. . . .

132 Interestingly in the one conversation between him and the aforementioned mystic Mordechai Rosenblatt, of which we have a record, Rav Kook is said to have answered Rosenblatt's query as to how he had been able to acquire advanced Kabbalistic knowledge at a young age by saying that "one might also be vouchsafed a revelation of Elijah, *by way of intellect* [emphasis added]." Neriah, *Sihot*, 191. The idea of a revelation of Elijah has a rich and complex history in Kabbalah and figured in Hasidic-Mitnagdic polemics as well; see briefly Maoz Kahana, "Ha-Hatam Sofer: Ha-Poseq be-Eyney 'Atzmo," *Tarbitz* 76, nos. 3-4 (2007): 519-556, esp. 533.

Midbar Shur: The Desert of Vision

His preoccupation with the relations between body and mind, on their own terms and as a prism through which to view the relationship between Jewish and gentile morality, is at the heart of *Midbar Shur* (the Desert of Shur, Ex. 15:22, and, in a Zoharic pun, the Desert of Vision).[133]

A collection of thirty-eight sermons, amounting to some 360 printed pages, written and/or delivered over two years from spring 1894 to the spring of 1896 in Zeimel,[134] it was not published until 1999.[135] Appended to the printed edition is an introduction entitled "Midbar Qedem" (literally, the Eastern Desert, but also, the Prefatory Desert), dated 1899, which I will discuss later on, and a detailed table of contents from Rav Kook's own hand listing the sermons' dates.[136]

It is unclear how accurately these long, Hebrew sermons reflect the sermons as, presumably, originally delivered in Yiddish.[137] In the 1899 introduction he writes that "some"

---

133 In Ex. 15:22, the Israelites, wandering in the Shur desert, could not find water, a standard rabbinic metaphor for Torah; *shur* also connotes visionary sight, as in Num. 24:17. As for the Zoharic pun, see Zohar II, 60a.

134 As previously noted the 1896 date given in the author's postscript to the manuscript is not easily squared with his arriving in Boisk in, by many conventional accounts, 1895. The manuscript also contains, at 322–347, a lengthy eulogy for Isaac Elhanan Spektor, who died on 21 Adar 5686/March 11, 1896.

135 The manuscript was stolen sometime during Rav Kook's first decade in Palestine; his son Zvi Yehudah Kook recounts that his father knew who had the manuscript but ordered on his deathbed not to try to have it published for fear of embarrassing the person who had taken it. This appears in the booklet published a year after Rav Kook's death containing his last will and testament and his son's reminiscences of his final illness *Nefesh Ha-Re'ayah* (Jerusalem: n.p., 1936), 21n2, 31. In 1962, the manuscript was returned to the office of Rav Kook's former attorney on the condition that neither the identity of the manuscript's possessor nor of the third party who facilitated the return to the attorney ever be made known. According to a newspaper account on the front page of *Ha-Aretz*, 8 Sivan 5722/June 10, 1962, on receiving the manuscript Zvi Yehudah "kissed each and every page and pressed it to his heart."

136 Kook, *Midbar Shur* (Jerusalem: Makhon Ha-Ratzyah Kook ztz"l, 1999), hereinafter MS. A photocopy of the manuscript is in the Schatz collection of the Scholem Library, NLI, Notebook 4. The editors of the printed edition, David Landau and Michael Hershkovitz, tell us in their brief preface that they have incorporated a later manuscript version of four of the sermons, though they do not tell us which. It is presumably the "revisions made in the Land of Israel" mentioned by Yeshahayu Hadari in his 1966 centennial exhibition catalogue *Re'ayah Kook: Me'ah Shanah le-Holadeto: Ta'arukhat Yovel, Catalogue, Elul 5726* (Jerusalem: Jewish Agency, 1966).

An English abridgement of *Midbar Shur* by Bezalel Naor with some notes and a brief Introduction was published under the title *In the Desert—A Vision* (Spring Valley: Orot, 2000). The translations here are entirely my own.

137 Thus, at MS 290 we find him introducing a comment with "And then I spoke about," indicating that he produced the written Hebrew text after the sermons were delivered. We find some references so *Midbar Shur in Metziot Qatan*. Other sermons of his from this period have very recently been published by Zuriel in volume 6 of *Otzarot Ha-Re'ayah*.

originated as public sermons, and that the constraints of time and work led him to present his ideas in sermonic rather than expository form.[138] Be that as it may, this work is no episodic collection, but a sustained outward-facing exercise in thought.

These sermons are deeply interesting for what they do contain and what they don't. In addition to wide-ranging citation from the Bible, Talmud, Midrash, and Zohar, we find a number of references to the works of Maharal, to Maimonides's *Guide* and Bahya's *Fara'id al-Qulub* in its canonical Hebrew translation *Hovot Ha-Levavot*, to Isaac Arama's *'Aqedat Yitzhaq*,[139] and Yehudah Ha-Levi's *Kuzari*. We also find, interestingly, reference to a Maskilic ethical classic, Naftali Herz Wessely's *Sefer Ha-Middot*.[140] Interestingly, Arama's *'Aqedat Yitzhaq*, Maimonides's *Guide*, and the works of Maharal, are the post-rabbinic sources cited most often in the text.[141] The Kabbalistic texts cited in *Midbar Shur* are relatively accessible: Yeshayahu Horowitz's *Shnei Luhot Ha-Berit*, Menahem Recanati's Torah commentary and Moshe Hayim Luzzatto's *Da'at Tevunot, Derekh 'Etz Hayim*, and *Mesillat Yesharim* (the Kabbalistic dimensions of which, if real, are subtle and below the surface).[142] In general, though, we find almost no use of Kabbalistic terminology.

This was, in other words, meant as a public, exoteric text. Yet while the philosophical infrastructure is striking, as we have already begun to see in the sermons on tefillin, and all with mounting force in the coming years, a similar scaffolding of mysticism onto a base of philosophy.

---

138 Interestingly, in the manuscript of the introduction, a photocopy of which is in my possession, he first wrote, and then crossed out, that "most" had originated as sermons.

139 As noted earlier, Arama, along with Maimonides and Albo, regularly appears in the memoirs of East European intellectuals as a formative philosophical text. An example of this is the commentary on Arama's treatment of Aristotle's *Ethics* in Israel Kitover, *Berurei Ha-Middot: Leva'er u-Levarer kol Davar be-Sefer 'Aqedat Yitzhaq u-ve-Yihud Divrei Sefer Ha-Middot* (Joszefof: Zesczer and Ra'anan, 1872).

140 Wessely's works, though decried by earlier generations of rabbis had become standard fare by the 1830s, see Moshe Samet, "M. Mendelssohn, N. H. Wessely ve-Rabbanei Doram," in *Mehqarim be-Toldot 'Am Yisrael ve-Eretz Yisrael le-Zekher Zvi Avneri*, ed. A. Gilboa et al. (Haifa: University of Haifa Press, 1970), 233–257. Rav Kook may have come to Wessely by way of Yosef Zekharia Stern, who was a latter-day admirer, see Samet, 255n116. For contemporary discussion of Wessely, see Litvak, *Haskalah*, 100ff.

   Both Rav Kook and the editors (in their table of citations) identify Wessely by his initials only. It seems safe to say that Rav Kook expected his readers to identify Wessely; as for his editors, this likely reflects the well-known practice among Zvi Yehudah Kook's disciples to downplay Rav Kook's knowledge and use of philosophical literature.

141 In the citation index at MS 381–382, references to Arama's *'Aqedat Yitzhaq* citations appear sixteen times, to various works of Maharal twenty times, and to Maimonides's *Guide* twenty times.

142 It perhaps bears noting that Rav Kook's ancestor Mordechai Jaffe, known as the Levush, authored a tripartite commentary to Recanati's Torah commentary (Lvov: Budweiser, 1880).

Moshe Hayim Luzzatto

It is at this point worth going into detail about Luzzatto (1707–1746), crucial for understanding Rav Kook, now and throughout his life. Luzzatto was a protean figure, his oeuvre and life story sufficiently capacious and complex to make him a culture hero for Kabbalists, Mussar adherents, and Maskilim, each of whom seized on different facets of his legacy.[143] And he figured as a villain in the minds of those who saw him and his disciples as Sabbatian heretics.[144] Our understanding of Luzzatto and his legacy has been deeply enriched by the recent studies of Jonathan Garb, who wonderfully contextualizes Luzzatto in terms of early modern intellectual history and the Kabbalistc tradition in general.[145] Luzzatto, Garb has shown, is a key inflection point for the emergence of distinctive features of modern Kabbalah, in particular psychologization and conceiving human history and even the political arena as a staging area of intradivine processes.[146] Complementing intellectual with social and cultural history in a series of studies, David Sclar has expertly woven Luzzatto and his circle into the fabric of their place and time, arguing that their distinctive mixing of mysticism, messianism, Pietism, radical elitism, and communal ethos (what he dubs "Italian Hasidism") both presaged and helped stimulate religious and communal changes well beyond mid-nineteenth century Padua.[147]

The text for which Luzzatto is best known, his later work *Mesillat Yesharim* (The Straight/Righteous Path), presents a graduated regimen of self-perfection, a *vade mecum* for a "pilgrim's progress" towards spiritual transfiguration. Unlike other examples of Kabbalistic Mussar, such as Vital's *Sha'arei Qedushah*, it does not use technical Kabbalistic terminology, which is one of the reasons for the work's overwhelming popularity (which is all the more striking for the severe criticism and ostracism Luzzatto engendered in his

---

143 Luzzatto's place in Maskilic culture derived in no small part from his play *La-Yesharim Tehillah*, which Rav Kook read in his youth; see Shmuel Verses's "Dimuyo shel Rabbi Moshe Hayim Luzzato," 3–24.

144 See chapters seven and eight of Isaiah Tishby, *Netivei Emunah ve-Minut* (Jerusalem: Hebrew University/Magnes, 1964).

145 See above all Garb, *Mequbal be-Lev Ha-Se'arah* and his other studies mentioned below.

146 On both these points, see Jonathan Garb, "Ha-Model Ha-Politi be-Qabbalah Ha-Modernit: 'Iyun be-Kitvei Ramhal u-bi-Sevivato Ha-Ra'ayonit," in *'Al Da'at Ha-Qahal: Dat u-Politika be-Hagut Yehudit*, ed. Benjamin Brown et al (Jerusalem: Israel Democracy Institute and Merkaz Shazar, 2012), 13–45.

147 See David Sclar, "Perfecting Community as 'One Man': Moses Hayim Luzzatto's Pietistic Confraternity in Eighteenth-Century Padua," *Journal of the History of Ideas* 81, no. 1 (2020): 45–66; idem, "Adaptation and Acceptance: Moses Hayim Luzzatto's Sojourn in Amsterdam among Portuguese Jews," *AJS Review* 40, no. 2 (2016): 335–358; idem, "The Rise of the 'Ramhal': Printing and Traditional Jewish Historiography in the 'After-Life' of Moses Hayyim Luzzatto," in *Ramhal: Pensiero ebraico e kabbalah tra Padova ed Eretz Israel*, ed. Gadi Luzzatto Voghera and Mauro Perani (Padua: Esedra editrice s. r. l., 2010), 139–153.

lifetime).[148] Crucially, it envisions the eventual dissolution, in holiness, of the boundary between body and soul.

A most significant dimension of Luzzatto's life and work was his translation of the fantastically mythic and deeply obscure terminology of Lurianic Kabbalah, about which more in a moment, into a coherent historiosophy and religious philosophy, laid out in carefully constructed treatises, and rendered in elegant Hebrew prose.[149] The Gaon of Vilna taught that Luzzatto had, in his allegorical reading of Lurianic mythology, penetrated to the truth of that corpus, and thus the study of Luzzatto's writings became a touchstone of Lithuanian Kabbalah. We will have much more to say on this later on.[150]

Luzzatto's work explores at length the dynamics of *tiqqun*, the longed-for telos of the Lurianic vision, which Joelle Hansel deftly translates as "reparation," connoting all at once restoration, retrieval, atonement, and repair.[151] The vast, complex, and deeply influential Lurianic corpus is itself a major and continually expanding field of scholarship that scarcely can be summarized here.[152] Briefly, Isaac Luria (1534–1572), known by his acro-

---

148 The work has gone through countless reprintings since its first appearance in the mid–eighteenth century. The most valuable edition is the one prepared by Yosef Avivi (Jerusalem: Ofeq, 1994), which includes a hitherto unknown manuscript, in which the work is written as a dialogue, and has valuable essays by Avivi.

149 Literary panache was a familial trademark; his ne'er-do-well cousin Ephraim was the originator of the modern Hebrew lyric. On this colorful figure, see David Mirsky, *The Life and Work of Ephraim Luzzatto* (New York: Ktav, 1987); Hebrew ed. (Jerusalem: Rubin Mass, 1994).

150 See on this Shuchat, "Ha-Parshanut Ha-Historiosofit," 125–152. As noted in the previous chapter, Shlomo Elyashiv took pains to have Luzzatto's work published, even though he disagreed with the latter's allegorizations.

    Luzzatto left a mark on Hasidic teachings as well, though he was not as central to that thought-world as he was to Lithuanian Kabbalah, see Isaiah Tishby, "'Iqvot Rabbi Moshe Hayim Luzzatto be-Mishnat He-Hasidut," *Tzion* 43 (1978): 201–234. For the printing and dissemination of Luzzatto's works in Eastern Europe, see Tishby's "Darkhei Hafatzatam shel Kitvei Kabbalah le-Ramhal be-Polin ve-Lita," *Qir'yat Sefer* 45 (1970): 127–155. Luzzatto's Kabbalistic works circulated clandestinely until well into the nineteenth century.

151 Joelle Hansel, *Moise Hayyim Luzzatto (1707–1746): Kabbale et Philosophie* (Paris: Patrimonies/ Les Editions du Cerf, 2004), 333.

152 The key text of the Lurianic canon is *Etz Hayim*, the massive treatise of his disciple Hayim Vital. The classic academic expositions of the fundamentals of Lurianic doctrine are Isaiah Tishby, *Torat Ha-Ra' ve-Ha-Qelippah be-Qabbalat Ha-Ari* (Jerusalem: Schocken, 1942) and the early chapters of Gershom Scholem, *Sabbatai Sevi: The Mystical Messiah* (Princeton: Bollingen, 1973). A recent scholarly biography of Luria is Lawrence Fine, *Physician of the Soul, Healer of the Cosmos: Isaac Luria and His Kabbalistic Fellowship* (Stanford: Stanford University Press, 2003). Yosef Avivi's monumental three-volume work, *Qabbalat Ha-Ari* (Jerusalem: Yad Ben-Tzvi, 2008) exhaustively traces the various iterations of Luria's teachings over successive generations, in manuscript and later in print, as well as working out the details of key doctrines and their histories. A very helpful discussion synthesizing twentieth-century scholarship on the Lurianic corpus and its relation to Zoharic literature as a whole is Pinchas Giller, *Reading the Zohar: The Sacred Text of the Kabbalah* (New York: Oxford University Press, 2001), esp. 21–27, 144–157.

nym *Ari* for *Ha-Elohi Rabbi Yitzhaq,* or "The Divine Rabbi Isaac," synthesized disparate cosmological, metaphysical, and theological doctrines of the Zoharic corpus into a myth of primordial creation as a great drama of divine withdrawal and resulting catastrophe which set in motion all of cosmic history. In the Lurianic myth, God, as it were, contracted Himself, leaving in the empty space thus created vestiges of divine light, contained in "vessels," nodal points of boundless divine energy, contained by a corresponding principle of restraint. Unable to contain the divine light, the vessels shattered, resulting in scattered sparks of divine goodness and the shells, *qelippot,* of the shattered vessels, which together comprise the forces of good and evil pulsating through the universe. The contest between these forces takes place over and over through aeons, on multiple levels of being—not least the human will—en route to the ultimate cosmic and meta-cosmic reparation, the *tiqqun.* This idea of *tiqqun* as theurgic human activity affecting and somehow benefiting the divine realm had been a Kabbalistic doctrine since the Geronese Kabbalists of the early thirteenth century, and certainly in the Zohar, but Luria endowed these doctrines with new sweep, pathos, and exacting detail.[153] Moreover, the astounding specificity and near-mechanistic detail of Luria's teachings (which at times amount to a cartography of the divine) were in many ways of a piece with emergent, early modern ways of exploring, cataloguing, and classifying the world.[154]

Lurianic language, like that of the Zohar itself, is explicitly—indeed, shockingly—mythic and anthropomorphic. Luzzatto translated this Lurianic imagery into philosophical terminology, a Neoplatonic synthesis of metaphysics and ethics, and a sacred history of the world.[155] A key term in Luzzatto's framework is *hanhagah,* governance or guidance, that is, divine guidance, as understood and experienced by human beings, which manifests itself in several forms: *hanhagat ha-tov ve-ha-ra',* the guidance of good and evil, the broad moral sphere, whose outer limits are demarcated by the divine Will, within which human beings discover their own wills, for good or ill; and *hanhagat ha-yihud,* the guidance of unity, the unseen Providence, hidden from the human will, which guides humanity and all of creation to its ultimate teleological perfection.[156] Adapting the Zoharic distinction between two principles of the diffusion of divine light, *'iggulim* and *yosher,* circles and lines, or cycles and linearity, Luzzatto identifies *hanhagah* with the latter, *yosher,* a divine plumb line inserted deep into the structure of the world, along which the world ascends as it is inexorably drawn back to its divine source, throughout the course of human history. *Yosher* is a principle of immanence, operating within historical time, a divine telos

---

153 For a very helpful survey of these ideas prior to Luria, see Morris M. Faierstein, "'God's Need for the Commandments' in Medieval Kabbalah," *Conservative Judaism* 36, no. 1 (1982): 45–59.

154 See on this, Roni Weinstein, *Kabbalah and Jewish Modernity* (Oxford: Littman, 2016).

155 See Rivka Schatz, "Ha-Metafisiqah shel Ramhal be-Heksherah Ha-'Eti: 'Iyun bi-Traktat Ha-Rishon shel 'Qalah Pithei Hokhmah,'" in *Sefer Ha-Yovel le-Shlomo Pines,* vol. 2, ed. Moshe Idel, Zev Harvey, and Eliezer Schweid, with Avriel Bar-Levav, *Mehqarei Yerushalayim be-Mahshevet Yisrael* 9 (1990): 361–396, esp. 378.

156 For explicit and pithy formulations of the doctrine, see Luzzatto's *Da'at Tevunot,* ed. Friedlander, 2nd ed. (Bnei Braq: n.p., 1975), 129–130, 183–184.

implanted in time. We have already noticed, and will increasingly see, that *yosher*, which is also synonymous with "righteousness," becomes a key term for Rav Kook, most clearly in his *'Eyn Ayah*.[157]

Luzzatto's historiosophy is presented in a trilogy *Adir ba-Marom* (*Awesome on High*, after Ps. 93:4), a detailed exegesis of the first pages of the Zoharic section known as *Idra Rabbah* (Zohar III, 126b–145a), and couched throughout in highly technical esoteric language; *Da'at Tevunot* (Insightful Knowledge, after Isa. 40:14), which presents the ideas as a straightforward philosophy of history via a dialogue in which the intellect educates the soul; and, in between, *Qalah Pithei Hokhmah* (*One Hundred and Thirty-Eight Apertures to Wisdom*), a synthesis of the two idioms (which may not have been written by him but reflects the ideas of his circle).[158] Luzzatto's influence is reflected in the teleological thrust of much of *Midbar Shur*.

Midbar Shur and the Pursuit of Perfection, Jewish and Universal

Thematically, *Midbar Shur* is preoccupied with the achievement of *shlemut*—the perfection, wholeness, and flourishing (all renderings of the Greek *eduaemonia*) of the individual and the cosmos. The task of perfection revolves around a series of concentric dualities—nature/choice; matter/form; action/thought; heart/mind; humanity/Israel—which find their resolution and apotheosis in the divine Will of whose workings they are a part. Self-perfection aims not to repress the creature, individual or national, but to realize its own divinely implanted telos. In *Midbar Shur*, Rav Kook integrates the concerns first articulated in *Metziot Qatan*, about the relations between body and mind, and the nations and Israel, into the central pursuit of the medieval philosophical tradition, human flourishing.

Again and again in *Midbar Shur*, Rav Kook revisits the relation of Jewish to general morality, which so occupied him in *Metziot Qatan*.[159] As East European Jewry tried to make its way in rapily changing times, this question was in the air; interestingly, this

---

157 It is also worth noting that *yosher* is the key term in Netziv's introduction to his commentary on Genesis, with which as we have seen Rav Kook was familiar. It was, he writes, the defining feature of the Biblical patriarchs, "who in their conduct with gentiles and even ugly idolaters, nonetheless acted with love and concern for their welfare, which is the maintenance of Creation." *Ha'ameq Davar*, 1:1.

158 On this point, see the exhaustive study by Jonathan Garb, "Ketavav Ha-Amitiyyim shel Ramhal be-Qabbalah," *Qabbalah* 25 (2011): 165–222.

159 The first stirrings of his interest in this problem were to be seen in his short-lived journal of 1888 *'Ittur Sofrim*. There, in a running commentary to his introduction to the journals' opening number, entitled *Lishkat Ha-Sha'ar* (Anteroom to the Gate). There, commenting on Deut. 4:6, that "for [the Torah] will be proof of your wisdom and discernment to other peoples," he says that each nation's talents come to light through that "branch of knowledge with which it is most engaged." And so Torah, and particularly its intensive study, demonstrates the Jewish people's distinctiveness. The approval of the Gentiles alluded to in the verse, he says, is by no means an end in itself, but that which indicates the distinctiveness of Israel's knowledge.

problem figures prominently in the writings of Netziv, perhaps most vividly in his commentary to Song of Songs, *Rinah shel Torah*, first published in 1887 and reissued posthumously in 1894, shortly before the sermons of *Midbar Shur* were first delivered.[160] There, Netziv repeatedly stresses a hierarchy of religious values in which interpersonal morality is essential but secondary to worship and Torah study, not least because it is natural and not revealed, and so, accessible to non-Jews.[161] By contrast, in *Midbar Shur*, Rav Kook, rather than denigrate a more universal morality, portrays it as the terrestrial handmaiden of transcendent Torah in the larger framework of redemption.

The very first sermon lays out the essential themes to follow: There are two kinds of perfection: that which is closer to natural virtue and is the estate of all humanity, as laid forth in the Noahide laws. This is ultimately nothing more than the realization of one's own nature as, in the words of Ecclesiastes, "God has made man upright/just [*yashar*]" (Eccles. 7:29). The perfection that is the particular patrimony of Israel involves exercising one's will to cling to divine virtues via Torah and mitzvot and, with effort, transform one's human nature into the angelic/divine.[162] (Indeed, he says elsewhere, Israel's very body is the matter for Torah's form.[163])

Citing the midrashic comment (cited by Rashi, Gen. 1:1) that the world was created "for the sake of Torah . . . and for the sake of Israel," he interprets the former term to mean Torah's achieving full actualization, and the latter, "for the sake of Israel," to mean that all existents receive His good in the telos (*takhlit*) of perfection: "and the perfection of man is built according to both these general goals: the keeping and study of Torah, and the straightening of one's character, *middot*."[164] The work of *imitatio dei* in the present is a preparation to the great perfection of the future, while Torah's full actualization will come

---

160 Naftali Zvi Yehudah Berlin, *Rinah shel Torah* (Warsaw: Halter & Eisenstadt, 1894). See also his introduction to Genesis in his Torah commentary, *Ha'ameq Davar*.

161 See, for instance, his comments to Sg. 1:3, 1:16–17, 2:3, 3:2, 7:1. At 3:6 he goes so far as to say that the lure of doing acts of kindness is a ruse of Satan to tempt scholars away from the study hall, a motif found in the early Mitnagdic treatise *Keter Torah* of Pinhas of Polotsk.

162 MS, 12:

ונבאר כי יש שני מיני שלמות לבעלי הבחירה, המה המין האנושי. השלמות האחת היא אשר חנן השי"ת אותו דעה והשכל ועשהו ישר, קרוב למעלת השלמות הראוי' להנהגה ישרה מצד מדות טבעיות שבו, בטבע נפשו, כמו שכתוב אשר עשה האלקים את האדם ישר, (קהלת ז:כט) . . . מין השלמות השני, הוא השלמות שהאדם מוכן לה להקנותה ע"י בחירתו הטובה, להיות דבק במעלות האלהיות שיקנה ע"י עמל התורה והמצות שנתן השי"ת לישראל עם קרובו . . . כלל ההבדל בין שני מיני השלמות הללו, הוא ההבדל שבין המעלה שזוכין לה כל באי עולם מבני נח ותעודתם ע"י שבע המצות שהם מוזהרין עליהן, שכולן דומות לטבע האדם הישר . . . להשלמות המיוחדת לזרע ישראל ע"י נחלת ד' שהנחילנו כל התורה כולה בתרי"ג מצותיה שהן למעלה מטבע האנושי . . . ולהפוך הטבע האנושי אל הפכו, לעלות ממצב האנושות למצב מלאכי אלקי . . . .

We will see that the verse he cites here from Ecclesiastes is a leitmotif of his aggadah commentary, *'Eyn Ayah*.

163 Ibid., 26:

שמצד קדושתו השפיע הכנה טבעית לפני (!) בניו של [של יעקב] שיהיו מוכנים אל התורה והיא כעין חומר לצורת התורה שבאה ע"י משה רבינו ע"ה . . . .

164 Ibid., 94:

ועל פי אלה שתי המטרות הכללות בנוי' שלמות האדם, בקיום התורה ותלמודה והישרת המדות.

in the *eschaton*.[165] At that time, Torah's interiority will be revealed in a new revelation and reception on the part of Israel.[166] *Tiqqun 'olam*, the final cosmic restoration and repair, is the effort to unify the disparate parts of creation, such that each seemingly distinctive creature be ready to reverse/transform its nature in order to fulfill God's encompassing Will.[167]

By way of answering Arama's question (*'Aqedat Yitzhaq* 1:10b) as to how it can be that Torah seems to be merely a means towards the end of human betterment, he writes that Torah exists qua form, independent of any other existent, and relates to other existents only in proportion to the divine flow directed through it to them, for the sake of their own perfection.[168] In practical terms, Torah is a matter of precepts, halakhot, and moral teachings, Mussarim. The former are vessels channeling action, strengthening in turn the inner life that is the province of Mussar, which itself serves to reinforce action, and so on.[169] Torah, he says, is the unification of all wisdom; individuals can receive its light only inasmuch as their own individual preparedness will allow; thus, in an early hint of a theme that will swell in his thought over time, one should follow one's own nature, with the caveat that one draws always from the light of Torah.[170] Mitzvot actualize the holiness that is already *in potentia* in the soul,[171] or, put a little differently, they rouse the divine states of mind, *de'ot*, engraved in Israel's soul.[172]

To what extent is perfection, then, a matter of the intellect?

---

165 Ibid., 99.

166 Ibid., 35.

167 Ibid., 15:

ודרך התאחדות הבריאה היא שלא יהיה כל דבר דוקא מיוחד בטבעו כ״א מוכן יהיה כל נמצא פרטי להעשות היפוך טבעו להשלים חפץ השי״ת הכולל.

168 Ibid., 92:

לא יערך אל הבריאה כ״א השפע הפרטי שהשפיע בה השי״ת למען הוציא את הבריאה אל הפועל, אבל כשהיא בעצמה, היא צורה נבחרת כוללת השלמות של הבריאה ויותר, וא״צ כלל לנושא של הבריאה.

He goes on to say that this is the meaning of the Zoharic passage (III:73a) that God, Torah, and Israel are each hidden and revealed. Interestingly, he does not cite the text directly but rather as it appears in the *Shelah* (*Toldot Adam*, intro.).

169 Ibid., 29:

והנה ההלכות מחזקות המעשים שהם החיצוניות ועי״ז מתחזקת הפנימיות והמוסרים מחזקים הפנימיות ועי״ז מתחזקים המעשים.

170 Ibid., 53–54:

עכ״פ לכך יצר השי״ת את כל אחד בטבע מיוחד והכנה מיוחדת כדי שיקבל ענייני השלמות לפי ענינו ובזה יושלם רצון השי״ת בכלל המציאות, שמקיבוץ כ״א להשלים את שלו תהא השלמות הכללית . . . אבל הדרך העיקרי בזה הוא שלא ילך בדרך טבעו לגמרי . . . אבל העיקר שתהי׳ קבלתו רק מאור התורה המיוחד ששם היא אחדות החכמה.

171 Ibid., 66:

והנה רצה הקב״ה לזכות אותנו שנעשה מצוה שבכחה לגלות קצת מהקדושה שבעצם כח נפשותינו.

172 Ibid., 128:

אמנם ישראל נתיחדו בציווויי המצות שבהן הטביע השי״ת בטבע נפשותיהם את כל קדושת הדעות שהמצות מיוסדות עליהן, אלא שהגוף גורם להשכיחן ועי״י המצות הן מתעוררות.

He tries, by examining the relationship between Jewish and universal morality, to clarify intellect's specific role in the cultivation of perfection. In sermon 19, seeking to explain the Biblical Isaac's seeming preference for Esau, he suggests the patriarch thought there are two kinds of perfection: one, by way of the intellect, which includes all interpersonal/ethical mitzvot, concrete societal needs and the broader notion of lovingkindness (*gemilut hasadim*); and a second, higher, perfection, of "divine service, above the human intellect."[173] Isaac mistakenly thought that the two kinds of perfection could not coexist within Jacob, for whom "the majority of interpersonal mitzvot which are the chiefly rational, *sikhli*, were below [Jacob's] level," but the matriarch Rebecca understood that Jacob was capable of both, indeed that's Jacob's being "burdened with the yoke of the world" is an affirmatively good thing. In the *eschaton*, though, the nations will assume the management and maintenance of the world, and Jacob will indeed have little need of interpersonal mitzvot, for there will be no poverty or injustice within Israel, though it will persist among the nations.[174]

One sermon in particular, 22, develops at greater length the relationship between intellect, ethics, and natural law, as he tries to navigate some of the tensions between the universality of reason and the election of Israel.[175]

The sermon begins with Jacob's bracing encounter, in Gen. 32, with the angel who changes his name to Israel. Abraham, Rav Kook says, first attained the knowledge of God via the human intellect; such prophecies as were given to him pertained, as the plain sense of the text says, to the destiny of Israel, "but as regards human conduct and the performance of mitzvot, the time had not yet come for Torah to be given on earth, and so he walked in the paths of justice and righteousness, according to rational practices [*tzedeq u-meisharim 'al pi nimusim sikhliyim*]."[176]

There is, of course, a lengthy history of rabbinic discussion regarding the nature and status of mitzvot before Sinai, much of it centering around the exegesis of Gen. 26:5, with many of the opinion that Abraham fulfilled the commandments entirely.[177] Rav Kook

---

173 Ibid., 177–178:

אלא שיצחק חשב הרי שני מיני שלמיות. יש שלמות האנושית מצד השכל האנושי, שנכללים בזה כל המצות שבין אדם לחבירו, וצדקה וגמ״ח וישובו של עולם להיטיב לבריות שזהו באמת בכלל גמ״ח כמו גשרים ושוקים וכיו״ב, ומעלת יעקב היתה למעלה מזה שיהי׳ איש אלקים מסור לעבודת השי״ת למעלה משכל האנושי.

174 Ibid., 178.

175 Ibid., 200–209.

176 Ibid., 201. Interestingly, in this work he does not cite Se'adyah for the distinction between *sikhliyot* and *shim'iyot* ('*aqlat wa-samiyyat*); when he uses the distinction, as in the next sermon we will discuss, it is as taken from Bahya.

177 See BT Kiddushin 82a, Yoma 28b for the view that Abraham observed all the mitzvot; and Nahmanides's commentary to Gen. ad loc, who argues that Abraham learned the entire Torah via the Holy Spirit, including its reasons and esoterica. Numerous sources on this are gathered and analyzed by Zvi Hirsch Chajes, *Torat Neviim* (Zolkiew: Hopfer, 1839). See also Netziv's comment, *Ha'ameq She'elah*, 35:1. For a discussion of this question in terms of contemporary jurisprudential debate, see Steven Wilf, *The Law Before the Law* (Lanham: Lexington Books, 2010).

here seems to be following the view of Bahya that the pre-Sinaitic figures were fortunately "possessed of clear intellects and weak passions and their souls followed their intellects and a few mitzvot sufficed them for the perfection of divine service."[178]

He then takes up one law that, he says, operates by the consensus of all humanity, with which Torah does agree—but for a higher reason in accord with divine righteousness (*yosher*)—and that is the law of national sovereignty. Ordinarily God does not desire division among peoples. Indeed, at Abraham's circumcision God told him that divisions among peoples are an abomination, for all are equal before Him. He continues:

> [T]rue righteousness is to make the success of the whole human race equal in the eyes of all. Yet, true success for the human species requires that there be one nation that is not mixed with the others, as by its nature intellect does not mix with matter, in order to work on the human species and improve it. Thus Israel must know that is has no permission at all to displace a nation for our own good and aggrandizement, but only according to the command of Torah, according to the divine plan for the end [*takhlit*] of *tiqqun 'olam*, which cannot be known with precision other than by divine guidance that teaches the way to the all-encompassing *eudaemonia*.[179]

Israel, he continues, abhors glory seeking. Through Torah, Israel seeks to do God's will for the perfection of the human species, and that requires Israel's maintaining its distinctiveness, in part by unique laws that are beyond human understanding.[180] When God changed Abram's name to Abraham, he could never use his old one, for God effectively said to him:

> I have raised you above the customary law, *hoq ha-nimus*, which is merely conventional, but not grounded in pure righteousness . . . *for you are a father to many peoples* (Gen. 17:5), you are the father of all the human race, you must seek the good of them all, and precisely that will give rise to a new separation so that you may be on a level devoted to the good of the whole world, which cannot come about other than by Israel's differentiation in purity.[181]

---

178 *Hovot Ha-Levavot, Sha'ar Ha-Perishut*, trans. Yehudah ibn Tibbon (Warsaw: n.p., 1852), chapter 7, pt. 2, 146.

179 MS, 202–203:

> והיושר האמיתי הוא להשוות בעיני כל איש את הצלחת המין האנושי. אלא שהההצלחה האמיתית למין האנושי בנויה היא ע״י בחירת עם נבחר שאינו מתערב עם כל העמים, כטבע השכל שאינו מתערב עם החומר, והוא יהי' פועל על כל המין האנושי לשכללו ולהציגו אל התכלית הטובה שהשי״ת מבקש ודורש ממנו. ע״כ החובה מוטלת על ישראל לדעת שלא ניתנה רשות כלל להדיח אומה מאתה למען טובת עצמנו והגדלת ממשלתנו, כי חק אחד הוא היוושר בין לרבים בין ליחיד. אלא שאנחנו עשינו בהגדלת האומה ואשרה ע״פ מצות התורה, כפי השיעור האלהי שיהי' לתכלית המביאה לתיקון העולם כולו ושכלולו, ודבר זה א״א לדעת בכיוון כ״א ע״פ הישרה אלהית המלמדת דעה מה הוא הדרך המביאה אל האושר הכללי.

180 Ibid.

181 Ibid., 204:

> כי אתה הגבתיך מחק הנימוס הזה שהוא רק מוסכם ולא מטעם היושר הטהור . . . *והי' שמך אברהם כי אב המון גוים* כולם, כל המין האנושי, לכולם אב אתה, את טובת כולם עליך לדרוש, ומזה, דוקא מזה, תולד לך בהפרדות חדשה כדי שתהי' מדרגה לבא לטובת כל העולם שאי אפשר כ״א ע״י התיחדות עם ישראל בטהרה. . . .

And so, Israel's isolation derives precisely from its ethical and spiritual mission to the whole of humanity. Jacob, the contemplative tent dweller, was a master of this isolation, and correspondingly recognized that if Torah were a matter of customary rational laws (*nimusim sikhliyyim*) Israel would assimilate and forfeit its divine mission.[182] Yet the self-love that runs intrinsically against righteousness, and is nonetheless the customary law of nations, is utterly contrary to the divine spirit that pulses in Jacob. Israel was unwilling to sacrifice itself for the sake of its distinctiveness—its peoplehood would indeed be just another of the imaginary lusts that have become acceptable by consensus.[183] The contribution of Israel's mind-centered, supernatural perfection, to the good of humanity as a whole, will become clear in the *eschaton*. Then, all will recognize that rational goals in and of themselves do not ensure final perfection, inextricable as they are from matter and its desires, "which blind the eye of intellect and righteousness (*ha-sekhel ve-ha-yosher*), which is the true Will of God."[184] The angel tells Jacob that he has wrestled *with gods and men* (Gen. 32:28)—the former are Esau's rational laws, the latter, Esau's brute strength.

Rav Kook is here making his own use of several concepts drawn from the philosophical literature of the Middle Ages: *nimus, sikhli, mefursamot*.

Maimonides, in *Guide*, 2:40, writes that man, as a political animal, recognizes that divine law "although it is not natural, enters into what is natural"—a law directed at establishing a just social order—but unconcerned with "the perfecting of the rational faculty . . . is a *nomos*."[185] Earlier in *Guide*, 1:2, he introduces the notion of consensus or convention as a basis of morality, distinguishing between the knowledge of true and false discerned by the intellect, and the knowledge of *al-hasan* and *al-qabih*, alternately translatable into English as "good and evil" or "fine and bad," a matter of convention.[186] In other words, the criterion for assessing necessary truths of metaphysics is whether they are, ultimately, true or false; moral truths, by contrast, are consensual and conventional.

Albo (*Sefer Ha-'Iqarim*, I:7) offers a threefold distinction between natural law, which reflects that which is necessary for the preservation of society; consensual law, identical to *nomos* (*ha-heskemi . . . o ha-dat ha-nimusit*), which determines the shape of rule in a given time and place; and divine law, like that set forth by prophets such as Adam, Noah, Abraham, or Moses, meant "to make men righteous (*lehayshir*) so that they obtain true success, which is the success of the soul and eternal immortality."

Arama, for his part (*'Aqedat Yitzhaq* §46, 121b–124a), offers a different threefold classification of laws: natural laws arrived at through a sense of natural justice shared by all

---

182 Ibid., 205.

183 Ibid., 207.

184 Ibid., 208.

185 Moses Maimonides, *Guide of the Perplexed*, trans. Shlomo Pines (Chicago: University of Chicago Press, 1963), 382–384. The Arabic phrase translated as *nomos* is *shari'ia namusiya*.

186 See on the history of this distinction, Shlomo Pines, "Truth and Falsehood Versus Good and Evil: A Study in Jewish and General Philosophy in Relation to the Guide of the Perplexed, 1:2," in *Harvard Judaic Texts and Studies*, vol. 9, *Studies in Maimonides*, ed. Isadore Twersky (Cambridge, MA: Harvard University Press, 1991), 95–157.

humanity, hence universal and eternal; human laws, created by legislation and thus neither natural, universal, nor eternal (including the rational laws of *Guide*, 2:40); and divine laws, which, like natural laws, are universal and eternal, but, more than that, are the very blueprint of creation, the notes for "the song of the world," in peace and harmony, and yielding humanity's greatest *eudaemonia*, eternal life.[187] Torah laws, for their part, build upon the foundation of natural law.[188]

Maharal of Prague dramatically differs from all these. For him, humanity is divorced from nature and participates in the divine eternal intellect as manifest in action; divine intellect prescribes human conduct in accordance with its own metaphysical laws; and that divine law is the only objectively commanding law. Israel, as a people, by its participation in divine intellect, the *sikhli* (on which more below), is removed from nature as gentiles are not; indeed Torah's utopian nature resides in its atemporality.[189]

Rav Kook in his discussion seemingly conflates *sikhli*, *nimus*, and *mefursam* and takes all of them to mean human, material, natural—and not partaking of the eternal good. At the same time, he makes a crucial point: mere prerogatives of national sovereignty are *mefursamot*, merely conventional, and not ultimately normative. Indeed, he takes pains to say that Israel's sovereignty is morally constrained and not on the bestial *mefursam* level. The intellect, though not material as such, is natural, and thus not divine. By extension, natural law and the laws derived from intellect will inevitably be bound by the limitations of humanity and mortality, and only a divine law can achieve the great longed-for cosmic synthesis of perfection.[190]

In sermon 28 he returns to the relation between intellect and Torah as vehicles of perfection, taking the "cave of *Makhpelah*," literally "doubled cave," in which Sarah is buried in Genesis 23, as a metaphor for the doubling of the human person into intellect and body in the service of God. He records the Talmudic debate (BT 'Eruvin 53a) as to whether the caves were one on top of the other, or one inside the other; the former would mean that intellect is atop the body, the latter, that the two are intertwined, and that is the position he develops.

He takes as his starting point Bahya's discussion of the role of intellect in rousing a human being to divine service.[191] The recognition of one's necessary gratitude towards God and, eventually, of one's external and interior obligation to Him is, Bahya says,

---

187 See the discussion in Heller-Wilensky, *Rabbi Yitzhak Arama u-Mishnato*, 186–188.

188 On this point, see Bernard Septimus, "Yitzhak Arama and Aristotle's Ethics," in *Jews and Conversos at the Time of the Expulsion*, ed. Yom Tov Assis and Yosef Kaplan (Jerusalem: Shazar Center, 1999), 1–24, esp. 13–14.

189 Rivka Schatz, "Ha-Tefisah Ha-Mishpatit shel Ha-Maharal—Antiteza Le-Hoq Ha-Tiv'i," *Da'at* 2–3 (1978–1979): 147–157. A similar point regarding Maharal's distancing of any religious law from nature, emerges, though less pointedly, from Byron Sherwin, *Mystical Theology and Social Dissent: The Life and Works of Judah Loew of Prague* (Rutherford: Fairleigh Dickinson University Press, Associated University Presses, 1982), 132.

190 It is worthwhile recalling his statement in one of the sermons of *Hevesh Pe'er* that Noahide laws are rooted in nature, while Torah laws are above nature.

191 Bahya *Hovot Ha-Levavot, Sha'ar 'Avodat Elohim*, 1–3, 72a–73a.

grounded both in the reason implanted in man, and in tradition (*be-derekh ha-shema'*), that is, Torah. Unaided reason is insufficient on three counts: man's corporeal desires; intellect's essential foreignness to the world, being "a spiritual essence derived from the upper spiritual world," as a result of which Torah commands many things which cut against the corporeal grain—such as fasting and prayer, and interestingly, acts of loving-kindness—and, finally, the intellect's episodic nature, no match for the relentless persistence of the body and its desires.[192]

Evincing, as he did in *Metizot Qatan*, a positive attitude towards the body, Rav Kook argues that Bahya has it backwards, and it is the performance of mitzvot that rouses the intellect "to pursue Torah and mitzvot according by the lights of one's own understanding (*'al pi hakarato ha-penimit*) so that one may attain the otherwise unattainable perfection."[193] The affirmation of the body continues:

> And once the insight of the intellect/mind attaches to human nature, when it does so with the arousal of Torah, it brings the bodily will to peace with the Torah's laws, and the body is perfected in sanctification through Torah in terms of its very nature, which would not have been possible without intellect's accompaniment by Torah. . . . Inasmuch as God has created man in His image, it is certainly His glory and will that man's body be sanctified and that the very body be fit for the supernal holiness.[194]

The dynamics of the self-sanctification of the body are "the arousal of the Torah which acts more on the external acts of the body and is thus sanctified, and the interiority is the arousal of the intellect which works on the body's sanctity by virtue of its virtues and interiority (*midotav u-penimiyuto*)."[195]

This is an interesting position: like an archetypal Mitnaged he values the exercise of the intellect as the highest religious act; yet unlike a Mitnaged he values the body too, seeing it as much more than a prison house for the soul.[196] At the same time, there is nothing here of the Lurianic raising of the sparks, nor of Hasidic doctrines of *'avodah be-gashmiyut* and the spiritualizing transformation of matter.

---

192 Implicit in his characterization of lovingkindness as an unnatural act is the powerful idea that lovingkindness expresses divine protest against the regularly inhumane logic of human affairs in this world.

193 MS, 260:

אלא שמעשי המצות שבתורה מעוררים את כח השכל לעסוק בתורה ובמצות ע"פ הכרתו הפנימית ואז ישתלם השכל שיגיע ע"י התורה אל שלמות מדרגתו מה שזולתה א"א שיעלה כלל לזאת המעלה.

194 Ibid.:

והנה עצם הערת השכל כיון שהוא דבק בטבע האדם, כשהוא דבק עם הערת התורה גורם שנעשה רצון הגוף שלם עם הערת התורה ומשתלם הגוף להתקדש בקדושת התורה מצד עצם טבעו. מה שלא היה כן אם לא התלוה השכל אל התורה הנה יקיים מצות התורה אבל הגוף יהי' מטבעו ההיפך מהמבוקש מצד התורה. והנה השי"ת שברא את האדם בצלמו ודאי זהו כבודו ורצונו שיתקדש גוף האדם ויהי' עצם הגוף מוכן לקדושה העליונה.

195 Ibid., 262.

196 On Mitnagdic devaluation of, and often even hatred for, the body, see Nadler, *The Faith of the Mithnagdim*, in particular 78–127.

He returns to Israel's moral relation to the gentiles in a sermon on the sin of the Golden Calf, which he interprets as a misguidedly exclusive focus on natural morality. He writes:

> The inclination to walk in good ways, to do good and lovingkindness by virtue of the internal feeling implanted in man's nature, to feel compassion towards the poor and do justice by the oppressed [*regesh ha-nafshi ha-natu'a be-lev ish lahamol 'al dal ve-la'asot la-'ashukim mishpat*] . . . is good and praiseworthy in its own right. Nonetheless, for Israel the obligation is great that this be done solely in order to give Him pleasure [*lema'an 'asot nahat ruah*]. It is indeed praiseworthy when a non-Jew performs the mitzvah of charity and all the *sikhliyot*, because of the soul-feeling implanted in him, and he has thus already achieved the telos of the virtue for which he is disposed. But an Israelite has not thus already merited all his due, until he does all these because they are the paths of God. And this flows from the fact that Israel's destiny in the world is for the sake of divine perfection. And for that, righteous *yashar* conduct via the intellect is insufficient, rather [one must] cling to God's ways because they are His supernal ways.[197]

While natural morality is God-given, it is not Godly, not divine, inasmuch as on its own terms it is not rooted in human recognition of the divine Will, a recognition which is necessary for God's own perfection, through Israel.[198] This last mention of God's own self-perfection underscores the Kabbalistic dimension to his ideas, that is, the *reparation of God* through the self-perfection of Israel.

Interestingly, here he no longer uses the terms *nimusim* or *mefursamot*, but rather *sikhliyot*, most famously known through the Hebrew translations of Sa'adya, and introduces the dimension of moral sentiment, *regesh* (about which we will have a great deal to say in chapter four).[199] We can read the absence of the former terms in two ways: simply that the particular moral laws he has in mind here are not the product of custom or consensus but rather arrived at by the intellect as such and/or moral feeling. Alternatively, we can see this as a more substantive devaluation of moral laws arrived at by mere custom and consensus, relative to those arrived at by intellect and moral feeling which, while not

---

197 MS, 300–301.

198 He continues that the cleansing of the serpent's filth that, according to BT Shabbat 146a, took place at Sinai was the cleansing of nature so that it would no longer oppose natural reason, and the preparation of the soul for virtue. But the final goal is that the desire to fulfill God's Will, which is God's own fulfillment, be as naturally rooted in man as the principles of natural morality. The sin of the Golden Calf qua an exclusive focus on natural morality leads to depending only on one's own unaided reason, which can be driven off by base desires and worldly cares, leaving us unraveled without wisdom or morality. MS, 301–302.

199 See Alexander Altmann's classic study, "Saadya's Conception of the Law," *Bulletin of the John Rylands Library* 28 (1944): 320–339; one fascinating feature of this study is Altmann's dialogue with the contemporaneous effort by Jacques Maritain and other Catholic thinkers to integrate medieval natural law doctrine into the then-burgeoning articulation of "human rights"; see, on that historical chapter, Samuel Moyn, *Christian Human Rights* (Philadelphia: University of Pennsylvania Press, 2015).

reflecting the divine Will as such, nonetheless reflect that Will's desired order here on earth.

That second reading seems to be suggested by the ensuing passage:

> The very act of doing good and kindness [*hesed*] is something that God nonetheless very much wants for its own sake. . . . Once matters were despoiled [that is, by the smashing of the first tables of the Law, which, as he sees it, represented the fulfillment of His Will for its own sake—Y. M.] the natural man will be more readily aroused by simple nature than the one who must act by the divine will that so few understand. . . . That is why God commanded the mitzvah of *sheqalim* [an annual tax for the upkeep of the Temple, commanded in the Torah shortly before the sin of the Golden Calf—Y. M.], so that this act of giving be sanctified in God's holiness until the heart of the doer be filled to do so only for His name. And this act of giving should work in its holy way, that all the acts of giving and all the *mitzvot sikhliyot*, all of which are broadly included in *tzedakah*, and are simply referred to as mitzvah as such in the Yerushalmi (Peah 8:8, Horayot 3:4) would all be raised in holiness, and performed because of God's will.[200] . . . Similarly, it ill befits Israel's political statecraft and warfare to be from the dimension of simple feeling of national strength that is found among every people and tongue, but rather and solely from His supernal Will.[201]

The love of kindness is the whole of human perfection; Israel's sin at the Golden Calf arose from thinking Torah had nothing more to add, and so they descended into the very depths. In repentance they saw that the love of God could work more deeply on Israel's hearts to rouse them to desire to do good than could unaided nature. In the *eschaton*, all will truly be done in order to do God's will.[202]

In his discussion of the divine Will he seems not to be discussing the virtue of obedience, but rather taking the Will in Luzzatto's sense as the manifestation of the living God in the sacred history of the world, as the emanated God made knowable to us, albeit only partially, via the sefirot.

The eschatological motif intensifies near the end of *Midbar Shur*, as he begins to speak in terms of a more historical teleology. Thus, in sermon 37 he writes that "holy" is all that is near the actualization of its telos, and "profane" is that which is far from it and not yet engaged in the connections of *tiqqun*. God's covenant with Israel—as demonstrated by the sanctification of months and festivals—is that in the end the great telos will be achieved. The elements of that telos are three; the innovations and transformations,

---

200 To these sources, in which mitzvah is taken to mean alms-giving, we can add *Devarim Rabbah*, ed. Saul Lieberman (Jerusalem: Bamberger & Wharman, 1940), 36n10, as well as those listed in Daniel Sperber, *A Commentary on Derekh Erez Zuta, Chapters Five to Eight* (Tel Aviv: Bar-Ilan University Press, 1990), 40. On the Geonic usage of the term, see Simha Assaf, *Teshuvot Ha-Ge'onim* (Jerusalem: Mekitzei Nirdamim, 1942), 124.

201 MS, 305.

202 Ibid., 309–310.

placed by God in the power of time;[203] the ability created by God for all these changes wrought by the times to reach the sacred goal; and Israel's God-given power to actualize the divinely directed holiness through the hidden holiness, this possibility that is latent in the changes of times.[204] These will come together in the *eschaton*, he says in conclusion, and be a great revelation to all, in joy.[205]

Throughout *Midbar Shur* we see a complex negotiation of mind, body and spirit, Torah and universal morality, Israel's distinctiveness and its universal mission. We also see the stirrings of the idea he will develop in his Boisk notebooks, the subject of the coming chapter, on the God-given nature of the individual personality and the divine writ of self-fulfillment. This stands in interesting counterpoint to his pronounced emphasis on the mind as the chief vessel of enlightenment. The deeper recesses and dynamics driving him towards an acceptance of individuality and subjective experience may have resided in part—bearing in mind appropriate interpretive caution and more—in his abiding sense of loss for his first wife, Bat-Sheva.

An Elegy for His First Wife

He seems deeply to have mourned his first wife years after her passing in 1889. One must tread gingerly here, as the evidence, though powerful, is limited, and because armchair psychologizing is just that. Nonetheless, the trauma of his first wife's death played, by the looks of it, a role in his inward turn not only, as we saw, in its immediate aftermath, but over time as well.[206] That he retained a deep personal connection to her father, Aderet, indeed a decisive one for his emigration to Palestine, is undoubted.[207]

In the early pages of the last spiritual diary he kept in Boisk, to be discussed in our final chapter, we find a number of poems, which were published by Zvi Yehudah Kook in 1970 under the title *Orot Ha-Re'ayah*. Contrary to his usual practice, Zvi Yehudah Kook published the poems in chronological order, with one striking—perhaps personally understandable—omission, an elegy to Rav Kook's first wife (bearing in mind that Zvi Yehudah was born of his father's second marriage). The poem, like the entirety of the notebook in which it appears, was published from manuscript in the late summer of

---

203 There is an echo here of Maharal's formulation that time is the medium of redemption, created by God for that purpose.

204 Ibid., 349–350.

205 Ibid., 358.

206 The detailed recounting of his wedding ceremony to his second wife in Even-Hen, *Rav u-Manhig*, 93–95, leaves one with the impression that this was much less than a happy occasion.

207 See, for instance, his letter to Aderet in *Igrot*, 1:10–12, dated 1900, that is, eleven years since his wife's death, signed "Your son-in-law like your own son, fused in soul-love."

חתנו כבנו דבק באהנ"פ.

2006.[208] It seems likely to have been written in 1894, that is, at least some five or six years after her death.[209]

The poem, entitled "The Perplexed One," begins: "Gloom surrounds me / And Darkness falls / My soul-fogs / Blacken for me the sun."[210] We are told why a few stanzas later: "The grave-sleeper / Yet lives / No end to the heartbreak / To anguish no stop . . . [ellipsis in original] / I cry out / I deafen ears / I breathe into the dust / And it rises to Heaven."[211] He ascends from the pit to the sun, to Torah, "whose face I had despaired of seeing."[212]

Yet this relief is short-lived, as he immediately writes: "My sought-after hope / From your pleasant company / Here it is burned / Like a pure sacrifice."[213] He describes the fiery sacrificial death for several stanzas "on an altar of tragedies / refusing to be forgotten / caused by sins."[214] It consumes "A loved soul / who like a floating pillar of light / so quickly passed, was no more / And before her sap ran / Gave birth to me a daughter."[215] In closing he says "The dew drops / My thoughts / Dripping from heaven / To you I have revealed— / Will they dissolve / On hard soil / Say the truth / Or give utterance ??? . . . . " (ellipsis in original).[216]

What were the sins for which he took his wife's death as punishment? His youthful arrogance and ambition? Some inattentiveness on his part? His having outshone his father at such an early age?[217] These questions are ultimately unanswerable. But this elegy to his wife, which unsurprisingly is more literarily compelling than most of his (frankly rather wooden) poetry, points, again, to his inward turn in these years, his moving from the intellectualism and mind-centeredness of his early years to a more interior vision of the

---

208 Ofan, *Qevatzim mi-Ketav Yad Qodsho*; the Boisk diary is from 15–73 (hereinafter Boisk Diary). I had been planning to publish portions of the manuscript based on the photocopy in the Rivka Schatz collection at NLI. My thanks to Rabbi Ofan for sharing his prepublication proofs with me.

209 In the diary the elegy is immediately preceded by a poem entitled "Masat Nafshi." In Zvi Yehudah Kook's edition of the poems *Orot Ha-Re'ayah* (Jerusalem: Mossad Ha-Rav Kook, 1970), that poem appears after the essay "Shalom be-Shem," which is expressly dated "Mar-Heshvan 5655," that is, autumn 1894. Ofan shares this assessment; see his comments at 11.

210 מחשכים סביבי \ וחושך ימש \ ערפלי עבי \ יקדירו לי שמש.

211 שוכב קבר \ עודנו חי\אין קץ לשבר \ למצוקה אין די . . . \ אזעק בקול \ אחריש אזנים\אפוח בחול\ויעל לשמים.

212 אשקד בתורה \ שראות פניה לא פללתי.

213 תקותי הנשקפת \ מחברתך הנעימה \ הניה נשרפת \ כעולה תמימה.

214 עלי מזבח \ של אסונות \ מאנו להשכח \ שגרמו עונות.

215 נפש נאהבת \ שכעמוד אור פורח \ חיש עברה חלדה \ וטרם נס לח \ לי בת ילדה.

216 ורסיסי טל \ שרעפי \ משמים מזל \ לך חשפתי - \ הילכו תמס \ עלי צחיח \ הגידה אמת \ או יתנו שיח.

217 For instance, in a letter dated 5 Tishrei 5653, September 26, 1892, shortly after turning twenty-seven, he apologizes to his father for not having yet provided him with the ghost-written sermon his father needed for his mendicant fund-raising, after mentioning his having spent some time relaxing in the resort of Dubbelen. This letter is printed in *Otzarot*, vol. 1, 2nd ed., 367. A more positive response to his father's query from later that year is at *Orah Mishpat* no. 49. For examples of halakhic queries sent to him at Zeimel and Boisk by his father see *Da'at Cohen*, nos. 222, 228.

religious life, a "religion of the heart," entailing acceptance and expression of the fullness of subjecrtive personality, of the individual, the collective and, eventually, the divine.[218]

Conclusion

During his years in Zeimel, Rav Kook underwent a passage to the interior life. He augmented his Talmudic erudition with wide-ranging study of Kabbalah. He began to explore the dynamics of self-cultivation, drawing heavily on the philosophical tradition, both for its emphasis on mind as well as for the idea of self-cultivation itself. In his personal writings, as well as in those meant for public consumption, he increasingly explored the relationship between mind and body, and, in parallel, Israel and the nations. These writings emphasize the primacy of the intellect within a hierarchically ordered conception of the perfected individual and Israel as the perfected nation. In the coming chapters we will see how, further pursuing his own developmental trajectory and responding to the Mussar controversies of the 1890s, that picture would change as he probed further inward, into the human person, and himself.

---

218 In using the term "religion of the heart" here, I am thinking of the general modern turn described by Ted A. Campbell's helpful study *The Religion of the Heart: A Study of European Religious Life in the Seventeenth and Eighteenth Centuries* (Columbia: University of South Carolina Press, 1991). While of course the metaphor of the heart well predates that—we need look no farther than *Hovot Ha-Levavot*— the peculiarly modern interiority we are talking about here is different from, though of course builds on, its premodern antecedents. I will have more to say on this later on.

Boisk: Turning Inward at the Crossroads of Mussar and *Tiqqun*

In 1896, Rav Kook moved from Zeimel to Boisk, where he was thrust into a larger, more cosmopolitan urban setting. All the while, the controversies swirling in the yeshivot of the time and in Jewish society in general were never far from view, as he worked to map the relations of the spiritual tradition to which he was heir—Lithuanian Talmudism, Kabbalah, Hasidism, Maimonidean philosophy—coming to see a need to augment Talmudism with study and reflection on the spiritual life and its relation to the world around him.

If as time went on Jewish nationalism and social radicalism were the contemporary movements that were the chief focal points for his complex explorations, in these years of the early to mid–1890s, the Mussar movement was crucial. Mussar's call for hard work on the inner life as an integral part of yeshiva culture resonated with him profoundly even as he parted company with Mussar on how to translate that intuition into reality; analogous to the way in which he later resonated deeply to Zionism's call for Jewish national renewal even as he parted company with it on how to translate that intuition into reality. During the 1890s he gave much and deep thought as to how to take Mussar's positive energies in hand, give them a more sustainable form, and integrate them with the Lurianic project of cosmic reparation, of *tiqqun*.

Yosef Avivi, Jonathan Garb, and Raphael Shuchat have argued persuasively, each from their own perspective (respectively, the Lurianic heritage, the history of ideas, and the Kabbalistic underpinnings of proto-Zionism) that Rav Kook's mature thought represents a further development of Luzzatto's ideas, building on and moving beyond their interpretation by the Vilna Gaon and his followers, and indeed, that the Gaon's circle is "the missing link" between Luzzatto and Rav Kook. The Gaon focused Luzzatto's sacred history of humanity onto the redemption of Israel, and took the comparatively naturalistic dimensions at play in his understanding of *tiqqun* as a warrant for concrete social and political activity, which would also be theurgic, and ultimately redemptive; Rav Kook in turn applied this template to modern secular nationalism.[1] I argue that the period I will look at in this chapter represents a step in this evolution, and is perhaps a "missing link" of its own between Rav Kook's historiosophic reading of modernity and another key feature of his mature thought, the celebration of the subjective self.

Crucially, I will try to reconstruct the evolution of Rav Kook's ideas on their own terms as he developed them, in his notebooks—published in recent years as *Pinqasim* 15 and 16, and as *Mahberot Qetanot Boisk* (*Little Notebooks of Boisk*)—and not as presented and published decades later by his editors. In particular, I will here refer not to the treatise posthumously edited and published in the 1940s as *Mussar Avikha,* but to the specific notebook, *Pinqas* 15, from which much, though not all, of that small but striking treatise was skillfully culled (and rearranged) by his son Zvi Yehudah.[2]

As we work through the writings of this period we will see the burgeoning of the idea of selfhood, of each individual having an essential core, unique to themselves, accessible only by their own reflection and introspection, whose actualization and expression is the truest expression of their own being, and of their place in the larger frame of being. It is this self that makes the individual a subject, a living being choosing and shaping their world alongside others. This idea has points of contact with premodern thought, but took on new and far-reaching meanings in modernity. In this chapter we will see Rav Kook explore subjectivity on the individual level—and, over time, his conceptions will expand to the subjectivity of the nation, the cosmos, and God.

A number of Maskilim, including traditionalists, had already affirmed the uniqueness of the individual self and the integrity of all its dimensions, as both a philosophic and pedagogical principle.[3] Rav Kook adapted some of these Maskilic ideas to Luzzatto's teleology of *tiqqun*, namely, that indeed each self is unique and each distinctive form of

---

1   Jonathan Garb, "Rabbi Kook and his Sources: From Kabbalistic Historiosophy to National Mysticism," in *Studies in Modern Religious Movements and the Babi-Baha'I Faiths*, ed. Moshe Sharon (Leiden: Brill, 2004), 77–96; idem, *The Chosen Will Become Herds: Studies in Twentieth-Century Kabbalah* (New Haven: Yale University Press, 2009); Yosef Avivi, "Historiyah Tzorekh Gevohah," in *Sefer Ha-Yovel li-Khvod Mordechai Breuer*, ed. Moshe Bar-Asher (Jerusalem: Aqademon, 1992), 709–771 and now his multivolume *Qabbalat ha-Re'ayah*; Raphael Shuchat, *Olam Nistar be-Meimadei Ha-Zman: Torat Ha-Ge'ulah shel Ha-Gra, Meqorotehah ve-Hashap'atah le-Dorot* (Ramat Gan: Bar-Ilan University Press, 2010). Tamar Ross's studies of Rav Kook are too numerous to mention here and a number will be cited in the course of this work; one which will not, but is foundational, is her "Musag Ha-Elohut shel Ha-Rav Kook," *Da'at* 8–9 (1982): 109–128, 39–74.

2   Unintentionally illustrating the vagaries of the editorial history of this corpus, Yohanan Fried, a keeper of some of Rav Kook's manuscripts, and editor of the fourth volume of *Orot Ha-Qodesh*, once told me that Zvi Yehudah Kook did not himself edit *Mussar Avikha* (phone conversation, January 22, 2007). Now that we have the notebooks in as close to their original form as is available for now, that view seems no longer tenable to say the least.

3   See chapter four of Harris Bor, "Moral Education in the Age of Jewish Enlightenment" (PhD diss., Cambridge University, 1996). My thanks to him for making a copy of his work available to me. Admittedly, Bor's work deals with an earlier time period than that under discussion here, yet a number of the Maskilic works discussed by Bor, dating to the eighteenth and

religious praxis has its own ordained role to play in the cosmic drama of restoration; by the same token, the primary forms of religious praxis—prayer, Torah study, mitzvot—are each of equal value. Earlier forms of Lurianic ethical writing embedded the individual in a broader cosmic drama in which they played a theurgic role.[4] Hasidic thought focused on the religious life of the individual qua individual, and in the process de-emphasized the individual's theurgic role in the Lurianic drama of *tiqqun* (even as Hasidism dramatically revised the theory and practice of religious community).[5] Rav Kook manages, over time, to integrate the individual qua individual, with one's own characteristics and bearings, into the Lurianic framework. This perspective also enabled Rav Kook to navigate among the spiritual traditions to which he was heir as well as the various ranks of society, such that each has its own time and place in the larger whole.

The chapter closes with the story of Rav Kook's relationship with his chief disciple in Boisk, Binyamin Menashe Levin, which opens a fascinating window onto his life at the time, and shows how his inward turn began to result in a celebration of personal expression. In other words Rav Kook's turn towards subjectivity, at least on the level of the individual, was well underway long before he stepped foot in Zion.

Unease in Zeimel and the Influence of Eliasberg

Not long after his arrival in Zeimel in 1888, Avraham Yitzhak Kook was looking for other postings beyond his small, fractious community, and had his eye on a position in Boisk (Bauska), a midsized town in Latvia. He was befriended by the rabbi there, Mordechai Eliasberg (1817–1889), friend of Aderet, a leading rabbinic figure in Hibat Tzion and rabbi of Boisk since 1861.[6] In later years, Rav Kook described Eliasberg as "a supreme exemplar of originality and of morality, one of a kind in a generation, or generations . . . as

---

early nineteenth centuries, were still being read in Rav Kook's time, indeed, he himself cites Wessely's *Sefer Ha-Middot* in his *Midbar Shur*.

4   This point is made by Joseph Dan, *Jewish Mysticism and Jewish Ethics*, 2nd ed. (Northvale: Jason Aronson, 2006), 110–111.

5   The place of the internalization of Kabbalistic ideas and symbols in Hasidism has generated much scholarly discussion, which I will discuss in chapter four.

6   In an letter to Aderet in 1889, less than a year after his arrival in Zeimel, Rav Kook discusses various possible rabbinical posts; he says he would not want to go to Kreisberg because 1) there is a Hasidic rabbinic authority in place there, 2) the rabbinate in that region is in a bad way, 3) he doesn't want to be in competition with the rabbi in nearby Jakobstadt (Jekabpils); but Lachovitz (Lyakhoichi, near Minsk), he says, sounds tempting. He adds that an unnamed former rabbi of Boisk has returned from Plotsk *en route* to liquidate his debts and settle the rent owed him by the community, see *Orah Mishpat,* Addenda 1. In a letter to Aderet from the summer of 1888, cited in Neriah, *Tal*, 125, he thanks the latter for sending him several Kabbalistic volumes, in particular Isaac Haver Wildman's *Binyan 'Olam*, adding that "ever since I saw them in the home of our friend Ha-Gaon Rabbi Mordechai [Eliasberg], the rabbinical judge of Boisk, my soul yearned to drink from the cool sacred fountains, streaming from sacred peaks." A halakhic query addressed by Kook to Eliasberg in 1889 is recorded at

though the Land of Israel was realized in his mind and thought. . . ."[7] Without overstating the degree of Eliasberg's influence on him, we offer a brief sketch of Eliasberg's ideas, and in particular his emphasis on internal Jewish harmony, as we will soon see Rav Kook's thinking increasingly hinging on the notion of reconciliation, of competing factions of the Jewish people, of the various spiritual traditions to which he was heir, and ultimately, in his response to Mussar, of the disparate elements of the religious life, and of the soul.

Eliasberg, an alumnus of Volozhin, was active in Hibat Tzion; yet unlike many of the Hibat Tzion rabbis he was deeply and pragmatically concerned with Jewish economic betterment, was broadly tolerant of freethinkers, and saw the experience of modern Western Jewry as a partial model for emulation.[8] Unlike Netziv, he opposed religious coercion in

---

'Ezrat Cohen, no. 78. In a letter to Aderet in the fall of 1888, Eliasberg addresses Aderet as *ahuvi yedidi*, "my beloved friend"; see *Igrot*, 535.

The reference to Haver's volume is interesting, inasmuch as Haver was regarded as a faithful transmitter and interpreter of the Kabbalistic traditions of the Gaon, not least of the Gaon's endorsement of Luzzatto's allegorization of Luria, in contrast to Shlomo Elyashiv, as will be discussed below. See the brief comments of Pachter, "Qabalat Ha-Gra be-Aspaqlariyah shel Shtei Mesorot," 119–136, 134–135.

Aderet unsuccessfully tried to have Rav Kook appointed as his successor in Ponevezh, which, as we saw in the previous chapter, had given him much grief when in 1894 he left that community for Mir; see Rav Kook's letter to his father in *Igrot*, 1:7.

At one point, Rav Kook wrote to Baron Simon Rothschild of Frankfurt, asking him to provide a stipend of ten rubles a week for his father-in-law and sending him a copy of the short-lived *'Ittur Sofrim*. The gesture is revealing in several ways: his care for his father-in-law, his interest in being recognized by a wider world, and the general unworldliness of his thinking. He reportedly got the idea on hearing that the Baron indeed supported a scholar in Minsk, the letter is reproduced in Neriah, *Tal*, 109–112.

7   This recollection is to be found in J. L. Fishman (Maimon), "Rabbi Mordechai Eliasberg (zl)," *Sinai* 6 (1940): 1–5, 2–3. Fishman (Maimon)'s own gloss on Rav Kook's characterization is worth noting: "Yet the reader of Rabbi Mordechai Eliasberg's articles and letters . . . recognizes and understands that this great genius *felt* [emphasis in original] more than wrote."

Reportedly after one of their conversations Eliasberg said to him "Zeimler Rov, iz vest zikh mit aikh a-mol opten groyse zakhen in Eretz Yisroel" (Rabbi of Zeimel, I'm sure that one day you'll do great things in the Land of Israel); Rabbiner, *Or Mufla'*, 972.

8   See Neriah, *Sihot*, 157–158. For a brief biography of Eliasberg accompanied by a number of his publicistic writings, see A. M. Genahovsky, "Ga'on Ha-Mahshava Ha-Tzionit," in Maimon, *Azkarah*, 453–555, later reprinted as a separate volume *Rav Mordechai Eliasberg: Toldotav, Mahshavotav ve-Helekh Ruho* (Jerusalem: n.p., 1937). Genahovsky also edited an anthology of his writings, *Ha-Rav Mordechai Eliasberg: Mivhar Ketavav* (Tel Aviv: Josef Srebrek, 1947). For a brief outline of Eliasberg's ideas, see David Shahar, "Tefisato Ha-Tzionit ve-Ha-Datit shel Ha-Rav Mordechai Eliasberg (1817–1889), *Kivvunim* 25 (1984): 93–112.

In addition to his writings in the Maskilic press, Eliasberg reportedly wrote some twenty-five book-length works, though only a few of his writings were published; a collection of Talmudic studies by himself and his son Yonatan (himself a distinguished scholar, who died comparatively young) and his *Shevil Ha-Zahav* from which I will quote presently. For his responsa and halakhic discourses, see Mordechai Eliasberg, *Terumat Yad* (Vilna: Dvorzetz, 1875).

the new settlements in Palestine.[9] An indication of Elisaberg's ecumenism can be seen from his having been eulogized at his death in the Gaon's *kloyz* in Vilna, in the modernized synagogues of St. Petersburg, Moscow, Odessa, and elsewhere, in student associations, and in print by Ahad Ha-Am himself.[10]

Eliasberg ceded some modern critiques of traditional society, and particularly its moral failings, which he attributed to the damage of exile, in which a corrosive individualism, stimulated by the Jews' economic situation, had taken hold, one which could be corrected by a return to the soil. He also took a strikingly positive view of Moses Mendelssohn, both his personal piety and the creativity he showed in redefining Jewish religious identity under the conditions of emancipation.[11] Like Pinhas Lintop, whom we mentioned in the previous chapter, though far more successfully, he carved out a principled stance of intra-Jewish toleration, at least as regards political and social activities, and a willingness to accept criticism, perhaps not of the tradition, but of traditional society. In the closing pages of his posthumous work, a collection of essays on contemporary affairs entitled *Shevil Ha-Zahav*, "The Golden Mean,"[12] he issued a heartfelt call for tolerance:

> And the special thing and a great principle, is that all Torah greats and pious men must be lovers of humanity, including those who are freethinkers in their actions too. . . . And to the Maskilim I say: love God and His Torah and do acts of kindness, let purity of character be your guiding principle. The Maskilim offer a chilly path, the zealots a path of fire, and we must walk in the middle, and God will pour His spirit upon us. [13]

Rav Kook did not share Eliasberg's interest in economics or, for that matter at the time, in Hibat Tzion. Yet Eliasberg does seem to have been, for the young Rav Kook, an older and unmistakably pious role model, working to synthesize traditionalist piety with qualified but genuine acceptance of some aspects of modernity and a broadly tolerant spirit. [14]

His influence on Rav Kook may be seen in an essay written in the fall of 1894, and never published in his lifetime. Entitled "Shalom be-Shem" (meaning both "Peace in [God's] Name" and "Among the Children of the Biblical Shem") it was meant to serve as

---

9   See Luz, *Maqbilim Nifgashim*, 107–108.

10 See Ahad Ha-Am (Asher Ginzberg), *Kol Kitvei Ahad Ha-Am* (Tel Aviv/Jerusalem: Devir/ Hotza'ah 'Ivrit, 1954), 41 (hereinafter *Kol Kitvei*). The well-known traditionalist Maskil S. Y. Fuenn had reportedly said of Eliasberg that he had never met another rabbi with "so clean a soul."

11 See the lengthy discussion in Eliasberg, *Shevil*, 20–30.

12 Ibid. The introductory essay to the latter is a source of much biographical information. A collection of his essays and letters is *Ha-Rav Mordechai Eliasberg: Mivhar Ma'amarav*, ed. A. M. Genahovsky (Tel Aviv: Serkes, 1947); hereinafter *Mivhar*.

13 Eliasberg, *Shevil*, 76–77. It is perhaps not ironic that Eliasberg's great-grandson Solomon Silberstam eventually became a famous Esperantist.

14 Indeed, Eliasberg was not a single-minded Talmudist; it is reported in a number of sources that he made a nearly nightly practice of rising at midnight, studying through the night and greeting the dawn with psalm-singing; see his son Yonatan's introduction to his father's posthumous publication, ibid., xxxiii.

the introduction to a series of publications entitled "Shalom la-'Am" (Peace to the People) that would preach a gospel of internal Jewish tolerance and unity.[15] Peace, he writes, is not merely the absence of discord. Rather:

> [T]he peace that we must pursue is the peace to be found in existence by virtue of its very wholeness and perfection, not by the passing of the problems that preceded its absence. Peace is the true relation that ought to obtain between the specific elements of the nation . . . [it is] the relation that ought to obtain between each Israelite and his fellow, to the point where it sets the relation as well between the counsel, strategy and well-intentioned thought, fast in the heart of multitudes of the pious faithful of Israel, and concrete action and realized existence.[16]

Reconciliation will be a key motif of his in this and coming chapters, of intellectual traditions, spiritual stances, and elements in the soul.

After Eliasberg's death in 1889, his successor in Boisk was Yehezqel Lifshitz (1862–1932), a man of some general education and broader interests, who served as both official and crown rabbi, as well as "spiritual rabbi."[17] Rav Kook had been one of Eliasberg's eulogists;[18] he was considered as a possible successor then, but did not receive the post at the time, due to his youth, and the perception among some townspeople that he was overly pious.[19] With Lifhshitz's departure in 1896, the post again became open. The people of Zeimel offered to raise Rav Kook's salary but relented on hearing the argument that their small town was no match for their young rabbi's talents and ambitions; reportedly the town porters, attached as they were to their rabbi, refused to help him move.[20] After taking his leave, Rav Kook assumed the post of spiritual leader—though not crown rabbi—of the Orthodox community of Boisk.[21]

---

15 "Shalom be-Shem" was first published in *Orot Ha-Re'ayah*, 16–19.

16 Ibid., 16–17:

שלום, השם הנערץ והנקדש הזה נמצאהו מושאל ברוב הפעמים רק לשלילת המחלוקת והמדנים, אבל לא זהו השלום שהוא אחד מעמודי העולם ולא על דבר של שלילה נוכל לומר שרק הוא יהיה הכלי האחד המחזיק ברכה לישראל, אבל השלום שאנחנו חייבים להיות רודפים אחריו הוא השלום המצוי במציאות מצד עצם שלימותו, לא עבור החסרונות הקודמים להעדרו. השלום הוא היחש (!) האמיתי שראוי להיות בין חלקי האומה הפרטיים . . . היחש (!) הראוי להמצא בין כל אחד מישראל לרעהו עד שיבא השלום להיות נותן יחש גם אל העצה והתחבולה והמחשבה הטובה, הכמוסה בלב רבבות אלפי ישראל שלמי אמונים, אל פעל ידים והמציאות הגמורה.

17 Lifshitz translated stories from German into Hebrew, published as *Galgal Ha-Hozer* (Warsaw: Unterhandler, 1886) and wrote under the pseudonym *Sofer Mahir*. He also published three volumes of sermons entitled, *Ha-Midrash ve-Ha-Ma'aseh*, 3 vols. (Pietrikov: Tzederbaum, 1901). On him, see Kagan, *Yiddishe Shtodt*, 231.

18 Maimon, 63.

19 Frankel, *Encyclopedia of Religious Zionism*.

20 This is based on Even-Hen, *Rav u-Manhig*, 96–97.

21 He did still stay in touch with Zeimel and was on at least one occasion drawn in to the resolution of a lingering halakhic question from his time there, see his query to Aderet in *Igrot*, 1:10–12, no. 10.

Boisk

Boisk (Bauska) was in Latvian Courland, on the Lyelufa River, a little north of the Lithuanian border. A relatively more cosmopolitan setting than Zeimel, it hosted two distinct minority groups, Jews and Germans.[22] Many of the Jews were educated; one of them, Lazar Niselovich, was a judge and eventually served as a deputy in the third Duma. Jews, Germans, and Latvians all worked in the liberal professions, trades and manufacture, with the Germans most prominently represented in the town's elite. The large, ornate main synagogue, built in the late nineteenth century, sat astride the main street, next door to a kosher abbatoir and directly across from the town's open-air market and city hall, with a smaller Hasidic synagogue some 1,000 yards away. Relations between Jews and non-Jews were essentially civil, aside from the standard run of stereotypes and prejudices.[23] In 1897, Boisk's population numbered 6,544, of whom 2,745, or forty-two percent, were Jews, some 300 of them craftsmen and artisans. The class divide between Latvian and Lithuanian Jews was pronounced, as the latter were predominantly poor, ineligible for civic relief, and thus heavily dependent on communal charities. The Jewish community at the time sponsored two private *hadarim* and a Talmud Torah; not many Jews studied in *gymnasia*. A number of Boisk's Jews eventually took part in the 1905 uprising, an indication of their movement with the currents of the time.[24]

A lengthy, informative, if frankly sentimental, portrait of Jewish Boisk in the years of Rav Kook's rabbinate there has been left to us by Zev Aryeh Rabbiner, whose father, Benjamin, taught in a yeshiva Rav Kook founded there.[25] He describes Boisk as a moderately well-off and well-kept community, with several synagogues, including separate ones for Hasidim and Mitnagdim, various charitable and social welfare societies, Zionist organizations and a Zionist library. Boisk's proximity to the rabbinic strongholds of

---

22 This paragraph draws on an unpublished 2004 lecture by Aigar Urtan of the Bauska Museum of Art and Regional Studies, "Bauska: The Late 19th and Early 20th Century." I am grateful to Dr. Urtan for sharing this with me, and to Pinhas Maurer for his help in translation from the Latvian. It is also based on observations during my visit to Boisk on December 14, 2004.

23 This observation draws on Dr. Urtan's paper.

24 "Boisk," in Levin, *Pinqas Ha-Kehillot*, 3–69. That a sizable number took part in the 1905 Revolution is a sign of some substantial acculturation, though not necessarily of radicalism, as the worsening conditions of Russian Jewry after 1903 eventually led Zionists, Bundists, and Liberals alike more openly to defend the interests of Russian Jews, to the point of moving, some cautiously, others less so, towards revolution; see Christoph Gassenschmidt, *Jewish Liberal Politics in Tsarist Russia, 1900–1914* (Oxford/London: St. Antony's/MacMillan, 1995), 1–18. My thanks to Professor Shaul Stampfer for directing me to this volume.

25 Zev Aryeh Rabbiner, "Shalosh Qehillot Qodesh," in *Yahadut Latvia: Sefer Zikaron*, ed. A. Ettingen, S. Lifshitz, M. Abramson, and M. Lavi (Tel Aviv: 'Igud Yotz'ei Latvia ve-Estonia be-Yisrael, 1953), 244–296. Benjamin Rabbiner, a descendant of Boisk's first rabbi, was an alumnus of Volozhin and close friend of Eliasberg's son Yonatan. Neriah mentions this essay in passing, though makes very little use of it. I have been unable to ascertain much about the yeshiva, and indeed I cannot say if it was much more than a traditional *beit midrash*, augmented by Rabbiner's presence, see the brief mention in Neriah, *Tal*, 152.

Lithuania gave it a more pronouncedly Orthodox cast than other Latvian communities, though it was a modern city and influenced by German culture, and a number of learned Jews were also in liberal professions.[26] Rav Kook, he writes, enjoyed a good relationship with the crown rabbi Yequtiel Ha-Levi Ephraimson and corresponded with his son, an Orthodox writer and intellectual named Ya'aqov.[27]

Rav Kook, Rabbiner says, distinguished himself, inter alia, by pawning his own valuables for the poor. In addition to the yeshiva (where Rav Kook gave the occasional lecture) he founded, with the help of his younger brother Shaul and his students Binyamin Menashe Levin (about whom more below) and Moshe Zeidel, a society for young men, workers, and students, a branch of the Orthodox Tiferet Bahurim network (also known as *Dem Rebbe's Gevardia*), which gathered to study Bible and (interestingly, as we shall see) Samson Raphael Hirsch's *Horev*, had a modest library, and occasionally mounted small productions.[28] On Shabbat afternoons Rav Kook would teach in his home a class from *Tze'na u-Re'na*, the Yiddish anthology of Torah commentary meant chiefly for Jewish women, to workingmen. He also founded a society called Linat Ha-Tzedeq for visiting the sick and loaning out medical supplies.[29] He kept up his studies as best he could, rising at five in the morning for prayers and then studying until noon, completing his quick review of the entire Babylonian Talmud once a year, while maintaining a regimen of in-depth study as well.[30]

---

26 Their names and backgrounds are given in ibid., 260–266.

27 Ya'aqov Efraimson, an admirer of the writings of S. R. Hirsch, published in *Der Israelit* and general newspapers, and also wrote for *Ha-Peles* under the pseudonyms *Ha-Tzofeh me-Har Efraim*, *Ben Efraim*, *Metushelah*, and others. Like Yonatan Eliasberg, he died young. I have thus far been unable to locate his correspondence with Rav Kook, though it should, if discoverable, be of great interest.

28 Rabbiner writes on p. 263 in "Shalosh Qehillot Qodesh" that in 1903 they put on a play in Rav Kook's home, written by Rabbi Yizhak Isaac Friedman, depicting the closing of Volozhin. Shaul Kook dressed up in his brother's coat and fur hat to play the role of the itinerant fundraiser of the yeshiva, who, we remember, was their father. (Rabbiner understandably omits this.)

For brief discussion of the formation of the Tiferet Bahurim network see Luz, *Maqbilim Nifgashim*, 291. These societies were founded under broadly anti-Zionist auspices; Rabbiner makes no mention of that, nor does he give any indication of the Boisk chapter's political orientation.

Rabbiner's tantalizing statement that the young Elhanan Wasserman—whose family lived in Boisk and whose father Naftali was the beadle of the synagogue—and who later emerged as one of the leading Lithuanian Talmudists and ultra-Orthodox ideologues of the twentieth century, studied with Rav Kook during these years, is likely an exaggeration. Wasserman, who was born in Birz in 1875, lived in Boisk from 1888 to 1892 and from there went off to Volozhin and thence to Telz; the most one can say is that he may well have availed himself of the yeshiva's *beit midrash* on his visits to his family, and may have heard Rav Kook offer the occasional lecture or sermon. For these dates see Mordechai Rabbiner, *Eleh Ezkerah*, vol. 1 (New York: Ha-Makhon Le-Heker Ba'ayot Ha-Yahadut Ha-Haredit, 1956), 83.

29 Efraim Zoref, *Hayei Ha-Rav Kook* (Jerusalem: M. Neuman, 1961), 54.

30 See Mordechai Rabbiner's memoirs recorded in Rabbiner, *Or Mufla*, 181–183. He writes that Rav Kook's study partner at the time, Mordechai Dat, said that Rav Kook displayed striking

He was, in brief, preoccupied with the work of a communal rabbi, which he approached with energy and, it seems, concern for a relatively broad range of people and their needs. During these years he began to be asked to contribute approbations, *haskamot*, to rabbinic works, usually, though not always, to those of a more aggadic or moralistic, and less strictly halakhic, bent.[31] As was the case in Zeimel, his halakhic writing reflects the concerns of the local rabbinate.[32]

At the same time, developments occurring in the yeshivot of the time most certainly did not escape his notice.

---

proficiency in the Jerusalem Talmud and in the philosophical works of Se'adyah, Yehudah Ha-Levi, Albo, Arama, and Maharal.

31 The volumes to which he contributed approbations in those years were: Simhah Kahane's aggadic commentary *Magen Ha-Talmud* (Warsaw, n.p. 1901); Kahane was a well-known preacher with a strikingly wide and varied range of admirers—among the others offering testimonials in that volume were Yitzhak Elhanan Spektor, Eliyahu Meisel, Hayim Berlin, Aderet, and Hayim Soloveitchik, as well as Ahad Ha-Am, Avraham Slutzky, Nahum Sokolov, and Zvi Hirsch Masliansky; Alexander Falk's *Sefat Emet* (Vilna: Garber, 1902), a polemic work defending basic principles of traditional Judaism; Eliyahu Halpern's volume of very brief comments on the Bible, *Hemdat Yisrael* (Jerusalem: n.p., 1950) (Rav Kook's approbation is dated to his time in Boisk); the Torah commentary *Ha-Ketav ve-Ha-Derash* of Aryeh Katzenellenbogen (Pietrkov: Rosengarten & Horovitz, 1909), a pious businessman from Mir and associate of Aderet, who turned to writing after his business failed (though published in 1909, the volume's approbations are dated earlier); the spiritual and moral treatise of Shimon Ha-Cohen of Mitowi, *Sha'ar Shimon* (Vilna: Garber, 1901), about which more below; and two volumes by Shaul Shohat, his Talmud commentary *Tiferet Shaul* (Pietrkov: Pinsky, 1899), and his responsa collection *Beit Yedidyah* (Pietrkov: Tzederbaum, 1904). In his approbation to the former volume, Rav Kook takes note of Shohat's straitened circumstances; Rav Kook's approbation to the latter was excised from the photo offset reprint edition done by Yitzhak Brakh (Brooklyn/Monsey: Copy Corner, 1992). For more on the excision of Rav Kook from reprints of various publications, see Marc B. Shapiro, *Changing the Immutable: How Orthodox Judaism Rewrites its History* (Oxford: Littman, 2015). His name also appears several times in Hillel David Ha-Cohen Travis's periodical *Ha-Pisgah* 3, 4, and 5 (1895–1904), a journal explicitly devoted to bringing out Torah scholarship of literary merit, as one of the rabbis subscribing to and supporting it. The rabbinical listings there are three: top-tier, middle, and lesser, and he appears in the middle.

32 A slight exception is *Da'at Cohen*, no. 140, an inconclusive discussion of *metzitzah be-peh*, oral suction at circumcision, relative to the science of the time; it was published in *Torah mi-Tzion* 4, no. 4 (1899—the dating in the Mossad Ha-Rav Kook edition seems off), a journal that usually showcased the writings of halakhists resident in Palestine. The following published responsa and sundry halakhic items in his printed response volumes date from his time in Boisk: *Da'at Cohen*, nos. 27, 29, 31, 35, 36, 74 (?), 139 (?), 140, 143 (?), 157, 162, 181, 182, 222, 228 (Dobbelen), 229 (to his father), *'Ezrat Cohen*, nos. 31, 101, final addendum on 486 (question posed to Yosef Zekharia Stern); *Orah Mishpat, Orah Hayim*, nos. 1, 19, 23, 32, 45 (46? and 47?), 82 (84?); *Mishpat Cohen*, nos. 29, 58, 115, 121.

Developments in Yeshiva Culture and the Mussar Movement

Toward the end of the nineteenth century, the traditional Russian rabbinate fell on hard times; ideological and class conflicts, the rise of state-sponsored crown rabbis who asserted their authority with varying degrees of success vis-à-vis traditional, so-called "spiritual" rabbis, increased Russification, urbanization, and immigration all led to severe economic and cultural pressures on communal rabbis, especially as rabbinic posts were increasingly obtained by inheritance.[33]

Meanwhile, the 1890s were a period of powerful ferment within Lithuanian yeshiva culture. Though Volozhin itself closed its doors in 1892, yeshivot founded along the Volozhin model, before and after its closing, grew in Radom, Mir, Lomza, Kletzk, Novaredok, Kamenetz, Slabodka, and Telz, with alumni of Volozhin regularly comprising much of the faculty and furthering the conceptual methods of study they had learned there.[34] While yeshivot were by no means the sole province of Talmudic study, they had an undeniably powerful effect on traditional Jewry.

---

33 These comments are based on Immanuel Etkes, "Beyn Lamdanut le-Rabbanut be-Yahadut Lita be-Me'ah Ha–19," 223–246 and the slightly expanded version of his essay in English "The Relationship Between Talmudic Scholarship and the Institution of the Rabbinate," 107–132; the increasing role of inheritance in Lithuanian rabbinic appointments is discussed in Shaul Stampfer, "Inheritance of the Rabbinate in Eastern Europe in the Modern Period," *Jewish History* 13, no. 1 (Spring 1999): 35–57. On the economic travails of the Lithuanian rabbinate, see Mordechai Zalkin, "Social Status," 174–187, as well as his "Issachar and Zebulun—A Profile of a Lithuanian Scholar of the 19th Century" [Heb.], *Gal-Ed* 18 (2002): 125–154; my thanks to Prof. Jay Harris for directing me to this latter article. Zalkin provides a fascinating discussion of the controversies surrounding forced conscription and accusations of rabbinic complicity therein in "Beyn 'Bnei Elohim' li-Vnei Adam': Rabbanim, Bahurei Yeshivot ve-ha-Giyus La-Tzava' Ha-Russi ba-Me'ah ha–19," in *Shalom u-Milhamah be-Tarbut Ha-Yehudit*, ed. Avriel Bar-Levav (Jerusalem/Haifa: Merkaz Shazar, University of Haifa, 2006), 165–222. On the crown rabbis of the period and the uneven "dual rabbinate," see Nathans, *Beyond the Pale*, 235–236. A generational profile of the second- and third-tier rabbis and preachers who eventually tried their luck with the mass migrations to America is to be found in Kimmy Caplan, *Ortodoksiyah be-'Olam He-Hadash: Rabbanim ve-Darshanut be-America, 1881–1924* (Jerusalem: Merkaz Shazar, 2002), 82–94. For a brief, helpful survey, see Tamar Kaplan Appel, "Crown Rabbi," in *Yivo Encyclopedia of Jews in Eastern Europe*, ed. Gershom David Hundert (New Haven: Yale University Press, 2008), https://yivoencyclopedia.org/article.aspx/ Crown_Rabbi.

34 For institutional histories, largely written by alumni, see the essays collected in Mirsky, *Mosdot Torah be-Europa be-Vinyanam u-ve-Hurbanam*. The yeshivot affiliated with the Mussar movement, about which more below, are the subject of Dov Katz's multivolume *Tenu'at Ha-Mussar* (Tel Aviv: Beitan Ha-Sefer, 1946–1956). Stampfer's *Ha-Yeshiva* focuses on the histories of Volozhin, Slabodka, and Telz. A great deal of fascinating information on Lithuanian yeshiva culture is gathered in Kamenetsky, *Making of a Godol*. A good deal of basic information is to be found in Abraham Menes, "Patterns of Jewish Scholarship in Eastern Europe," in *The Jews: Their History, Culture and Religion*, vol. 1, ed. Louis Finkelstein (New York: Harper, 1960), 376–392. My thanks to Prof. Jay Harris for directing me to this last source.

One major feature of that ferment was the Mussar movement, Rav Kook's relationship to which was deeper than is generally thought. Indeed, I think that much of his early writing can best be understood against the background of the Mussar movement, and represents his attempt to further Mussar's emphasis on self-cultivation from within traditional textual and institutional structures, and without recourse to the new and regularly contentious patterns of Mussar yeshivot.

Mussar's institutionalization in the yeshivot was accompanied by significant shifts in the content of Mussar teachings as well. Salanter had, for his part, drawn in no small measure on the medieval rationalist tradition, and urged the cultivation of the intellect as crucial to the cultivation, in turn, of the will;[35] his adaptation, especially via the works of Menahem Mendel Lefin, of the Enlightenment's deployment of instrumental, and even technological, rationality over the self, nonetheless comported well with elements of the medieval tradition.[36] By contrast, his disciples progressively rejected autonomous intellect and reason as religious values, eschewing abstraction and intellectualization in favor of concerted discipline and intense attention to the details of religious life.[37] Crucially, while Salanter often saw himself as a reformer for Jewish society at large, his disciples focused their energies on the more circumscribed, if very intense, ambit of the yeshivot.[38]

Mordechai Zalkin has characterized Mussar as a third way between Hasidism and Lithuanian Talmuism, integrating fervor with monastic study, while avoiding both metaphysics and Kabbalah in favor of cultivating obeisance to the law, and moral character.[39]

---

35 Salanter's use of the medieval tradition emerges most strongly in his essays in the journal he founded, tellingly named *Ha-Tevunah*, particularly in his *Beirurei Ha-Middot*, which were reprinted in Sidarsky, *Imrei Binah*, 5–32, and in Pachter, *Kitvei Rabbi Yisrael Salanter*, 125–159.

36 On Lefin see Nancy Sinkoff, "Strategy and Ruse in the Haskalah of Mendel Lefin of Satanow," in Feiner and Sorkin, *New Perspectives on the Haskalah*, 86–102.

37 For instance, Simha Zissel Braude of Kelm (1829–1898), in whose writings we find the first articulation of a distinctively post-Salanter Mussar path, taught a subdued, introverted path of lifelong self-cultivation based on humility, self-observation, and introspection, whose goal was an independent mind and moral self that would of its own accord adhere to Torah and the commandments.

38 On these developments, see Tamar Ross, "Ha-Megamah Ha-Anti-Ratziyonalit be-Tenu'at Ha-Mussar," in *'Alei Shefer: Alexander Safran Festschrift*, ed. Moshe Hallamish (Ramat Gan Bar-Ilan University Press, 1990), 145–162, and Yehudah Mirsky, "Mussar after Salanter," in *Yivo Encyclopedia of Jews in Eastern Europe*, 1:924, 2:1214–1216, with accompanying bibliography. For lengthy discussion of the issue of the will and its weaknesses, *akrasia*, in post-Salanter Mussar, see Tamar Ross, "Ha-Mahshavah ha-I'yunit be-Ktivei Mamshikhav shel Rabbi Yisrael Salanter be-Tenu'at Ha-Mussar" (PhD diss., Hebrew University, 1986).

39 Mordechai Zalkin, "Beyn Ga'on le-Eglon—Morashtah Ha-Tarbutit shel Yahadut Lita," *Gesher* 43, no. 136 (Winter 1997): 73–82, esp. 74–75. Scholars have differed on the extent of Kabbalah in the thought of Salanter and his disciples. Benjamin Brown offers a careful survey of the evidence and convincingly argues that Kabbalah was of little moment there. See his "'Eynnenu Shayakh li ki Eyni 'Oseq ba-Zeh': Yahaso shel Rabbi Yisrael Salnter le-Qabbalah," in *Ve-Zot li-Yehudah: Yehudah Liebes Festschrift*, ed. Maren Niehoff, Ronit Meroz, and Jonathan Garb (Jerusalem: Hebrew University and Mossad Bialik, 2012), 420–439. On the place of Kabbalah in the post-Salanter movement, see Mordechai Pachter, "Tenu'at Ha-Mussar ve-Ha-Kabbalah,"

Within the Mussar yeshivot, the formal study of moral texts, such as Luzzatto's *Mesilat Yesharim* and Bahya ibn Paquda's *Hovot Ha-Levavot*, though something of a departure from the strictly Talmudic curriculum, was less a scandal than was the ecstatic mode of text study which gave a Mussar yeshiva its distinctive ambience.[40] As one student at Slabodka, where Mussar took center stage,[41] later recalled:

> The study of Mussar was organized as follows: Twice a week an ascetic from the town of Weisgal would preach on a chapter of *Mesillat Yesharim*, and the other days of the week each would study a Mussar volume of his choosing. Some would call up Mussar-matter from whatever was on their tongues, others would take the saying "If I am not for me, who will be for me" (Avot 1:14) and like the cow that chews its cud, would chew and chew it a hundred times. Who can imagine, who can depict, Mussar study in all its colors? If a stranger suddenly were to appear in the Mussar house and hear with his ears and see with his eyes the shouts, the sighs, the grimaces, the fists pounding the walls, he would justly think he had come to an insane asylum, a hospital for the mentally ill. After the Mussar they would pray the evening

---

in *Yashan Mipnei Hadash: Emanuel Etkes Festschrift*, ed. David Assaf and Ada Rapoport-Albert (Jerusalem: Mercaz Shazar, 2009), 223-250. Yehi'el Ya'aqov Weinberg (1884–1966), alumnus of Slabodka and towering Talmudist, observed that Mussar study afforded Lithuanian students an opportunity for Hasidic-style ecstasies, see the comment in his *Seridei Esh*, 4:284.

40 An interesting illustration of *Hovot Ha-Levavot*'s honored place as a traditional subject of study is provided by Elimelekh Ozer Bodek's compilation of every reference to it in the works of none other than Hatam Sofer, *Bo'u She'arav: Divrei Hatam Sofer 'al Sefer Hovot Ha-Levavot* (Brooklyn: n.p., 1999).

41 The Slabodka yeshiva was founded in a suburb of Kovno (Kaunas) in 1881 by Nathan Zvi Finkel (1849–1927), a third-generation adherent of Mussar and disciple of Simhah Zissel of Kelm. Finkel himself took a less severe view of the religious life than his contemporaries in the Mussar movement and repeatedly in his homilies stressed respect for human dignity and the cultivation of a positive self-image. Volume 3 of Dov Katz's *Tenu'at Ha-Mussar*, first published in 1956, is entirely given over to a full-length biography of Finkel. Citations to this multivolume work of Katz's will refer to the reprint edition (Jerusalem: Feldheim, 1966). On Slabodka's history up to 1905, see Stampfer, *Ha-Yeshivah*, 221–251. Finkel published next to nothing in his lifetime; a handful of student notes of his homilies, some from the nineteenth century, were published in *Sihot Ha-Sabba mi-Slabodka*, ed. Zvi Kaplan (Tel Aviv: Avraham Zioni, 1955), and a more extensive collection from his later years, organized around passages from the books of Genesis and Exodus, was published in two volumes under the title *Or Ha-Tzafun*, 2 vols. (Jerusalem: Haskel/Yeshivat Hevron, 1959–1968) It is a measure of Finkel's self-confidence and humility that he engaged a greater Talmudist than he, some seventeen years his junior, Moshe Mordechai Epstein (1866–1933), to give the Talmud lectures and designated himself as merely the yeshiva administrator. See as well on Slabodka, Marc B. Shapiro, *Between the Yeshiva World and Modern Orthodoxy: The Life and Works of Rabbi Jehiel Jacob Weinberg, 1884–1966* (London: Littman, 1999), and more recently, Shlomo Tickochinski, *Lamdanut Mussar ve-Elitizm: Yeshivat Slabodka mi-Lita le-Eretz Yisrael* (Jerusalem: Merkaz Shazar, 2016).

prayer, go to their homes to eat dinner and gather again to the *beit midrash* and continue their learning until eleven at night.[42]

The inner conflicts fueling the transports of Mussar sessions are captured in another student's recollection of the tension between the ecstasies of Mussar and the pull of Kovno's Hebrew library:

> The battle with Satan's forces lying in ambush roused my young imagination and enchanted me with a mysterious charm of heavenly sanctity. The hundreds of ecstatic young men spouting in a frenzy lines from *Mesillat Yesharim* . . . in those hours the heart seethed with wondrous sadness and it was so good to be in the company of those young men of torch-lit faces and flaming souls . . . but, O, there would rise the desire for the little books, drenched with rousing and intoxicating nectars and caressing your soul like snakes.[43]

Through the 1890s, reaction to Mussar from more traditional rabbinic quarters gathered steam, culminating in the spring of 1897 with the publication in *Ha-Melitz*, a newspaper broadly circulated among nonrabbinic circles, of a declaration by eight prominent Lithuanian rabbis against the study of Mussar.[44] They argued that while of course the study of moral texts was a venerable if distinctly limited element of Torah study, the sainted Salanter himself surely had had no intention of overturning those priorities, and certainly not of creating a new self-satisfied sect that replaced text study with frenzied chanting. The Mussar adherents, the rabbis argued, concoct shameful and embarrassing practices, denigrate established Torah scholars, aggrandize themselves while neglecting meaningful study, encourage their disciples arrogantly to impose themselves on other communities, and unwittingly contribute to the collapse of Jewish life that they claim to combat.[45]

A series of similar declarations and counter-declarations ensued; one, in support of the study of Mussar, appearing in *Ha-Melitz*, had Aderet as one of its nine principal signatories, and his former son-in-law, Rav Kook, was one of thirty others adding their support to a reprint of that declaration, in *Ha-Tzefirah*.[46] That latter declaration attested to the scholarship and piety of the rabbis instituting the study of Mussar, which was characterized as "a mere half hour of study before evening prayers of some Mussar books laid down by the immortal patriarchs, pietists of old, resting in Eden." This innocuous characterization of Mussar study skirted the issues raised in the original polemic, which was chiefly concerned not with the character of the rabbis of the Mussar yeshivot but with the deliberately outrageous and unconventional character of Mussar study by the students.[47]

---

42 Joshua Leib Rados, *Zikhrones*, cited in Etkes and Tykochinski, *Yeshivot Lita: Pirkei Zikhronot*, 338.

43 Nathan Greenblatt, cited in Stampfer, *Ha-Yeshivah*, 236–237.

44 The controversy is detailed in Dov Katz, *Pulmus Ha-Mussar* (Jerusalem: Weiss, 1972).

45 The declaration is reproduced in ibid., 104–112.

46 These are reprinted in ibid., 144–148.

47 It is also interesting to note that *Mesillat Yesharim*, the basic study text of Mussar, was by no means ancient or even medieval, but composed a mere 150 years before this polemic.

Those issues were joined in two letters to the editor of *Ha-Tzefirah* by none other than Berdyczewsky, who was fiercely critical of the anti-Mussar rabbis:

> We need not exactly be Mussar adherents ourselves to know and feel what they want; and that it is their prerogative to desire and listen to the echo of their feeling souls . . . which can no longer suffice with the dry crumbs of the halakhists who have forgotten in their unthinking innocence that there is a spirit in man.[48]

As we saw with regards to *'Ittur Sofrim*, here too Rav Kook was moved by the same currents as was Berdyczewsky, yet unlike him tried to stay within, and articulate a response from the resources of, the rabbinic tradition. At the time, though, ensconced as he was in Boisk and removed from the yeshivot, he did not personally figure in these disputes as more than a signatory. Interestingly, in 1903, Eliezer Gordon (1841–1910), dean of the Telz yeshiva, itself wracked by internal controversies over the study of Mussar, offered Rav Kook the position of *mashgiah*, or moral tutor. He visited the yeshiva for several days, before turning the position down; several suggestions have been offered as to why; the likeliest, put forth by Zev Rabbiner (and echoed by Zvi Yehudah Kook) is that the rabbinical post in Jaffa was simply more attractive.[49] Rav Kook did suggest to Gordon that he institute a curriculum of Bible, midrash, Zohar, Ha-Levi's *Kuzari*, Se'adyah's *Emunot Ve-De'ot*, Maimonides's *Eight Chapters*, and Bahya's *Hovot Ha-Levavot*.[50] Interestingly, the position remained unfilled, perhaps indicating that Rav Kook's mix of theology and Talmud was uncommon among Lithuanian Talmudists of his generation.

To be sure, as Mordechai Zalkin has persuasively argued, the undoubtedly colorful story of the yeshivot, and the intense and often romantic memories they fostered in their alumni, have contributed to a picture of East European Jewry which scants the fact that most Talmud study of the time took place not in yeshivot but in the more traditional,

---

This is further striking testament to its acceptance as a canonical text, despite the massive controversies that swirled around its author Moshe Hayim Luzzatto.

48 Holzman, *Kitvei Micha Josef Berdyczewski*, vol. 5, 81–83, esp. 82 and 107–109. This excerpt is from the first letter, which appeared in *Ha-Tzefirah* 24, no. 163, July 30, 1897, 812–813.

49 Zev Aryeh Rabbiner, *Ha-Ga'on Rabbi Eliezer Gordon* (Tel Aviv: n.p., 1968), 67, 192. Another version has it that Rav Kook's wanting to teach theology ended his chances, but that is likely a conflation of the aftermath of the two pieces of information recorded by Rabbiner. According to yet another version, the offer was rescinded because Rav Kook's practice of helping his wife in the kitchen on Friday afternoons was considered conduct unbecoming a rabbinical authority. This story, derived from Rabbi Yeshayahu Hadari, was related to me by Rabbi Nathan Kamenetsky, author of *Making of a Godol*, in a phone conversation, Jerusalem, Sunday, April 27, 2003.

The multiple versions of the story are perhaps related to Rav Kook's own preference for a yeshiva position over the rabbinate. In a letter dating from 1907, three years after his move to Palestine, *Igrot*, 1:89, Rav Kook expresses an interest in leaving the Jaffa post and succeeding the recently deceased Isaac Blazer (one of Salanter's leading disciples) as head of the Kollel Vilna in Jerusalem, because he doesn't want to be a working rabbi but rather to study and teach.

50 Rabbiner, *Ha-Ga'on Rabbi Eliezer Gordon*, 216.

smaller, local *batei midrash* (such as those in which the youthful Rav Kook had himself received the lion's share of his education) as well as in the study circles, *kloyzen*, of the cities.[51] Much of the hold exercised by the great yeshivot on the historical imagination, he says, derives from their sheer innovativeness and from their character as total and totalizing institutions, organizing every aspect of their student's lives (or trying to) and impressing upon them a powerful ideological commitment to *Torah li-Shmah* as enacted in the yeshivot. Indeed, Rav Kook's position alongside, but not inside, the yeshivot, forcing him to engage with a broader range of people and keep touch with a range of spiritual and intellectual traditions, helped shape his complex response to Mussar.

The Turn to Interiority as a Defining Theme of this Period

A fascinating, little-known essay by Rav Kook written during this period casts much light on his preoccupations and the way in which he tried to navigate the various spiritual traditions to which he was heir.[52] This essay, like the unpublished 1894 essay on peace, focuses on reconciliation, this time not among broad swathes of the Jewish people but within the rabbinic fraternity, between Hasidim, Mitnagdim, Maimonidean philosophers, and the new social force that had come to the fore in the intervening years, the latter-day adherents of Salanter's Mussar movement.

The untitled essay purports to explain the role of philosophy and centrality of Kabbalistic study in the pursuit of perfection, the reasons for the decline in its study in modern times, the mutual estrangements of the Hasidic disciples of the Ba'al Shem Tov (Besht) and the Mitnagdic followers of the Vilna Gaon, and the achievements and pitfalls of Mussar; from all these he tries to craft a spiritual stance of his own.

It is known to all, he says, that Torah study is the central feature of human perfection, and that the higher and deeper the subject of study the greater the perfection to be derived therefrom. Thus, inasmuch as Kabbalah deals with "the ways of God and the ordered structures of His sacred universes, the pure lights," it is necessarily compulsory study for one who is capable of it.[53] Maimonides, he says, was simply unaware of the Kabbalistic

---

51 See Mordechai Zalkin, "'Ir shel Torah—Torah ve-Limudah ba-Merhav Ha-'Ironi Ha-Litai ba-Me'ah Ha–19," in *Yeshivot u-Vatei Midrashot*, ed. Immanuel Etkes (Jerusalem: Merkaz Shazar, 2006), 131–161.

52 The essay was published for the first time in *Otzarot*, 2:303–312. Page numbers refer to that edition. Zuriel provides the title "Return to the Study of the Interiority of Torah for the Sake of Human Perfection." Zuriel's dating of the text to shortly before Rav Kook's departure for Palestine in 1904 period reflects his conversation with Ben-Zion Shapira, the manuscript's owner and disciple of Zvi Yehudah Kook, from whom he received it. (Related by Zuriel to me in conversation, summer 2005.) Beyond that we cannot be certain of its exact date. It is my sense that this essay is earlier than that, as it does not sound the themes of expressiveness and subjectivity that characterized his later years in Boisk.

53 *Otzarot*, 2:304:

כי העסק בדרכי האל ית' ובסדרי מערכות עולמיו הקדושים המאורות הטהורות הוא יותר נשגב מכל עסק זולת זה וראוי להחליט שמי שהשיגה ידו שכלו לעסוק בזה אין לו רשות להזניחו.

tradition, but, recognizing the higher nature of philosophical study, placed that pursuit above the study of halakhah in the scale of Torah study, and indeed saw philosophy as itself the very substance of Torah.[54]

He offers several reasons for the sages' discomfort with Maimonides's identification of philosophy with the highest form of Torah. The first, echoing the major theme of *Midbar Shur*, is that the universality of philosophy is at odds with the distinctiveness of the divine revelation of Torah to Israel. The others are that philosophy as such is unrelated to the mitzvot, and that "Torah's words are the true words of God, while the words of philosophy are thoughts of the human heart, founded in dust."[55] Certainly, once the Kabbalah had been revealed, and with it, not only God's own paths, but the profound underlying rationales of the mitzvot, it is the ultimate guide to the perfection of the soul; it (and not, by implication, Maimonidean philosophy) holds the key to the discourse of seeking reasons for the commandments, *ta'amei ha-mitzvot* (about which we will have more to say later on). All the other parts of Torah (presumably including the halakhah) are the matter to Kabbalah's form.[56]

Turning to Hasidism, he writes that the Besht's casting Lurianic Kabbalah in psychological terms as "a parable . . . of man created in the divine image, from whose powers and the light of whose soul we may understand a sort of model of that which is on high,"[57] was a pedagogic device meant to render Kabbalistic teachings more accessible to the people of his time, but by no means intended to exhaust the meaning of Kabbalistic ideas, and certainly not to confine the meaning of *tiqqun* to the individual's own subjective sense of his own love and fear of God, "for the essence of *tiqqunim* literally is that the human repairs and restores the supernal Glory, and even if he doesn't feel it, yet he does his *tiqqun*."[58] Yet that, he says, was precisely the error of the Besht's disciples, who understood

---

54 This was a common apologetic explanatory formula among Lithuanian Kabbalists, and in particular with Isaac Haver; see Nadler, "The 'Rambam Revival,'" 36–61, 51–52.

55 *Otzarot*, 2:305:

ובאמת אין ללימודי הפילוסופיא ערך אל לימוד התורה כלל, כי דברי תורה הם דבר ה' אמת המה ודברי הפילוסופיא הגות לבב בן אדם אשר בעפר יסודם. . . .

56 Ibid., 306:

א"כ אחרי שנגלה אור ה' והקבלה הנאמנה בסודות האלוהות המורים דרכי השם ית' . . . והם הם דברי תורה ועיקר תורה, שעליהם בנויים כל עמקי טעמי מצוות ופרטיהם שרשי האמונה ומיוחסים לישראל ביחוד . . . א"כ ודאי זהו החלק המיוחד בתורה שאליו ראוי לכסוף לשומו עיקרי, עם שמירת שאר חלקי התורה שהם כמו חומר לצורה נגד ערך הלימוד המרומם הזה.

57 Ibid.:

והנה הבעש"ט ז"ל ראה שאין דברי האר"י ז"ל מובנים לבני הדור ללמוד בהם, מצא לו משל קרוב שכל גופי תורה תלויים עליו, הוא האדם הנברא בצלם, שבכל כוחותיו ואור נפשו נבין מעין דוגמא של מעלה.

The nature and extent of the Besht's psychologization, or what Scholem termed "internalization" of Kabbalistic ideas has been the subject of lively scholarly discussion; see the full-length study by Ron Margolin, *Miqdash Adam: Ha-Hafnamah Ha-Datit ve-'Itzuv Hayei Ha-Dat Ha-Penimiyim be-Rei'shit Ha-Hasidut* (Jerusalem: Hebrew University/Magnes, 2005). I will have more to say on this in the coming chapter.

58 *Otzarot*, 2:307:

כי עיקרי התיקונים תיקונים ממש המה שהאדם מתקן הכבוד העליון, ואע"פ שאינו מרגיש, מכל מקום תיקונו עושה.

Kabbalah to be nothing more than a vessel for the repair of the individual's own soul, an error reinforced paradoxically by Kabbalah's very success at positively reforming their spiritual lives. This emphasis on prayer and excited or ecstatic worship (*tefillah ve-'avodah murgeshet*) also entailed neglect of the intellectual study of Kabbalah—the pursuit of his Mitnagdic Kabbalist teachers and, one recalls, the Habad preachers of his youth—which he takes pains to distinguish from the intellectual pursuit of philosophy: "We have found no path other than the perfection of true knowledge, which is man's very form. Yet this is not the perfection of philosophical study, for human intellect cannot grasp the truth, but the knowledge of Torah, all of whose words are true, is incompatible with the nature of transitory perfection."[59]

Interestingly, here he is employing against the Besht an inflection of the argumentative vein that had been directed by Shlomo Elyashiv, his most prominent Kabbalistic tutor, against Luzzatto, that is, that Luzzatto's allegorizations had undermined the meaning and significance of *tiqqun* as the reparation of God and the cosmos.[60]

This error of the Hasidim led to not only the neglect of serious Talmud study but, far more seriously, of the study of true Kabbalah, and of that study's role in the cosmic *tiqqun*. Contrary to popular belief, it was that latter failing, he says, which animated the Gaon's deepest polemic with Hasidism. The polemics around Hasidism further compounded the situation, he writes, perhaps reflecting Eliasberg's influence, and in something of a departure from the combative tone of his own earliest articles, since "it is in the nature of noise to confuse opinion, and anger leads to error."[61] Now that the fury of polemic between Hasidim and their opponents has cooled, for reasons good and bad (the latter presumably being their shared opposition to the onslaught of modernity) it is time for brothers to reunite and embrace in peace. Moreover, the excesses of pilpulistic Talmud study have resulted, he says, from the absence of proper outlets for intellectual exercise resulting from the eclipse of serious Kabbalistic study, and the inability of the masses to integrate philosophy with piety.[62] This must be remedied, with each form of study assuming its proper role:

The specific term he uses here, *tiqqun ha-kavod*, is a leitmotif of Meir ibn Gabbai's (1480/81–1544?) *'Avodat ha-Qodesh*, signifying the theurgical effect of mitzvot, see therein at, for example, 1:17, 1:24, 2:1, 2:17.

59 *Otzarot*, 2:307:

אבל לא מצינו . . . שיהיה דרך עיקרי זולת שלמות הידיעה האמיתית, שהיא עצם צורת האדם. אלא שאין השלמות בהן מעיון הפילוסופיא מפני ששכל האנושי אינו משיג האמת אבל ידיעת התורה שכל דבריה אמת ודאי א"א בטבע השלמות שמתחלף.

60 See Wachs, "Peraqim be-Mishnato Ha-Qabalit shel Ha-Rav Shlomo Elyashiv," 21–34; Hallamish, Rivlin, and Schuchat, *The Vilna Gaon and His Disciples*, 119–136, 124ff.

61 *Otzarot*, 2:309:

טבע הרעש לבלבל את הדעות והכעס מביא לידי טעות.

62 I am here, and in many similar contexts, translating the word *yirah* as "piety," or "reverence." Admittedly, this does somewhat elide a primary meaning of the word as "fear," that is, fear of divine punishment, which is central to the term's semantic range in rabbinic literature, especially when juxtaposed to "love." (See, for instance, the first two sections of Eliyahu de

Pietist studies, when well-founded, strengthen the soul and purify thoughts, halakhic studies strengthen the intellect and accustom it to diligence, the Wisdom of Truth [that is, Kabbalah] illumines every darkness and guides the intellect on the true contemplative path, and raises the soul to direct the heart to the ways of God . . . and from this emerges the telos of all, which is the cleaving [*devequt*] of the soul to the supernal light and the love of His great name and the fear of His Blessed exaltedness and greatness, and the recognition of the great value of Torah and mitzvot and the knowledge of the truth of faith and the special virtue of God's nation and their grace, and all things that are the essentials of perfection for those who *fear God and contemplate His Name, Blessed is He* [after Mal. 3:17].[63]

He then cites the emergence of the works of Luzzatto as a great help in these times, precisely because they unite all these seemingly disparate spiritual and intellectual traditions; he goes on to urge, presumably in light of the great controversies surrounding those texts, that they be studied in the context of pious Jewish literature as a whole. The goal is *devequt*, the ideal of *unio mystica*, the key value of Corodvero's teachings (relative to Luria's emphasis on *tiqqun*), which is central to Hasidism, and which in the Lithuanian tradition was achieved intellectually through Torah study and contemplation.[64]

Turning to the question of pedagogy in the yeshivot, he writes that pietistic study, when studied along with the words of the rabbis of the Talmud and scripture, is itself truly Torah study and thus not a deviation from the ideal of *Torah li-Shmah*. But, he says, regarding Mussar, "the rousing of the heart to storms is not study at all, for it is not beneficial to wisdom or knowledge, it is just a particular form of worship which one may need

---

Vidas's sixteenth-century classic *Reishit Hokhmah*.) That primal layer remains in Rav Kook's use of *yirah* but I believe his intention is broader than that. In the helpful terms laid out by Jacob Agus, the sense of *yirah* as fear captures "the virtue of obedience" and, in the broader inflection I am suggesting here, the "infinite dimension of piety"; see his *The Vision and the Way: An Interpretation of Jewish Ethics* (New York: Frederick Ungar, 1966), 194–220.

63 *Otzarot*, 2:310:

לימודי חכמת היראה כשהם במכונם מחזקים את הנפש ומטהרים את המחשבות, לימודי ההלכה מחזקים את השכל ומרגלים אותו בחריצות, חכמת האמת מאירה כל מחשך ומנהגת את השכל בדרך עיוני האמת, ומגדלת את הנפש להגיה לב בדרכי ה'. . . . ומזה יוצא תכלית הכל, שהוא דבקות הנשמה באור העליון ואהבת שמו הגדול ויראת רוממותו וגדלו ב"ה, והכרת גודל ערך מעלת התורה והמצוות, וידיעת אמיתת האמונה ויתרון עם ד" וסגולתם, וכל הדברים שהם עיקרי השלמות ליראי ד" וחושבי שמו ב"ה.

64 This is a very large subject. On the idea of *devequt* generally, and in particular for the ways in which it emerged in part via the philosophical tradition, including the Aristotelian, see Moshe Idel, *Kabbalah: New Perspectives* (New Haven: Yale University Press, 1988), 39–42, and Adam Afterman's book-length study, *Devequt* (Los Angeles: Cherub Press, 2011). For brief, illustrative references to *devequt* by the Gaon, see his commentary to Prov. 16:15, 27:19. See also Raphael Shuchat, "Yesodot Meshihiyyim u-Mistiyyim be-Limud Torah be-Veit Midrasho shel Ha-Gra: Hebet Hadash 'al Ha-Mashber be-Limud ba-Me'ah Ha-18 u-Musag Ha-Devequt," in Hallamish, Rivlin, and Schuchat, *The Vilna Gaon and His Disciples*, 155–172, 166–168; Alan Brill, "The Mystical Path of the Vilna Gaon," *Journal of Jewish Thought and Philosophy* 3 (1993): 131–151. Hayim of Volozhin proceeded from the Gaon in making his revolutionary argument that *devequt* was attainable by exoteric Torah study in itself; see his *Nefesh Ha-Hayim*, 4:10–11.

per his nature, and maybe not."[65] Salanter's efforts to found the study of piety as a broad-based discipline were ultimately unsuccessful, because he spoke only about soul-feeling and storm-spirit, emphasizing only the fear of divine punishment. Yet fear of punishment is insufficient for those whose minds are capable of plumbing the depths of the Talmud. Once the study of piety is well founded, which itself is impossible in the absence of Kabbalistic study, each individual will be able to find the proper sort of spiritual direction they require. And, he writes, this requires the writing of books that will meet that need;[66] his diarykeeping was, to say the least, a major step in that direction.

In general, Rav Kook's relationship to Mussar was richer and more complex than is generally thought. (And a number of his contemporaries engaged Mussar on their own terms as well.)[67] Smadar Sherlo has wisely pointed out a number of passages in Rav Kook's later writings which indicate a polemic, largely on pedagogic grounds, with the Mussar movement, especially as developed by Salanter's latter-day disciples.[68] Above all, in 1946 Zvi Yehudah Kook published a brief collection he had edited from his father's journals,

---

65 *Otzarot*, 2:311:

אבל ההסערה של הלב אינו בכלל לימוד כלל, שאינו מועיל עי׳׳ז [ל]חכמה וידיעה, רק היא עבודה מיוחדת, אפשר שיצטרך לאחד לפי טבעו ואפשר שלא תצטרך.

66 In a brief letter to Aderet from the summer of 1904, he tries to win him over to this way of thinking, and says he hopes to discuss with him the necessity of fixed and deep study of the moral (*Mussari*) part of Torah, which, he says, consists of the details of the mitzvot of *Hovot Ha-Levavot*. The letter is reprinted in *Otzarot*, 2:313.

67 Mordechai Eliasberg's son Yehonatan (?–1898) prefaced his own collection of Talmudic studies *Darkhei Horaah* (Vilna: Metz, 1884) with a treatise on Talmudic study as a contemplative-ethical practice entitled *Darkah shel Torah*. Rav Kook's younger contemporary Avraham Yeshayahu Karelitz (1878–1953), later known as Hazon Ish, in writings likely authored during his years in Eastern Europe prior to his emigration to Palestine in 1933, posthumously edited and published by Shlomo Greineman in 1954 under the title *Emunah u-Vitahon*, argued that Mussar's broader, legitimate goals can and must be realized only within the framework of classic Talmudic study and halakhic reasoning. Moreover, the broader project of Israel Meir Kagan (1838–1933), also known as Hafetz Hayim, seems at least to some extent to have been the articulation of the values of Mussar via halakhic literature and categories. Both Rav Kook and his father wrote glosses to Kagan's *Hafetz Hayim*.

68 Smadar Sherlo (Cherlow), "Pulmus Ha-Mussar Ha-Sheni: Beyn Shitat Ha-Mussar shel Ha-Rav Kook le-Shitato shel Rabbi Yisrael mi-Salant" (master's thesis, Touro College, Jerusalem, 1996). To the texts Sherlo brings in here, we may add *Da'at Cohen*, nos. 133–134. Amihai Kinnarati has recently gathered Rav Kook's various statements on the Mussar movement and his relationships with some of its figures, in "Yahas Ha-Reay"ah li-Tenu'at Ha-Mussar," in *Otzarot*, 7:496–517. In his magnum opus on the history of yeshivot, Mordechai Breuer touches on a possible relationship between the Mussar movement and Rav Kook's program of study in the yeshivot he went on to found, but concludes, not unreasonably on the face of it, that given Rav Kook's emphasis on study with joy, and the absence of formal Mussar study in Volozhin, such a connection is unlikely; see his *'Ohalei Torah: Ha-Yeshivah: Tavnitah ve-Toldotehah* (Jerusalem: Merkaz Shazar, 2003), 157–158. It should become clear from this and the subsequent chapter that this, admittedly tentative, conclusion of Breuer's, needs to be revised. Interestingly, here Neriah's hagiographic instincts and anecdotal information, which yield his regularly linking Rav Kook with the influence of Salanter, seem closer to the mark.

under the title *Mussar Avikha*, about which more presently.[69] Yet Rav Kook's engagement with Mussar, I argue, went far deeper than that. His aggadah commentary, the subject of our next chapter, was in several ways meant as a study text for Mussar. Rav Kook took seriously Mussar's emphasis on self-cultivation, but sought to anchor that undertaking in classic halakhic, philosophic, and Kabbalistic, texts. *'Eyn Ayah* was Rav Kook's public, pedagogic response to Mussar, while his private responses were in his notebooks.[70]

In his landmark study of Salanter, Immanuel Etkes has pointed out that one of Salanter's great departures from the earlier pietist traditions was his psychological emphasis, and concomitant devaluation of the cosmic processes which in the traditional literature were of a piece with the individual's own moral and spiritual progress.[71] Salanter nonetheless drew greatly on the rationalist tradition as well as on Maskilic ideas;[72] yet, as noted above, earlier, most of Salanter's successors became progressively antirationalist.[73] Rav Kook for his part undertook the personal, detailed psychological self-examination called for by Salanter, yet reintegrated it into broader Kabbalistic themes of cosmic *tiqqun*. Against the backdrop of Mussar introspection and Maskilic ideas of the uniqueness of the individual soul with all its complementary faculties, he applies Luzzatto's understanding of redemptive teleology to the inner life of the individual, namely, that only by bringing

---

69 I know of few sustained scholarly treatments of this treatise; one is Yehudah Bitti, "Beyn Mussar Avikha le-Mussar Ha-Qodesh" (master's thesis, Hebrew University, 1998), esp. 29–40. Bitti's fundamental insight—that this text rewards careful study its own right and as a window into a stage in Rav Kook's thinking that is qualitatively different from his better-known mature writings—is certainly correct. Bitti also correctly notes the primacy of the intellect and its mastery of the body and of the emotions, correlative to an ordered world, structured by the divine mind as the touchstone of the work. He characterizes this, at 37, as a "moderate rationalism." Bitti only briefly, but perceptively, touches on the Kabbalistic traces in the work, at 38–39; though I think he may be overstating, at 33, the reflection here of Rav Kook's later existentialist, subjectivist thinking.

An interesting set of close readings of select passages in *Mussar Avikha* which lead to distinctive halakhic conclusions is Hayim Yehudah Daum, "'Iyunei Halakhah be-'Mussar Avikha,'" in Neriah, Stern, and Gutel, *Berurim be-Hilkhot Ha-Re'ayah*, 479–487. Though Daum doesn't say this in so many words, it seems the tendency in the three cases he examines is to expand halakhic prohibitions to include intangibles of character and personal morality. The three cruxes he examines are the suggestion that a rabbinic enactment (*seyag*) will sometimes be promulgated not just as a prophylactic but also because if an act is itself objectionable, so too are all its causes and component parts (Rav Kook uses here explicitly philosophical language of cause and effect); that language conducive to sin is forbidden in itself; and that the prohibition of placing a stumbling block before another (*lifnei 'iver*) also attaches to actions and words that might somehow degrade another's morals in general.

70 Admittedly, *'Eyn Ayah* was not published in full until more than half a century after Rav Kook's death; yet, as we will see in the chapter devoted to it, he fully intended it to be published at the time.

71 Etkes, *Rabbi Yisrael Salanter ve-Rei'shitah shel Tenu'at Ha-Mussar*, 102–106.

72 For Salanter's use of Haskalah ideas see §7.2 of Bor, "Moral Education in the Age of Jewish Enlightenment."

73 See Ross, "Ha-Megamah Ha-Anti-Ratziyonalit be-Tenu'at Ha-Mussar," 145–162.

all the God-given elements of one's personality to expression will one do one's part in the great *tiqqun*.[74]

In his preface to the 1946 publication of *Mussar Avikha*, Zvi Yehudah Kook wrote that it was composed at a stroke sometime during the 1890s.[75] Owing to the recent publications of Rav Kook's notebooks in their original form (bearing in mind that we do not have access to the manuscripts themselves), we now know it was written during his time in Boisk, as, or not long after, the Mussar controversy came to a head in 1897.[76] Most of it, that is, as some passages are from elsewhere in Rav Kook's corpus, while others are in manuscripts not yet available to the reading public.

In the following I will try to reconstruct the discussion as it emerges from the notebooks themselves, without reference to Zvi Yehudah's editorial reworking (readers interested in those details are encouraged to consult the chart in the footnotes).[77]

This book is especially helpful as regards our understanding of what the word "Mussar"—the one term that appears more than any other in his corpus—meant for Rav Kook at this stage of his thinking. It is the dimension of religious life, of Torah and

---

74 For ideas of the soul in the writings of traditionalist Maskilim, see Bor, "Moral Education in the Age of Jewish Enlightenment," chapter 4. Rav Kook does not here, though, work with their categories of faculty psychology, that is, he accepts the various parts of the soul as given and does not try to map their relations with the external senses. (It's worth recalling Rav Kook's citation of Wessely's *Sefer Ha-Middot* in his *Midbar Shur*.)

75 In his brief preface to the first edition of 1946, Zvi Yehudah Kook says, "these sacred words of his were written roughly a jubilee ago, during the '*nunim*' [in the 1890s] nearly all in one consecutive period" (*kim'at be-pereq zeman ehad*). *Mussar Avikha* (Jerusalem: Ha-Yeshiva Ha-Merkazit Ha-'Olamit, 1946). *Mussar Avikha* was reprinted by Mossad Ha-Rav Kook in 1971 along with brief passages on the cultivation of character and piety entitled *Middot Ha-Re'ayah*. Our pagination follows the 1971 edition (hereinafter MA); we will not discuss the *Middot* passages, as they nearly all date from after Rav Kook's arrival in Palestine in 1904; see the indices to Rav Kook's *Shemonah Qevatzim*.

   Avikha is an acronym, that is, **AV**raham **Y**itzhak Ha-**Cohen**.

76 They are published in *Pinqasei Ha-Re'ayah*, vol. 3, ed. Ben-Zion Shapira and Zev Neuman (Jerusalem: Makhon Ha-Ratzyah Kook ztz"l, 2008).

   The sermons of *Midbar Shur* were composed between 1894 and 1896, that is, before the explosive Mussar controversies of 1897, and the word "Mussar" does not often appear in its pages, certainly not with the stunning frequency we will find here and in Rav Kook's aggadic commentary *'Eyn Ayah*. Yet the introduction to *Midbar Shur*, written in 1889, does contain implicit criticism of Mussar, that in the cultivation of piety "it is not fit to neglect the essential, which is understanding," MS, 6. The additions in square brackets are those of the editors of the printed edition.

   ובאמת חלק האגדה בעקרו ודאי מטרתו היא לרומם את רוח [האדם ואת] הכרתו המוסרית וכאשר ראיתי רבים מהספרים [העוסקים] בדרוש לא שמו להם קו להרחיב את גבול חכמת המוסר, רק לה[ציג] הדברים הטובים הידועים ע"פ ביאורים בדברי חז"ל ובמקרא[ות]. אמנם דבר זה גם הוא רצוי ומקובל כי בהרחבת הדברים י[כנסו] בלב להיות שמורים ופועלים על הטבע והמדות, אבל אין ראוי להזני[ח] העיקר, והוא הדעת.

77 I have prepared a chart laying out the passages from Rav Kook's relevant notebooks and their placement in Zvi Yehudah Kook's *Mussar Avikhah*. I have left blank those passages whose source has not yet been made known to the reading public.

mitzvot, relating to the cultivation of one's own personality in light of one's relation to God's Will, which is His revelation in the world.

Passage in *Mussar Avikha*, ed. Zvi Yehudah Kook	Source in *Pinqasim* 15 and 16
Preface	
1	
2	15:72, 15:66
3	
Chapter 1—The Mitzvah of Yirat Ha-Shem	
1	16:27
2	15:64
3	ibid.
4	
5	15:18
6	15:74
7	16:28
8	15:65
Chapter 2—The Organization of the Self's Energies (Kokhot Ha-Nefesh) in the Paths of Serving God	
1	
2	15:58
3	
4	
5	16:33
Chapter 3—Sifting the Attributes of One's Self	
1	
2	15:18
3	
4	15:18 [*sic*], 15:21
5	15:20
Chapter 4	
1	15:67
2	
3	15:17
4	

Lithuanian Kabbalah

It is time to introduce Lithuanian Kabbalah at some greater length. As always, one must be wary of catchall terms, and in speaking here of Lithuanian Kabbalah my intention is not to convey a single unified school, but a network of thinkers and ideas in contact with one another, sharing not only geography but tendencies, clusters of texts, ideas, and authorities, above all the Gaon of Vilna.[78]

One characteristic of Lithuanian Kabbalah, in keeping with Lithuanian rabbinical culture's scholastic tenor, was its pronounced emphasis on exegesis, and in its textual corpus, Luzzatto's works figure prominently along with the Gaon's own writings. Another characteristic was an overarchimg emphasis on the dimension of Mind. It is a Kabbalah of study, in terms of method, praxis, and teaching. In this it seems it may be better, or more precisely, referred to as Mitnagdic Kabbalah. Central to the Gaon's Kabbalistic legacy is his relationship to the teachings of Luria and, closer to him in time, Luzzatto; the latter's authority was not unquestioningly accepted by the Gaon, nor for that matter was Luria's. But it was Luria as understood by Luzzatto who framed the school's questions and its points of inquiry and departure.

Yosef Avivi, in his seminal 1993 work *Qabbalat Ha-Gra*, carefully detailed what he saw as consistent differences between the Gaon and Luria on a range of issues, which he traces to a cardinal disagreement as to the order of emanation, the intricate process by which the infinitude of God contracted and constrained itself to create and be present in the dimensions of space, time, and, eventually, human consciousness.[79]

In Avivi's painstaking reconstruction, the Gaon, basing himself on the plain sense of *Sefer Yetzirah*'s triumvirate of *sfar*, *sefer*, and *sippur*, unpacks the process of emanation as simple/hidden thought, manifest (unvocalized) writing and manifest speech. This triad is at work in the creation of the world (from the hidden divine thought underlying the Torah that is blueprint for the world and the divine utterances of Genesis 1) and in the revelation the Torah towards humanity (from the hidden divine thought to the written text to its transmission in divine speech).

The Zohar seems to suggest that within the world of emanation there are two kinds of union between the high sefirot of *Hokhmah* and *Binah*—in the higher configuration of *Arikh Anpin*. But of what sort?[80]

---

78 Jonatan Meir forcefully cautions against over-generalizing about Lithuanian Kabbalah, in "Ha-Kabbalah Ha-Eqleqtit shel Rabbi Shimon Zvi Horowitz (He'arah Biqortit 'al Ha-Munah 'Kabbalah Litait')," *Qabbalah* 31 (2014): 411–420.

79 Yosef Avivi, *Qabbalat Ha-Gra* (Jerusalem: Makhon Qerem Eliyahu, 1993).

80 This idea's roots are to be found in a seeming contradiction in the Zohar—discerned by Cordovero (*Pardes*, 8:13–14). The Zohar says there are two unions in the universe of emanations, the ceaseless one of *Abba* and *Ima*, and the occasional one of *Ze'ir* and *Nuqvah*, in which human agency plays a role (Zohar III, 4a; see also III, 290b). Yet in *Tiqqunei Zohar* we read that the union of *Hokhmah* and *Binah*, too, is dependent on the deeds of Israel (intro, 1b). (Cordovero's own suggested resolution was that the union of *Abba* and *Ima* ceases only at the crisis point of *hurban*, but not episodically at the root, as is the case with *Ze'ir* and *Nuqvah*.)

For Luria, one is an unending union of *Hokhmah* and *Binah*, providing all of existence with a necessary foundation; along with another, episodic union, dependent on
human action, and ultimately more important and complete—as it is that episodic union
that brings forth souls. The Gaon accepts that there are two kinds of union, one unending
and the other episodic, but reverses their order and importance. For the Gaon, the unending union of *Hokhmah* and *Binah* is the union that is superior and whole, since without
it there would be no life force and no souls at all. The episodic union, by contrast, which
yields angels and the power of speech in creatures, simply cannot exist without the union
unending.

These seemingly abstruse debates and distinctions make a profound difference for
basic understandings of human personhood and its relation to God. Since for the Gaon
it is the unending union that produces souls, the soul, *neshamah*, is moored to its divine
source, hidden, a gift that even its receiver cannot perceive, as it permeates one's existence. Only the other dimensions of personhood, spirit and self, *ruah* and *nefesh*, can be
disclosed and known. The soul is the mind, whose unceasing work sustains the life force.
Hence the utter primacy of Torah study, which sustains the supernal union of *Hohkmah*
and *Binah* and thus the universe—while the cosmic energies generated by performing
mitzvot are as episodic as the performances themselves. These questions of metaphysics and theology were, for Mitngdic and Hasidic Kabbalists both, tied to Luria's status
as an authority, and the related question of how one ought to study and understand his
teachings.

Eliezer Baumgarten has shown that Shneur Zalman of Liady, following Ramhal,
saw Luria's teachings as rooted in revelation and thus not susceptible to challenge. (And
the centrality for the Besht of "ascent of the soul" as a source of teachings, indicates he
thought the same.) This, for Shneur Zalman of Liady, was one of the essential divisions
between Hasidim on the one hand, and their opponents—and the latter's celebrated Vilna
master—on the other. For the Gaon, by contrast, Luria, great as he was, was ultimately,
ontologically, a sage, whose ideas can respectfully be disagreed with like any other. (This
in turn relates to the Gaon's self-understanding of not only himself, but of all post-Tal-
mudic scholars, as interpreters of earlier texts, and no more—bearing in mind that for
him the Zohar was itself a Mishnaic text—and helps explain why almost all the Gaon's
own works were commentaries.)[81] Baumgarten perceptively observes that the stakes here
go beyond Luria's status as such, and speak to the shape of the Kabbalistic ideal and the
source of the Kabbalist opposition: prophecy versus wisdom.

A crucial aspect of both the Gaon's and, a few decades earlier, Luzzatto's legacies was
their reading Luria's shockingly anthropomorphic language as *mashal*, parable, or metaphor. Reading Luria in this light was a defining feature for perhaps most, though not all,
Lithuanian Kabbalists.

---

81 Eliezer Baumgarten, "Samkhuto shel Ha-Ari eitzel Ha-Gra ve-Talmidav," *Da'at* 71 (Summer
2011): 53–74.

Baumgarten notes that though the Gaon takes the idea of Lurianic text as metaphor from Luzzatto, he wields it differently, to wit, Luzzatto saw himself as an interpreter of Luria and himself a revelatory generator of new metaphors, while the Gaon saw himself as an interpreter of the metaphors revealed to others, and in particular, of the pre-Lurianic Kabbalistic classics. Hence for the Gaon, Luria's authority is not that of a prophet, but of a sagacious interpreter of earlier revelations. While Luria may indeed, for the Gaon, have been vouchsafed revelation—those revelations were not authoritative, per se, and certainly not more so than teachings generated by the mind, through the act of interpretation. Thus one could accept that Luria had indeed been vouchsafed revelation, without necessarily agreeing that that revelation constituted a binding interpretation of the Zohar.

There were, to be sure, significant differences among leading nineteenth-century Kabbalists who saw themselves as the Gaon's disciples.[82] Menahem Mendel of Shklov (d. 1827) and his own student Yizhak Isaac Haver Wildman (1789–1853) sought to harmonize disagreements between Luria and the Gaon each in their way. Menahem Mendel emphasized the nonsemantic aspects of the Torah text (letters, vocalizations, etc.) detached from its nomistic freight. His form of interpretation is distinctly theurgic and experiential (even if, as Baumgarten points out, the experience is not ecstatic *devekut*, but in Lithuanian fashion, Torah study). He drew on sources other than the Gaon, such as Emanuel Hai Ricci and Ashkenazic traditions of commentary on Luria, especially after his migration to Palestine in 1808. By contrast, Isaac Haver emphasized Torah as idea and its cerebral study. He read Luria's system as a complex revelation of various facets of Torah, in particular the Written Torah, which he identifies with *Ze'ir Anpin* (such that the "shattering of the vessels" is none other than the Fall of Torah) and was indebted to Yisrael Saruq's doctrine of the supernal universe of *malbush* (garment), about which more below. Haver also follows Luzzatto in seeing Luria's complex doctrine of emanations as providing a sacred historiosophy. Haver, Baumgarten suggests, responding as he was to the nineteenth century's multiple onslaughts on tradition, was less concerned than his teacher Menachem Mendel had been with harmonizing Luria and the Gaon, seeing them both as chapters in the transmission of the tradition, a tradition which needs to be both preserved in its entirely and subject to disciplined study, which is, after all, the heart of Torah and summit of the religious life, and superior to prophecy, in matters of theology as it is in halakhah.[83]

---

82   Hallamish, Rivlin, and Schuchat, *The Vilna Gaon and His Disciples*, 119–136.

83   Eliezer Baumgarten, "Ha-Kabbalah be-Hug Talmidei Ha-Gra" (PhD diss., Ben-Gurion University, 2010). For Haver's influence on Rav Kook's later writings, see Elhanan Shilo, "Hashpa'ato shel Rabbi Yitzhak Haver 'al Parshanuto shel Ha-Rav Kook le-Qabbalah," *Da'at* 79–80 (2005): 95–117. Shilo has also written on Haver's points of disagreement with Luzzatto—see his "Ma'amad Ha-'Olam lifnei Hithavut 'Am Yisrael: Beyn Ha-Ramhal le-Rabbi Yitzhak Isaac Haver," *Qabbalah* 37 (2017): 251–270.

A different leading latter-day disciple, whom we have already met, was Shlomo Elyashiv (1841–1926). [84] In a number of ways, Baumgarten suggests, Elyashiv was a school all his own, not least in his demurral from the allegoric readings of Luzzatto's teachings that characterized the Gaon's school (though he did not criticize Luzzatto himself). For Elyashiv, metaphor was the necessary tool for understanding the world of emanation, but not the lower four worlds, which make up the subject matter of "wisdom of truth," *hokhmat ha-emet.*

Key to Luzzatto's innovation was seeing human history as the arena for the working out of the intradivine processes limned by the Kabbalah. But how should this be worked out? Haver, alone among the Gaon's disciples, made extensive use of Luzzatto's two forms of Providence, training focus on practical action in this world, which would bring about Luzzatto's understanding of *tiqqun* as the reparation, rectification of all history. Elyashiv, by contrast, focused on theurgic action in worlds up above. For Elyashiv the allegorical dimension of Luria applies only to the truly inaccessible world of emanation, and he subscribed to the idea of divine contraction in its literal sense, *tzimtzum ki-feshuto,* on which he had strong disagreement with Pinhas Lintop.

The Gaon's Kabbalistic legacy as interpreted by these various disciples, and their respective emphases on the workings of the mind and of history, set the terms for Rav Kook's own explorations in his notebooks (even if, at this stage at least, the Gaon's Messianic ideas did not). We will look at two notebooks from this period, published in recent years as *Pinqasim* 15 and 16, from which Zvi Yehudah Kook nearly a half century later culled much, though not all, of *Mussar Avikha.* As noted above, we will here not follow Zvi Yehudah's reorganization, skillful though it is, but rather trace the developmental arc of his ideas on the axis of time.

The psychologization of Kabbalistic terminology is usually thought of as a feature of Hasidic thought, and indeed we have seen Rav Kook say as much in his essay on interiority. Yet in this notebook we will see his using Lithuanian Kabbalah as a means of mapping the individual soul, without reference to Hasidic doctrines or Hasidism's valorization of prayer and ecstasy, but with a Litvak's emphasis on mind.

Pinqas 15 is preoccupied with several themes: a) the place of the mind in perfecting character and realizing God's will; b) Israel's vocation in the world; c) the place of feelings in the religious life; d) the meaning of *yirat shamayim,* that is, reverence, or piety; and e) the relations of body and soul.[85]

---

84 See Eliezer Baumgarten, "Historiyah ve-Historiosophia be-Mishnato shel Rav Shlomo Elyashiv" (master's thesis, Ben-Gurion University, 2006), as well as the work of Wachs cited earlier. A very helpful survey is Joey Rosenfeld, "A Tribute to Rav Shlomo Elyashiv, Author of Leshem Shevo v-Achloma: On his Ninetieth Yahrzeit," *The Seforim Blog* (Blog), last modified March 10, 2016, http://seforim.blogspot.com/2016/03/a-tribute-to-rav-shlomo-elyashiv-author.html.

85 It is printed in Ben-Zion Shapira and Zev Neuman, eds., Pinqasei Ha-*Re'ayah*, vol. 3 (Jerusalem: Makhon Ha-Ratzyah Kook ztz"l, 2011), and page numbers follow that edition.

Taken together, we see here a meeting of Lithuanian Kabbalah, preoccupations of the Mussar movement, and concerns arising in relation to currents working through Jewish Eastern Europe—universalism and nationalism. Of course, the term "Mussar" had a central place well before Salanter, to say the very least—and it is precisely the multiple resonances of the term Mussar that bridge the concern for personal development of the Mussar movement, and the historiosophy of Luzzatto in Rav Kook's burgeoning thought.[86]

Pinqas 15: The Self and *Tiqqun*

The second, lengthy entry in *Pinqas* 15 deserves close inspection, not least for its high-lighting his shared preoccupations with Mussar and Lithuanian Kabbalah—the relation-ships between the divine mind as revealed in and through Torah, its workings on human consciousness and thus, eventually, on human character.[87] *Pinqas* 15:2 takes up the rela-tion between mind and character (*sekhel* and *middot*); the mind vivifies traits, "but sins stop up the heart, so that the light of understanding in the brain not enter the heart, and this necessarily ruins characteristics."[88] The crucial slippages occur between exultant moments of enlivened understanding and those moments when the mind is called upon to direct the person, by which time the moment of understanding is but a memory.[89] The possibility of this slippage is rooted in the primeval Fall of Adam, which was the Fall of Mind. Prelapsarian Adam's intellect was continually flowing and shining—but when the serpent tempted him into imagining evil, the flow was stopped, mind turned into recol-lection, memory was born and sin made possible. The present time, evil having taken root in the human person—and seemingly echoing both the Gaon's view that the soul created by unending union must necessarily be inaccessible, and Haver's understanding the Fall in Eden as the Fall of Torah—a ceaseless flow of light would be fatal, and so the episodic flowing of *sekhel* is a divine grace.[90]

Now, human perfection is the union of Mind and Will.[91] Torah study draws down the light which is *or 'atzmi*, a self-sufficient light, while memory is but the matter of *Hokhmah* without its form, and is by its own terms incapable of giving life; its necessity is a result

---

86 Here I differ respectfully with the late Eitam Henkin's suggestion that my focus on the Mussar movement is overstated, as it is both unnecessary to explain the frequent use of the term in the texts published as *Mussar Avikha*, and is also a staple of Luzzatto's teachings. See his "Li-Nevukhei Ha-Dor shel Ha-Re'ayah Kook: Mavo' le-Hibur she-lo Hushlam," *'Aqdamot* 25 (2010): 171–188. Henkin's observation is well-taken, and yet the ways in which *Mussar* figures in relation to Rav Kook's exploration of the dynamics of the inner life seems to me very much of a piece with the Mussar movement and its concerns.

87 Shapira and Neuman, *Pinqasei Ha-Re'ayah*, 13–35. It also appears in *Meorot Ha-Re'ayah*, *Shavuot* (Jerusalem: Makhon Ha-Ratzyah, 1994), 263

88 Shapira and Neuman, *Pinqasei Ha-Re'ayah*, 16.

89 Ibid., 19.

90 Ibid., 20.

91 Ibid., 21.

of Adam's sin, prior to which the mind and the body were one. [92] The degree of effort one puts into Torah study and mitzvot itself determines how much light memory casts; memory comes from faith; and it is this light of Torah that accounts for the new, vivified spirit one experiences at times.[93] The Gaon had written that in this world we can't know our own souls, only our spirit and divinely given self (*ruah* and *nefesh*). Rav Kook writes that to the extent we can perceive our selves, we can only do so dimly.[94] But we can know that our inability to see our souls' true luminosity is because of the occluding matter that is the garment of the soul

Turning these insights to the ends of Mussar, Rav Kook continues that the Torah, its general character aside, has within it a particular holiness (*qedushah pratit*), that is aimed at each individual and all the powers of one's own self, from which we divine the *hanhagah* of all our energies. The Torah itself does not fluctuate with human fluctuation, since it is, he says, echoing the terminology of Maharal, "set apart," *nivdelet*. Rather—in keeping with the language of *malbushim*—one adorns oneself with the Torah it and it fits the human who takes it on.[95]

He seems here to be working with the ideas of Israel Saruq (who flourished at the turn of the seventeeth centry and is credited with bringing Luria's ideas to Europe from Palestine) which were current in the circles of Lithuanian Kabbalah.[96] In Saruq's teaching, between the originary contraction/emanation of *tzimtzum* and the emergence of the Universe of *Adam Qadmon*, Primordial Man, is an intervening Universe, a Primordial Torah, comprised of 231 variations on the first two letters of the Hebrew alphabet (per the 231 gates mentioned in *Sefer Yetzirah*), known as *malbush*, garment; it is this primordial Torah itself that sets in motion the contraction and emanation yielding *Adam Qadmon*. The Torah is thus the very stuff of emanation—hence, the theological relevance of Saruq's ideas for the ethos of Torah study at the heart of Lithuanian Kabbalah.

With these ideas in hand, Rav Kook explores the difference between Wisdom and Knowledge, *Hokhmah* and *Da'at*; or, in the Gaon's terms, between Torah itself at its point of emanation/revelation, the divine made manifest in the triad of prophecy, Torah, and mitzvot and *mohin,* consciousness, ushering in the power of speech—and making Torah manifest in human experience.[97] Wisdom, he says, is understanding something and willingly being drawn to it; while knowledge is to cleave to that object with all one's abilities

---

92 Ibid., 22–24.

93 Ibid., 27.

94 Ibid., 28. On the soul's hiddenness in the Gaon's teachings, see Avivi, *Qabbalat Ha-GRA*, 43.

95 While the term *nivdelet* appears in the Hebrew translations of *Kuzari* (part 5) and Maimonides's *Guide* (for instance, 2:35 and 39 as regards Moses's prophecy), as well as Luzzatto (for example, *Derekh Ha-Shem* 1:5, 3:1), by far its most ubiquitous appearance as a central idea, and certainly regarding the Torah, is in the works of Maharal.

96 See Moshe Idel, "Beyn Kabbalat Yerushalayim le-Kabbalat Rabbi Yisrael Saruq," *Shalem* 6 (1992): 165–173. Idel argues that Saruq's ideas are not, as was thought, neoplatonic, but rather derive from a synthesis of Lurianic ideas with ideas of the created *kavod* derived from Hasidei Ashkenaz and elements of magical traditions.

97 See Avivi, *Qabbalat Ha-Gra*, 87.

other than the understanding, and with one's will.[98] With telling Mitnagdic caution, he says one must not for the sake of knowledge take the risk of cleaving to evil, as this was the seduction of the serpent in the Garden, and eating from the Tree of Knowledge, because then *devekut* was towards both good and bad.[99]

While this caution might reasonably tend towards a rejection of the body and its works, he proceeds instead to a meditation on the body and its functions, which he positively affirms, to the extent to which they are disciplined by Torah.

Take, for instance, eating. *Hokhmah*, Wisdom, tells us we need food to live. Consciousness, *Da'at*, tells us it's enjoyable, and so we do too much of it. Thus what should be a revitalization of ourselves, a *tiqqun*, becomes their ruination, *qilqul*—not because the material world is bad in itself, but because we take in a greater light of enjoyment, a pleasure of consciousness, than the vessel, that is, matter, can bear and so the vessel shatters.[100] The Lurianc terminology here is unmistakable—and recalls the Gaon's teachings that the primordial shattering was due to a deficiency of *mohin*.[101] (This, in halakhic terms, he says, is then the deep reason for the *asher yatzar* blessing on bodily functions, in that God allows material filth, *zuhama*, to diffuse through the human body and be expelled, so that one can gradually be repaired, as every sin can only gradually be repaired, "as it depends on the light clinging to the vessel and being well tied to it.")[102]

This idea of gradual improvement reappears further on in this journal, as he writes:

> [O]ne ought not to seek from any act, thought, or object of learning more elevation and holiness than one's own preparation makes possible.[103] Torah, mitzvot, and prayer are themselves a form of perfection. But one who seeks immediate spiritual gratification in prayer, or great intellectual insights and Torah knowledge all the time, and great illumination in every good deed, robs himself of joy and good-heartedness in his labor and will find many obstacles on the road to perfection.[104]

The Israelite soul, he writes, is particularly suited for a rushing influx of holy spirit.

> There is power in the sanctity of the Israelite soul in particular to merit the holy spirit, and thus grasp clear, true things, without onerous searching and (truth) emerging drop by drop.
> . . . But as long as one is empty of Torah, *like me, in my sinfulness* [emphasis added—Y. M.],

---

98 Interestingly, he cites the verse from Prov. 5:19, on delirious love of wisdom, which figures so prominently in Maimonides's depiction of the summit of the love of God in his *Code—Hilkhot Teshuvah* 10:3, at *Pinqas* 30.

99 Ibid., 30.

100 Ibid., 31.

101 Avivi, *Qabbalat Ha-Gra*, 88.

102 *Pinqas* 15, 32–33. The word *zuhama* brings an inescapable allusion to the serpent who, in midrashic tradition, implanted his filth into Eve, BT Shabbat 146a.

103 MA, 81. *Pinqas* 15:17, 51:

הפרט הוא, שלא יבקש משום מעשה ושום לימוד ושום מחשבה שיצטיירו בלבו ציורי מעלה וקודש יותר ממה שהוכן בו מקודם לזה.

104 MA, 81–82. *Pinqas* 15, ibid.

then this desire to think thoughts from the depth of the heart requires great watchfulness, for the vessels of the heart and intellect are not in a sufficient state of repair such that that which emerges from them is of the essence of Torah.[105]

The different facets of religious life speak to the different facets of *tiqqun*. What are the relative merits and demands of prayer, Torah study and acts of kindness (the celebrated three pillars of existence of Mishnah Avot 1:2)? Hasidism had, from early on, called into question the primacy accorded to Torah study over prayer in the traditional rabbinic hierarchy of values, a primacy which Mitnagdism championed and took to new heights.[106] The relationship of both prayer and study to concrete deeds was itself a major subject of Mussar literature from *Hovot Ha-Levavot* onwards. (It is perhaps tempting—if ultimately unverifiable—to wonder if in discussing "acts of kindness" Rav Kook had in mind the burgeoning social and political activism of his time. It stands to reason that his concern with integrating the three reflects his living in a more complex religious milieu than that of the yeshivot.) Rav Kook here tries to squares these circles via a novel reading of the Book of Proverbs' injunction (Prov. 3:6) to "Know Him with all your ways," that is, when you study, *study*; when you pray, *pray*; when doing kindness, focus on the *good of the other*.[107] This is no Polonius-like nostrum but a reflection of the basic structure of the universe, created by God's self-contraction the stately procession of *tiqqun*:

> The "with" of the verse means "within," that in the very paths themselves he will come to know God. That is why this verse is *a small teaching*,[108] for the commandment therein isn't greatness and expansion of wisdom and thought, to the contrary, contraction *tzimtzum* onto just the one thing with which one is occupied, on which all of Torah necessarily depends, for then everything will be done in proper measure, and God's presence be manifest to the fullest . . . and one should understand this [*ve-havein*].[109]

At 15:67 he redefines *heshbon ha-nefesh*, literally "soul reckoning," the practice of introspection that was a staple of Mussar, as an intellectual negotiation over all the affairs of one's soul and the obligation of divine service, not a matter of imagination but a lucid, discriminating act of intellect, which, like all wisdom, requires a base of knowledge.[110]

---

105 MA, 82. *Pinqas* 15, ibid.:

יש בכח קדושת נשמת האדם הישראלי ביחוד לזכות למעלת רוח-הקדש . . . שישכיל דברי אמת ברורים בלא טורח חיפוש הקדמות ויציאת טיפין טיפין . . . אבל כל-זמן שהאדם ריק מהתורה, כערכי בעוה"ר, אז כשהתשוקה הזאת מתעוררת לחשוב מחשבות מעומק הלב צריך שמירה יתרה, שעדיין אין כלי הלב והשכל מתוקנים כ"כ עד שיהיו הדברים היוצאים מהם גופי תורה.

106 See generally, Nadler, *The Faith of the Mithnagdim*, 50–77.

107 MA, 39, 15:58, 103–104.

108 He is referring here to BT Berakhot 63a, which understands that verse from Proverbs as "a small teaching on which the entire body of Torah depends."

109 *Pinqas* 15:58, 104.

110 MA, 77:

מהות חשבון הנפש היא שיהי' האדם נושא-ונותן בשכל על כל עניני נפשו וחיוב עבודתו לאלהים ית'. אבל ראוי שלא לשכח כי אין החשבון מענין המדמה אלא ענין שכלי צרוף ומבורר, וכמו שבכל חכמה וידיעה שבעולם אי

Proceeding without proper study of the words of the sages and good sense leads to despair.[111]

This idea that every form of the religious life has its own integrity and its rootedness in metaphysics yields, in turn, a rich notion of the self. He says we see in nature that everything seeks to realize itself, and so one who has some special strength or talent must realize it as best one can, and if not, greatly damages oneself. Thus each must seek out their own special strengths in order to develop them to the full, and failing to do so disturbs the order of things in God's world.[112] One cannot escape the impression that Rav Kook is here working to understand and in some way justify himself.[113] In this and the coming chapter we will increasingly see how his struggle to accept the fact that he was not a standard Lithuanian Talmudist, and indeed that the study of aggadah spoke more deeply to him than the halakhah, was crucial to his articulation of this kind of individualism.

Again, and crucially, this evolving view of the place of selfhood in religious life is rooted in the metaphysics of Lithuanian Kabbalah. Expressly taking up the well-known distinction between outer and inner light and as discussed by Issac Haver, he says the former is the teleological perspective, while the former is the good will in action in each individuum. The former is the Torah, the latter is the individual cultivation of virtue—which requires that one *feel* divine service, most keenly in prayer.[114]

A little further on he addresses a defining tension between the Mitnagdic emphasis on study and the intellect, and Hasidism's emphasis on prayer. One cannot attain flourishing, perfection, *shlemut*, he says, without exercising the mind in understanding the truths of metaphysics and theology and their relation to Israel; at the same time the reason why prayer must be the focal point of one's energies is that it serves as a kind of prism through which one observes one's own approximations of perfection—of thought and feeling both.[115]

What is the goal of this knowledge, this self-understanding? Piety, which, properly understood, synthesizes will and intellect, bringing us into alignment with the divine mind, which is the fount of all actions:

אפשר לישא וליתן בה כי-אם כשתהי' לו מתחילה ידיעה מבוררת ברוב פינותי' העיקריות. . . .

111 MA, 78.

112 MA, 83. *Pinqas* 15:67, 113–114:

זה נראה בטבע המציאות, שכל כח שנמצא בכל דבר וטבעו לפעול הוא פועל בהכרח, וכיון שהוא פועל אם יזדמנו לו מצבים שפעולתו תהי' מסודרת אל השלמות ותכלית הנרצה יפעל טוב, ואם לא יתנהג כפי הסדר והתכלית יפעול הריסות ורע ע"י תנועתו . . . לכן יש ללמוד, שכל מי שיש בו איזה כח מיוחד צריך להוציאו לשלמותו כפי האפשר לו, ואם לאו הרי לא די שאינו מוציא ממנו תועלת אלא הוא פועל בלבול סדרים והפסדים גדולים בכל דרכי הנהגתו. . . .

113 As has become clear by now, this work of self-understanding was central to his ideas' development.

114 *Pinqas* 15:70, 119.

115 MA, 17–19, *Pinqas* 15:72. The subjects one must penetrate are the respective truths of faith as a category, of God's existence, of the written and oral Torah, of Kabbalah's necessary existence and study and its manifold benefits, and the greatness of the human soul in general and of Israel and its land and redemption.

Every act of piety . . . all its deeds and guidances [*hanhagot*] are clothed in the structures of supreme wisdom flowing downward from Him. . . . Thus every good act as defined by Torah, draws down upon the doer, by virtue of his good choice and consenting intellect, a flow of *devequt* from the treasury of life and goodness. This is because one's mind is thus aligned with the mind that radiates downward from Him so that one may bask in the light of His countenance, and thus one is complete and perfect in oneself. . . . And should he ruin his ways he draws down on himself a form that is precisely the opposite of the perfect supreme wisdom . . . and he will become embittered, for everything is painful when it is reversed.[116]

The religious life is situated in a universe through which course the positive energy of the divine intellect and its dialectical opposites. The pious life is that which aligns itself with, and draws life-giving intellect from, the former, and sin is that which aligns itself with, and allows itself to be shaped by, the latter.

Of particular interest here is the word he uses for "practices"—*hanhagot*. In the Hasidic tradition, it means individualized spiritual practices, and that is its primary meaning here.[117] Yet it is also, of course, a key term for Luzzatto, denoting the working of Providence whereby the shattered body of God is reconstituted in the great *tiqqun*, by human action. His use of this term with its multiple resonances further highlights that the individual is to achieve his own divinely ordained perfection, his alignment with the great divine mind, as part of the process of *tiqqun*.

The great emphasis on Mind recalls the Maimonidean engagement, and the rationalistic thrust, that we have seen in some of Rav Kook's earlier writings. Yet the *study* of piety here is different from the analytic study of Talmud or the intellectual exertions of philosophy; it is very much an intellectual-spiritual practice of the sort identified by Pierre Hadot, a transformative engagement of one's mental powers.[118] While for Maimonides the summit of the spiritual practice was reaching the final limit of one's intellectual abilities and finding equanimity at that stopping point,[119] for Rav Kook, emerging from the Kabbalistic tradition, the final end of intellectual exertion is the mix of self-realization and self-dissolution that is *devequt*. But again this exertion is not merely cerebral. Earlier, in discussing his essay of this period on the need for interiority in Torah study, I noted his use of the term *devequt* in the intellectual sense that characterized mainstream Lithuanian

---

116 MA, 28, *Pinqas* 15:74:

כל פעולה . . . וכל מעשי' והנהגתה מלובשים בסדרי החכמה העליונה המושפעת ממנו ית' . . . ע"כ כל פעל שהוא טוב לפי התורה ממשיך על העושה אותו, בבחירתו הטובה ושכלו המסכים לזה, משך דבקות מאוצר החיים והטוב. כי ימצא שכלו מוטבע באופן שוה עם השכל המושפע ממנו ית' ליהנות ממאור פניו ית', ונמצא שלם הוא בעצמו . . . ואם קלקל דרכיו הנה המשיך על עצמו צורה מוטבעת היפך החכמה העליונה השלמה . . . וגם יהי' לו למורת רוח מאד, כי כל דבר מצטער בהפכו.

117 See Zev Gries, *Sifrut Ha-Hanhagot: Toldotehah u-Meqomah be-Hayei Hasidei Rabbi Yisrael Ba'al Shem Tov* (Jerusalem: Mossad Bialik, 1989).

118 I have already discussed Hadot and his relevance for our inquiry in the introduction.

119 See, for this characterization, Stern, "Maimonides on the Growth of Knowledge and the Limitations of the Intellect," 143–191, in particular part 4, and Levy and Rashed, "Maimonides' Epistemology," 105–133, 127–129.

teachings. Here he is adding another dimension, namely action—*devequt* is still a union with the divine mind, but one attained via the performance of actions which reflect and give embodiment to that divine mind. As his reflections proceed, he will further try to work out the respective relations among action, study and the road to *unio mystica* preferred by Hasidism, prayer.[120]

Pinqas 16—Kabbalah and Self-Understanding

In turning to the next journal of this period, we see its chief drama is a dual integration of the metaphyiscs of Lithuanian Kabbalah—into the concrete practices of rabbinic culture and his own self-understanding.

By way of preface he offers a series of rhymed epigrams, addressed to an imagined reader, but also, one senses, to himself. They begin with a didactic tone—"Rejoice my soul, be happy, rejoice / Just don't forget the One who guards your Soul"—and so on for a number of lines.[121] But as it proceeds we get a glimpse of his sense of the workings of his own mind:

> Always the mind
> working and splitting
> with no rest
> its light shines.
> The seer of deceptions
> and superficial conversations
> the precious thing
> he crushingly enslaves
> for his destiny
> yea, his object
> and all his success
> is his wisdom.[122]

And then, a deeper wellspring of this feverish mental activity:

> With thought-crafted wisdom
> he'll imprison sadness
> and like scorching fire

---

120 He does not, though, in this work have recourse to the Hasidic idea of *'avodah be-gashmiyut*—a consistent absence.

121 *Pinqas* 16, 131:

שיש נפשי גילי ושמחי / רק נוצר נשמתך אל תשכחי.

122 Ibid., 131–132:

תמיד המח / עובד ופולח / באפס מנוח / אורו זורח. / חוזה מהתלות / ושיחות נקלות / יקר הערך / יעביד בפרך /

כי תעודתו / אף מטרתו / וכל הצלחתו / היא חכמתו.

despair is gone.[123]

And so:

> Engrave in the book
> a word of law set in stone
> think and go deep
> to elucidate and untangle
> your eyes shining
> your fountains gushing.[124]

We have come a long way from the writerly self-confidence with which he'd announced the launch of *'Ittur Sofrim* roughly a decade before. He still burns to write, though is by now more self-conscious, both of the temptations of writerly myopia and of the mounting force of his own ideas.

And many of those ideas are explicitly metaphysical, and Kabbalistic; at the notebook's beginning we find an exploration of whether or not *Eyn Sof* and *Keter* are the same. This seemingly recondite question is deeply consequential, for at stake is whether or not infinity itself is even a little present in the world that humans can know.

Rav Kook follows Cordovero's view, that *Eyn Sof* and *Keter* are not the same—which he understands in terms of Luzzatto's view that all we can possibly know of God is His Will, and what He wills us to see from *Keter* on down; in other words, God set the terms, the frameworks of human consciousness and understanding, by His own untrammeled Will. *Eyn Sof*, though, God's Endless Infinitude, is utterly unconstrained, pure potentiality, free even of the idea of necessity. And so it cannot be identical to *Keter*, which, exalted as it is, is still trammeled up in creation. [125]

This meditation ends with an apologia: "And in His mercies may he atone for my allowing my mouth to burst into discourse, for my soul desires the interiority of Torah (after BT Yevamot 63b), and in His kindnesses may He not shade from me a word of truth, and enable me to be enlightened with His truth."[126]

Earlier, in *Metziot Qatan*, we saw him reflect on his desire to study aggadah, contra the conventions of Lithuanian rabbinic culture. Here, his internal struggle to give himself permission not only to study but to innovate in Kabbalah is abundantly clear. As the notebook continues, he theorizes this struggle in terms of Kabbalistic teachings, in particular, the Lurianic *mayin nuqvin*, literally "feminine waters," the principle of feminine creativity, from below. In the Kabbalah's profoundly essentialist view of gender, womanhood is,

---

123 Ibid.:

בחכמת מחשבת / יכלא עצבת / וכאש צורבת / בטלה מדאבת.

124 Ibid., 132:

בספר חקק/ דבר חק / חשב והעמק / לברר ולפרק / יאירו עיניך / ויפוצו מעינותיך.

125 *Pinqas* 16:2, 134–135.

126 Ibid., 135:

וברחמיו יכפר על התירי פי לפצות שיח, כי פנימיות נפשי חשקה בתורה, ובחסדיו אל יצל מפי דבר אמת, ויזכני להשכיל באמיתו.

fundamentally, openness and receptivity, and feminine creativity is the desire to receive—an arousal of desire which, when met by the male principle of transmission, brings forth life.[127] Just as the feminine supernal principle of *nuqva*, which is to say an emptiness that is to be filled, and the source of failures and disappointments, indeed rises to the level of *Eyn Sof* and with that union beomes God's garland in the world, so too does spiritual progress unfold in a human self:

> And so whatever seeks to become more whole, feels within a lack before fulfillment, and that is the place of self-perfection. How so? One who is ready to study *halakhot* will find in himself a sense of lack of *halakhot* . . . and so find a sense of desire in himself. One who is ready for the interiority of Torah will find his soul desirous of it and if he doesn't fulfill it, will find a sense of lack, such that his virtues cannot flourish without it. . . . We find, then, that so deep the lack, so great the elevation in its fulfillment. And this absence, preventing fulfillment, is the principle of *nuqva* in one's self, and when he fills it, *becomes a cornerstone* [after Ps. 118:22], and that [precisely—Y. M.] for its descent to the dust, its ascent is to the stars.[128]

Following on from the conjugal metaphors, he theorizes different kinds of marital unions and the kinds of creativity they bring. The rabbis referred to marriage as both finding one's soul mate, and also as no less taxing a miracle than parting the Red Sea; the former, one passage says, refers to one's first marriage, the latter to one's second (BT Sotah 2a). Sometimes, Rav Kook says, our natural talents will abandon us, and this inability to receive, a form of departure of the Shekhinah, is the metaphysical-psychological correlative of the death of one's first wife, at which, as the Talmud says, one's thoughtfulness falls away (BT Sanhedrin 22a). All is not lost, he says, but one's second conjugal union, so to

---

127 See, for example, Ramhal, *Qalah Pithei Hokhmah* §138.

128 *Pinqas* 16:3:

כשם שבחינת נוק' מושרש בה ענין הקלקולים, בחי' ב"ן, כמו כן בנפש האדם. וכשם דסלקא עד א"ס, עטרת בעלה בעולמו, כמ"כ באדם. ביאור זה, הנה חז"ל אמרו, ע"פ כ"א בתורת ד' חפצו לעולם ילמד אדם ממה שלבו חפץ. והנה, כ"ד שצריך להשתלם, יש בו הרגשת חסרון קודם שישתלם, והוא מקום להההשתלמות. כיצד, מי שמוכן ללמוד הלכות, ימצא בנפשו ענין חסירה להלכות, וכשלא ישלים זה, יסבבו לו חסרון בהנהגתו ובדרכי יראתו, וימצא ג"כ תשוקה לזה בטבע נפשו. ומי שמוכן לפנימיות התורה, ימצא בנפשו חשק לזה, ואם לא ישלים, ימצא חסרון, שלא יוכלו מדותיו להשתלם בלא זה, ולא תוכל יראתו להתכונן עמו למה שמוכן . . . החסרון הזה בעצמו הוא הכנתו להההשתלמה. נמצא, שכפי עומק החסרון כה תגדל המעלה בהשלמה. והחסרון במניעת ההשלמה היא בחי' נוקבא שבנפשו, וכשממלאה, היתה לראש פנה, ובזמן שהם יורדים עד עפר, לכן עלייתם עד לכוכבים . . . והנה ע"פ רוב, הטבע הראשונה היא נקודת האמת הישרה, וזו היא אשתו הראשונה וכ"א יכול ע"י הרגל לשנות תשוקתו וטבעו, אבל לא יצליח בשינוי שבא ע"י ההרגל כמו שהי' מצליח בהיותו מתנהג כפי עצם תכונתו . . . רק אם מוצא טבעו חושק לעשות עיקר מחכמות חיצוניות, אות הוא ששם השי"ת זה בטבעו כדי לבטל טבעו . . . וזהו מציאת ערות דבר שמצוה לגרשה . . . אך לפעמים ע"פ ההשגחה העליונה מסתלק ממנו כשרון הטבעו שלו, והוא שמסולק ממנו החסרון וההכנה לקבל, ובגדר סילוק השכינה, וזוהי מיתת אשתו הראשונה, שפסיעותיו מקוצרות ולא יעלה כ"כ בקל ממדרגה למדרגה, ועצתו נופלת (ע' סנהדרין כא) . . . וכשכבר אין עזרת טבעו בו, לפעמים לא יצליח בעצה וצריך רחמים רבים, ועולם חשך בעדו, בכלל אין השגתו בהירה כ"כ, וכאילו נחרב ביהמ"ק בימיו . . . אבל זיווג שני אינו בטבע ותלוי רק ע"פ מעשה, כי אם יזכך מעשיו, ד' יתן חכמה מפיו לחכימין, ובכלל עומד ע"פ נס ולא בחק הטבע, והיינו קשה לזווגן כקי"ס. (סוטה ב.)

speak, does not come about naturally, only through one's own deeds and exertions; and that is why it is as hard as parting the Red Sea—a miracle.[129]

In other words, achieving *shlemut* takes a complex balancing act between recognizing one's own ontological emptiness and a commitment to develop oneself with all the work that entails. And much of this notebook discusses religious exertions of different kinds, regularly in Kabbalistic terms.[130] And he expressly contends with the emotionalized study practices of the Mussar movement. The arousal of the emotions is a striking—but deceptive—by-product of the early stages of the study of piety:

And because all study rouses the forces of the soul a bit, and even more so the study of piety . . . one in whom the love of searching for truth, which is the search after His Name, is not well-established . . . finds himself with a stormy heart—[aroused to] joy in matters dealing with love [of God] and to trembling in matters dealing with fear [of God]—and thinks that with that he has completed his due and thus sloughs off true knowledge . . . [yet] with the passing of his storm he will find nothing in his soul, and thereby come, God forbid, to denigrate the matter of piety, and nonetheless flee to those studies in which his intellect finds room to exercise itself.[131]

It is thus incumbent on all who can, to write pietist texts that will challenge the intellect as well as nourish the soul. The great contemporary advances in Talmudic methodology, he says, in a striking criticism of Lithuanian yeshiva culture, have led to the denigration of the seemingly less challenging study of prayer and the fear of God; reinvigorating the study of these subjects is thus all the more imperative.[132] He then sets out to do just that.

---

129 To see here a reflection of the experience of his second marriage is as speculative as it is inevitable.

130 For instance, at 16:4 *Adam Qadmon*'s physiognomy—in which hair are the vessels of *Dinim*, while the brain itself is the seat of interiority—leads to a discussion of the external and internal in mitzvot and in Torah study (the lesser form of which is *pilpul*) and the great Torah of the future, of which the present is a pale shadow.

131 MA, 29–31, *Pinqas* 16:28:

כי סערת הלב והתפעלות הנפש מתנגדת לגמרי לחכמה שתתישב באדם, ואם כי טובה היא לפעמים התפעלות טובה וקדושה אינה כ״א לקבוע ביותר בעומק הנפש את קנין הדעת שכבר קנתה, אז ישתרש יותר ויוכר יותר, אבל קביעות דעת והשכל בתחילתה מנוחה שלמה דרושה לה . . . . מצד בחינת השכל בבטחון שלם על האלהים ית׳ והשכלת טובו ואז יצליח. ומפני שטבע כל לימוד להסעיר מעט את כוחות הנפש, והרבה יותר מטבע כל לימוד הוא בענין לימוד היראה . . . דבר זה גורם למי שאין אהבת בקשת האמת, שהיא דרישת השם ית׳, קבועה בו היטיב . . . אם מוצא הוא בעצמו שלבבו נסער, שמחה בעניני אהבה או לחרדה בעניני היראה, הוא סובר שבזה הוא משלים חוקו, והרי הוא מתרפה בעצמו מהידיעה האמיתית . . . שכאשר סערתו עוברת אינו מוצא בנפשו מאומה, ובא מזה ח״ו להבזות בלבבו כל ענין היראה, ועכ״פ יברח יותר ללימודים שמוצא שכלו מקום להתגדר בהם להבין ולהשכיל.

132 Ibid., 31. See also *Pinqas* 16:28. In his 1902 *Ha-Peles* essay "'Etzot me-Rahoq," in which he issued a similar call, the halakhic works he cited as having reinvigorated intellectual Talmudic study are *Tumim* [sic], *Noda' Bi-Yehudah*, *Haflaah*, *Qetzot ha-Hoshen*, *Netivot* [sic], and the works of Aqiva Eger. His inclusion of Eybeschutz's *Urim ve-Tumim* reminds us that he does cite Eybeschutz in various sermons of the period. This list is interesting in that these works were

The Religious Life and the Telos within the Self

At *Pinqas* 16:31, we find lengthy glosses to perhaps the central text of the Mussar Movement, Luzzatto's *Mesilat Yesharim*. Not a commentary as such, his glosses to Luzzatto are more the starting points for his own explorations.

Luzzatto famously wrote in his introduction that he had come to explain nothing more than one's obligations in this world. This, Rav Kook says, points to two essential principles. We are obligated in all the good deeds we do, virtues we acquire, and true beliefs we attain, en route to true comprehension of God and His guidance of the world, *hanhagah*. The point of all this is not to satisfy our own desire for knowledge, but rather to please God. But what does that mean? After all, we can no more understand the divine good vouchsafed for us in eternity than a babe can understand all the good that God has laid up for him.

On further reflection, he says, we see that the path of the mind has no perfection but righteousness, *yosher*, and the achievments of mind and righteousness are the perfection of the soul as life is perfection of the body.[133] And so as we work to fulfill God's will it is God's will that we come to perfection not for our benefit, but for its and His own sake.

Moreover, when we reflect on what perfection is, we see that all of life is, necessarily, will and cognition.[134] The perfection of cognition means understanding the very highest of things, which is God. Being human, though, the best we can hope for is understanding His *hanhagah* and His wisdom in fashioning all worlds, and perfecting the will, which is to make one's own will like God's who is the Will of all.[135]

All of life is consciousness and will, understanding Him and making our will align with His. And His Will is to do good; God's perfection is His bestowing goodness on others, and that is what He wants us to do. This is the deepest meaning of *'avodah tzorekh gevohah*, worship as fulfilling divine need, God's need to do good, through us, and is the deepest meaning of the psalmist's *the world is built on love* (Ps. 89:3). The virtue most necessary for this work is humility—because as one clings to the narrow straits of the self, one cannot be a vessel for God's Will, which gives life to everyone and everything.

As the passage proceeds, a spiritual exercise unolds. It is hard, he says, for us to grasp nothingness, let alone the nothingness of ourselves. And here Maimonides's (*Guide*, 3:10–11) notion of evil as privation, absence, is helpful, forcing us as it does to think about vast nothingness, and of one's own emptiness as a result.[136] Shifting from Maimonides to an explicitly Kabbalistic vein, he writes that once we see that all existence is moving towards perfection—and even the philosophers understand this—the final endless *shlemut* is the knowledge of God (*yedi'at Ha-Shem*) and since we know perfection is of both wisdom

---

important for the analytic methodology of Hayim Soloveitchik and were not consequential for Netziv; I am indebted for this observation to Prof. Jay Harris.

133 Ibid., 196.
134 Ibid., 197.
135 Ibid., 198.
136 Ibid., 200.

and will, both must be perfected, boundlessly, which can only be done through God's own Wisdom and Will.

Now, if existence were necessary in itself as some philosophers say (one assumes he means Spinoza) there would be no room for perfection of the will.[137] The perfection of the human will has its source in God, and is consequently unbound by necessity. And so, the foundation of creation, and its perfection, depend on humility before God. This means, first, that one's own will not count for anything vis-à-vis God's; and, second, understanding that there is no existence beside God. Taken together, reverence arises in us from His Wisdom, *Hokhmah*, and humility from His Will.[138] And Will, *Ratzon* (a synonym for *Keter*—Y. M.), is greater than *Hokhmah*, for the latter is a vessel through which the former is revealed. Everything in our lives is part of His Will, just as a single drop is part of the ocean.[139] That is why "the one who says Amen is greater than the one who says the blessing (BT Berakhot 53a)—because the blessing is God's, "and for that one should desire.""[140] And this is why the Rabbis said (BT Shabbat 119b) that saying Amen is itself the opening of the Gates of Eden.[141]

Like Maimonides, Rav Kook is trying to explore what God could mean when He is, by definition, at the very limits of thought and language. Maimonidean ethics is a personal drama, whose outcome does not as such affect the larger metahistorical or metaphysical forces through which God governs the world. By contrast, the Lurianic ethics that Rav Kook is forging here is the site of a drama of cosmic proportions. At the same time, and Lurianic though he may be, he is not here directly speaking in the theurgical terms of much Kabbalistic amd Lurianic ethics, but in an idiom more personal and introspective.[142]

He is, in other words, trying to synthesize the introspection of Mussar with the Lurianic framework of cosmic *tiqqun* as formulated by Luzzatto, for whom the divine telos is implanted in the world, and he locates that telos within the self.

He is, in some respects, taking a cue from Salanter, but with a difference. Salanter, in an essay in *Ha-Tevunah* in 1861–1862, with which Rav Kook was familiar, reprinted

---

137 Ibid., 201.

138 Ibid., 202:

ונמצא שיראה היא מצד חכמה וענוה מצד רצונו.

139 Ibid., 204:

נמצא, שבכלל מילוי רצונו, הכל בכלל. כמו שטיפת המים בכלל מי הים היא. ובחינת החסד היא רק על הידיעה המושגת לנו, שאם לא היתה מושפעת לנו ידיעה מאתו ית' באופן זה הנעלה... לא היינו באים לזאת המעלה... ועיקר הבקשה והתשוקה היא שתהי' לפי הכרת השכל והיושר, והם מורים ומלמדים אותנו שאין ראוי לבקש ולחפוץ כ"א עשיית רצונו ית'.

140 Ibid., 205.

141 Ibid., 206.

142 See, for instance, Bracha Sack's discussion of perhaps the greatest Kabbalistic ethical tract, Moshe Cordovero's *Tomer Devorah*, in her *Be-Sha'arei Ha-Qabbalah shel Rabbi Moshe Cordovero* (Beersheba: Ben-Gurion University Press, 1995), 214–229. Sack strongly brings out the theurgic dimension of that work, though, to my mind, scants the profoundly interpersonally moralizing thrust of Cordovero's work.

in 1878 under the title "Berurei Ha-Middot"[143] (Siftings of Traits), had written that one should identify and make use of the lesser elements of personality, such as the emotions, to root in one's heart a commitment to subdue one's evil inclination. This is the prelude to what Salanter calls *tiqqun ha-yetzer*, the repair of one's inclinations, resulting in joyous worship, itself the prelude to the highest level of worship, "with intellectual contemplation, in accord with the process of worship and one's own situation, to establish for worship a steady foundation which not all the winds of the world will stir from their place."[144] For Salanter, the sifting of qualities of the soul—all of which fall under a broad heading of feeling and intellect—is meant to give each its proper due within a well-defined hierarchy, resulting in a controlled will under the sovereign intellect. This process takes place within the individual and partakes of the intellectual nature of divine reality, but is unconnected to any larger metaphysical dynamic, and certainly not to any of the involved processes which, in the Kabbalistic tradition, take place within the highly ramified and multidimensional realm of the divine.[145]

Introspection for Rav Kook, by contrast, is meant to discover that personal telos and bring it to expression for the sake of *tiqqun*. This introspection yields a dynamic soul, whose parts are in reciprocal, creative tension, and correlative of a larger metaphysical process.[146]

---

143 Pachter, *Kitvei Rabbi Yisrael Salanter*, 125–159. It was reprinted in 1878 in *Imrei Binah*, ed. David Sidarsky (Warsaw: Izhak Goldman, 1878), 5–32, and in that edition received its title; for the bibliographic information see Pachter, *Kitvei Rabbi Yisrael Salanter*, 65. Rav Kook explicitly cites from the *Ha-Tevunah* essays, which he presumably knew from the 1878 volume, at *'Eyn Ayah* to BT Berakhot 4:10, 112.

One might also note the title of Yisrael Kitover's populatization of Arama's *'Aqedat Yitzhaq*.

144 Pachter, *Kitvei Rabbi Yisrael Salanter*, 157:

הב' היא העיקרית, בהתבוננות שכלית, לפי דרכי תהלוכות העבודה ומצב תכונת האדם, לקבוע להעבודה יתד נאמן אשר כל הרוחות שבעולם לא יזיזו אותו ממקומו.

145 This essay, in which Salanter quotes from Maimonides throughout, demonstrates inter alia, his own indebtedness to the philosophical tradition, in contrast with his disciples in late nineteenth-century Mussar.

146 This acceptance of the range of one's traits did, in his view, have its limits. Thus in the late nineteenth-century controversy over Yisrael Lipschutz's reference in his commentary *Tiferet Yisrael* at Mishnah Qiddushin 4:4, to a legend, circulating in Hasidic circles, that Moses overcame an innately nasty disposition, Rav Kook took the side of those criticizing Lipschtuz, as did Aderet. On the controversy see Sid Z. Leiman, "R. Israel Lipschutz and the Portrait of Moses Controversy," in *Danzig Between East and West: Aspects of Modern Jewish History*, ed. Isadore Twersky (Cambridge, MA; Harvard University Press, 1985), 51–63, 53n10; my thanks for this reference to the indefatigable Menachem Butler.

Rav Kook's comments appear in a letter to Shimon Ha-Cohen of Mitovi, printed in the latter's *Sha'ar Shimon* (Vilna: Garber, 1902), 53. Interestingly he cites both Luria and Philo, the former for the proposition that Moses's soul had no need of *tiqqun* and was sent to this world for the sake of Israel, and the latter for his comments on Moses's virtuous character from childhood onward "and so ancient an author clearly had reliable sources."

We have here perhaps the first articulation *in nuce* of the subjective expressive—and nationalist—doctrines which Rav Kook would later develop, with such profound consequences.

But for now, he was in Boisk. Just what that might look like, what sort of rhetorical and affective power this perspective might unleash, emerged in conversation with his disciples there.

"The Rustlings of My Heart": Rav Kook and B. M. Levin

Among his students in Boisk, two stand out—Moshe Zeidel and Binyamin Menashe Levin. Both went on to scholarly careers, though Levin is more accurately described as a scholarly giant. Zeidel (1886–1971), a native of Boisk, studied in Telz, and became, at Rav Kook's suggestion, a Semitic philologist and important teacher and scholar of Bible, integrating the findings of modern scholarship with reverence.[147] He is perhaps chiefly remembered, though, for Rav Kook's letters to him from the latter's years in Palestine, which touch on a broad range of subjects and are written with great paternal and pedagogic care.[148] Levin (1879–1944) eventually founded modern scholarship of Geonic halakhah, and is best remembered for his massive, multivolume anthology of Geonic Talmudic commentary *Otzar Ha-Geonim*, the product of decades of painstaking research.[149] Rav Kook's deep and decades-long friendship with each also yielded some of his most significant

---

147 A bibliography of his works is to be found in the *Festschrift* for him, ed. Eliezer Eliner (Jerusalem: Israel Bible Society, 1962). A number of his articles, along with a brief appreciation by Yehudah Kil, appeared as *Hiqrei Miqra* (Jerusalem: Mossad Ha-Rav Kook, 1978). He was also an editor of the *Da'at Miqra* series. For more on Zeidel, and Rav Kook's influence on his scholarly path, see Ari Shvat, "Mivhanim Ma'asiyim ha-Mevatim et Ahadat Ha-Rav Kook le-Limud Torah Biqorti-Mada'i," *'Asif* 4 (2017): 297–329, esp. 314–317.

148 They are to be found in *Igrot*, 1, nos. 20, 90, 91, 93, 108, 134, 164, 283; *Igrot*, 2, nos. 379, 478, 645, 706, 719, 775, 776; *Igrot*, 3, nos. 748, 846, 871, 924, 968.

149 Two autobiographical essays by Levin appeared in *Sinai* 14 (1944): 185–203 (hereafter *Levin*). An abridged version of his memoir as it relates to Rav Kook appeared in *Ba-Mishor* 1, no. 33 (September 9, 1940), 3–4.

A bibliography of Levin's works up to 1940 along with appreciations by Y. M. Harlap, J. L. Fishman, and the noted writer Rebbe Binyomin (Joshua Radler-Feldman) are to be found in the festschrift *Sefer Ha-Yovel Mugash le-Doctor Binyamin Menashe Levin le-Yovlo Ha-Shishim*, ed. J. L. Maimon (Jerusalem: Mossad Ha-Rav Kook, 1940). A biographical essay by Yitzhak Refael marking the tenth anniversary of his death appears in *Sinai* 35 (1954): 66–73. An appreciation and assessment of Levin's scholarly work is provided by Neil Danzig, "Geonic Jurisprudence from the Cairo Genizah: An Appreciation of Early Scholarship," *Proceedings of the American Academy for Jewish Research* 63 (2001): 1–47.

Rebbe Binyomin in his essay calls attention to Levin's deep individualism: "By his nature he walked and worked alone. . . . He differed from others in everything, and then resembled them in this or that and you don't know which is the fixed, standing principle . . . today he appears gentle as Hillel, tomorrow exacting as Shammai . . . without his feeling that in these two visages he is different from others, he just desires what he sees as natural"; Maimon, *Sefer Ha-Yovel*, 8.

correspondences, and Levin and Zeidel both later edited some of Rav Kook's works.[150] In particular, his relationship with Levin, seven years Zeidel's elder and in his twenties during Rav Kook's time in Boisk, is a richly informative chapter in Rav Kook's life and development at the time.

Levin, a Talmudic prodigy and alumnus of the yeshiva in Telz, had earlier studied in Bobroysk with the iconoclastic Shmuel Alexandrov (1865–1941), whom he later introduced to Rav Kook, with significant results, which we will discuss in a later chapter.[151] Alexandrov was, in addition to being an accomplished Talmudist, an autodidact intellectual, consumer of academic scholarship and a no-holds-barred participant in the various social, political, and intellectual polemics of the day, a critic of both left and right.[152] A mystic, cultural nationalist, and anarchist, he saw himself as a Jewish current of the stream of contemporary Russian Idealism for whom Nietzsche's critique of dessicated religion pointed the way to a new kind of God-seeking.[153]

Levin made Rav Kook's acquaintance in the resort of Dubbelen (Dubulti), where in the summer of 1899 the young scholar found himself managing, on behalf of the non-Jewish owner, a local inn favored by the rabbinic clientele, after the regular manager, a Hasid from Dvinsk, absconded with the till.[154] Rav Kook and Levin were so taken with each other that Rav Kook invited Levin to move to Boisk and live with the Kook family, and he became, along with Zeidel, Zvi Yehudah Kook's tutor. Levin's acerbic reminiscences of Boisk are less rose-tinted than those of Zev Rabbiner. He says he found only a few scholars, and not many Maskilim worth talking to.

Levin recalled that on meeting Rav Kook he was drawn to him "especially after I began to stand before him and present my questions on contemporary matters of faith with which he was occupying himself and about which he would give and take with others in order to clarify every aspect thereof, as in a halakhic disputation."[155] This broad-mindedness was not to the liking of the other rabbis staying at the inn, who, Levin says, subjected Rav Kook to a public grilling on Talmudic minutiae, which he not only passed but

---

150 See the rich documentation in Meir, "Orot ve-Kelim ": 163–247, 223–231.

151 On this fascinating figure, see Ehud Luz, "Spiritualism ve-Anarkhism Dati be-Mishnato shel Shmuel Alexandrov," *Da'at* 7 (1981): 121–138; Geulah Bat-Yehudah, "Rabbi Shmuel Alexandrov," *Sinai* 100 (1987): 195–221; Yitzhak (Tsachi) Slater, *Leumiyut Universalit: Dat u-Leumiyut be-Haguto shel Shmuel Alexandrov* (MA Thesis, Ben-Gurion University, 2014); and idem, "Those Who Yearn for the Divine: Rabbi Shmuel Alexandrov and the Russian Religious-Philosophical Renaissance," *Judaica Petropolitana* 5 (2016): 55-67.

152 Levin quotes Rav Kook as saying that "Alexandrov is a great thinker, but in his desire to penetrate the divine curtain he has left himself outside and only just up to it." Levin assured the reader that Alexandrov for his part had no doubt that he had managed to get behind the curtain (*Levin*, 189).

153 Alexandrov's correspondence with Rav Kook was one of the conduits through which the latter engaged the ideas of Nietzsche, Solovyev, Tolstoy, and other thinkers of that stream.

154 The date of the meeting is given by Levin in the abridged memoir. Also see Rav Kook's brief letter to his father from Dubbelen, dated at the end of summer 1899; *Igrot*, 1, nos. 7 and 9.

155 *Levin*, 198.

turned into an impromptu lecture, to the consternation of his inquisitors. "His beliefs and ideas," Levin writes, "were strange to his fellow rabbis, who were, to be sure, masterful Torah scholars . . . but whose beliefs and opinions had not taken wing, and they remained like children. . . . And there was a special charm to him in his extraordinary humility and his proceeding with a particular grace among all men."[156] Levin became attached to him and the two went for long daily walks. In a different reminiscence, Levin recounted that Rav Kook was strikingly up to date on the literature and journalism of the time, and once tried to write his own version of a story of David Frischman's.[157] It seems that Rav Kook, whose somewhat heterodox ideas aroused the suspicions of his more conventional colleagues, felt something of an affinity with the disciple of the iconoclastic Alexandrov.

Rav Kook and Levin regularly took their walks along the shores of the Baltic. His description of their conversations conveys what seems best described as the synthetic workings of Rav Kook's mind:[158]

> To the questions and contradictions with which I would attack he wouldn't, like most, respond with answer after answer, but would begin to encompass the sphere of the question from all sides, from idea to idea, stringing thought to thought and image to image, near and far, until all would come together. . . . By the waves, rising, falling and rising again, his spirit would rise upward and he'd precede his high-flown answer thus: The waves of questions and doubts that we always encounter, they have a center, from which flow the changes and transformations in our spirit and burst out. Ours is none other than to encompass all those waves and their turnings and seek their center and then we'll find that all were but the outcomes of that one great central question, and deep in the very depth of that question the many others will dissolve by themselves.[159]

Their conversations continued in Boisk; Rav Kook for his part would later recount these talks as: "those times when I would speak in your ears the rustlings of my heart from the flow of Godly light that is the light of true Torah; I can see your gentle soul that absorbed in high love every utterance and thought."[160]

---

156 Ibid.

157 This was in a talk Levin gave to the Jerusalem Jewish Studies Society on the first anniversary of Rav Kook's death, a summary of which appeared in *Ha-Tzofeh*, August 21, 1936, and is reprinted in Beeri, *'Oved Yisrael bi-Qedushah*, 5:124–126. Significantly, there Levin also notes, as emerges from this study, that Rav Kook's celebrated tolerance was a later development in his personality.

158 My characterization of Rav Kook's as a synthetic mind is drawn from the pithy observations of him by Isaac Breuer (1883–1946), reprinted in Rivka Horovitz, *Yitzhak Breuer: 'Iyunim be-Mishnato* (Ramat-Gan: Bar-Ilan University Press, 1988), 182–188.

159 *Levin*, 199.

160 From a letter dated 4 Tevet 5668/December 9, 1907; *Igrot*, 1, nos. 102, 122. "True Torah" is presumably a reference to Kabbalah.

Conclusion

We have seen in these years Rav Kook self-consciously articulating and theorizing his attempted navigation of a range of spiritual traditions, and his reworking of some of them, in particular Luzzatto's Kabbalah, in light of the Mussar controversies of the late 1890s; along the way he has begun to articulate some rich understandings of selfhood, using the concepts and categories of Kabbalah both to understand theology and to make sense of his own, at times unexpected, inner life. At the same time, he developed not in isolation but very much in dialogue with some currents of his time.

In the coming chapter we will look at his dialogue with the past, in his aggadic commentary *'Eyn Ayah*, which he began while still in Zeimel and on which he labored during these years. In it he further developed his ideas, along with a distinctive and personal style of writing; by attending to both we will clearly see his trajectory from a hierarchically ordered, rationalistic view of the self and the religious life, to a more ramified and expressive picture of each, as philosophical ideas provide the scaffolding for his Kabbalistic explorations of selfhood—his own and that of the world around him.

'Eyn Ayah: Intellect, Imagination, Self-Expression, Prophecy

We turn now to 'Eyn Ayah, Rav Kook's commentary to the aggadic (nonlegal) passages of Tractate Berakhot of the Babylonian Talmud. (The commentary as a whole covers the first two Talmudic tractates, Berakhot and Shabbat, and several intervening Mishnaic tractates.)[1] This large work runs to some thousand, densely printed, folio pages. Rav Kook began this commentary sometime during his years in Zeimel (that is, before 1896), completed some two-thirds of it by 1906 and worked on it intermittently throughout the rest of his life, occasionally revising earlier passages.[2] It was published in full over a number

1   Hereinafter 'Eyn Ayah to BT Berakhot will be designated EAB. Individual passages will be cited by volume and page number as well as by their chapter and *pisqa*/paragraph in the printed edition, for example, EAB 3:1 would mean 'Eyn Ayah to BT Berakhot, chapter 3, paragraph 1. Volume and page numbers refer to the edition edited by Ya'aqov Filber and published in four volumes in Jerusalem by Makhon Ha-Ratzy"ah Kook zt"l, between the years 1987–2000; volumes 1 and 2 of that edition cover tractate Berakhot and selected comments on the Mishnaic order of Zera'im; and volumes 3 and 4 cover Tractate Shabbat. Talmudic folio pages are, unless otherwise stated, from BT Berakhot.

   The name 'Eyn Ayah, literally "falcon's eye," after Job 28:7, is of course a pun, that is, the 'Eyn of **A**vraham **Y**itzhak **Ha**-Cohen. He first used it as a pseudonym for the fragment on Song of Songs published in *Ha-Mizrahi* in 1903, which is discussed below in chapter six, note 134; the title also appears on the fragments published in his lifetime.

2   In a letter dated 22 Iyar 5666/May 17, 1906, some two years after his arrival in Palestine, he writes that he is up to the fifth chapter of BT Shabbat, the letter is cited in Filber's preface to vol. 1, iv. Two years later he writes that he is unable to publish the work for lack of resources—*Igrot*, 1, no. 142. He continued to work on it throughout his life, and in the last passage; commenting on a passage in the fourteenth chapter of Shabbat, there is a note reading "'Eyn Ayah on rabbinic aggadot. Last volume—Jerusalem 5694 (1934). Unfinished! [*sic*]."

   In Meir Berlin (Bar-Ilan)'s preface to the prospectus of the association for the publication of Rav Kook's writings, he quotes Rav Kook as saying that the commentary was meant "to be a pair of glasses," which Berlin took to mean, "clearly to see the inner and essential content of the Sages' words in aggadah." See his *Prospeqt le-Hotza'at Kitvei Rabbeinu Ha-Gadol*, 5.

of years, from 1995 to 2000, and has slowly been receiving scholarly attention.[3] A detailed treatment of *'Eyn Ayah* as a whole is a major project, easily a volume in itself and perhaps several.[4] While I cannot provide such a treatment here, I will try to sketch some cartographic lines of orientation across this sprawling work.

Yuval Sherlo (Cherlow) has argued that *'Eyn Ayah* be viewed as a central text in Rav Kook's oeuvre because it represents the most accessible expression of a number of Rav Kook's positions, and vividly shows theological discussion emerging in the literary spontaneity sparked by direct encounter with the classic texts.[5] I would add that its being a sustained writing project spanning decades, from the 1890s until shortly before his death, opens a valuable window onto the development of his ideas over time. Like his diaries, and in some ways more deeply, *'Eyn Ayah* brings us into Rav Kook's *atelier*, as the work of commenting on line after line of Talmud forces him to revisit his ideas again and again, and bring them into dialogue with the classic texts. Of course, here, as nearly everywhere in Rav Kook studies, the inaccessibility of the manuscript to academic researchers makes it hard to draw ironclad conclusions regarding the history of the text. Yet we can, as we read, discern a definite procession of ideas evolving over time, interesting in its own right, and showing that indeed the published text reflects the text as written over the decades.

Throughout *'Eyn Ayah*, as elsewhere in Rav Kook's corpus, his ideas unmistakably develop but not in a strictly linear fashion. Rather, he works with a cluster of related concepts that change over time, such that by the end of the book we are dealing with a different picture than at the beginning. Yet the earlier layers remain, pools and eddies of ideas shifting over the progressing surface of the text, against which he tests himself over and over, his repertoire of concepts in hand, concepts that he reworks in turn. His interpretations work in concentric circles, bringing fundamental ideas to bear, and as their semantic-ideational range grows, they encompass increasingly broader swathes of religious experience, and of world history.

---

3   Early scholarly works on it are the writings of Yuval and Smadar Sherlo (Cherlow), to be discussed presently, and Michal Lanir's dissertation (the later volume), which makes some use of *'Eyn Ayah* in her work on the evolution of Rav Kook's thinking on nationalism, and this writer's 2007 dissertation on which the present volume is based. Within the avowedly Orthodox and sectarian circles of Rav Kook's latter-day adherents, *'Eyn Ayah* appears regularly in the writings of Zvi Tau; as an exoteric text it well suits an educational agenda committed both to propagating Rav Kook's teachings, while maintaining a strong esotericism at variance with the practices of moderate Religious Zionism and academia.

4   Smadar Sherlo (Cherlow) astutely noted the difference between the rationalism of its early chapters, and what she terms the *Lebensphilosophie* reflected in the second version of those early chapters which Rav Kook undertook after his move to Palestine. My study here differs from hers, as I attempt to plumb particular ideas in depth and chart the developments she observed in the broader context of Rav Kook's development at the time; see her "Hitpathut Shitat Ha-Musssar shel Ha-Rav Kook be-Hibbur 'Eyn Ayah," *Da'at* 43 (1999): 95–123.

5   Yuval Sherlo (Cherlow), *Ve-Erastikh li le-'Olam: Demutu Ha-Ruhanit shel Ha-Adam Mi-Yisrael bi-'Et Ha-Tehiya Be-Mishnat Ha-Rav Kook* (Hispin: Yeshivat Ha-Golan, 1996), 255–288.

Here we will see Rav Kook take up some issues we have already discerned observed—the concern with prophecy in 'Ittur Sofrim, the idea of perfection in Midbar Shur, the role of each personality in the Lurianic teleology as developed in Pinqasim 15 and 16—as he brings them into dialogue with each other and tries to manage the tensions in his thought generated by that very dialogue.

We have traced how in his early writings Rav Kook developed a picture of the religious life, indebted to the philosophical tradition, the Mussar movement, and the writings of Luzzatto. In this he projected an ethos of self-cultivation stressing the primacy of the mind and embedded in a teleology of tiqqun, whereby the individual's cultivation to perfection of his distinctive personality is itself a part of the Lurianic drama of divine reparation. In this chapter, we will see him begin 'Eyn Ayah with that structure and move steadily towards an expressive picture of the religious life with great emphasis on feeling, alongside, and at times over, the intellect.[6] We will see how he takes ideas and constructs from the medieval tradition, in particular the relations between intellect and imagination, transmutes them into a modern idiom of feeling, expression, and subjectivity, and has recourse to dialectic as a means of holding this increasingly tensile structure together. We will also see his deepening internalization of Kabbalah, his mounting sense that the individual soul is part of greater currents sweeping through and beyond time and space. He takes Luzzatto's notion of the teleological movement of the divine through all things en route to redemption and links it to the expressive inner life of the individual, which, too, is part of the great cosmic process. (He also joins this dynamic to some Hasidic ideas, particularly those associated with Habad.) We see here the beginnings of a leitmotif of Rav Kook's mature thought, his projection of the individual, and indeed the cosmos, as navigating poles of intellect and feeling.[7] Later on we will relate this to the development of his thinking on nationalism; but for now we will explore the literary emergence of this tension in his religious life between theosophy and ecstasy.[8]

Stylistically, here as elsewhere we see his passage through the genres; in these early decades he experimented with a number of forms—commentary, sermons, essays, poetry—until finding several years after his arrival in Jaffa that the genre which was his most congenial and expressive vehicle, was the spiritual diary. As 'Eyn Ayah progresses, we see a more expressive form of writing take shape, in both ideas and style, which steadily becomes more associative, less controlled, and less thematically uniform, if enduringly

---

6   As noted above, Smadar Sherlo (Cherlow) has discussed 'Eyn Ayah in terms of rationalism and Lebensphilosophie. I am, as will become clear, in agreement with her on the broad arc of Rav Kook's development, even as I take a different interpretive tack, as noted above.

7   This is obvious to all readers of his work; the point is made throughout Benjamin Ish-Shalom, Ha-Rav Kook: Beyn Ratziyonalism le-Mistiqah (Tel Aviv: 'Am 'Oved, 1990), and most explicitly and memorably therein at p. 213. On the role of imagination in Rav Kook's later writings, see Lawrence Kaplan, "Rav Kook and the Jewish Philosophical Tradition," in Kaplan and Shatz, Rabbi Abraham Isaac Kook and Jewish Spirituality, 41–77.

8   On this dichotomy as a defining duality of the mystic tradition, see Moshe Idel, "Yofyah shel Ishah: Le-Toldotehah shel Ha-Mistiqah Ha-Yehudit," in Immanuel Etkes et al., Be-Ma'agalei Hasidim, 317–334.

consistent in its underlying concerns. Berel Lang has distinguished between three modes of philosophical writing: the expository, the performative, and the reflexive that works to mediate between the two.[9] *'Eyn Ayah* begins as a philosophical commentary in an expository mode, then becomes increasingly performative-reflexive, that is, the text increasingly dramatizes Rav Kook's internal conversation, much of which is his attempt to reflect on the increasingly expressivist stances he works to articulate. Passages become longer, more digressive and poetic, increasingly reacting with greater immediacy to the Talmudic passages at hand.

If the notebooks were the arena of his private response to Mussar, *'Eyn Ayah* was, in no small part to be his public, pedagogic response, that would channel the positive energies of the Mussar movement—its call for moral and spiritual renewal within the framework of Lithuanian Talmudism—into a sustainable direction by creating a text with two aims: First, a rabbinic text, whose study could achieve Mussar's goals without recourse to the then-current Mussar methodologies of ecstatic reading. And, second, a text that would recast Mussar's program in the terms of the self-cultivation traditions of medieval Jewish philosophy and pietism. In *'Eyn Ayah*'s pages the religious life is presented not, as the Mussar movement then had it, as a lonely battle against the evil inclination, the *yetzer ha-ra'*, for the sake of avoiding divine wrath, but rather as part of a lifelong effort at self-cultivation aimed at bringing one's own morals and intellect into alignment with the divine ethos structuring and sustaining the universe.[10]

Yet while begun as an alternative Mussar text, *'Eyn Ayah* became something different, a sort of textual laboratory in which Rav Kook developed his increasingly expressive and subjective religious ethos. Crucial to this development is his use and transformation of medieval categories; in particular, we will focus on his use and transformation of the idea of the faculty of the imagination, as developed by the medieval philosophers, to gain some purchase on the development of his ideas. This is far from the only vein to be mined in the rich lodes of *'Eyn Ayah*, but one that is particularly crucial and revealing. Strikingly, in light of Rav Kook's post-1904 thought, one theological category that hardly figures here is the Land of Israel.[11]

We will explore the development of his ideas as regards intellect, imagination and feeling with an eye to some broader themes in the history of modernity and, in particular,

---

9   See Berel Lang, "Space, Time and Philosophical Style," in Lang, *Philosophical Style*, 144–172.

10   Jonathan Garb has suggested that my characterization of Rav Kook's critique of ecstatic Mussar may be overstated. For Rav Kook, he suggests, the ecstasies of Mussar are not invalid, but rather are better seen not as the province of study, but of prayer. This seems reasonable to me. This astute observation of Garb's notwithstanding, the force of *'Eyn Ayah* as a study-text for Mussar still, I think, stands. See his *Yearnings of the Soul: Psychological Thought in Modern Kabbalah* (Chicago: University of Chicago Press, 2015), 99.

11   Among the other categories developed through *'Eyn Ayah* are what I would characterize as Israel and humanity, prayer, moral sentiments, ethics, and eschatology. I will have more to say about the latter category in later chapters.

the emergence of the subject and the expressive turn described at length by Charles Taylor, about which a few more words now.[12]

'Eyn Ayah and Modernity's Expressivist Turn

Thomas Dixon has written at length on the process by which over the course of the eighteenth and nineteenth centuries the all-inclusive category of "emotions" replaced the more supple headings "passions," "sentiments," and "affections."[13] Central to Dixon's account is secularization. While "passion" and "affection" were part of a network of terms prominent in Christian ethics, such as soul, conscience, sin, grace, spirit, will, and self-love, "emotion," he says, was part of a different semantic network of psychology, organism, brain, nerves, expression, and behavior. At the same time, as a relatively new term, "emotion" could serve multiple uses. Thus the shift from "passions" and "affections" to "emotions" was a shift from the Christian realist view (the will and intellect are two principal faculties of a substantial soul) to a nonrealist view ("will" is not a power or faculty, but a feeling, indeed there are no autonomous faculties, nor is there an autonomous self, but rather a stream of impressions, feelings and ideas).

The trajectory we will observe while walking through 'Eyn Ayah relates to these broader trends. We will see Rav Kook increasingly using one form or other of the verb R-G-Sh to describe a broad range of affective and expressive states, emotions, feelings, intuitions, sensations (moral sense included), themselves rooted in larger cosmic forces.[14] While Rav Kook was by no means searching for a secular vocabulary, he was seeking some immediate source of religious knowledge, knowledge that increasingly opened up towards experience, and, by creative use of medieval philosophical categories, he found such a vehicle in the idea of feeling.

---

12 Taylor, *Sources of the Self.*

13 Thomas Dixon, *From Passions to Emotions: The Creation of a Secular Psychological Category* (Cambridge: Cambridge University Press, 2003); Dixon focuses extensively on the English-speaking world, though he also devotes great attention to the Augustinian and Thomist accounts of passions, as well as German philosophy of the eighteenth century. His story fittingly culminates with William James.

14 Throughout, for better or worse, I generally translate *R-G-Sh* as "feeling," since that seems best to capture the multiple senses of sentiment, perception, moral sense, intuition, and emotion; moreover, this serves as a marker for the English reader of the basic terminological shift I am trying to chronicle. In Hebrew philosophical texts of the nineteenth and twentieth centuries, one form or other of *R-G-Sh* was regularly used to translate *Empfindung*. For instance, in the late eighteenth-century Hebrew philosophical popularizations of Naftali Herz Ullmann, which received the approval of Moses Mendelssohn, as well as in the works of Solomon Maimon, *hargashah* was used to translate *Empfindung*; see Shalom Rosenberg and Alexander Even-Hen, "Hidush Ha-Minuah Ha-Filosofi Ha-'Ivri be-Shilhei Ha-Me'ah Ha–18," *'Iyun* 37 (1988): 263–270, 265; see as well Avraham Zaltzman, "Munahim Filosofiyyim 'al pi Sefer 'Otzar Ha-Hokhmah' le-Julius Barasch," *'Iyun* 3 (1952): 151–168, 158, 163.

The Work: Genre, Method and the Study of Aggadah in Rabbinic Circles

Though to this writer's knowledge we have next to no available external sources to help us date the composition of *'Eyn Ayah*, it seems not unreasonable to think that *'Eyn Ayah* to Berakhot was near completion by 1902.[15] As noted earlier, by 1906, two years after his arrival in Jaffa, Rav Kook had reached the fifth chapter of Tractate Shabbat and kept working on it until shortly before his death in 1935. Portions were published in his lifetime and thereafter and large portions were published by Zvi Yehudah Kook, without identification as to where they came from, and, at times with editorial liberties, as parts of the prayerbook commentary *'Olat Re'ayah*, which appeared between 1939 and 1949.[16]

---

15   One of the few external references to the work is in a letter written in the summer of that year, in which his father-in-law offers practical advice on how to make the *'Eyn Ya'aqov* publishing venture more remunerative, or at least not as costly as *'Ittur Sofrim* and *Hevesh Pe'er*, and urges him to publish halakhic material as well. See *Igrot Ha-Aderet*, no. 8, in *Eder Ha-Yaqar* (Jerusalem: Mossad Ha-Rav Kook, 1967), 83–85. One surmises that EAB was the volume in mind. A comparison of the shifts in tone from EAB to *Eyn Ayah* to BT Shabbat will, I think, support this working hypothesis.

16   Moshe Zuriel lists which *'Eyn Ayah* passages were published in *'Olat Re'ayah* throughout his lengthy summary of the latter. See *Otzarot*, 3:413–517—and he offers his own recommended textual emendations and explanatory notes to a number of passages at *Otzarot*, 5:187–192. For illustrative examples of Zvi Yehudah Kook's editorial changes, see *'Olat Re'ayah*, 1:291 and compare with EAB 2:54, 81; similarly comparison of the celebrated passage EAB 9:361, 397 with *'Olat Re'ayah*, 330, shows that he has added *da'at Torah* to the attributes of the sages listed therein. The only indication he gives as to the texts' original provenance is an elliptical comment that his father "was greatly occupied with Shelah's Siddur commentary during the years he wrote those passages."

In Rav Kook's lifetime, excerpts were published in *Ha-Devir* 3, nos. 7–9 (1921), in the compilation of his writings undertaken by Isaiah Shapira (1891–1945) (also called *Ha-Admor He-Halutz*, brother of Kalonymous Shapira of Pieczysna and Warsaw), *Eretz Hefetz* (Jerusalem: Darom, 1930), *Netivah* 5, no. 7 (1930), and in the Harry Fischel Festschrift. Some passages were published in a booklet *Qovetz Ma'amarim*, published in the fall of 1935 by *Ha-Yesod*, which also reprinted Rav Kook's articles in that venue from 1932 to 1935, to mark the first month after his passing, at 41–48. They appear in the printed edition as *'Eyn Ayah* to Shabbat 3:112–116, 133–136. A comparison of the two shows that Filber has reprinted the original faithfully, apart from some very minor changes to bring the text in line with some contemporary conventions of Hebrew usage and spelling.

A fascinating glimpse into some of the editorial decisions at work here is offered by the protocol of the society to publish Rav Kook's writings, which functioned briefly after his death. See Neriah Gutel, "Protoqol 'Ha-Agudah le-Hotza'at Kitvei Ha-Rav Kook,'" *Sinai* 126–127 (2000–2001): 340–353. At 349, we read that the questions of how to publish *'Eyn Ayah*, and whether to publish it now or give precedence to the Siddur commentary begun by Rav Kook in response to the Balfour Declaration, was discussed at the second (and next-to-last) meeting of the group, chaired by Meir Bar-Ilan, on 4 Tevet 5697/December 18, 1936. Rav Kook's brother Dov wanted to publish *'Eyn Ayah*, which was a bona fide commentary, while the Siddur commentary was incomplete, consisting simply of ideas attached to well-known prayers. Berlin took his points but said the Siddur has "a special suasion" and suggested that Zvi Yehudah Kook could fill in the lacunae. The latter, interestingly, said that the Siddur is

'Eyn Ayah is structured as a commentary to 'Eyn Ya'aqov, the canonical anthology of the aggadot of the Babylonian Talmud, edited by the fifteenth to sixteenth-century scholar and Spanish exile Jacob ibn Habib of Salonika.[17] Rav Kook's commentary stands at the confluence of multiple trends: the interest in aggadah generated by the Gaon of Vilna's agenda of broadening the rabbinic bookshelf beyond the Babylonian Talmud (indeed he himself authored aggadic commentaries, including to Tractate Berakhot);[18] Maskilic interest in philosophy; and late nineteenth-century yeshiva culture—not least the Mussar controversies of the 1890s.

Early nineteenth-century Lithuania saw the devotion of great energies to the study of aggadah and midrash. Some of this was undertaken by self-identified followers of the Gaon. As Gil Perl has recently shown, interest in midrash went well beyond the Gaon's circles and spoke to the concerns of Maskilim, rabbinic scholars, and roving preachers. These broader circles of early nineteenth-century rabbinic students of midrash and aggadah in Vilna and Volozhin, inter alia, crucially influenced the deep midrashic interests of Rav Kook's own venerated teacher, Netziv.[19]

Aggadah's unsystematic, often anthropomorphic and regularly hyperbolic—at times fantastic—tenor made it a focal point of Enlightenment polemics, Jewish apologetics, and

---

a commentary in every respect, while 'Eyn Ayah needed editing and work. In the end, his view prevailed and thus was born the Siddur commentary 'Olat Reay'ah and its multitude of unsourced—and thus regularly abstruse—citations from 'Eyn Ayah. In my view, Dov Kook had the better argument, since, detached from their exegetical contexts, much of the 'Eyn Ayah materials in the Siddur commentary make for disorienting reading.

17   Ibn Habib's anthology was meant as a study text, the mirror image of the canonical medieval Talmudic digests of Isaac Alfasi and Asher ben Yehiel, who had simply omitted the aggadah; yet unlike them, ibn Habib simply presented the text without inserting any comments of his own. For a lengthy study of 'Eyn Ya'aqov and its reception, see Marjorie Lehman, *The En Ya'aqov: Jacob ibn Habib's Search for Faith in the Talmudic Corpus* (Detroit: Wayne State University Press, 2011). 'Eyn Ya'aqov was widely reprinted, up to and during Rav Kook's lifetime (and after); for instance, the Vilna 1883 edition contained a number of commentaries and supercommentaries, as well as citations to passages discussed in Arama's *'Aqedat Yitzhaq*. That the text used by ibn Habib was based on the medieval compilation Haggadot Ha-Talmud, has been demonstrated by Stephen G. Wald, *Pereq Eylu 'Ovrin: Bavli Pesahim Pereq Shlishi, Mahadurah Biqortit 'im Bei'yur Maqif* (New York and Jerusalem: Jewish Theological Seminary, 2000), 357–385.

18   The Gaon's largely Kabbalistic commentary to aggadic passages of Berakhot was published in two slightly different versions, as *Yad Eliyahu* (Warsaw: Kutler, 1882) and, along with commentaries to aggadic passages in Tractates Bava Qama and Megilah, and with commentary by the Gaon's son Avraham, as *Beurei Aggadot* (Warsaw: Goldman, 1886). The latter serves as the basis for Yosef Movshovitz's edition of the commentary to Berakhot, *Hidushei Ha-Gra: Be'urei Aggadot* (Jerusalem: Mossad Ha-Rav Kook, 2007). On the Gaon's agenda for rabbinic literature see generally Harris, "Rabbinic Literature in Lithuania After the Death of the Gaon," 88–95.

19   See Perl, *The Pillar of Volozhin*, esp. 163–167.

various strategies of reading.[20] Thus for instance, Samson Rafael Hirsch argued that aggadah, never canonized or made normative like the halakhic dimension of the Babylonian Talmud, represents only individual viewpoints and, moreover, one cannot easily distinguish between aggadic passages that are exegetical and those that are poetic-literary.[21] For their part, the circles of Vilna Maskilim of the mid-nineteenth century produced several works attempting to allay modern readers' discomfort with the seemingly fantastic and improbable language of many aggadic passages.[22]

While, as we saw in our discussion of 'Ittur Sofrim, Rav Kook had absorbed some elements of Maskilic discussion of rabbinic literature and may well have heard of these works,[23] of no less concern to him, and likely more, was the uncertain and regularly problematic place of aggadah in yeshiva curricula, over the centuries and certainly in the late nineteenth century.[24] Long looked down upon for its seemingly simple nature, in contrast

---

20 See Jay M. Harris, *Nachman Krochmal: Guiding the Perplexed of the Modern Age* (New York: New York University Press, 1991), 277–282, and esp. note 7 therein.

21 Hirsch lays out his views in the introduction to his *Horev*; however, the introduction was not translated into Hebrew until 1965, and then only partially, such that Rav Kook would not have read it. For a fuller discussion of Hirsch's views that draws on hitherto unpublished manuscripts, see Mordechai Breuer, "Ma'amar Rabbi Shimshon Refael Hirsch ztz"l 'al Aggadot Hazal," *Ha-Ma'ayan* 17, no. 2 (Winter 1975–1976): 1–16.

22 Thus Kalman Shulman, *Havatzelet Ha-Sharon* (Vilna: Romm, 1861) dealt with problematic aggadot by using Josephus and similar sources to show that Hazal were current on the science and history of their time. Moshe Aharon Shatzkes, *Ha-Mafteah/Hamafteach oder der Schlussel*, vol. 1 (Warsaw: n.p., 1866); vol 2 (Warsaw: n.p., 1869), offered naturalizing, rationalistic, and moralizing readings of aggadot, which utterly denuded the aggadot of their plain sense. His volumes, written in a florid and self-dramatizing style, generated several critical responses; see the spirited polemics of Yisrael David Miller, *Sefer Milhemet Sofrim* (Vilna: Dvorez, 1871) and Avraham Dov Duvzevitz, *Lo Dubim ve-lo Ya'ar* (Berdiczew: Sheftel, 1890).

Duvzevitz himself authored a work of his own, *Ha-Metzaref* (Odessa: Beilinison, 1870), in which he painstakingly tried to interpret difficult and fantastic aggadot by collating variant readings, intra-rabbinic philological researches and parallel passages to arrive at the most reasonable readings. Of the various works in this vein, Yehudah Edel Sharshevsky's *Kur le-Zahav*, vol. 1 (Vilna: Romm, 1858), vol. 2 (Vilna: Fuenn & Rosenkranz, 1866), a philosophically minded commentary, seems particularly interesting, in its own right, and as the one work of this type that I know of which seems partially akin to that of Rav Kook's.

23 According to Hayim Czernowitz (Rav Tzair), who, like the young Avraham Yitzhak Kook, was part of Ya'aqov Rabinowitz's quasi-Maskilic study circle in Lyutsin, albeit several years later, Shatzkes's works were "half-kosher" among yeshiva students there; see his *Pirqei Hayim* (New York: Bitzaron, 1954), 79, 81.

24 A characteristic statement is Yair Hayim Bachrach's (1638–1702) depiction of 'Eyn Ya'aqov and Midrash Rabbah as "pleasant for youngsters like appetizers before a meal and a beautiful thing for those who might hear him [sic] when he offers some homily or interrupts an elder's sermon to display his own learning and understanding." This appears in his responsa *Havot Yair* no. 124, which offers an interesting pedagogic presentation along with a classic anti-pilpul polemic. Rav Kook himself conformed to this pattern; at age eleven he studied the 'Eyn Ya'aqov commentary of Aryeh de Modena (Neriah, *Tal*, 44). For a very helpful survey of the

to the bracing complexities of Talmudic legal passages, aggadah's being a standard object of study by laymen did little to enhance its status in the rabbinic fraternity.[25]

Aggadah was indeed studied in Volozhin, in keeping with the broader curricular practice of studying the entire Babylonian Talmud from beginning to end rather than picking and choosing tractates or themes, as was regularly the practice elsewhere. Yet, in an 1887 essay, Rav Kook's Volozhin classmate Berdyczewsky describes the low esteem, bordering on derision, in which study of aggadah was held among the students there.[26] Some years later, partially overlapping with the composition of 'Eyn Ayah, Berdyczewsky himself turned to the study and dissemination of aggadah as part of a search for Jewish literary sources that that would rejuvenate what he had come to see as a desiccated tradition.[27]

Berdyczewsky's looking to aggadah as a repository of vibrant religious energy emerges as yet another parallel between him and Rav Kook; here as elsewhere in the kindred growth of these two figures, Rav Kook worked to articulate his aggadic interests as an invigorated element of, and not as an alternative to, the rabbinic tradition. In this respect he resembles other contemporaries whom he knew or read and turned to aggadah as a source of philosophic reflection: Yosef Zekharia Stern, with whom, as we have found,

---

status of aggadah in rabbinic circles through the centuries, see Yair Lorberbaum, "Reflection on the Halakhic Status of Aggadah," *Dine Israel* (2007): 29–64.

25　See, for instance, the passage from Mendele Mokher Seforim's 1899 "Shlomo Reb Hazins," cited in Gershon Hundert, "The Library of the Study Hall in Volozhin," in Lempertas, *The Gaon of Vilnius and the Annals of Jewish Culture*, 247–256, 251.

　　As I noted in an earlier chapter, Rav Kook taught *Tze'nah u-Re'nah* to a group of laymen in Boisk, which indicates that he was somewhat free of the usual inhibitions of the Talmudic elite where pedagogy was concerned.

26　"Olam Ha-Atzilut: Hashkafah 'al Yeshivat Volozhin be-Hamisha Peraqim," which appeared in *Ha-Qerem* in 1887 and is reprinted in Holzman's *Kitvei Micha Josef Berdyczewski*, vol. 1, 78–97, 82:

האם לא צחוק מכאיב לב הוא, שכל התלמידים הרבים בעת יבואו לפרקי האגדות—אשר המה המפתחות לפתוח אוצר התלמוד—ידלגו עליהם כעל דברים שאין בהם צורך; והראשים עומדים ומחשים, ולא יעוררו אותם—כי אם יעמיקו בהם יגלו לפניהם מושבי היהדות והאומה. העבודה! שבאזני שמעתי מעילויי הישיבה, החושבים כי כל העולם לא נברא אלא בשבילם, אומרים: "לו היינו מדפיסים, אז דילגנו על האגדות ולא הדפסנום כלל, כי איזה תועלת יביאו? האגדות לא נבראו אלא בשביל בעלי הבתים הפשוטים, המה צריכים ללמוד 'עין יעקב,' אבל לא לנו." הדברים האלה יתנו להקורא מושג נאמן מהשקפת רוב בני הישיבה על היהדות והאומה בכלל.

27　Between 1903 and 1905 Berdyczewsky worked on two anthologies, one of Talmudic, the other of Hasidic texts; he returned to the project a decade later and, from 1906 to 1914, compiled *Me-Otzar Ha-Aggadah*, which contains 533 legends. He regarded the expanded edition *Tzefunot Ha-Aggadot* as his masterpiece. In both, the legends are reworked, in an attempted fusion of folk tradition and literature, and his later *Mi-Meqor Yisrael* faithfully reproduces these texts. See Zipora Kagan, "*Homo Anthologicus*: Micha Josef Berdyczewski and the Anthological Genre," *Prooftexts: A Journal of Jewish Literary History* 19, no. 1 (1999): 41–57.

Rav Kook corresponded on halakhic matters, and whose son contributed to Rav Kook's short-lived journal *'Ittur Sofrim*;[28] and Yehoshua Yosef Preil.[29]

Rav Kook's own reading strategy in *'Eyn Ayah* takes a leaf, and more, from the great seventeenth-century figure Maharal (Judah Loew) of Prague (1525–1609), to whose works we saw he was likely first exposed in his teens during his time in Lyutzin. This indebtedness to Maharal is made explicit in his 1899 introduction to *Midbar Shur*, wherein he writes that he has learned from Maharal how to read aggadah "with deep reasoning" (*be-'omeq ha-higayon*). Maharal's method of reading synthesized two interpretive traditions: the Franco-German tradition in which the teachings of the sages were studied word for word as rich with significances in every detail; and the Spanish-Provencal philosophic tradition, whose best-known exponent was Maimonides, for whom the details of nonlegal rabbinic statements are less significant than their broader figurative, poetic, or allegorical articulations of philosophic truths.[30] Like the Franco-Germans, Maharal scrutinizes every detail of rabbinic aggadot for their meaning; like Maimonides, and unlike commentators

---

28 Stern's *Tahalukhot Ha-Aggadot* (Warsaw: Meir Yehiel Halter & Partners, 5662/1902), running to forty-one folio pages, is part of his Talmud commentary *Zekher Yehosef*, published as an appendix to volume four of his reponsa on *Orah Hayim* of the same name. The introduction to it was published in the introduction to volume one of the responsa collection of the same name (Vilna: Dov Berish Torsch Nalkavy, 5659/1898 [*sic*]), 3–4; vol. 2 (Vilna: Yehudah Leib son of Eliezer Lipman Metz, 1899); vol. 3 (Vilna: Pyrzhnykov, 1901). Rav Kook specifically requested Stern's "new book," presumably these first two volumes; see the postscript to his letter to Stern of 20 Sivan 5659/May 29, 1899, reprinted as addendum to *'Ezrat Cohen*, 486 (1969 edition).

　　Stern says in the introduction to his aggadah commentary that one should study aggadot for the essentials of faith—reward and punishment, resurrection, universal revelation at the end of days—for piety, and for righteous interpersonal behavior. Just as one cannot study astronomy (*tekhunah*), geometry (*medidah*), or algebra without preparation, so too, he says, is the case with aggadot. In the remainder of *Tahalukhot* he continues to develop the notion of the inherently oral character of aggadah as accounting for many of its allusions, peculiar features, etc.

　　Interestingly, at 6b he uses language strikingly reminiscent of Rav Kook's emphasis on *yosher*, writing that all God's desire is for man to man straighten himself out, for his own benefit (*haysharat ha-adam derakhav le-oshro*). This is also true for ritual mitzvot, *beyn adam la-maqom*, which mean to rouse man to recognize God's greatness and goodness and desire for the betterment of His creatures.

29 See Preil's *Eglei Tal*. Throughout that somewhat idiosyncratic work Preil tackles problematic aggadot by reading them as working out issues of metaphysics, theology, and Biblical exegesis in the terms of medieval Jewish philosophy. Interestingly, Preil wrote of "feeling" as the necessary prerequisite for Jewish revival, in terms resembling those of Rav Kook; see his posthumous essay printed in Moshe Zvi Greenberg, *Mo'etzot va-Da'at* (Odessa: Beilinson, 1897), 40ff.

30 Maimonides's view is laid out in his introduction to his Mishnah Commentary, and at *Guide*, 3:43. See therein at 3:26, 30 for examples of his dismissing rabbinic statements which seem to defy science, or, alternatively, unwittingly lead in the direction of Aristotle's doctrine of eternity. For a survey of medieval strategies for reading aggadah, see Jacob Elbaum's introduction to his anthology *Lehavin Divrei Hakhamim: Mivhar Divrei Mavo' le-Aggadah u-Midrash mi-shel Hakhmei Yemei Ha-Beynayim* (Jerusalem: Mossad Bialik, 2000), 13–41.

who elucidate the text philologically, intertextually, within the rabbinic corpus or within each textual unit, he understands the true meanings of aggadot to be embedded within a broader philosophical and metaphysical framework.[31] Another key characteristic of Maharal's exegeses greatly shaped those of Rav Kook: Maharal resolutely, consistently, and, it may be said, with no little ingenuity, returns to the same cluster of ideas no matter what text he is discussing. His detailed reading of a text becomes a springboard for, or illustration of, a specific set of moral and theological points, to which he turns again and again almost without exception. The same is very true of *'Eyn Ayah*.

Rav Kook's attempt to establish an honored place for the study of aggadah in yeshiva curricula (an argument we will shortly see him making in his introduction to the work) is of more than educational and theological significance.[32] His argument, made explicitly at times and implicitly on every page, that the desire to study aggadah is as legitimate as the study of halakhah, is of a piece with his arguing for a richer, more expressive, religious vocabulary, as well as an acceptance of the stirrings of the particular student. His need to justify his own study of and love for aggadah is thus part of the larger drama of the age.

Aggadah Between Living Waters and Commentary

In a sense, we have two introductions to *'Eyn Ayah*, one written in medias res, in his 1899 introduction to *Midbar Shur*, the other his formal introduction to the work itself, written sometime, to my mind, about 1902, after much of the work was completed.[33] In his introduction to *Midbar Shur*, he acknowledges the lesser status of aggadic study in rabbinic curricula and says he means to publish this aggadic/sermonic work before any of his halakhic works because he feels that his own halakhic writing is merely conventional, in the realm of thought he is charting a new course: "[T]o expand the bounds of deep thought reflected in honest examination of the depths of rabbinic and Biblical texts, with the addition of the general moral force drawn from the roots of Torah and piety and their

---

31 See Jacob Elbaum, "Rabbi Judah Loew of Prague and His Attitude to the Aggadah," *Scripta Hierosolymitana* 22 (1971): 28–47, and esp. 35–42 therein. Elsewhere, Elbaum sets Maharal's aggadic commentary in the context of the approaches to aggadic commentary in his own milieu, including his differences with that of his successor Samuel Edels, also called Maharsha, whose very different, more classically exegetical commentary became canonical; see Elbaum, *Beyn Petihut Le-Histagrut: Ha-Yetzirah Ha-Ruhanit-Sifrutit be-Polin u-ve-Artzot Ashkenaz be-Shilhei Ha-Me'ah Ha-Shesh-'Esreh* (Jerusalem: Magnes, 1990), 95–142.

32 The pedagogic dimension of Rav Kook's aggadic program is, inter alia, another reflection of the influence of Maharal; see Aharon Fritz Kleinberger, *Ha-Mahshavah Ha-Pedagogit shel Ha-Maharal mi-Prag* (Jerusalem: Hebrew University/Magnes, 1962), esp. 143–145; for a brief English version of the volume, see idem, "The Didactics of Rabbi Loew of Prague," *Scripta Hierosolymitana* 13 (1963): 32–55, which explicitly discusses Maharal's ideas in the context of contemporary humanist pedagogic trends.

33 This timing is reinforced by the appearance of a key idea, *bi'ur*, as a fount of revelation, in his *Mahberot Qetanot Boisk* 1:21, whose entries overall, as I will discuss in a later chapter, reflect the germs of his ideas in his *Ha-Peles* essays of 1901–1904.

branches," hopefully expanding the reader's heart and study of morality/Mussar, which is a sine qua non of the faithful life.[34] Presumably seeking to distinguish his own take on Mussar from that of others, he emphasizes that inasmuch as the point of studying aggadot, is their "rais[ing] of the spirit of one's moral awareness," it is all well and good that most sermonic literature expounds on the conventional teachings of the rabbis and scripture, since "with the expansion of things they will enter the heart where they will be preserved and will act upon [one's] nature and morals," but, he continues, "it is not fit to neglect the essential, which is knowledge, da'at."[35] This is also an implicit critique of the Mussar movement and its emphasis on religious behavior to the point of neglect of the cultivation of the mind; moreover, while for Salanter the cultivation of the mind was a means towards the control of the will, he posits it as an end in itself.

'Eyn Ayah was largely intended as a study text for Mussar, one which would take the positive educational, moral, and spiritual energies of the Mussar movement and channel them into text study.[36] This is clear from the lengthy introduction to the work itself, an apologia for his project and an exploration of its larger meaning, likely written at the close of his work on Berakhot.[37] In it, he reflects on his own reading and exegetical practice, and the tension therein between expansiveness, to the point of new revelation, and the structures of rabbinic tradition. Though the fruit of reflection on writing he had already completed, reading it now is a helpful prolepsis for us to the themes that will gradually emerge as we make our way through the text of the commentary itself.

The introduction begins with the statement that just as there are no true accidents in the natural world, but rather all things unfold according to their deepest natures, so too in the world of the spirit and the development of the corpus of Torah over time.[38]

---

34 MS, 5–6:

להרחיב גבול הגיוני לב המושקפים על פי הבחנה ישרה בעומק דברי חז"ל וכתבי הקודש, בצירוף הכח המוסרי הכללי הנלקט משרשי התורה והיראה וענפיהם. אשר אקוה כי מי שיבחון בדברי אלה ברעיון של בינה ישרה וחודרת, ימצא בהם דברים המרחיבים את הלב ומגדילים את תורת המוסר, הנחוצה לכל איש אמונים אשר ישר הולך.

35 Ibid., 6. The additions in square brackets are those of the editors of the printed edition.

ובאמת חלק האגדה בעדרו ודאי מטרתו היא לרומם את רוח [האדם ואת] הכרתו המוסרית וכאשר ראיתי רבים מהספרים [העוסקים] בדרוש לא שמו להם קו להרחיב את גבול חכמת המוסר, רק לה[ציג] הדברים הטובים הידועים ע"פ ביאורים בדברי חז"ל ובמקרא[ות]. אמנם דבר זה גם הוא רצוי ומקובל כי בהרחבת הדברים י[כנסו] בלב להיות שמורים ופועלים על הטבע והמדות, אבל אין ראוי להזני[ח] העיקר, והוא הדעת.

36 The notebooks we surveyed in the previous chapter, much of which found their way into *Mussar Avikhah*, were a private response. 'Eyn Ayah, by contrast, was meant as a public, pedagogic response.

37 In the introduction, at 13, he references his commentary to a passage in the penultimate chapter of Berakhot, EAB 8:1. A portion of the introduction, up to passages corresponding to p. xvii in the printed edition, was published in *Ha-Devir* 3, nos. 7–9 (1921): 1–5, as part of a series of publications of his there, aimed to bolster his election to the chief rabbinate.

38 It is worth noting that he is here following the expository pattern of Ahad Ha-Am's essays, see Alan Mintz, "Ahad Ha-Am and the Essay: The Vicissitudes of Reason," in *At the Crossroads: Essays on Ahad Ha-Am*, ed. Jacques Kornberg (Albany: State University of New York Press, 1983), 3–11.

He draws a distinction between *be'ur*, exposition, and *perush*, commentary. Punning on *be'ur* and *be'er*, that is, a well, he writes that the former category represents the source of living waters, namely, the way in which every idea has the power to work its way through the mind and bring forth new things, and is to be associated with the self-assured, primal Torah of Moses. By contrast, *perush*, commentary, is the rabbinic tradition as instituted by Ezra, battered by destruction and proceeding in the shadow of exile.[39] Within the Talmudic corpus, it is within the aggadot that *be'ur*, the *élan vital* of revelation, is to be found: "As regards the aggadot, those things *given over to men's hearts* [after BT Bava Metzia 58b] which reveal more of the general principles in nature than the details, we still may join the power of *be'ur* with that of *perush*, and walk broadly as an 'open-ended utterance' . . . and that is *the light that has been sown* (for the righteous) [after Ps. 97:11]."

In other words, aggadah as a sacred text offers a more primal and less strictly legal revelation, one that speaks to, and is interpreted from, the interiority of the student and is thus an "open-ended utterance," which as we will presently see, means that it is more universal than the halakhah peculiar to Israel. The imagery from Ps. 97, of light sprouting out of the ground, conjures up the emergence of this knowledge from the depths; at the same time, in Zoharic literature that verse is taken to refer to the primordial light that was secreted away for the righteous from before creation, to be revealed in the *eschaton*;[40] in *Hovot Ha-Levavot* it represents the prophecy to be attained through and beyond the enlightenment of the mind.[41] The study of aggadah is thus the portal to mystical enlightenment and prophecy, and its study may be of universal mystical significance. He then connects the aggadah to the study of Mussar as he defines that term:

> The rabbinic aggadot are rooted in the moral [*Mussari*] dimensions of Torah, as well as the dimensions that deal with beliefs, opinions, and all spiritual concepts. This dimension of study must be strengthened in every generation, even more than that of practical Torah. Since time immemorial all the giants have roused the hearts of the wise men of Israel who occupy themselves with Torah to pay heed to the spiritual part of Torah, the wisdom of Mussar, its theological morals [*de'ot*] and Duties of the Heart, *Hovot Ha-Levavot*, which overall is stored up in the living treasure of the words of the Rabbis in aggadot.[42]

---

39 We see here an early adumbration of the distinction between the primal, prophetic Torah of the Land of Israel and the alienated, ratiocinating Torah of Exile, which was to figure prominently in his later writings. See Avinoam Rosenak, "'Torat Eretz Yisrael' Ha-Nevu'it be-Mishnat Ha-Re'ayah Kook," in Ravitzky, *Eretz Yisrael be-Hagut Ha-Yehudit be-Me'ah Ha-'Esrim*, 26–70.

40 See, for example, Zohar I, 32a, II, 220b, III, 93a.

41 *Hovot Ha-Levavot*, s.v. *ve-Ha-Hamishi.*

42 EAB, vol. 1, xvii.

והנה שרשי אגדות חז״ל המה פתוחים על חלק המוסרי שבתורה, על החלק של האמונות והדעות וכל המושגים הרוחניים. חלק הלימוד הזה היה היה צריך חיזוק בכל דור ודור עוד יותר מחלק הלימוד של חלק התורה המעשית. וכל גדולי הדורות מעולם העירו את לב חכמי ישראל העוסקים בתורה לשום לב אל חלק הרוחני שבתורה אל חכמת המוסר הדיעות וחובות הלבבות שבכללה היא אצורה באוצר חיים של דברי חז״ל באגדות. . . .

This passage is key to our understanding of what he means by "Mussar," which appears in these pages a staggering number of times.[43] We have already assayed some understanding of the term in his notebooks of the period some of which were likely written after he had already begun work on *'Eyn Ayah*; It may well be that he was himself unclear at the outset as to just what he meant by Mussar; indeed later in his career he seems to have become aware of the extraordinarily broad semantic range of his usage of the term.[44] But in these early writings, Mussar is the interior dimension, intellectual and spiritual, of the religious life, as expressed in action. And the classics of medieval philosophy (as we see, this brief passage alludes to Se'adyah, Bahya and Maimonides) are the starting point for discussion. In a brief letter to Aderet in the summer of 1904, in which he tries to win him over to this way of thinking on religious issues overall, he says he hopes to discuss with him the necessity of fixed and deep study of the moral (*Mussari*) part of Torah, "the details of the mitzvot of *Hovot Ha-Levavot*."[45] Mussar, in other words, consists of the duties of the heart, made manifest in action.[46]

In a pedagogic and more mundane tone, he writes that sustained study of, and writing on, aggadah should speak to two pressings needs: first, the explosion of publishing and the availability to youth of easily readable books on a wide range of subjects, which has yielded a contrasting dearth of compelling spiritual works for young people; and second, the broad public perception of rabbis as people of uncertain character, a challenge which the moral growth to be attained via aggadic study may help meet.[47]

---

43 A search of *Kitvei Ha-Re'ayah Ha-Memuhshavim* (Jerusalem: 2000), a CD-ROM concordance of Rav Kook's writings compiled by Dror Shilo, yielded no fewer than 1223 uses of the word "Mussar," in one form or another, in the first three volumes of *'Eyn Ayah*.

44 In this light we can assay a new interpretation of a key passage, that with which Ha-Nazir opens volume three of *Orot Ha-Qodesh*, entitled *Mussar Ha-Qodesh*, wherein Rav Kook writes that an introduction to the study of Mussar/morality-cum-ethics must needs distinguish between eighteen different kinds of Mussar (*Orot Ha-Qodesh*, 3:19; the original is found in *Qevatzim*, 1:683 and was written around 1910). While Ha-Nazir places it at the outset of his discussion of ethics, this dissertation places it after decades of writing by Rav Kook, chiefly in Eastern Europe, about the meaning of Mussar, that is, this passage reflects his own recognition of the extraordinarily broad range of meanings he had hitherto been assigning the term.

45 The letter is reprinted in *Otzarot*, 2:313.

46 In these pages I periodically translate "Mussar" as morality; while the parsing of the distinctions, such as they are, between "morality" and "ethics" are many and varied, I particularly appreciate George Fletcher's characterization of "morality" as a general orientation of the self, while "ethics" speaks to the duties devolving on oneself in specific situations; see his *Basic Concepts of Legal Thought* (New York: Oxford University Press, 1996). Fletcher's categories reflect the Hegelian distinction distinction between *Moralität* as personal morality and *Sittlichkeit* as socially based (my thanks for this observation to Prof. Jay Harris).

In Julius Barasch's 1816 century philosophic encyclopedia, which was endorsed by Shlomo Yehudah Rappoport, *Otzar Ha-Hokhmah*, "Mussar" is used generally to translate various forms of *Moralität* but also *Ethik* and duty, *Pflicht*. See Zaltzman, "Munahim Filosofiyyim 'al pi Sefer 'Otzar Ha-Hokhmah' le-Julius Barasch," 151–168, 163–165.

47 EAB, vol. 1, xviii–xix.

By way of clarifying the distinction between halakhah and aggadah, and how aggadah's open-ended nature does not detract from its place in the Torah's scale of values, he recurs to the distinction mentioned earlier between an open and sealed utterance, a Talmudic locution (BT Shabbat 104a) with a distinguished history, especially in Hasidic sources.[48] "From the sealed utterance proceeds the Torah of practice, the mitzvot, statutes and laws, the words of God and His testimonies. Only when those [words of God] are safeguarded by that which arises from the sealed utterance (i.e. by the law – ym) will the words illuminate and joyously open the gates of righteousness with the open utterance."[49] Moreover, the sealed utterance is peculiar to Israel, who have nothing to learn from non-Jews by way of praxis; the open utterance, by contrast, opens up as well to the broader reaches of humanity. The failure to maintain this distinction, he says, is a major source of confusion.[50]

In sum, then, there are two complementary ontological facets to the Oral Law's revelation, *aggadah,* aka *bi'ur.* Thus *bi'ur* is aggadah in open utterance, "open" in its endless expansion of meanings and its reaching towards humanity as a whole, and the law (*perush*) is sealed, seeking precise definitions and unique to Israel.

He then addresses the Mussar controversies of his day. There are those who say that the study of Musssar and aggadah will distance students from deep and intensive study of Talmud and halakhah. This is perhaps true of study by way of enthusiasm, *hitragshut,* which disturbs the equanimity that ought to obtain in soul-feelings (and was a distinctive practice of the Mussar yeshivot). But not when it proceeds by an organized, systematic and thoroughgoing course of study.[51] As we have seen previously he tries again to mediate among the various spiritual traditions he has inherited, in particular medieval philosophy and the Kabbalah. Each tradition has its place he says, "and we in this later generation will gather in joy that which they sowed in tears" (after Ps. 126:5).[52] Now, he says, that the great storms around Hasidism have passed, that spiritual tradition can be drawn upon as

---

48　The phrase first appears in BT Shabbat 104a as regards two possible orthographies of the letter *mem,* Rashi *ad loc.* adds that "closed things" are esoterica such as *ma'aseh merkavah,* which one may not freely discuss. A most striking anticipation of the usage here is in the writings of the early Hasidic master Nahum of Chernobyl (1730–1797), who says that the "open utterance" is both the revealed Torah, as well as its soul and inner meaning; see *Meor 'Eynayim,* rev. ed. (Jerusalem: n.p., 1989), 215. The other places in his published writings where discussion of "open and closed utterance" are later—in *'Eyn Ayah* to Berakhot 2:247, and in a talk transcribed by Neriah very shortly before Rav Kook's death appearing in *Meorot Ha-Re'ayah* to Shavu'ot, 259–261, which is preceded by an undated fragment at 258, which seems later as well.

49　EAB, vol. 1, xx.

מהמאמר-הסתום תצא תורה למעשה, המצות החקים והמשפטים, דברי ד' ועדותיו. רק כשיהיו נשמרים כל אלה
ע"פ העולה מהמאמר-הסתום יהיו הדברים מאירים ושמחים לפתח שערי צדק במאמר הפתוח.

50　Ibid., xxi.

51　Ibid., xxii.

52　Ibid., xxiii:

. . . ואנחנו בדור אחרון נאסוף ברינה את אשר זרעו הם בדמעה.

well.[53] Yet all this requires careful, painstaking work and study, which is what he proposes to undertake here and in the books he hopes to pen in the future.

As seen earlier, notwithstanding Salanter's use of the philosophical tradition and emphasis on the cultivation of the intellect in a number of his writings (of which Rav Kook was aware),[54] the Mussar movement as a whole was by the 1890s characterized by mistrust, if not hostility, towards rationalism, and emphasized emphasis on emotional exertion aimed at repression of the self.[55] While taking to heart the Mussar movement's objective of strengthening piety and the moral life—and indeed the word "Mussar" figures several times on every page of 'Eyn Ayah, and regularly in contexts where terms such as yirah or qedushah or ruah would do—'Eyn Ayah aims to further these objectives by a renewed engagement with the philosophical tradition, and along the methodological—and at times theological—lines of aggadic study laid out by Maharal of Prague, whose works were a constant companion to him in those years. That the one figure cited nearly as often as Maimonides is Bahya ibn Paquda, further points to the work's dual nature as a philosophically inflected Mussar text, albeit one in which intellectual perfection was to be met with devotion to a very personal God.

Self-Perfection

Throughout 'Eyn Ayah to Berakhot, as in his notebooks, we find a preoccupation with the cultivation of shlemut, or self-perfection, a driving theme of the philosophical-moral literature of the Middle Ages and of the Maskilic literature that succeeded it.[56] He does

---

53 Ibid., xxiv.

54 See the essays gathered in Pachter, Kitvei Rabbi Yisrael Salanter, particularly 125–159, which were written for Salanter's journal Tevunah (Reason) and reprinted in 1878 in Sidarsky, ed. Imrei Binah, 5–32. That Rav Kook knew these writings is attested to at EAB 4:10, vol. 1, 111–112.

55 See Ross, "Ha-Megamah Ha-Anti-Ratziyonalit be-Tenu'at Ha-Mussar," 145–162. Slabodka Mussar is something of an exception here, both in Finkel's emphasis on "human dignity" as well as in the striking accomplishments of the yeshiva's analytic-minded Talmudists, such as Isser Zalman Meltzer and Shimon Shkop; yet there too the medieval rationalist tradition and its variety of self-cultivation was not looked to as a model. Though Shkop did have recourse to some basic concepts of natural law in his Talmudic work—see his explicit formulation in his Sha'arei Yosher, 5:1, vol. 2, 4—his was a complex position, in which natural reason takes its place as a part of the broader revelation of Torah of which it is itself a part; see the discussion in Shai Aqiva Wozner, Hashivah Mishpatit bi-Yeshivot Lita: 'Iyunim be-Mishnato shel Ha-Rav Shimon Shkop (Jerusalem: Magnes, 2016), particularly chapter five.

56 On perfection in Maimonides see, inter alia, Guide, 3:13; Menachem Kellner, Brown Judaic Studies, vol. 202, Maimonides on Human Perfection (Atlanta: Scholars Press, 1990); Howard Kreisel, "Imitatio Dei in Maimonides' Guide of the Perplexed," AJS Review 19 (1994): 169–211; Kenneth Seeskin, Searching for a Distant God: The Legacy of Maimonides (New York: Oxford University Press, 2000), 96–123. The debate between Leo Strauss and Hermann Cohen on the meaning of perfection for Maimonides need not detain us here; Rav Kook's inclusion of Maimonidean ideals in this work, meant for a broad, if learned, audience, indicates that he

not make much use of traditional terminology of love and fear of God.[57] Rather, he speaks in terms of the philosophical category of *shlemut*, perfection, and of *yosher*, natural right-eousness, which has its own integrity and, contra standard Mitnagdic asceticism and as we have already seen, makes possible an affirmation of the body as a vehicle of religious service.[58] He follows Arama in his seeing religious and natural perfection as distinct yet progressive, with the former a necessary stepping-stone to the latter.[59] At the same time, read in light of his *Pinqasim*, some of the Kabbalistic meanings of *yosher* echo in these pages.[60]

The theme of perfection is sounded early on, at 1:5. Discussing the disagreement (3a)[61] as to whether the night is, for liturgical (and heavenly) purposes, divided into three or four watches, and after a lengthy apologia for presuming to discuss such weighty matters despite his youthful shallowness, he says:

> When we examine the elements of perfection fitting to man in general and in particular the legatees of God's Torah,[62] we see that they are divided into four: first, the perfection

---

did not see Maimonides's teachings as meant for an esoteric elite. This is not to say that he did not believe in esotericism—rather, in the manner of Lithuanian Kabbalists he practiced his esotericism with regards to the study of Kabbalah, at least at this early stage of his career.

The ways in which traditionalist Jewish Maskilim interpreted the philosophical ideal of perfection is one of the threads running through Bor, "Moral Education in the Age of the Jewish Enlightenment."

57 When he does it can be interesting: at EAB 2:36, vol. 1, 79–80 we read that love of God comes from *imitatio dei*, but fear of God comes from contemplating God's great ways; hence love of God is love of Torah, whose essence is to foster *imitatio dei*, while fear of God is fear of Heaven, that is, of His greatness.

58 For uses of *yosher* connoting natural righteousness, see, for example, EAB 1:52, 1:101, 1:126, 3:5, 3:31, 3:33, 3:41, 5:35, 5:67, 5:75, 5:76.

The meaning of *yosher* as the foundation of natural righteousness and the necessary steppingstone to mystical enlightenment emerges clearly from Pinhas Eliyahu of Vilna's massive treatise of natural science and metaphysics *Sefer Ha-Berit*, first published in 1797 and republished frequently throughout the nineteenth century, the first volume of which is entitled *Ketav Yosher*, while the second, metaphysical volume is entitled *Ketav Emet*. For an insightful discussion of this work and its overall place in nineteenth-century Orthodox thought, see Ira Robinson, "Kabbalah and Science in *Sefer Ha-Berit*: A Modernization Strategy for Orthodox Jews," *Modern Judaism* 9, no. 3 (1989): 275–288; for details on how widely the work was read, see 285n4, and more generally, David B. Ruderman, *A Best-Selling Hebrew Book of the Modern Era: The Book of the Covenant of Pinhas Hurwitz and its Remarkable Legacy* (Seattle: University of Washington Press, 2014).

59 Arama's critique of Maimonides on this point is discussed by Heller-Wilensky, *Rabbi Yitzhaq Arama u-Mishnato*, 193–196.

60 At *Pinqas* 16:23 he says that the the difference between *tzadiq* and *yashar* is the following: the former is one who masters their will, but the latter are those who have entirely merged their will with God's and they can grasp joy in its essence.

61 Once again, unless otherwise stated, all Talmudic page numbers here refer to BT Berakhot.

62 Rav Kook's use of the masculine throughout is no accident of usage but also reflects his own very gendered view of intellect, feeling and human capability—see, for example, EAB 1:147,

of worship in practice, fulfilling all the mitzvot and guarding oneself from all that He has proscribed; second, the perfection of moral virtues, to walk in His blessed ways, of which the Rabbis said [BT Avodah Zarah 20b] *hasidut* is the greatest . . . as the Hasid [Luzzatto—Y. M.] explained in *Mesillat Yesharim*; third, perfection in knowing the revealed [exoteric Torah] in all its details so that one may thereby fulfill all the mitzvot, and also perfect his soul with the decoration of the Intelligibles of Torah . . . and fourth, the seal and telos of the first three, to know God, attain the love of Him and awe of his exaltedness and to know His ways, which is the telos of human perfection.[63]

He is here essentially reworking the four perfections outlined at the close of Maimonides's *Guide*, 3:54. In Maimonides's scheme, the progressive perfections are those of one's relation to possessions, one's relation to one's own body, the perfection of the moral virtues, and, finally, the true perfection of the conception of intelligibles. The first three are but preparatory steps towards this last perfection; and this apprehension of God's ways and Providence at the very limit of human understanding will then manifest itself in a life of *imitatio dei*, characterized by kindness, justice, and good judgment. Here, Rav Kook conflates the bodily reference of the first two perfections and gives it an explicitly religious inflection in his first perfection, that of practical mitzvot; Maimonides's third perfection, the cultivation of virtue, is his second; and he divides Maimonides's fourth perfection, that of the intellect, into two, reflecting the two faces of Torah study, the esoteric and exoteric; or in terms of two traditions to which Rav Kook was heir, Mitnagdic Talmudism and Kabbalistic contemplation.[64]

He thus fuses the Maimonidean structure of self-perfection with the pietistic concern of Luzzatto's *Mesillat Yesharim*. Intellectual perfection, exoteric and esoteric both, is the summit of an ascent of both man and cosmos, from mitzvot to virtue to Torah study to, finally, knowledge of God. He is not, however, a Maimonidean rationalist through and through; alongside intellectual perfection there is still piety, *hasidut*, which draws on different human resources. Indeed, from the outset of the work we see an oscillation, and regularly, tension, between intellectual perfection and piety, which in turn correlates with

---

2:65, 7:46–47, and the discussion in this chapter of 9:191. I will translate him accordingly, however discordant that may sound to contemporary ears.

63   EAB, vol. 1, 2–3:

והנה כשנבחין חלקי השלמות הראוים לאדם, ובפרט לנוחלי תורת ה' נמצאם חלוקים לארבע מחלקות: הא' הוא שלמות העבודה בפועל, לקיים כל מצות השי"ת ולהשמר מכל אשר הזהיר. והב' הוא שלמות המדות ללכת בדרכיו ית' אשר ע"פ דחז"ל שאמרו חסידות גדולה מכולם . . . וכמו שביאר בזה החסיד במסילת ישרים. הג' הוא שלמות ידיעת התורה הנגלית בכל פרטי' שעי"ז ידע לקיים כל המצות כולן, גם ישלים את נפשו בקשוטי מושכלות התורה . . . . הד', הוא החותם והתכלית של כל שלש המעלות הקדומות והפרי היוצא מהן, שהוא לדעת את השי"ת, כדי להגיע לאהבתו ויראת רוממותו ולדעת דרכיו ית' שהוא תכלית שלמות האדם.

64   While he does not explicitly cite *Guide*, 3:54, he does cite *Guide*, 3:51 for the proposition that "the final telos is the knowledge of God which is the perfecting of man" and is best arrived at via the three actions outlined above:

כי זו התכלית האחרונה שהיא ידיעת השם יתברך שהיא השלמת האדם.

his regularly shifting the respective prioritizations of mind vis-à-vis imagination-feeling. This tension is both a matter of practice, as well as of different textual and spiritual traditions.

Regarding practice, he says, apropos of the relative merits of the angels Michael and Gabriel (4b), that human, and especially Israelite, perfection can be attained in two ways: the way of wisdom and philosophizing culminating in the realization of the truth by way of demonstration, and "the path of simplicity and righteousness derived from the righteous heart and path, from which comes perfect faith."[65] Ha-Levi's *Kuzari*, he notes, correctly praises the latter over the former.[66] Indeed, the path of simplicity is the greater, not because obedience as such is a virtue, but "because the natural inclination is something immanent/intrinsic to the human self, requiring nothing external to rouse it to perfection, while understanding and wisdom are extrinsic to it . . . they are separate (*nivdalim*) and one who follows that path will require an external stimulus to rouse him to perfection."[67] The relationship of this question to different textual traditions is made explicit further when he straightforwardly asks—and leaves open—whether essential perfection is to be found in the intellect, per Maimonides, or via moral cultivation and worship, per Bahya's *Hovot Ha-Levavot*.[68]

This tension between the religion of the mind and the religion of the heart is central to *'Eyn Ayah*. The axis around which his discussion thereof evolves is through the medieval categorization of intellect and imagination; that word's first appearances in the text connote "sensation," but he gradually unmoors it and uses it in a distinctly modern sense as a mix of intuition and emotion, and thus as a point of entry from within the philosophic tradition for discussion of the affective, and increasingly expressive, religious life.

Intellect, Imagination, Feeling

We have already seen his early interest in the Maimonidean doctrine of prophecy in *'Ittur Sofrim*, where he tried to soften some of that doctrine's naturalistic edges. That interest

---

65   החכמה והתפלספות . . . התמימות והמישרים מצד ישרות הלב והנטיה הישרה שממנה באה האמונה השלמה.

66   See *Kuzari* 2:26.

    In terms of the Talmudic passage at hand, he writes, the angel Michael, who is said (BT Berakhot 4b) to be greater than Gabriel, stands only for Israel, representing the path of simple righteousness, while Gabriel, who has a more diffuse function, is appointed over knowledge (see Deut. 9:22–23) and the seventy tongues of the world (BT Sotah 36b).

67   כי הנטי' הטבעית שבלב היא דבר עצמי בנפש האדם, וא"צ דבר מחוצה לה שיעיר אותה אל שלמותה, אבל ההשגה והחכמה הם דברים נבדלים מהאדם, וצריך הערה חיצונה להעיר אותו על השלמתו.

68   EAB 1:75, vol. 1, 32–33:
נראה דפליגי על מרכז השלמות האנושית אם הוא השכל, כדעת הרמב"ם שיחס הכל אל הידיעה, או המוסר והעבודה כד' חובת הלבבות.

returns here in *'Eyn Ayah*, as Maimonides's doctrine of prophecy becomes the starting point for an exploration of the affective dimension of the religious life.[69]

Maimonides lays out his doctrine of non-Mosaic prophecy at *Guide*, 2:36. There he writes that the perfection of the imaginative faculty through natural disposition is—along with intellectual perfection through study and of morals through self-discipline—a prerequisite for prophecy. Prophecy is an abundant flow from God via the Active Intellect towards, first, the rational faculty and thence toward the faculty of the imagination. It is the ultimate perfection of the imagination, which itself is of the body, retaining, reordering and imitating sensual perceptions. The Active Intellect courses through the imagination, and thus, linked as the latter is to the senses, enables the prophet to clothe abstract truths in representational language and thus facilitate community, by forging a shared social imaginary, held together by law.

Rav Kook recurs to this Maimonidean passage several times in *'Eyn Ayah* to Berakhot.[70] Yet, the conception he develops of the human faculty which bridges between abstract metaphysical truth, on the one hand, and sensible perception and expression on the other, seems more akin to that of Yehudah Ha-Levi, who, interestingly, he does not directly quote on this point. At *Kuzari* 4:3, Ha-Levi writes that prophecy—superior to philosophy and expressing of the divine Will in apprehensible form—is facilitated by a kind of inner sense perception which is able to grasp nonmaterial, spiritual entities, even if it is not able to penetrate to their very essences (the same way that sense perception grasps the existence of sensate entities even if it does not penetrate to their essences).[71] Ha-Levi calls this an "internal eye" (in the original Arabic, *'ayn batinah*), through which prophets look at this world. While Ha-Levi himself says that this "internal eye" is "nearly"—but not identical to—the imagination, ibn Tibbon, in the canonical translation which was the source of Rav Kook's knowledge of *Kuzari*, writes "and it may be that this eye is the imaginative faculty."[72]

Crucially, while for Maimonides the imagination is a tool for the expression of truths received through and shaped by the intellect, for Ha-Levi imagination is itself the medium through which spiritual truths are immediately perceived. We will see that Rav Kook adds to intellect and imagination an element akin to Ha-Levi's "third eye," namely feeling, which can intuit religious truths, and through *'Eyn Ayah* he keeps trying to work out the respective relations of this trio of intellect, imagination, and feeling.

---

69 A number of the points made in this section are summarized in my "Ha-Re'ayah ve-Ha-Rambam: 'Iyun Mehudash," in *'Iggud* 1 (2008): 397–405.

70 See EAB 3:16, 9:72, 9:112, 9:203.

71 See Zev Harvey, "Torat Ha-Nevu'ah Ha-Synesteti shel Rihal ve-He'arah 'al Sefer Ha-Zohar," in *Mehqarei Yerushalayim be-Mahshevet Yisrael* 2, no. 12 (1996): 141–155. For a discussion of the differences between the respective views of Maimonides and Ha-Levi on prophecy see Harry Wolfson, "Maimonides and Hallevi on Prophecy."

72 This is pointed out by Harvey, "Torat Ha-Nevu'ah Ha-Synesteti shel Rihal ve-He'arah 'al Sefer Ha-Zohar," 143n5. Qafih's translation follows ibn Tibbon; see his edition, 156. The phrase "inner eye" appears in other medieval Jewish thinkers in the Islamicate orbit; see Abraham ibn Ezra on Ps. 19:4.

Thus, after beginning with the Maimonidean hierarchy of intellect-imagination-body he will shift to intellect-feeling-body with feeling coming eventually to rival intellect in sovereign status in defining human personhood. This is of a piece with a general shift in moral-psychological vocabulary in the late nineteenth and early twentieth centuries, and, as we will see, contrasts interestingly with how these categories are worked in Lithuanian Kabbalah and in the writings of Nahman of Bratslav.

In early passages Rav Kook discusses *hergesh*—whose semantic range is somewhere between sensate perception, sentiment, instinct and the modern notion of feeling, as a power that one must arouse for the pursuit of divine service, as it leaves a greater impress on the soul than does intellectual knowledge.[73] A little later, he writes that all activities divide into one of three, for good or ill—intellect, deed, and feeling.[74] Feeling is hand-maiden to intellect, and—harking back to his discussions of the intellect's cognition of particulars which we saw in his sermons around *Hevesh Pe'er*—if one is inclined to intel-lect his feelings will tend towards universal and disinterested principles like justice and righteousness.[75]

In a central passage, 1:127, he introduces Maimonides's concept of the faculty of the imagination as a way of gaining some purchase on the idea of feeling. However, he pits intellect and imagination against each other, seemingly opening a window onto some of his own conflicts. Apropos the comment (10a) that only King David was uniquely able to sing no matter the world of experience in which he found himself:

> Two things are necessary for human perfection, intellect and feeling. The origin of intellect is in demonstrable knowledge and wisdom, learned and experiential, and has nothing to do with the feelings of the heart. And the origin of feeling is the imaginative faculty and the strengthening of the poetic faculty in the human soul, as it feels the sublime, until the end of her ascent is the love of the Name of God.

Yet the relation between these two faculties is essentially antagonistic.

> Now these two wondrous forces generally oppress one another, since when the intellect is busy with gathering its cold facts to reckon all things, the sentiment is not awake, and cannot long for the holy and sublime in the deepest outpourings of the soul. And at the moment that the heart is enflamed to holy feelings, the judging faculty of the intellect is unable to function.[76]

A little more background is helpful here. In Maimonides's presentation, the faculty of the imagination is clearly subordinate to the intellect, as prophecy proceeds from the Active Intellect towards the human intellect, and is then translated downwards towards the masses by the prophet's imaginative power. For other medieval thinkers, by contrast, imagination is necessary for prophetic revelation itself as the prophet himself depends on

---

73 EAB 1:24, 1:31.
74 Ibid. 1:33.
75 Ibid. 1:46.
76 The full translation of this passage appears at the close of our discussion.

material images for the perception of metaphysical truths.[77] Arama wrote that while both imagination and intellect have roles to play in devotion, which I will discuss later on, neither is essential for prophecy, which is in any case a freely given grace of God; if anything is the sine qua non of prophecy it is a synthesis of love of God, moral perfection, and religious obedience.[78] Ha-Levi argues both that the "inner eye" mentioned above is the faculty of prophetic inspiration, and that philosophy's disparagement of the imagination is misplaced, as human feeling can be deepened most effectively by sensory representations and symbols.[79]

Importantly—in the medieval philosophic spectrum, intellect and the imagination are not depicted as antagonists.[80] Nor do we find this in such Kabbalistic classics as the Zoharic literature of Cordovero's *Pardes Rimonim*, wherein imagination is identified with the lowest, tenth sefirah, *Malkhut*, and thus with the *Shekhinah*, an identification with which Rav Kook was familiar.[81]

We do, however, find it in Lithuanian Kabbalah. In the writings of Menahem Mendel of Shklov (d. 1827), a premier disciple of the Gaon of Vilna, we find the following description of a fundamental conflict *au fond* in the emanation process of the sefirot: "these are the two currents: they are the inner meaning of *Hokhmah* and *Binah*, of the reflection and the likeness, Abel and Cain, thought and imagination."[82] The invocation of Cain and Abel highlights like nothing else the conflictual nature of this relation.

---

77 This was the view of the late fourteenth- to mid-fifteenth-century thinker Zerahia Ha-Levi Saladin; see the discussion in Ari Ackerman, "The Philosophic Sermons of R. Zerahia Ha-Levi Saladin" (PhD diss., Hebrew University, 2000), 103–115. Almost none of Zerahia's work was printed until the present day and so Rav Kook would not have been aware of him. Looking at Zerahia does, though, usefully illustrate the range of ways in which the imaginative faculty was thought of as figuring in prophecy.

78 See Heller-Wilensky, *Rabbi Yitzhaq Arama u-Mishnato*, 171–176.

79 See *Kuzari* 4:5 and Ackerman's discussion in "The Philosophic Sermons of R. Zerahia Ha-Levi Saladin."

80 Spinoza, for his part, regards imagination as distinctly inferior to and inherently at odds with reason, which grasps things in terms of their necessity and eternity; see *Ethics* 3:18 et seq., and see Harry Wolfson's succinct formulation in his *The Philosophy of Spinoza*, vol. 2 (Cambridge, MA: Harvard University Press, 1934), 160–161. I do not know if Rav Kook was aware of Spinoza's position on this at this time. See as well Jose Faur, "Intuitive Knowledge of God in Medieval Jewish Theology," *Jewish Quarterly Review* 67 nos. 2-3 (1976-1977): 90-110.

81 See *Tiqqunei Zohar* 18, 31b; 22, 65a; 30, 74b; *Ra'ya Mehemna*, Zohar II, 42b; 3:280b; see Cordovero's *Pardes Rimonin* 23, s.v. *dimyon*. See Rav Kook's comment at *Pinqas* 16:17, see also his comment in *Pinqas* 14, §41 and in EAB 9:151. See also Eliot R. Wolfson, *Through a Speculum That Shines: Vision and Imagination in Medieval Jewish Mysticism* (Princeton: Princeton University Press, 1994), 306. For Luzzatto, the truths of Kabbalah were themselves the stuff of visual revelation, and his status as an ostensible prophet was a key factor in the controversies swirling around him; see Eliezer Baumgarten, "Hinei 'Eyn Ha-Navi Ye-Dameh: Nevuah, Qabbalah ve-Dimuy Haziti etzel Ramhal," *Pe'amim* 150-152 (2017): 289-321.

82 אלין תרין משיכן: הם סוד חו''ב, הצלם והדמות, הבל וקין, מחשבת והדמיון.
    This passage appears in Menahem Mendel's *Mayim Adirim*, published in Warsaw in 1886 with Isaac Haver Wildman's glosses, and is cited in Moshe Idel, "Beyn Ha-Kabbalah Ha-Nevu'it

Turning to a different tradition, a fraught relationship between intellect and imagination is found in the writings of Menahem Mendel's Hasidic contemporary, Nahman of Bratslav (1772–1810). There we find the striking idea that because faith is itself a form of prophecy, depending as it does on an immediate sense of the presence of God, the faculty of the imagination is no less than a key ingredient of faith; indeed the cultivation of the imagination is the first step towards an ultimate desideratum of attaining the degree of prophecy greater even that that of Moses. That in turn involves the "casting away" of intellect, and the content of that prophecy is the answer to the problem of theodicy.[83] The imagination thus enables a degree of prophecy higher than the intellect, perhaps even opposed to it, in its embrace of paradox and contradiction.

Nahman's ideas reflect to no small degree the complex and often dramatic dynamics of his own internal religious life, even as he is also working as a commentator on received traditions and ideas. Here Rav Kook for his part strikes what seems a remarkably self-referential note of his own in working out the relations between intellect and imagination-feeling.

> But there are distinguished individuals, in whom the two forces can be perfected entirely, they will know true knowledge by the intellect and its analogies and experiments, and that will give birth in them to perfection of the feeling of majesty that is in the work of God which comes from the wondrous understanding of His love and kindness.

To be sure, this feeling is not untutored but is itself the product of cultivation.

> This kind of feeling does not come from a simple natural source but rather from effort and deep knowledge, which is the conjunction of the Torah of Hesed, from which emerges feeling and song, with the fountain of wisdom, to know and reckon the regimen of deeds on which feeling is built.[84]

---

le-Kabbalat Rabbi Menahem Mendel mi-Shklov," in Hallamish, Rivlin, and Schuchat, *The Vilna Gaon and His Disciples*, 173–184, 177. Idel noted that this was to his knowledge a sui generis depiction of "imagination" as an intradivine activity in the Kabbalistic tradition, and that Menahem Mendel is synthesizing traditions associated with both Abraham Abulafia and the Gaon.

83 See the penetrating analysis of Zvi Mark, *Mistiqah ve-Shiga'on bi-Yetzirat Rabbi Nahman mi-Breslov* (Jerusalem/Tel Aviv: Hartman Institute/'Am 'Oved, 2003), 86–114.

84 EAB 1:127:

שני דברים ישנם הדרושים (!) לשלמות האדם, השכל והרגש. מקור השכל הוא הידיעה המופתית והחכמה הלימודית והנסיונית שדבר אין לה עם רגשי הלב. והרגש מוצאו מכח המדמה והתגברות הכח הפיוטי שבנפש האדם, בהרגישה את הנשגב, עד שתכלית מעלתה היא אהבת שם ה' ית'. והנה ע"פ רוב אלה שני הכוחות הנפלאים הם מעיקים זה ע"ז, כי בהיות השכל טרוד בקיבוץ ידיעותיו הקרות, להביא חשבון את כל הנעשה, אין הרגש ער להתגעגע בעומק השתפכות הנפש אל הקדוש והמרומם. ובשעה שהלב מתלהב לרגשי קודש לא יוכל כח השופט השכלי לפעול. אמנם אנשים מצוינים נמצאים שבהם [ובהם] ישתלמו שני הכוחות בשלמותם, יכירו את הידיעה האמיתית ע"פ השכל והקישיו ונסיונותיו, ומזה תולד להם בשלמות הרגשת ההוד ההוא במעשה האלהים שיסודה היא אהבת ד' הבאה מהכרה נפלאה באהבתו וחסדיו . . . רגש כזה אינו בא ממקור רגש טבעי פשוט כ"א אחרי עמל וידיעה עמוקה, והוא החיבור של תורת חסד שממנה תוצאות לרגש ושירה עם מקור חכמה, לדעת ולהבין בחשבון את משטר המעשים, שעליהם הרגש בנוי.

We see here the emergence of the tension between intellect and feeling that is a leitmotif of Rav Kook's mature thought.[85] Unlike Nahman, Rav Kook refuses throughout *'Eyn Ayah*, and in his later writings as well, ever finally to privilege one over the another, but maintains the integrity of each, at times agonistically, as did Menahem Mendel of Shklov, at times attempting synthesis. And this synthesis will be a key ingredient in his eventual embrace of dialectic as a metaphysical principle with which to untangle the knots of modernity.

As Alain Touraine helpfully put it, a defining element of modernity is "the tension between reason and the subject."[86] He writes: "As we enter modernity, religion shatters, but its component elements do not vanish. When it ceases to be divine or to be defined as Reason, the subject becomes human and personal. It becomes a specific type of relation of individuals or groups to themselves."[87] As Rav Kook's thought develops in these pages we will see that tension vigorously expressing itself, and—given his ongoing commitment to the ontological reality of Mind and its human realization in the intellect—with mounting force and growing complexity.

Rav Kook's positive valuation of imagination, which in the Maimonidean scheme bridges between the mind and the body, is related to the generally positive valuation of the body reflected in a number of the early passages of *'Eyn Ayah*, which in turn deepens our understanding of what we have earlier seen in his *Metziot Qatan* and *Midbar Shur*. Thus he writes at 1:148 that holiness is transcendence from within the body, a self-transformation such that the discipline of intellect is unnecessary since the body seeks the good of its own accord. Indeed, he says at 1:165 that the diminution of one's own powers is only in the passage to perfection, but on coming truly to know God, one will feel the strength of all his faculties. (Relatedly, in *Pinqas,* 16:20 we read that sin comes from man's being separated from the light of the mind, and that comes from arrogance—and that which does the separating is imagination.)

If so, what is the problem with a religious life based on imagination? Reading Abaye's dictum (17a) that "one must be naked in piety, answering softly and deflecting anger, speaking words of peace" to mean that one must strip away imagination, he writes that one whose representation of piety is based on imagination will be spiritually solipsistic—so filled will one's heart be with piety that there will be no room there for the "human obligations" of humanity, sociability and human dignity. By contrast, one whose piety proceeds via the intellect will see that the goal of piety is to repair all one's ways by the

---

85 This is obvious to all readers of his work; the point is made throughout Ish-Shalom, *Ha-Rav Kook: Beyn Ratziyonalism le-Mistiqah,* and most explicitly and powerfully therein at 213.

86 Alain Touraine, *Critique of Modernity*, trans. David Macey, 2nd ed. (Oxford: Blackwell, 1995). There are points of contact here to Eisenstadt and Taylor's understandings of modernity woven throughout this work.

87 Ibid., 306.

greater *tiqqun* and see that the truest outgrowths of piety are human dignity and ways of peace and sociability.[88]

He is unsure as to what hierarchical relations should obtain, if any, between intellect and imagination. Even though at 3:16 he straightforwardly cites Maimonides's *Guide* 2:36 for the proposition that "the faculty of imagination is the foundation and preparation to the intellectual faculty," a little later on, at 3:35, commenting on the passage (20a) as to why miracles happened to earlier generations who sanctified God's Name, he reverses the sequencing and makes the intellect the steppingstone to the imagination, which latter is not governed by logical principles of necessity and is thus an arena in which there can be miracles, which themselves express the free, unbounded will of God:

> True perfection requires perfection of both the intellect and the imagination, from which derive all traits and acts. Torah perfects the intellect and prayer is based in the heart. . . . Now the divine acceptance of prayer in particular and changes in the natural order in general are all miracles, whose possibility cannot be apprehended by the intellect and if they are apprehended at all [by the intellect it will be] in only a limited way, for the intellect regularly perceives the necessity of those obstacles which make them (i.e., miracles) impossible. But by representation and the imaginative faculty everything is possible. . . . And so, miracles will more likely occur to one who paves his way by his deeds and thus broadens the perfection of the imaginative faculty, after he has perfected his intellect. . . . And then he will be drawn to all worship and holiness in a path higher than his mind and without reckonings and questions will do all that touches on God's service with wondrous energy and exalted feeling.

The passage closes with a hint of ambivalence, which he mediates interestingly: "And even if at times some error may arise therefrom in the worldly order, yet of this it is written *be forever mad with her love* (Prov. 5:19)."[89]

The verse in Proverbs, whose subject is the love of wisdom, and which served none other than Maimonides (*Hilkhot Teshuvah* 10:6) to characterize the fullest worship of God, offers a bit of Scriptural reassurance that there is a place for love in the life of the

---

88 EAB 2:60, vol. 1, 84:

יש הבדל בין מי שמתנהג בציור יראת ד' כפי השכל, או שמתנהג בה כפי הדמיון וכח המדמה לבד. כי בראשית ההשקפה הדמיונית, אין עם יראת ד' דבר כ"א ציור היראה האלהית לבד, ואין עמה מקום לדרך ארץ, לאנושיות וכבוד הבריות. כיון שיראת ד' ממלאת את לבבו וכל רגשותיו, איפה יכנסו אלה החיובים האנושיים בלבבו. אבל מי שמסתכל ביראת ד' בשכל, יכיר כי מטרת יראת ד' היא לתקן כל דרכיו ע"ד התיקון היותר שלם ויותר נאה . . א"כ לא ילך אחר הציור הדמיוני, כ"א אחר עצת השכל בפרטי היראה, אז ישכיל כי גדולי ענפי היראה האמיתית היא כבוד הבריות ודרכי שלום ודרך ארץ.

89 Ibid., vol. 1, 100–101:

לשלימות האדם צריך שישתלם בשני חלקיו, שלמות השכל ושלימות הכח המדמה, שממנו נובעים כל המדות והמעשים . . . .התורה משלמת את השכל והתפילה יסודה בלב. . . . והנה קבלת התפילה בפרט ושינויי הטבע בכלל, שהם כל הניסים, לפי כח השכל לא תושג אפשרותם, ואם תושג תהי' מוגבלת מאד. כי השכל משיג לפעמים נמנעות חיוביות שמסלק אותן מגדר היכולת אמנם לפי הציור והמדמה הכל אפשר . . . ע"כ יותר קרוב שיעשו ניסים לאדם ושתתרבה תפילתו אז יפלס נתיבו בהליכותיו בהרחבת שלימות כח המדמה, אחרי שישלם שכלו. . . . ואז ימשך אל העבודה והקדושה באורח נעלה משכלו ובלא שאלת פי החשבון יעשה כל דבר הנוגע לעבודת ד' בזירוז מופלא ורגש נשגב. ואף אם לפעמים אפשר לבא מזה איזו שגיאה שלה בסדרי עולם אבל ע"ז נאמר באהבתה תשגה תמיד.

mind and that the system itself acknowledges the delirium of divine love and its inevitable disequilibria.

Rav Kook's attempted resolutions of this ambivalence, however, last only as long as his encounter with the Talmudic passage at hand, and the ambivalence persists as he makes his way through the text of Tractate Berakhot. Thus at 4:32, commenting on Rabbi Eliezer's deathbed exhortation (28b) to his disciples to "know before Whom you pray," he oscillates between a celebration of feeling and anxiety over its possible excesses:

> Prayer is worship founded in emotion and the arousal of the imaginative faculty as well, and if not joined with the intellect it can take a man and his desire out of the world and make life unbearable. So conjoin in your emotional ascent the light of the mind, know, with mindfulness and understanding, before Whom you pray, and do not depend on feeling alone.

What is the practical difference between a religious life grounded in intellect and one grounded in feeling?

> For feeling longs only for the end in its purity and does not grasp the value of the means, but intellect will guide, teach that the means are of the essence of the ends, and the means to the end of eternal life of the mind are to be found only in the ordering of earthly life here on the ground, *with knowledge and skill* (after Eccles. 2:21).[90]

Feeling brings immediate knowledge of the telos and thus provides more immediate access to the divine; yet intellect and its means are not feeling's handmaidens but, as he writes, are "of the essence of the ends." He later writes that when an appropriate feeling is absent, then intellectual perfection is lacking in that regard as well.[91] He is affirming mitzvot as themselves the vessels of ongoing contact with the divine, and we can see here an early contention with what he took as the otherworldliness of Christianity, something we will take up in further detail in chapter six.[92]

As the work continues he keeps trying to work out the relations between intellect and imagination/feeling—the former a principle of universal ordering, the latter a more immediate source of divine knowledge, as immediate as it is potentially disruptive. The frame of reference steadily expands beyond the individual, and he will eventually have recourse to dialectic to hold this increasingly tensile vision together.

---

90 Ibid., vol. 1, 118:

התפילה היא עבודה שיסודתה בהרגש ובהתעוררות הכח המדמה ג"כ ואם לא יחובר עמה השכל תוכל לגרום שיצא האדם בחשקו מן העולם ויהיו החיים לו לזרא. ע"כ תשתתפו בהתעלות הרגש גם את אור השכל דעו בדעת והבנה לפני מי אתם מתפללים ולא תסמכו על הרגש לבד . . . כי הרגש יערוג רק אל התכלית גם בטהרתו ולא יבין ערך האמצעיים אבל השכל ינחהו להורות לו כי האמצעים המה עקרים של התכלית ואמצעים לתכלית חיי השכל הנצחיים רק בסיקור החיים הארציים פה עלי אדמות בדעת ובכשרון.

91 Ibid. 4:36, 119.

92 See an earlier adumbration of this comment at ibid. 1:162.

Perfection of the Individual and the Whole and the Internalization of Kabbalah

As 'Eyn Ayah to Berakhot progresses, the angle of vision steadily widens, from the individual's pursuit of his own perfection via self-discipline, towards broader public, historical, and eventually cosmic horizons. Ultimately, the reciprocal relations of intellect and feeling within the individual personality reflect in microcosm the ordering of all the facets of being towards the goal of realizing the divine Will. Over time, intellect and imagination/feeling become in his hands not merely faculties of individual perception—and their reciprocity not merely a religious anthropology—but the manifestations of larger forces coursing through the universe; the human person and his facets are themselves part of this interaction of forces. Moreover, in a central shift, that which imagination/feeling perceives is not something external to the individual but rather something that wells up from within the recesses of one's own, divinely ordained, soul, in all its complexity.

This mythologized worldview, in which the universe is an arena of forces contending with and complementing each other, reflects, I submit, Rav Kook's steady internalizing of Kabbalistic ideas as a map to the inner life, a development in his thinking that would take on increasingly large and complex proportions in his later writing.[93] At the same time, his writing here steadily becomes more lyrical and expressive, the aggadic texts of Tractate Berakhot serving as occasions for encounter with his own inner life.

In the previous chapter we saw the long-unpublished essay in which he said the flaw of Hasidism was its overemphasis on the meaning of Kabbalistic concepts as reflections of the inner life. Throughout this work, 'Eyn Ayah, we will see Rav Kook's working to internalize Kabbalistic concepts but trying to do so in a way that does not deprive them of a referent external to the self. This becomes clearer when we look at similar processes in Hasidic thought. Internalization of Kabbalistic metaphysics and theosophy has figured prominently in discussions of Hasidism ever since Scholem characterized Hasidism as the internalization of Messianism.[94] This notion has undergone significant scholarly refinement in recent decades; as Moshe Idel has put it, here as elsewhere, internalization was not an innovation of Hasidism but rather a reorganization of earlier psychologically oriented concepts, leading to a de-emphasis of theosophy and the theurgic repair of the divine in favor of anthroposophy and the repair of man; this in turn led Hasidic thinkers to cultivate a more dynamic, subjective conception of the human person and of religious acts. "[I]t is the inner vitality that serves as the bridge between the *Deus Absconditus* and

---

93 On the Kabbalistic rendering of perfection and the process of perfection in his later writing, see Yosef Ben-Shlomo, "Shlemut ve-Hishtalmut be-Torat Ha-Elohut shel Ha-Rav Kook," *'Iyun* 33, nos. 1–2 (1984): 289–309. Ben-Shlomo identifies the self-perfection of the cosmos through historical dialectics as a, and perhaps the, distinctive element in Rav Kook's mature thought. Of particular interest is his comment on 309 and 309n41, where he notes that this historical emphasis and its affirmation of human agency pushes strongly against the a-cosmism of Habad, and he cites Samuel Hugo Bergmann for that proposition as well.

94 This is the theme of the final chapter of Scholem's classic *Major Trends in Jewish Mysticism* (New York: Schocken, 1946).

the mystic. It is not the multiplicity of the sefirotic system that is fathomed by means of the human anatomy, but the vitality of the divine reality that is traced by introspection."[95]

Ron Margolin subsequently offered a lengthy discussion and helpful typology of forms of internalization in mystical literature in general and Hasidism in particular.[96] By Margolin's typology, the internalizations at work in Rav Kook here are conceptual rather than ritual. In other words, we see here a new rendering of mythic concepts in terms of inner experience, rather than the intensification of ritual acts; we also see what Margolin calls "internalization in awareness," what Taylor would characterize as a neo-Augustinian turn in which everything we learn about God and the world is something we learn about ourselves. Most helpful here is Margolin's observation that likely catalysts for internalization are the advent of rationalist and skeptical currents which undermine myth, social changes in the direction of individuation, reformation struggles vis-à-vis an outmoded establishment, and the introduction into a culture of new ideas which generate dissonance with the traditional way of life.[97] Every one of those factors was present in Jewish society in late nineteenth-century Russia.

Mind , Imagination, Cosmic Flow, and History

In the following passage, at 5:70, commenting on the Talmudic understanding (32a) of God's saying to Moses (after the latter's having once again successfully saved Israel from divine wrath) "by My Life" (Num. 14:21) as "you, Moses, have enlivened me through your words," Rav Kook asserts the primacy of the Mind, but within an *élan vital* coursing through the structure of the universe as a whole, in a manner reminiscent of the sefirotic structure of the Kabbalah, in which the divine flow animates the entire sefirotic structure, at the pinnacle of which stands *Hokhmah*.

> The force of life is the unification of all individual organs into one body, such that by the sovereign intellect life governs even the tiniest details of the body; so too the final end of perfected existence is that all its parts be unified by the divine light . . . it is by this knowledge that the perfected end of Israel's election is that all the human race be brought to its perfection, and it is through this that He is called "alive," that by His Blessed Light there be joined to life and to one center of perfection all the disparate elements of the human race, until there be left not a single one un-encompassed by the sacred center, that all will cleave at the end of days to the living God.[98]

---

95 Idel, *Hasidism: Between Ecstasy and Magic*, Appendix A, 227–238, 236.

96 Margolin, *Miqdash Adam*, 55–122.

97 Ibid., 116.

98 EAB 1:147:

כח החיים הוא התאחדות כל פרטי האברים והחלקים שבגוף למרכז אחד שע"י שליטת השכל שולט[ים] החיים בכל
פרטי פרטיות (!) הקטנים שבגוף, כמו כן תכלית שלימות המציאות היא שיהיו כל חלקיה נאחדים ע"י אור ד' . . .
ע"י הידיעה זו שתכלית השלימות של בחירת ישראל היא שיבא כל המין אנושי אל שלימותו בזה ית' נקרא "חי"
שע"י אורו ית' יקשר לחיים ולמרכז שלימות אחד את כל החלקים הנפזרים של המין האנושי עד שלא ישאר חלק
אחד שלא יכלל תחת זה המרכז המקודש שיהיו כולם דבקים בסוף הימים באלהים חיים.

As Rav Kook's lenses widen, he incorporates Luzzatto's redemptive historiosophy into his anthropology. Imagination figures in Luzzatto's system as the principle of the mutability of perception, or put a little differently, of perspective. The mutability of perception that imagination presents is what accounts for the two perspectives by which the divine emanation is perceived—'*iggulim* and *yosher*, the cyclical and the linear, the reciprocal divine energies which eternally endure outside of time and which work inside of time. As he puts it in *Pinqas* 16:6, '*iggulim* are reflected in moral disposition and virtue, whose textual-spiritual correlative is aggadah, and *yosher* is reflected in divine commands, whose textual spiritual correlative is halakhah.[99]

While until now the dramas of the manifestation of Mind in intellect and imagination in '*Eyn Ayah* have been a matter of the individual's own religious life Rav Kook now begins to cast them as protagonists in a larger historical drama. The potentially destructive excesses of the imagination are themselves a function of the current, unredeemed phase of world history.

Thus the Temple in Jerusalem represents the perfect alignment of imagination and intellect, and its destruction inaugurated an era of imbalance in the human soul. Discussing the Talmudic statement (32b) that since the Temple's destruction all heavenly gates have been sealed, save the gate of tears, citing as its prooftext: "Hear, O God my prayer and give ear to my cry, be not deaf to my tears" (Ps. 39:13):

> But since the Temple's destruction and with it the tie that bound imaginative faculties—which are the constitutive principles of humanity—to the light of intellect, the gates of prayer have been sealed. For every individual certainly has a hard time raising his imaginative faculty to the heights of the mind, and at times the ascendance of the imaginative faculty leads one astray from the path of the intellect and via overexcitement oversteps the bounds of natural righteousness.... The House of Life is the imaginative faculty, which is the axis around which human life revolves with all its desires and inclinations, and the true Presence, *kavod*, is the pure divine intellect, *Presence is none other than Torah* [Avot 6:3].[100]

At this point, within this very same paragraph, intellect is itself the steppingstone to feeling, roused from within yet ultimately coming from without, expressing itself in the human person:

> Yet when one's good forces are strengthened without his choosing but by virtue of all the good intellectual paths with which he continuously disciplines himself, and when the powers of his soul reach a central point, there is roused in man a feeling greater than his own power,

---

99   See also Ramhal's teaching in *Qalah Pithei Hokhmah* §8, and the discussion of Schatz, "Ha-Metafisiqa shel Ramhal be-Heksherah Ha-'Eti," 361–396, 372.

100 EAB 5:75, vol. 1, 149 :

אבל מיום שחרב ביהמ״ק ובטל מרכז הכללי של הקישור של הכוחות הדמיוניים שהם חקי הנפש האנושית אל אור השכל נגעלו שערי תפילה. כי כל יחיד ודאי יקשה לו מאד לרומם כחו המדמה לבדו אל מרומי השכל ולפעמים בהתגברות [כח] המדמה יטעה [היחיד] מדרך השכל וע״י ההתרגשות יצא (משורה הישרה) [משורת היושר] . . . בית החיים הוא [פילבר מוסיף פה ״מצד״ ונ״ל שא״צ—ים] הכח המדמה שהוא הציר שעליו יסובו כל חיי האדם בתשוקותיהם ונטיותיהם והכבוד האמיתי הוא השכל האלהי הטהור ״אין כבוד אלא תורה.״ [אבות ו:ג].

and the tears flow from his great longings for the good of divine loving grace. *My soul thirsts for God, a living God* [Ps. 42:3]. . . . Hence the gates of tears have never been shut, as the verse says *be not deaf to my tears*. [Ps. 39:13].[101]

He expresses here something akin to prophetic experience, generated, as in the Maimonidean model by intellect, but an experience whose content is not imaginative representation, as such, but feeling.

Strategies of Containment, or, What Does the Faculty of the Imagination Imagine?

Alert as he is to the dangers of, as he puts it, overstepping the bounds of righteousness, Rav Kook adopts different strategies for containing this swelling, at times seemingly Promethean, sense of self—as much a temptation of the intellect as it is of the imagination—within the framework of tradition and an appropriately humbled self. One such strategy, a sort of half-Kantianism, is seeing one's own concepts not as absolutes but as relative—not relative in terms of their connection to metaphysical truth, which they do indeed reflect, but in terms of any individual's ability to grasp the ultimate essence of concepts and the totality of concepts as a whole.

> At times one will seek enlightenment through true concepts but will try to represent them in terms of how they exist externally to oneself and thereby fail to realize the deep point of true understanding, for one is unfit to know any sublime thing other than as it appears in relation to oneself. And so those seekers of divine enlightenment who place their standpoint outside themselves will find their wisdom overtaking their piety . . . (The pious man) realizes that the point of truth is to be found only in his internal relation to every concept, and so the telos of all concepts, which is the knowledge of God, must be established within, in terms of one's own relationship to it, and this will be the deep truth of enlightenment.[102]

What is the telos? Or to put it a little differently, just what is it that the faculty of the imagination is imagining? At 45a, the Talmud brings two alternate prooftexts for the call and response of Grace after Meals, requiring a quorum of three: Ps. 34:4, "O magnify the Lord with me, and let us exalt His Name together," and Deut. 32:3, "Because I will call God's Name, render greatness to our Lord." Rav Kook writes:

---

101 אמנם בשעה שמתגברים על האדם ציוריו לטובה בלי בחירתו ונטיותיו הבחיריות כ"א כענין תולדה מכל הדרכים הטובים השכליים, שמתאמץ תמיד להדריך בהם את נפשו, וכשבאים הכחות [ש]בנפש לידי נקודה מרכזית מתעורר האדם ברגש נעלה מכחו והדמעות משתפכות מרוב געגועיו לטוב ולחסד עליון "צמאה נפשי לאלהים לאל חי." . . . ע"כ שערי דמעות לעולם לא ננעלו כמקרא שכתוב אל דמעתי אל תחרש. . . .

102 EAB 5:108, vol. 1, 162 :

> יש שישכיל אדם בהשכלות אמתיות אבל ישתדל לציירן לפי מה שהן עומדות מחוץ לנפש, ובזה עוד לא יבא לתכלית העומק של ההכרה האמיתית, מפני שאין האדם מוכשר לדעת כל נשגב כ"א כפי הערך שהדבר מצויר ביחושו לנפשו. וע"כ המשכילים בהשגה אלהית, והם קובעים את נקודת השקפתם מחוץ לנפשם, בהם תגדל מעלת החכמה על מעלת היראה . . . ובהיותו משיג שנקודת האמת תימצא רק ביחוסו הפנימי אל כל השגה, א"כ התכלית של כל ההשגות, שהיא הדעת [את] אלהים, צריכה ודאי להיות נקבעת בתוכו מצד יחסו אלי', וזה יהי' עומק האמת בהשגה.

The foundation of recognizing God's ways resides in knowing divine Providence and the exalted paths of Governance. This necessarily requires three perspectives: the order of all things *au fond*, how they are arrayed in the wisdom and divine grace of a living God, good and doing good; the second is all the causalities that are the means towards the lovely supernal end which we grasp as the perfection of all creatures for their own good to the ultimate degree; and the final supernal end, greater than everything and endlessly sublime.[103]

The vision is one of the extraordinary linkage of all things, but one with a direction, a telos realizable in time, perhaps in, or at the end, of historical time, but the result of a process within time.

Thus, the three-person quorum of Grace reflects a progressive, threefold, awareness of God. The first prooftext, from Ps. 34, reflects the first two forms of awareness. Recognizing God's *greatness* is the result of intellectual inquiry, and *exalting* His name results from an influx of the holy spirit, "which sometimes lofts the soul above individual concepts and understands its Maker and His sublime paths . . . and thus call out."[104] The verse from Deuteronomy reflects the third; a prophecy higher than intellect and the holy spirit, which is none other than the prophecy of Moses, which is the very aim of all Torah, culminating in *imitatio Dei*. While he does not explicitly reference Maimonides here, we recall that in Maimonides's scheme, Moses's prophecy was uniquely beyond imagination and uniquely lawgiving; by the same token, on a decidedly non-Maimonidean note, more reminiscent of Luzzatto, Moses's prophetic lawgiving, scaling the highest summit of perfection, is able to attain, in the saying of Grace, the sanctification of the most bodily of functions, eating. At this vertical summit, a sweeping horizontal vista opens up as well.

And when we reflect further we will attain a more wondrous perspective, that one who looks out with a clear perspective on all the paths of actions will see how they are fused into one great chain, and one will no longer wonder about the relation of the end and the means, and all one's actions will be sanctified as parts of the great sublime telos, and so one will always be none other than *calling out in the Name of God*.[105]

The individual subject is intimately bound up with the great telos. As *Eyn Ayah* Berakhot progresses, the earlier passages about perfection as involving the whole of one's person

---

103 Ibid. 7:2, 200 :

יסוד הכרת דרכי ד' הוא ידיעת ההשגחה העליונה ודרכי ההנהגה הרוממה. ובזה יש בהכרח חלוקה של שלש השקפות: השקפה על התחלת כל המעשים כולם, איך הם ערוכים בחכמה ובחסד-אל, אלהים חיים, הטוב והמטיב ב"ה. והשקפה שני' על כל הסיבובים הגדולים שהם בתור אמצעיים להפיק תכלית נחמד העליון, שאנו משיגים אותו בתור השלמת כל הברואים כולם לטוב להם בתכלית המעלה והטוב. והשלישית גמר תכלית המטרה העליונה שהיא עולה על הכל ונשגבה באין תכלית.

104 Ibid., 201.
105 Ibid.

וכשנתבונן ביותר תבא לנו השקפה יותר מופלאה, שהמסתכל בידיעה ברורה בכל דרכי המעשים כולם איך הם מתרתקים לשלשלת אחת נכבדה, הוא לא יפליא עוד בין המטרה אל התכלית, וכל מעשיו כולם קדושים לו כי הם חלקים מחלקי התכלית העליון, ע"כ הוא תמיד רק קורא בשם ד'.

increasingly lead him to celebrate freedom as itself the telos, insofar as one chooses the good in freedom.[106] With time, the sense of self is greatly strengthened and contained at the same time, by seeing it as constituted, in all its variety, by larger forces. The world stirs with life, and the individual self with it.

This brings us to discussion of a key passage. Discussing the Talmudic statement (43b) regarding what sort of illumination counts as protection while walking in the night, "Rav Zutra said in the name of Rav, a torch is like two (companions) and the moon is like three."

> The reality of all the wondrous things in the world, as the rabbis have taught us in their divine wisdom, is that they are vital, living things. This is as it should be, for the very ground of creation is the reception of God's light and goodness, and who can receive kindness and good but the living, who know their own existence and feel their own good? Thus there is nothing, even the lowest rung of existence, into which some *élan vital* cannot enter, for God's loving kindness truly fills the world.[107]

This dynamic, Kabbalistically inflected picture, seeing every single thing as pulsing with *élan vital*, does, though, introduce another, darker, even demonic element into his worldview.

> Forces acting for good are insufficient, since the evil forces are also required for creation as a whole, and so they too have powers, and creatures activated via their life force, such that even via the evil portion of existence, which comes in order to perfect and refine the good, there too will the supernal dimension of loving kindness find a place to bestow its goodness.[108]

If the early passages in *'Eyn Ayah* reflected a philosophical world picture in which the complexities of the world are ordered in a stately procession of the mind, he is here operating in the mythologized world picture of the Kabbalah, in which there are a multiplicity of contending wills, perhaps all deriving from the divine Will, but with drives all their own. One of the multiple arenas within which those forces contend is none other than our inner life.

---

106 See also EAB 6:7, vol. 2, 173—the telos of existence is the emergence into actuality of the good choice of doing good and wisdom in utter freedom, from internal will and desire; at 6:43 he says absolute freedom is the highest telos. He also evinces a recognition that this telos is not identical to or subsumed in halakhah as such. At 6:47 he discusses a "natural moral feeling," *regesh ha-yashar*, which is not identical with Torah; see also ibid. 6:54.

107 Ibid. 7:53, vol. 2, 233:
מציאות כל הדברים הנפלאים בעולם, לפי מה שהורונו חז"ל בחכמתם האלהית, המה דברים חיים. וכך היא המדה, שהרי יסוד הבריאה הוא לקבל אור ד' וטובו, ומי יוכל לקבל חסד וטוב הלא רק החיים, היודעים את מציאותם ומרגישים את טובם. ע"כ אין מדריגה היותר נמוכה בכל המציאות, שרק אפשר להתכנס שמה כח של חיים, שלא יהי' נמצא, כי חסד ד' מלאה הארץ.

108 Ibid.:
ולא די בכוחות הפועלים טוב, כ"א גם הכוחות הרעים כיון שנצרכים לכלל הבריאה, ע"כ גם להם ישנם כוחות ובריות פועלים ע"י חייהם, כדי שאפי' ע"י החלק הרע שבמציאות, שבא להשלים את הטוב ולשכללו, ג"כ תמצא מקום מדת החסד העליונה להשביע מטובה.

Thus one should bear in mind that as one establishes his intellect in all its purity, as he directs his virtues, efforts and contemplative ability so as to grasp the truth of existence, he is actively being worked upon by forces of life full of good and kindness, light and wisdom. And when one is drawn to false imaginings, engendered by his own debased ways, via his rotten morals, when one neglects true knowledge, he is thus readying his representations to be acted upon by life forces akin to the counterfeit for which he has outfitted himself.[109]

How is one to draw down upon oneself the good forces and ward off the bad? By intellect of course but, more powerfully, by feeling. Reason, in the form of philosophy, offers some, but unpersuasive, resistance to the evil forces afoot in the world. Philosophy's fatal weakness rests with its incomplete picture of the human person, who is as much a feeling as a thinking creature.

Of a piece with this mounting primacy of what we immediately feel and live, rather than analogically and artificially think, is of a piece with the shift in Rav Kook's writing style; experiential, increasingly associative, at times running away with him in an associative train of allusions from Talmudic, Kabbalistic and philosophic literature, leaving normal grammar and syntax behind.

The artificial means of guarding against the darkness of bad moral ideas is the wisdom of analogy built on the synthesis of philosophical investigations, yet it is unable entirely to erase every idea that is damaging and destructive to the fundaments of the soul's peace . . . that is *the torch* composed of lone lights to light up the night, *which are two*. But *the moon* is the natural light, the heart's heat, in a flame of piety and pure simple faith, *the eccelsia of Israel is named for you*, said God to the moon. True union with the ecclesia of Israel and accepting the yoke of Heaven, the heat of simplicity, the light of the moon, the speculum that does not shine.[110] That is *like three*, erasing from the heart every bad image and every tremor of bad thought, to the point of invisibility and harmlessness, for *they will not wreak evil and destruction in all My holy mountain* [Isa. 11:9], *Israel is sacred unto God* [Jer. 2:3], and *Jacob the simple man* [Gen. 25:27], *God stood over him* [Gen. 28:13] to guard him from the flies as in the Rabbis' parable in Genesis Rabbah and the *'Aqedah* there.[111]

---

109 Ibid., 234:

ע"כ ראוי לדעת שהאדם בהיותו מכונן שכלו על טהרתו, בהכינו לזה מדותיו והשתדלותו ועיונו בהשכילו את המציאות לאמתתה, הוא נפעל מכחות חיים מלאי חסד וטוב אורה וחכמה. ובהיותו נמשך אחרי דמיונות כוזבים, בהיותו גורם לזה בדרכיו הנלוזים, במוסרו הנפסד, בהתרשלו בידיעה אמתית, הנהו מכין ציורו להיות נפעל מכחות חיים הדומים לאותו הזיוף וההפסד שהוא מוכשר לקבלו.

110 This somewhat obscure reference will be explained presently.

111 EAB 7:53:

ההגנה המלאכותית נגד חושך של דיעות רעות בנוגע למוסריות, היא החכמה ההקישית הבנוי' מהרכבת הקדמות עיוניות, שהם אמנם אין בידם למחות כליל כל רעיון מזיק ומהרס אשיות השלום הנפשי . . . זאת האבוקה, המורכבת מאורים בודדים להאיר את הלילה, שהיא כשנים. אמנם ירח הוא האור הטבעי, חום הלב, בלבת אש יראת אלהים ואמונה תמימה טהורה כנסת ישראל נקרי' על שמך, א"ל קוב"ה לירח. הדבקות האמתית בכנס"י ובקבלת עול מ"ש, חום התמימות, אור הירח אספקלריא דלא נהרא. זוהי כשלשה, המוחק מהלב כל צל ציור רע וכל נדנוד מחשבה רעה, עד שאינו נראה ולא מזיק, כי 'לא ירעו ולא ישחיתו בכל הר קדשי', 'קודש ישראל לד'' ו'יעקב איש תם' 'והנה ד' נצב עליו' לשמרו מהזבובים כמשל חז"ל בב"ר וכד' העקידה שם.

Unpacking these allusions will yield a powerful interpretive dividend. According to a celebrated Talmudic saying (BT Yevamot 49b), while "all the prophets looked through a speculum that did not shine, Moses looked through a speculum that shone." The spectral, moonlike speculum appears repeatedly in the Zoharic corpus. In Habad literature, the advantage of the speculum that does not shine is "that one can see oneself and one can see behind oneself . . . and the matter of the speculum that does not shine is (loving God) *with all one's might* (Deut. 6:5), which is to say by the soul's descent into the body, a descent for the sake of ascent to transform the animal soul."[112] The moon-like speculum casts a spectral, penetrating light that is the plaintive human love for God that will transform the material world.

His reference to Arama is worth noting. Contra Maimonides, Arama thought that prophetic experience, unless scripture states otherwise, is not the product of the prophet's imagination but an actually occurring event external to the prophet, even if visible only to him.[113] The *'Aqedat Yitzhaq* passage to which Rav Kook is referring here, §25:1 (1:203a–211b) centers on Jacob's dream (Gen. 28:10–22) and takes as its starting point the midrashic parable that Jacob was like an infant whose nursemaid swats away the flies buzzing around him. In Arama's reading, Jacob was a philosophically minded seeker after God, who found himself surrounded by foggy and uncertain concepts (the flies), hence his vision seemed dreamlike to him. More broadly, Arama argues that while reason and analogy may bring one to a formal understanding of the truth, in the absence of imagination one cannot grasp truth's reality, in the same way that a denizen of the tropics cannot grasp the reality of ice and snow no matter how well he understands the concepts. Similarly, Arama writes, though intellection is a necessary prerequisite to knowledge of God, by reason alone one will not be able to grasp His true reality, including seemingly nonrational features of the divine, such as His designating a specific place for His temple, or His preference for the weak and the poor. Once Jacob achieved intellectual perfection

> by way of many and distinguished contemplations beautifully constructed on true intellectual premises (including) the existence of God and His unity and simplicity and the manner of His Providence and governance of this existence as much as the intellect can perceive, this

---

112 See Shneur Zalman of Liady, *Torah Ohr, Miqetz*, 33a:

אמנם יש באספקלריא שאינה מאירה מעלה א' גבוה במדרגה שיכולין לראות עצמו וגם לראות מאחוריו כידוע מה שאין יכולין לראות באספקלריא המאירה וזהו ארץ קדמה ודו"ק. ועד"ז תירצו בגמ' ביבמות (ספ"ד) דישעיה שאמר ואראה את ה' היינו באספקלריא שאינה מאירה שבה יוכל לראות את ה'. משא"כ באספקלריא המאירה כתיב כי לא יראני כו'. ועניין אספקלריא דלא נהרא הוא בחי' בכל מאדך היינו עניין ירידת הנשמה בגוף ירידה צורך עלייה להפך נה"ב.

113 See on this Pearl, *The Medieval Jewish Mind*, 146–150. For a thorough discussion of Arama's differences with both Maimonides and Ha-Levi as to the doctrine of prophecy, see chapter eight of Heller-Wilensky, *Rabbi Yitzhaq Arama u-Mishnato*. While Arama's conception of prophecy is far less naturalistic than that of Maimonides and closer to that of Ha-Levi, it is interesting to note that, unlike Ha-Levi, he does not restrict the possibility of prophecy to the people or land of Israel.

perfection brought him to receive a spirit from on high to grasp and understand great and wondrous things.[114]

I believe we see through this thicket of allusions Rav Kook's own sense that he is being vouchsafed some sort of revelation. At this point it is worth recalling the allusions to prophetic revelation via the study of aggadah that we saw in his introduction, which as I said, was composed after he had gone through the process of writing this commentary.

In the Boisk notebooks (later published as *Mussar Avikha*), he applied Luzzatto's understanding of redemptive teleology to the inner life of the individual, namely, that only by bringing all the God-given elements of one's personality to expression will one do one's part in the great *tiqqun*. That theme appears here in *'Eyn Ayah* too, but charged with a far more dynamic, at times tempestuous and farther-reaching expressive conception of the individual. This embrace of the self is an acceptance of feeling, which was no small thing for a Lithuanian Talmudist.

In this acceptance of oneself intellect can become something not only to be transcended, but evaded and even overcome—and here he is beginning to sound a bit like Nahman of Bratslav—with the difference that while Nahman urges the casting away of intellect across the board, here he limits it to the time of prayer.

Commenting on the dictum (54b) that "lengthening and looking into prayer bring heartache in the end" he writes

> *Eudaemonia* consists of the realization that all one's energies and all the paths one must take in the course of his life, by virtue of his temperament, his physical and spiritual nature, are all ordered by the Fashioner of All in wisdom, and all fit his own flourishing and that of the whole, temporal and eternal. So when one is aggrieved by sorrow, from the pain disturbing his world in his own private situation, or the human condition in general, and lofts prayer to God from pure-hearted feeling, that prayer will yield a great good in his own moral state and renewed *élan vital* for all his feelings.

Prayer *in extremis* moves the divine Will because the individual's own *Sturm und Drang* is, at its deepest level, divinely ordained.

> And one needn't be troubled by philosophy's questioning how prayer can effectuate change in God's unchanging Will. That question arises merely from an inability to understand that the inner makeup of every created thing, and all the particulars and general things that bring one to his perfection, all derive from the divine wisdom, which lacks for nothing. Thus when one finds nearness to God via his inner feelings, his soul will blossom and his moral forces develop by their fitting nature. And so all things necessary to direct all one's interiority towards its perfection are themselves part of the broader order of creation. One who understands this will seek from prayer none other than the very task of feeling which is that his honest heart

---

114 Arama, *'Aqedat Yitzhaq*, 1:206a.

act in him by his own nature. The honest man's nature is for his soul to pour itself out from longings for its saving God, and thus prayer actualizes itself and finds its task.[115]

The Renewal of Prophecy and the Mission of the Artist

We noted at the outset of our discussion his interest in prophecy; here too the shifts continue. Earlier in *'Eyn Ayah* prophecy was discussed in fairly straightforward Maimonidean terms as a function of individual perfection.[116] As the work proceeds the discussion of prophecy takes on a more richly textured cast.

For Rav Kook, as for other fin-de-siècle figures, the artist beckoned as a prophet-like alternative to the sage as a model of religious life. This notion of the artist as prophet was of course a staple of Romantic poets such as Wordsworth and Whitman, and of Idealist thinkers with whose ideas Rav Kook was, even at this stage, familiar, such as Schelling and Soloviev.[117] For Jewish thinkers this notion of prophecy was especially appealing; a full discussion of the subject is well beyond our purview here.[118] Suffice it to say that it could meet modernity's epistemological, ethical, and historicizing challenges to religious traditions. Epistemologically, prophecy offers the possibility of an experiential grounding for religious truth, or if you will, a channel whose immediacy can restore the access to truth seemingly sealed off by Kant. Inasmuch as the modern awareness of historical change—and nineteenth-century beliefs in the progressive (in both senses) unfolding of meaning and even revelation through history—seemed to undermine the law's aspiration to timeless authority, prophecy beckoned, as validating change in the law when it fails to meet ethical standards, and legitimating a progressive reading of history. Finally, the heritage of Biblical prophecy beckoned as a source of universal ethics, and a critique of desiccated legalism, from within the very heart of the tradition.

---

115 EAB 9:23, vol. 2, 257:

הצלחת האדם היא שישכיל שכל כוחותיו וכל הדרכים שצריך שיתגלגל בהם בסדרי חייו, מפני מזגו וטבעו הנפשי, כולם הם ערוכים מיוצר כל בחכמה, וכולם מתאימים להצלחתו הפרטית והכללית, הזמנית והנצחית. ע"כ כאשר יתחמץ לב האדם בקרבו, מעוצר רעה ויגון שפוגע בעולמו מצד מצבו הפרטי, או מצד המצב האנושי הכללי, ומרגש לב טהור ישא תפילה לד', תהי' תוצאות התפלה הטבה גדולה במצב מוסרו וחליפת כח חיים לכל רגשותיו. ואין צריך שיבהללוהו שאלות הפילוסופיא אם אין לפני השם יתעלה שינוי רצון איך תועיל התפילה כאלו כל תועלת התפלה היא רק להפוך רצון עליון. זאת השאלה באה רק מקוצר דעת להבין, כי כל מערכות לב-כל-נוצר וכל פרטי וכללי הדברים שיביאו את האדם לידי השלמתו, הנה זאת היא מכלל החכמה האלהית שלא יחסר כל בה. . . . ע"כ באשר האדם כשימצא קרבת אלהים לפי רגשותיו הפנימיים, אז תפרח משמתו וכוחותיו המוסריים יתפתחו ע"פ טבעם הנאות. ע"כ כל הדברים הצריכים להזמין את המערכה הפנימית של נפש האדם שתהיה מכוונת להשלמתה הם מכללי סדרי הבריאה. המבין כן לא יבקש בתפילה כ"א תעודת הרגש, שיהיה לבו הישר פועל בו ע"פ טבעו. טבע האדם הישר הוא שתהי' נפשו משתפכת בגעגועים לאלהי ישעו, ובזה תצא התפילה לפעולה ובזה תמצא ג"כ פעולתה.

116 See, for example, EAB 1:136–138, 174; 5:66, 69, 108, 118, 120–122; 6:36.

117 Davidson, "Vladimir Soloviev and the Ideal of Prophecy," 643–670; Bergmann, *Toldot Ha-Philosophia He-Hadashah*, 185–186.

118 An important survey of the centrality of prophecy to the work of a striking range of modern Jewish thinkers is Schweid, *Neviim le-'Amam u-le-Enoshut*.

In the coming years, Rav Kook would explore the idea of the renewal of prophecy in its latter two senses, the historical and ethical.[119] His focus here seems more on what I have called prophecy's epistemological sense, an experience offering immediate, unmediated access to divine knowledge; I don't necessarily mean to imply that his interest in prophecy arose from his being troubled by Kantian epistemology as such, though we have seen that Kantian ideas and *problematiques* were indeed on his horizon. Rav Kook was certainly heir to elements of prophetic Kabbalistic tradition, which as we saw earlier were preserved within Lithuanian Kabbalah. But the identification of the prophet with the artist, and the invocation of prophecy not, or not only, as a result of mystical technique, but as an upswelling from within, albeit from within a God-given interiority, are distinctively modern.

Talmudic discussion (55b) of the Biblical artisan charged with crafting the Tabernacle, Bezalel, leads Rav Kook to a series of reflections on the artist.

> The natural feeling of the artist is for his representation to be natural and strong. His inner feeling is his chief talent and it must guide his work, not let him draw anything contrary to the way and path befitting his own quality; much in the way that a musician will physically be unable to bear dissonance.

The artist, to be sure, is not the sage.

> The artist and the sage will naturally have differing conceptions of order. The latter will order things by wisdom and morality, the former by correspondence to reality. The sublime wisdom and absolute justice must be joined by the natural feeling of the pure soul to perfect the power of vision.[120]

He increasingly tries to negotiate the tension between this burgeoning individualism and the nomian submission to community. *Crucially, he is not urging an autonomous self, but rather an expressive self.* The self does not give itself the law. Indeed, to submit to the community is precisely to be true to oneself, since the normative claims of morality are themselves revealed to us by the inner voice of conscience. Commenting on the statement (55b) that one who has had a disturbing dream should convene a council of three for the ceremony of dream-healing:[121]

> The first step in strengthening one's force of justice is to habituate oneself not to disavow inner feeling, for often it is the voice of God calling to him from the walls of his heart to desist from evil and cast off injustice. And so one should habituate oneself not to trample on the internal stirrings of his soul, and then he truly will draw therefrom the intention directed towards God, who so created the soul that it will at times be greatly disturbed by evildoing and distortion of the just path. . . . And since submission to the community's consensus brings one

---

119 See Rosenak, "'Torat Eretz Yisrael' Ha-Nevu'it be-Mishnat Ha-Re'ayah Kook," 26–70.
120 EAB 9:29, vol. 2, 263.
121 The particulars of the ceremony as it evolved over time are briefly found in *Shulhan 'Arukh, Orakh Hayim* §220:1.

to the good and just path, it is thus a feature of morality itself. . . . And the moral deficiency which Providence has sent the dream to fill will in turn be filled by inner recognition in proportion to the preciousness of society and loving fellowship.[122]

That this is no mere bromide about the joys of fraternity but an expression of his trying to square the circle of an increasingly robust sense of the individual with his powerful commitment to the community and its laws becomes clear not much further down the road. Commenting in a distinctly Rousseauian tone on the Talmudic saying (57b) that pleasant voice, view, and smell "restore one's mind," he writes that:

> *God has created man's soul naturally righteous* [after Eccles. 7:29], rejoicing in life and finding ease in its feelings . . . but the contentious hand of society distances man from his natural feelings of health and his mind becomes sullied as well. And so that which will restore him to his natural equanimity is his sharing in nature's tranquility, the kindness of God that fills all creation, the song of the birds *singing among the branches* [Ps. 104:12], the majestic vista of Carmel and Sharon in their delicate blooms.[123]

Yet nature left to its own devices will never spur one to the desire for the advancement of humanity or the nation or for that matter existence as a whole. "Those longings arise only from one's individual cultivation, not only by restoring one's equanimity but by expanding one's own mind." [124]

We will have more to say about the Rousseauian element in *'Eyn Ayah* presently. By this point his thinking reflects a complex mix of a burgeoning individual expression, fealty to the community and to law, and a corresponding or correlative tension between feeling and mind as constitutive elements of personality and points of contact with the divine.

---

122 EAB 9:48, vol. 2, 270:

ראשית דרכי חיזוק כח הצדק באדם הוא שירגיל עצמו שלא ישים אל רגשו הפנימי, כי פעמים רבות קול אלהים הוא הקורא לו מקירות לבו לסור מדרך רעה ושלא להחזיק בעול. ע"כ ראוי שירגיל האדם את הנהגתו שלא לרמוס ברגל גאוה על המית נפשו הפנימית, ואז באמת ימשיך מזה הכונה המכוונת לשם ית' שיצר ועשה את הנפש הזאת באופן שתתרגש לפעמים מעסקי רשע וסילוף דרך ישרה . . . וכיון שההכנעה אל הסכמת הכלל מביאה את האדם לדרך טובה וישרה, כבר היא אחת מחלקי המוסר . . . והחסרון המוסרי שלמלאותו בא החלום ע"פ יסוד ההשגחה העליונה, יתמלא ע"י ההכרה הפנימית שיתוסף לחלום בערך יקרת החברה ואהבת הרעים.

123 Ibid., 296–297:

נפש האדם בראה אלהים ישרה, שמחה בחייה ומוצאת נחת ברגשותיה . . . אמנם בתגרת יד החברה האנושית, התרחק האדם מרגשות הטבע הטהורים ונעכרה ג"כ דעתו. ע"כ המדה שתשיבהו אל ישוב דעתו הטבעית היא הקורת רוח הכללית המשותפת שימצא האדם בטבע, חסד ד' המלא כל היקום, קול זמרת הצפרים מבין עפאים יתנו קול, מראה הדר הכרמל והשרון בפרחיהם הנחמדים. . . .

See also *Pinqas* 16:11, 23.

124 Ibid.:

. . . כי הטבע אף שיהי' מישר את דרך האדם ביושר פנימי, לא תעוז להחכם להתגדל מעל לגבול, ולשאוף בכל לב ונפש לטובת הכלל האנושי או הלאומי, ומכש"כ כל כל המציאות מעשה ד' אשר ברא לשכלל ולהעלות. אלה התשוקות אינם באות כ"א בדרך הגידול הפרטי שבאדם, לא לבד ע"י השבת דעתו של אדם כ"א ע"י הרחבת דעתו.

The Emergence of Dialectic and the Theodicy of History

As *'Eyn Ayah* Berakhot proceeds, he works to resolve or at least manage these inherently unstable relations by a conception of dialectic, of opposites competing with, and at the same time reinforcing and complementing, each other in an integrated whole. This is in contrast to the hierarchical ordering with which he began, under the impress of the medieval philosophical tradition, and the stately structures of Lithuanian Kabbalah, wherein each principle or potency, in the soul and in the world, is held in place, contained by the mind; in dialectic each expresses itself to the utmost, pushing against the limits set to it by the other.

By way of the comment (58b) that without Orion's warmth the world would not endure the Pleiades' chill, and vice versa, he writes:

> The foundation of the world's existence and its improvement is always dependent on opposing forces working on each other by affirmation and negation. This is the deepest demonstration of the insight of the Creator of all in wisdom, who unifies all opposites in the unity of his supernal rule.[125]

His use of the tern "unification of opposites," which figures prominently his post-1904 writings, alludes both to Schelling and to "the reversal of opposites" which is a standard term in Habad literature.[126] This bit of cultural synthesis is striking, but, again, less so for the terminology as such than for the role this idea plays in his evolving thinking, in the position to which he has been driven, standing in a different moral universe than the one in which he began.

> Just as combinations of opposing and contradictory forces work on our feelings and thoughts . . . we similarly ascend to moral values in the sense of governance, both general and particular.[127]

And these forces are not all benign:

> There are orders of evil forces, in which the wisdom, knowledge and light of divine Providence is felt, they meet precisely one who befits them by his lesser morality.[128]

Will these evil forces triumph? Hopefully not:

---

125 Ibid. 9:130, 307:

יסוד קיומו של עולם ושכלולו תלוי תמיד בכוחות מנוגדים הפועלים אלה על אלה בדרך חיוב ושלילה. וזהו המורה
ביותר על עצה עמוקה של היוצר כל בחכמה, המאחד כל ההפכים באחדות שליטתו העליונה.

126 See Rachel Elior, *Torat Ahdut Ha-Hafakhim: Ha-Teosofia Ha-Mistit shel Habad* (Jerusalem: Mossad Bialik, 1992), and in particular chapter 10, 187–203.

127 EAB 9:131, vol. 2, 307:

כשם שחיבורם של הכוחות המתנגדים וסותרים זא''ז פועל על הרגשתינו והבנתינו . . . כן עולים אנחנו מזה גם אל
הערכים המוסריים בחוש ההנהגה הכללית והפרטית.

128 Ibid., 308:

. . . ישנם מערכת של כחות רעים, שבהם יש תבונה ודעת ואור ההשגחה האלהית המורגש בהם, הם נפגשים דוקא
במי שראוי לכך לפי מוסרו הפחות. . . .

> Because all is reckoned and of the sublime mind, we are promised the perfect good and utter loving-kindness that will flow outwards from all these combinations, the depths of whose meaning our bleary eyes cannot see. *How precious is your loving-kindness O God.* (Ps. 36:8)[129]

Stylistically, this is not the first time we see him end a passage with an arresting Biblical citation, a consistent feature of his later writing in his spiritual diaries, but it does start to happen with greater frequency, and is a complex gesture in its own right.[130] His writing is becoming freer, more associative, and the directions in which he is starting to move, increasingly lyrical. In terms of the history of Jewish rhetoric, the device of ending a long passage with the citation of verse of course recalls the *petihtot* or proem-invocations of early midrashic collections such as Lamentations Rabbah. He also seems to be recalling the Gaon's ambition to ground, and in some sense restore, the multiple exegetical layers of the tradition to the plain sense of the text.[131] At the same time, the striking invocation of an unadorned Biblical verse at the close of a soaring passage bespeaks a conjuring of prophecy, and the contrast between the undulations of his writing and the austerity of the verses is regularly electrifying.

One way to mediate the anxieties of this seemingly threatening and unstable world-view is to reemphasize the primacy of mind. And, indeed, he does once again introduce the mind, to which the life of feeling is necessary preparation. Commenting on the phrase (59a) "a lone bolt of lightning," he says:

> Maimonides, in his Introduction to the *Guide,* discussed at length the analogy between the illumination of wisdom from the recesses of divinity in the souls who walk in darkness, and the lightning that lights a great path in the darkness. . . . The simple light must always proceed in a manner akin to natural human feeling so that it will hew to good actions proceeding from the dimension of feeling, and not be too abstract and intellectual. Though feeling and natural inclination are clouded and a little occluded next to the simple light, that is precisely its advantage. . . . For the internal understanding transcending all speech will pave clear, simple intellectual paths precisely via representations near to sentiment of the heart and natural inclination in a path of justice, simplicity and honesty.[132]

---

129 Ibid.:

ומתוך שהכל הוא בחשבון ובדעת עליון, אנו מובטחים על הטובה השלמה והחסד הגמור שיהיה נשפע ע״י המון כל
אלה ההרכבות, שעינינו הטרוטות לא יוכלו להביט אל עומק ערכם. "מה יקר חסדך אלהים."

130 For an earlier example, see ibid. 2:43. I have briefly discussed this element of his writing in "Kook, Abraham Isaac," in *Encyclopedia of the Bible and Its Reception* (Berlin: De Gruyter, 2017), vol. 15, 452–454. It has recently been treated at length by Dov Weisbard, *Parshanut Ha-Miqra be-Haguto shel Ha-Rav Kook* (PhD diss., Bar-Ilan University, 2020).

131 This is too large a subject to go into here; for now, see Krumbein, "El Ha-Maqor" and our earlier discussion of the Gaon's glosses to *Shulhan 'Arukh*, as well as the comments by Menahem Mendel of Shklov in his introduction to the Gaon's commentary to *Avot de-Rabbi Natan* (Shklov: n.p., 1894):

. . . והעולה על כולם כי ליכא מידי בשיטות הש״ס ומדרשים ורזי דרזין דלא הוי רמיז ליה באורייתא על כל קוץ
ותלי תילין.

132 EAB 9:151, vol. 2, 315–316.

In terms of the oscillations we have seen throughout this chapter between the respective places of mind and imagination-feeling, he echoes his earlier position in which the latter is preparatory to the former. We noted earlier that in Zoharic literature and Cordovero's writings imagination is identified with *Shekhinah*; now he says that "The knowledge of God in terms of internal feeling, with all other great and fundamental things, is, in the language of the Sage, *Shekhinah*." Noting the Talmudic comment (BT Bava Batra, 25a) that the *Shekhinah* is in the west, the place of sunset, he writes: "The inner feeling wells up in man by his nature, when he takes solitude in his private world, in the chambers of his soul. When he detaches himself from the tumult of the world, gathers his feelings unto himself and goes deep into the world of feeling and intimate conversation."

The delicate relations of mind and feeling as metaphysical principles figure in his emergent historical theodicy of modernity, an understanding, and perhaps justification, of how such massive rebellion against tradition could emerge in a world guided by divine Providence. Moral ideas, he writes, straighten hearts with the goal of "embodying the divine intellectual light in men's hearts."[133] But when in a given historical period new energies proceed from God—and by His Providence—before people are ready for them the result can be general moral collapse. And this is why (as the Mishnah Sotah 9:15 famously declared) in the time of the footsteps of the Messiah, impudence and arrogance will swell—"because by imaginative arousal to seek a new light not yet revealed to them, many will lose their way in terms of familiar moral ideas."[134] These are the "morning clouds with no substance" (59a).

We see here the beginnings of his theodicy of modernity—by which, in a recapitulation of the Lurianic myth of the primordial shattering, the outbreak of heresy is the revelation of a new, higher morality, but one that cannot be contained in normal vessels.

Near the Tractate's end, the Talmudic discussion (61a) of the primal Adam having been created with two countenances (*du-partzufin*) leads to yet another attempt on his part to work out the relations between intellect and imagination-feeling (which latter embraces aesthetics) as he asserts that at a fundamental, prelapsarian level they are one and the same, complementary expressions of the divine Will flowing through humanity towards the great *tiqqun*.

> Feeling, the power of creativity and imagination, determining taste and grace, and the intellect which penetrates, and observes with judgment and reckoning, each possess a complete structure. Man is composed of a song that flows from the depth of the power of creativity and feeling, and an intellectual perspective that flows from the source of judgment.

---

133 Ibid. 9:152, 317:

כן העניינים השכליים המיישרים את הלבבות, היינו הציורים המוסריים שהם גוררים מדות טובות והדרכות ישרות . . . ותכלית כל אלה הוא שיתגשם האור השכלי האלהי בלבבות.

134 Ibid.:

. . . אמנם לעת תחל תקופה חדשה בעם, וכחות חדשים יבאו לכל מקום, שהמה הולכים ע״פ השגחת השם יתברך מ״מ בהתחלה, קודם בוא האורה והכוחות צריכות להתחזק, אז מתמוטטות הצעות רבות ונפילה מוסרית מוכנת. ע״כ בעקבא דמשיחא . . . חוצפא יסגא, והם חבלי משיח, שע״י ההתעוררות הדמיונית לחפש אור חדש שעוד לא נגלה להם, יאבדו רבים את דרכם במושגים של ציורי המוסר הרגילים.

Feeling flows upward from the depths, and mind, downward from the summit, correlating with their respective roles as the ideational dimensions of, respectively, matter and form. Matter is not inert and has an integrity all its own. All the same, it is still within a hierarchy, inasmuch as the two are gendered, befitting the two faces of the primal Adam.

> Now male and female are distinct in the qualities of their souls, males are fashioned to prevail with their minds over feeling and aesthetic taste, female is constructed by the powers of her soul to be founded on a feeling heart and good taste, like the rule of all energies which when commingled hinder each other and prevent each other's perfection. But when each emerges into actualization as though it had its very own realm then each energy is entirely resplendent and destined to effect perfect good.[135]

Yet a few lines later he seems to say that their relations are indeed not as hierarchical as they might seem. Commenting on the verse in Psalms, which, in the Talmudic reading, suggests the dual-countenance of primal Adam, "You have fashioned me front and back" (Ps. 139:5):

> Feeling is to intellect as the back is to the front, to the extent that it seeks recognition on its own right and not as a handmaiden to intellect. Yet inasmuch as nearness to God in deed and worship can only be founded on the quality of feeling, which is also God's handiwork, and man's meeting his Creator on his own terms via feeling is the desired worship on which many elements of Torah are founded . . . the human form is not to be characterized qua intellect and feeling in terms of front and back, but rather as one complete form of higher and lesser degrees, like the head and feet. Yet the front and back stand in a unitary structure and each is perfect in itself.[136]

---

135 Ibid. 9:191, 332:

הרגש, כח המצייר והמדמה בעל הטעם והחן, והשכל החודר ומשקיף במשפט וחשבון, לשניהם יש מערכה שלמה. האדם הוא מורכב משירה הנובעת מעומק כח המצייר והרגש, והשקפה שכלית הנובעת ממקור המשפט. והנה האיש והאשה מחולקים בזה בתכונות נפשותיהם, האיש מיוחד להיות גובר בשכלו ע"פ (?) הרגש והטעם הציורי, האשה בנויה בכוחות נפשה להיות מבונה בלב רגש וטוב טעם, במשפט כל הכחות שכשהם מתערבים יחד הם מעכבים זע"ז ומונעים כ"א השלמת זולתו. אמנם כאשר כ"א יצא בפני עצמו לפעל הגמור כאילו הי' לו תחום בפ"ע יצא כל כח כלול בהדרו, ולמקום שימושו יהי' עתיד להשפיע טובה שלמה.

136 Ibid. 9:193, 332:

הרגש הוא ערך אחור לגבי השכל שהוא הפנים, הקדם. וכ"ז הוא בהיותו מוכר בתור תכונה שלמה משמשת לעצמה ולא בתור כח נחלש של השכל. וכאשר קרבת אלהים במעשים ועבודה לאדם אפשר ליסד רק ע"פ תכונת הרגש, שהוא ג"כ יצור כפיו של יוצר כל, והקבלת האדם את קונו לפי ערכו בטעם הרגש היא העבודה הרצויה שהרבה פינות התורה נוסדו עליה. . . אין לתאר את היצירה האנושית מצד השכל והרגש בשם אחור וקדם, כ"א יצירה אחת שלמה בעלת מעלות עליונות ומעלות שפלות, כערך ראש ורגלים. אמנם האחור והקדם עומדים במערכה אחת וכ"א שלם בכחו העצמי.

The Problem of Self-Love

Throughout '*Eyn Ayah* he recurs to a problem that he characterizes in Rousseau's terms, of *amour propre*, self-love, *ahavah 'atzmit*.[137] Just how Rav Kook came to be familiar with Rousseau through the Hebrew press is less germane than seeing how and why Rousseauian ideals were congenial to him.[138] For Rousseau, the General Will is necessary as the only thing that can reconcile duty and inclination and save society from the self-love into which individuals may fall in the full experience of freedom.[139] Similarly for Rav Kook, his burgeoning concept of the individual is so expansive that it requires a submersion into a larger reality, the ecclesia of Israel, which is the expression of the divinely ordained telos, in order to contain its otherwise destructive, self-loving tendencies. Like Rousseau, he follows what, after Taylor, we call a neo-Augustinian trajectory, of looking for the truth not outside, but within oneself. Indeed, he is more Augustinian than Rousseau in his believing that conscience is not the afterimage of a vanished God, but the voice of God Himself.[140] Thus one should feel great self-love in all its power, which will only intensify the force of the dissolution of oneself in the telos and love of the whole.[141]

This heightening of the love of self as a necessary step towards its dissolution also leads him to an increasingly immanentist theology and to an acceptance of something like the Hasidic doctrine of *bitul ha-yesh* via '*avodah be-gashmiyut*.[142] This stance, well-removed from Mitnagdic spirituality,[143] nonetheless has roots of its own in the writings of Luzzatto.[144] Rav Kook, following Habad, does not limit this form of divine service to the individual *tzadiq*.

> It is fitting that one savor the taste of self-love in all its strength, and with all the depth of his feeling of self-love dissolve his individual love for the sake and telos of love of all, and then there emerges the true light of human righteousness with great effects for doing good

---

137 See ibid. 1:160, 1:175, 2:20, 2:59, 3:40, 3:51, 9:42, 9:225, 9:292.

138 Rousseau often appeared in the Hebrew press of the time, including in the writings of Hillel Zeitlin and Berdyczewsky. Rousseau's importance for Rav Kook is a prominent theme in the groundbreaking work of Shlomo Fischer. See, for now, Shlomo Fischer, "Self-Expression and Democracy in Radical Religious Zionist Ideology" (PhD diss., Hebrew University, 2007).

139 On this dimension of Rousseau, scanted by Taylor, see Judith N. Shklar, *Men and Citizens: A Study of Rousseau's Social Theory* (Cambridge: Cambridge University Press, 1969), 57–74, 184–197.

140 For Rousseau's neo-Augustinian turn, see Taylor, *Sources of the Self*, 356–362.

141 EAB 9:225, vol. 2, 342:
אמנם ראוי הוא שיהי' האדם חש טעם אהבת עצמו בכל תקפו, ועם כל עומק הרגשתו באהבת עצמו יהי' מבטל אהבתו הפרטית לצורך ותכלית אהבת הכלל, אז יצא האור האמיתי בצדקת האדם שממנה תוצאות גדולות למעשה הטוב ודרך ד'.

142 Ada Rapoport-Albert, "God and the Zaddik as the Two Focal Points of Hasidic Worship," *History of Religions* 18, no. 4 (1979): 296–325. And see at greater length *Be-Khol Derakhekah Da'ehu* by the the late, much lamented Tsippi Kaufmann.

143 See part 3 of Hayim of Volozhin's *Nefesh Ha-Hayim*.

144 See Tishby, "'Iqvot Rabbi Moshe Hayim Luzzatto be-Mishnat Ha-Hasidut": 201–234.

and the Godly path. . . . The love of materiality is not bad in and of itself; indeed it is a great virtue for the civilizing and and betterment of the world, the deficiency is that generally the human heart is not broad enough to accept in all their perfection and power the two loves, of materiality and spirituality. But the true virtue is so to perfect oneself that there be in oneself a love of materiality and inclination to civilization . . . and so he will do great deeds in matters material and repairing the world (*tiqqunei 'olam*) and be so noble and ethereal a person, a divine saint and servant in great holiness for the sake of His blessed Name, till his turning to spirituality is itself so great that he seems as if he is one who has nothing at all to do with materiality.[145]

The Study of Aggadah and Spiritual Individualism

I noted at the outset of this chapter that the study of aggadah held a comparatively inferior place in the rabbinic curriculum of the time. Thus Rav Kook's drive to study aggadah was not without its complications, indeed one surmises that no small part of the affirmation of the self in *'Eyn Ayah* arose in no small part from his efforts to accept his own love of aggadah, which he identified with a religion of the heart well removed from Lithuanian Talmudism.

One should listen to the voice of his inner feelings, which have been created by God in order to protect us and guide us, regarding matters of both body and soul. For instance . . . at times one's intention and intellectual readiness will incline more towards the practical study of halakhah, and at times his soul will incline more towards liturgical poetry and aggadah, to *devequt* with God and sacred feelings of love and pure piety, which are the general principles of aggadah . . . one should preserve *a time for every desire* (Eccles. 3:1) of his internal desiring, which points to the soul's inclination by its nature to long for that which it lacks.[146]

---

145 EAB 9:225, vol. 2, 342:

אמנם ראוי הוא שיהי' האדם חש טעם אהבת עצמו בכל תקפו, ועם כל עומק הרגשתו באהבת עצמו יהי' מבטל אהבתו הפרטית לצורך ותכלית אהבת הכלל, אז יצא האור האמיתי בצדקת האדם שממנה תוצאות גדולות למעשה הטוב ודרך ד'. . . . ובכלל אין אהבת החומריות מצד עצמה שום חסרון כ"א מעלה גדולה לישובה של עולם ותיקונו, והחסרון האחד הוא מפני שע"פ רוב לבו של אדם אינו רחב לקבל בכל שלימות ותוקף שתי האהבות, אהבת החומריות ואהבת הרוחניות בכל שלימותם. אבל המעלה האמיתית היא שישתלם האדם כ"כ, עד שתהי' בו אהבת החומריות ונטיה רבה לישובה של עולם גדולה כ"כ, כמו שתצוייר להיות באיש אשר לא יתערב בו שום אהבה רוחנית המונעתו מהתמכרות לאהבת החומריות. ע"כ יהיו מעשיו גדולים בעניני החומריות ותיקוני העולם, ויהי כ"כ איש נאצל, קדוש אלהים ועובד ברוב קדושה לשם השם ית', עד שתהיה פנייתו לצד הרוחניות גדולה כ"כ, עד שתתראה לפנינו כאילו הוא איש שאין לו דבר עם החומריות.

146 Ibid. 9:254, 352–353:

ראוי לאדם להאזין לקול הרגשותיו הפנימיות, שהם נוסדו מיוצר כל ב"ה כדי לשמרנו מכל רע ולהדריכנו בדרך חיים, והדברים כוללים עניני הגוף ועניני הנפש. דוגמת אלה בעניני הנפש . . . לפעמים יהי' נוטה דעתו והכשר שכלו אל דברים של עיון מעשיים כעניני הלכה . . . ולפעמים ימצא את נפשו נוטה לעניני פיוט ואגדה, לדבקות בד' ית' ורגשי קודש של אהבה ויראה טהורה, שהם כללי האגדה . . . ראוי לו לאדם לשמור עת לכל חפץ כחפצו הפנימי, שמורה על נטיית הנפש בטבעה להשתוקק אל אשר יחסר לה. . . .

If individual inclination in some sense reveals where it is that the divine Will wants to go, so do differences among individuals. Commenting on Rav Hamnuna's dictum (58a) that on seeing a multitude of Israel one is to recite the blessing "Blessed be the Sage of mysteries," he paraphrases the gloss on this saying found in Midrash Tanhuma, that just as countenances differ, so do minds, each one distinct.[147] He continues:

> The deeper one looks into the souls of men the more one is astounded by the variety of differences among them. . . . Yet precisely via these differences they join in a single goal, of fashioning the world by its proper destiny. Indeed, one must marvel on the sublime wisdom which, by internal secrets known and revealed only to God, ties and relates all these opposites to one another, until by the conjoining of all the varied minds and countenances there emerges a singularly pleasing, harmonious structure. [148]

Why, though, should this knowledge of deep linkage within human diversity be, by the terms of the blessing, esoteric, known only to God?

> And if men were to know of their inner equality, then each would not zealously exert his own sphere, individuality would thus wither, and with it the material that will build the whole. And so God thus implanted in nature that each individual person relate to the world and define himself in it by his own particularity and thus he will perfect that which he should.

This in turn leads to a question implied rather than stated: how to explain Rav Kook's own insight into this divine mystery of human concord-in-diversity?

> Thus all these revealed differences stand in full force, even as they are unified in the deep secrets of divine wisdom, until the end when human education will be complete, and this individuality will no longer have need of this protective cover, *I will restore to the nations lucid speech that all should call in the name of God and serve Him shoulder to shoulder.* (Zeph. 3:9)

In other words, the increasingly Messianic tenor of the times makes possible the insight into an ultimate unity within diversity; indeed the seeming multiplication of diversity and discord in modernity is itself a sign of the approaching millennium.[149] In this regard

---

147 Midrash Tanhuma, Warsaw ed., *Pinhas* §10:

ילמדנו רבינו הרואה בני אדם משונין כיצד מברך. . . אבל אם ראה אוכלסין הרבה של בני אדם (!) [לאו דווקא ישראל—ים] אומר ברוך חכם הרזים, כשם שאין פרצופותיהם (!) שוין זה לזה כך אין דעתם שוין זה לזה, אלא כל אחד ואחד יש לו דעת בפני עצמו וכן אומר (איוב כח: כה) לעשות לרוח משקל ומים תכן במדה, כל בריה ובריה יש לו דעת בפני עצמו. . . .

148 EAB 9:284, vol. 2 , 370:

כל שיסתכל יותר האדם בתוכן הנפשות הפרטיות של בנ"א יותר ישתומם על ההבדל הגדול שיש בין תכונה לתכונה . . . ומ"מ דוקא ע"י השינויים הם מתאחדים כולה למטרה אחת, לבנין העולם בתעודתו הראויה לו. הרי יש להתפלאות על החכמה העליונה, שע"י הרזים הפנימים הידועים וגלויים רק לפניו ית' מתקשרים ומתיחסים כל אלו ההפכים זה לזה, עד שע"פ צירוף כל הדיעות והפרצופים השונים יצא בנין הרמוני מתאים מאד.

149 While this may put the reader in mind of Netziv's well-known reading of the story of the Tower of Babel as a reminder that human minds are diverse, and indeed that reading of Netziv's may have played some germinating role in Rav Kook's thinking here, there are profound differences between the two. Netziv is making an essentially empirical observation (perhaps deriving

it is worth noting that he follows the reading of the Midrash Tanhuma, which, unlike the Talmud, extends this idea not only to Israel but to all of humanity.

The Talmud's citations (58a) of the verse in 1 Chronicles 29:11 ("Yours, O God, is the greatness, and the power, and the glory, and the victory, and the majesty: for all that is in the heaven and in the earth is Yours; Yours is the kingdom, O God, and You are exalted as head above all.") whose ten designations of God provided early Kabbalists with a, perhaps the, canonical names of the ten sefirot,[150] occasion his own rendering of the cosmic principles represented by the sefirot, and here his adoption of dialectic as a mediating concept emerges clearly.[151]

Thus *Gedulah/Hesed* is the universal work of creation and the sweeping forces of nature, *Gevurah/Din* is detailed Providence and the universe of details; *Tiferet* is beauty, which is the balanced relation of particulars, such as are seen in the rhythms of sun and moon; *Netzah* is the dialectical motion, things moving with their opposites in a manner that gives them strength towards an ultimate goal—a metonym for the history of Israel; *Hod* is a non-dialectical encounter where the lesser gives way to the greater of its own volition, out of recognition of the latter's greater sanctity.

These relationships' dialectical nature means that they are not ultimately at odds. Thus the statement (63a) that on seeing a fallen woman one should take the Nazirite's vow, elicits his comment that

> Human connection is a wondrous thing, to the point where the acts and customs of the farthest social order work an impression of sorts on the people at the far end of the other. . . . Nothing restrains the human spirit, such that by many mediations in the varied paths of life, one meets even another in a far and exalted place.[152]

In the case of Israel, this deep connectedness is related to feeling.

---

from his reading in Enlightenment literature) with pragmatic consequences for legislation, and limited consequences as far as the requirements and prerogatives of halakhic authority are concerned. His ideas of tolerance, even if striking for a major Lithuanian halakhist, are not grounded in anything like Rav Kook's encompassing Kabbalistic metaphysic or his teleological and increasingly dialectical view of history. On Netziv's views, see Perl, "'No Two Minds are Alike': Tolerance and Pluralism in the Work of Netziv": 74–98. For a thorough presentation of Rav Kook's ideas of tolerance as developed in his later writings, see Tamar Ross, "Between Metaphysical and Liberal Pluralism: A Reappraisal of Rabbi A. I. Kook's Espousal of Toleration," *AJS Review* 21, no. 1 (1996): 61–110; she well characterizes him, at 95, as a "harmonistic pluralist," rather than the classic liberal he sometimes seems to be, and which many of his readers wish he were.

150 See, for example, Zohar II, 42b–43a, Nahmanides's Commentary to *Sefer Yetzirah* §1, s.v. *'omeq*; Pseudo-Rabad's Commentary to *Sefer Yetzirah*, introduction; Yosef Gikatilla, *Sha'arei Orah* §3–4.

151 EAB 9:305–314, vol. 2, 378–380.

152 Ibid. 9:317, 381:

יחש נפלא יחש לבנ׳׳א זה עם זה, עד שפעולות ומנהגים של השדרה היותר רחוקה מקצה מזה פועלת איזה רושם גם על האנשים הרחוקים הרבה משדרה זו . . . כי אין מעצור לרוח האדם, שע׳׳י הרבה מיצועים שבדרכי החיים השונים יהיו פוגשים גם במי שעומד במצב רם ורחוק.

One must never forget the central truth that Israel's distinctiveness, its separation from others by the bounds of Torah law, flows from none other than a feeling of simple religiosity, which explains itself to man by his efforts to draw nearer to his Creator in his ways, deeds and thoughts.

He adds, in a note which reveals his burgeoning interest in Zionism:

And the deep quality by which every individual will truly attain his own soul before his Maker emerges only from the great charity that Israel will do with the entire world, via the establishment of Israel as a strong people by all its virtues, which will return to it precisely in the ancestral land given to it by a divine word, everlasting. [153]

Yet feeling does not have the last word in *'Eyn Ayah* Berakhot, indeed he is not wedded to the idea that feeling is ultimately communal. Turning to the closing three passages in the work, we see the themes that have been in play throughout, reaching a kind of equilibrium. Thus, commenting on (64a) the dictum that one who exits the synagogue for the *beit midrash* will be vouchsafed an encounter with the divine Presence, he writes that:

Prayer will bring one near his God only to the extent of his inner sense, per the soul-feelings he has already acquired within, for that is the Torah of feeling on which prayer is founded. Torah will indeed give one knowledge and insight, introducing into him knowledge greater than his individual feeling; it brings into his inner soul those kinds of knowledge that are external to himself . . . thus Torah has need of prayer too, albeit at times, hence *one who leaves the synagogue*, and perfects his internal feeling, *and enters the beit midrash* and occupies himself with Torah to perfect his power of intellect in the terms external to himself *merits an encounter with the divine Presence*.[154]

It is unclear if the Torah he is referring to here is Mitnagdic Talmudic study, or philosophic, mystic study. My sense is that it is the latter. But of course for him, basic Talmudic and halakhic study was the necessary, bread-and-butter prerequisite to higher study and enlightenment. These multiple senses of Torah study come together as his commentary to this Tractate nears its close.

---

153 Ibid. 9:329, 384–385:

לעולם צריך שיהי' נשמר העיקר, כי טעם היות ישראל חטיבה בפ"ע ומובדל מכל העמים בגדרי תורה חקים ומשפטים, אינו נובע כ"א מיסוד רגש של דת פשוטה, המתבארת לאדם ע"פ השתדלותו להיות יותר קרוב לבוראו בדרכיו מעשיו ודיעותיו . . . והתכונה העמוקה שבזה יזכה כל יחיד את נפשו לפני קונו, היא מסתעפת רק מהצדקה הגדולה שיעשה עם ישראל ועם כל העולם כולו, בהעמדת ישראל לגוי איתן ע"פ כל סגולותיו, שישובו אליו דוקא בארץ אבות הנתונה לו למורשה בדבר ד' שיקום לעד.

154 Ibid. 9:359, 396:

שמצד התפילה יתקרב האדם אל אלהיו רק ע"פ חושו הפנימי הפרטי, כפי רגשי נפשו ודעותיו הקנויות לו מכבר בקנין נפשו פנימה, כי זאת היא תורת הרגש שעליו התפילה נוסדת. התורה אמנם תתן לאדם דעת והשכל להכניס בתוכו ידיעות יתירות על ההרגשה הפרטית שלו, היא מכנסת לו את המדעים שמחוץ לנפשו אל נפשו פנימה.... ע"כ התורה צריכה ג"כ אל התפילה, עכ"פ לפרקים. ע"כ היוצא מביהכ"נ, ומשלים את כח רגשו הפנימי, ונכנס לביהמ"ד ועוסק בתורה להשלים כח שכלו בערך החיצוני שחוץ לנפשו, זוכה להקביל פני שכינה. . . .

At 64a, the Talmud writes that the sages know no rest, neither in this world nor the next. This is not, he says, as grim a verdict as it seems. The soul has active and passive qualities, the former is fulfilled when acting, the latter when receiving; thus sages are never at rest because their very quality is to act upon themselves and constantly to be reaching outward to others—and their greatest pleasure is ceaseless motion.[155] Given what we have seen of the restless nature of his own thinking one surmises that he is here also talking about himself.

Commenting on the dictum (64a) that sages multiply peace in the world, he writes:

> There are those who erroneously think that world peace will only come from a common character of opinions and qualities. . . . But no—true peace will come to the world precisely by multiplying it . . . and that comes from all the opinions and perspectives of wisdom becoming visible, which clarifies how all have their place, each according to its place, value and meaning.[156]

Up to now this is a straightforward recitation of the procedural ethics of argument that are a standard feature of rabbinic discourse from antiquity on.[157] But, the passage and his comments continue:

> It is precisely by the multiplication of forces and their opponents that life will be found. But this to the extent that the difference and opposition is structured appropriately, that all foster one goal. Thus we find *tranquility in your palaces*, peace and tranquility in the place that seeks quiet, in the center of the telos. *For the sake of my brothers and friends* that all find a space for their labor, the labor of intellect, and the labor of inclination and feeling . . . *may God grant His people strength* may He give them life full of relation, which is strength, and when life is full of relation, it is full of many sides and built from the syntheses of many forces. . . . *May God bless His people with peace* . . . this is the peace of the unification of all opposites. But there must be opposites, so that there be those who labor and that which they will unify. . . . Hence peace is the name of God, who is the master of all the forces, omnipotent and gathering them all, may His great Name be blessed forever and ever.[158]

---

155 Ibid. 9:360, 397.

156 Ibid. 9:361, 397–398. The passage was printed by Zvi Yehudah Kook in *'Olat Re'ayah*, vol. 1, 330–331, with some editorial changes. The text given here is the original.

יש טועים שחושבים שהשלום העולמי לא יבנה כ"א ע"י צביון אחד בדיעות ותכונות. א"כ כשרואים ת"ח חוקרים בחכמה וע"י המחקר מתרבים הצדדים והשיטות, חושבים שבזה הם גורמים למחלוקת והפך השלום. ובאמת אינו כן, כי השלום האמיתי א"א שיבא לעולם כ"א דוקא ע"י ריבוי השלום . . . הוא שיתראו כל הצדדים וכל השיטות שיש בחכמה, ויתבררו איך כולם יש להם מקום כל דבר לפי מקומו ערכו וענינו.

157 For the classic statements, see Mishnah 'Eduyot 1:5–6, BT 'Eruvin 13b.

158 כי דוקא ע"י ריבוי הכחות והתנגדותם, ימצא החיים. אלא שנערך ההבדל וההתנגדות בערך מתאים, שכולם מובילים למטרה אחת, ע"כ נמצא שלוה בארמנותיך, שקט ושלוה במקום הדרוש שקט, במרכז התכלית. למען אחי ורעי שלכולם יהי' מקום לעבודה, עבודת שכל ונטית רגש . . . ד' עז לעמו יתן, יתן להם חיים מלאים ענין, שהם עז, וכשהחיים מלאים ענין, מלאים הם צדדים רבים ונבנים מהרכבות של כחות רבים . . . ד' יברך את עמו בשלום . . . היא השלום של התאחדות כל ההפכים. אבל צריך שימצאו שימצאו הפכים כדי שיהי' מי שיעבוד ומה שיתאחדו . . . ע"כ שלום הוא שמו של הקב"ה שהוא בעל הכחות כולם, הכל יכול וכוללם יחד, יהי שמו הגדול מבורך מן העולם ועד העולם.

As I mentioned earlier, in Hasidism in general and especially Habad we find the concept of the unification of opposites as a supreme religious act; Rav Kook's monumental, modernist innovation here is that the opposites which are being united are concrete, and antagonistic, social groups and ideologies.

He brings 'Eyn Ayah to Berakhot to a close with a prayer, in which he asks God, inter alia, to "save me from snare and error in halakhah and aggadah . . . and grant that I may realize the desires of my heart, for the honor of your sacred Name, from *in potentia* to actualization."[159]

Concluding Remarks on Expressivism and Subjectivity

In many ways, the course of 'Eyn Ayah neatly recapitulates the "expressivist turn" which Charles Taylor presents as a key feature in the evolution of modern identity. In Taylor's view, Romanticism, rather than being simply a reaction to the overweening technocratic rationalism of the Enlightenment (itself a somewhat overstated characterization) represents a neo-Augustinian attempt to find the truth of existence within oneself and one's own relation to a supreme, external good. Indeed, whereas for Aristotle, sentiments served as a spur to virtue, for the Neo-Platonist Augustine they can be and at times are points of contact with the good, and with God. If for the Deists, nature, human nature included, is the articulation of a divine plan, for the Romantics it is the reservoir of the good, and our own access to goodness is thus dependent on our access to our inner selves.[160] Later, the high Modernists moved through this charged sense of self to a critique of what they saw as Romanticism's own attempted holism and articulated a more fragmented self; Postmodernism moved even further, finding the locus of meaning, if it is to be found anywhere at all, in the interstices between subjects.[161] Rav Kook shared in this expressivist turn; moreover, his turns towards internalization, and his seizing on the elements of the Kabbalistic tradition lending themselves to a recognition and even celebration of the distinctive selfhood of each facet of existence, seems part of his response to the steady fragmentation of Jewish society in his time.

---

159 This closing prayer appears at the close of the introduction as well and it was presumably written originally for that venue; at any rate, as I have said, the introduction was likely written at the end of his work on *Eyn Ayah* to Berakhot. See EAB, vol. 2 , 398:

. . . ותצילני מכל מכשול ושגיאה בהלכה ובאגדה . . . ותזכני להוציא מאויי לבבי, למען כבוד שם קדשך, מן הכח אל הפועל. . . . .

160 See Taylor, "The Expressivist Turn" [chapter 21], in *Sources of the Self*.

161 See ibid., chapter 24, "Epiphanies of Modernism," as well as Jerrold Seigel, "Problematizing the Self," in *Beyond the Cultural Turn: New Directions in the Study of Society and Culture*, ed. Victoria E. Bonnell and Lynn Hunt (Berkeley: University of California Press, 1999), 281–314, and Zygmunt Bauman, *Postmodern Ethics* (Cambridge: Blackwell, 1993). Postmodernism is a large subject and I find Bauman's effort to salvage genuine ethical content from it most valuable; some basic reflections of mine on certain Postmodern currents as a kind of Gnosticism, unmoored from theology and hence ethics, are in my "Mi-Tahat la-Harisot," *Eretz Aheret* 15 (April, 2003): 26-29.

What makes Rav Kook riveting here is his struggle with the tension between reason and the subject, his attempt to synthesize various several spiritual traditions, drawing on them in order to explain both his own inner life, and, increasingly, the life of his times. He saw the competing and conflicting trends in his own inner life as a reflection of a larger drama and similarly reframed the great social and cultural fragmentation of Russian Jewry as a powerful array of subjectivities held together in dialectical encounter.[162] As we have seen in this chapter, his basic preoccupations, categories and contradictions abide but he deploys them in increasingly wider spheres of significance and thus subtly transforms them.

It often makes more sense to speak of someone's religious and metaphysical stances less as a narrow assertion of specific positions than as part of a general worldview, consisting of ontological, epistemological and textual commitments and the relations and patterns obtaining among them.[163] In this light, we can say that as Rav Kook's own *episteme* moved to encompass and at times assert the primacy of feeling, his ontology shifted towards increasing dynamism, and with it a deepened commitment to the Kabbalah, which afforded him not only a vocabulary for a dynamic and often contradictory sense of experience, but a means of giving that experience an ontological grounding in its mythologized worldview. Kabbalah's way of seeing the individual as the locus of larger forces also helps ease another set of anxieties. A strong sense of self at the least pushes against, if not downright threatens, the highly structured, deeply nomian, order of rabbinic Judaism. By casting the self in Kabbalistic terms, the self emerges only to be dissolved, indeed it can only exist as an independent entity if it is ultimately to be dissolved. Via the idea of a phantom self, which is a self en route to its dissolution, Rav Kook is able to incorporate a concern with the subjective self, as a locus of both cognition and expression, into his halakhic worldview.

Finally, Alain Touraine, in noting the distinctively modern tensions between reason and the subject, has observed that the agent of potential union between reason and the subject is the social movement which transforms the personal and collective subject into a collective action towards liberation.[164] Rav Kook, for his part, eventually found resolution of the subject by an embrace of nationalism, one which did not come to full realization until his emigration to Palestine. Indeed, his writings on nationalism from his Eastern European years are very distinct from his later, more celebrated writings, and it is to them that we now turn.

---

162 Compare this to Abrams, *Natural Supernaturalism*, 185: "[W]hat was most distinctive in Romantic thought was the . . . organized unity in which all individuation and diversity survive, in Coleridge's terms, as distinctions without division." See also Arthur O. Lovejoy, *The Great Chain of Being: A Study of the History of an Idea* (Cambridge, MA: Harvard University Press, 1936), chapter 10, esp. 294–297.

163 Dixon, *From Passions to Emotions*, 240.

164 Touraine, *Critique of Modernity*, 374.

5

The Turn Towards Nationalism: Between Ideology and Utopia, or, Ethics and Eschatology

Up to now, we have not discussed Rav Kook's pre-Jaffan thoughts on nationalism and the Land of Israel much, not least because these questions were of little concern or interest to him. In the mid- to late 1890s, that began to change. It is time, then, to trace the stirrings and evolution of his thinking on Jewish nationalism, first sketched out in his *Mahberot Qetanot Boisk* (Little Notebooks of Boisk) of these years, culminating in the series of essays in the Orthodox rabbinic journal *Ha-Peles* of 1901-1904, in which he emerged as a qualified supporter of Jewish nationalism in general and Zionism in particular, on his own distinctive terms. In the next chapter we will unearth the roots of his thinking on these questions in his grappling with the broader crisis of religion of the time, as reflected in his recently published notebooks and his long-unpublished work recently issued as *For the Perplexed of the Generation*. As elsewhere, so too here he imaginatively reworked themes drawn from medieval philosophy—especially the role of the mind in our moral cultivation and the Kabbalistic ideas of Luzzatto, shifting them into a distinctively modern key of historical progress towards a radiant human future, in which Jewish nationalism has its own role to play.

Unlike almost all of Rav Kook other pre-Palestine writings, his early writings on nationalism did receive some scholarly attention over the years.[1] This is not surprising,

---

1 The academic studies which seriously treat this period are, in alphabetical order, Reuven Gerber, "Hitpathut Hazon Ha-Tehiyah Ha-Leu'mit be-Mishnat Ha-Re'ayah Kook" (PhD diss., Hebrew University, 1991), 29–39, and more recently, 43–48 of his *Mahapekhat Ha-Hearah: Darko Ha-Ruhanit shel Ha-Re'ayah Kook* (Jerusalem: Ha-Sifriyah Ha-Tzionit, 2005); Goldman, "Tzionut Hilonit, Te'udat Yisrael ve-Takhlit Ha-Torah"; Lanir, *Ha-Re'ayah Kook ve-Ha-Tzionut*, 55–126 (a largely unrevised printing of her dissertation of 2000); Ravitzky, *Ha-Qetz Ha-Megulah*, 119–134; as well as Michal Lanir's work to be discussed below.

Hagi Ben-Artzi offers close and interesting reading of the essays on nationalism in "Biqoret Ha-Dat u-Derakhim le-Hithadshutah be-Haguto Ha-Muqdemet shel Ha-Rav Kook"

not only for their being in the public domain, but also for his stature as the rabbinic trib-une of Jewish nationalism. Even so, much remains to be said, especially for tracing the development of his thinking over time.[2]

In these years and afterwards, Rav Kook in many ways subscribed more to nationhood than to nationalism qua "ism," to "nation" as a category of experience and understanding, and less as political ideology. Nations are the vessels in and through which people receive their formative ideals and culture. In a sense, there is for him only one nation in the fullest sense, that is, an ethnic entity whose very existence qua corporate body is morally mean-ingful, serving as the incarnation of, and ontologically grounded in, something larger than itself—and that is Israel. As we will see, he takes pains to differentiate Jewish nation-alism from what he characterizes as the dangerously chauvinistic delusion of, as he refers to it, *Nationalismus*. If he thinks that other nations have unique and particular contribu-tions to make to the progress of humankind, he doesn't say so. To him, Jewish nationhood properly understood is Torah nationhood, which is to say a nationhood in which national feeling is disciplined by intellect. This disciplining would take the form, most basically of halakhah, of course, but not be limited to that. Rather, the nation is the matter to the Torah's form, to be guided by universal principles of order, much in the same way that the individual is to discipline himself by the exercise of his intellect, which leads to halakhic practice in the first instance, but beyond, to the alignment of one's own higher, and gov-erning faculties, with the divine mind governing the universe. In this respect his thinking on nationalism is an interesting and unexpected legacy of his Maimonidean concerns, a merger of his thinking on Mussar and nationalism, in striking contrast to the expressive Romantic nationalism of his later, more celebrated writings. Here, as elsewhere, he tries to balance the particular and universal, threading his way through a number of competing currents of the time. Casting Jewish nationhood in larger historiosophical terms would come after his arrival in Jaffa.

(master's thesis, Hebrew University, 1991). By contrast, in his "He-Yashan Yithadesh ve-He-Hadash Yitqadesh": Biqoret Ha-Dat u-Derakhim le-Hithadshutah be-Haguto Ha-Muqdemet shel Ha-Rav Kook," *Aqdamot* 3 (September 1997): 9–28, he argues unconvincingly that nearly all the elements of Rav Kook's mature thought are present in the essays in *Ha-Peles* and indeed that that thought straightforwardly reflects the priorities of latter-day Religious Zionism. His subsequent exchange with Aryeh Weinman over whether Rav Kook ought to be labeled "Zionist" is strictly semantic, ideologically driven on both sides, and illuminates little; it appears in *Aqdamot* 6 (January 1999): 69–71, 73–75.

Of all these treatments, Goldman's is particularly astute and he, inter alia, perceptively notices the multiple roles of the medieval philosophical tradition in the *Ha-Peles* essays.

2   The longest treatment of the essays—and a very valuable one—is that of Michal Lanir; while she carefully and thoughtfully teases out a number of themes, she regularly blurs the distinction between this and later periods in Rav Kook's thought, and in particular sees at work here the later themes that are the focus of the work of her advisor, the great scholar Yosef Ben-Shlomo.

Jewish Nationalism in Eastern Europe

The rich and complicated history of Jewish nationalism in general, and Zionism in particular, has been told many times and we will concentrate here only on some elements crucial to our story.[3] Nascent Jewish settlement efforts in Palestine began in the early nineteenth century, spurred in no small measure by latter-day disciples of the Gaon of Vilna (the significance of which for Rav Kook will become part of our story in the subsequent chapter).[4] Lone nationalist thinkers of different stripes in varying locales (for example, religious figures such as Zvi Hirsch Kalischer,[5] the socialist thinker Moses Hess,[6] both of whom exercised influence on Rav Kook) appeared in mid-century. Yet it was not until the late nineteenth century that Jewish nationalism emerged in Eastern Europe with the rudiments of a social and cultural program with the creation of Hibat Tzion. And a bona fide political program for nationalism moving beyond efforts at settlement and cultural renewal in the direction of diplomacy and statecraft did not appear until Theodore Herzl. In Jacob Katz's characteristically judicious formulation (an historian's restatement of Ahad Ha-Am's powerful distinction between "the problem of the Jews" and "the problem of Judaism"), while it was the failure of emancipation that stirred Western Zionists, it was the collapse of traditional society that moved the proto-Zionist rabbis Kalischer and

---

3   The list of books is nearly endless and I will spare the reader. Key to my thinking throughout has been Arthur Hertzberg's still-extraordinary introductory essay to his *The Zionist Idea: A Historical Analysis and Reader* (New York: Atheneun, 1976) [1959].

   As we will see, there are some points of contact between Rav Kook's thinking in this period and that of his contemporary Simon Dubnow, particularly as regards embedding Jewish nationalism in a universal moral framework; see the essays of Dubnow's from this period gathered and translated in his *Nationalism and History: Essays on Old and New Judaism*, ed. Koppel S. Pinson (Philadelphia: Jewish Publication Society, 1958) and the other works referenced below.

4   The role of the Gaon's followers in laying the foundations for later Zionist activity has been the subject of lively scholarly debate; the view that they were proto-Zionist has been championed by Arie Morgenstern, *Geʾulah be-Derekh Ha-Tevaʿ: Talmidei Ha-Gra be-Eretz Yisrael, 1800–1840*, 2nd ed. (Jerusalem: Maʾor, 1997), 1–28; therein, Morgenstern rehearses the Gaon's basic theological and historical arguments; it originally appeared in *Cathedra* 24 (1982): 51–69, 76–78, with responses by Menachem Friedman, Jacob Katz, and Isaiah Tishby. See also Morgenstern's exchanges with Israel Bartal, reprinted in the latter's *Galut Ba-Aretz: Yishuv Eretz Yisrael be-Terem Ha-Tzionut* (Jerusalem: Ha-Sifriyah Ha-Tzionit, 1995), 250–295, and, for the fullest statement of the contraty view, most recently Etkes, *Ha-Tzionut Ha-Meshihit shel Ha-Gaʾon mi-Vilna*. However one characterizes these efforts in the sweep of Zionist history, it seems fair to say that Rav Kook saw these earlier efforts as precursors to his.

5   On Kalischer, see Jody Myers, *Seeking Zion: Modernity and Messianic Activism in the Writings of Tsevi Hirsch Kalischer* (Oxford and Portland: Littman, 2003).

6   On Hess, see Shlomo Avineri, *Moses Hess: Prophet of Communism and Zionism* (New York: New York University Press, 1985), and more recently Ken Koltun-Fromm, *Moses Hess and Modern Jewish Identity* (Bloomington: Indiana University Press, 2001).

Alkalay, and in any case it was not until the multiple crises of the 1880s that their ideas conjoined with the social realities of Eastern Europe to create anything like a movement. [7]

Hibat Tzion arose, as we have seen, as one response to the failure of Russian liberalism and sought to ameliorate Russian Jewry's civic, cultural, and economic crises by encouraging immigration and settlement efforts in Palestine; it elicited mixed reactions among the rabbis of Eastern Europe.[8] While it, and Zionism later, met with near total rejection by Hasidic rabbis, some non-Hasidic rabbis showed some openness to it, both for the practical possibilities it offered for the amelioration of Jewish economic and political disability in the Russian Empire, and, to a lesser extent, for the possible rapprochement it offered with moderate Haskalah. This *modus vivendi* was challenged by the secular but deeply cultural and moralistic nationalism of Ahad Ha-Am (the pen name of Asher Ginzberg, 1856–1927), and made nearly untenable by the advent in 1897 of political Zionism, with its claim to activist representation of the entire Jewish world by avowedly assimilated Western Jews.

More than Herzl, it was Ahad Ha-Am who challenged traditionalists with a plausible set of alternatives to religion. In a nutshell, Ahad Ha-Am's doctrine of nationalism is that every nation has its own peculiar national spirit, which is one particular manifestation of the broader human spirit; Israel's peculiar spirit is reflected in its concern with morality.[9] Moral intuition, feeling, is for him the defining feature of Israel's sprit. Interestingly, for Ahad Ha-Am feeling is the vehicle of moral progress, that is, through the course of multiple evolutions that we call history, moral intuition tests itself against, and inevitably critiques, the status quo. When that intuition cannot square its critiques with received metaphysical truths, it reinterprets and mythologizes them and thus is born and developed the complex interplay of religious traditions.[10] Alfred Gottschalk points out that while for Krochmal Spirit is a metaphysical entity capable of ultimate realization as Absolute, Ahad Ha-Am's more naturalized national spirit does not partake of metaphysics.[11] Rather, national spirit is an inner, creative energy that makes itself concretely manifest in Israel's national life and culture. At the same time Rina Hevlin sees at work in

---

7   See his *Le'umiyut Yehudit: Masot u-Mehqarim* (Jerusalem: Ha-Sifriyah Ha-Tzionit, 1979), 10, 22–25.

8   This paragraph draws heavily on Luz's extraordinary history, *Maqbilim Nifgashim*. Much of this ground is covered by the various works of Yosef Salmon, which are rich and valuable sources of information and texts, but rarely reach Luz's historical-sociological sweep and philosophical insight.

9   This is put succinctly in his brief 1898 review "Iyov ve-Prometheus," reprinted in Ahad Ha-Am, *Kol Kitvei*, 280–281.

10   The clearest statement of this is Ahad Ha-Am's 1899 essay "Li-She'elot Ha-Yom, 5," reprinted as "Ha-Mussar Ha-Le'umi," in *Kol Kitvei*, 159–164. (A little embarrassingly in retrospect, the essay closes with a rousing endorsement of Felix Adler's ethical culture movement.) His insistence on morality as constitutive of Jewish identity emerges clearly in his polemic with the Nietzschean Berdichewsky; see his "Shinui Ha-'Arakhin," in *Kol Kitvei*, 154–156.

11   See Yehiel Alfred Gottschalk (with Hillel Agranat), *Ahad Ha-Am ve-Ha-Ruah Ha-Leumi* (Jerusalem: Ha-Sifriayh Ha-Tzionit/Mossad Bialik, 1992), esp. 161.

Ahad Ha-Am, Gottschalk's observation notwithstanding, Hegelian concepts of concrete self-realization by the subject, in this case, the national subject, in a form that is expressive of its own essence, metaphysical or not.[12]

Those rabbis who continued to support the Herzlian Zionist movement as the preferred vehicle of Jewish political and economic betterment concluded that these limited goals were best served by keeping religious issues and debates (and certainly Messianic longings) out of the business of Zionism. Herzl, for his part, was made keenly aware of the divisive nature of religious issues through the torments he suffered at the hands of the "Democratic Fraction" and its *enfant terrible* leader, Chaim Weizmann, who urged the Zionist movement actively to engage in "cultural" work. Herzl well appreciated the rabbis' willingness to bracket religious issues for the foreseeable future and beyond, and repaid them with his support. In 1902, the Zionist rabbis, led by Yitzhak Ya'aqov Reines (1839–1915), formed the Mizrahi, which aimed to function as a religious party within the Zionist movement as a whole.[13]

Rav Kook was uninvolved in these developments, surprising though that may sound in light of his later career. He had ties to rabbis who were active to varying degrees in Hibat Tzion, such as Aderet, Netziv, Eliasberg, and Mordechai Gimpel Jaffe, and to rabbis who were uninvolved in and even hostile to, Hibat Tzion and, later, Zionism, such as Eliezer Gordon, who offered Rav Kook the position of spiritual director of his yeshiva at Telz.[14] He was not listed among the rabbinic supporters of Zionism in a well-publicized open letter of 1900.[15] Indeed, one looks in vain for mention of Rav Kook in the contem-

---

12 Rina Hevlin, *Mehuyavut Kefulah: Zehut Yehudit beyn Masoret le-Hilun be-Haguto shel Ahad Ha-Am* (Tel Aviv: Ha-Kibbutz Ha-Meuhad, 2001), 109. Hevlin says that for Ahad Ha-Am the various manifestations of Jewish identity emerging over time are not hierarchically arrayed; this seems difficult to square with his privileging of morality as the defining Jewish value.

Ahad Ha-Am's disciple Klausner rejected Hegelian determinism and its seeing nations as following inevitable paths of growth and decline; Herzl for his part *qua* political leader spoke in both voluntarist and deterministic terms; see Shmuel Almog, *Tzionut ve-Historiyah* (Jerusalem: Hebrew University/Magnes, 1982), 51–52.

13 The term "Mizrahi" itself had arisen in 1893 when Shmuel Mohilever created in Bialystok a *merkaz ruhani* to agitate for Hibat Tzion among religious Jews.

14 For the little that is known about this incident see above in chapter three. Whatever the reasons for Rav Kook's not taking the position, it would never have been offered him had he been thought of as an avowed supporter of Zionism. For Gordon's attitudes towards Zionism, see Salmon, *Dat ve-Tzionut*, 296–297.

Yosef Zekharia Stern was, on the one hand, listed as a signatory to the pro-Zionist declaration in *Ha-Melitz* to be discussed immediately following, yet in the anti-Zionist volume *Or la-Yesharim*, which will be discussed below, he is quoted as saying that he regrets the association of his name with Zionism, even though he did not provide a signed statement for the volume. It will be recalled that Stern maintained good ties and wide-ranging correspondence, with a strikingly broad range of rabbinic colleagues on a number of matters; see Hamiel, "Yahasei RY"Z Stern ve-Rabbanei Doro be-Shu"t." My thanks to Dr. Yehuda Galinsky for directing me to this source.

15 The declaration was published in *Ha-Melitz*, 13 Nisan 5660/March 30, 1900, 1.

poraneous and historical depictions of Hibat Tzion and early Zionism (though he did on occasion raise money "for the benefit of the workers" in the Land of Israel).[16] Moreover, the Tiferet Bahurim society which, as we saw earlier, he created in Boisk, was presumably part of the Tiferet Bahurim network created in 1901 as part of Orthodox anti-Zionist activism. [17]

The point was powerfully made by a leading Religious Zionist activist, Yitzhak Nissenbaum, writing in his memoirs about his reaction on hearing of Rav Kook's appointment as rabbi of Jaffa: "This rabbi [that is, Kook] never interested me in particular. He took no part in Hibat Tzion, and, later, Zionism. He hadn't written important books by then, and so what would I have to do with him?"[18] His absence from the periodical press of the time, aside from a few brief halakhic pieces, is striking especially given the literary ambitions he displayed in the years 1886–1888, and his torrent of writing as the years went by. As we have seen, most of his energies in the 1880s–1890s were taken up with his rabbinic posts, and what I have characterized as an inward turn in the wake of his wife's death and his arrival in Zeimel, and the contemporary movement that most exercised him was not Hibat Tzion but Mussar. When in 1894 he wrote the unpublished essay discussed earlier in chapter three, on the need for peace among the contending Jewish parties of the time, he mentioned Hovevei Zion only at the very end of a long list of splintered elements of Jewish life, alongside supporters of settlement in Argentina.[19]

It may well be that precisely because he had so little direct experience with Zionists that, in the essays we will be looking at, he could talk about them as hopefully, and regularly naively, as he did.[20]

---

16 See the notices in *Ha-Melitz*, 20 Tammuz 5602/July 25, 1902, and 28 Shevat 5663/February 25, 1903; the latter donation was the result of an appeal on Yom Kippur. My thanks to the late Rabbi Yehoshua Mondschein for bringing these sources to my attention.

17 On the societies, see Luz, *Maqbilim Nifgashim*, 291. On his creating one in Boisk, see Rabbiner, "Shalosh Qehillot Qodesh," 244–296, 263 (admittedly Rabbiner's description leaves some doubt as to whether the Boisk chapter was itself anti-Zionist).

18 Nissebaum, *'Alei Heldi*, 188. This sentence is interestingly, and tellingly, omitted from Neriah's citation of Nissenbaum's other, extremely flattering comments about Rav Kook, see Neriah, *Sihot*, 302. Nissenbaum was, inter alia, Shmuel Mohilever's personal secretary and thus at the center of Hibat Tzion activities.

19 The essay "Shalom be-Shem" was published in 1970 in *Orot Ha-Re'ayah*, 16–19, and was meant to be the introduction to a series of publications arguing for internal Jewish concord; to the best of my knowledge none were ever written or published. The pertinent passage is:
ועתה אחינו בשרנו קהל עדת ישורון הגוי כולו לכל מפלגותיו וכוחותיו, לכל חברותיו ואגודותיו, גאוניו צדיקיו ויראיו, חכמיו ומשכיליו, חובשי בתי מדרשיו לתורה ולתעודה ולוקחי לקח בתי מדע וחכמה, רופאיו ורוקחיו, מוריו ופקידיו, חרשיו וסוחריו, חנוניו וסרסוריו, תומכי תורה ושוקדי מלאכה, חובבי ציון ומאשרי ארגנטינה . . .

20 In this regard, his experience contrasts interestingly with that of his contemporary Aharon Shmuel Tamares (1869–1931), who wrote under the pseudonym "one of the feeling rabbis." Tamares shared Rav Kook's moralist interests, embraced Zionism at first, and then broke with it after his experience as a delegate to the Fourth Zionist Congress of 1901 convinced him that the movement was becoming hopelessly bureaucratic and largely unconcerned with broader issues of, as he put it, "justice and freedom." On this fascinating figure see Ehud Luz, *Pasifism*

Early Mentions of Nationalism and Hints of Apocalypse

We do have, in a letter by Rav Kook to Aderet in the fall of 1889, one very early, private adumbration of his later view that the modern world's chaotic mixture of extraordinary material progress and spiritual collapse itself might be a sign of its Messianic or at least apocalyptic tenor.[21] A few years later, in 1893, we find him writing of his decision to undertake the regular study of laws pertaining to the Temple and its accompanying sacrificial and tithing practices, out of an explicit desire to rouse a longing for the Temple that would, in a kind of theurgic Torah study, itself rouse divine favor.[22] Be that as it may,

---

le-'Or Ha-Torah: Mikhtavei Ehad Ha-Rabbanim Ha-Margishim (Jerusalem: Merkaz Dinur, 1992). Luz offers a sampling of his writings as well as his autobiographic essay, in both the Yiddish original and Hebrew translation. An alternative Hebrew translation by Avraham Bick (Shauly) appears in Refael, ed., Sefer Shragai, 162–174. Shalom Rosenberg compares Tamares's thinking on social justice with that of Rav Kook in his "Stirot ve-Dialektikah be-Mussar Ha-Hevrati e-Hagutam shel Ha-Re'ayah Kook ve-shel Ha-Rav A. S. Tamares," in Hevrah ve-Historiyah, ed. Yehezqel Cohen (Jerusalem: Misrad Ha-Hinukh, 1980), 137–154.

21 This is found in his OM, addendum 4, 248. Written during the High Holy Days, after halakhic give and take and a request for forgiveness in anticipation of Yom Kippur, he adds:

אגלה אוזן הדר"ג מר שי' אע"ג דמהסתם לא חדת היא לו דמיסתפינא מהך דספרי האזינו ותמלא ארצו וגו' והוא בסמך ע"פ שמנת עוית וגו' שהוא ג' דורות לפני ביאת המשיח ואדוני יבין מחשבתי מ"מ יעשה הקב"ה למען שמו ויקרב קץ ישעו וונשגב ד' לבדו ביום ההוא.

I will reveal to [your] ear, though it is probably not news [to you] that if I may dare to say so, unless I am mistaken the text of the Sifrei in Haazinu, and he will fill his land [Isa. 2:7–8] which is adjacent to the verse you have grown fat and gross etc. [Deut. 32:15] refers to three generations before the advent of the Messiah, and my master will understand my thought, at any rate, may God act for His name and hasten the end of his redemption, and God alone will be exalted on that day [Isa. 2:11].

The text he is referring to is the Tannaitic Midrash Sifrei's gloss to Deut. 32:15, "But Yeshurun grew fat and kicked, you were fat, you were gross, you were gorged, forsook the God that made him." The midrashic passage, which assigns the dire prophecies of Moses's valediction in Deut. 32 to various phases of Biblical history, says on this verse: "These are the three generations preceding the Messianic days, as is written: Their land is full of silver and gold, there is no limit to their treasures; their land is full of horses, there is no limit to their their chariots. And their land is full of idols. The bow down to the work of their hands, to what their fingers have wrought. (Isa. 2:7–8).

The Sifrei passage is to be found at paragraph 318 (Finkelstein edition, 363). Earlier, at paragraph 310, the Sifrei introduces the idea that the Messianic age will last for three generations, based on the verse "They shall see you with the sun, and before the moon, generation and generations" (Ps. 72:5; Finkelstein edition, 351). See the notes therein for parallel passages in rabbinic literature.

22 His motivation is given in the brief essay of 1893 published posthumously as the introduction to Mishpat Cohen. For these halakhic discussions of his from that period see there, nos. 29, 39, 55, 56, 58, 98, 115, and 121. Also interesting is no. 58, which is a discussion of the early attempts to circumvent the sabbatical year, an issue which would later become a defining cause celebre of his career, and no. 147, which discusses the permissibility of ever leaving the Land of Israel once one has settled there.

neither of these brief comments have anything to do with the phenomenon of Hibat Tzion as such.

As noted above, in his unpublished 1894 essay he sees Hibat Tzion as but one of the many factions into which the Jewish world has divided. In a poem written at this time he voices a similar concern, as spokesman for the sacred people; *El Hiki Shofar* ("To my palette, O ram's horn!" after Hos. 8:1): "Would that I had a voice like the raging sea/I would shout to the ends of the earth. . . . About the wars of words . . . that turn fast lovers to hatred."[23] The solution to this discord, he says, is not to criticize but to strive towards remedying each other's deficiencies: "Let us know that each one is but a particular element of our community." Stanza after stanza extols the merits and necessity of each camp, its abilities and preoccupations. Talmudists, physicians, poets, Maskilim, artisans, each have their part to play. Strikingly, rather than giving primacy to the Orthodox in his call for unity, they come after men of liberal professions, Maskilim and artisans, and before Hebraists and workers.[24] He closes with the exhortation: "Let each one take care to adore and cherish / the value of the calling which is not his own / and not defile with ridicule or even criticism / that which is his colleague's goal."

As we have seen in our earlier discussions of *Metziot Qatan* and *Midbar Shur*, he did in the early mid 1890s begin to give serious thought to Israel's place among the nations, with Israel tutoring the latter in those forms of material and moral perfection available to them, though Jewish nationalism as a basis of identity is, in those texts, nowhere to be found.

First Responses to the Zionist Movement

Interestingly, he not only reacted with enthusiasm, at least privately, to the first Zionist Congress, but saw it as perhaps creating the possibility of sustainable halakhic change. In 1898, he wrote an essay responding to the new Zionist movement, the only extant part of which is a lengthy discussion of the relationship between Zionism and halakhic change.[25]

---

23 *Orot Ha-Reʾayah*, 25–28. The poem also appears with the group of poems in his notebook from Boisk, which I will discuss in the last chapter, published in Ofan, *Qevatzim mi-Ketav Yad Qodsho*.

24 This choice is not necessitated in the poem by the rhyme or meter (which are in any case uneven), and may reflect an intuitive sense on his part that the first two groups require greater exhortation than the others to stay within the fold.

25 The essay was not published until the 1920, when it appeared in a religious Zionist monthly, as part of a series of hitherto unpublished writings of Rav Kook's, whose publication was meant to advance his candidacy for the then-in-formation chief rabbinate. It was published under the title "On Zionism" in *Ha-Devir* (1920), 7–9, 10–12, 29–33, and 33–38. An editor's note accompanying the first installment says that "Our Rabbi wrote this 22 years ago, at the outset of the Zionist movement, the earlier chapters have been lost." The essay is reprinted in *Otzarot*, 2:235–244, and the references here follow that edition.

In this he has recourse to Maimonides's jurisprudence, echoing some of his earlier essays in 'Ittur Sofrim.[26]

The polemics on halakhic change in the 1860s had ended in the shelving of the question by the rabbinic leadership. The question of halakhic development in the context of Eastern European Jewish nationalism had recently, in 1894, been broached by Ahad Ha-Am in an exchange with Mordechai Eliasberg's son Yonatan; Ahad Ha-Am contrasted the idea of "development," an unconscious, natural process, to the artificial and doomed idea of Reform.[27] Development, he says, "is dependent on the moral understanding of the heart, which latter depends on the development of life in general amidst the nation"; the loss of Jewish political freedom has dulled this sense, the law has become "petrified" as a result, and the vehicle for its restoration is the movement known as Hibat Tzion.[28]

Rav Kook too articulates a critique of Reform, but with a difference; in contrast to Ahad Ha-Am, he sees a place for institutional changes, but within an ideal halakhic process, which will be restored with the end of exile. Indeed, he writes, the deepest error of the Reform movement is its accepting exile as the truth of Jewish existence, thereby relinquishing the idea of a return to the Land, and with it a restoration of the free and just legal institutions envisioned by the Torah, including the great legislating Sanhedrin, or in Maimonides's formulation, the Bet Din Ha-Gadol. A return to the Land by natural means of immigration and statecraft, and certainly with the consent of the international community, violates no dogma. Of course, he writes, one may not abrogate a single letter of the written Torah, and much of the Oral Torah has a similar normative force, whether by virtue of its origin in the properly constituted legal authorities of Temple times, or its rootedness in the Talmud and acceptance by all of Israel. But there is no reason to assume that any and every precedent or stringency that has accrued over time is immutable; the great Sanhedrin to be established in Jerusalem will sift the halakhic wheat from the chaff. The need to staff the Sanhedrin and the lower courts it will oversee will itself require a shift in rabbinic curricula, along the lines of the great legal faculties of the world. Indeed, this will finally bring to a close the battles over Haskalah, since the Rabbis themselves will have to become the true Maskilim.

Necessary changes are already *in potentia* within the halakhah, he says, prepared by God to be roused by the moral and material needs of changing times—and by no means in an obvious, shallow, direction of leniency. Indeed, new stringencies may be necessary in these new times, but they will be facilitated by a process willing to reopen those elements of halakhah which are neither black letter Talmudic law, nor rabbinic enactments

---

26 The key Maimonidean texts are the introduction to his *Mishneh Torah*, and therein at Hil. Mamrim, chapters 1–2. Much has been written on this; for now see Ya'aqov (Gerald) Blidstein, *Samkhut u-Meri be-Hilkhot Ha-Rambam* (Tel Aviv: Ha-Kibbutz Ha-Meuchad, 2002).

27 Ahad Ha-Am, "Divrei Shalom," in *Kol Kitvei*, 56–60, esp. 59–60. Yonatan Eliasberg's interesting and always respectful letters to him are to be found in NLI, Ahad Ha-Am archive, 4° 791/59.

28 *Kol Kitvei*, 60.

accepted unanimously. Issues that have been the subject of principled rabbinic disagreement over time would be considered properly left open for revisiting by a renewed Sanhedrin.

> The national aspiration is powerful and its moral strength is great as well. But withal it needs a moral fount, from which it may draw vivifying plenitude. For every nation and tongue, that is the humane love of humanity as a whole; for us it is in the broader sense the love of God, for the eternal Torah must encompass the perfection extending to the end of all generations, until that felicitous time when man will have fulfilled his obligations in love of humanity to its apex. Then he will lift his heart for the good of all creatures, God's handiwork all.[29]

Interestingly, this leads directly into a discussion of the issues of sacrifices and vegetarianism that, we will see, came increasingly to preoccupy him in these years, and became the prism through which he first explored ideas of the moral progress of humanity, and of Torah. Isaiah's vision of the wolf and the lamb, he says, may actually be brought about by humanity; but "giving untimely precedence to animals, at the time when human blood is spilled like water for national desires, is a cheap illusion."[30] Torah encompasses all the highest developments of culture that will unfold over time, but only over time.

The need for a religiously disciplined nationalism is driven home for him by the negative example of France where nationalism unanchored in the divine spirit led to mass bestiality, intellectual pretensions to the liberation of humanity notwithstanding.

> Nationalism alone, when it strikes root deep in the nation's heart, may degrade and animalize its spirit the same way that it can elevate it. Witness patriotic France, which enlightened wise men took to be the redemption of humanity, and go see what became of them! Our nationalism is protected against this wildness, but only when guided by its nature, which is God's spirit that is upon us, as promised by our Prophets *that it will not depart from our offspring and theirs, says God, from now and forever* (after Isa. 59:21).[31]

---

29   *Otzarot*, ibid., 241.

השאיפה הלאומית היא רבת אונים וכוחה המוסרי ג"כ גדול. אבל בכל זאת היא צריכה מעין מוסרי להיות יונקת
ממנו שפע חיים, אצל כל עם ולשון היא ההומנית אהבת האנושית הכללית ואצלנו במובן יותר רחב אהבת השם
יתברך, כי התורה הנצחית צריכה להיות כוללת ההשתלמות עד סוף כל הדורות, עד העת המאושרה שכבר יצא
האדם ידי חובתו, בהאהבה האנושית, עד מרום קצה, אז ירום לבבו לטובת כל הנבראים כולם מעשי ד'.

30   Ibid.:

לא נפלאת היא אחי, להכיר כי גם בתעודה העליונה של וגר זאב עם כבש אינה צריכה להיות משל, כ"א דברים
כמשמען וגם היא תעשה ע"י האנושיות. הזיה טפילה היא להקדים הרחמים המרובים על בע"ח בלא עת, בעת אשר
דמי אדם נגררים כמים עבור חפץ עממי.

31   Ibid., 242:

הלאומיות לבדה, כשהיא מכה שורש עמוק בלב העם, היא עלולה גם להשפיל רוחו ולבהמתן, כמו שתוכל לרומם
אותו. עדה היא צרפת הפטריוטית אשר חכמים נאורים חשבוה לגאולת האנושיות, ופוק חזי מאי סלקא בהו!
לאומיותנו אנו היא שמורה מפראות כאלה, אבל רק בהיותה מתנהלת על פי טבעה שהיא רוח ד' אשר עלינו, ושאנו
מובטחים מפי נביאינו שלא תמוש מפי זרענו ומפי זרע זרענו אמר ד' מעתה ועד עולם.

   It is not clear if he has in mind the Terror of the revolution, the antisemitism of the Dreyfuss affair, or, more likely, both.

In closing, he urges the religious not to segregate themselves into a separate party, but to join the Zionist movement and shape it from within, even if that means adopting the occasional halakhic leniency.

Aviezer Ravitzky, one of the few scholars of Rav Kook to discuss this essay, sees it as following the so-called "forerunners of Zionism" (such as Kalischer or Alkalay) in ascribing religious significance to Jewish nationalism, and notes his casting of Messiah as an historical process, one that will bring about a religious renewal.[32] Ravitzky draws attention to the Maimonidean elements here, most notably the idea of the great Sanhedrin as the fulcrum of legal dynamism. He also notes the undeniably utopian elements of Rav Kook's sense of how a putative Sanhedrin would relate to other sovereign institutions. In sum, Ravitzky well-characterizes Rav Kook's views here as an activist conception of Messianism; intellectual audacity that doesn't deal much with particulars; an organismic conception of Jewish peoplehood and religion and a denial of Jewish freethinking on its own terms. Crucially absent here, as elsewhere in these years, are the large theological, cosmological, and historiosophical concerns of his later writing.

In a letter to his father from the summer of 1899, Rav Kook mentions in passing that he seeks to found a network of societies called "Torah-Keeping Zionists," but we have no records of anything coming of this.[33] A further whiff, though not much more than that, of a Messianic reading of the times appeared in 1900, when, on behalf of Aderet, Rav Kook wrote an approbation to the *Liqutei Halakhot*, a volume by the celebrated sage and saint Israel Meir Kagan (aka Hafetz Hayim) on the laws of Temple sacrifices, understandably a less-visited precinct of Talmudic study.[34] After setting forth familiar themes about the need for sages to immerse themselves in this topic as the appropriately rabbinic form of Messianic longing, he adds: "And this is God's desire from us in this morbid exile, *and all the more so during the footstep of the Messiah, in this our present generation*" (emphasis added).[35]

First Response to Orthodox Anti-Zionism

In 1900 Ya'aqov Lifshitz, a skillful and tireless Orthodox activist and publicist, published a volume entitled *Or la-Yesharim*, containing anti-Zionist declarations by some of the most prominent rabbis of the time, including Eliezer Gordon, Hayim Soloveitchik, Eliyahu Hayim Meisel (with whom, we recall, Shlomo Zalman Kook had studied in his youth), and Shalom Ber Schneerson, the Lubavitcher rebbe (the latter's presence being a striking

---

32 Ravitzky, *Ha-Qetz Ha-Megulah*, 120–129; see also Lanir, *Ha-Re'ayah Kook ve-Ha-Tzionut*, 58.

33 *Igrot*, 1:9.

34 Israel Meir Kagan, *Liqutei Halakhot* (Warsaw/Pietrkov: Baumritter 1900); the approbation is reprinted in Shvat and Halamish, *Haskamot Ha-Re'ayah*, 1–4. For Aderet's request that he draft it, see Neriah, *Sihot*, 183.

35 Shvat and Halamish, *Haskamot Ha-Re'ayah*, 3:

הנה זאת היא חפץ ה' ית"ש מאתנו בגלות החל הזה וביותר בעקבא דמשיחא בדורנו הנוכחי. . . .

advance for Hasidic-Mitnagdic cooperation).[36] The various contributors had themselves shown varying degrees of support for Hibat Tzion and other nationalist activities over the years, but now saw Zionism as a straightforward threat to traditional Judaism, a movement whose true goals were not the Jews' political and economic betterment, but their widespread assimilation under the aegis of a pernicious simulacrum of Jewish identity, one that made promises it could not hope to fulfill.[37]

Rav Kook drafted a critical response to *Or la-Yesharim*, never published in his lifetime.[38] While he urged his rabbinic colleagues not to abandon the nationalist project, gone is the optimism of the 1898 essay that Zionism will bring about a Messianic restoration and revitalization of the halakhic process. Rather we find here argumentation akin to that of the rabbis of Hibat Tzion, arguing for nationalism as a vehicle for Jewish unity and identity and supporting the program of settlement in Palestine in largely utilitarian terms.

Throughout the essay, he takes pains to distance himself from the writings of Ahad Ha-Am, Lilienblum, and Smolenskin—whose cultural critiques of political Zionism he nonetheless seems at times to endorse. He contends that the nationalist impulse, and the settlement project it is bringing forth, itself springs from essential elements of Judaism, and that the rabbinic fraternity abandons nationalism at its own peril. The fact that we find heretics among supporters of nationalism is no more reason to abandon it than would the existence of ethically minded heretics be reason to abandon ethics.[39] The respective historical controversies over Maimonideanism and Hasidism, two ostensible heresies which eventually became mainstream teachings, sound a cautionary note against too hasty a condemnation of new ideas.[40] Indeed, he strikingly notes, Bahya's *Hovot Ha-Levavot* openly borrowed from the moral teachings of other religions (such as Islam) and enriched Judaism in the process.[41]

There is nothing, he says, inherently sinful or rebellious in the project of settling Palestine as such and rabbis should take a hand in it. Moreover, if redemption should come about from this, then the rejuvenation of mitzvot would necessarily ensue (indeed,

---

36 A detailed discussion of the volume is to be found in Salmon, *Dat ve-Tzionut*, 284–300. Lifshitz astutely kept his own, controversial, name out of *Or la-Yesharim*.

    Lifshitz's historical writing is the subject of Israel Bartal, "'Zikhron Ya'aqov' le-Ya'aqov Lifshitz: Historiografiyah Ortodoksit?," *Mileit* 2 (1984): 409–414; see also Bartal, "True Knowledge and Wisdom," 178–192. For a fascinating discussion of Lifhsitz's role in the exemption of yeshiva students from conscription into the tsarist army, an episode with significant ramifications to the present day, see Zalkin, "Beyn 'Bnei Elohim' li-Vnei Adam,'" 165–222, 200ff.

    Ehud Luz has pointed out that the volume effectively served as the antithesis to Druyanov's collection, *Hibat Tzion*, published eight years before.

37 Luz's discussion is at *Maqbilim Nifgashim*, 276–279.

38 It was published in Ben-Zion Shapira, ed., *Ginzei Re'ayah*, vol. 3 (Jerusalem: Qeren 'al-shem Ha-Ratzya"h Kook, 1985), 24–28.

39 Ibid., 24.

40 Ibid., 25.

41 Ibid., 26–27.

he says, this surely must have been the intent of Kalischer's support of nationalism).[42] Towards the end he lays out some tentative ideas about Jewish nationalism. "The national spirit is no foreign plant in Israel, but a natural and refined spirit, just as the love of children is planted in parents' hearts, and so it requires no express mitzvah, for the national spirit is something natural, good and lovely."[43] Zionism is not the corrosive Haskalah of Mendelssohn, since "those Maskilim sought to disavow their people, destroy all its sacred institutions, mock its future hopes, while Zionism works to enhance the nation's strength, strengthen its future hope."[44]

In the previous chapter, we saw that in his picture of the religious life he begins with Maimonides's picture of the human person as composed of body-imagination-mind, and at some point substitutes feeling for imagination. His writing here would seem to indicate a point at which he has recourse to feeling as a bridging category between body and mind, even if feeling is not yet for him on parity with the mind. This second, unpublished, essay marks a retreat from the optimism of the first, as the Zionist movement had in the interim shown itself to be resolutely secular. And as ever, Rav Kook strives to stay within the consensus of the rabbinic fraternity, even as he creatively explores the currents of his time.

That neither of these two essays was published at the time indicates some hesitation before publicly emerging as a supporter, or more precisely friendly critic, of secular Jewish nationalism. But that he finally did, in *Ha-Peles*.

Ha-Peles

Ha-Peles (literally, *The Scale*) was founded in 1901 by Eliyahu Aqiva Rabinowitz, rabbi of Poltava, a vigorous, independent-minded writer, who after gingerly supporting Zionism broke with it after the second Zionist Congress rejected his call for a rabbinic supervisory council to oversee the movement's spiritual health.[45] Published in Berlin, and thus free of tsarist censorship, *Ha-Peles* announced itself on its masthead as: "A Rabbinic Monthly for Torah, Worship, and Lovingkindness, and for the Weighing of All that Israel Does in All the Lands of its Dispersion on the Scales of Truth, Law, and Peace."[46] In the publisher's letter of the first issue, Rabinowitz writes that the journal's goal is to return Israel to Torah,

---

42 Ibid., 27.
43 Ibid., 28.
44 Ibid.
45 On Rabinowitz, see Luz, *Maqbilim Nifgashim*, 201–202, 276–277, 289–292. A fascinating autobiographical essay by him appears in the introduction to a volume of responsa by his father Dov Ber Rabinowitz—*Devar Emet* (Poltava: Rabinowitz, 1913). Shmuel Almog slyly points out that Rabinowitz's parodies of Zionists' anti-rabbinic polemics are so vividly rendered (see Rabinowitz's *Tzion be-Mishpat*, 65–66) that one could almost be forgiven for thinking that he himself believed them, Almog, *Tzionut ve-Historiyah*, 127–128. For more biographical information on Rabinowitz, see Rivka Blau, *Learn Torah, Live Torah, Love Torah: HaRav Mordechai Pinchas Teitz, the Quintessential Rabbi* (Hoboken: Ktav, 2001), 3–8.
46 הפלס והוא ירחון רבני לתורה לעבודה ולגמילות חסדים ולשקול כל אשר יעשה ישראל בכל ארצות פזוריו במאזני האמת הדין והשלום.

which can only be accomplished by peaceful unity within the religious camp. While the journal will brook no assertion contrary to Torah, it will do its utmost to avoid personal attacks. The journal published pieces on a wide variety of subjects by a range of Orthodox rabbis, scholars, writers, and activists, including the occasional woman.[47]

Over the years 1901–1904, Rav Kook published three essays in the pages of *Ha-Peles*, the first and third particularly lengthy and consequential, in which he came out as a supporter of Zionist nationalism, on his own qualified and distinctive terms.[48] They are well removed from his later writings, so much so that Zvi Yehudah Kook cast doubt on their complete authenticity and did his best to see that they were not reprinted.[49]

Rabinowitz was a cousin of Rav Kook's by marriage. Even so, exactly why Rav Kook chose this venue—as unlikely a journal as any to reach the secular nationalist readership to which the essays are explicitly addressed—is unclear, and indeed whether he himself was entirely comfortable with this choice is open to question.[50] Maimon writes that he

---

47 Inter alia, it was there that David Zvi Hoffmann published, in many installments, his pioneering edition of *Mekhilta de-Rashbi*. In the book version (Frankfurt: Kaufmann, 1905) he does not credit *Ha-Peles* in the introduction, though he thanks the Jüdische Literaturgesellschaft for their financial support. Hoffmann published other items there: see *Ha-Peles* 1 (1901): 268; 2 (1902): 121, 266–267. Sarah Feiga Nimtzowicz of Bialystok published a poetic elegy to Rabbi Yonatan Abelman in *Ha-Peles* 3 (1903–1904): 634.

48 They are: "Te'udat Yisrael u-Leumiyuto," *Ha-Peles* 1 (1901): 45–52, 82–94, 154–161, 223–228, 428–433; "'Etzot me-Rahoq," *Ha-Peles* 2 (1902): 457–464, 530–532; and "Afiqim ba-Negev," *Ha-Peles* 3 (1903–1904): 596–604,655–663, 714–722, and 4 (1904): 19–26, 73–80, 138–144. These essays are reprinted in *Otzarot*, 2:25–130, and my citations reflect the pagination there.

49 When portions of the third essay (all had long been out of print) were published by Michael Zvi Nehorai in "Medinat Yisrael be-Mishnato shel Ha-Rav Kook," *'Amudim* 23, no. 12 (Elul 1975): 409–417, as part of a broader argument that Rav Kook's acceptance of nationalism was entirely conditioned on its fostering a just social order and a life of mitzvot, Zvi Yehudah Kook was not long in responding; see his "Le-Verurei Devarim Yesodiyim bi-Temimutam," *'Amudim* 24, no. 2 (Heshvan 5736/1975): 40. He bitterly and somewhat crassly denounced *Ha-Peles* (it was not a *yarhon* [monthly], but a *sirahon* [stink], he says) and suggests—on the basis of no preferred evidence—that Rabinowitz may have tampered with his father's text. As for his directive to his disciples not to reprint the essays, Elisha Aviner (Langenauer) writes in his 1984 preface to MH, xiv, that Zvi Yehudah Kook explicitly directed him not to reprint the *Ha-Peles* essays. For one illustration of why he felt it necessary to keep these essays under wraps, see the uses made of them in the avowedly anti-Zionist Haredi polemic of Zvi Wineman, *Ve-Da' Mah she-Tashiv* (Jerusalem: Vatikin, 2001), 17–18, 24. Moreover, the essays, as we will see, are well removed from the mystic historiosophy of Rav Kook's later writings, and scarcely mention the Land of Israel *qua* religious category as such.

50 The poet Yosef Zvi Rimon, with whom Rav Kook became close later in Palestine, writes that their publication there was "not entirely to the author's will"; see his *'Atzei Hayim: Devarim 'al Gedolei Ha-Umah* (Jerusalem: Mossad Ha-Rav Kook, 1946), 99:

בשני המאמרים האלה, שנתפרסמו לא לגמרי ברצון מחברם, בירחון, שיש בו התנגדות גמורה לציונות, והוא עודו רב צעיר באחת מערי השדה שברוסיה. . . .

In a 1934 letter to the Mizrahi rabbinic leader Moshe Avigdor 'Amiel, Rav Kook wrote that he had written the essays to counter the pernicious idea that "Zionism has nothing to do with religion," by which he meant the efforts by political Zionists to exclude discussion of Jewish

published there at the urging of his former father-in-law Aderet; indeed the latter published several halakhic glosses there himself.[51] While the odds of his essays being read by their intended Zionist readership were slim, he may have been trying to offer rabbinic peers a way of thinking and speaking about Zionism that would join their concerns to those of progressive secular nationalists.[52]

One of his major contentions in these essays is adumbrated in a poem of his from this period. "Walk about Zion, Circle It," dated "Boisk 1900–1903," is a long series of variations on Ps. 48.[53] Attend, he says, to the towers of Jerusalem, which have kept a sorrowful watch over all of Jewish history, reminding Israel of its eternal heritage. In a rebuke to early Zionists, he reminds us that it is Torah that preserves Jewish identity: "There is a quality to our nationalism that is distinct [*nivdelet*] . . . Torah's laws of life / The Torah of the living God / Rock of Israel, awesome Deity / He it is who chose Zion and Jerusalem." Other religions, he says, only weaken their bearers' national spirit: "When their nationalism rises up / Religion brings them low / Folded up in church spires."[54] Non-Jewish nationalism is thus no model for Jewish nationalism, and a return to Torah is the necessary condition of national renewal. This poem is also interesting for its invocation of the Land of Israel, missing from the essays in *Ha-Peles* and more generally from his writings of the period.

While other commentators have read the three essays as all of a piece, I prefer, as I have throughout, to closely read them in chronological order to trace the developmental arc of his ideas, and see the twists and occasional contortions into which he argues himself at times.

But first, a word about the notebooks in which he sketched the ideas that would emerge in the essays.

The Little Notebooks of Boisk

The year 2008 saw the publication of two notebooks from Boisk, which Zvi Yehudah Kook had designated *Mahberot Qetanot* (*Little Notebooks*)—hereafter MQB, for *Mahberot*

---

culture and religion from the Zionist movement. In point of fact, and ironically enough, Herzl and his allies took this tack precisely in order to keep the Mizrahi inside the Zionist tent. The letter was reprinted in the second, 1947, edition of Zvi Yehudah Kook's *Li-Sheloshah be-Elul* (Jerusalem: Ha-Makhon 'al-shem-Ha-Ratzya"h Kook, 2003), 106–107.

51 They appear in *Ha-Peles* 1 (1901): 15, 68–70, 3 (1903–1904): 390–392.

52 Ben-Artzi, "Biqoret Ha-Dat u-Derakhim le-Hithadshutah be-Haguto Ha-Muqdemet shel Ha-Rav Kook" compellingly argues that throughout the essays Rav Kook critiques both secular nationalism and Haredi Judaism along three parallel axes: inadequate appreciation of nationalism, educational failure and ethical insensitivity, and that he sees literature as the key ingredient in revival. On this basis he suggests that Rav Kook published the essays in the particular venue of *Ha-Peles* precisely because the critique of Orthodox society mattered more to him than did the critique of secular nationalism.

53 *Orot Ha-Re'ayah*, 29–35, *Qevatzim mi-Ketav Yad Qodsho*, 25–31.

54 This is perhaps Rav Kook's first echoing of Nietzsche; his classmate and contemporary Berdyczewsky had begun to cite Nietzsche in his writings as early as 1894; see Holzman, *El Ha-Qer'a She-ba-Lev*, 194–195.

Qetanot Boisk. They also appeared in 2011, the third part of *Pinqasei Ha-Re'ayah*, with very substantial omissions and several additions, and we here follow the 2008 volume edited by Bezalel Ofan.[55]

The entries in these notebooks (which also contain scattered Talmudic and halakhic novellae) reflect Rav Kook's burgeoning interests in national identity, history, and eschatology, as well as their relation to principled rebellion against Jewish tradition. He also explores ideas like the compatibility of seemingly miraculous future changes and the progress promised by modern science and the theory of evolution.

Above all, we see in these pages nationhood becoming a new lens on his familiar themes. Thus, for instance, he writes that the Gaon of Vilna's argument with then-emergent Hasidism's taking halakhic liberties (presumably referring to the well-known discomfort with Hasidism's perceived willingness to postpone prayer time for the sake of meditative focus) was rooted less in legal deviance as such than by the fear that focusing on the spiritual virtuoso comes at a cost to "the nation's coming to perfection."[56]

This is a striking reframing of eighteenth-century debates over halakhic and spiritual priorities in fin-de-siècle terms of the relationship between the individual and the nation, and in terms of his explorations of his own place as a spiritual virtuoso tied to the broader ranks of society. All the more striking in this discussion of Hasidism and nationhood is his omitting Hasidism's profoundly communal character as it developed through the nineteenth century; still a disciple of the Gaon, he's presumably reluctant to endorse the Hasidic doctrine of the *tzadiq*, trying to see nationhood, and not Hasidic communal sectarianism, as the new vessel of Jewish collective belonging.

Turning to eschatology, he says, we see that human life spans are lengthening, because there are fewer wars; similarly, resurrection is tied to the evolution of the human spirit, and human wisdom will swell such that there may indeed be knowledge of how to bring the dead back to life. Moreover, the worship of God in the *eschaton* will entail bringing even mute beasts to His service, and thus raise them from their lowliness.[57]

Crucially, though, and keeping with his fundamentally positive valuation of the body, the *eschaton* will still be a time of religious praxis, and not of spiritual worship. Indeed, the

---

55 They will be referred to here as MQB 1 and MQB 2, and we follow *Qevatzim mi-Ketav Yad Qodsho*, vol. 2; they appear there at 11–40. The 2011 edition is in Shapira and Neuman, *Pinqasei Ha-Re'ayah*.

There is an opening paragraph to MQB 1 in the *Pinqasei* edition missing in *Qevatzim*, as well as two concluding paragraphs in MQB 2. On the other hand, the following paragraphs in *Qevatzim* are missing from the 2011 edition: 1: 5–7, 9–15, 18–19; and 2: 16–18, 24–34.

56 MQB 1:2:

יסוד המחלוקת שהקים הגר"א ז"ל נגד החסידים בעיקרה הוא שהרים ראש החסידים הכונה על המעשה, והיתרון ליחיד סגולה להתנהג לפעמים במעשה על פי ראות עינם לצאת מדרכה של תורה, היא בנוי' על יסוד של שלימות היחיד, אבל ההשלמה הלאומית צריכה שתעשה עיקר המעשה, והיחיד אפילו יהי' גדול מאד צריך שיגרר אחרי הציבור בכל דבר שנחתם במנין, כמו פסוקות (!) של דברי חז"ל במשנה וגמרא.

57 Ibid. 1:5, 6, 7. These paragraphs are omitted in the 2011 edition. Further, at ibid. 1:11 he writes that the overpopulation likely to be generated by mass resurrection may indeed be alleviated by new technologies of space travel.

error of the Talmudic arch-heretic, Elisha Ben Avuyah, was his seeing mitzvot as goal-oriented and not meaningful on their own embodied terms. To the contrary, it is through bodily praxis that all will rise over time, because, in God, past, present and future are one.[58]

The foundation of Torah, he writes, is the continued existence of the nation, it engages the individual only as part of the collective, and the individual's energies help the nation achieve self-realization; individuals may find rest among the nations, but the nation itself cannot.[59] The Jewish people itself is in flux, in a rhythm, like one finds in material entities, of contraction and differentiation, of coming together and expansion, and, in Israel's case, of Torah and gentile civilization and knowledge, whose seeming conflict is in essence a disequilibrium due to the nation's not-yet-stable foundation.[60] Indeed, he writes further on, heresy and rebellion arise in our time because the images and ideas of the knowledge of God are imperfect and incomplete, and this restlessness itself is part of the Messianic awakening.[61]

In the second of the "little notebooks," he further tries to work out this dual attitude towards incipient heresy—that it is a threat to the the nation and, at the same time, an understandable reaction to the insufficiency of contemporary religious thought. Indeed, he writes, it is obligatory in the present time calmly to plumb the depths of heresy and show that the heretics' own ideas lead them to Torah and mitzvot, indispensable for the their own national identity.[62] He starts in this notebook to work with the medieval philosophical tradition of *ta'amei ha-mitzvot*, the meanings of commandments, which are to be understood in terms meaningful to both Israel and all of humanity.[63] In a passage seemingly aimed at quieting doubts about expounding the meaning of Torah in terms of contemporary thought and historical development, he writes that there is no true change in Creation, only in terms of human understanding. We understand the present the way we do, because that is the specific kind of light that God has sent us.[64] In a passage linking

---

58 Ibid. 1:8:

‏. . . וזה הי' מקור תרבות הרעה דאחר, שחשב שמצות יש להן יחש מוגבל ותכליתי, חשב שבאמת אפשר להתעלות‎
‏מהמעשים, גם בלא עת, ובאמת הכל אחדות יחיד, היה, הוה והיהי', וכל עת וזמן את חובותי' נשמור בלא נדנוד צל‎
‏ופקפוק. . . .‎

59 Ibid. 1:17.

60 Ibid. 1:18. This passage was omitted in the 2011 edition:

‏בהוויית החומרים יש התכנסות והתפשטות, וב' הכוחות הם ערוכים לסדר החומרי במדה הממוזגת, כחק המשקל‎
‏האמיתי המתוקן, כמו כן בקיום האומה הישראלית ביחוד, ההתפשטות היא בהתפשטות ידיעות חול וחכמות חיצוניות‎
‏ומדות מתוקנות משאר אומות העולם, וההתכנסות היא ההתיחדות בדרכי תורה ומצות. וטרם שהתבססה האומה‎
‏בכללה שני הכוחות מתגוששים זה בזה, וכשתבוא השלימות יבנה האושר על ידי מיזוג שניהם גם יחד.‎

61 Ibid. 1:22.

62 Ibid. 2:11–12:

‏חובתנו בדורנו לרדת לסוף דעת הכפירה לכל צדדיה ולהראות דפיה, ולא להתבהל כלל, כי ד' אלוקינו אתנו, והאמת‎
‏נר לרגלינו . . . ראוי להשכיל כי פריקת עול התורה והמצות הוא חורבן לאומה, חלילה . . . על כן אפילו רק מצד‎
‏המבט הלאומי לבדו ראוי לאיתן התורה והמצות כולן . . . אם כן כבר עולה בידו על ידי הלאומי רגשי דת. . . .‎

63 Ibid. 2:2.

64 Ibid. 2:6.

this mounting historical consciousness with his efforts to understand his own spiritual quest, he writes that there's great comfort to be found in this very understanding of the partiality of our understanding.

> If one thinks he can comprehend all the truths, he will become sad in the realization, weighing heavily on him as it will, that he has not reached his *telos*, and sadness itself is contrary to the nature of flourishing. But when he decides it is utterly impossible for him to reach the truths, but rather the representation most fitting to his constitution, then all his flourishing is the searching itself, and he will be glad at heart always.[65]

In an early entry in the first "little notebook" this relationship between eternal truths in themselves and how they may be grasped is put in explicitly Lurianic terms, of "inner," and "outer" light: the "light within," *or penimi*, consists of "concepts as they are understood in terms of the perceivers," while the "encompassing light," *or maqif*, is what they are in themselves, "and to contemplation, there is no end."[66]

It was in these "little notebooks" that he sketched out the ideas he would expound at length in the essays of *Ha-Peles*, his first significant intervention into the debates of his day on Jewish nationalism and youth's ethical critique of religion. These essays are his major statement on the subject in this period. As we will see, in the first essay Rav Kook argues that nationhood, and the concomitant *feeling* of nationhood, is a fundamental category of Jewish identity and is part of Israel's broader mission to the whole of humanity. In the second, he refines his conception of the relationship between Jewish and other nationalisms. In the third, he picks up the themes of the first, but now places the Torah within a framework of human moral development—namely, the Torah stands at the end of history, offering a higher morality than humanity is capable of at present. The way towards the Torah of the future is lighted in the present by halakhah and mitzvot, which comprise a system of moral and spiritual education to the *eschaton*. In that essay, he evinces a striking willingness to judge contemporary halakhic practice by a higher moral standard, which he defers to, or sees as rooted in, a Messianic future. And he tries, by casting halakhah in a vanguard role in the moral progress of humanity as a whole, to create a halakhic vision that would appeal to progressive nationalists themselves.

---

65 Ibid. 2:8:

אם יחשב אדם שיוכל להשיג כל האמתיות, יתעצב בהשגה, כי יכבד עליו שלא הגיע לתכליתו, והעצבון הוא נגד טבע הלשימות. אמנם בהיותו מחליט כי ההגעה להאמיתיות אי אפשר לו בהחלט, כי אם ציור היותר נאות לפי חוקו, אם כן כל שלימותו הוא עסק הדרישה, על כן הוא תמיד בטוב לבב.

66 Ibid. 1:1:

אור פנימי ואור מקיף. מובן המושגים מצד המשיגים כפי ציורם בנפש הוא האור הפנימי, והמושגים מצד היותם בעצמם חוץ לנפש הוא האור המקיף. ויש עוד ציורים רבים, ואין קץ להתבוננות.

The First Essay: Israel's Universal Mission

The first essay, "Te'udat Yisrael u-Leumiyuto," is best translated as "Israel's Mission and Its Nationhood."[67] The absence of the word *takhlit* (telos), so pervasive in *'Eyn Ayah* and elsewhere, likely reflects the wide use of *te'udah* in Zionist writings and, perhaps, given the universal terms in which he casts Jewish nationalism, alludes to a mission of witness to non-Jews.[68] Throughout, he consciously uses the idea of "mission" to cast both Zionism and Jewish peoplehood into a larger universal framework, a striking posture for an avowedly traditionalist rabbi.

Indeed, the term *te'udah* figured in a well-known controversy of the time that echoes in his essays. In Ahad Ha-Am's 1898 philosophical—and pointedly intergenerational—polemic with Berdyczewsky over the latter's embrace of Nietzsche's withering critique of the very idea of stable bodies of knowledge, and of the *Übermensch* as an ideal, he wrote at length about Israel's *te'udah* in terms of moral obligation, as the end (*takhlit*) towards which chosenness is the means.[69] Ahad Ha-Am was no theist, but he did, unlike the Nietzschean Berdyczewsky, think that Jewish identity and morality exhibited stable characteristics over time.[70] Berdyczewsky for his part saw nationalism, even of the moralizing variety, as a self-ghettoization that would sever the Jewish people both from humanity and from the greater *élan vital* coursing through the world. This *problematique* of moralized Jewish nationalism and its relation to humanity at large is joined in Rav Kook's *Ha-Peles* essays to themes we have seen him developing, that is, the casting of Israel's election in terms of a mission to the rest of humanity, which we saw at work in *Midbar Shur*, and the defining, tensile, relationship between intellect and feeling that was so central to *'Eyn Ayah*. But while in those works these dynamics played out in the arena of individual perfection, here they are a central element in the burgeoning drama of Jewish nationalism. There are echoes of Moses Hess, of Ahad Ha-Am, and also of Valdimir Soloviev, in whose writings nations are divinely ordained vessels of a universal ethical mission, vessels which

---

67 Rav Kook drew on the 1899 Hebrew version of Hess's *Rom und Jerusalem*, which appeared as Moshe Hess, *Roma ve-Yerushalayim*, trans. David Tzemah (Warsaw: Tushiyah/Halter, 1899). There, *Beruf* is translated as *yi'ud* and *bestimmung* as *te'udah* (cf. the 1899 ed, pp. 55, 47 and Hess, *Rom und Jerusalem* (Tel Aviv: n.p., 1935), pp. 47, 63. I do think that the "mission" here could also be translated as "a witnessing destiny."

68 The very first publisher's letter by Rabinowitz in *Ha-Peles* was titled "Ve-Zot Ha-Te'udah be-Yisrael" (after Ruth 4:7). Yehudah Leib Tzirelson also had recourse to the term in "Shtei Terufot," an essay appearing in *Ha-Peles* 1 (1901): 350ff, which we will discuss below.

69 *Kol Kitvei*, 156–157. For other appearances of the term see ibid., 34, 48.

70 I am indebted for this formulation to Arnold J. Band, "The Ahad Ha-Am and Berdyczewski Polarity," in *At the Crossroads: Essays on Ahad Ha-Am*, ed. Jacques Kornberg (Albany: State University of New York Press, 1983), 49–59. For a powerful summary of Berdyczewsky's critique of Ahad Ha-Am, see Steven J. Zipperstein, *Elusive Prophet: Ahad Ha'am and the Origins of Zionism* (Berkeley: University of California Press, 1993), 122–123, as well as Yosef Goldstein, *Ahad Ha-Am: Biografiyah* (Jerusalem: Keter, 1992), 226–233.

must strenuously resist the temptations of self-love (the Rousseauian *problematique* discussed in the previous chapter, to which, as we will see, Rav Kook regularly recurs).[71]

Rav Kook says at the outset:

> Our destiny and mission . . . accompanies the mission of nature in general, which is to improve all existents and bring them to the summit of perfection. And so we must guard (this mission) well for the sake of our collective life contained therein, and for the sake of the human race as a whole and its moral development, whose fate is tied to the fate of our existence. And there can be no doubt that our ascending development depends on the ascent of our people in general by virtue of our collective national strength.[72]

Nationhood is, for most peoples, a function of their political life and its various exigencies, but not for Israel, whose national feeling has been dulled by many centuries of collective absence from the political arena. Such outbreaks of feeling as have occurred in Jewish history spoke to and solely fulfilled individual moral and spiritual yearnings. Paradoxically, the very catastrophe of secularism has led to the arousal of national feeling, as Jews who had become alienated from their Jewishness came to sense something missing from their lives and turn to national identity.[73] Here he is following Kalischer in seeing Zionism as a movement of repentance, but in the very different context of a full-blown international Zionist movement, led by secular Jews.

"The foundations of national love are in intellect and the rule of justice and righteousness, but its branches rise to heated and stormy feeling, and because it is founded on enduring nature it does not pass or die away, but rather stays and endures."[74] Thus, as long as the leaders of Zionism refuse to recognize that Torah and mitzvot—the peculiarly Jewish iterations of intellect and righteousness—are essential to the development of national feeling, they will get nowhere; moreover, the rabbis who act tolerantly towards them will be disingenuously and corrosively repressing genuine and justified

---

71 On Soloviev's moralized nationalism see Greg Gaut, "Can a Christian Be a Nationalist? Vladimir Solov'ev's Critique of Nationalism," *Slavic Review* 57, no. 1 (Spring 1998): 77–94. For his widespread reception among Jewish intellectuals of the time, and in particular his 1895 essay "Nationality from a Moral Point of View," see Bar-Yosef, "The Jewish Reception of Vladimir Solov'ev," 363–392, and, more recently, Horowitz, "Vladimir Solov'ev and the Jews," 198-214. William Kluback, "Israel in the Thought of Vladimir Soloviev," *Midstream* 36, no. 5 (June–July 1990): 28–31, briefly summarizes Soloviev's philosemitic views in terms of his theory of Incarnation. Soloviev also figures in Rav Kook's correspondence with Alexandrov, which will be discussed below, and he refers to Soloviev in a 1905 open letter to Eliezer Ben-Yehudah, *Igrot*, 1:1, no. 18.

72 *Otzarot*, vol 2., 26.

73 Ibid., 26–27.

74 Ibid., 28.

disagreement.[75] Rabbis and Zionists alike must realize that the broad national spirit pervades the Torah and mitzvot in many and varied ways.[76]

How does this work and how does it accord with universalism? The future of humanity depends on a universal, familial, feeling of fraternity and shared responsibility for the other, irrespective of race or nationality.[77] This in turn requires the clear knowledge that God is the Creator and sole ruler and sustainer of the world, indeed that knowledge is the sine qua non of all humanity's development, and it is the task that Israel has taken upon itself.[78] This, then, is why Torah and mitzvot are so central: "Only they make the national spirit within us fit for enduring life, only they elicit the great love with which we must love our fellow, not a *pro forma* love, but true love as befits brothers of the same actual father."[79]

In the next sentence he makes a crucial move. The argument until now would seem to be meaningful with regard to ethical, interpersonal mitzvot; but what about the vast corpus of mitzvot that are cultic and ritual?

Well, one objective of mitzvot is the development of fraternity through uniformity: "And in truth how can we really feel that we are brothers, sons of a single father, and that we owe special and wondrous love to our fellow, if not by all being equal through the Torah's laws and paths?" He then inflects "equality" with uniformity of practice, or perhaps, equality before the law: "For moral equality is the sole source that gives birth to great love that has no comparison to conventional norms of equality, as we always see that men who are equal in their moral ideas and traits grow fond of and love one another. And so, we must habituate ourselves and others of our people to act only according to Torah and mitzvah."[80] Israel, which carries the banner of God's unity, must also carry the banner of peace and concretely explain to the world by its own conduct the meaning of pure, fraternal national love.[81] Thus the Torah commands manifold observances in food, dress,

---

75 Ibid., 30.

76 Ibid., 31–32.

In the spirit of his unpublished thoughts on the Sanhedrin, he goes on to say that Haskalah is dangerous as long as Torah and mitzvot are based only on sentiment, but once placed on a solid natural footing Torah will be conjoined with all the spheres of life and there will be nothing to fear, and this will be for the good of humanity as a whole.

77 Ibid., 33:

התפתחות שלום המין האנושי כמו שעתיד להיות . . . היא שכפי אותו החלק שהאדם נוטל בחיים הכלליים כן עליו למלא את החובה הכללית: שיהיה כל המין האנושי חי חיי משפחה אחת שלמה שכל אחד יכיר וידע שראוי לו לשקוד על טובת חברו ושחובה לאהוב ולכבד את חברו בלי הבדל בין גזע ואומה.

78 Ibid.:

הידיעה הברורה שד' אחד הוא אדון העולם הבורא ומשגיח המחיה ומקיים ומידו מוטל הכל—רק בידו מוטל גורל השלמת האנושות כולה וכאשר יבאו בני האדם לשלמות הידיעה וההכרה הזאת רק אז יכירו וידעו כי אחים אנחנו כלנו . . . ועל כן הדבר מבואר גם בהשקפה קלה כי יסוד ידיעת ד' והגחתו היא תעודת התפתחות האנושית כולה. תעודה זאת נטלה עליה היהדות. . . .

79 Ibid., 34.

80 Ibid.:

כי רק שווי המוסר הוא המקור היחידי המוליד אהבה רבה שאין לו בכל חוקי השווי, וכמו שהננו רואים תמיד אנשים השוים בדעותיהם ובמדותיהם מחבבים ואוהבים זה את זה.

81 Ibid., 36.

family life, and so on, to bring about "an equality of wills."[82] In other words, fraternity means equality means uniformity.

Before plunging into the particulars, he pauses to say that Jewish nationhood, Judaism and world peace as a whole are ever-expanding concentric circles. This recognition can lead to great lyric heights, but requires the discipline of mitzvot once that ecstasy has passed and the hard work of building the national spirit begins.[83] As for individual morality, its goals in this framework are twofold: for each individual to perfect himself as best he can and realize himself in relation to the whole, and reciprocally, to work for the betterment of the whole as best he can.[84] All the mitzvot come to help us perfect our national spirit, which in turn is impossible so long as we have not perfected ourselves by trying to perfect and complete one another.[85] (It is at this point that he makes his sole reference in this essay to the Land of Israel, as the only place where the national spirit can develop and be "a light to the world.")

He then proceeds to walk through a variety of mitzvot and explain them by reference to their ostensible deepening of national solidarity. Thus the laws of kashrut bring about uniformity in the fellowship of the table;[86] the laws against shaving one's sidelocks and beard are meant to encourage a uniform personal aesthetic (among men, of course);[87] Sabbath observance of course reminds Israel of Creation and its providential role in the progressive unfolding of Creation over time, and its many laws serve to deepen that national commitment.[88] These national-based understandings of mitzvot were obvious once, he writes, so much so that they weren't talked about, and thus fell into desuetude; much in the same way, he says—echoing the pedagogic concerns that animated his *Eyn Ayah*—that the "duties of the heart" ceased to be an object of proper study and reflection.

He is drawing here on the medieval genre of *ta'amei ha-mitzvot*, seeking reasons for the mitzvot.[89] As Steven Schwarzschild succinctly noted, a fundamental premise of the genre is "that Jewish doctrine must be derived from Jewish law, not vice-versa, and not from any other source."[90] Recourse to this genre certainly reflects his immersion in and engagement with Maimonides, which will become particularly clear when we address the

---

82 Ibid., 37.

83 Ibid., 39.

84 Ibid., 40:

ע"כ שתים הנה מטרות המוסר הפרטי הראוי לכל איש מאישי המין האנושי, להשלים עצמו כפי ערכו בעצמו ויותר נכון כפי ערך חלקו ביחס אל הכלל, ויחסו אל הכלל בתור פועל לטובת כל הכלל כולו כפי יכולתו.

85 Ibid., 41.

86 Ibid., 42–44.

87 Ibid., 47–48.

88 Ibid., 50–52.

89 The classic treatment remains Isaac Heinemann, *Ta'amei Ha-Mitzvot be-Sifrut Yisrael*, 2 vols., 3rd ed. (Jerusalem: Jewish Agency Press, 1954); see also Josef Stern, *Problems and Parables of Law: Maimonides and Nahmanides on Reasons for the Commandments* (Albany: State University of New York Press, 1998).

90 This is in his review of Gersion Appel, *A Philosophy of Mitzvot* (New York: Ktav, 1975) in *Journal of Biblical Literature* 95, no. 3 (September 1976): 519–520, 520.

third essay in the series.[91] There, he will develop this genre in interesting and unexpected ways, deeply inflected by the Kabbalah.[92] Yet at this point he seems to be working with the terms of another, modern, exponent of the genre, Samson Rafael Hirsch, whose *Horev* we saw in an earlier chapter was taught by Rav Kook to a class in Boisk.[93]

One of Hirsch's categories, *'Edot*, denotes symbolic observances meant to illustrate and solidify Israel's unique peoplehood. Rav Kook adopts that category, though the specific commandments which he discusses were dealt with by Hirsch under a different category, *huqim*. Though that latter term had long designated ostensibly a-rational commandments, for Hirsch it denotes human responsibility for lower, natural orders. That concept of responsibility towards the nonhuman in turn will, as we shall see, be used by Rav Kook in his own development of *ta'amei ha-mitzvot* in the third essay, though in dynamic, historically oriented terms well removed from Hirsch's rather static symbolism.[94]

These passages are couched in an impassioned, hortatory tone, beseeching secular Jews to assume a life of mitzvot for the sake of their own nationalist ideals. Their effect on the reader is, in truth, puzzling. The sheer unlikelihood of fin-de-siècle Jewish nationalists submitting themselves to the rigors of halakhic life and rabbinic authority for the sake of national unity defined as external uniformity, much less their doing so on the basis of an essay written in the pages of an Orthodox rabbinic journal whose editor was avowedly anti-Zionist, deepens the suspicion that Rav Kook at this point had limited understanding of the motivations of political Zionists, certainly not those who were Western, assimilated Jews, like Herzl and Nordau.[95] Again and again, Rav Kook shows himself to be naïve or at best unconcerned about the political and economic realities of Zionism.[96] The contor-

---

91 See the texts reprinted in *Otzarot*, 2:499–520.

92 Don Seeman has written a wonderful study of the place of *ta'amei ha-mitzvot* in Rav Kook's thought, see his "Evolutionary Ethics: The Ta'amei Ha-Mitzvot of Rav Kook," *Hakirah* 26 (2019): 13–55. We will have more to say on this presently and in the coming chapter.

93 See Hirsch's magnum opus *Horev* [1837], trans. Isadore Grunfeld (New York, London, and Jerusalem: Soncino, 1962); for a survey and analysis of Hirsch's work see Noah H. Rosenbloom, *Tradition in an Age of Reform: The Religious Philosophy of Samson Rafael Hirsch* (Philadelphia: Jewish Publication Society, 1976). The problems with Rosenbloom's work on the biographical front have been vivdly criticized by Mordechai Breuer in *Tradition* 16, no. 4 (Summer 1977): 140-149. Yet Rosenbloom's analysis of Hirsch's philosophy does, I think, have real merit. For Rav Kook's teaching *Horev* during this period, see Rabbiner, "Shalosh Qehillot Qodesh," 244–296, 253.

94 My characterization of Hirsch's symbolism as "static" is taken from the lengthy and penetrating discussion to be found in Arnold M. Eisen, *Rethinking Modern Judaism: Ritual, Commandment, Community* (Chicago: University of Chicago Press, 1998), chapter five.

95 Reuven Gerber argues that this rhetoric was less naïve than we might think, given the *narodniki*, "back to the people," sentiments of the younger East European Zionists of the time; Gerber, *Mahapekhat Ha-Hearah*, 48. Yet the vast majority of Zionists who became freethinkers stayed that way, and it is seems unlikely that his halakhic *narodniki* arguments, if that is what they were, would have swayed many.

96 It is thus not surprising that, like most Jewish nationalist thinkers of the time, he does not at all discuss the many issues posed by the existence of Palestine's non-Jewish inhabitants; it seems

tions of his argument perhaps reflect the difficulties of the position he tried to stake out between the rabbis and the Zionists.

Yet just at the point when the essay strains the reader's credulity to the breaking point, he offers a powerful moral critique of Herzlian Zionism's drive for normalization, abandoning a specifically Jewish mission to the world, and adopting an entirely secularized nationalism unmoored in any larger religious or moral ideas.

> So long as national feeling proceeds from the well of nature alone it cannot but become mixed with gross love, disproportionate self-love . . . and now it properly ought to return to us not as a natural feeling alone, but as a pure intellectual concept from the very fount of Israel, fittingly joined to the telos of our witnessing mission to all of humanity.[97]

After making clear that he is addressing himself not only to freethinking nationalists, but also to those Orthodox Jews who neglect the national dimension of Torah,[98] he continues:

> Our nationalism in the spirit of Torah is saved from the riot-causing idiocy of *Nationalismus* divorced from the righteous path, easily becoming self-love. Nationalism which has no feeling more exalted than itself from which to draw life and light can easily turn into self-love in a gross and ugly way. But our nationalism is built on the most exalted foundation of moral philosophy and that is gratitude . . . the love of parents which is the most beautifully sublime feeling of humanity is but a single flame to the torch of national love, the goods we receive from our people . . . God's desire for the development of all humanity, by our perfection, so that there may follow in its train the development of every creature, and the paths of Torah, which alone can secure our special qualities, they alone are the paths leading to the exalted mission of Israel which is God's desire in our world. [99]

---

safe to say that he likely shared what Derek J. Penslar has well characterized as this, to put it mildly, major lacuna in early Zionist thought, as Herzl's "humanitarian (albeit Eurocentric, condescending and paternalistic) [parentheses in original—Y. M.]" perspective, one "riddled with ambiguities and absences, depicted with benevolence and condescension;" see his "Herzl and the Palestinian Arabs: Myth and Counter-Myth," *Journal of Israeli History* 24, no. 1 (2005): 65–78. For Rav Kook's later views on the matter, see Avneri, "Ha-Rav Avraham Yitzhak Ha-Cohen Kook ve-She'elat Yahasei Yehudim-'Aravim be-Eretz Yisrael, 1904–1935," 331–338, and my *Rav Kook*, 83, 196-202

97 *Otzarot*, 2:57:

והנה כל זמן שנמשכה ההרגשה הלאומית ממקור הטבע אי אפשר שלא תהיה מעורבת באהבה גסה, אהבת עצמו יותר מדאי . . . ועכשיו ראויה היא שתשוב אלינו לא בתור הרגשה טבעית לבדה כי אם בתור מושג טהור שכלי ממקור ישראל מחובר כראוי עם תכלית תעודתנו לכלל האנושות.

98 Ibid., 58.

99 Ibid., 59:

לאומיותנו ברוח התורה נשמרת היא מטמטום המוח שתוכל לגרום מהומה של הנאצינואליזמוס כשהיא יוצאת מדרך הישרה. הלאומיות, שאון לה רגש יותר נעלה ממנה לשאוב ממנו חיים ואורה, יכולה בנקל להתהפך לאהבה עצמית במדה גסה וכעורה. אבל לאומיותנו בנויה היא על היסוד היותר נשגב שבתורת המוסר היותר גבוה, הוא יסוד הכרת טובה . . . אהבת הורים שהוא הרגש היותר נעלה לתפארת האנושות הוא רק כ'נר כ'נר לפני האבוקה' נגד האהבה הלאומית, נגד הטובות שאנו מקבלים מלאומנו . . . חפץ ד' להתפתחות האנושות כולה, על ידי השלמתנו

In closing, he draws an interesting analogy: out of the fear of heresy (i.e., Christianity), Jews stopped reciting the Ten Commandments, "to the heartache of every true lover of his people," and stopped teaching schoolchildren the Bible. Today out of the fear of heresy "many lovers of Zion have refrained from becoming Hovevei Tzion."[100] This must end. Rouse the proper national love; then, "the light of Torah and knowledge, piety, will illuminate all the dark places and all the shadows will flee."[101]

Comparing his essay to another which appeared that same year in *Ha-Peles*, Yehudah Leib Tzirelson's "Shtei Terufot" (Two Remedies), sharpens the picture.[102] Tzirelson, Rav Kook's contemporary (1860–1941), rabbi of Priulki from 1878 to 1908 and thereafter rabbi of Kishinev, was a leading rabbi and gifted writer, and, moreover, had the broad secular learning in European languages which Rav Kook lacked.[103] His vivid essay, like Rav Kook's, begins with an assertion of Israel's *te'udah* as the herald of divine morality to the world, followed by a withering attack on the Zionist movement, and in particular its aspirations to "culture," which he characterizes as a thinly veiled aping of Christianity. Unlike Rav Kook, he is less exercised by the homegrown nationalists of Eastern Europe than he is by the cosmopolitan Zionists of Western Europe, whom he characterizes as "homeopaths" (hence the "remedies" of the title), who seek the cure to Jewish troubles in imitation of the Gentiles. Tzirelson excoriates and delegitimizes them, unlike Rav Kook who tries, however awkwardly, to make them see mitzvot as essential to the realization of their national ideals. Tzirelson's sole audience is the rabbinic fraternity, whom he calls to arms in frankly aggressive battle against the Zionists, and, interestingly, against their

---

אנו, למען אשר אחריה תמשיך התפתחות כל היצור, ודרכי התורה שרק המה שומרים את סגולותינו המה הדרכים
המובילים אל התעודה הרוממה של ישראל שהוא חפץ ד' בעולמו.

100 Ibid., 64.

101 Ibid., 65.

102 Yehudah Leib Tzirelson, "Shtei Terufot," *Ha-Peles* 1 (1900): 350–356, 407–421.

103 A brief biography and appreciation of Tzirelson is Mordekhai Sliyfoy, *Ha-Ga'on Rabbi Yehudah Leib Tzirelson: Hayyav u-Fe'ulato* (Tel Aviv: Netzah, 1944). Widely learned and proficient in a number of languages, he wrote, in addition to Talmudic novellae and responsa, prose and poetry. In the words of a contemporary, "as he was learned in the ways of the world and knew how to walk with life, loved truth and hated lucre, he won the love of the hearts of Jews and Christians alike." Eisenstadt, *Dor Rabbanav u-Sofrav*, 38. His certification as a crown rabbi and his receiving honors from the tsar despite his staunch traditionalism were impressive testament to his worldliness. He gathered a number of his journalistic essays and poems in a volume entitled *Derekh Selulah* (Priulki: Mirov, 1902); in it he argued that traditionalists are the true Zionists, he supported the development of Palestine, though not at irreligious Rothschildian hands, and called on his fellow rabbis to participate in journalism. Thanking Tzirelson in late 1906 for sending him a volume of his, presumably his responsa collection, *Gevul Yehudah* (Pietrkov: Rosengarten,1906), Rav Kook writes that he "very much enjoyed its style and organization, straight talk, pristine analysis and tranquil way, and the use of exact science where appropriate." *Da'at Cohen*, no. 96, 196–197. A particularly warm and fulsome letter from Tzirelson to Rav Kook from 1926 is to be found in *Igrot la-Re'ayah*, 328 and 329.

own moral failings and corruption, which he lists in powerful detail.[104] Rather than urging Zionists to rejoin the fold he closes with a call for a new, combative rabbinic organization that will send preachers throughout the Russian Empire. In sum, in Tzirelson we see an acculturated rabbinic figure uninterested in discovering and engaging with secular Zionists' underlying spiritual longings, as was Rav Kook, but also displaying a more lucid understanding of secular (and certainly Western European) Zionists on their own terms.

Eliezer Goldman, following Rivka Schatz, has pointed out Rav Kook's indebtedness in these essays to Moses Hess, and in particular to the 1899 Hebrew translation of the latter's *Rom und Jerusalem*.[105] Goldman points to Hess's influence as regards Israel's role as God's historical instrument for the moral and ethical perfection of the family of humanity and its future-oriented destiny. The law of development, Hess writes, is common to all natural beings, yet a morally free being is only the one who lives by his destiny (translated in the Hebrew editions as *te'udato)* and who uses his mind and will to make his will like God's; this necessary development will result in a life of justice and righteousness.[106] Goldman also points to significant differences between the two, particularly in Hess's denial of transcendence and sin (and with it of the idea of repentance as an historical category).[107]

To these observations of Goldman's we would add another element of Hess's influence, one especially pertinent in light of the previous chapter's discussion, and that is the role of feeling. Hess writes that "Jewish national feeling . . . is a natural feeling,"[108] whose irreducible and ineradicable character gives it a sounder foundation than the merely "religious," and which gives birth to a knowledge of God which develops within the individual and humanity at large, and reaches beyond the narrow bounds of religious law.[109] We have seen how in this essay, and will see in those that follow, Rav Kook works with feeling as the essential basis of nationalism, while seeking to discipline it via the mind. As for Israel's historic destiny, while this essay still casts that element in Hess' relatively naturalistic terms, the idea will, by the third essay, take on a more Kabbalistic cast. And the nexus of feeling and nationalism goes some, perhaps a long, way towards our understanding

---

104 Thus, Tzirelson urges rabbis ("Shtei Terufot": 417) to minimize discord among their congregants, more strictly regulate business ethics, stop selling rabbinic posts to the highest bidder, stop looking the other way as regards trafficking in women, stop performing marriages unless they can prove that the groom is actually unmarried, and to use bans and excommunications towards these ends.

105 I had reached a similar conclusion, independently of Goldman, and my citations to Hess follow the Warsaw 1899 edition.

106 Hess, *Roma ve-Yerushalayim*, 75–77.

107 Goldman, *Mehqarim ve-'Iyunim*, 171–174.

108 Hess, *Roma ve-Yerushalayim*, 23.

109 Ibid., 48. Ken Koltun-Fromm has characterized Jewish racial identity's role for Hess as what Charles Taylor has called an "inescapable framework" (Taylor, *Sources of the Self*, 3), a basic category of identity and thus of epistemology, setting the terms of our moral lives; Koltun-Fromm, *Moses Hess and Modern Jewish Identity*, chapter 4. Avineri, *Moses Hess*, 201–202, has pointed out that for Hess, "race" variously signified ethnicity, culture, descent, language, or physical characteristics.

Rav Kook's increasing clustering of his ideas and experiences around that term in his *'Eyn Ayah*.

For Reines, the leading rabbinic figure of the Mizrahi, such human moral progress as has been made in history is the result of Providence's reordering of the material world so as to make morality necessary for survival.[110] For Rav Kook, at this stage, by contrast, moral progress results from the moral education of Torah and its expansive, edifying effects on the human race.

Rav Kook's according a central religious role to nationalism was prefigured nearly a decade earlier by the maverick rabbi Shmuel Alexandrov, to whom he was introduced, as we have previously seen, by Binyamin Menashe Levin, and with whom he carried out a lively correspondence. In 1891, Alexandrov published an essay entitled "Esh Dat ve-Ruah Leumi," in which he argued that "religion" as such is simply an earlier historical iteration of the larger idea of God, one rooted in piety and awe, which expression now finds in national identity, an affective stance of reaching towards one's fellow-man and thence to God.[111] Rav Kook shares Alexandrov's seeing religion and nationalism as arrayed along a continuum, even if he reverses the directions, with the affective bonds of nationalism leading to mitzvot.

Interlude: Creation of the Mizraḥi

Rav Kook's written response to the formation of Mizrahi in 1902, yet another fragment never published in his lifetime, is an additional valuable window onto his thinking.[112] Notwithstanding his affinity to Mizrahi's willingness to engage, as religious Jews, with the

---

110 There is a burgeoning literature on Reines, who is still an understudied figure. A most perceptive analysis is that of Eliezer Schweid, "Teologiyah Le'umit-Tzionit be-Rei'shitah—'Al Mishnato shel Ha-Rav Yitzhak Ya'aqov Reines," in *Mehqarim be-Qabbalah, be-Filosofiyah Yehudit u-ve-Sifrut Ha-Mussar Mugashim le-Yeshayah Tishby bi-Mel'ot Lo Shiv'im ve-Hamesh Shanim*, ed. Joseph Dan and Joseph Hacker (Jerusalem: Hebrew University/Magnes, 1986), 689–720. Reines too accords a role for feeling, namely, matter rouses feeling which then vitalizes action. See Schweid, 709n36.

111 The essay appeared in installments in *Ha-Maggid* 19, 20, 21, 23, 24, 25, 31, 33 (1891). In addition to the original publication, Rav Kook may have become aware of these ideas via Mordechai Eliasberg who drew on Alexandrov's language without citing directly to him in a letter to Ahad Ha-Am, see *Kol Kitvei*, 56.

112 It was published by Yitzhak Refael in the volume he edited, *Zikhron Ha-Re'ayah* (Jerusalem: Mossad Ha-Rav Kook, 1986), 5–14, and we follow that pagination, notwithstanding the fact that Refael misidentified the text's provenance as having been written in 1912; Menahem Klein has argued persuasively that the text was indeed written in 1902 in response to the creation of the Mizrahi. See his "Teyotah Ne'elamah mi-Kitvei Ha-Shaharut shel Ha-Rav Kook odot Ha-Tzionut Ha-Hilonit," in *Masuot: Mehqarim be-Sifrut Ha-Qabbalah u-Mahshevet Yisrael Muqdashim le-Zikhro shel Professor Ephraim Gottlieb z"l* , ed. Mikhal Oron and Amos Goldreich (Jerusalem/Tel Aviv: Mossad Bialik/Tel Aviv University, 1994), 395–413. Klein believes it was a draft of the *Ha-Peles* essay "'Etzot mi-Rahoq," which I will discuss shortly.

Zionist movement, he didn't join then, and was ambivalent towards the Mizrahi all his life.[113]

He notes at the outset that (as the reader has likely noticed by now) he is not concerned with Zionism's political and economic dimensions but rather with Zionism's religious effect on youth. The religious community has divided into three camps, those who deny Zionism outright, those who call for active engagement within the ranks of the movement, and those who urge a division of labor, and the concomitant creation of a separate religious Zionist party. That is the path embarked upon by the newly created Mizrahi, and it is doomed to failure, as it diminishes not by a whit the primacy of free-thinkers within the Zionist mainstream. Indeed, should the Zionist enterprise eventually succeed this religious self-segregation will lead to disaster. "No parties. Nor special fractions of religious parties do we seek. That is not the way to bring us to the goal we long for, our Torah and faith are our very life-breath and the light of our lives and so they must penetrate all the limbs of our people."[114]

What then is to be done? Religious people should join every Zionist federation and they will certainly bring secular Zionists to repent. Literature must mobilize to spiritualize Zionism. Indeed, Zionism will come to see that it needs religion, no less than it needs a connection to Jewish language and history.

Menahem Klein has pointed out that this fragment shares common features with the essays in *Ha-Peles*: attention to secular literature; an argument that Zionism's role as a vehicle of cultural renewal must similarly stimulate the religious camp; opposition to the creation of a religious party within the Zionist movement; a call to Zionism to undo its secular character; and the argument that the religious camp must effect its goals by education and persuasion, and not by coercion. He also points out a significant difference, that while this text basically assumes the eventual success of Zionism's political territorial program, the essays are more skeptical, and argue that Zionism's success depends on its changing its secular stripes.[115]

To this I would add that Rav Kook is, on the one hand, terribly naïve about the ability of religious Zionists to transform the Zionist movement from within and, on the other, comparatively astute in the recognition, which he shared with Ahad Ha-Am as well as some younger activists such as CChaim Weizmannn—that a political Zionism unconnected to Jewish culture was basing itself on perilously unsustainable foundations.[116]

---

113 Judah Leib Fishman (Maimon) writes that the first *Ha-Peles* essay left a deep impression on Mizrahi's founders, including Zev Yavetz (with whom Rav Kook broke late in life); see his "Toldot Ha-Mizrahi ve-Hitpathuto," in *Sefer Ha-Mizrahi*, ed. J. L. Fishman (Jerusalem: Mossad Ha-Rav Kook, 1946), 5–381, 98. For Rav Kook's ambivalence towards Mizrahi in his public career see my *Rav Kook*, 149-152, 161-165, 192-194.

114 Refael, *Zikhron*, 11.

115 Klein, "Teyotah Ne'elamah mi-Kitvei Ha-Shaharut shel Ha-Rav Kook odot Ha-Tzionut Ha-Hilonit," 411.

116 See Luz, *Maqbilim Nifgashim*, 231–268.

The Second Essay: Mobilizing Literature

The second essay of Rav Kook's to appear in *Ha-Peles*, "'Etzot me-Rahoq" (literally, "Counsels from Afar," taken from Isaiah 25:1), deals primarily with the Zeitgeist wars as played out in the periodical press of the time. He argues that the sarcasm and cynicism of freethinkers ought not be responded to by Orthodox writers in kind,[117] nor by protestations of simple faith, however fervent.[118] The former will just breed further conflict, the latter, distanced from actual knowledge of and engagement with the spirit of the times, are doomed to failure.

What is needed is a measured, powerful response that will deal with the tribulations of secular modernity from within, and he turns for role models, once again, to the medieval philosophers.

> The measure of courage is to be full of courage and perfect tranquility in one's soul. . . . Such were our medieval heroes Se'adyah Gaon, the *Kuzari* [sic], Maimonides and *Ha-'Iqarim* [sic]; they saw their people's sufferings, saw the foe soaring like an eagle in the Zeitgeist . . . and fought, in tranquility and bravery, were neither enthusiastic nor overwrought . . . engaging with tranquility and the equanimity of the righteous the words of those who denied the existence of God, Providence, prophecy, divine revelation, the truth of tradition and the Oral Law, shattering their words like potsherds, without a sign of anger or vexation., without a sigh or sign of worry but rather with a joyfully gracious countenance and a spirit of courage and strength.[119]

Elaborating on the pedagogic concerns that animated his *'Eyn Ayah*, he argues that while modern times have seen great advances in Talmudic methodology which have, inter alia, made Talmud study more engaging and attractive to youth, there has been no corresponding creative work in Jewish theology and ethics.[120] While one may argue about the specific techniques employed by the Mussar movement, none can gainsay the need for exhaustive study of Jewish moral and philosophical literature. Today, the masses turn to literature for aesthetic enjoyment and moral guidance, yet the community of Torah scholars has failed to provide them with suitable works. What is needed is an explosion of literary creativity, of a range of books of varying lengths and formats, in Hebrew, Yiddish, and other languages. [121]

---

117 *Otzarot*, 2:66.

118 Ibid., 67.

119 Ibid., 68.

120 Ibid., 69. The examples he gives of halakhic creativity are the the *Tumim* of Yonatan Eibeschutz, the works of Aqiva Eger, Yehezqel Landau's *Noda' bi-Yehudah*, Aryeh Leib Ha-Cohen's *Qetzot Ha-Hoshen*, Jacob of Lisa's *Netivot Ha-Mishpat* and Pinhas Horovitz's *Hafla'ah*. As noted earlier, these are not works generally associated with the methodology of Netziv; they are, though, works that in some respects partake of more critical and analytic forms of Talmud study.

121 Ibid., 71.

At this point he recurs to the theme he explored in the earlier essay and which he worked to develop in *'Eyn Ayah*, the relationship between feeling and reason: "'natural feeling'" [quotation marks in original—Y. M.] is a good and beautiful thing, but like every other natural thing requires cultivation. All the work of creation must be repaired. . . . So too the natural feeling of pure piety of zealotry for God . . . heaven forbid that we leave it to its nature . . . rather we must educate it by Torah and intellect."[122] The need for the reasoned study of theology and morals is not simply to fortify unmodified traditional religiosity or package it more attractively:

> When piety works in the heart only by nature, it stands ready to make war with everything that seems at first glance to run counter to piety . . . yet it is often the case that when we look deeper into the halakhot of moral attitudes and obligations of the heart [the reference to Maimonides and Bahya is obvious—Y. M.] we find in them things that are good and attractive, such that not only ought we not distance ourselves and combat them, but rather it is our great duty to support them and bring them near.[123]

Indeed, rabbinic authors only lose their credibility with the masses when they fail to concede the legitimacy of those well-founded critiques of the status quo propounded by free-thinking writers. Only a reasoned response that discerningly separates the wheat from the chaff of those critiques will pass muster.[124]

In the next installment of the essay, he immediately assures his readers that he by no means identifies with the freethinkers.[125]

> Those who deal with the broad questions facing our people must necessarily recognize and know that the chief essential that keeps our people from assimilating among the other nations is religion. . . . Indeed the difference within our community between those who keep the Torah and those who leave religion is greater than the difference between Israel and the nations. We are separated from the other nations in religion, but only separated; we are enjoined to love and honor them. But the guilty among our people who cast off the yoke of Torah we are commanded to hate and expel.[126]

---

122 Ibid., 71–72.

123 Ibid., 72:

כשיראת שמים פועלת בלב רק ע״פ טבעה, אז היא עומדת להלחם על כל דבר הנראה לו לאדם בהשקפה הראשונה נגד רגילות בציור יראת ד׳ . . . אבל כשנעמיק בהלכות היראה בהלכות דעות וחובות הלבבות, גם אם שהם דברים טובים ויפים עד שלא די שאין עלינו להרחיקן ולעמוד כנגדם כ״א חובתנו גדולה גם לתמכם ולקרבם.

124 Ibid.

125 This installment of the essay appears much later in the publication year than do its earlier installments, in *Ha-Peles* 2 (1902): 530ff., and one speculates (though not much more than that) whether the striking and strident shift in tone is the result of his own considered ambivalences, or critical reactions he may have received to the relative tolerance of the first part of the essay.

126 *Otzarot*, 2:73–74:

הם העסוקים בשאלות הכלליות של עמנו, על כרחם צריכים להכיר ולדעת שכל העיקר שאינו מניח את עמנו להתבולל בין גויי הארץ הוא הדת . . . כי גדול הוא יותר ההבדל הפנימי שבין שומרי תורה לעוזבי דת, מאותו

One senses here the tensions with which he is struggling, between keeping freethinking nationalists within the camp while feeling compelled as a representative of halakhic tradition and rabbinic authority to excoriate them at the same time.

Turning to the recent creation of Mizrahi, which he doesn't mention by name: as in the fragment we looked at earlier, he rejects the self-segregation and self-designation of the Orthodox as one party among others, denounces "the strange consensus that our nation must split into parties, the Orthodox and the enlightened, which is to say, those who keep the Torah and those who abandon her." Indeed, the secular party is essentially "the sick man's party," sick with rebellion and adolescent fury, and they must be brought back to health.[127] "Useless is the confidence that the national idea by itself will suffice us in our present state, without land or sovereignty, to resurrect the dry bones and breathe into them the spirit of life."[128]

He writes in closing:

> In truth, nothing is more dangerous to Israel . . . than this mistaken religious tolerance. . . . We must call out in God's name and declare that we do not accept the distinction between separate camps of Orthodox and enlightened. We know only that there are righteous, sinners, and the middling sort between the two.[129] And all our desire is to change the sinners into at least middling, and the middling to raise them ever higher until they become righteous, as is written *and your whole nation is righteous* (Isa. 60:21).[130]

He is, unlike other rabbis, willing to work with nationalists, and even accord their project a greater moral and spiritual significance than they themselves know, but always on his own traditional terms.

The Third Essay: Ethics, History, and Eschatology

In this last, and longest, of the three essays, "Afiqim ba-Negev" (Watercourses in the Southern Desert [after Ps. 126:4, "Restore, O God, our captivity, like watercourses in the southern desert"]),[131] he presents the possibility that Zionism not only affords an avenue of return to tradition, but positively opens a new horizon for the tradition itself, one along which the immanent moral forces of the tradition would emerge. He takes on the issue of

---

ההבדל שבין ישראל לעמים. אנחנו מובדלים מן העמים בדת, אבל רק מובדלים אנחנו. אבל הלא אנו מוזהרים
לאהבם ולכבדם. אולם את הרשעים פורקי עול תורה מעמנו אנו חייבים לשנוא ולהרחיק.

127 Ibid., 74.

128 Ibid., 75.

129 This classification is taken from Maimonides, *Hilkhot Teshuvah* 3:1.

130 *Otzarot*, 2:75:

ובאמת אין לך דבר שהוא מסוכן כ"כ לישראל . . . כהסבלנות המוטעית הזאת . . . נקרא בשם ד' ונודיע גלוי לכל
שאין אנו מכירים כלל בעמנו מפלגות של 'חרדים' ו 'נאורים.' אנו יודעים שיש רק צדיקים, בינונים ורשעים, וכל
משאת נפשנו הוא לעשות את הרשעים לבינונים לכל הפחות והבינונים להעלותם במעלה יותר רמה עד אשר יהיו
לצדיקים, ככתוב 'ועמך כולם צדיקים' (ישעיה ס,כא).

131 The title is perhaps an allusion to the 1880s pogroms (referred to as "storms in the southern desert," so as to avoid tsarist censorship) that had spurred the activity of Hibat Tzion.

halakhic change first broached in his 1898 essay, but, having been persuaded by events of the past years to take *la longue durée*, looks less to short-term institutional reforms and more to the broader tides of history.

As we saw, his first written (albeit unpublished) response to the emergence of Herzlian Zionism placed that development in the context of halakhic development, which he cast into a neo-Maimonidean institutional framework of the recreation of the Bet Din Ha-Gadol. In this essay, he returns to the issue of halakhic development—but now as part of the moral evolution of humanity.

He begins with an exploration of the very idea of mission and destiny, adumbrated in the first essay, opening with the well-known, dramatic rabbinic statement that humanity would have been better off never to have been created at all (BT Eruvin 13b). The very idea of destiny, rooted in our very human nature, arises out of the present miseries of the human condition.

> Since the overall balance arising from the tears of the oppressed, the sighs of embittered souls and the cries of the destitute far outweighs the cheers of the joyous at heart . . . and there too will be found little light and many shadows, sad feelings, fear, anguish and dread. . . . Because such is the present condition of life, thus life itself turns, even without the presumption of any broader perspective, towards the search for its destiny."[132]

The future calls to the present: The power of justice that chastises existence, *the angel that beats it and says 'grow!'*,[133] sends its shafts of light from amidst the great, gracious and wondrous light of the future, and with them illuminating the darkened existence of the present."[134] Indeed, he says, in a first stirring of his later organismic thinking, "neither obstacles, nor glooms, nor shortsightedness will restrain the current of life."[135]

All theology derives from a universal drive towards the moral improvement of humanity; yet the best that human culture can do by its own devices is offer a negative morality of "don't"s, as exemplified by the Noahide laws. Unless, that is, it chooses to ask an existential question: "If 'to be or not to be' [sic] were to emerge as a question from the chambers of the human heart in general, this narrowness would not suffice."[136] Turning from the individual towards the group, he writes, a materially successful nation will not worry much about its mission or destiny, while an unsuccessful nation, let alone one which is poor and downtrodden, which fails to provide for its members' well-being, the

---

132 Ibid., 77:

> כיון שהמשקל הכללי העולה מדמעות העשוקים, מאנחות מרי נפש ומיללות של קשי יום, עולה מונים רבים יותר
> מצהלות עליזי לב . . . וגם שם ימצא אור מעט וצללים מרובים, רגשי עצב, פחד, יגון וחרדה . . . וכיון שכך הוא
> מצב ההווה שבחיים, ע״כ החיים עצמם פונים, גם בלא התנשאות של השקפה יותר רחבה מעצמותם, אל בקשת
> התעודה.

133 This is a reference to the celebrated midrash (Genesis Rabbah §10), according to which every blade of grass is whipped by an angel who commands it to grow.

134 *Otzarot*, 2:77.

135 Ibid., 78.

136 Ibid.

raison d'être of any group, will not likely survive. In other words, he concludes, Israel's continued existence can only be explained by its part in some mission larger than itself.

The radiant justice of the future illuminates the present and brings the individual to give himself to Israel in its path towards fulfillment. Is this mere sentiment? No, it is a powerful vision of mind and feeling working together along a divinely ordained path to make a better world.

> And God forbid that the foundation of justice, the general yearning for the future, which bears *in potentia* all the higher moral value, which bears within it the elevation of the human soul— be built only on feeling, whose foundation is in imagination alone, which when reckoning and investigation come to inspect it will find it to be empty and a vain illusion, founded as it is merely in enthusiasm and poetry. . . . Just as the foundation of Judaism. . . . God's unity conjoins soft, warm feeling with clarified thought, with reason clear, and even dry. . . . Thus truly *the foundation of foundations and pillar of wisdom* [the opening words of Maimonides's Code—Y. M.] works upon human culture in a wondrous manner, to educate and make wise, uplift and elevate, make delicate and refine all the forces of the soul all at once—the be all and end all, a whole and perfect world, not in parts, without rupture or fracture. That is the truth of existence, and the very foundation of the moral world, the soul of the scales [after BT Bava Mezia 89a] of human life. As the foundation, so too the branches, fostering justice for all at the right hand of truth and righteousness, between the pillars of intellect and feeling, clear thinking, judgment and justice, and the stormy feeling, hot and flaming and *rising in the sparks of the God-flame* [after Sg. 8:6].[137]

All this can come to pass, he says, in a transposition of the Aristotelian-Maimonidean doctrine of the mean to nationalist discourse, only when both the individual and the group strike a healthy balance that avoids the extremes of self-love and self-hatred.[138] The individual and the whole must similarly be integrated in their shared turning towards the future. The experience of exile, he says, contra Ahad Ha-Am, did not create any new qualities in the Jewish people, but rather led them to realize their inner qualities, and above all, that they are a forward-looking people, whose present draws almost entirely on their future, a future "pregnant with Ideals."[139]

---

137 Ibid, 80:

וחלילה שיהיה יסוד הצדק, השאיפה הכללית לעתיד, שהוא נושא בתוכו את כל הערך המוסרי היותר רם, הכולל בתוכו את עליית הנשמה האנושית – –בנוי רק על רגש שיסודו בכח הדמיון לבדו, וכבוא החשבון וההגיון לחקור עליו ימצאהו שהוא דבר ריק ומקסם שוא, כי יסודו הוא רק התלהבות השירה. . . . . . כשם שיסוד היהדות. . . אחדות השם יתברך, הוא מתאים את הרגש הלח והחם עם המדע המבורר, עם ההגיון הזך ויבש. . . . על כן הוא באמת ''יסוד היסודות ועמוד החכמות'' פועל על הקולטורה האנושית באופן מפליא, לפקח ולהחכים, לרומם ולעלה, לעדן ולפנק את כל כחות הנפש גם יחד – –חזות הכל, עולם שלם, לא קטעים, ולא שברים וקרעים. זאת היא אמיתת המציאות, הוא הוא יסודו של העולם המוסרי, נפש המאזנים של החיים האנושיים. כהיסוד, כן הענפים מתאימים יחד, מוליכים את הצדק הכללי לימין האמת והיושר, בין עמודי השכל והרגש, המדע המבורר החשבון הצדק, והרגש הסוער החם הנלהב ומתרומם ברשפי אש שלהבתיה.

138 Ibid., 80–81.

139 Ibid., 83–84. This passage also includes a reference to Schelling's *Weltseele*.

He then returns to a theme he developed in the first essay, that is, *ta'amei ha-mitzvot* as creating the basis for integration of modern nationalism into Jewish peoplehood; but while in the first essay this was presented in static fashion, with frankly unconvincing appeals to Zionists to assume uniformity of dress and behavior, and peoplehood consisting of little more than mere belonging, here he has—up to a point, but genuinely—internalized progressive ideas of forward historical movement. If in the first essay he allowed some practical critiques of traditional society, here he goes so far as to say that the halakhah does not represent the last word in ethical sensibility, and that it itself points towards a future animated by higher ethical standards than those of the present.

> The very essence of *ta'amei ha-mitzvot* is a hidden divine science. But our goal is to understand how mitzvot work their impress on our mental faculty. We will see their present and future action, as appears to a simple and healthy mind . . . there suffices for us an impression, *a bit of an ear* (after Amos 3:12), a clouded point where there is to be found the footprints of the wonderful future, human righteousness at the utmost to which it can be expanded, refined, indulged and beautified.[140]

The future is the development of natural human righteousness to the utmost. He then integrates this view of history with Lithuanian Kabbalah, in perhaps one of the first passages in his corpus to put forward a Kabbalistic historiosophy of progress, and the beginnings of a sweeping vision of the future integrated with the metaphors of light which featured so prominently in his later work:

> It [the future] will always be the *line of measure*,[141] the vessel with which to receive the few fragments of light which we can receive from the great light waiting to shine, from the ideals of Torah, from that source of light, which has already shown its work in illuminating many darknesses.[142]

Torah seeks the highest elevation of human culture, which includes both freedom and democracy, albeit by a particular understanding: "True democracy, utter equality, negates the overlordship of even a spiritual intelligentsia, but does not make its way in haste, and thus bring woe and darkness and many troubles, but securely: by preparing the recipients of freedom for their freedom."[143] This preparation will lead to the liberation not only of the human race but of all existence, physical and metaphysical. God has arranged to bring these noblest longings of humanity to their realization through the observance of mitzvot in the present.

> Thus it is that (those longings) are composed of a moving force that pushes and rises towards the heights of aspiration, and a force that restrains and halts. The one longs to actualize things

---

140 Ibid., 86.
141 This term features in Zoharic literature (see, for instance, *Zohar Hadash* 57a) and represents a principle of cosmic balance within the realm of the Sefirot.
142 *Otzarot*, 2:86.
143 Ibid., 87.

as their time comes, and the other works that they not emerge so long as their time has not brought it about, so long as humanity is not yet ready, limiting the "light" so it not overwhelm the vessels lest "they shatter" [quotation marks in the original—Y. M.].[144]

We see his harnessing the Lurianic idea of the shattering of the vessels in the process of creation as signaling a fact of human history in all its facets, metaphysical, moral, and mundane, that a premature moral aspiration can bring disastrous results. Indeed, he says, it is a well-observed phenomenon in human history that immoderate and unrestrained progress brings immoderate and unrestrained reaction. And the dialectical push and pull that he explored within lone religious consciousness in *'Eyn Ayah* he now sees in the workings of contemporary history.

Now he proceeds to concrete examples, specifically to the contemporary trend in some circles towards vegetarianism. This is surprising; there are few precedents for vegetarianism within rabbinic tradition, and in the Jewish philosophical tradition Joseph Albo was practically its only advocate.[145] Vegetarianism did come to the notice of some Eastern European Maskilim;[146] and a likely proximate influence here is Tolstoy's vegetarianism, which became known in 1892 with the publication of his *The First Step*.[147] At the same time, discussing progress through the prism of vegetarianism has the frankly apologetic advantage of dealing with the ethical critiques of halakhah in terms of humanity's relation to the natural order without having to broach the more challenging issues of politics and economics, which, as we saw in our discussion above of the 1902 fragment, Rav Kook chose not to address. He may also have been responding to the discussion of sacrifices in the closing chapters of Hess's *Rom und Jerusalem*.

---

144 Ibid., 87.

145 Nahmanides in his commentary to Gen. 1:29 points out the limited but genuine similarities between man and animal, namely the exercise of (albeit limited) choice and the deliberate avoidance of pain, while fully endorsing human carnivorousness (and see Zohar I, 89b). See at greater length Albo, *'Iqarim* III:15, Abravanel to Ex. 16:4 and Isa. 11:7, 11:9, 65:25. For halakhic and theological discussions of the ethical status of animals see Menahem Salai, *Hayto Eretz* (Jerusalem: Shem, 1988), and, more recently, Natan Slifkin, *Man and Beast: Our Relationships with Animals in Jewish Life and Thought* (New York: Yashar, 2006).

146 The polymath writer Solomon Rubin (1823–1910) published a lengthy essay entitled "Adam u-Vehemah, O, Tzaʿar Baʿalei Hayim," in *Melitz Ehad Minei Alef: Meʾasef Maʾamarim ve-Shirim le-Gilyon Ha-Elef me-az Hehel Ha-Melitz*, ed. Alexander Zederbaum (St. Petersburg: Zederbaum, 1884), in which he discusses cruelty to animals in both Jewish sources and the evolving science of the day and endorses vegetarianism; interestingly for our purposes, he says that while cool reason leads to vivisection, warm feeling leads to vegetarianism. Rubin was a fascinating character, a Maskil who wrote widely on many subjects and was a significant popularizer of Spinoza. See Daniel B. Schwartz, *The First Modern Jew: Spinoza and the History of an Image* (Princeton: Princeton University Press, 2012), 81-112. For more sources on Jewish vegetarians of the time, see Rina Li, *Agnon ve-Ha-Tzimhonut* (Tel Aviv: Reshafim, 1993), 222.

147 See Colin Spencer, *The Heretic's Feast: A History of Vegetarianism* (Hanover: University Press of New England, 1995), 275–290.

It is clear to any rational being, Rav Kook writes, that man's dominion over the natural and animal worlds is not a writ for despotism. Torah seeks to bring about a process of human education, rousing reason to its perfection.[148] But that perfected reason is for now given only to individuals and not to humanity as a whole.[149] Meat eating, from its very inception in the wake of the Flood (Gen. 9:1–8), is a temporary concession to man's sinful appetites. Yet it must not be renounced before its time.

> How ridiculous it is, if while one is still besotted with impurity, he were to remove his claws and reach for the far path of charity, to do kindness to animals, as if he has closed his accounts with men created in God's image, as if he had already set everything aright, already done away with the dominion of evil and lies, hatred between peoples and jealousy among nations, race-hatred and family feuds, which mow down many corpses and spill rivers of blood—as if all that had already vanished from the earth, such that that "humane" pietist[150] had nothing left with which to justify himself except proving his righteousness by way of animals![151]

He then—in a swipe at Kantian ethics—says that so long as men are incapable of teaching themselves morality and righteousness from within they require many hedges and restrictions; indeed they may even need, for the sake of their own moral disciplining and education, to forego what seem to be compelling moral claims in the present in order to prepare themselves for a higher level; this is a grave and complicated matter and none of this can be decided by anyone other than God, through His divinely revealed law. Thus, so long as human self-love stands ready with all its destructiveness, man must keep his distance from the animals, so that he not come to see himself as one of them;[152] that is until such time as he achieves his moral potential and the world may be sustained not by the concessions of mercy but even by the very line of the law (*middat ha-din*). Undisciplined moral passion may lead to awful results, as one could imagine a bloodthirsty, yet vegetarian despot.[153]

"And so the divine discretion, which alone can pave a road deep into men's hearts, saw fit to snap the cord tying man to animals, so that human moral focus could center on his particular good, and then, and only then, successfully bring him to his *eudaemonia* at the end of days."[154] And interestingly, the moral law to emerge at that time will be the work

---

148 He cites Bahya (*Sha'ar 'Avodat Ha-Shem* 5, no. 3 [5]) on human illumination by Torah and by reason.

149 *Otzarot*, 2:88.

150 He uses the word *hasidah*, a pun on Hasid and the word "stork," presumably alluding to the rabbinic comment that the stork is merciful to its own and merciless to others. See Lev. 11:19 and BT Hullin 63a.

151 *Otzarot*, 2:89–90.

152 Ibid., 90.

153 There is here an eerie premonition of Hitler; see Janet Flanner's profile of him in *The New Yorker*, February 29, 1936.

154 *Otzarot*, 2:90:

עי"כ ראתה ההסכמה האלוהית, שרק היא יכולה לסול מסילות בקרב כליות ולב, לנתק את פתיל החבור בין האדם לבע"ח, למען יתרכז מרכז המוסרי האנושי בטובתו המיוחדת ואז, רק אז, יצליח להביא לו את אשרו בקץ הימים.

of the free human mind, having been educated by Torah to its freedom, a *summum bonum* which he describes both in Maimonidean terms as the universal knowledge of God, and in Luzzatto's terms as the transfiguring sanctification of human life.

> And when humanity arrives at the goal of its *eudaemonia* and perfect freedom, when it attains the high summit of perfected and purified knowledge of God, the sanctity of life in all its dimensions, then will come the turn of the "arousal of the mind" which is an edifice built upon the foundation of the "arousal of Torah," which preceded humanity as a whole, and then man will recognize his relation to his fellows in creation, living creatures all, as it should be, in terms of the pure morality which no longer has any need for the concessions of necessity, for the conjoining of mercy and law in his own particular case, the concessions which Torah made only by way of dealing with the evil inclination [after BT Qiddushin 21b]. But rather then he will go in a path of absolute good. *And I will make a covenant with them on that day, with the beast of the field and the bird of the sky and the insect of the ground, and bow and sword and war I will banish from the earth* [Hos. 2:20].[155]

This remarkable passage synthesizes a number of themes: The idea found in rabbinic texts that speak of halakhic change in the *eschaton*;[156] Maimonides's view of halakhah as a system of moral and spiritual education, which, however, Maimonides did not attach to a moralizing reinterpretation of halakhah (the farthest he goes is the projected restoration of good lawmaking procedure in the Bet Din Ha-Gadol in Jerusalem); Luzzatto's visions of self-perfection as transformative sanctification; and Luzzatto's historiosophy pitched in a moral key, in tune with Gotthold Lessing's notion of Enlightenment as the progressive education of the human race.

There is, though, a real difference between the ideas presented here and Rav Kook's later post-1904 views: while in his later views present and eschatological time exist along a continuum, here there is still a divide to be crossed between the halakhah of the present day and the moralized law of the *eschaton*. Nor does he express here, as he does, we will see, in his diary of this time and even more in his later writings, any justification for

---

155 Ibid., 90–91:

ובבא האנושות למטרת אשרה וחופשה השלם, בבואה עד מרום פסגת ההשלמה של דעת אלהים צרופה, אל קדושת החיים המלאים בצביונם, אז יגיע תור "הערת השכל" שהוא בבנין נוסד על יסוד "הערת התורה" שקדמתה לכלל האנושיות, ויכיר אז האדם את יחשו אל חבריו ביצירה בעה"ח כולם, אך הוא ראוי להיות מצד המוסר הטהור שאינו נזקק עוד לוויתורים של דוחק, לצירוף של מדת הרחמים עם מדת הדין ביחס אליו הפרטי, לוויתורים שלא דברה בהם תורה אלא אלא כנגד יצה"ר. כי אם ללכת בארח טוב מוחלט, וכרתי להם ברית ביום ההוא עם חית השדה ועוף השמים ורמש האדמה וקשת וחרב ומלחמה אשבור מן הארץ.

156 A number of these texts are gathered by Abraham Joshua Heschel in the posthumous final volume of his *Torah min Ha-Shamayim be-Aspaqlariyah shel Ha-Dorot*, vol. 3 (Jerusalem: Beit Ha-Midrash Le-Rabbanim be-America, 1995), 54–81. (Reverberations of these ideas in later mystical and Hasidic sources are therein at 69–74.) Heschel, in keeping with his own liberalizing halakhic ideology, downplays the darkly apocalyptic strain of this rabbinic cluster of associations, and for instance does not mention the well-known passages along those lines from Mishnah Sotah 9:15 and BT Sanhedrin 97a which, we will see in the final chapter, figured prominently in Rav Kook's thinking on these matters at this time.

halakhic rebellion in the present as part of the Messianic drama. Indeed, in these essays, the *eschaton* is well in the future.

Pursuing this train of thought, of present-day halakhah as education for the transformed morality of the future, he offers moralizing readings of a number of mitzvot: Sabbath observance, the practice of covering the blood of slaughtered fowl and domestic animals with dirt; the prohibition of certain fats, mixing meat and milk in food and wool and linen in dress, and eating meat not slaughtered in halakhic fashion.[157] All are meant to elevate the human spirit, teach kindness and mercy in an as-yet-unredeemed world; the divinely driven nature of this process means that it can never be said to reach "a final summit" in the dimension of human time.[158]

This, he says, is the meaning of God's telling Moses that His name is *I will be what I will be* (Ex. 3:14), that is, the mission of Israel and of humanity is always developing, growing towards the future in which human culture develops; the reasons of the mitzvot serve to light the way towards the future.[159] Like Maimonides and Se'adyah, he says that there are no a-rational commandments; but whereas for those thinkers their seeming a-rationality arises from the—severe but not in principle insuperable—limitations of human intellect, and their meaning conceivably is discoverable in the present (*Guide*, 3:26), for Rav Kook, "there are laws whose reasons may not be revealed, because they point towards a great future, the details of whose characteristics are hidden from us."[160] They fill humankind with the knowledge of God in their tracing a more perfect morality, in which there will hold sway the prophecies of Isaiah; yet not before their time.[161] "In a soft, still voice Israel's wisdom says that 'the animals of the future will be at the level of speaking beings today via the transformative ascent of the universe.'"[162] Until then, man the carnivore will need the practice of animal sacrifices (in the rebuilt Temple) to internalize a feeling of gratitude and dependence on God. He continues, with distinctly Nietzschean overtones, that when man achieves morality not out of weakness of soul or mercies born of a quaking heart, but from a deep awareness of God's essential justice, his "enlightenment by reason" (using Bahya's phrase) will teach him the foolishness of meat eating for merely mundane purposes. Until then, one's qualms at meat eating serve not only as a reminder of the higher morality to come, but as a goad to overcome one's own weaknesses when it comes to showing gratitude to God.[163] All of life's pains and sorrows are meant to bring us to the state of *Teshuvah*, of repentance and ontological restoration, which, the Talmud says (BT

---

157 *Otzarot*, Vol. 2, 92–101.

158 Ibid., 94.

159 Ibid., 96.

160 Ibid., 97:

‎. . . נערכו בתורה מערכה של חוקים שאי אפשר שיהיה טעמן גלוי, מפני שהם פונים אל העתיד הגדול שפרטי צביוניו נעלמו מאתנו.

161 Ibid., 100.

162 Ibid. 101. Zuriel points out that he is quoting from Hayim Vital's *Sha'ar Ha-Mitzvot, Parshat va-Yetzei*.

163 Ibid., 102.

Pesahim 54a) preceded all of Creation.[164] Indeed, death itself will be vanquished in the *eschaton*.[165] Every single religious life is part of this broader religious life of humanity;[166] in sum, the mitzvot as we know them now, play matter to the form of humanity's later greater destiny. And so—as we finally cycle back to the question of burgeoning Jewish nationalism—only by keeping the Torah and mitzvot, in all their details, can one participate in Israel's historic mission for the liberation of all humanity.[167]

This, he says, is why political Zionism's eschewal of religion is doomed to failure; not for its forfeiting rabbinical political support, but, more cuttingly, because in eschewing religion Zionism alienates itself from the deepest wellsprings of Jewish identity in the past and Israel's historic mission in the future, an alienation for which no act of diplomacy, however skillful, will compensate.[168] Yet we ought not forsake the Zionist movement, for who knows if perhaps God, in His unfathomable wisdom, has ordained that redemption should proceed precisely by our own efforts; and so no opening towards redemption should be foregone.[169]

Withal, returning to notes he sounded in the first essay, Israel must not simply mimic non-Jewish nationalism. His illustration of this point perhaps points to some of his ambivalence about political Zionism's presenting itself as a junior partner in the colonial enterprise. A merely mimetic nationalism will, he writes, make Israel as ridiculous as a primitive tribe dressing itself up in the finery of their European masters; and by mere fineries he means language, history, poetry, arts, and literature, which are at best harmless, but nowhere near as substantial as the great and thoroughgoing structures of Torah and mitzvot.[170] And that is why the Jewish soul must be poured into the organic body of Jewish nationalism without delay; and no single Mizrahi party can do the job—the movement must be converted as a whole.[171]

Antisemitism, central as it was to Zionism, hardly figured in Rav Kook's thinking, now, or later. It does make a rare appearance here—to reinforce the centrality of his spiritual concerns: antisemitism is insufficient to win the goodwill of the nations, only Israel's universal moralizing mission can do that.[172] And, he writes in a statement that would shock many of his latter-day disciples, it is the higher universal moral calling of Israel's nationalism that makes the land worth striving for.[173] Zionism's restoration, not of some phantom ethnic feeling, but of true, that is, sacred feeling, and a concomitant

---

164 Ibid., 104.
165 Ibid., 104.
166 Ibid., 105.
167 Ibid., 106.
168 In a swipe at Herzl and Nordau, he says that "those who have come from elsewhere" are simply incapable of appreciating Israel's rich spiritual endowment.
169 *Otzarot*, vol. 2:111.
170 Ibid., 113.
171 Ibid., 116–117.
172 Ibid., 119.
173 Ibid., 120. Some, but not all, as we will see in our discussion of Yehuda Amital in this work's conclusion.

return to mitzvot, will be that calling's truest test.[174] Harking back to his unpublished essay of 1898, he writes that Zionism may create the conditions for halakhic rethinking via the agency of a renewed Sanhedrin, which would offer leniencies as regards outmoded halakhic practices and new stringencies as may be made necessary by the times. This in turn will lead to a great outpouring of goodwill towards the Jewish people.[175] He asks in closing: "When already will Zionism recognize itself, that it could be so beloved, so holy, when it recognizes that very thing which is in truth all the existence of its life, its light and soul, when the name of Heaven will always be on its lips, and *oh so desirous of His Torah and mitzvot* [after Ps. 112:1]."[176]

Alexandrov's Response: Rav Kook and Ahad Ha-Am

Rav Kook shared a prepublication copy of this essay with the independent-minded rabbi and intellectual Shmuel Alexandrov and the latter's response is instructive. In a letter a year earlier, Alexandrov had noted the similarities between Rav Kook's thinking and that of Ahad Ha-Am, with the difference being that "while Ahad Ha-Am's explorations flow from historical 'necessity' and the springs of heresy, those of (your) heart flow from a pure source, from the free, primal divine 'will.'"[177] He now reasserts an essential similarity between the two, and a key difference: "Ahad Ha-Am, too, finds the eternality of Judaism only in its high ethics . . . but the difference is that Ahad Ha-Am sees the beauty of ethics only in its general principles, while (you) see the beauty of Hebrew ethics also in its details and at times in the minor details." There is an even deeper essential dichotomy between the two. "[B]oth of you want to see in the Zionist movement an answer to the moral and spiritual question of the Hebrew nation standing now at the crossroads."[178] But while Ahad Ha-Am seeks an artificial content for terms that that have emptied themselves of substance, "[you] have already found that content close to hand in the reasons and details of the sacred Torah." He also expresses astonishment at Rav Kook's publishing the essay in the frankly reactionary and, as he sees it, less-than-moral *Ha-Peles* and notes, accurately, that Rav Kook is addressing himself to a rabbinic fraternity hardly interested in listening to "his gentle feelings and delicate longings."[179]

---

174 Ibid., 126.

175 Ibid., 128.

176 Ibid., 130:

אימתי כבר תכיר הציונות את עצמה, כי יכולה היא להיות כ"כ אהובה, כל כך קדושה, כשתכיר אותו הדבר, שהוא באמת כל מציאותה חייה אורה ונשמתה, כשיהיה שם שמים שגור על פיה, ובתורתו ומצוותיו חפץ מאד!

177 Alexandrov's letters to Rav Kook are printed in the former's *Mikhtavei Mehqar u-Viqoret*, vol. 1 (Vilna: Romm, 1907), 6. Sadly we do not have Rav Kook's side of his very fruitful correspondences with Alexandrov from this period. Hillel Alexandrov, the rabbi's son, was an historian and archivist in St. Petersburg, and associate professor at the university, and perhaps some of his father's papers can be found there.

178 Ibid., 12.

179 Ibid., 13.

Indeed, an examination of passages in Rav Kook's contemporaneous aggadah commentary, *'Eyn Ayah* to tractate Berakhot, illuminates some of the metaphysical underpinnings of his third essay in *Ha-Peles* and indicates just how well-advised he was to keep that scaffolding from the view of his rabbinic peers.

History, Ethics, and Eschatology in *'Eyn Ayah*

In the course of *'Eyn Ayah* we see the development of his attitudes toward historical development and historical time as a medium of divine disclosure. Later passages reveal the metaphysical underpinnings of his third essay, including traces of Luzzatto's historiosophy, as divine Providence works on multiple—and at times dialectical—levels to achieve the perfection and purification of the world.[180]

At the outset of *'Eyn Ayah* he says that chronologies (in that case the sequencing of chapters of Psalms) are essentially accidents "and we should not expect it to teach us anything of moral value that will address our faults."[181] In good Maimonidean terms, history is a procession of accidents, meaningful, if at all, as the story of reason's coming to actualization in perfected individuals, such as Abraham and Moses.[182] As with individuals, so too with nations. Thus in the early passages of *'Eyn Ayah* to Berakhot, and in keeping with the ideas Rav Kook expressed in his *Midbar Shur*, nations, through history, perfect themselves, as though they were individuals writ large.[183] He does at one point say, following Maharal, that exile has had positive effects for humanity—namely, had Israel not sinned, its light would not have spread and the perfection of humanity would have taken much longer; and this gives meaning to Israel's sufferings.[184]

In one very significant passage in *'Eyn Ayah* to Berakhot 6:40, he speaks of the secular settlers of the Land of Israel—in far more glowing terms than he does in *Ha-Peles*—and cites the well-known Talmudic passage on the "oaths" by which Israel renounces occupying the land by force, a passage which was and is a major focal point of Orthodox

---

180 It stands to reason that no small part of his keeping Luzzatto's Kabbalistic terminology out of the *Ha-Peles* essays was the exoteric thrust and deeply Mitnagdic orientation of the journal's readership; indeed, even those readers of *Ha-Peles* who may have engaged in Kabbalistic study, would presumably, in keeping with Lithuanian tradition, have been surprised and more to see Kabbalistic theology in a periodical aimed at a broad readership.

181 EAB 1:125, vol. 1, 49:

כי אין לנו לתלות במקרה כל דבר שממנו נוכל לשאוב תועלת מוסרית המשלימה את חסרונותינו.

182 Salo Baron, in his classic 1935 essay "The Historical Outlook of Maimonides," reprinted in his *History and Jewish Historians* (Philadelphia: Jewish Publication Society, 1964), 109–163, has written, at 160: "[T]he truth of an historical fact is for him [that is, Maimonides], as for every true scholastic, based chiefly upon reasoning rather than documentary evidence." See also Amos Funkenstein's essay "Tefisato Ha-Historit ve-ha-Meshihit shel ha-Rambam," in his *Tadmit ve-Toda'ah Historit be-Yahadut u-ve-Sevivatah ha-Tarbutit* (Tel Aviv: 'Am 'Oved, 1991), 103–156. See also my comments in the introduction to this volume.

183 See EAB 1:126, vol. 1, 50; 1:172, vol. 1, 68; 5:13, vol. 1, 130.

184 Ibid. 5:59, 145.

anti-Zionist polemics.[185] Two sorts of people, he writes, love the Land of Israel—those who love it for its inherent spiritual properties, which redound to the benefit of humanity as a whole, and those who love it for the concrete well-being it brings to the people. While the former is preferable, he says, the latter is not to be denigrated or dismissed, since the settlement of the Land grounds the collective, whose broader horizons in turn transform the narrowly material into the spiritual.[186] Continuing in this vein, he writes that concrete settlement of the land will provide the foundation for the proper acquisition of the land by the Torah:

> And we will walk in Your ways to merit the land by the path of Torah, with love and peace, *not to scale the walls and not to rebel against the nations* [BT Ketubot 111a], but rather to foster inner strength and power, even if it be material, for that will bring us the spiritual discipline, which is the goal *not by might and not by force but by My word, says the Lord* [Zech. 4:6].[187]

Later on in *'Eyn Ayah* to Berakhot, Rav Kook begins to depict history in terms of a world of contending forces, sweeping through individuals and nations, uniting material with spiritual causalities (the latter residing in the soulful wills of men).[188] (He increasingly has recourse to Kabbalistic terminology such as *'olamot*) He speaks less of nations needing to discipline themselves as though they were large individuals and more about their playing roles within a universe of contending metaphysical forces. And as the work

---

185 The locus classicus of the oaths is BT Ketubot 111a, where their number is given as three; elsewhere, at Song of Songs Rabbah 2:7, their number is given as four. For extended discussion of this motif through Jewish intellectual history and to the present, see Ravitzky, *Ha-Qetz Ha-Megulah*, 277–305.

186 EAB 6:40, vol. 2, 185–186. The Talmudic text at hand, 41b, discusses the order in which one recites blessings over those foods listed in Deut. 8:8, and the rabbinic difference of opinion as to whether the verse contains two distinct lists, or one. Rav Kook's comment is an elaboration of the former view, which he reads as suggesting two different ways of loving the Land of Israel:

ובאשר חבת הארץ מחולקת היא לפי מעלת האנשים והכרתם, כי יש מי שמחבב ארה"ק בשביל סגולותיה היקרות, וצמא מאד לרצות אבני' ולחונן עפרה כדי לקיים המצות התלויות בארץ ובשביל התכלית העליונה הנמצאת בה לכלל ישראל ולכלל העולם במעלתם הרוחנית. ויש מי שמחבב ארה"ק וישתדל בישובה ובדירתה בשביל שמכיר בה התכלית של המנוחה החומרית לכלל ישראל, שהוא ג"כ דבר טוב ונשגב, ובכ"ז לא בא עד המעלה הראשונה למי שמכיר יסוד התכלית העליונה שבחבת הארץ . . . ולמדנו מכאן כמה גדולה היא המעלה של מי שמשתוקק לישב ארה"ק אפי' לשם התכלית החומרית של הכלל, כי אצל הכלל יהפך תמיד כל ענין גשמי לרוחני, והתכלית העליונה בא תבוא ע"י חבור עם ד' בארץ ד'.

187 Ibid.:

ונלך בדרכך איך לזכות לזה ע"פ דרכה של תורה, באהבה ושלו' שלא לעלות בחומה ולא למרוד באוה"ע, כ"א להרבות כח ועצמה פנימית, אפי' גשמית, כי זאת תביא לנו המשמעת הרוחנית, שהיא המטרה, לא בחיל ולא בכח כ"א ברוחי אמר ד'.

A highly edited version of this passage, deleting the citation from BT Ketubot, appeared in the anthology of Rav Kook's writings compiled and published in Rav Kook's lifetime by Yeshayahu Shapira (He-Admor He-Halutz, the brother of Kalonymous Shapira), *Eretz Hefetz*, vol. 1 (Jerusalem: Darom, 1930), 11, 23. Interestingly, Zvi Yehudah Kook reprinted this passage in full; see *'Olat Re'ayah*, 1:374–376.

188 EAB 9:56, vol. 2, 273.

further proceeds those forces complement each other dialectically, and find their resolution in God.[189]

Then, at 9:152, we read—in his allegorical reading of "the insubstantial clouds of morning" (BT Berakhot 59a)—that while divinely directed moral ideas work to infuse human intellect with divine light, in a given historical period new moral energies may proceed before their appointed time, and result in general moral collapse.[190] We see here a theme we have noticed before (especially in his invocations of the Mishnah Sotah 9:15) and will see at greater length in the coming chapter, of his creating an historical theodicy of modernity by recasting its moral crises in terms of the Lurianic myth of the primordial shattering of the vessels of the divine light. He says in the immediately following paragraph, and echoing his essays in *Ha-Peles*, at 9:153, that moral destiny (*te'udah*) is the most clearly seen thread of divine Providence running through the world, for the most exalted thing in existence is the good done by people.[191]

Thus, he writes later on, the righteous and the wicked both serve the general telos of the world and both are necessary—but woe to the wicked who has chosen to have the telos emerge from him via things that do ill to himself and others, and blessed be the *tzadiq* who chooses to serve the telos via the good. Indeed, he adds in yet another unmistakably Nietzschean note, and in a striking inversion of Habad terminology, that the fullness of creation requires men of great souls, while the middling (*beynonim*) who blow with the wind are not men of perfection.[192] And how does a great soul conduct himself? "One should feel the taste of great self-love in all its power, and with all the deep feeling of his self-love should dissolve his particular love into the need and telos of love of the whole, and then the light of truth will emerge in human righteousness to great effect for good action and the path of God."[193]

As I said, we see the beginnings here of his historical theodicy of modernity, or what I think of as his "ethnodicy," that is, the need to justify the acts of his fellow Jews who are as morally idealistic as they are halakhically rebellious. His first muted suggestion in 1889

---

189 See ibid. 9:130–138.

190 Ibid. 9:152, 317–318:

כן העניינים השכליים המיישבים את הלבבות, היינו הציורים המוסריים שהם גוררים מדות טובות והדרכות ישרות,
והם מתפשטים על דרכי החיים להרחיב ההדרכות התוריות . . . אמנם לעת תחל תקופה חדשה בעם, וכוחות חדשים
יבואו לכל מקום, שהמה הולכים ע״פ השגחת השם יתברך . . . מ״מ בהתחלה, קודם בוא האורה והכוחות צריכות
להתחזק, אז מתמוטטות הצעות רבות ונפילה מוסרית מוכנת. ע״כ בעקבא דמשיחא, שאז יתעוררו כחות רבים
בישראל להיות מוכנים להתנער ולאור באור החיים, באור ד׳ . . . חוצפא יסגא, והם חבלי משיח. . . .

191 Ibid. 9:153, 318:

ההשקפה היותר ברורה על תעודת המציאות בכללה היא התעודה המוסרית, כי מציאות נפשות יקרות פועלות
צדקות ועז היא המציאות היותר מפוארה ונשגבה בעולם.

192 Ibid. 9:224, 341–342.

193 Ibid. 9:225, 342:

אמנם ראוי הוא שיהי׳ האדם חש טעם אהבת עצמו בכל תקפו, ועם כל עומק הרגשתו באהבת עצמו יהי׳ מבטל
אהבתו הפרטית לצורך ותכלית אהבת הכלל, אז יצא האור האמיתי בצדקת האדם שממנה תוצאות גדולות למעשה
הטוב ודרך ד׳.

that the travails of modernity might have Messianic import has matured into a historiosophy of morally driven rebellion against Torah as part of the Messianic drama.

Assessing the Essays: Ideology and Utopia

As we have seen, political and economic issues simply do not figure in these writings. Rav Kook sees the problem of Zionism in terms of cultural identity, which in turn is inextricably tied to morality and spirituality. Unlike other early religious Zionist thinkers, such as Eliasberg or Reines, making Jews economically productive was not of interest to Rav Kook; though he did share Reines's concern with making Talmud study more relevant and broadening yeshiva curricula, and certainly came to care more about this after 1904.[194] Nor was he particularly concerned with antisemitism. Rav Kook's real interlocutors here are the cultural Zionists who developed the pan-national idea that nationalism was the defining feature of Jewish identity throughout history.[195]

Shmuel Almog, in his study of the idea of history in early Zionism, points out that in debates of the time Zionism was viewed as either Messianic for good or ill, or luckily non-Messianic, though nobody argued that its being non-Messianic would be a bad thing.[196] Here, Rav Kook is something of an exception. While the tone of the *Ha-Peles* essays is still well removed from the full Messianic cry of his later writings, there is an unmistakable sense that without a sense of a larger destiny anchored in the moral apotheosis of humanity Zionism will lose its way and dangerously fracture Jewry in the process.

In terms of some of the larger themes we have been tracing, in these essays on nationalism there is a progress analogous to that which we have already seen in his explorations of the religious and moral life. Starting with medieval concepts of self-cultivation and perfection, applied in *Midbar Shur* to Israel's stance towards other nations, he links them in the *Ha-Peles* essays to modern ideas of universal development through nationalism (with Hess playing a crucial role) with emotion as a driving force, proceeding in delicate tandem with the intellect. In the third *Ha-Peles* essay he uses the radiant ethics of the future and the moral passion it engenders to critique current halakhah and push towards the future. In the passages from *'Eyn Ayah* we see that this is linked to Kabbalistic ideas of a moral energy, nearly at times uncontrollable, which drives good and wicked alike to the greater good.

---

194 For Reines the answer was refashioning Talmudic study as the deduction of formal logical rules, while for Rav Kook, at this stage of his thinking, the answer was to inject it with moral and spiritual meaning via aggadic study. (I will have more to say on this in the conclusion.) One might add that for Hayim Soloveitchik it was to refashion it as a dialectic of abstract legal concepts, while for Netziv it was to broaden the rabbinic bookshelf beyond the Babylonian Talmud. Reines also introduced secular studies in his yeshiva in Lida.

195 Almog, *Tzionut ve-Historiyah*, 122–124.

196 Ibid., 45.

The title of this chapter alludes to Karl Mannheim's classic study *Ideology and Utopia*.[197] In Mannheim's formulation, ideology denotes the ideals of the class currently representing the status quo, ideals which are never fully realizable in the present, while utopia posits goals which transcend, and are simply unrealizable within, the current social order. Mannheim writes that the two are dialectically related: "Every age allows to arise (in differently located social groups) [parentheses in original—Y. M.] those ideas and values in which are contained in condensed form the unrealized and unfulfilled tendencies which represent the needs of each age. These intellectual elements then become the explosive material for bursting the limits of the existing order."[198]

In his early writings on nationalism, above all in the first *Ha-Peles* essay, Rav Kook tries to assimilate Zionism to the existing rabbinic order, urging Zionists to channel, and indeed constrain their impulses (the nobly humanitarian thrust of which he is willing to concede) through the workings of an unmodified halakhah. By the third essay, his position has shifted and he sees Zionism's deepest promise in its drive to actualize moral ideals that are by definition unrealizable in the present. In so doing he allows the future to stand in judgment over the halakhic ideology of the present and is willing to join the march to utopia.

This march took him to the Land of Israel, as we will see in the forthcoming chapter. Indeed, the absence of the Land of Israel in these early writings of his is frankly astonishing in light of his later teachings and reveals the deepest wellsprings of his thought. It is to his transit to the land, and his increasing reflection on the ostensible heretics in whose company he would be making that journey, that we now turn.

---

197 Karl Mannheim, *Ideology and Utopia: An Introduction to the Sociology of Knowledge*, trans. Louis Wirth and Edward Shils [1936] (San Diego and New York: Harcourt, 1985), see esp. 193–204.

198 Ibid., 199.

6

"The New Guide of the Perplexed" and "The Last in Boisk": Making Sense of Heresy en Route to Zion

Rav Kook's decision to emigrate to Palestine was by no means inevitable. His thinking on Jewish nationalism in general, and Zionism in particular, prior to his arrival in Jaffa and in many ways long thereafter, was part of a larger project to make sense of ethical and intellectual critiques of rabbinic authority through philosophic and mystical study, and attention to the multiple currents coursing through his own inner life. Unlike almost all his rabbinic peers, he saw opportunities for the revitalization of tradition precisely from within the storms of modernity, guided by subtle divine Will.

As he began his move to Palestine, he made a great effort to start thinking through the generational cohort he would find there, many of whose driving concerns and passions spoke to him. This becomes clear when looking at two texts published out of manuscript in recent years, one originally meant by him for public consumption—"The New Guide of the Perplexed," (in particular of those perplexed by modern intellectual trends such as ethical universalism, comparative religion, and the theory of evolution) and one written for himself, a diary on whose cover we find the legend, in Zvi Yehudah Kook's hand, "The Last in Boisk."[1]

---

1 The cover legend is *aharon be-Boisk*, and hereinafter it will be referred to as PAB, that is, *Pinqas Aharon be-Boisk*. It was published from manuscript by Boaz Ofan, along with four other hitherto unpublished diaries, in *Qevatzim mi-Ketav Yad Qodsho*. A photocopy of the manuscript is available in the Rivka Schatz collection within the Gershom Scholem collection at the Jewish National and University Library in Jerusalem (for some reason, this goes unmentioned). I myself had planned to publish this manuscript and can vouch for the reliability of Ofan's edition. My sincere thanks to Boaz Ofan for having shared his prepublication proofs with me. It was listed by Zvi Yehudah Kook as "Notebook 14" (*Pinqas* 14). That numbering is not dispositive for dating as the one chronologically following it was designated by him "Notebook 13" (*Pinqas* 13).

Both texts are preoccupied with the emergence of mass rebellion and heresy, especially among idealistic youth—and his response is a theodicy of modernity, discerning in these alarming, unsettling rejections of traditional practice and authority, the hand of Providence. Crucially, Rav Kook's Messianism, so historically consequential, was not sparked in the first instance by Zionism; it emerged as he tried to explain the catastrophic collapse of Jewish society and the rise of principled heretics who were committed both to Jewish nationalism and universal ethics. Eschatology became a framework through which he could contain the incommensurables of contemporary Jewish life, and of world history. That—and not Zionism as such—was the crucible out of which his Messianic reading of modernity emerged. He came to see this heresy as not only something to be coped with but as revealing its own religious truths—a truly revolutionary proposition. In the process he undertook a complex internal negotiation with the challenges of contemporary religious rebellion, and with their points of contact with Christian critiques of Judaism and the antinomian spirituality of Sabbatianism too. His move to Palestine was not solely responsible for the centrality of these issues to him—we have seen him throughout preoccupied with these moral and intellectual questions—but his impending migration certainly deepened his attention and raised the stakes.

1904, the year of Rav Kook's arrival, has long been taken in Zionist historiography as the beginning of the legendary "Second Aliyah," though that periodiation and lionization has far more to do with the younger thinkers and activists who came at that time than with him as such.[2]

Why were they coming? The years 1903 and 1904 saw the terrible Kishinev pogroms, and the further radicalization of Jewish youth.[3] Rabbinic responses in the Russian Empire to this radicalization, David Fishman has shown, ranged from reaffirming monarchism, emphasizing the religious value of obedience to civil authority, to pragmatic quietism. Unlike their counterparts in Austro-Hungary, where socialists were a legitimate parliamentary force, few if any traditionalist Russian rabbis of standing supported the right of Jewish radicals to express their views, let alone support their ideas. The Mizrahi took pains in their founding document to distance themselves from Jewish radicalism, the only Zionist faction to do so. Many rabbis saw Jewish radicalism and the calamities it was sure to bring in its wake as yet more bitter fruit of the Haskalah.[4]

---

2   On the Zionist historiographical scheme of various Aliyot and their role in defining who was and who was not considered part of the Zionist vanguard, see Hizky Shoham, "From 'Great History' to 'Small History': The Genesis of the Zionist Periodization," *Israel Studies* 18, no. 1 (2013): 31–55.

3   Steven J. Zipperstein's remarkable work *Pogrom: Kishinev and the Tilt of History* (New York: Liveright/Norton, 2018), draws together the multiple strands of 1903's Kishinev pogrom, not least its epochal influence on Bialik and his highly influential critique of Diaspora Judaism.

4   David E. Fishman, ""The Kingdom on Earth is like the Kingdom in Heaven": Orthodox Responses to the Rise of Jewish Radicalism in Russia," in *"Let the Old Make Way for the New": Studies in the Social and Cultural History of Eastern European Jewry, Presented to Immanuel Etkes*, vol. 2, ed. David Assaf and Ada Rapoport-Albert (Jerusalem: Merkaz Shazar, 2009), 227–259.

Rav Kook was planning a different response. He wrote a treatise whose starting point was taking the radicals seriously on their own terms, arguing that their commitments to social justice and universal ethics were not only compatible with Jewish teachings, but their fruition. As we will see, this public stance was rooted not only in his reading in and sharing the experiences of the times, but his reading of the Kabbalah.

To Jaffa and Palestine

In 1901, Eliyahu David Rabinowitz-Teomim (Aderet), Rav Kook's former father-in-law, to whom he remained especially close, was appointed as deputy and successor to Shmuel Salant (1816–1909), the venerable and ailing rabbi of the Ashkenazi community in Jerusalem. Salant sought, by importing a distinguished and comparatively moderate Lithuanian Talmudist, to shore up his community, battered by economic want and the absence of advanced yeshivot, and assert his authority over the Hasidim of Jerusalem. (Salant further tried to placate the local Hasidim by giving them a larger share of various charitable funds and communal emoluments.) Aderet has left us, in a letter to Rav Kook, a moving account of his travels; a glimpse of the piety and humility that his son-in-law, like so many, found so inspiring in him can be sensed by his genuine anguish over the honors bestowed upon him on arrival.[5] Aderet, never a political animal to begin with, and now having to deal with the fractious Jerusalem community, soon found himself tragically out of his depth; he never became a significant presence, suffered further from his lifelong ill health, and passed away in 1905; Shmuel Salant outlived him by four years.[6]

Meanwhile, in the spring of 1902, the rabbinic post in Jaffa opened up with the passing of Naftali Hertz Ha-Levi (Weidemann) (1853–1902). Jaffa was poised between the old and new, an ancient city with its own traditions, and the urban center of the burgeoning Jewish agricultural settlements that were the cutting edge of change in Jewish Palestine. Jaffa had for some years been wracked by conflicts between staunch traditionalists and comparative modernists, which came to a head in elections for the town council in 1900.[7] Ha-Levi was a Lithuanian pietist and Kabbalist of gentle disposition; intellectually, he was, Eliezer Baumgarten has shown, an independent and innovative thinker who took a characteristic Lithuanian stance of taking Luria's mythic imagery metaphorically—not only as revealing the truth of history, but of natural science, for which he was criticized

---

5   The letter is reproduced in *Igrot la-Re'ayah*, 37–41, no. 17.

6   See Menachem Friedman, *Hevrah be-Mashber Legitimatzyah: Ha-Yishuv Ha-Yashan Ha-Ashkenazi, 1900–1917* (Jerusalem: Mossad Bialik, 2001), 101–105 .

     The extent to which Aderet was unprepared for the situation in which he found himself becomes clear from the above-cited letter in which he relates that when Yitzhak Suvalski queried him as to why he had taken on such a difficult job he replied that "here there is hardly any quarrel or discord, God forbid, as people think in the diaspora." Ibid., 40.

7   See Hannah Ram, "Mahloqet bi-Qerev Hanhagat Ha-'Edah Ha-Yehudit be-Yafo," *Cathedra* 64 (1992): 103–126.

by Shlomo Elyashiv.[8] Politically, though, he had arrayed himself alongside his colleagues in the Jerusalem rabbinate as a foe of the modernizing trends represented by the Zionists; his followers immediately tried to put in his place a similarly conservative successor.[9] Rav Kook appealed to those seeking a more forward-looking alternative.[10] At the same time, his identification with, and sponsorship by, Aderet served to placate more traditional elements.

He was first brought to the attention of the community of Jaffa by Yoel Moshe Salomon (Solomon) (1838–1912), who had met, and been impressed by, the young Rav Kook on a visit to Boisk in 1896. Salomon was a Talmudist, printer, journalist, activist, developer, one of the founders of the new city of Jerusalem and of the first independent Jewish agricultural settlement Petah Tiqva.[11] His grandfather, Avraham Shlomo Zalman Zoref (1786–1851) had emigrated from Lithuania with the "Aliyah of the Students of the Gaon" in 1811. The precise nature of that group, the extent of their contribution to settlement efforts in Palestine and the extent of their Messianic consciousness is a subject of lively scholarly argument to this day.[12] Be that as it may, they did see themselves as latter-day inheritors of the Gaon's program, in their traditions, institution-building and their nascent, naturalistic Messianism, and it is thus not insignificant that a leading figure in that circle, and one of its most practical-minded activists, recognized in the young Rav Kook a kindred spirit.

---

8   See Eliezer Baumgarten, "Hadshanut ve-Shamranut be-Qabbalat Rabbi Naftali Hertz Ha-Levi," *Da'at*: 79–80 (2015): 205–219.

9   See Friedman, *Hevrah be-Mashber Legitimatzyah*, 84–85.

10   See Avneri, "Ha-Rav Avraham Yitzhak Ha-Cohen Kook, Rabbah shel Yafo (1904–1914)," 49–82, 51–54. The expectations that Rav Kook's supporters had of him are indicated by a letter to him by a local supporter in the mercantile community, Elazar Rokah, urging him to pass on his way to Palestine through Paris, so that he might meet the comparatively moderate and cosmopolitan Chief Rabbi Zadok Kahn, reproduced by Avneri at 55.

11   A full-length study of Salomon remains a desideratum. For a long while we were dependent on memoirs of his son and other descendants, above all Mordechai Salomon, *Sheloshah Dorot ba-Yishuv* (Jerusalem: Salomon Press, 1939), and the 1950 essay, "Le-Toldot R' Yoel Moshe Salomon," in Eliezer Rephael Malachi, *Mi-Neged Tir'eh*, ed. Elhanan Reiner and Haggai Ben-Shammai (Jerusalem: Yad Ben-Tzvi, 2001), 229–248. The scholarly literature on Salomon has progressed considerably with the publication of Shimon Shamir and Israel Bartal, eds., *Beit Solomon: Shloshah Dorot shel Mehadshei Ha-Yishuv* (Jerusalem: Merkaz Shazar, 2014). Salomon's essays from his short-lived newspaper *Yehudah ve-Yerushalayim* of the 1860s, were gathered in a volume of the same name, edited by Gedalyahu Kressel and published by Mossad Ha-Rav Kook in 1955; Salomon's halakhic correspondence with Aderet dating from 1902 is to be found in *Sefer Torah mi-Tzion*, ed. Simha Mandelbaum (Jerusalem: Lyna, 1995), 181–187.

12   See the exchange between Arie Morgenstern and Israel Bartal in the latter's *Galut ba-Aretz* (Jerusalem: Ha-Sifriyah Ha-Tzionit, 1995), 236–295, and most recently, Etkes, *Ha-Tzionut Ha-Meshihit shel Ha-Ga'on mi-Vilna*.

Salomon took it upon himself to secure the position in Jaffa for Rav Kook, and not long after Ha-Levi's death approached Aderet as a first step.[13] This was a magnanimous gesture, in that one of Aderet's first actions on taking up his Jerusalem post had been to fire Salomon, his erstwhile patron, from the board of Jerusalem's leading Jewish hospital, Biqur Holim, on which Salomon served as representative of the Lithuanians, a move which earned Aderet the ire of Lithuanians, Hasidim, and modernizers alike, as well as of his own patron Salant.[14] (Salomon was soon reappointed to the Board as the representative of the Hasidim.) Salomon offered Aderet not only to support his former son-in-law's candidacy but to underwrite the shortfall between the Jaffa community's salary and Rav Kook's remaining debts; Aderet wrote to Rav Kook that day, urging him to take the position.

Salomon went to work at putting together a coalition that would further Rav Kook's candidacy.[15] He enlisted the aid of Shimon Rokah (1863–1922), a leading Jaffa businessman and public figure,[16] of Bezalel Lapin (1856–1939), a young communal leader in Jaffa and the son of a colleague in his Jerusalem development efforts,[17] and of Pinhas Lintop (whose friendship with Rav Kook, it will be recalled, dated to the latter's tefillin pilgrimage of the early 1890s), who had since migrated to Palestine and enjoyed close ties with Jaffa's community of Habad Hasidim; this was a deft bit of maneuvering as Rokah was also a fierce Mitnaged, who had underwritten the publication of a prayer book according to the rite of the Gaon, with commentary by Jaffa's late Rabbi Hertz Ha-Levi.[18]

While the course of Rav Kook's later career makes his decision to move to Palestine seem inevitable in retrospect, it was not an obvious move. He had not been involved in Hibat Tzion, or, later, Mizrahi. The Land of Israel was not a significant theological category for him in his writings of those years (unlike Jewish peoplehood which, as we have seen, always loomed large). He was a Talmudist and thinker, uninvolved in public affairs

---

13 See Aderet's letter 12, reprinted in *Eder Ha-Yaqar*, 90–91. The letter is undated but reprinted between one dated 15 Iyar 5662/May 22, 1902 and another dated "the fourth day of Emor" 5662, which places it roughly in late Spring. A truncated version of the letter, omitting discussion of Rav Kook's financial troubles, appears in *Igrot*, 1:372.

   The position had first been unsuccessfully offered to Netziv's son Hayim Berlin, and to Mordechai Rosenblatt of Ashmina, though we do not know how Salomon stood on their candidacies. Berlin eventually succeeded Salant in Jerusalem, serving as rabbi from 1906 until his own death in 1912; while a capable and respected figure, he never attained the stature of his predecessor; see Friedman, *Hevrah be-Mashber Legitimatzyah*, 105–106.

14 Ibid., 104.

15 See Neriah, *Sihot*, 294–300.

16 On Rokah, see the essay "Elazar Rokah," by Hannah Ram in *Ha-'Aliyah Ha-Sheniyah*, 3 vols., ed. Israel Bartal, Zvi Zahor, and Yehoshua Kaniel (Jerusalem: Yad Ben-Tzvi, 1997), 2:331–335 (hereinafter *Ha-'Aliyah Ha-Sheniya*).

17 On Lapin, see *EJ* 10:1427.

18 *Seder Ha-Gra: Yakhil Shnei Halaqim, Heleq Ha-Nigleh ve-Heleq Ha-Nistar* (Jerusalem: Yitzhak Nahum Loewy, 1895–1898). The introduction of this prayer book into Jaffa's Ashkenazi synagogues, which followed the Lurianic rite, itself contributed to Jaffa's communal tensions.

beyond the confines of Boisk, who longed for the study hall; moving to Jaffa not only meant taking on responsibilities of a greater order of magnitude but also putting himself in a setting where there were no yeshivot of any stature, certainly nothing comparable to what was available to him in the Lithuanian cultural region.[19]

He seems to have entertained thoughts of taking other posts—as mentioned earlier, he entertained the possibility of becoming mashgiah, or spiritual tutor, of the Telz yeshiva; in 1902 the community of Boisk raised his salary to ten rubles as week and generally did their best to keep him.[20] Meanwhile, in a letter from early 1903, Salomon discusses Rav Kook's negotiations with Jaffa, and says the latter is concerned both about whether his salary will cover the rent, and whether he will meet with resentment on the part of his predecessor's heirs.[21]

Zev Yavetz (Javitz), the historian and publicist who had emigrated to Palestine as a Hibat Tzion activist in 1888 and left in disappointment in 1894, urged Rav Kook not to take the job.[22] Jaffa, he wrote him, is "a metropolis of desolate sin. . . . I must warn him lest he render his soul over to the fierce conflict in which not even one as strong as he can prevail." Interestingly, Yavetz says he has in mind here not only the freethinkers, but the abuse that the late Rabbi Hertz Ha-Levi had suffered at the hands of the city's Hasidim to his dying day. If indeed Rav Kook seeks the religious satisfaction of living in the land of Israel, he would do well to opt for the more staid precincts of Petah Tiqva; but if he wants to promote a religious awakening, Yavetz continues, then he "one of the last, perhaps

---

19 In a letter to Y. M. Tyckoczynsky, dated 14 Av 5667/July 25, 1907, some three years after his arrival in Jaffa, he says that with Isaac Blazer's passing he wants to go to Jerusalem and head up the Vilna Zamosc kollel until then led by Blazer, "without the public burden of [halakhic] ruling . . . and without the yoke of matters of rabbinate and ruling." *Igrot*, 1:89, no. 84.

20 See *Igrot Ha-Aderet*, no. 8, 83. The people of Boisk seem to have interfered with Rav Kook's correspondence with Aderet as part of their efforts to frustrate his travel plans, see ibid., no. 14, 93, n. 4. For the Telz episode, see above, chapter three.

21 A transcription of the letter, made by Samuel K. Mirsky, is in my possession.
    Hertz Halevy's son Yoseph was himself an accomplished scholar, with particular expertise in the laws regarding tithes and other halakhic issues relating to the Land of Israel, see Aderet's reference to him in *Igrot Ha-Aderet*, no. 6, 81.

22 The letter, dated 11 Kislev 5664/November 30, 1903, appears as part of a group of his letters to Rav Kook from 1904 to 1924, reprinted in *Sinai* 29, nos. 7–8 (1951): 109–121; this particular letter appears at 109–110.
    Yavetz (1847–1924), brother-in-law of Y. M. Pines, was a mix of traditional scholar and historian, whose histories had a wide readership. See on him *EJ* 9:1303–1304, and Asaf Yedidya, *Le-Gadel Tarbut 'Ivriyah—Hayav u-Mishnato shel Zev Yavetz* (Jerusalem: Mossad Bialik, 2015). A biography and series of appreciations is to be found in a memorial volume published a decade after his passing—S. Ernst, ed., *Sefer Yavetz* (Tel Aviv: Ahiever, 1934) and in that volume, at 34–35, we find a brief encomium by Rav Kook from 1925, who holds up Yavetz as a model for combining religious piety with humanist scholarship. Rav Kook's last published writings in his lifetime were occasioned by the Maimonides octocentennial of 1935 and were sallies against Yavetz's bifurcation of Maimonides the halakhist and philosopher into two distinct personae.

the sole remnant who knows what Judaism needs," should stay in Eastern Europe. He invites Rav Kook to participate in the activities of the Mizrahi, underscoring that Rav Kook simply was not involved in Zionist activities in Eastern Europe. Indeed, one gets the sense from Yavetz's letter that Rav Kook's own motives in moving to Jaffa were themselves unclear, at least to outside observers, and indeed perhaps they were unclear to himself as well.[23] Aderet offered Rav Kook some guidance as to conditions in Jerusalem and rabbinical activities, but none as regards the politics of the place.[24]

With his decision to move, Rav Kook became a member of the large and influential cohort of migrants to Palestine which later became known as the Second Aliyah.

The Second Aliyah

The Second Aliyah (1904–1914) looms large in Zionist historiography, both because so many of its members became prominent political leaders (the most obvious examples being David Ben-Gurion and Berl Katznelson) and because of the intensity and pathos with which its literary figures (such as Yosef Hayim Brenner and Rachel Bluwstein) registered their impressions and experiences.[25] Of course, much of the mythic quality of the Second Aliyah was generated by its members themselves, who sought to distinguish themselves both from earlier, traditionalist settlers (like Yoel Moshe Salomon), from the settlement efforts sponsored by the Rothschilds and other philanthropists in previous decades, and the so-called "First Aliyah," and by the many migrants who didn't share their class or ideological positions.[26]

Contrary to popular conceptions, as Gur Alroey has shown, the majority of immigrants to Palestine were driven less by ideology than by the financial and other hardships of life in the Pale.[27] Of the 20,000 or so migrants of the Second Aliyah, only a relatively

---

23 Yavetz also writes that he declines to publish in *Ha-Mizrah*, the journal he edited, an article by Rav Kook entitled "Le-Zarot u-le-Havar," saying that "it deals with the critique of a book by a man who is not great . . . though the article itself seems good to us, it befits some other good writer but from His Honor we request something distinguished which others do not fit: something on Zionism and Mizrahi-ism generally, on their use, destiny and future, and his judgment on them." I do not know what this article was about; I can speculate that it may have been about Lilienblum's "Orhot Ha-Talmud," published in 1868, in which the title phrase appears: s.v. *Adonai Ha-Rabanim*. As we will see, Rav Kook later read and was sometimes exercised by Lilienblum's work.

24 In a letter to Rav Kook dated 15 Iyar 5662/May 22, 1902, presumably in response to a question, Aderet writes obscurely "as for Zionism, here one knows no more than in the Diaspora." *Igrot Ha-Aderet*, no. 11, 90 :

בדבר הציוניות אין לדעת פה יותר מבחו"ל.

25 See the comprehensive three-volume series, *Ha-'Aliyah Ha-Sheniyah*.

26 For discussion of the complicated historiographical and ideological issues involved, see Israel Bartal, "'Yishuv Yashan' ve-'Yishuv Hadash'—Ha-Dimuy ve-Ha-Metzi'ut," in his *Galut ba-Aretz*, 74–89.

27 Gur Alroey, *Immigrantim: Ha-Hagirah Ha-Yehudit le-Eretz Yisrael bi-Rei'shit Ha-Me'ah Ha-'Esrim* (Jerusalem: Yad Ben-Tzvi, 2004).

small percentage were members of the ideological hard core who in later years were to assume commanding roles in the development of Jewish Palestine and give the Second Aliyah its mythic character in official history and public imagination. Yet as we will see, this group, or more accurately, the elements of Russian Jewish youth who cast off tradition in principled terms and sought some new, higher, dispensation, loomed large in Rav Kook's own reading of the times, and of himself.

The radicals of the Second Aliyah carried with them their ideological and identity struggles in Eastern Europe, which they articulated in formal stances ranging from Tolstyoan *narodniki* utopian self-realization, to Marxism, social democracy, and secular nationalism.[28] Unlike Herzlian Zionists, they were animated less by power, politics, and diplomacy than by grassroots activism and qustions of economic justice and class struggle.[29] They were countercultural and their stances towards the traditional Judaism in which they'd been raised ranged from ambivalence to deep hostility, drawing variously from the conceptual frames of Haskalah, the anticlericalism of the labor movement, and Russian radicalism.[30] Though overwhelmingly Yiddish-speaking, those who emigrated were committed to the creation of a new, Hebrew culture as a vital alternative to the desiccated Jewish identity of the Diaspora; though Berdyczewsky never migrated himself, he well captured the existential stance of many who did, as needing to choose to become "the last Jews or the first Hebrews." They were nationalists, and even their Socialism was informed by the categories of Jewish national identity, which they identified both with the needs of the Jewish working class and with prophetic ideals of social justice; indeed, the ways in which they rejected tradition reflected a deep, if deeply argumentative, engagement with that tradition.[31] As their chief latter-day interpreter has put it, the principal axes of this group as a whole were: revolution and Zionism, generational conflict, the search for new community hand in hand with thorough self-criticism, commitment to

---

28 A brief, incisive, and marvelously lucid portrait of the ideologically charged young workers of the Second Aliyah is to be found in chapter seven of Ben Halpern and Jehuda Reinharz, *Zionism and the Creation of a New Society* (Hanover: Brandeis University Press/University Press of New England, 2000).

29 Shmuel Ettinger, "Ha-Ideologiyah shel Ha-'Aliyah Ha-Sheniyah," in *Ha-'Aliyah Ha-Sheniyah*, 1:3–10.

30 See Shmuel Almog, "The Role of Religious Values in the Second Aliyah," in *Zionism and Religion*, ed. Shmuel Almog, Jehuda Reinharz, and Anita Shapira (Hanover: University Press of New England/Brandeis University Press, 1998), 237–250. A powerfully evocative description of the broader Russian Jewish radical culture of which they were a part is to be found in chapter three of Yuri Slezkine, *The Jewish Century* (Princeton: Princeton University Press, 2004), though as noted earlier, religion is entirely absent from this book.

31 See Luz, *Maqbilim Nifgashim*, chapter seven and in particular 252–268. On this cohort's self-conscious rejection of passivity and the cultivation of quasi-martial values see Israel Bartal, "Cossack ve-Bedouin: 'Olam Ha-Dimuyim Ha-Le'umi Ha-Hadash," in *Ha-'Aliyah Ha-Sheniyah*, 1:482–493.

labor (at least as a matter of ideology, even if hard to realize in practice), and men and women working together.[32]

Rav Kook was, at thirty-eight at the time of his move, somewhat older than most migrants, though not by much.[33] (By contrast, Aharon David Gordon, who also emigrated in 1904, was already forty-eight years old at the time.) These were of course not the only intellectually minded, religiously rebellious Jewish youth in Russia. [34] But they were the ones who mattered to him.[35] It was their principled critiques of Judaism—some of whose critiques he understood and more—that preoccupied him as he moved to cast his lot with theirs in Palestine. And he had been working on a response.

"The New Guide of the Perplexed"—*Li-Nevukhei Ha-Dor*—From Philosophy to History, and Polemic to Understanding

In the years immediately preceding his move, Rav Kook wrote a treatise, published only in recent years, in which he attempted to formulate a compelling rabbinic reply to the Jewish radicalism of the time, and in particular to the challenges to tradition posed by secular nationalism, Zionism, ethical universalism, modern science, and critical scholarship. When finally published and annotated from manuscript in 2014, Shahar Rahmani gave it the title *Li-Nevukhei Ha-Dor (*For the Perplexed of the Generation), echoing both Maimonides's monumental *Guide of the Perplexed* and the less canonical but highly influential work by Nahman Krochmal (1785–1840) *Moreh-Nevukhei Ha-Zman* (Guide of the Perplexed of the Age).[36] Rahmani's title is well-chosen: Rav Kook's own immediate disciples had referred to a work of his Eastern European years "The New Guide of the Perplexed," which Rahmani takes as his subtitle.[37] But though he takes some cues from

---

32 Muki Tzur, "Anshei Ha-'Aliyah Ha-Sheniyah, Tipusei Ha-'Olim ve-Deyuqonam Ha-Hevrati-Tarbuti," in ibid., 1:282–293.

33 See Alroey, *Immigrantim*, 119; the migrants of the Second Aliyah divided evenly across a range of age groups (unlike Jewish immigrants to the United States in the same period, almost none of whom were older than forty-five).

34 On the Jewish student culture in Russian universities of the time, see Nathans, *Beyond the Pale*, 234–256, as well as Slezkine, *The Jewish Century*.

35 A possible exception may have been the Boisk Jews who eventually participated in the 1905 Revolution, but that is at this stage of research no more than speculation.

36 Avraham Yitzhak Ha-Cohen Kook, *Li-Nevukhei Ha-Dor, Ha-Mekhuneh Moreh Nevukhim He-Hadash*, ed. Shahar Rahmani (Tel Aviv: Yediot Aharonot, 2014)—hereinafter LNH.

37 This latter is a detective story all of its own. In an unsigned biographical essay (which I would guess was written by Yehoshua Hutner) in the collection of Rav Kook's writings on Zionism entitled *Hazon Ha-Geulah* (Jerusalem: Ha-Agudah le-Hotza'at Sifrei Ha-Re'ayah Kook z"l, 1941), we read at 14:

בספר מיוחד, הנמצא עדיין בכת"י, שתלמידיו כנוהו בשם: מורה נבוכים חדש, נגש לברר בהרצאה מקיפה ומפורטה את מקום הדת והמדע בתפיסת העולם הישראלית, מתוך מגמה לאחד את הקצוות ולאחות את הקרעים.

It is listed among forthcoming publications of Rav Kook's works in the 1937 *Prospeqt le-Hotza'at Kitvei*, 11. Of all the works listed, this is the only one not published in one form or another, and, unlike the others, it was not discussed at all in the text of the prospectus

Maimonides, particularly in his openness to contemporary secular philosophy, seemingly heretical doctrines, universal ethical ideas, and Krochmal, in looking to the Jewish nation as the bearer, through history, of those ideals, Rav Kook stakes out his own independent path.

Rahmani concludes, after careful investigation, that Rav Kook began to write the work not before the latter part of 1902, and completed it sometime before his move to Palestine in May of 1904, and elements of it appear in his 1906 *Eder Ha-Yaqar*. It was, in other words, largely written after the articles in *Ha-Peles* and while actively contemplating a move to Palestine.[38]

The burden of the work is to demonstrate the compatibility of Torah—rightly understood—with contemporary intellectual and moral challenges, and in particular: the theory of evolution, Biblical criticism, universalist ethics, and comparative religion. As in *'Eyn Ayah*, the medieval philosophical tradition provides the internal scaffolding for a distinctively modern exploration—in this case of the idea of historical development—drawing on the Kabbalah.

Of these four themes, one of them, his interest in understanding the relationship between Jewish and gentile morality, we have seen before, especially in *Metziot Qatan* and *Midbar Shur*. In comparing those earlier works, composed nearly a decade earlier or more, to *Li-Nevukhei Ha-Dor*, several salient differences emerge. The earlier works focused on the development of the individual, did not relate non-Jewish ethics and morals to the question of comparative religion in general, approached the question very much through the prism of the relationships of body and soul, and cast ethical teachings as timeless. *Li-Nevukhei Ha-Dor*, by contrast, takes as its subject the moral lives of nations, relates them to religion, does not deal much with the relations of body and soul, and frames ethics in an explicitly temporal framework of evolution over time. In that latter respect there are points of contact with his *Ha-Peles* essays, and his discussions of vegetarianism in particular. His taking up evolution, Bible criticism and comparative religion, though, are new.

The first chapter of the work sets out key themes—human dignity, mind, intellect, development, science, freedom and the religious life.

---

written by the group's chair Meir Berlin (Bar-Ilan). Neriah Gutel suggested reasonably that the projected work was to be based on the texts regarding *ta'amei ha-mitzvot*, which have been reprinted in *Otzarot*, 2:499–520; see Gutel, "Protocol 'Ha-Agudah le-Hotza'at Kitvei Ha-Rav Kook,'" 340–353, 343n9. At the same time, the late Rabbi Yeshayahu Hadari told me, in a lengthy and generous conversation, that his master Zvi Yehudah Kook had told him that no such work ever existed (interview in Jerusalem, May 15, 2005). This seems to have been of a piece with his general minimization of his father's pre-Aliyah writings.

38 The work began to circulate online in May of 2010, and was also published in bowdlerized form in *Pinqasei Ha-Re'ayah*, vol. 2 (Jerusalem: Ha-Makhon 'al-shem Ha-Ratzya"h, 2010). Working from the versions then available, the late, much lamented, Eitam Henkin, surveyed the work, noted the passages that appeared in *Eder Ha-Yaqar* and elsewhere and offered valuable observations. See his "Li-Nevukhei Ha-Dor shel Ha-Re'ayah Kook," 171–188.

That man has been created in God's image is the foundation of the Torah. The central feature of that image is the absolute freedom we find in man, by which he has choice. And were it not for choice there would be no place for Torah, as Maimonides said in *Hilkhot Teshuvah*. If so, choice is the foundation of Torah in practice. And the knowledge that man is made in the divine image thus comes to teach that the perfection of utter freedom must be found in the true perfect being, Bless His Name—is the conceptual foundation of the entire Torah, on which all deeds depend.[39]

These opening lines well convey what is to follow: in substance, that human dignity is integral to Torah and, hermeneutically, as cardinal teachings of medieval philosophy (on choice and necessity), and subtly shift to a distinctively modern, yet Kabbalistic, register, of freedom.

As Maimonides and Se'adyah dealt with the intellectual challenges of their time, he says, so he will face the challenges of his.[40] Far more central, though, to today's challenges than the logical questions preoccupying the medievals, is something more abiding, namely longings for righteousness (*yosher*) and justice.

Those longings, he says, take different shapes over time—and another central contemporary challenge is making sense of change and development over time, not least as articulated in the contemporary theory of evolution; which is, philosophically, but the latest iteration of the challenge known to the medievals as the doctrine of the eternity of matter and its corollary, determinism.[41] But that challenge will dissolve

---

39 LNH, 27:

שהאדם נברא בצלם אלהים זה הוא יסוד התורה. עיקר הצלם הוא החופש הגמור שאנו מוצאים באדם, שעל כן הוא בעל בחירה. ולולא הבחירה לא היה מקום לתורה, כדברי הרמב״ם בה׳ תשובה. אם כן, הבחירה היא יסוד התורה במעשה. והידיעה שהאדם הוא עשוי בצלם אלהים, אם כן הרי (זה) [היא]באה ללמד ששלימות החופש הגמור מוכרחה להמצא בעצם השלם האמיתי יתברך שמו—היא היסוד העיוני של כל התורה כולה, שכל המעשים נסמכים עליו.

Rahmani notes in his preface, 22–23, that he has at times brought Rav Kook's grammatical usages into line with those of contemporary Hebrew, and that, in places where the manuscript seemed unclear or incomplete, provided parentheses, and his own suggestions in brackets.

40 LNH, 30.

41 Darwin and Spencer's ideas were very much in circulation among Eastern Europe's Jewish readers; see Yaacov Shavit and Jehuda Reinharz, *Darwin ve-Khama mi-Bnei Mino: Evolutziyah, Geza', Sevivah ve-Tarbut—Yehudim Qorim et Darwin, Spencer, Buckle ve-Renan* (Tel Aviv: Ha-Kibbutz Ha-Meuhad, 2009), as well as Stern, *Jewish Materialism*. A full-length exploration of Rav Kook's ideas on the theory of evolution and their relationship to the Kabbalah is presented in Dov Berger, "Mishnato Ha-Hitpathutit shel Ha-Re'ayah Kook ve-Torat Ha-Evolutziyah" (PhD diss., Bar Ilan University, 2015). Berger amasses a wealth of citations and helpfully explains how and why Rav Kook found the theory of evolution as he understood it to be congenial with various doctrines of the Kabbalah. His work, though, does not reckon with the development of Rav Kook's ideas over time, and his presentation is straightforwardly theological and celebratory.

A similar argument that medieval discussions of determinism are helpful resources for such early twenty-first-century challenges to ethics from issues like neuroethics and social

when we come to see that nature's laws—and the laws of moral development—are joined at the source.[42]

As for the theory of evolution itself, he says, we've long known, not least from Maimonides, that the opening chapters of Genesis are not meant to be understood literally.[43] Human creation evolves under God's direction—and it evolves whole. In other words, human moral evolution is, too, woven into the fabric of the universe, to the point of human beings one day achieving immortality.[44]

He is here clearly reading a teleology into the theory of evolution that Darwin's theory of natural selection most certainly did not intend. He does, though, seem to be echoing the ideas of Herbert Spencer, for whom evolution was progress by another, and more all-encompassing and biologically determined name.

Does the idea of development extend to Torah as well—especially inasmuch as the very idea of the Oral Torah seems to lend itself to that? No, because while matter develops at a sluggish pace, "the sweep of the mind is unfathomably swift, especially when it comes to the 'Master of the Prophets,' Moses."[45] Moreover, the central facet of revelation is its acceptance by the people—which though cumulative over time, is grounded in revelation itself.[46]

Turning to nationalism, he says, every nation has the right to exist and develop by the lights of its own character and fraternity, so long as they mutually recognize one another and learn from one another, as they all contribute to the betterment of the world.[47] Every nation has its own vocation, and Israel's is divine wisdom and ethics, beautiful deeds, and divine service.[48] There is indeed no other nation whose religion is so deeply tied to its nationalism—because other nations will come to the worship of God precisely through that which they will learn from Israel. It is through the process of reciprocal learning that nations will come to see one another as one large family with a division of moral and material labors, and come, eventually, to peace.[49]

But the nations do have religions, and they must be reckoned with. Some are compelling, others are mistaken. Moses's prophecy, free of the dross of imagination, provides the guidance people need to reach their destiny when religion ascends beyond every limited idea and faith.[50] That destiny, life's ultimate *tiqqun*, is the Resurrection of the Dead, when each and every one will be a prophet, and mitzvot as we know them may perhaps no

---

theories, is intelligently pursued in Alan Mittleman, *Human Nature and Jewish Thought* (Princeton: Princeton University Press, 2015), 111, 141–144.

42   LNH, 34–6.
43   Ibid., 38.
44   Ibid., 45.
45   Ibid., 46.
46   Ibid., 48–9.
47   Ibid., 50–51.
48   Ibid.
49   Ibid., 52
50   Ibid., 53.

longer apply.[51] Only monotheism can bring about the *eschaton*, hence the evil of idolatry; any religion, though, that can bring out respect for morality is worthy of respect in its own right and ought not to be defected from.[52]

He then turns, as he did in the essays in *Ha-Peles*, to *ta'amei ha-mitzvot*. The details of mitzvot, he says, serve two aims, one negative, or prophylactic, the other positive, and future-oriented: that the moral posture of God's presence (*Kavod Elohim*) take root in the world (and avert descending into gross corporeality), improving society and individual character over time.[53] The intellectual work of *ta'amei ha-mitzvot* today, then, is to explain their place in the moral progress of the Jews and humanity.[54] Extending his approach in *Ha-Peles* to vegetarianism as a step in the moral development of humanity to other mitzvot, he writes that Temple sacrifices, for instance, are meant to school us in gratitude, and remind us that there still need to be coercion and stern judgement (*middat ha-din*) in this world. (Of course, the Bet Din Ha-Gadol will eventually be able to rule all sacrifices to be from grains.) The seemingly a-rational prohibition on Sha'atnez is, for its part, meant to inculcate respect for the integrity of species and creatures.[55]

Paradoxical as it may sound—precisely because the moral teaching of Torah is future-oriented its details cannot change.[56] Departing from the approach of Samson Rafael Hirsch and of allegorists through the ages, he says mitzvot are not merely symbols, such that they could take most any form and be merely about obedience.[57] Their truth is in their details.

Here again, Rav Kook's discussion invites comparison with Hirsch's enterprise.[58] In some respects there are similarities—both explicate and justify the details of *mitzvot* and the sharp distinctions they draw between Jews and non-Jews, in ways that would nonetheless be intelligible to a modern intellectual (if not necessarily philosophical) sensibility. And for Hirsch, as for Rav Kook in this particular work, the mitzvot are meant as a system of moral and spiritual education, and less as a vehicle for intimacy between the human and the divine.

---

51 Ibid., 55.

52 Ibid., 58. That being said, he adds, Jews can accept converts, who presumably are genuinely pained by the alienation of humanity into different peoples, and seek to join the one people dedicated entirely to the repair of all humanity, namely Israel.

53 Ibid., 60.

54 Ibid., 63.

55 Ibid., 71–72. Much has been written on Rav Kook's attitudes towards sacrifices in the Messianic Age. See David Sperber, "Qorbanot le-'Atid la-Vo' be-Mishnat Ha-Rav Kook," in *Re'ayot Re'ayah: Masot u-Mehqarim be-Torato shel Ha-Rav Kook*, ed. Shmuel Sperber (Jerusalem: Beit Ha-Rav, 1992), 97–112.

56 LNH, 80.

57 Ibid., 82. Seeman, "Evolutionary Ethics," 36 draws attention to Rav Kook's implicit polemic here with Abraham Geiger.

58 My comments on Hirsch draw heavily on the very helpful discussion in Eisen, *Rethinking Modern Judaism*, 135–155.

Yet there are differences, and they become clearer here—in Rav Kook's affirmation of nationalism, of historical development, and above all, of critiques of traditional Judaism as being ethically incomplete in the present, a farther move than Hirsch would ever make; though, to be sure, at this point at least, he maintains that the Judaism that contemporaries are criticizing, and its place in world history, are imperfectly understood and lived, not only by its critics but also by its adherents.

Torah and Other Religions

Earlier, in *Midbar Shur* and elsewhere, Rav Kook had discussed Jewish and gentile morality in broad terms, though not in terms of non-Jewish religious traditions. He does, though, present Torah as in a dynamic relationship with other faith traditions here; one needn't, he says, dismiss other faiths in order to maintain complete faith in Torah, which is, he says, separate and distinct, and, in the terms of secular scholars of religion and (perhaps echoing accounts he may have read of the World Parliament of Religions of 1893) "the mistress of religions."[59]

There is a hierarchy among world religions. At the bottom is idolatry, which doesn't acknowledge a lone Creator; a notch above that are those religions that do, but have yet to rid themselves of idolatry—presumably Christianity; above them, those that are rid of idolatry, but without Torah—presumably Islam. Towards idolatry one must be intolerant, save for those that have "a spark of morality." He seems here to be taking a leaf from the position of Menachem Ha-Meiri, for whom nations that provide the basis for civilized society are not necessarily to be thought of idolaters for purposes of halakhah.[60]

Judaism, of course, mandates separation between Jews and adherents of other religions—but this is to be regarded, he says,

> as akin to the distancing one puts between oneself and another's wife, not out of jealousy or resentment, God forbid, but from purity of soul and sanctity of virtues and deeds. . . . With our distancing from another woman, we love her as a person, and work for her good. So too the paths of morality, and the ways that virtues rooted in fear of Heaven, are acquired, are

---

59 LNH, 99.

והנה אנו צריכים לחלק את כללות האמונות הנמצאות בעולם לשלשה חלקים, חוץ מתורת ישראל, שגם לפי דברי
חוקרי הדתות החפשיים היא גברת הדתות.

At the 1893 World Parliament of Religions, Rabbi Henry Berkowitz of Philadelphia gave an address entitled "The Voice of the Mother of Religions on the Social Question," reprinted in *Judaism at the World's Parliament of Religions* (Cincinnati: Robert Clarke and Union of American Hebrew Congregations, 1894), 367–372. I have at this point been unable to ascertain if that phrase appeared in Hebrew and Yiddish reports of the Parliament, though that is my surmise.

60 Meiri's position has been much discussed in the last decades; for a relatively recent, and very interesting presentation, see Yaakov Elman, "Meiri and the Non-Jew: A Comparative Investigation," in *New Perspectives on Jewish-Christian Relations*, ed. Elisheva Carlebach and Jacob J. Schachter (Leiden: E. J. Brill, 2011), 266–296.

distributed to every nation by the workings of its fortunes, by its race, land, and whatever befalls it, be it in matter or the spirit, and that which impresses the majesty of God's light and the honor of Heaven in this one nation, doesn't do so for another.[61]

This commonality is possible because there is no qualitative difference between morals as understood by human accord (in the language of medieval Hebrew philosophy, *mefur-samim*) "which one naturally feels in the soul," and the laws of Torah—rather Torah, being divine, offers teachings and laws of farther depth and reach over time than humans' limitation could attain.[62]

> The instruction of Torah serves three purposes, in ascending order: maintaining national character in its moral dimension, doing good for the benefit of humanity, and a relationship to All That Is, that all will come to delight in heavenly grace.[63]
>
> Indeed, man with all his powers is one of the disclosures of God's powers, for via all that encompasses him, from moral dispositions [*de'ot*], virtues, thoughts and deeds, antinomies and contradictions, inclinations good and bad, times when one overpowers the other, from all of them proceed the justice supreme, good to all.[64]

The Dialectics of Change

One senses here a shift towards the dialectic, the understanding of change as happening by entities' own complex composition's giving rise to their opposites, which, in the

---

61 LNH, 104:

את השמירה וההרחקה שראוי לכל אדם מישראל ביחוד להיות מרחיק עצמו מכל קירוב של נימוסי דתות אחרות במנהגים ומוסרים דתיים, ראוי לשקול תמיד כערך ההרחקה של הצניעות מאשת רעהו, שאינה באה מתוך קנאה וצרות עין חלילה, כי אם מתוך טהרת הנפש וקדושת המדות והמעשים . . . ועם התרחקותינו מאשה זרה, הננו אוהבים אותה בתור אדם, ומשתדלים בטובתה. כן ארחות המוסר, והדרכים שהמדות הטובות ששרשם היא יראת שמים, נקנים בהם, הם מחולקים בכל אומה על פי מקריה, על פי גזעה, ארצה, והעוברות עליה בין בעניניה החומריים הין בעניניה הרוחניים, ומה שמרשם הוד אור ד' וכבוד שמים באומה זו, אינו פועל על אחרת.

62 Ibid., 108:

וכשנשתכל (!) יפה, נמצא שאין שום הפרש כלל, בין חיובי המוסר המוסכמים שהאדם מרגיש בטבע נפשו, לחיובי התורה היותר חוקים, אלא בין הכמות, דהיינו [ב]יסוד החיוב הוא הצדק והיושר. אמנם, האדם לא יוכל להרגיש חובת יושר כי אם על החוג הצר שלו, אבל צפיה האלהית היא מקפת את היושר הכללי, בכל הדורות ובכל הזמנים, ועל פיו נבנו כל חיובי התורה שהם לפי ההשקפה—חוקים. וקרוב הדבר שאפילו במצות היושר הפשוט, נמצא גם כן עמקי השקפות שמתאימות להיושר העמוק, שאין לו דרך כי אם על ידי הצפיה האלהית הכוללת, ובשביל כך נמצאים פרטים חוקים גם כן בתוך כללי המשפטים.

Though he uses the term *muskamim*, with Maimonidean connotations of convention, he seems more to be following Se'adyah's moral sense theory, as explicated by Alexander Altmann, "Saadya's Conception of the Law," *Bulletin of the John Rylands Library* 28 (1944): 320–339.

63 LNH, 110.

64 Ibid.:

אמנם האדם הוא עם כל כחותיו אחד מגילויי הכוחות האלהיים, שעל פי כל הדברים הסובבים אותו, מדעות, מדות, מחשבות ומעשים, ניגודים סתירות, יצרים טובים ורעים, עתות ההגברה לצד אחד ולמשנהו, מכולם יצא המשפט העליוני, הטוב לכל.

fullness of time, emerge as the entity's richer fulfillment. The human wellspring driving that dialectic starts to emerge more clearly as the work proceeds.

The concern, keening within us, to help all of humanity "is the divine spark in the human soul." One must develop this and as ideas rush in, one must bring them to light, "pour them on to the page so that they will at any rate be of benefit to others, to rouse them too to goodwill. And with time, ability will join goodwill, *and to he who comes to be purified, they will come to aid him* (BT Shabbat 104a)."[65] The personal note here is inescapable—and in this one paragraph we see the more personal tone of his journal, and his signature closing a reflection with a citation to a classic text.

The dialectical vein continues—as he is starting to see this process unfold in his own time. The worst thing, he says, is everyone thinking that their own set of ideas—moral, practical, scientific, political, personal—rooted in the limits of one's own perspective, encompasses the truth. Even when contending with other views, we should try to build up and not destroy, and try to see our own opposition as rooted in our own limitations—as hopefully our opponents will too.[66] Indeed, we shouldn't wish for any worthwhile thing to be banished from the world, but rather to be expanded and improved.[67]

This idea of equilibrium applies well beyond the world of polemics and pertains to the very meaning of a well-balanced life, of both the general and the particular, which takes five forces: healthy body and mind; human powers of spiritual enjoyment (beauty, poetry, healthy imagination, social graces—the *derekh eretz* that precedes the Torah); national feeling; religious feeling, which includes morality; opening of the mind, philosophy, science in its broader sense, and understanding. Health is the balance of them all.[68]

The echoes here of Aristotle's doctrine of the mean, via Maimonides's *Hilkhot De'ot*, are unmistakable, but there are telling differences too. Maimonides speaks of contending drives or dispositions within the individual, but not within and among nations, religions, and cultures. Moreover, Maimonides directs his therapeutic *via media* towards virtues and vices of disposition and behavior; he does not speak of religious, let alone national, feeling, nor is philosophy for him a facet of endeavor alongside others. Moreover, for Rav Kook, as we saw in *'Eyn Ayah*, these contending drives express forces larger than themselves, aiming towards a kind of equilibrium not only individual, but global (and perhaps, cosmic). And, once again, we see how a scaffolding of the medieval philosophical tradition is becoming the platform for a different set of explorations, themselves reflecting the more conflicted, and affectively bristling, world of the Kabbalah.

Indeed, he immediately launches into discussion of metaphysics, by way of contention with a thinker who also took early Maimonidean influences into a much different direction, Spinoza.[69] A truly free man, Rav Kook writes, will see two potential ways to

---

65 Ibid., 117.
66 Ibid., 124.
67 Ibid., 127.
68 Ibid., 132–133.
69 For a marvelous summary of Spinoza's image in modern Jewish culture, see Daniel B. Schwartz, *The First Modern Jew: Spinoza and the History of an Image* (Princeton: Princeton University Press, 2012).

solve the riddle of existence—"the dark path of *apiqorsut* [by which he seems to mean radical empiricism or mere nihilism—Y. M.], which truly offers no solution, but *envelops the eyes* [after Isa. 6:10] so as not to think deeply . . . [or] the path of light, recognizing the source of life, wisdom and kindness, of order and system, of will and ability in general," in other words, God. Yet this recognition itself can take two forms: "to recognize divinity as an exalted self, encompassing all in its power, renewing and inaugurating existence outside Him," or, "as Spinoza's doctrine, that there is no existence but divine existence, such that any particular existence is nothing but a revealed image per the particular perception of the perceiving soul . . . such that it seems that everything is but one particular, in and to itself."[70] To be sure, he says, there is truth here, inasmuch as any revelation is but a divine flash relative to the particular truth being revealed, be it of science or morals. But this is a partial view, to be complimented by "Lurianic Kabbalah, at its deepest," that individual perceptions are not new in themselves, but rather come from "a diminution of revealed divinity in general." In other words, *tzimtzum*—though, interestingly, he refrains from using that term.[71] Indeed, the Hasidic masters, he says, were able to turn these ideas into teachings for the masses. "But at any rate," he says, "the conclusions of the most rationalist philosophy, in truth concur with the substance of Torah, and simple faith."[72]

Yet Spinoza and his successors are not entirely off the hook here; as no religious heretic seems driven as he to deny the Jews' national identity. Biblical criticism is the "most virulent symptom" of that (and in Spinoza's case, though Rav Kook doesn't say so explicitly, the link between Biblical criticism and the disavowal of Jewish national identity in the present is explicit.)[73] Indeed, to deny one's nation is effectively to deny one's own parents.

To be sure, he says, healthy national feeling requires all parts of the nation acknowledging each other—just as Hasidim and Mitnagdim in their time were essentially arguing

---

70 LNH, 134:

כאשר יהיה אדם בן חורין באמת . . . וישים נגד עיניו שהנה יש שני דרכים לפניו בפתרון השאלה הגדולה, חידת עולמים של המציאות. האחת—היא דרך החושך של האפיקורסות, שבאמת אינה נותנת שום פתרון כי אם היא משעת את העינים שלא להתבונן, שלא לחזות בגיאות ד' . . . והשניה היא דרך האורה הכרת מקור החיים, החכמה והחסד, מקור הסדר והמשטר, החפץ והיכולת הכלליים . . . אמנם ההכרה הבהירה הזאת תוכל גם היא להתפצל לשני דרכים: או שיכיר את האלהות בתור עצם נשגב, הכולל הכל בכחו, ומחדש ומחולל את המציאות מחוצה לו, או שיכיר כשיטה השפינוצית, שאין שם שום מציאות אחרת כי אם מציאות האלהות, שהמציאות הפרטית איננה כי אם התגלות חזיונית שלפי ההכרה הפרטית של הנפש המכרת, שהיא גם כן איננה דבר אחר כי אם התגלות פרטית של ההתנוצצות האלהית, נדמה לה כי כל דבר ועניו לפרט מיוחד ודבר מצוי לעצמו.

71 In an as-yet-unpublished paper "Spinoza and the Kabbalah: From the *Gate of Heaven* to the 'Field of Holy Apples,'" forthcoming in *Early Modern Philosophy and the Kabbalah*, ed. Cristina Ciucu, Yitzhak Melamed shows that Spinoza, in his *Short Treatise on God, Man and his Well-Being*, takes pains to make clear that he thinks *tzimtzum* is an impossibility, as substance, by definition cannot limit itself. My thanks to him for sharing this with me.

72 LNH, 135:

לפי הביאור המשלים של שיטה זאת, יש עמה מקום לתור למצות ואמונה תמימה, והיא מסעיית בדברי קבלה, וקבלת האריז"ל העמוקה יותר, שהחזיונות הפרטיים אינם חדשים בעצם, כי אם באים ממיעוט התגלות האלהות הכללית . . . הלימודים הללו שהם המסקנות של הפילוסופיא היותר רציונלית, הם באמת מסכימים לתוכן התורה ואמונה תמימה.

73 LNH, 137.

over two equally necessary and legitimate ends, study and feeling, and were able to bury the hatchet with humility, so too should we in the present.[74] Tolerance, wrongly understood, is to have little belief in anything; correctly understood, it is recognizing both the good and bad sides of those engaged in that which "adds *tiqqun* and builds the nation."[75] On walking into a hospital, you see people doing things in seeming defiance of natural, bodily well-being; the discerning physician knows that that is just what long-term health requires. "Only he who understands the two impressions in the soul can make peace between them." Humanity is ailing, and the Jews too, and a reconciliation of body and mind is required, along with those with the discernment to effect it.[76] Further shifting from polemics to understanding, he says: "And so, rather than denying natural longings, we should sift them."[77] This sifting looks towards the future—and as he did in his discussions of *ta'amei ha-mitzvot*, a future orientation enables him to find a place for contemporary criticism of the law, absorbing contemporary criticisms, while shifting them up and forward to an eschatological horizon.[78]

The final end of humanity is love; the laws of morals derive from that ultimate end, and more than our presently degraded condition can allow us to know - that discrepancy between that end and our present drives the descent of many into wildness and destruction. [79] And he means Nietzsche.[80] There are those, he says, who characterize saintliness as "slave morality." And "[w]e well recognize from whence this illness and mad genius flow. They issue from the high souls of the world of *Tohu* (primordial chaos—Gen. 1:2), who surge forth to receive a light greater than their vessels, and fall to the depths of evil and the *qelippot*. This is the solution that the wisdom of Israel gives us to the strange sight of the *ascending to establish visions and floundering* (Deut. 11:14) in humanity at large."[81]

Rav Kook's employing this striking image of "souls of the world of primordial chaos" to describe a point in social criticism where madness meets genius, something he will

---

74 Ibid., 140.

75 Ibid., 141.

76 Ibid., 145:

שרק הוא יוכל לעשות שלום ביניהם, הוא מי שמרגיש את עומקן של שתי הרשימות הנפשיות. . .

77 Ibid., 146:

על כן, אין ראוי להכחיש את השאיפות הטבעיות, כי אם לברר מהן הפסולת.

78 In "Evolutionary Ethics," his essay on *ta'amei ha-mitzvot*, Seeman suggests I have overstated the difference between Rav Kook's concern here and his increasingly Kabbalistic turn after 1904; see p. 15. I don't mean to suggest that after 1904 Rav Kook leaves medieval philosophy behind, rather that the Kabbalistic framing he builds on it predominates, and makes possible a historiosophical orientation that the medieval project would not provide.

79 LNH, 149–150.

80 I will have much more to say on Nietzsche's place in Rav Kook's writings of this period later on in this chapter.

81 Ibid., 152:

אנו מכירים היטב את החלי (!) והשגעון הגאוני הזה מאין הוא נובע. הם תוצאות נשמות גבוהות של עולם התוהו, המתפרצות לקבל אור מרובה על מדת הכלים שלהן, הן נופלות לעמקי הרע והקליפות. זהו הפתרון שתתן לנו חכמת ישראל על המחזה המוזר של המתנשאים להעמיד חזון ונכשלים בכלל האנושות.

increasingly do in later years, is, as Elhanan Shilo has brilliantly shown, a remarkable synthesis of the different Kabbalistic schools to which Rav Kook was heir. The phrase itself originated with Naftali Bakhrakh's 1648 work *'Emeq Ha-Melekh*; in discussing the "shattering of the vessels" of Lurianic myth, Bakhrakh identified these souls with the impudent. Shneur Zalman of Liady went one step further, and said that these souls are more powerful than those of the righteous from the universe of *tiqqun*. And, from Lithuanian Kabbalah, Rav Kook takes the idea that precisely these souls will appear at the time of the Messianic advent.[82] We will have more to say on this later on.

To be sure, mercy, grace, justice, compassion—all the kinds of morality that Nietzsche derides—can only sweeten a little the bitterness of life, poverty, bereavement. True hope requires ascent beyond natural moral sentiments to a vision of divine unity, a divine light bringing illumination to all humanity.[83] Why, then, is Israel central to this drama? Because Israel's nationhood is an answer to a philosophical problem—finding a solid foundation for ethics and truth beyond the vagaries of human comprehension. Philosophy does not know how to combine God's unity with absolute justice without bringing in some third, bridging term, like moral sense, too thin a reed on which to establish both social order and real justice.[84] Hence the need for the Jews, a living people whose entire existence, of enslavement and wilderness, drives them to ethics.[85] And the power of truth that is in Israel is all the stronger when it knows "it is a legacy for all those created in the image of God, *for God made man righteous* (Eccles. 7:29)—and then when the (world) situation collapsed, they become a cause for building the world, its establishment, and destiny in the end."[86]

Turning to Biblical criticism—the spiritual lives of other nations have left their deposits in Israel's history and sciences like Assyriology are helpful to the faithful—and injurious to those of shallow understanding.[87] Torah reads in parts like ancient Near Eastern codes, yes, because it was revealed in that time and place; parallels to Biblical tales, like Gilgamesh, derive to their, unsurprisingly, having been known in the ancient world, if corrupted by other retellings.[88] More cuttingly, idolatrous religions corrupted the universal truths of the rational commandments, which Se'adyah called *sikhliyot*, and those he

---

82 Shilo, "Hashpa'ato shel Rabbi Yitzhak Isaac Haver 'al Parshanuto shel Ha-Rav Kook le-Qabbalah," 95–117.

83 LNH, 152–153.

84 Ibid., 161.

85 Ibid., 163.

86 Ibid., 168:

. . . ואדרבא, כח האמת, שהיא הנחלה האמיתית לישראל, הוא מתגבר ועולה בהיותו מתברר שבמקורו הוא נחלה לכל הנבראים בצלם אלהים, כי אלקים עשה את האדם ישר—ואחר כך כשנתמוטט המצב, נעשו הם סבה לבנין העולם והקמתו ותעודתו באחרית.

87 This motif that idolatrous relics endure in monotheistic traditions appears in the pioneering anthropological work of E. B. Tylor, who in turn derived it in part from readers of Maimonides in Latin translation; see Jonathan Decter, "Survivals, Debris and Relics: E. B. Tylor, the Orientalist Inheritance, and Medieval Polemic," *History of Humanities* 5, no. 1 (2020): 251-271.

88 Ibid., 170–171.

called *shim'iyot* reflect human wisdom predating Sinai. Rather than diminish our ties to Torah, the parallels we find should only deepen them. "Those who think that it ill befits man's spirit and independent abilities for some of the Torah's sanctity and majesty to be found there don't grasp the majesty of the divine image with which the Creator of man formed him."[89]

Yet, Israel is not the same as other nations—and, he says in a dig at political Zionism, any attempt to base Jewish nationalism on anything other than ideals, is doomed to failure.[90] Indeed, he hardly refers to antisemitism as a motive force for Jewish nationalism, or in history in general; in a rare mention of antisemitism he suggests it first arose among gentiles, raised on the less moral idolatries and ill-equipped for affinity towards Israel.[91] (One can't help but note this, to put it mildly, highly ethereal understanding of antisemitism, so dramatically different from the sociological analyses to be found in the writings of Pinsker, Herzl, Dubnow, and other thinkers associated with political Jewish nationalism.)

There were, though, non-Jews with deep affinities for Israel, including Jesus and Muhammad. Regarding the former, those who saw God in one human being because he so profoundly wanted to do good for others, will, in time, be ready to understand how God's presence transcends any human being, no matter who profoundly well-intentioned.[92] As for the latter—though he mentions neither Islam nor its Prophet by name, referring to them as "the second branch" (*ha-se'if ha-sheni*)—there are indeed degrees of prophecy, which, if not as great as those of Moses, "can build the house of righteousness and the good, and the purification of thoughts by their (adherents') measure, and prepare them for the great, general, unifying light."[93]

Here too, he follows Maimonides, who, in *Hilkhot Melakhim* 11:4, saw Christianity and Islam as paving the way for the reach of the Messianic advent to humanity, but again, with a difference.[94] For Maimonides the role of the other monotheisms is, so to speak,

---

89 Ibid., 174:

ואותם שחושבים, שראוי הוא שלא ימצא ברוח האדם וכשרונו העצמי מאומה מקדושתה והודה של תורה, אינם מכירים את ההוד של צלם אלהים אשר יצר אותו בו יוצר האדם.

90 Ibid., 185.

91 Ibid., 196.

92 Ibid., 197.

93 Ibid.:

וכן היה עם הסעיף השני, לפי ערך מושפעיו היה נשפע ונעזר עזר אלקי, והרי כמה מדרגות ישנן גם כן בנבואה, ואם לא עלה שום אחד למעלה כללית של שינויי סדרים בכללות הבריאה כמשה רבינו ע"ה, הוא מפני מיעוט מדרגתם ומיעוט הצורך להשפעה רוחנית אדירה, אבל החפץ הכללי חפץ ד' הוא. ועם הזהירות הרבה להבדיל בין הקודש האמיתי למה שהוא לערכנו חול וגם טמא, לא נבהל לחשוב תועה, שאי אפשר להתאים עם דעה ומוסר טוב לערכם את הציורים הדתיים שלהם ואת המנהגים המסתעפים, שהם בונים את בית היושר והטוב וזיכוך המחשבות להם לפי מדתם, והם מכשירים אותם לאור הגדול האחדותי הכללי.

94 That particular passage was censored from printed editions of *Mishneh Torah* available in Eastern Europe, though did appear in the Constantinople printing of 1509 and some may have known of it. It was mentioned by Ya'aqov Emden, who expressed views along these lines in several works, with which Rav Kook may well hae been familiar; see Jacob J. Schachter, "Rabbi Jacob Emden, Sabbatianism and Frankism: Attitudes Towards Christianity in the Eighteenth

informational, introducing to humanity the laws of the Torah, so that when the Messiah comes they will not be unfamiliar. For Rav Kook, Jesus and Mohammed are genuine, if limited, prophets, and their followers participate alongside Israel in the evolving religious life of humanity, a process to reach fruition in the *eschaton*—with the difference that Jews do so as a nation and non-Jews as individuals. In terms of the super-typology of Jewish approaches to other religious traditions developed by Alan Brill and Rori Picker-Neiss, this stance is "inclusivist," as opposed to "universalist," "pluralist," or "exclusivist."[95] Yet helpful as this characterization is, it needs to be augmented by consideration of a more combustible dimension in Rav Kook's thought—namely, history.

Israel and the Education of Humanity

This historical process of the education of humanity will be a reciprocal effort of Israel and the other religions, who will develop "the broad ideas that become one with the deep intention of the Torah and her mitzvot in the knottiest details."[96] The religious wars plaguing human history result from the mediocrity of the theological concepts of religious functionaries.[97]

But the historical denouement already in process will not be serene. Indeed God has introduced the "*hutzpah* of the footsteps of the Messiah" of the Mishnah (Sotah 9:15) to enflame people's hearts and quicken the pious.[98] Thus the current rebellions against God and traditional religion are none other than the work of God Himself. Writing in explicitly Hegelian fashion, he says: "And the final end is realized by the opposition and strengthening which will purify the dross and establish thoughts, from period to period and era to era, to their purification."[99]

Who, exactly, is opposing whom? He identifies three contending groups within the Jewish people: liberals seeking human rights qua individuals, rather than as a national collective (an idea which left to its own devices is "dangerous" as it leads to Reform Judaism); those seeking rights qua national minority rights in the Diaspora; and those extending that claim in a different direction, seeking for Jews a land of their own. Until the Land of Israel is available, "any place that we may find" will do (in a nod to the Uganda plan), while still founding in the Land of Israel "a supreme spiritual center" (in a nod to Ahad

---

Century," in *New Perspectives on Jewish-Christian Relations in Honor of David Berger*, ed. Elisheva Carlebach and Jacob J. Schachter (Leiden/Boston: Brill, 2012), 359–396, esp. 366.

95   See Alan Brill and Rori Picker-Neiss, "Jewish Views of World Religions: Four Models," in *Jewish Theology and World Religions*, ed. Alon Goshen-Gottstein and Eugene Korn (Oxford: Littman, 2012), 41–60.

96   LNH, 198.

97   Ibid., 199.

98   Ibid., 206.

99   Ibid., 207:

והתכלית תבא מתוך ההתנגדות וההתגברות שתטהר את הסיגים ותעמיד את הרעיונות, מפרק לפרק ומתקופה לתקופה, על מצב טהרתם.

Ha-Am).[100] This passage is interesting, and even startling, for what he does and does not say. Squaring the circles of liberalism and nationalism, he affirms the idea of human rights within a society that recognizes Jewish national rights in the Land of Israel, while engaging the ideas of Diaspora nationalists like Dubnow, Territorialists like Israel Zangwill, and cultural Zionists too. Missing here is just what form this polity might take, and whether it would entail a state, a lacuna in keeping with his general lack of interest in government and statecraft, as well as his Krochmal-mediated Hegelianism; that is, the nation, rather than the state as such, is the earthly vessel for the realization of the spirit.[101] His omission of the Land of startling (and helps explain Zvi Yehudah's reluctance to publish his father's pre-Jaffan writings).[102]

Whatever form this Jewish collective may take, the goal is freedom, by which he means that the individual, and the nation, should live by their own nature.[103] His understanding of freedom here here clearly is that which Isaiah Berlin famously characterized as "positive freedom," the ability most fully to realize oneself, as part of some larger whole, as distinct from "negative freedom," the absence of restraint, and hallmark of the liberal state.[104] Just how far Rav Kook is from the vision of the liberal state becomes clear when he argues that while the work of culture is the adaptation of universal norms to the particulars of every nation, for Israel the Oral Torah is the very foundation of national self-rule and whoever would undo it is calling for slavery in the name of illusory freedom.[105] Once

---

100 Ibid., 211–212:

המחשבה האחת, להגן עבור הכלל גם כן במצב הגלות, גם בארצות אויב, לדרוש משפט וזכויות אדם בנימוס ודין . . . .(מ)המחשבה הזאת . . . יצא הריפורם . . . עוד מחשבה אחת יש, שרוחה נמצא בראשונה . . . . כי גם בארץ אויב איננו עוד מבקשים זכויות אדם בשכר ביטול הצורה הלאומית שלנו, כי אם בתור עם..וזה, אמנם, יביא למחשבה . . . להשתדל עם זה לרכש לנו אחוזה בתור עם לבדד, במקום שנוכל להתרומם ולהתעודד כראוי, כי איך שיהיה, יש גבול לדרישות הלאומיות בגלות גם מצד המשפט, אף על פי שכמעט אין גבול לדרישת היחידים בתור זכות אדם. . . . אבל המחשבה הזאת לא תאמר די. שהרי אין לנו ארץ שנוכל למצא את ערכנו האמיתי כראוי . . . . אם לא נשוב למקור חיינו, לציון . . . . על כן, אף על פי שאי אפשר לנו לעכב כלל את הפעולה להתאזר בעז עם בעל ארץ נושבת ועז שלטון פנימי, בכל מקום שימצא לנו, כיון שאין ארץ ישראל עדיין מוכנת לנו, מכל מקום, אנחנו צריכים להתקשר הרבה לארה"ק על ידי יסוד מרכזי רוחני עליון, באופן שהישוב הקטן שבארץ ישראל יכלול בקרבו את שלש המחשבות גם יחד. . . .

101 Recent years have seen a wave of scholarship on Diaspora nationalism in this time, some of which also calls into question the assumed links between all forms of Zionism and the drive for independent statehood. See Simon Rabinovich, *Jewish Rights, National Rites: Nationalism and Autonomy in Late Imperial and Revolutionary Russia* (Stanford: Stanford University Press, 2014) and Shumsky, *Beyond the Nation-State: The Zionist Political Imagination from Pinsker to Ben-Gurion.*

102 One cannnot read this passage without thinking of his famous comments in his Jaffan years about the three forces wrestling in Jewry—liberalism, nationalism, and Orthodoxy; SQ 3:1-2, *Orot*, 70-72. We will say more on this in our conclusion.

103 LNH, 222.

104 Isaiah Berlin, "Two Concepts of Liberty," in his *Four Essays on Liberty* (London: Oxford University Press, 1969); Berlin's classic essay was first written in 1958.

105 LNH, 225.

Zionism understands this it will find its rightful place in Israel, and among the nations.[106] It is precisely adherence to the Oral Torah arising from the divinely Written Torah's interaction with Israel—that will enable the Jewish people to fulfill its universalist mission of bringing to fruition the best that is in the other families of humanity, as all religions, in purified form, will come to see their shared truth, however variously they live it.[107]

The particular and universal forms of ethics will always naturally be intertwined with one another in the life of nations.[108] The distinctive form of Jewish ethics is Torah, whose "goal is to lift up the human spirit . . . to the point where even if one were to be acting only on the basis of one's own heart, one would be ascending in paths of life that bring a good end, and hope to oneself and the world."[109] The fact that Torah has come to seem so oppressive to so many is itself a sign of the Messianic advent: "The basis of the spiritual pangs of the Messiah" comes from exilic generations having accepted Torah as a yoke even when contra their innate moral sense. Now as their moral senses are reviving, the true, forward looking, reasons for the mitzvot must be revealed.[110]

He enunciates this forward-looking view in the book's closing chapter, whose opening line alludes to the Maimonidean spirit animating this work with, as we have seen, crucial differences: most perplexities come to the world "because people satisfy themselves with fixed and limited opinions" and don't "roam in all the expanse of the idea in its pure nature."[111] As a result, their conclusions lead to division. That is why Israel must "expand the laws of moral opinions and beliefs [*hilkhot ha-de'ot ve-ha-emunot*—a nod to both Se'adyah and Maimonides that subtly preserves the primacy of the latter—Y. M.] . . . and thus remove the confusion and darkened imagination from the conventional opinions of the nation . . . and (through Torah) raises all the forces of the good and upright to the highest summit of ethics, exalted and majestic."[112]

How much of *Li-Nevukhei Ha-Dor* is apologetics and how much a program for rethinking rabbinic Judaism's own understandings of its place and mission? Turning now to this last notebook in Boisk, we can see just how much of *Li-Nevukhei Ha-Dori* is the exoteric expression of his own esoteric and expansive thinking. The mental climate of this notebook is far stormier than the treatise, as regards the rebellious generation on whom he's reflecting, and himself.

---

106 Ibid., 231.
107 Ibid, 234.
108 Ibid, 246.
109 Ibid, 249:
תכלית התורה היא לרומם את הלב האנושי, לעדנו להביאו למעלתו הראויה לו, שאפילו אם יעזב להיות מתנהג כולו על פי נטיית לבו לבדו, ילך הולך ועולה בדרכי חיים שיהיו מביאים אחרית ותקוה, לו ולעולם.
110 Ibid, 252.
111 Ibid, 259.
112 Ibid, 260.

"The Last in Boisk": Heresy, Nietzsche, Apocalypse

Underlying the ideas he confidently expressed in *'Eyn Ayah*, the essays in *Ha-Peles* and *Li-Nevukhei Ha-Dor* were raw, personal, tentative, and at times, shockingly unorthodox explorations—all on display in the last journal he kept during his time in Boisk. In its pages, as we have seen time and again, he starts in a structured register that increasingly gives ways to a more associative writing, as he comes to see himself and the experiences of his times as the manifestations of larger mythic forces sweeping through the cosmos, to whose hidden dynamics the Kabbalah holds the key.

This notebook reveals just how preoccupied he was with freethinking, to which he refers using the classic term for heresy, *kefirah*. While in *Li-Nevukhei Ha-Dor* he addresses critiques of religion as an open-minded rabbi, in this journal he confronts the full, experiential force of rebellion, engaging a remarkable range of ideas and longings.

These pages reveal Rav Kook's complex negotiations with the heretics of his time; the depth of his wrestling with their ideas and sympathy for their critiques not only of popular religion, but of Talmud study and halakhah is, for an upstanding member of the Lithuanian rabbinic fraternity nothing short of astonishing. Placing himself in the middle of both Nietzschean critiques of religion and Christian critiques of Jewish ethics he provisionally accepts both—as the metahistorical frame in which all these negotiations are taking place is proto-Messianic, with even some proto-Sabbatian ideas appearing on the horizon.

As I have elsewhere put it, he undertakes an historical theodicy of modernity, justifying the mass defections from tradition as the hand of Providence, purging the dross of Judaism before the final coming of the Messiah. And here as elsewhere in his pre-Palestine corpus, the Land of Israel hardly figures at all in his analyses qua category, all the more strikingly in light of his impending emigration.

Central to the climate of opinion he was trying to understand was Nietzsche, who was introduced to the Hebrew readership of the time in 1892 by none other than Rav Kook's classmate, Berdyczewsky.[113] Nietzsche's image and his ideas were in the ensuing years taken up by a number of writers, including Ahad Ha-Am, Hillel Zeitlin, and Rav Kook's correspondent Shmuel Alexandrov. Much and heated argument swirled through the Hebrew press around Berdyczewsky's own provocative uses of Nietzsche.[114] Menahem Brinker has pointed out that Hebrew writers of the time encountered Nietzsche on three

---

113 See the collection edited by Shmuel Golomb, *Nietzsche be-Tarbut Ha-'Ivrit* (Jerusalem: Hebrew University/Magnes, 2002). Therein at 383ff., Golomb provides a detailed bibliography of Nietzsche's appearances in Hebrew. In the same collection, Smadar Sherlo offers an astute reading of Rav Kook's engagements with Nietzsche in his later career.

114 See Shmuel Alexandrov's "Zeman Matan Toratenu," *Ha-Maggid* 9, no. 22 (May 1900): 249–250, a biting attack on Berdyczewsky; he writes, inter alia, that Berdyczewsky seeks sanction for his halakhic deviance in the writings of Nietzsche. Alexandrov's sarcasm contrasts dramatically with Rav Kook's attitudes here. For discussions by others, see, for instance, Shimon Bernfeld's article on Schopenhauer and Nietzsche in *Ha-Shiloah* 5 (January–June 1899); another essay of Bernfeld's resembles much of the language and ideas of *'Eyn Ayah* to Berakhot; see his essays

levels: as a fashionable cultural cliché; through a broad impression garnered from secondary discussion; and finally, and most rarely, via genuine acquaintance with the man and his ideas. At all three levels he stimulated debate like nobody else, to the point where even avowed anti-Nietzscheans like Ahad Ha-Am and Bialik spoke in his terms.[115]

Here, too, Berdyczewsky provides an interesting foil to Rav Kook. The leading scholar of Berdyczewsky, Avner Holzman, has argued that Berdyczewsky was expressing his "Nietzschean" ideas well before he ever read him, that is, that Nietzsche simply reinforced the tendency in which he had been headed.[116] Put a little differently, talking about Nietzsche gave people a way of focusing on key themes—such as self-assertion, the denigration of traditional ethics, the radical critique of tradition and a corresponding ethos of self-creation—perhaps analogously to the way earlier generations had argued over whether Mendelssohn was a Spinozist, using a seminal thinker as a helpful shorthand for registering a number of trends.

Nietzsche is key to a major theme of this study, the evolution of modern subjectivity. Charles Taylor notes that, while he argues for self-overcoming like Kierkegaard and Dostoevsky, he departs from them by locating its sources entirely within, that is, the power to say "yes!" resides within us. This far-reaching internalization leads to his thoroughgoing critique of traditional morality and its subjection of the self to debilitating rules.[117] This critique is itself of a piece with his project of breaking and reconstructing the notion of power—not merely criticizing, but unmasking and undoing the very idea of transcendence. Even as unconventional a rabbi as Rav Kook would, it seems, have little to discuss with such an original and powerful atheist. Yet, while Nietzsche radically revises Western ethics and metaphysics, he does not entirely repudiate them and is, in his assertion of value, removed from the nihilism of his latter-day exponents. As Taylor puts it, there is "a saving inconsistency of Nietzsche, from whom there emerged, out of the uncompromising recognition of the flux, something which deserved affirmation, yea-saying. For Derrida [by contrast—Y. M.], there is nothing but deconstruction . . . nothing emerges from this flux worth affirming."[118]

Taken together, the centrality of Nietzsche in the Hebrew press of the time, and the power of that critique, lent further impetus to Rav Kook's seeing modern freethinking as the apocalypse that would precede the Messianic advent.

Crucial to his thinking, as we have noted and will now further examine, is the rabbinic tradition projecting widespread religious disobedience in the pre-Messianic time, a theme first occurring in his writings, as we have seen, as early as 1889. In Mishnah Sotah 9:15, "at the time of the footsteps of the Messiah, impudence will wax strong" and

---

on Hayyim Shteintal under the title "Torat Hayim" in *Ha-Shiloah* 6 (1899): 97–107, 193–206, 385–396.

115 See Menahem Brinker's essay in Golomb, *Nietzsche be-Tarbut Ha-'Ivrit*, esp. 134–135.

116 See Avner Holzman in ibid., 161–179.

117 Taylor, *Sources of the Self*, 452–455.

118 Ibid., 489. This reading of Nietzsche is argued compellingly at length by Peter Berkowitz, *Nietzsche: The Ethics of an Immoralist* (Cambridge, MA: Harvard University Press, 1995).

religious and social order will collapse. According to a Talmudic passage (Sanhedrin 97a), the Messianic time will be characterized by mass sinfulness, sexual immorality, and the eclipse of rabbinic authority. These passages played no small role in the antinomianism of the Sabbatian movement.[119]

A naturalized reading of the apocalypse of heresy, or at least of mass sinfulness, is offered by Maharal in his *Netzah Yisrael*: inasmuch as every new form of being represents the passing, and superseding, of a predecessor, there must be absence, or privation of being in the world before the Messiah. This is why the generation before the Messiah's advent will be deeply sinful (per BT Sanhedrin 97a), that is, in order to create the dialectical springboard for a new being; thus these privations in the form of sin are themselves a new existence since they create the reality that will in turn lead to the great Messianic restoration.[120]

Here, once again, Luzzatto's ideas are crucial to our story. Luzzatto's Messianic doctrine—not to mention the manifold controversies regarding the perceptions of his own Messianic role outside his circle—is too vast a subject to be rendered here. Most crucial for us is his contention that redemption unfolds within historical time, and that the true Messianic advent must be universal and not limited to Israel (*Qalah Pithei Hokhmah* §30, ed. Friedlander, 95); indeed, as we have already seen, the relation between Israel's national destiny and universal ethics is a key touchstone of Rav Kook's attempt to understand the mission of contemporary Jewish nationalism.

Finally, and interestingly—unlike in his earliest notebook *Metziot Qatan*—here Rav Kook seldom explicitly cites the texts on which he draws as he forges his own mystical-theological style and language.

Critique of Conventional Religious Thought

The journal's very first entry engages modern philosophy, recast in Kabbalistic terms:

> The likeness that reality presents to us in our internal representations is more significant to us than its truth in and of itself, for that [truth—Y. M.] we cannot perceive, and it is in our representations that we live and sense.

---

119 The literature here is vast. See, of course, Gershom Scholem, *Sabbatai Sevi: The Mystical Messiah, 1626–1676*, trans. R. J. Z. Werblowsky (Princeton: Princeton University Press, 1973, 2017). In Scholem's classic 1937 essay "Redemption through Sin," reprinted in his *The Messianic Idea in Judaism and Other Essays on Jewish Spirituality* (New York: Schocken, 1971), 78–141; at 98 he cites the Sabbatian uses of the passage in Sanhedrin to explain Shabtai's apostasy. See also the title essay therein, as well as "Crisis and Tradition in Jewish Messianism." For a marvelous survey of Scholem's work on Sabbatianism, its reception, and the research of the decades since, see Yaacob Dweck's introduction to the 2017 Princeton volume, xxix–lxv.

120 Maharal, *Netzah Yisrael*, chapter 35 158–160 (London edition). The word that I am translating as "privations" is *hefsedim*.

This seems a straightforward acceptance of Kantian epistemology.[121] But in the following sentence he characterizes human forms of perception in Kabbalistic metaphors.

> And so all the hues in which reality comes to be represented, throughout time, are the garments of reality in relation to man, who had best pay attention to them and discern their effects.[122]

"Hues" are a classic characterization of the sefirot; "garments" are in Kabbalistic literature, as Pinhas Giller has put it, "a central metaphor for the dimensional nature of existence . . . [a]s the body is a garment of the soul, so all of reality is multilayered, a series of aspects hidden within each other. Such is the case with the most hidden thing, the Torah, whose exoteric nature is merely the garment for its inner meaning."[123]

This is no mere point of epistemology—it speaks to the waves of heresy sweeping through Jewry in modern times; this perspective, he writes, enables us to see contemporary heretics not as simple deviants but as perceptive, if flawed, critics of popular religious conceptions.

> Spiritual concepts regarding faith and essentials of Torah are usually mistakenly drawn by the masses, but at any rate elicit good behavior. In truth this is not an absolute error, since all know that the very truth of sublime things is not to be represented *for no human can see Me and live* [Ex. 33:20]. As for those who have cast off the yoke and their thoughts damaged, that generally happens because they have sensed the confusion of the mass conception, but their wisdom is insufficient, nor have they worked to construct a sophisticated conception in place of that of the masses, which could elicit all the good deeds that at the least are elicited by the mass conception, and even higher, as befits those of purified minds.[124]

---

121 This recalls what I characterized as the half-Kantian position he expressed at ʿEyn Ayah to Berakhot 5:108.

I say "Kantian" because unlike the Maimonidean *via negativa*, which argued for the inaccessibility of ultimate metaphysical knowledge but admitted genuine empirical knowledge, he is articulating here a relativization of all knowledge, including empirical knowledge. On Maimonides's position, see Levy and Rashed, "Maimonides' Epistemology," 105–133, 116–119. In a 1907 letter to Shmuel Alexandrov, Rav Kook protested that we have no need of Kant to teach us the relativity of all concepts, inasmuch as our basic perceptions are a function of the tenth and lowest sefirah, *Malkhut*, "which has nothing in and of itself [*let lei mi-garmei kelum*]"; see *Igrot*, 1:47–48. That being said, it is unlikely that he would have used that Kabbalistic concept in this particular, and very modern, epistemological context, had he not been acquainted with Kant in one form or another.

122 PAB 1, 36:

הדמיון שבמציאות מצוייר בו בציורינו הפנימי, הוא יותר חשוב אצלינו מאמתתו כשהוא לעצמו, כי את אמתתו לעצמו אין אנו יכולים להשיג, ובציורינו הלא נחיה ונחוש. על כן כל הגוונים השונים שמצטייר בו המציאות, בכל הדורות כולם הם לבושים אל המציאות ביחש האדם, שכדאי לשום אליהם לב ולהשכיל לתוצאותיהם.

123 Pinchas Giller, *Reading the Zohar: The Sacred Text of the Kabbalah* (New York: Oxford University Press, 2001), 53.

124 PAB 3, 36–37:

המושגים הרוחניים שנוגעים באמונות ועקרי תורה, הם על פי רוב מצויירים בשבוש אצל המון רב, ומכל מקום הם

In the story of Orthodox perceptions of the nonobservant, this attribution of mass defection to the intellectual inadequacy of conventional religious thinking was something new. Distancing from nonobservant Jews, in theory and practice, was a central feature in the emergence of Orthodoxy in the nineteenth century, in response to the emergence of what Adam Ferziger suitably characterizes as the novel phenomenon of "normative nonobservance."[125] In Western Europe, where non-Jewish society's relative openness to acculturated Jews helped facilitate mass defections from traditional Judaism, traditionalist leaders adopted a circumscribed but varied range of ideological positions vis-à-vis the growing numbers of nonobservant Jews, from outright exclusion to a hierarchical distinction between more and less observant Jews.[126] In the Russian Empire, where mass defection proceeded more slowly and unevenly than in the West, and the surrounding non-Jewish society was less welcoming of even assimilated Jews, we find, even alongside virulent polemics against nonobservance, less forthright ideological exclusion of the nonobservant. Netziv, for his part, had a comparatively nuanced position, expressing some understanding for—though certainly not approval of—some forms of halakhic deviance, and urging cooperation with nonobservant Jews on communal issues, even while, for example, ruling against praying in the company of secular Jewish nationalists.[127]

Rav Kook might at first blush seem not that distant from Hirsch, whose rejection of nonobservance as a legitimate category did not preclude engaging high secular culture and, in particular, Hegel. Indeed, implicit in Hirsch's public educational and publishing enterprises is the recognition that halakhic Judaism's continued suasion depended on its reformulation in terms of contemporary philosophic language. But Rav Kook moves in the pages of the journal well beyond Hirsch, and beyond his own *Li-Nevukhei Ha-Dor*, according legitimacy, and even some metaphysical status, to secular Jewish nationalism.

Messiah ben Joseph: Redemption, National and Universal

His first broaching of nationalism in this journal is an arresting reinterpretation of the doctrine of Messiah ben Joseph, the proto-Messianic figure who in rabbinic tradition complements his superior and successor Messiah ben David, and, according to some

---

ממשיכים את ההדרכה הטובה. ובאמת אין זה שיבוש החלטי, מאחר שהכל יודעים שאמתת האמת בדברים הנשגבים אין לצייר, כי לא יראני האדם וחי. אמנם אותם שפרקו עול ונפגעו בדיעות, הדבר נובע על פי רוב מפני שהרגישו בשיבוש הציור ההמוני, ולא הספיקה חכמתם, ולא עמלו לבנות תמורת ציור ההמוני ציור מוחכם, שיוכל להמשיך את כל המעשים הטובים שציור ההמוני ממשיך לפחות, ועד ביותר מעלה, כראוי למי שדיעותיו זכות.

125 See Adam S. Ferziger, *Exclusion and Hierarchy: Orthodoxy, Nonobservance and the Emergence of Modern Jewish Identity* (Philadelphia: University of Pennsylvania Press, 2005).

126 Thus Samson Rafael Hirsch of Frankfurt took a more exclusionary stance, while the comparatively more accommodating David Zvi Hoffmann and Azriel Hildesheimer of Berlin had recourse to notions of hierarchy.

127 See Howard S. Joseph, "As Swords Thrust Through the Body: The Netziv's Rejection of Separatism," *Edah Journal* 1, no. 1 (2000), http://www.edah.org/backend/JournalArticle/joseph.pdf and Perl, "'No Two Minds are Alike'": 74–98. Netziv's ruling on praying in the company of members of Bilu is found in his responsa collection *Meshiv Davar*, part 1, no. 9.

traditions, is fated to be killed in a prelude to the final Messianic advent.[128] Indeed, Yehudah Liebes has concluded that traditions of Messiah ben Joseph themselves played a role in the formation of Christianity; we will return to that association later on.[129]

Messiah ben-Joseph, Rav Kook writes, represents the particularist dimension of Jewish nationalism without regard to Israel's larger mission to the rest of humanity, represented by the Messiahship of the House of David, and that lower form of nationalism must be extinguished en route to Israel's higher mission. Indeed, he goes on to say, when no less a figure than Hillel said Israel has no messiah (BT Sanhedrin 92b) it was because monarchy was, for him, a sign of deficient morality, an exigency for which Israel would have no need. But that is to misread Israel's deepest longings, which are for the universal ethical kingship of David.

These ideas of Rav Kook's took on greater significance when, shortly after his arrival in Palestine, Theodor Herzl died on July 3, 1904. Rav Kook's journal entry responding to that event, the basis of his eulogy for Herzl, casts Herzlian Zionism in the role of Messiah ben Joseph, in even broader terms than here, as the historiosophical resolution of a dialectic of body and soul.[130] We see from the passage at hand that Herzl's sudden and untimely death made such a deep impression on Rav Kook in part because it seemed to confirm Herzl's role in Rav Kook's evolving historiosophy of Jewish nationalism. Herzl's death electrifyingly confirmed his earlier intuition that secular nationalism was indeed none other than the incarnation of the Messiah ben-Joseph. We will return to the figure of Messiah ben Joseph later on, in the context of Rav Kook's explicit invocations of Shabtai Zvi and Nietzsche.

As we saw in the *Ha-Peles* essays, drawn to Jewish nationalism as he was, Rav Kook took takes pains to moralize it, and thus distinguish it, from non-Jewish nationalism. In *'Eyn Ayah* we saw how his mounting assertion of the individual subject and its drive to self-realization elicited in his thinking a set of anxieties which he discussed in the Rousseauian idiom of self-love and its moral pitfalls. These two strains come together here:

> Among the bases of the prohibitions on incest is the intensification of love in the individual self, for familial love is an expanded self-love, thus the foundation of the expansion of the concept of love for another is grounded in the notion of generation, the unification of parts, *thus shall a man leave his father and mother and cleave to his wife* (Gen. 2:24). . . . But proper self-love is a very foundation of morality, albeit one that requires great care lest it lead to a dissolution of one's own sense of self, this especially when it comes to Israel, whose sacred

---

128 See, for example, BT Sukah 52a.

129 Yehudah Liebes, "Yonah ben Amitai ke-Mashiah ben Yosef," *Mehqarei Yerushalayim bi-Mahshevet Yisrael* 3, nos. 1–2 (1983–1984): 269–311.

130 It appears in the same volume as does this journal—*Qevatzim mi-Ketav Yad Qodsho*, 109–116, and was reprinted in *Sinai* 47, and in MH, 94–99. See the discussion of this episode in my *Rav Kook*, 48–50, where I discuss the public context of this, as well as his subtle dialogue therein with Ahad Ha-Am.

Abrahamic tendency is to spread loving-kindness through the world, without distinction of race or nation. So Israel left to its own devices had no instinct of national self-preservation without an admixture of self-love, which required some foreign grafting, and that is why David's kingship had to derive from Moab and Amon, Moab representing the love of race and Amon the love of nation. . . . Though from the divine perspective there are no divisions of race or people . . . yet God had to set aside one pure place in order to preserve the internal point for the sake of the whole, so that selfhood not be dissolved, and for its own sake that deserves to be loved and cherished, He had to establish a foundation *by a far place* (Zohar III, 98b), *purity from defilement* (Job 14:4), *the wondrous paths of wisdom* (after *Sefer Yetzirah* §1).[131]

He identifies the individual subject and its legitimate, indeed divinely ordained, drive for self-realization with the collective, national subject while working to square the morally problematic assertion of subjectivity, personal and collective, with a more universal ethics. This he does by making the unique subjectivity of Israel secondary to ethics—namely, Israel's uniqueness is justified by reference to its universal ethical mission, and such self-love as it needs to cultivate for the sake of that mission is a necessary evil towards that good end. In saying that self-love is foreign to Israel's national character and had to be imported, he is trying somehow to cordon off self-love from Israel's most immediate and penetrating self-understanding (notwithstanding the apologies the contemporary reader may feel the need to make on his behalf to the latter-day descendants of Amon and Moab).

Expressivism and the Song of Songs

The entry immediately following, the result of an extraordinary conversation with his disciple Binyamin Menashe Levin, would eventually become one of Rav Kook's most famous essays.[132] Practically the only entry the circumstance of whose composition is known to us, it shows how the idea of self-love and its temptations were, for him, no mere figure of speech. One day, Levin tells us, on one of their walks on the outskirts of Boisk, Rav Kook began to discuss the Song of Songs, and in particular the famous comment of Rabbi Aqiva recorded in the Mishnah that "if all scripture is holy, the Song of Songs is

---

131 PAB 10, 39–40:

מיסודי איסורי עריות הוא התעצמות האהבה רק בעצמות הפרט, כי גם אהבת המשפחה היא אהבה עצמית נרחבת, על כן יסוד התרחבות מושג האהבה לזולתו יכונן מיסוד תולדות, מהתאחדות החלקים. על כן יעזוב איש את אביו ואת אמו ודבק באשתו . . . אמנם אהבת עצמו במדה הראויה, היא מיסודי חקי המוסר. אמנם שמירה גדולה צריך שלא יבא לביטול העצמיות, ביחוד בישראל, כי נטיית הקודש מאברהם אבינו ע"ה הי' להתפשטות החסד בעולם, שלא להתגדר לא בגזע ולא בלאם. על כן לא הי' נטיות שמירה כלל לצביון הלאומי לולא עירוב כח אהבת עצמו, שצריך הי' להרכבה זרה, על כן מלכות בית דוד הי' צריך להיות ממואב ועמון, מואב אהבת הגזע, עמון אהבת האומה . . . אף על פי שלגבי היסוד העליון אין הבדל בין גזע ועם . . . מכל מקום כדי לבא לשמירת הנקודה התוכיית שלא יתבלע העצמות עבור השימוש שיש לו אל ערך הכלל, ועבור חשיבות עצמו שראוי הוא להיות נאהב ונחבב, הי' צריך ליסד יסוד על ידי אתר רחיקא, טהור מטמא, פליאות נתיבות חכמה.

132 PAB 11–12, 40–42.

the holy of holies" (M. Yadayim 3:5). Levin produced a pencil, Rav Kook began to write[133] and the result was published anonmymously in Zev Yavetz's *Ha-Mizrah* in 1903.[134] It is perhaps the first expression of some themes that would come to characterize the later periods of Rav Kook's thought: a theology of politics and secular culture that tries to unite Romanticism, personal subjectivity, and nationalism in a poetic idiom rooted in classical tradition, aware of its own testing of traditional boundaries, or its redrawing them around a new understanding of the sacred:

> Literature, painting and sculpture aim to bring to realization all the spiritual concepts impressed deep in the human soul. And so long as even one etching hidden in the depth of the thinking and feeling soul is missing and unexpressed the labor of art has an obligation to bring it out. Of course, only those treasures whose exposure perfumes the air of existence are to be opened . . . and woe to him who works his spade for perverse action, simply to tarry with women. The soul-upheavals accompanying feelings of natural love, which take up much of existence, morality and life, are best interpreted by literature via all the dimensions through which she actualizes the hidden things, but with the highest vigilance from the tendency to drunkenness that accompanies such feelings. . . . How great is the void when those high and exalted upheavals, which work, have worked and will work so much on all good men and on especially the ecclesia of Israel, flowing from the love of The Master of All Works, Fount of Good and Kindness—when those beloved feelings go missing and are not properly engraved

---

133 In a brief prefatory comment to a reprint of the essay in an annual he edited, *'Alumah* (Jerusalem: Rubin Mass, 1936), 1, 43–44, Levin writes that the conversation took place during a walk on the outskirts of Boisk in 1901, and that Rav Kook wrote the essay while sitting on one of the ruins of the town's old wall. He later told a more colorful version, placed on the shores of the Baltic, to Moshe Zvi Neriah, recorded in the latter's *Mo'adei Ha-Re'ayah*, 334 (Tel Aviv: Merkaz Yeshivot Bnei Aqiva: 1980). "I knew that other waves of thought would soon follow and feared that these gems would be forgotten, and wanted to write them down. But we had no writing instruments at all. I asked the rabbi to wait a bit and I ran to bring pencil and paper." The *'Alumah* version seems the more authentic, yet I wonder if the essay may have been written later than 1901. It appears fairly early in the notebook and its not being printed until 1903, if not dispositive, nonetheless lends credence to a later dating.

134 The piece appears in *Ha-Mizrah* 1, no. 6 (1903): 352–354. In the table of contents it is titled "From the *'Eyn Ayah* Notebook,"—"Mi-Pinqas 'Eyn Ayah," literally, "From the Notebook of the Falcon's Eye," punning on Job 28:7 and Rav Kook's acronym Ayah, that is, **A**vraham **Y**itzhak **Ha**-Kohen, while the piece itself is titled "The Falcon's Knowing Glance" ("Tevi'at 'Eyn Ayah"). We have here, in other words, the first appearance of the title of Rav Kook's aggadic commentary. At the end of the piece we find "given to print by Binyamin Menashe Levin of Horodetz." The piece appears in the canonical writings of Rav Kook as an introduction to Song of Songs in the commentary to the Siddur begun by Rav Kook in London during World War I, and posthumously issued by Zvi Yehudah Kook with selections from then-unpublished writings as *'Olat Re'ayah*, vol. 2 (Jerusalem: Mossad Ha-Rav Kook, 1939), 3–4. Zvi Yehudah Kook characteristically sandwiched this essay into a longer compilation of passages from his father's work, with no indication of its distinct provenance, and took significant liberties with the editing. For example, he replaced "sculpture," *ha-hituv*, with *ve-hituvah*, that is, "her [literature's] shaping."

in writing. . . . This void is filled for us in that love song which is the holy of holies, *the Song of Songs that is Solomon's* (Sg. 1:1).[135]

We have come a long way from his essay on the art of writing in the first issue of *'Ittur Sofrim* in 1888; from an exercise in sociology of knowledge on the role of writing in transmitting traditions, to the art of writing as the expression of a unique self. [136]

It is precisely the sage Aqiva, he continues, who declares the utter sanctity of the Song, as it was he who, according to the Talmud, accepted his own martyrdom at the hands of the Romans as the apotheosis of the commandment to love God, and was, in his patronage of the nationalist leader of his day Bar-Kokhba, the apostle of national love.[137] He then draws on two other sets of association to Aqiva, that is, romantic love and nationalism.[138]

> Yet, like a drop from the ocean, like a single spark from a tongue of flame that shoots to the sky, like one letter from a broad and vast book, one whose soul is so great will also value individual natural love in its pure worth, and will have pure natural love, and enlightened national love, and sacred divine love, full of splendor, all in array *like the tower of David nobly built* (Sg. 4:4).[139]

---

135 PAB 11, 40–42:

הספרות, הציור והחיטוב עומדים להוציא אל הפעל כל המושגים הרוחניים הצבורים בעומק הנפש האנושית. וכל זמן שחסר גם שרטוט אחד הגנוז בעומק הנפש החושבת והמרגשת, שלא יצא אל הפעל, עוד יש חובה על עבודת האמנות להוציאו. מובן הדבר שרק את אותם האוצרות שבהפתחם מבסמים הם את אויר המציאות טוב ויפה לפתח . . . ואוי למי שמשתמש ביתדו פעולה הפכית למען הרבות באשה. זעזועי הנפש שמצד רגשי האהבה הטבעית, שנוטלת חלק גדול במציאות, במוסר ובחיים, הם ראויים להתפרש על ידי הספרות בכל הצדדים שבהם היא מוציאה אל הפעל את הגניזות, אבל בשמירה היותר מעולה מנטיה לצד השכרון שיש באלה הרגשות . . . כמה ראוי לחשב לחסרון אם אותם הזעזועים הרמים והנשאים שכל כך פועלים ופעלו, ועתידים לפעול על כל טובי בני אדם, ועל כנסת ישראל ביחוד, הנובעים מאהבת אדון כל המעשים מקור הטוב והחסד, אם יפקדו אלה הרגשות ולא יחוקו בספר . . . החסרון הזה אמנם נמלא לנו בשיר האהבה אותו שהוא קודש קדשים הוא שיר השירים אשר לשלמה.

136 Shaul Magid largely concurs with this reading and suggests that Rav Kook is here positioning himself in counterpoint to his rabbinic peers. See his "Allegory Unbound: Rav Kook, Rabbi Akiva, Song of Songs, and the Rabbinic (Anti)Hero," *Kabbalah* 32 (2014): 57–82. This may indeed account for his having published this text anonymously.

137 The celebrated tale of Aqiva's martyrdom at BT Menahot 29b has generated an extraordinary amount of commentary over the centuries. A particularly well-done discussion of the reverberations of the love motif of the story in the mystical tradition is Michael A. Fishbane, *The Kiss of God: Spiritual and Mystical Death in Judaism* (Seattle: University of Washington Press, 1994). Aqiva recommends himself as a figure of nationalism within rabbinic tradition for the story of his ill-fated support of the Bar Kokhba rebellion of 135 CE. The best-known Talmudic passage in this regard is JT Ta'anit 4:3.

138 The historicity of Aqiva's support for Bar Kohba is uncertain; see Peter Schafer, "Bar Kokhba and the Rabbis," in *The Bar Kokhba War Reconsidered*, ed. Peter Schafer (Tubingen: Mohr Siebeck, 2003), 1–22.

139 PAB, 41:

אמנם כנטף מים מני ים, כזיק אחד מלהב אש שעד לב השמים, כאות אחד מספר גדול ורחב ידים, ידע איש אשר כה רמה נפשו גם כן להעריך את האהבה הפרטית הטבעית בערכה הטהור והיו לו האהבה הטהורה הטבעית והאהבה הלאומית הנאורה והאהבה האלהית הקדושה ומלאה הוד עורכות במערכה 'כמגדל דוד בנוי לתלפיות.'

The presence of the qualifying adjective in the phrase "*enlightened* national love" in a passage of otherwise unbridled lyricism (as well as his choosing to publish this text anonymously) points to a characteristic tension for Rav Kook as he sought to integrate the subjective self—and the subjective nation—into the normative precincts of the tradition.

While Rav Kook celebrates the expressive power of literature, he takes pains to distinguish himself from "mere" literary enthusiasm. Recent authors, he says, are drawn to the seemingly pastoral simplicity of the tale of Aqiva's love for his wife;[140] but the pure at heart will see Aqiva's greatness in his famous elation at seeing in the fulfillment of Biblical prophecies of doom the guarantee of prophecies of deliverance.[141]

> The luxuriant love elicited by the certain future vision will so fill his pure heart that there will be no place for the horrifying present, which he will see as but a light cloud passing over the sun, clear in the sky; only from the fount of that one whose soul expired at "One!" could there flow the decision that all the writings are sacred and the Song of Songs is the holy of holies![142]

As the journal proceeds the expressivist ethos reemerges in his discussion of the unstable relations between intellect and feeling, a key theme in *'Eyn Ayah*. The following rollicking, somewhat tortured, passage rings the changes on a series of increasingly unstable dichotomies between intellect and feeling, heresy and piety, complex belief and simple faith, Israel and the nations:

> Heart feeling, the foundation of faith, flows from the special gift of Israel; it is analogous to the barley offering [made on the second day on Passover—Y. M.] consisting of food for an animal, which is instinctively drawn only to natural feeling. Above this is the elevation of the mind. And man needs every one of his powers to emerge in full force, and yet it happens that— from human weakness—his talent for philosophical inquiry will weaken the foundations of instinctual feeling, the feeling in the heart, the foundation of faith, so too it happens that when he is a perfect believer he is prone to betray enlightenment and inner wisdom. In truth that is not the straight path, that one faculty should diminish the other; rather each should be complete as if it alone held sway. The power of faith should be so perfect that there is no room

---

140 In *'Alumah*, 44, we find in parentheses "in the manner of one of the older writes in *Luah Ahi'asaf*." This, according to Levin, was none other than Lilienblum, who in an essay entitled "Divrei Zemer," *Luah Ahi'asaf* 5 (1898): 19–24, 22, unfavorably contrasts the involved *schwarmerei* of contemporary poems with the rustic simplicity of the Aqiva story and the Song of Songs.

   The story of Rabbi Aqiva's love for his wife, another classic tale, appears in two versions, at BT Nedarim 50a and BT Ketubot 62b–63a. A sensitive reading of the differences between the two versions is to be found in Shulamit Valler, *Nashim ve-Nashiyut be-Sippurei Ha-Talmud* (Tel Aviv: Ha-Kibbutz Ha-Meuhad, 1993); on the evolution of the legend through its multiple sources, see Shamma Friedman, "A Good Story Deserves Retelling—The Unfolding of the Akiva Legend," *JSIJ* 3 (2004): 55–93.

141 He is here referring to the celebrated tale recounted at BT Makkot 24b.

142 האהבה בתענוגים למחזה העתיד הודאי מלאה כל כך את לבבו הטהור עד כי לא הניחה לו מקום גם לאנחת לב על הווה המרעיד, שהכירו רק כעב קל העובר על פני החמה הברה בשחקים הוא יכיר. רק ממקור אותו הנפש שנשמתו יצאתה באחד, נובעת ההחלטה שכל הכתובים קודש ושיר השירים קודש קדשים.

for philosophical inquiry. That is the dimension of *"man and beast" cunning in knowledge and comporting themselves like animals* [BT Hullin 5b, commenting on Ps. 36:6]. And this is the legacy distinct to Israel, whose abiding in faith comes naturally to them from the manifest inheritance of the revelation of the Shekhinah *has God ever deigned to take Himself a nation among the nations* [Deut. 4:34].[143]

Seemingly following Yehudah Ha-Levi's essentialist reading of Israel's election he modifies it with a twist at the end—Israel's innate faithfulness is not strictly genetic as such, but comes from its being the collective inheritor of revelation. For Ha-Levi that collective witness vouchsafes the truth of revelation but is not itself the basis for Israel's independently existing sanctity. Rav Kook modifies that essentialist reading of Israel's sanctity, not as inborn but as a result of having witnessed the revelation at Sinai.

While earlier in this notebook he saw heresy as a healthy reaction to vulgar popular religion, here he sees it as an unnatural delirium of willfulness and lust: "And on the other hand, heresy is unnatural, possible only by an impudence of intoxication from willfulness or lusts."[144] This helps him account for the fact that many Gentiles, perhaps more than many Jews, are believers.

> And the opposite is true of the gentiles, for them faith is precisely through delirium, for great sensible things were not revealed to them as the foundation of their faith, and so human nature does not decree faith, but rather achieves power, and consensus intoxicates as does assent to every convention.[145]

He is here using "consensus" in its rich Maimonidean sense (*Guide*, 1:2) as the principle of consent that accounts for most conventional morality: "And so it is very good for Israel that faith be simple, for its simplicity shines like a clear day, bright as the sun." But this resolution doesn't last for long. In the very next sentence:

> Yet even so the power of wisdom must be so elevated and energized as if there were no power of faith in the soul at all. And the two powers in their perfection, when they are gathered in the soul, do their work O, so beautifully. That is why Passover is joined to Pentecost by the counting of the Omer, which joins the barley offering, animal feed, feeling, to wheat, food, *the*

---

143 PAB 20, 44:

רגש הלב, יסוד האמונה, נובע מסגולה שבנפש ישראל. לעומתו הוא קרבן בעומר שעורים, מאכל בהמה, הנוטה רק לרגש הטבעי. למעלה מזה הוא העילוי בשכלי שבא אחר כך. והאדם צריך שכל כח יצא אצלו אל הפועל בכל עזו, על כן באשר מצד חולשת האדם מזדמן שבהיותו מוכשר למחקר יוחלש בו היסוד של רגש הנטיה, הרגש שבלב, היסוד האמוני, ובהיותו מאמין שלם הוא עלול למעול בהשכלה וחכמת לב. ובאמת לא זו דרך הישר שכל אחד ימעיט את חבירו, כי אם כל כח צריך שיהי' שלם כאילו הוא השולט לבדו, כה האמונה צריך שיהיה שלם כל כך, כאילו אין לו שום אפשריות של מחקר. זוהי מדרגת אדם ובהמה, ערומים בדעת ומשימים עצמם כבהמה, וזאת היא מורשה מיוחדת לישראל, שהעמידה באמונה היא אצלם טבעית מצד המורשה הגלויה של גילוי שכינה. הניסה אלקים לבא לקחת לו גוי מקרב גוי.

144 Ibid.; see Hebrew text below.

145 Ibid.; see Hebrew text below.

Tree of Knowledge was wheat [BT Berakhot 40a]. Yet distinct it is because of the teaching that each particular must exert itself to its fullest as if nothing else restrained it at all.[146]

Vital energies of all kinds must come to expression, strain one another's limits though they will.

Heresy and Eschatology

After a brief interval of just a few lines he comes at heresy again, neither as a fundamentally correct but misguided critique of vulgar religious ideas, nor a kind of delirium, but as part of a more sweeping apocalyptic movement, to which the Mishnah in Sotah once again holds the key.

The impudence of the footsteps of the Messiah is preparation for the light that is to be revealed. For true perfection must be revealed in all its full powers, even the bad ones must attain their full strength but after they repent they must be repaired and restored so that they may fittingly be used. And when they are still in their raw state they are defiled and evil and must be defended against by the force of good, with Torah and fear of God. And so it was fitting that the beginning of the renewal of Israel's kingdom be precisely from *a generation that judges its judges* [BT Bava Batra 15b] and this willfulness then be transformed into the perfect courage of *the one* [Judah—Y. M.] *who hunches, crouches like a lion* [Gen. 49:9].[147]

We first saw him suggest pre-Messianic impudence as a way to understand the confusions of modernity in his 1889 letter to Aderet, with no reference to heresy or nationalism. Here, though, he relates the power of heresy to both; he does not, though, uncritically embrace nationalism, which is as morally problematic as it is tempting.

The relationship between Jewish and gentile nationalism is, again, as we saw in *Ha-Peles*, related to the relationship between Jewish and gentile ethics. He has a problem: there is no denying the trenchancy of universal ethics and its corollary in natural law

---

146 Ibid.:

ולהיפוך (!), הכפירה היא בלתי טבעית, רק אפשרית על ידי העזה של שכרון מעקשות או תאוות. ובאומות העולם להיפוך (!), האמונה היא דוקא על ידי שכרון, כי לא נגלה להם דברים מוחשים גדולים על יסודי אמונותיהם, על כן אין הטבע האנושי גוזר להאמין, כי אם ההתגברות וההסכמה משכרת כמו שמשכרת המודה כל דבר מוסכם. על כן טוב מאד לישראל שתהיה האמונה פשוטה, מפני שפשטותה היא גם כן מאירה כיום בהיר, ברה כחמה. אף על כן (!) צריך שיהיה כח החכמה כל כך מעולה ומזורז כמו לא היה כלל כח של אמונה בנפש. ושני הכחות בשלמותם, כשמתכנסים בנפש, עושים הם את פעולתם יפה יפה. על כן מחובר הוא פסח לעצרת על ידי ספירת העומר, המחבר מנחת השעורים, מאכל בהמה, הרגש, לחיטים, האוכל, מאכל אדם, עץ הדעת חטה היה. אמנם מובדל הוא גם כן, מפני ההוראה שכל ענין יתעצם בשלימותו כאילו אין לו שום דבר מעיק כלל וכלל.

Avner Holzman

147 Ibid. 22, 44–45.

החוצפא שבעיקבא דמשיחא היא ההכנה לאור הבא להגלות. כי השלמות האמיתי צריך שיתגלה בכל כחותיו המלאים, על כן גם אותם הכחות הרעים צריכים שישובו לשלמות גבורתם, אלא שאחר שישובו צריכים הם להיות נתקנים להשתמש בהם כראוי להם. ובעודם במצבם הגולמי הם בערך הטומאה והרע, שצריך להגן מפניהם בכח הטוב, בתורה ויראת ד'. על כן גם התחלת צמיחת מלכות ישראל היתה ראויה לבא דוקא בדור ששופט את שופטיו, והשרירות הזאת נהפכה אחר כך לגבורה שלמה של כרע רבץ כאריה.

traditions, yet how are they to be squared with the exclusive revelation of Torah to Israel? He says, in terms reminiscent of his discussion some years earlier in *Metziot Qatan* and *Midbar Shur*, that while non-Jewish ethics are indeed good for human betterment in the here and now they do not elevate the spiritual condition of humanity over the long term. Natural ethics at best ease the grimmer necessities of existence; Torah transforms that existence into a positive good. But while in *Midbar Shur* this was couched in the straightforward terms of self-perfection derived from the medieval philosophical tradition, and in *Metziot Qatan*, of Kabbalistic ethics, now he casts this idea in terms of a broader drama of universal redemption. From this perspective, base nationalism and its lure of self-love is a warning of where nationalism and ethics can go if not rooted in Israel's vision of cosmic redemption.

He begins with the midrash (Exodus Rabbah 28:1) that God made Moses look like Abraham in order to appease the angels during his heavenly ascent to receive the Torah. Abraham, he writes, is the spiritual man of charity, preaching and spreading human fellowship, his Torah was thus spiritual and intellectual, and deeply human. Though Moses's Torah and its laws do not seem to be directed towards recognizably human ends, they aim at the same Abrahamic telos of creaturely peace and kindness; the difference is that Abrahamic/Noahide laws are immediately and obviously beneficial to the world, while Torah's positive effects will be revealed only in the *eschaton*, which will include every existent being. Thus, he writes, Moses's visage is truly ultimately the same as Abraham's, indeed, as Hillel famously said (BT Sabbath 31a) the essence of Moses's Torah is "love thy neighbor." Natural morality as such lacks the means truly to elevate the world as high as the longings of the soul seek to go. But Israel's Torah is all one large preparation for bringing the world to those practical paths on which are based the nature of longings for the good. Because the sacral mitzvot are educational means towards the higher morality of the future, they are of as much ethical import as are the simple kindnesses of the present. The new heavens and new earth of the future are eternally present before God even if mortal man cannot grasp them.[148]

What then is the need for those mitzvot that are not immediately translatable into universal ethical terms?

> Interpersonal mitzvot are meant to lighten the yoke of existence as it is now, within the ambit of *man would have been better off never to have been created at all* [BT Eruvin 13b].... But the sacral mitzvot [*beyn adam la-maqom*] are meant to raise us to a reality so exalted that for its sake life deserves to exist in some other existence that has not yet come to pass.[149]

In our discussion of *'Eyn Ayah* we saw how he moved to a position of the unification of opposites in language akin both to that of Schelling and Habad. There, unification was a

---

148 Ibid. 24, 45–47.
149 Ibid. 26, 47:

כלל המצות שבין אדם לחבירו הוא להקל את עול החיים מאחר שכבר הוא נמצא . . . אבל עבודת ד' שבמצות שבין אדם למקום, הם מוכנים להרים את החיים שיבואו למעלה שהיא כל כך נשגבה, שבעבורה הם כדאים להיות נמצאים במציאות אחר שלא היו.

balance of forces coursing through the world, with a strong mythic inflection. In the following passage, we see this notion of unification in a simpler personal vein, engaging that tension with explicit reference to his mounting self-perception as a leader.

> Perfection entails the unification of opposites. And so, simple faith must be well-rooted along with the love of wisdom and philosophical inquiry, as became clear to us elsewhere with regards to the relationship between the barley offering of the *Omer* and the wheat offering of Pentecost and their connection by the counting of the Omer. The same is true of love, the love of creatures by the broadest reaches of the virtue of a good heart, along with zealotry for God's Name and His Torah as a necessary result of the hatred of evil that must be fixed deep deep in the soul, though they seem like opposites, and they must be joined in the heart that desires the perfect way of our holy Torah, especially for one who is fit to be the leader of a community.[150]

This unification is not the hazy dissolution of differences in some sort of Romantic *schwarmerei*. The ontological distinctions are real and need to be maintained.

Indeed, the very next entry begins: "The foundation of knowledge is distinction—between holy and profane, light and dark, impure and pure, Israel and the nations."[151] He then proceeds to a lengthy, associative, densely allusive, and not always coherent set of musings on the significance of Moses's having been buried by God "facing the House of Pe'or" (Deut. 34:6), Pe'or being in rabbinic tradition the most obviously disgusting and nonsensical of ancient idolatries.[152] The occultation of Moses, like the various other mystifications and occultations of the world, is the work of God, and necessary in order to let every form of exile come to expression, for the purpose of serving the greater light that is to come.[153] This will in the end bring the destruction of the evil idolatries.[154] In the twists and turns of this passage one feels his struggle and perhaps unease with his own ideas; to borrow the Greek adage made famous by Isaiah Berlin, his increasingly fox-like

---

150 Ibid. 28, 49–50:

> השלימות היא מכילה התאחדות ההפכים. על כן האמונה היותר פשוטה ותמימה צריכה להיות קבועה בלב עם האהבה אל החכמה והמחקר השלם והברור, כאשר נתבאר לנו במקום אחר בענין יחש עומר דשעורין לב' הלחם שמן החיטים, וקישורם זה לזה על ידי הספירה. והוא הדין האהבה, אהבת הבריות על פי התוצאות היותר רחבות של מדת לב טוב, עם הקנאה לשם ד' ותורתו כתולדה מחוייבת מצד שנאת הרע הצריכה להיות קבועה בנפש עמוק עמוק, שנראים כהפכים, והם צריכים להתאחד בלב החפץ בדרך השלמות של תורתנו הקדושה, ביחוד למי שראוי להיות מנהיג לעדה.

151 Ibid. 29, 50:

> יסוד הדעה היא ההבדלה, הבדלה בין קודש לחול, בין אור לחשך, בין טמא לטהור, בין ישראל לעמים.

152 See the dramatically scatological characterization of the Pe'or cult in BT Sanhedrin 64a.

153 Ibid., 50:

> והנה ההעלם הזה צריך הוא לעולם, כדי ליתן מקום לכל הנסיונות והצרות של הגלויות. על כן לא הי' ראוי כלל שיעלם אורו של משה רבינו ע"ה ביסוד קבורתו על ידי בני אדם, כי אי אפשר כלל שיושג לאדם תכלית מהעלם אורו של משה רבינו ע"ה באופן שיכנס בכלל דבר טוב, ומצד הצד היותר מעולה שבחכמה היותר גבוהה שבאדם ראוי הדבר לכסוף לגילוי האורה. אבל השי"ת, אדון כל המעשים, הוא יודע כמה טובה תבא לעולם מהעלם האורה, וכמה טובות והכנות לאור יותר גדול יביא החושך השולט לשעה, על כן על פי ד' גנזו.

154 Ibid. 29–30, 50–51.

understanding of and appreciation for the diversity of things, including of religious opinions, strains against the ultimate, unshakeable hedgehog-like commitment to the one Truth of God and Torah and God's permeating presence in history and the world.[155]

An entry a little further down the road takes off on the verse "God has made all for Himself" (Prov. 16:4) He does not cite, but presumably also had in mind, the second half of the verse: "even the wicked for the day of evil."[156] Luzzatto read that verse as referring to 'Olam Ha-Nequdim, the primal emanated universe which spreads Being, as it were, horizontally, and thus contains within it the potentiality of every existent, metaphysical and physical, ontologically prior to their vertical descent and differentiation into the multiple and conflicting manifestations of existence.[157]

Rav Kook synthesizes this reading of Luzzatto's with an eschatological reading of the verse, hinted at in the Gaon's commentary to Proverbs.[158] In the Gaon's reading, the first half of the verse refers to the fifty gates of insight into God which are hidden in the world along with their rewards (fifty being the numerical equivalent of kol [all]), the last and fiftieth of which will be revealed at the eschaton, which is the "day of evil" of the verse's second half: "for the Sitra Ahrah has naught but the forty-nine gates of defilement, a fiftieth he does not have, and when his forty-nine are all filled up then he will be burned out of the world." Rav Kook takes the verse to mean that the eschaton will reveal the latent spiritual energies of all existents, including the seemingly evil.

> Even the worst things have a broader utility, moral or material, and all is of a piece with the tiqqun of the world, to the point where King David realized the usefulness of madness in the world by the situation in which he found himself.[159]

Thus, many bad moral dispositions and ideas have their place; indeed, the rabbis "hinted" that the Temple sacrifices entail an offering to the evil dimension of things.[160] Taking this idea further, the existence of "gross heresy" serves two purposes: the first is as a prophylactic against the inevitable imperfections of religious language.

---

155 Berlin's 1953 essay has been reprinted many times; see in particular the edition edited by Henry Hardy for Princeton University Press in 2013.

156 PAB 35, 53–54.

157 Ramhal, Qalah Pithei Hokhmah §39, 149.

158 Yisrael Vidovsky, ed., Sefer Mishlei 'im Perush Ha-Gra (Jerusalem: Even Yisrael, 1994), 198–200. This edition follows the standard printed edition which was available in Rav Kook's time: ואמר פעל שהוא נסתר והוא השכר הטוב הצפון . . . כי חמשים שערי בינה נבראו בעולם, ושער החמשים לא נתגלה עד ביאת הגואל, שהוא סוד עלמא דחרות; והינו כי להסטרא אחרא אינו רק מ''ט שערי טמאה, שער החמשים אין לו, וכאשר נתמלא כל המ''ט שלו אז יתבער הוא מן העולם.

159 PAB 35, 50:
כל פעל ד' למענהו. גם הדברים היותר רעים יש בהם תועלת כללי, מוסרי או חומרי, הכל בכלל תיקונו של עולם הוא, עד שעמד דוד המלך ע''ה גם בן על תועלת מציאות השגעון בעולם על ידי מעשה הבא לידיו.
He is referring to the incident described in 1 Sam. 21:16.

160 He refers to the passage in BT Yoma 21b that the altar faced north; a direction traditionally associated with evil, following Jer. 1:14.

Faithless human imagination, and its accompanying descent, brings rust onto spiritual ideas, because they represent them in false imaginings. . . . Yet humanity cannot be brought to its telos other than by the purification of spiritual concepts by knowing God and His ways in pure knowledge, clear language. . . . That is why heresy is found in every holy thing in the human race because the heretics lack the existence of spiritual concepts in their uncircumcised hearts and so there will be no place for false imaginings either.[161]

This movement of heresy in turn helps the pious refine their own religious ideas. Heresy is no mere deviance, it is a kind of purging, something suffered by the corporate body of Israel and by the human spirit as a whole.

And heresy exudes this negative quality of the negation of false imaginings until it helps those who know God and quake at His word to strip their true concepts from the *qelippot* of delusion. . . . For just as a vessel can be cleaned and scrubbed and restored to its purity, and the human soul similarly scourged and cleansed, so too the broad spiritual concept within Israel suffers terribly at the hand of evil, the general heresy, from whom suffers the general posture of faith which is the root of holiness in the world as a whole. But this suffering will not wreak evil on the true, enduring foundation of pure, sacred ideas that are the light of the world.[162]

Later, after his arrival in Palestine, Rav Kook famously developed the idea that the heretics of his time, in particular, the idealists of the Second Aliyah, were in their commitments to Jewish peoplehood and socialism the unwitting instruments of a larger truth; in his celebrated essay "The Generation," one of his more Nietzschean statements, he stated even more explicitly than he did in the unpublished *Li-Nevukhei Ha-Dor*, that they were "souls from the world of chaos" articulating a higher morality.[163] We see that idea *in nuce* here but in a wholly negative light. Through this passage he wrestles with the compelling sides of tempestuous heresy, yet in the end uses it as a reminder of the comforts, material and spiritual, of the *eudaemonia* of the medieval philosophical tradition.

---

161 PAB, 54:

המציאות של הכפירה הגסה . . . צריכה היא לשני שימושים. האחת, מפני שהציורים האמיתיים, המביאים את האדם למעלתו באהבת תורה ויראת שמים, מצד כח הדמיון הכוזב של האדם והשיקוע היתר שבכלל האנושי בענינים החמריים על ידי זה, מעלים חלודה גם כן על המושגים הרוחניים, מפני שהם מציירים אותם בדמיונות כוזבים . . . אבל אי אפשר להביא את האנושיות לתכליתה כי אם על ידי צירוף המושגים הרוחניים בדעת ד' ודרכיו בדעה טהורה, בשפה ברורה . . . על כן נמצאת הכפירה בכל קודש במין האנושי, מפני שאצל הכופרים הוא מפני העדר מציאות המושגים הרוחניים בלבבם הערל, ולכן אין מקום גם כן לדמיונות כוזבות שלהם להמצא.

162 Ibid., 53–54:

ואותה התכונה של השלילה של הדמיונות, משפעת היא הכפירה בכחה השלילי, עד שיעזרו על ידה יודעי ד' והחרדים אל דברו להפשיט את מושגהם האמיתיים מקליפות הדמיונות. . . . והנה כמו שעל ידי מריקה ושטיפה מתמרק הכלי מלכלוכו ועומד על טהרתו, והנפש האנושי על ידי יסורין הממרקין אותה נדמית לזה, כמו כן המושג הרוחני הכללי שבישראל סובל הרבה יסורין מיד הרשעה, הכפירה הכללית, שסובל ממנה כלל כח הנטיה האמונית שהיא שורש הקדושה בעולם כולו.

163 The essay appeared in his 1906 collection *'Iqvei Ha-Tzion* (Jerusalem: Shmuel Ha-Cohen Kook, 1906), 1-15.

And so the widespread heresy is useful, because when a God-fearing man beholds the depth of the evil and potential descent to be found in souls far from God, he becomes settled in his mind to put his own soul at rest even if he may not have achieved fear and love of God as much as he desires inside, and thus he follows the good median path, which is the true path of God, *the King to whom peace belongs* [Sifra Shemini 1] who desires the good of His creatures, their *eudaemonia*, joy, material and spiritual good all linked together.[164]

Hc is willing to accept real earthly conflicts because he sees them enacting larger cosmic conflicts, between forces which each must exercise themselves to the fullest to make their necessary points.

Ethics, Jesus, Shabtai Zvi, Nietzsche, *Qelippah*

Several entries on, he moves beyond discussions of universal morality to articulate a critique of Christian ethics, in sharp contrast to the broad ecumenism of *Li-Nevukhei Ha-Dor*, coming to arresting conclusions about Christian ethics' strongest contemporary critic.

Abel was [the hypostasis of] excessive mercies, as is written in the Zohar [I: 36b, 54a], and so he was not part of *tiqqun ha-'olam* as was Seth who was in man's likeness and image, composed of a mixture of characteristics, and Cain killed him because he is the zealotry of impurity, an excess of the power of judgment. Yet the two forces conjoin over time and in proper balance by Moses, whose diffusion proceeds in every generation [*Tiqqunei Zohar* §69, 114a]. And from the dimension of Abel, excessive mercies, came he who sought to blur the world, to expand the bounds of Torah's influence where it simply could not establish itself because of their [sic] evil foundation, and may perhaps be repaired by the ascent of Israel. But the attempt to exercise influence there, brings about many troubles for Israel, and thus for the world.[165]

Back in Zeimel, Rav Kook, in his commentary on the Rabbah bar bar Hannah tales, took Jesus as a simple antinomian. Here, the picture is far more complex, echoing the classic Christian typology of Abel as the prefiguration of Jesus (see Hebrews 12:22–25), while

---

164 PAB, 54:

על כן מועילה הכפירה הכללית, שמתוך שמסתכל הירא לדבר ד' את עומק הרע והירידה האפשרית להמצא בנפשות הרחוקות מגאון ד', הוא מתישב בדעתו לשום מנוחה לנפשו אף על פי שלא עלתה בידו להתגבר ביראת ד' ואהבתו בכל חפצו הפנימי, ומתוך כך הוא הולך בדרך טובה ממוצעת, שהיא דרך ד' באמת, מלך שהשלום שלו, החפץ בטובת בריותיו, באשרם, שמחתם, וטובם החמרי והרוחני העולים בחוברת.

165 Ibid. 38, 55–56:

הבל הי' רחמי יתירי, כדכתיב בזוהר, ולא הי' גם כן בכלל תיקון העולם כמו שת שהי כדמות וצלם אדם, כלול במדות ממוזגות, וקין הרגו מפני שהוא קינא דמסאבותא, דין יתר. אמנם במשך הדורות מתחברים ב' הכוחות ועומדים על משקלם, על ידי משה דאתפשטותי' בכל דור ודור. ומסטרא דהבל, רחמי יתיר, בא מי שביקש לטשטש את העולם, להרחיב גבול ההשפעה של התורה במקום שאי אפשר כלל שתתכונן בהם מפני יסודם הרע, ורק במשך דורות רבים אפשר שיתוקנו על ידי שגובן של ישראל. אמנם ההתאמצות להשפיע שמה, מסבבת צרות רבות לישראל, וממילא גם כן לעולם.

turning it on its head. Jesus, acting out of an excess of love, extended Torah's reach farther than the world could bear, to catastrophic result. Critical of Jesus though he is, he also understands Jesus's life and message as a recapitulation of the Lurianic myth of the primordial shattering of the vessels. Indeed, Jesus, in Rav Kook's reading, seems not unlike one of the "souls of *Tohu*." Moreover, Rav Kook's own feelings about Jesus are not entirely negative; he immediately proceeds to expresses his admiration, and more, in a dense series of Messianic allusions.

> *And the sons proceeding from Cain were elevated to the hewn chamber* [seat of the Great Sanhedrin—Y. M.] [BT Sotah 11a] *the Tirathites, the Shimeathites, and Suchathites* [these are the Kenites, 1 Chr 2: 55]. They set in motion the sacred execution, *and in place of the thorn will rise a myrtle* [Isa. 55:13], *a man whose name is Tzemah* [literally, growth or shoot, Zec. 7:12], *righteousness will girdle his loins, faith girdle his hips and he will judge the poor with justice and render with equity for the meek of the earth, not for the evil or arrogant, and he will smite the earth with the rod of his mouth and with the breath of his lips slay the wicked* [after Isa. 11:3–5] *and drive the defiled spirit out of the land* [Zec 12:2]. *Law will return to justice, and all the righteous in train.* [Ps. 94:15][166]

He seems to see Jesus as a failed, proto-Messiah, and the idea of Jesus as moral teacher fires his imagination, which runs away with him in the train of verses. In 1909, some five years after writing this entry, Rav Kook published an article in which he said that Jesus "possessed wondrous personal strength, his soul powerfully flowed, but he didn't escape the idolatrous weakness, the intensifying of the soul's flow, devoid of education, in morality and study."[167] In other words, Jesus was not a Christian, that is, not a foe of Judaism, but rather one whose spiritual *élan vital* overcame him, much like the freethinkers of Rav Kook's own time.

A number of East European Jewish intellectuals felt the need somehow to come to terms with Jesus and incorporate him into their understanding of Jewish history. Thus, Rav Kook's contemporary (and in some ways Hasidic doppelganger) Hillel Zeitlin, in his lengthy series of essays on good and evil in *Ha-Shiloah*, expressed admiration for Jesus and his early followers as inheritors of a prophetic ethos of radical acceptance of God's will, including the acceptance of suffering, and a correspondingly radical ethical demand.[168] Though Rav Kook sees Jesus differently, not as self-abnegating but as brim-

---

166 Ibid. 55:

והבנים הבאים מקין הם נתעלו לשבת בלשכת הגזית, תרעתים שמעתים שוכתים. מכחם נסתבב שנהרג במשפט קדוש, ותחת הסרפד יעלה הדס, איש צמח שמו, שיהי' צדק אזור מתניו והאמונה אזור חלציו, ושפט בצדק דלים והוכיח במישור לענוי ארץ, לא לרשעים וגאים. והכה ארץ בשבט פיו וברוח שפתיו ימית רשע, להעביר רוח הטומאה מן הארץ. ועד צדק ישוב משפט ואחריו כל ישרי לב.

167 The essay appeared in *Ha-Nir* 1, no. 1 (1909): 1-11, esp. 7. and is reprinted in *Ma'amarei Ha-Re'ayah*, 1-9, esp. 5–6.

168 Zeitlin's essays, a lengthy treatment of pessimism east and west, appeared in seven installments from vol. 5 (January–June 1899) through vol. 8 (July–December 1901), and Rav Kook may have read at least some of them. The discussion of Jesus and Christianity there is summarized in Shraga Bar-Sela', *Beyn Sa'ar li-Demamah: Hayav u-Mishnato shel Hillel Zeitlin* (Tel Aviv:

ming with *élan vital*, he shares (here at least) Zeitlin's view of Jesus as a radical moralist in deep continuity—and perhaps more—with Torah. This is an extraordinary statement for someone of Rav Kook's station to make, even if he made it, at this stage, only to himself.

In the entry immediately following, continuing his effort to formulate the proper balance between worldliness and godliness, he notes that according to the conventional wisdom of Mussar one cannot love both this world and the next, as was argued in *Hovot Ha-Levavot*.[169] But, he says, there is a more perfect way whereby love of this world is rightfully full and with it love of the next, albeit from an understanding of the latter's superiority and its diminution of the former. This was the way of the patriarchs, who were *yesharim*, that is, embodied natural righteousness. He endorses Nietzsche's critique of the otherworldliness of Christian ethics—a critique he would more fully develop in the coming years, and most vehemently during World War I[170]—and Nietzsche's characterization of Judaism as a comparatively more life-affirming ethic, while using the terms of Netziv's characterization of the patriarchs as naturally righteous. [171]

The immediately following, two-line entry, is stunning.

> Sh"z [Shabtai Zvi], may the name of the evil rot, was the image of Nietzsche in the Jewish religion's analogy to humanity, and just as one lost his mind, the other lost his religion. One *qelippah* relates to the footsteps of the Messiah.[172]

Ha-Kibbutz Ha-Meuhad, 1999), 35–37. Berdyczewsky, in a sketch entitled "Yeshu ben Hanan," not published until 1979, presented Jesus as merely a simple farmer who prophesied the destruction of the Temple and nothing more; perhaps this was in keeping with his Nietzscheanism and his denigration of Christian ethics, though that is not much more than speculation. The sketch was recently reprinted in *Oto Ha-Ish: Yehudim Mesaprim 'al Yeshu*, ed. Avigdor Shinan (Tel Aviv: Yediot/Hemed, 1999), 201–209. The best-known attempts to Judaize Jesus by a member of this cohort are those of Joseph Klausner. And Yosef Hayim Brenner famously elicited massive controversy in the years 1911–1913 with his essays on Jesus; see Nurit Govrin, *Meora' Brenner* (Jerusalem: Yad Ben Zvi, 1985).

169 He is referring to *Sha'ar Heshbon Ha-Nefesh* 8:3 (s.v. *ve-ha-'esrim ve-hamesh*).

170 I have discussed this at length in an unpublished lecture, 'A Halfway Despair': Rav Kook's Critique of Christianity in World War I" (lecture, Association for Jewish Studies, Washington, DC, December 17, 2005), and in chapter three of my book. See also Jason Rappoport, "Rav Kook and Nietzsche: A Preliminary Comparison of their Ideas on Religions, Christianity, Buddhism and Atheism," *Torah u-Madda Journal* 12 (2004): 99–129; and Karma Ben Johanan, "Wreaking Judgment on Mount Esau: Christianity in R. Kook's Thought," *Jewish Quarterly Review* 106, no. 1 (Winter 2016): 76–100.

171 As we noted earlier, *yosher* is the key term in Netziv's introduction to his commentary on Genesis, the defining feature of the Biblical patriarchs, "who in their conduct with gentiles and even ugly idolaters, nonetheless acted with love and concern for their welfare, which is the maintenance of Creation." *Ha-'ameq Davar*, 1:1.

172 PAB 40, 56:

ש״צ שר״י הי' דמותו של ניצ'א בערך דת היהדות לאנושיות, וכשם שזה נטרפה דעתו, כן זה יצא מדתו. קליפה אחת מתיחסת לעקבא דמשיחא.

Nietzsche's insanity, like Shabtai Zvi's apostasy, resulted from an antinomian nihilism that is no mere deviance but itself tied to the pre-Messianic apocalypse. In our earlier discussion of *Li-Nevukhei Ha-Dor,* we saw Rav Kook casting Nietzschean madness in a mystical light—and here it is an eschatological light too.

Briefly, by "one *qelippah*" I believe he intends *Qelippat Nogah*, literally, "the radiant/penumbral *qelippah*," the dimension of evil which is closest to the holy, and is, in Rav Kook's view, the hypostasis of Messiah ben Joseph. But first some words of explanation.

In an earlier Boisk notebook, briefly discussing the phenomenon of heresy, he says that "the evildoers make use of the *qelippah* itself, and will fall silent in the dark, *and the path of the righteous is like radiant light [ke-or nogah]*, precisely, *radiant*" (Prov. 4:18).[173]

Qelippot, literally "husks" or "shells," are, in Kabbalistic doctrine, the ontological membranes preventing contact with the sacred.[174] For Cordovero, the *qelippot* result from the thickening of evanescent spirit in its descent, taking up layer upon layer, and necessarily, extrusions.[175] In the Lurianic myth, the *qelippot* are deformities, excrescences of holiness resulting from the primordial catastrophic shattering of the divine, their residual power exercising a malign influence throughout human and cosmic history.[176] A central feature of Luria's Messianic doctrine was the descent of the Messiah into the realm of the *qelippot* to do final battle with them, a doctrine which came to figure prominently in Sabbatianism.

Luzzatto for his part shared the Sabbatian notion of the Messiah as a figure who descends to the realm of *qelippot* for a battle in which he himself is defeated. But he regarded Sabbatianism's chief error as its projecting this struggle into the realm of visible reality in this world—to catastrophic antinomian effect—when, in fact, it takes place in an entirely spiritual realm.[177] Luzzatto, unlike Luria, laid great emphasis on the ideal of *unio*

---

173 *Mahberot Qetanot Boisk,* 1:4, in *Qevatzim mi-Ketav Yad Qodsho,* volume 2, p. 14.

174 The basic idea is, I believe, very helpfully formulated in Isaiah Horowitz's *Shnei Luhot Ha-Berit*:

ספר השל"ה—ספר בראשית—פרשת תולדות תורה אור (ה)

כבר כתבתי בפרשת חיי שרה ענין בכל מכל כל, מאברהם יצא קליפת ישמעאל, ובן בנו הוא עשו, ומיצחק יצא קליפת עשו. וענין יציאת הקליפות מאבות הקדושים, הוא כמו קדימת הקליפה לפרי, שאי אפשר לפרי בלא הקדמת קליפה שהוא הנץ והפרח, ויעקב הוא הפרי. אבל יש סוד בדבר, כי הקליפה יש לה אחיזה בקדושה בשרשה, ובשרשה למעלה נדבקת בקדושה, והטומאה היא בהתפשטותא. ולעתיד תחזור ותטהר על ידי הצדיקים הקדושים המכניעים אותה, בסוד איזהו גבור הכובש את יצרו (אבות ד, א), שבארתי בכמה מקומות שהענין הוא אינו הורג את יצרו הרע רק כובשו תחתיו ומטהרו, שלוקח מדת היצר הרע ומשתמש בהם עבודת השם יתברך. כגון קנאה קנאת סופרים, חמדת חומד חמודה גנוזה, וכיוצא באלה הרבה. וזהו ענין שאמרו לאברהם אבינו נשיא אלהים אתה בתוכינו, כלומר בתוכיות שלנו, דהיינו בשרשינו אתה נשיא, ועל ידך נטהר לעתיד. וכל האומות הודו לזה.

175 See Bracha Sack's essay "Qelippah Tzorekh Qedushah," reprinted as chapter two of her *Be-Sha'arei Ha-Qabbalah shel Rabbi Moshe Cordovero* (Beersheva: Ben-Gurion University Press, 1995). Cordovero does have a doctrine of "*qelippah* for the sake of the sacred," akin to some of the ideas developed by Rav Kook, articulated in manuscripts with which Rav Kook would presumably not have been familiar.

176 See *'Etz Hayim, Sha'ar Ha-Gilgulim,* introduction, 23, s.v. *ve-hi be-'inyan 'onesh hivut ha-qever.*

177 See Isaiah Tishby, "Yahaso shel Ramhal el Ha-Shabtaut," in his *Netivei Emunah ve-Minut* (Jerusalem: Hebrew University/Magnes, 1964), 169–185.

mystica, and, in Moshe Idel's formulation thus "integrates the mythical-Messianic element and the spiritual element of the religious life."[178]

As for the phrase *qelippah ahat,* it appears in Yosef Gikatilla's foundational thirteenth-century treatise, *Sha'arei Orah* (chapter 5, s.v. *De'u Yisrael*). In Gikatilla's book, the four winds of Ezekiel's vision (Ezek. 1:4) are correlated to the four *qelippot,* there meaning "membranes" that separate God from Israel. The fourth wind, and the thinnest, is the one that in Ezekiel's vision has "a glowing aura," that is, *nogah.*[179] In Meir Ibn Gabbai's 1531 treatise *'Avodat Ha-Qodesh,* a comprehensive presentation of pre-Lurianic Kabbalisitic doctrine, *Qelippat Nogah* is described as "one thin shell, a divide close to the Holy."[180] It is the only "thin" *qelippah,* and the Davidic Messiah will dissolve all four *qelippot* and restore them to their original spiritual purity.[181] For Luzzatto as well, *Qelippat Nogah* is the closest to the holy.[182] And a central feature of the *eschaton* is that "the evil is peeled away from the *qelippah* and that which remains will be restored to the service of the holy and all will recognize that the holy is the true root and master of all."[183]

In his study of Messiah Ben-Joseph, Yehudah Liebes discusses at length this figure's role in the writings of the seventeenth-century Polish Kabbalists Natan Shapira and Samson Ostropoler, with which I believe Rav Kook was at least somewhat familiar.[184] And

---

178 Moshe Idel, *Messianic Mystics* (New Haven: Yale University Press, 1998), 207.

179 *Sha'arei Orah*, chapter 5, s.v. *De'u Yisrael*:

דעו ישראל כי הד' הקליפות הקשות אני רואה אותן שמבדילות ביניכם ובין יהו"ה, לפיכך אתם בגלות בבל. כיצד? בתחילה.

אמר: נפתחו השמים ואראה מראות אלהים (יחזקאל א, א), ואחר כך פירש ואמר כי מראות אלהים שראה, לא ראה אותן מיד אבל ראה ראה קודם לכן אלו הקליפות מפסיקות בינו ובין מראות אלהים. ומשום הכי פירש ואמר; ואראה והנה רוח סערה באה מן הצפון, הרי קליפה אחת; חזר ואמר 'ענן גדול', הרי קליפה שנייה; 'ואש מתלקחת', הרי קליפה שלישית; 'ונוגה לו סביב' הרי קליפה רביעית הדקה שאמרנו. ואחר כך התחיל לומר סוד ה', ואמר: ומתוכה כעין החשמל, ובסוף פירש ואמר: הוא מראה דמות כבוד יהו"ה. הרי לך אלו הארבע קליפות הן מפסיקות בין ישראל ובין יהו"ה.

180 Meir ibn Gabbai, *'Avodat Ha-Qodesh* 4:19:

ונוגה לו קליפה אחת דקה והיא מחיצה קרובה אל הקדש.

181 Ibid. 3:61:

שלשה קליפות קשות ואחת דקה בסוד ונגה לו סביב, וכשיגלה משיח בן דוד יבער רוח הטומאה מן העולם שהם הקליפות האלה, ויתגלו הארבע רוחות הקדושות הכוללות כל המעלות וישרו עליו, והנה בכאן ששה מעלות חכמה בינה עצה גבורה דעת יראת ד', וארבע רוחות והנה היו בשלמותם קודם חטא אדם.

182 See Shalom Ullman, *Sefer Maftehot Ha-Hokhmah* (Jerusalem: Mesorah, 1987), 126–127.

183 Luzzatto, *Ma'amar Ha-Ge'ulah*, ed. Mordechai Shriqi (Jerusalem: Makhon Ha-Ramhal, 1998), 41.

ולע"ל יוסר הרע מן הקליפה ומה שישאר ממנה ישוב תחת עבודת הקדושה ויכירו הכל כי הקדושה היא השורש האמיתי ואדון הכל.

This work was first published in Warsaw in 1891 and Rav Kook may have known of it.

184 See Rav Kook's first spiritual diary from Jaffa, written not long after this one, §43, 99 (ed. Ofan), where he cites Samson of Ostropol on the doctrine of qelipot in reference to Jesus; Ofan believes he is referring to Samson's *Dan Yadin,* in his commentary to Aharon ben Avraham of Cardona's *Sefer Qarnayim* (Amsterdam: press, 1747), 2a. I have not been able to find that edition, but did see this in the Zhitomir edition (1805), 8.

there we find an excerpt from Natan Shapira's *Megaleh 'Amuqot* in which Shapira identifies Messiah Ben-Joseph in his various incarnations as deriving from *Qelippat Nogah*.[185]

In other words, in this passage Rav Kook sees the advent of Nietzscheanism as of a piece with Sabbatianism, in its principled antinomianism, fracturing of all conventional religious ethics and ultimate descent into madness. Moreover both phenomena do not represent mere deviance but a principled revolt preaching liberation, a lesser liberation—that of Sabbatian antinomianism, Nietzschean *Übermenschlichkeit* and, I would submit, the lesser, merely material redemption of secular nationalism—that sets in play a grand meta-historical drama and in its eventual death sets the stage for the final Messianic redemption. And the Messianic cast of the drama demands that the realm of the *qelippot* be engaged by the truly righteous, and perhaps by those who would truly herald the Messiah.

The significance of this brief, profoundly suggestive passage for Rav Kook's thinking cannot be overstated. He forcefully registers the power of Pauline Christianity's critique of the law, perhaps of Sabbatianism's critique too, and certainly by contemporary critics of halakhah—and rather than simply rejecting that critique or seeing it as a failure of pedagogy, internalizing it, casting it as nothing less than a prelude to redemption.

A few entries later, he returns to Nietzsche's critique of ethics as chafing against the unbridled, free, divine spirit.

> At the end of days, near the Redemption, it is written *And they shall make confession for their sins and the sin of their fathers* [Lev. 25:40]. Presumably the ancestors' failing was idolatry, but we have already rid ourselves of that, and what place is there for our confession? Idolatry destroys the soul in that it renders it unreceptive to pure divine concepts and the ability to live by them, and this destructiveness works upon later generations. That is why behavioral morality must especially grow, and since it is foreign to human nature—which is made to be enlightened and free, rejoicing in God, delighting in knowledge of the truth and rejoicing in the presence of the Maker of all, God—the winds storm and those who do not grasp the telos of this necessity loom over him [sic], abuse Torah scholars and despise laws and many rules, and are destructive, and they are themselves the wreckers of the vineyard. But when we confess to the fathers' sins we recognize the negative reasons that caused us to need this long practical path of ours and we willingly accept it as medicine, and they become sweet to us.[186]

185 Liebes, "Yonah ben Amitai ke-Mashiah ben Yosef," 275.
186 PAB 44, 58–59:

באחרית הימים, קרוב לגאולה, נאמר והתודו את עונם ואת עון אבותם. ולכאורה מגרעון אבות הי' עבודה זרה, וכבר ניקינו ממנו, ומה מקום לוידויינו? אמנם עבודה זרה נקראת השחתה, שמשחתת את הנפש באופן שלא תוכל לקבל מושגים טהורים בדעת אלהים ולחיות בהם, וזאת ההשחתה פועלת על דורות הבאים. ומתוך כך הדבר גורם שהמוסר החיצוני המעשי צריך להתגדל ביותר, וכיון שהוא חוץ מטבע האדם, שהוא נועד להיות משכיל ובן חורין, מתענג על ד' ומתעלס בידיעת האמת ושמח בכבוד יוצר כל, על כן הרוחות סוערות, ומי שאינם משיגים את תכלית ההכרה הזה הם עומדים עליו, ומבזים תלמידי חכמים ומואסים במשפטים ודינים רבים, והם הם משחיתי הכרם. אמנם בהתודות עון אבות נכיר את הסיבות הרעות שגרמו שאנו צריכים לאורך מעשי כזה, ונקבל דברים אלה באהבה בתור רפואה, ויערבו לנו.

This is an extraordinary thing for a Lithuanian Talmudist to say. The law is a necessary second best to the ideal, which is to live by the light of pure divine concepts. It is, though, necessary, something which Christianity has forgotten at its peril.

> Of this it was said that '*He has placed me in darkness*' [Lam. 3:6] *refers to the Talmud of Babylonia* [BT Sanhedrin 24a]. And yet withal the midrash says '*The nation that walks in darkness*' [Isa. 9:1] *refers to those who preoccupy themselves with Talmud* [Midrash Tanhuma, Noah 3, Warsaw ed.] precisely they have seen a great light. And the Ecclesia of Israel says to its adversary who fixes his calendar by the sun,[187] and thinks he can absorb the general principles without recourse to the exacting details, which they have never achieved at all, and at the bidding of their unjust souls enact unjust laws and pervert the rights of the poor, and their deeds are oppression, banditry, murder and vile—*Do not rejoice in me O my foe, if I fall, I rise, if I sit in darkness, God is my light.* [Mic. 6:8][188]

The oppressive halakhic and spiritual problems of the present are real, and will be resolved in the *eschaton*—precisely by the receptivity of the halakhically committed to principled rebellion.

Working with Heresy, Reworking Torah Study and Theology

The problem of religious representation and language, which seemed at the outset a question of epistemological refinement and the varying perceptions of the enlightened and the masses is now part of the drama of the *eschaton* and its reworking of theology and law.

Fear of God's greatness and the corresponding reluctance to investigate the eternal mysteries by one's own devices, he writes, was a necessary historical stage, but has led to the total neglect of theology, a development he decries, since "so much darkness it brings to the world and many pathetic souls fall away from Judaism, go roving in foreign pastures, with none to bring them back." By the same token, severe asceticism was once a necessary response to "drunken sunkenness in matter." Now, though, in the near pre-*eschaton*, vital life energies reassert themselves—both for each individual and for the collective, as different energies are needed to complement and strengthen one another. It

---

187 He is here alluding to Genesis Rabbah 6, to Gen. 1:16, which says that Jacob calculates the calendar by moon and Esau, by the sun. For a survey of the identification of Esau with the Church in rabbinic tradition, see the classic essay by Gerson D. Cohen, "Esau as Symbol in Early Medieval Thought," in *Jewish Medieval and Renaissance Studies*, ed. Alexander Altmann (Cambridge, MA: Harvard University Press, 1967), 19–48.

188 PAB, 59:

> ועל זה אמרו במחשכים הושיבני זו תלמודה של בבל, ועם כל זה אמרו במדרש העם ההולכים בחושך אלו העוסקים בתלמוד דוקא הם ראו אור גדול. וכנסת ישראל אומרת לאוייבתה המונה לחמה וסוברת שיכולים כבר לקלוט את היסודות הכלליות מבלי היזקק לפרטים דקדוקיים, מה שבאמת לא עלתה בידם כלל, והם הולכים אחרי הוות נפשם לחק חקקי און ולהטות משפט דלים, וחמס ושוד רצח ונבלה מעלליהם—אל תשמחי אויבתי לי, כי נפלתי קמתי, כי אשב בחושך ד' אור לי.

was that equanimity at which Esau struck when he left Jacob limping, and that equanimity is an ultimate truth which God will restore.[189]

The fieriness of the freethinkers is not only a necessary historical stage, but something he admires. The acceptance he advocates goes beyond tolerance and the liberal acceptance of difference, and looks towards a powerful dialectical clash; the spiritual virtuoso is one who can relish the play of combat as he sees that it rounds out the Great Chain of Being to its fullest.

> Only one who can take in all of knowledge from a sweeping divine perspective can see how the details fit into a greater perfect whole. And only thus can tolerance in its broader, higher way establish itself in the heart. Imaginary tolerance only diminishes the [divine] image and the *élan vital*. . . . Conventionally tolerant people want to cool the hot feeling of faith, and with it the depth of knowing God and quaking at His word. But thus the world will not be built. The fruit of life won't emerge from diminishing the power of good. True tolerance will only come on the heels of the comprehensive, clear knowledge of how each and every existent completes the other, all the ideas are one chain stringing together all the links in one existence. Evil delineates the good.[190]

The entry immediately following dramatically depicts the extent of his willingness to accept the freethinkers' critique of religion:

> From the absence of education/enlightenment in knowing God which is the basic reason for exile. . . there have emerged disordered ideas regarding the true meaning of Torah. . . . And there is no remedy for this but to find masters of negation emptied of every sacred idea. Their being devoid of any religious ideas means they are devoid of the mistaken ones too. And so when the *élan vital* brings them to experience the clashing of different human forces, though they may engender some evils and pains by their *formlessness and void* [Gen. 1:2], the result of privation and emptiness, yet much good will also come, to purify the field of sacred ideas from vain imagining and every alien tendency.[191]

---

189 PAB 47, 60–61.
190 Ibid. 48, 62:

המשקיף על כללות המחשבה הסוקרת מתחילה ועד סוף בצפיה האלהית, רק הוא ישכיל איך כל הפרטים מתאחדים לכלל גדול שאי אפשר שיחסר ממנו מאומה. רק על ידי ההשקפה הכללית הזאת יבא מעמד הסבלנות בלבבות במובנה היותר רחב ויותר רם. הסבלנות הדמיונית היא רק ממעטת את הדמות, מקטנת אל כח החיים של כל נטיה. . כפי הרגיל, חפצים בעלי הסבלנות לקרר את חם רגש האמונה, את עמק רעיון דעת ד' והחרדות אל דבריו. אבל לא באופן כזה יבנה העולם. לא ממיעוט כח טוב אפשר להוציא פרי חיים. אמנם הסבלנות שהיא אמיתית, תבא רק לרגלי ידיעה הכוללת והברורה איך שכל המצוי כלו מתאחד ומשלים איש את רעהו, כל הרעיונות כולם הם כשלשלת אחת המחרזת את כל פרטי החוליות למציאות הזאת. הרע מבחין את הטוב. . . .

On his later views on tolerance, see Ross, "Between Metaphysical and Liberal Pluralism": 61–110. I have discussed this in my "Ha-Havayah Ha-Sovlanit le-Sugehah," *Aqdamot* 23 (2009): 219–228.

191 PAB 49, 62–63:

מתוך חסרון ההשכלה בדעת ד', שהוא יסוד סיבת הגלות . . . נמשכו כמה שיבושים בציורים הנוגעים לאמתת דיעות התורה . . . על כן איך להטהר מזה אי אפשר כי אם על ידי מציאות בעלי השלילה שהם מנוערים מכל רעיון קודש. מחסרון הציורים הרוחניים שבנפשם אין מקום גם כן לציורם דמיוניים להתערב בהם, על כן בהתערבם על ידי אותו

He has not, to be sure, become antinomian. He asserts the law and recognizes that the temptations of antinomianism predate Christianity: "How venerable is the idea that one could attain true knowledge and abiding ideals only through deeds especially founded in the divine compass of Torah. Philo in his day did battle with those who would destroy praxis."[192]

Turning to present day ideologies, while nationalism's rise has resulted from the diffusion of Jewish ideas, it will come to naught if not grounded in the law. Indeed, the contemporary trend of freethinking must itself pass away.

> And now we see that the Jewish spirit is on every tongue, national ideals are common currency, but how can they become firmly established in the nation over time, if not by Torah and her mitzvot? And so there must be a return to Torah which is only possible through faith and deep religious feeling and a pure heart. And so we must cast off all the *hutzpah* and antinomianism and its causes and find a way to make life pleasant in a way that brings with it the yoke of Torah.[193]

There follows this poignant reflection on his own difficulties with the study of halakhah:

> Many have fallen away because they betrayed their own character. How? Let's say someone is talented at aggadah, and constant focus on halakhic matters ill suits him . . . but because he does not recognize this talent of his he immerses himself in Talmud and commentaries because he sees that that is the custom, and he comes to feel a hatred in his heart for that in which he works, because in truth the immersion in this runs counter to his nature. And if he had found a role that had him deal with the subject fitting his soul, then he would immediately feel that the *nausea* [emphasis added—Y. M.][194] that comes over him when dealing with halakhah doesn't derive from some deficiency in those sacred and necessary studies but because his soul doesn't incline after them.[195]

הכח החיים שמערב ומפעיל כחות האנושיות אלו מאלו, אף על פי שכמה רעות ומכאובים הם מסבבים על ידי התוהו ובוהו שלהם, על ידי ההעדר והריקנות, מכל מקום הטובה גם כן באה, לזכך את האויר של המקומות ששם הציורים הקדושים נמצאים מכל דמיון וכל נטיה זרה . . . .

192 Ibid. 51, 63–64:

מה ישנה היא הדעה שאי אפשר להגיע לקנין של דיעות אמתיות ואידיאלים קבועים כי אם על ידי המעשים שהם נוסדו להם ביחוד במחוגה האלהית שבתורה. כבר נלחם פילון היהודי בזה עם המהרסים המעשיים בימיו.

193 Ibid:

ועכשיו הנה רוח היהדות שגור על כל לשון, האידיאליים הלאומיים עוברים לסוחר, אמנם במה יהיו נקבעים ונקנים באומה לדורותיה, הלא רק במעשים, בקיום התורה ומצותיה. אם כן הלא החובה גלויה לשוב לתורה, ואי אפשר גם כן התשובה אל התורה כי אם באמונה בעומק רגש הדת בלב שלם. אם כן הלא צריכים לזרות הלאה כל פריצות ופריקת עול וכל הגורם לזה, ולבקש דרך להנעים את החיים באופן המושך עמו את עולה של תורה.

194 When Zvi Yehudah Kook reprinted this passage in *Orot Ha-Torah* 9:6 he substituted "oppositional feeling," *hargashah nigudit*, for "nausea."

195 PAB, 64:

הרבה יצאו לתרבות רעה מפני שבגדו בתכונתם. כיצד, הרי שאחד מוכשר לדברי אגדה, ועניני הלכה אינם לפי תכונתו להיות עסוק בהם בקביעות, ומתוך שאינו מכיר כשרונו הוא משתקע בגמרא ומפרשים מפני שרואה שכן הוא המנהג, והוא מרגיש בנפשו שינאה למה שעוסק בהם, כיון שבאמת אין ההשתקעות באלו הענינים לפי טבעו. ואם הי' מוצא את תפקידו להתעסק באותו המקצוע המקביל לתכונת נפשו, אז הי' מרגיש מיד שאותה הבחילה שבאה

This passage also serves as a jarring reminder that all the while Rav Kook was writing this notebook he was working as an active halakhist and communal rabbi; this seems trivial but is worth recalling given the far-reaching ideas he engaged. And also reminds us how crucial for the emergence of his dialectical perspective was his own reckoning and self-understanding.

This observation about the need to tailor one's study to the specific contours of personality is not only pedagogical, but metaphysical. The individual's own nature is God-given, is part of God's plan for the world, of a teleology of cosmic repentance and return. In the journal's penultimate entry we read.[196]

> *Repentance preceded the world* [BT Pesahim 54a] because perfected life is precisely natural and nature is blind, and so sin is necessary, since *there is no mortal who does not sin* [Eccles. 7:20] and repentance repairs the damage. But that a man be free of sin because he has undone natural life, that is the greater sin. *And he shall atone for sinning against his soul* [Num. 6:11].[197] And so the foundation of the world is repentance, the world of freedom *'olam ha-herut*, for whose sake God's Name is called "life."[198]

We saw in *Li-Nevukhei Ha-Dor*, his affirmation of the religious value of, in Isaiah Berlin's terms, positive freedom; here, the roots of that affirmation in classic Kabbalistic ideas is made clear, in his association of repentance with "freedom" and with the appellation "living God."[199] In the Kabbalah, freedom, identified with the sefirah of *Binah*, denotes a realm of being that is free of sin and free of the ordinary causalities that trammel human beings in the sinful lower world of the law. And yet one cannot help concluding that the semantic range of "freedom" has in the course of this diary been widened to include both the political, existential and antinomian claims of freedom by contemporary freethinkers. The rebellions of secular nationalists and socialists, their assertion of freedom, as well as

---

לו בעסקו בהלכה לא באה מצד איזה חסרון עצמי באופן של הלימודים הקדושים והנחוצים הללו, אלא מפני שנפשו אינו נוטה להם. . . . .

196 It is worth nothing that the entry preceding this, PAB 55, 66–67, discusses the theory of evolution, so pronounced in *Li-Nevukhei Ha-Dor*, but assimilated here into the development of the cosmos.

197 He presumably has in mind the Talmudic comment (BT Nedarim 10a) that this refers to the Nazirite who has assumed a supererogatory vow of asceticism.

198 PAB 56, 67–68:

התשובה קדמה לעולם, מפני שהחיים השלמים הם דוקא על פי הטבע, והטבע אינו בעל הסתכלות, על כן החטא מוכרח, אין אדם צדיק בארץ אשר יעשה טוב ולא יחטא (!): והתשובה מתקנת הקלקול. אבל שיהיה האדם בלתי חוטא מפני שיבטל החיים בטבעם, זהו עצמו החטא היותר גדול. וכפר עליו מאשר חטא על הנפש. על כן יסוד העולם היא התשובה, עולם החירות, שעל שם כך מכנים שם ד' אלהים חיים.

Zvi Yehudah Kook reprinted this text in *Orot Ha-Teshuvah* 5:6, with substantial changes.

199 Moshe Cordovero, *Pardes Rimonim* 23:8:

חירות הוא בבינה כי משם יוצא החפשיות והחירות.

Ibid., 23:1:

אלהים חיים יתייחס לפעמים אל הבינה מטעם שהיא משפעת חיים לכל הספירות.

The association of *Binah* with repentance is of course a staple of Zoharic literature. For Cordovero's own formulation see *Pardes Rimonim* 23:22.

their assertion of Jewish political freedom, is not the anti-Jewish catastrophe it seems but itself part of the Messianic *denouement* of history.

The last, brief, entry seems a comment on the act of his writing the diary as a whole: "Sensible things are a kind of shorthand abbreviation for thoughts grasped in speech and writing, and they themselves are a shorthand abbreviation for the inner thought."[200]

In the course of this notebook he makes almost no mention of the Land of Israel. And yet he has come to cast the religious deviance of his time as nothing less than the opening stage of the Messianic drama, a stage which requires engagement. Would he have come to this conclusion if he were not en route to Palestine? Possibly, as Jewish life in fin-de-siècle Russia provided more than enough ferment to fire the imagination. And we have seen his lengthy discussions in *Li-Nevukhei Ha-Dor* proceeding with little reference to Zionism. We do, though, see here how deeply that ferment registered on him, and how rich a conception of the subject he had attained, before his arrival in Jaffa.

And we see how deep ran the esoteric roots of his public-facing writings, in *Ha-Peles* and *Li-Nevukhei Ha-Dor*, and how more far-reaching his private musings were.

Leaving Boisk

By the late fall of 1903 he was making preparations to leave Boisk, but still there were delays.[201] He finally left on the first day of Parashat Emor 1904 (9 Iyar 5664/April 24, 1904). Many townspeople accompanied his carriage, and for a long distance. Eventually he stopped, stood up and gave one last homily. He cited the well-known rabbinic dictum (BT Berakhot 34a) that one ought to take leave of a friend with a word of Torah. From this, he said, we learn that the real pain of separation is the interruption in Torah, which life sometimes demands. But because our inner connection remains, he said, we are never truly separate from one another. God, he said, has commanded us to leave for the Land of Israel, but we do so with the faith that we will meet again when God redeems His people.[202]

Directly from Boisk he proceeded to the regional capital of Jelgava (Yiddish, Mitoi; German, Mitau) in order to obtain a passport, thence to Riga, on to Dvinsk (near his hometown of Griva), and from there to Vilna, where Isaac Blazer, a leading disciple of Salanter, who would soon to move to Palestine himself, visited him in the train station. A planned side trip to Paris fell through and so the Kook family proceeded to Odessa.[203] There he waited for three days till boarding the boat which, after stops in Istanbul, Izmir,

---

200 PAB 57, 68:

המוחשים הם בערך נוטריקון להמחשבות הנתפסות בדיבור ובמכתב, והם נערכין לנוטריקון להמחשבה הפנימית.

201 See his letter to his brother, *Igrot*, 1:13–14.

202 This is recounted in Yehudah Gershuni, *Sha'arei Tzedeq* (Jerusalem: n.p., 1994), 206, Even-Hen, *Rav u-Manhig*, 127.

203 As noted above, Shimon Rokah thought it wise for Rav Kook to meet the moderate chief rabbi of France, Zadok Kahn; Zvi Yehudah Kook says that the motivation for trying to travel to Paris was the hope of meeting with Baron Rothschild.

and Beirut,[204] steamed for Palestine. The next day, Friday, May 13, 1904, he laid anchor in Jaffa; Shimon Rokah, Bezalel Lappin, and Yoel Moshe Salomon rowed out to meet him and in their company he came ashore and took his first steps on the Land of Israel, bending low to kiss the ground.[205]

---

204 In Izmir he visited the Palagi rabbinical family, and in Beirut he stayed overnight with a family named Elshtein, in-laws of Bezalel Lefin, a local Jaffa figure and one of his supporters.

205 This account by Zvi Yehudah Kook is recounted in *Shivhei Ha-Reʿayah*, 74, and reprinted in Neriah, *Tal*, 190–191. For a discussion of Rav Kook's first days in Jaffa and the newspaper accounts of his arrival, see Neriah, *Sihot*, 310–312, and, in greater detail A. R. Malachi, "Ha-Pulmus ʿal Ha-Rav Kook ve-Sifro *Eder Ha-Yaqar*," ʿ*Or Ha-Mizrah* 15, no. 3 (1965): 136–144.

Conclusion

We are all mysteries to others, as to ourselves, and great thinkers retain their hold on us in no small measure because of the sense of mystery they evoke, receding as they do before our grasping analyses. But we do the best we can.

Transformations in the Land of Israel

We are, at the close of our inquiry, better able to appreciate significant developments in Rav Kook's later thought, how his early years laid foundations for his heroic decades, and what decisively changed. Some key foundations of his thought—his concern for the relations of body and soul, his sensitivity to the unique truths of self-expression and subjectivity, his receptivity to principled critiques of tradition, his seeing the social and political movements of his time enacting a Messianic drama whose dialectics reflected the dialectics he had learned to appreciate by observing his own complicated and conflicted soul—were indeed in place before his move to Jaffa. Other key features of his thought came later.

Seven Shifts: From Top-Down to Bottom-Up

What, then, changed after his arrival in Jaffa?[1] First, as we have seen, while Jewish peoplehood was from the beginning a very significant category of analysis for him, the Land of Israel was not in itself a distinct category through which he analyzed multiple dimensions of the religious life. This changed dramatically after his arrival in Jaffa, and deepened in his exile from the Land during World War I. Second, his understanding of Jewish peoplehood became, for lack of a better word, increasingly essentialist, as did his understanding of the Land of Israel, taking on fixed, ontological characteristics, as their this-worldly manifestations are entirely collapsed into very abstract metaphysical categories.

---

1 My presentation here in many ways concurs with that put forth by Bin-Nun in his wonderful *Ha-Maqor Ha-Kaful*, 205–210, though I am parsing it with some differing emphases and in relation to the currents of modern thought we have been looking at throughout. Moreover, Bin-Nun comes close to endorsing a kind of essentializing monistic thinking about religious and secular Jewry that is at cross-purposes with the humane polity he hopes his reading of Rav Kook's ideas can help bring about.

Of course, nations have always been with us—the question posed by the rise of nationalism is how do we understand nationhood and what are the political stakes of those understandings? There are thinkers, and Rav Kook was one of them, for whom nationalism appeals, not just as a helpful program, but as an answer to pressing theological questions. In Rav Kook's case, questions of the relationship of body and soul, the universal and the particular, and the enduring meaning of Jewish peoplehood in an age when so many of its young arise against it in idealistic rebellion, find an answer in the project of Jewish national rebirth and revival.

A key feature of the secularized dispensation of modernity is the distinction between religion and politics, not merely as discrete functions or as, in Augustine's doctrine of the "two cities," two parallel moral realms, but as different ontological realms: one—namely, politics—necessary; the other—religion—ontologically unnecessary, contingent, safely nestled, or, depending on your preference, walled in from the monopoly of legitimate violence claimed by the modern state.[2] As a result, moderns can meaningfully question the existence or nonexistence of God in the abstract, while questioning the existence of politics and society is literally inconceivable. Nationalist religion undoes that distinction, giving religion and its transworldly claims the ontological necessity of politics.[3] Rav Kook married the ontological necessity of the nation to the ontological necessities of God and the world—and to the ontological necessity of the universally minded ethical teachings of God's Torah. That exhilarating and electrifying mix is hard to sustain outside a Messianic framework, and even harder when it fails to make room, as Rav Kook ultimately failed to do, for the truly darkest human impulses towards violence and the will to power.

Rav Kook arrived in Jaffa with his burgeoning ideas of subjectivity in hand. He then projected them or, if you will, expanded their frame of reference onto the nation, endowing the nation with the dynamic, tensile subjectivity of the individual, and reciprocally charging the individual's subjectivity with the vastly richer being of the nation.[4] The strongly universalist dimension we saw in his early writings persisted, and became even more intense, yet it did so in a conceptual field more electrically charged in all directions.

---

2   For a brief, penetrating discussion of this large subject, see Leora Batnitzky, *How Judaism Became a Religion* (Princeton: Princeton University Press, 2011), esp. chapters one and three.

3   See my "What is a Nation-State For?" in *Defining Israel: The Jewish State, Democracy and the Law*, ed. Simon Rabinovich (Cincinnati: Hebrew Union College Press, 2018), 299-311, as well as my "Reflections on the Nationalization of Religion after Balfour" (lecture given at Harvard University, Cambridge, MA, November 5, 2017), https://brandeis.academia.edu/YehudahMirsky. The large debates over the constructedness of nationalism I leave for another time. For now, suffice it to say I follow the views of Anthony Smith, Azar Gat, and others who see modern nationalism as a modernization of preexistent forms of identity.

4   This central feature of Rav Kook's thought is explored at length and insightfully by Dov Schwartz, *The Religious Genius in Rav Kook's Thought; National "Saint?"* (Boston: Academic Studies Press, 2014). I largely concur with Schwartz's presentation, though see more tension running through those ideas, and would suggest greater attention to how they shifted over time and their emerging out of his pre-nationalist metaphysics and theology.

Third, the dialectical worldview which he developed as a means of managing the relations of intellect, feeling, and imagination, was also increasingly projected by him onto the stage of history and onto concrete historical epochs. In this, he increasingly followed Krochmal, both in the latter's broad Hegelianism and in seeing history as an object of contemplation and source of revelation, in the way that natural science and physics were for Maimonidean philosophers.[5]

These three shifts did much to shift the stance that I have described as an historical theodicy of modernity into full-blown Messianism and the integration of *leumiyut* into the heart of his thought. They also open the possibility that Orthodoxy itself is but a phase of human history en route to resolution in a higher synthesis.[6]

The deep political meanings—to the present day—of these three shifts go well beyond our scope here. Suffice it to say that he did not foresee the disturbingly chauvinistic and violent uses to which these notions of his would be put. It is worth recalling that nationalism was transformed after World War I from a moral claim asserted by minority groups against empires into claims which they asserted against each other. The degree to which he recognized that shift is unclear. Moreover, he very much needed Messianism to rescue some meaning from the chaos of modernity. The Messianic perspective provided a kind of gravitational energy which enabled him to hold together the seeming incommensurables of the spiritual and sociopolitical conflicts of his time, and this well before he began seriously to engage with Zionism. He seems not to have known that he was playing with fire.

In saying this, I am well aware that many of his latter-day disciples argue that these chauvinist and violent interpretations are precisely what he intended and that they are simply faithfully following their master's teachings. I would argue in response that Rav Kook was and is a large and capacious thinker, whose ideas admit of multiple interpretations, interpretations which are themselves moral choices.[7]

---

5   A helpful treatment of Rav Kook's historiosophy is Yosef Ben-Shlomo, "Historiyah ve-Utopia be-Mishnatam shel Ha-Maharal ve-shel Ha-Re'ayah Kook," in *Historiosofiyah u-Mada'ei Ha-Yahadut*, ed. Michael F. Mach and Yoram Jacobson (Tel Aviv: Tel Aviv University Press, 2005), 37–65. On Krochmal's historiosophy, see Harris, *Nachman Krochmal*, chapters 8–10. For the latter point on history as the object of contemplation, see Micah Goodman, "Beyn Mevukhat Ha-Zeman le-Limud Qor'ot Ha-Zeman: 'Iyun Mehudash bi-Tefisat Ha-Historiyah shel Ranak," *Da'at* 57–59 (2006): 210–228. Rav Kook regularly downplayed Krochmal, and I think that was because he wanted to root his own historiosophy, its Hegelianism notwithstanding, firmly in the Kabbalah.

6   Thus the "three camps" into which he divides the Jews of *Li-Nevukhei-Ha-Dor*—liberals, Diaspoara nationalists and Land of Israel Zionists—are reconfigured as liberals, nationalists, and Orthodoxy. See LNH, 211-212, SQ 3:1-2, *Orot*, 70-72.

7   The idea of interpretation as a moral choice deserves further exploration; for now see Hanoch Ben-Pazi, *Ha-Parshanut ke-Ma'aseh Mussari: Ha-Hermeneutica shel Emmanuel Levinas* (Tel Aviv: Resling, 2012).

To take just one example, Zvi Tau, a leading contemporary figure, argues, in part on the basis of passages we have seen in *Midbar Shur* regarding Esau's martial qualities being innate while Jacob's are acquired, that nothing that Israel does, when acting in its corporate, national

That Messianic nationalism need not be the only reading of Rav Kook from within the religious Zionist rabbinic fraternity is illustrated by the trajectory of Yehudah Amital (b. 1924). Amital smuggled an anthology of Rav Kook's writings into a Nazi labor camp, emigrated to Israel, founded a leading yeshivat hesder in Gush Etzion, emerged as a leader of Gush Emunim, and eventually became the spiritual leader of Israel's small religious peace movement. Further, in the wake of the Rabin assassination, he became a cabinet member in the Labor government, all the while rooting his ideas in the teachings of Rav Kook.[8] And other careful readers of Rav Kook, inside and outside the academy, offer self-reflective readings of ways in which his teachings can serve as sources for moral reflection in terms congenial to humanism, feminism, and more.[9]

Fourth, we see in his post-1904 thought a crucial, Kabbalistically inflected, theologizing of all human history, and this by the daring transformation, terminologically and

---

capacity and for the sake of its national-metaphysical telos, no matter how violent, can properly be regarded as unethical, since Israel's very essence is moral by definition. See his *Le-Emunat 'Itenu*, vol. 4 (Jerusalem: Hosen Yeshu'ot, 2001), 55–92. For discussion of all these figures, see Fischer's magnificent "Self-Expression and Democracy in Radical Religious Zionist Ideology" and Ahituv, "Erkei Mussar u-Le'umiyut be-Hugei Merkaz Ha-Rav," 279–306 and the other studies of Fischer's mentioned in this work's introduction. For a remarkably penetrating discussion of how Rav Kook's ideas in many ways cut against the theological justifications of violence offered by Rabbi Yitzhak Ginsburg, see Don Seeman, "Violence, Ethics and Divine Honor in Modern Jewish Thought," *Journal of the American Academy of Religion* 73, no. 4 (2005): 1015–48.

8   See Yehudah Amital, "Mashma'utah shel Mishnat Ha-Rav Kook le-Doreynu," in Ish-Shalom and Rosenberg, eds., *Yovel Orot*, 333–341, and, more generally, Alan Brill, "Worlds Destroyed, Worlds Rebuilt: The Religious Thought of R. Yehudah Amital," *Edah Journal* 5, no. 2 (2006), https://library.yctorah.org/files/2016/09/Worlds-Destroyed-Worlds-Rebuilt-The-Religious-Thought-of-Yehudah-Amital.pdf; and Yehudah Mirsky and Reuven Ziegler, "Torah and Humanity in a Time of Rebirth: Rabbi Yehuda Amital as Educator and Thinker," in *Torah and Western Thought: Intellectual Portraits of Orthodoxy and Modernity*, ed. Meir Y. Soloveichik, Stuart W. Halpern, and Shlomo Zuckier (Jerusalem/New York: Maggid Books/the Straus Center for Torah and Western Thought, 2015), 179–217.

     Amital's Messianic period is reflected in his *Ha-Ma'alot mi-Ma'amaqim* (Alon Shvut: Yeshivat Har Etzion, 1978); his later views are to be found in *Ve-Ha-Aretz Natan li-Vnei Adam* (Alon Shvut: Herzog College and Tevunot, 2005), which also gives a good idea of his educational philosophy. A discussion of Amital's views on the Holocaust and his explicit disagreements theron with Zvi Yehudah is provided by Moshe Mayah, *'Olam Banuy ve-Harev u-Vanuy: Ha-Rav Yehudah Amital le-Nokhah Zikhron Ha-Shoah* (Alon Shvut: Herzog College, 2002). His halakhic writings are gathered in his *Resisei Tal* (Alon Shvut: Yeshivat Har Etzion, 2005). See also Kalman Neuman, *Quntres Re'ayah Shelemah* (Jerusalem: Meimad, 1994).

9   In some respects, the volume of essays on Rav Kook coedited by Kaplan and Shatz, *Rabbi Abraham Isaac Kook and Jewish Spirituality*, drawing as it does on American scholarship on Rav Kook and liberal-minded Israeli academics, presents to some extent a collective picture of Rav Kook somewhat at variance with that usually found in Israeli writings. Similarly, Ben-Zion Bokser's anthology and translation *Abraham Isaac Kook* (New York: Paulist Press, 1978) highlights the more universalist dimensions of the teachings. Zohar Maor discusses Rav Kook's influence on some of the activists of the the Brit Shalom bi-nationalism movement of

conceptually, of "ideals" into "Divine Ideals," by which he means the sefirot qua divinely energized vessels of the metaphysical, epistemological, moral, and historical categories of human understanding and action.[10] Thus, at a stroke he synthesized the Kantian Idealism of Hermann Cohen with his own decidedly un-Kantian celebration of personal subjectivity and emerging philosophy of history.[11]

Fifth, we see him turn towards Hasidic teachings, in several ways. Above all, he came to see himself as a *tzadiq* in that concept's meaning in Hasidism, that is, as the individual who is the conduit for spiritual energy to his time and place, and whose own spiritual ups and downs both mirror and affect the ups and downs of the time.[12] At the same time, this conception was also married to issues of Messianism, and eventually prophecy, not to mention nationalism and the tides of history, well beyond the range of most Hasidic thought.[13]

In some ways, his mountingly immanentist ideas seem to resemble Hasidic ideas of *'avodah be-gashmiyut*, worship through the corporeal, and *ha'alat nitzotzot*, the raising of the fallen sparks of divinity latent in the material world via direct engagement with that very material world. Yet, as observed, he was preoccupied with the idea of the body even in his early years, and from within the terms of Lithuanian Kabbalah.[14] Not only did he not need Hasidic terminology given how much was available to him through Lithuanian Kabbalah, it did not give him the historical teleology he needed—something for which Hasidic thought would await until Menachem Mendel Schneersohn, the seventh, and final rebbe of Habad.[15] Habad theology shaped his later metaphysics and he crucially had

---

the 1930s and 1940s in his "Beyn Anti-Kolonializm le-Post-Kolonializm: Orientalizm, Biqoret ve-Ha-Hilun shel Brit Shalom," *Theoriyah u-Viqoret* 30 (2007): 13–38.

A different sort of liberalizing reading of Rav Kook is provided by Tamar Ross in those writings of hers which use Rav Kook's ideas as a basis for Jewish feminist theology (Rav Kook's own decidedly un- and anti-feminist halakhic rulings notwithstanding); see her *Expanding the Palace of Torah: Orthodoxy and Women* (Hanover: University Press of New England and Brandeis University Press, 2004) and "Hebeitim Feministiyyim be-Mishnato Ha-Utopit shel Ha-Rav Kook," in *Derekh Ha-Ruah: Sefer Ha-Yovel le-Eliezer Schweid*, vol. 2, ed. Yehoyada' 'Amir (Jerusalem: Hebrew University/Van Leer Institute, 2005), 717–752.

10   On this see Yosef Ben-Shlomo, "'Ha-Idealim Ha-Elohiyyim be-Torato shel Ha-Rav Kook," *Bar-Ilan Annual of Jewish Studies* 23 (1988): 73–86, and Ben-Shlomo, "Shlemut ve-Hishtalmut be-Torat Ha-Elohut shel Ha-Rav Kook," *'Iyun* 33, nos. 1–2 (1984): 289–309.

11   The connection to Cohen was first mentioned by Zvi Yehudah Kook in a letter to Yosef Hayim Brenner, and is carefully unpacked in Avivi, "Aqdamot."

12   See, at length, Sherlo, *Tzadiq Yesod 'Olam*.

13   There are a number of studies of Rav Kook's relationship to Hasidic thought in the Tamar Ross festschrift *Ruah Hadashah be-Armon Ha-Torah*, ed. Ronit Ir-Shai and Dov Schwartz (Ramat Gan: Bar-Ilan University Press, 2018).

14   For brief discussion comparing his ideas to the Hasidic teachings, see the wonderful work by the tragically late Tsippi Kaufmann *Be-Khol Derakhekah Da'ehu*, 125n108.

15   Much has been written on Schneersohn—for a brief, excellent summary of his historiosophy and its practical ramifications, see Tomer Persico, "Chabad's Lost Messiah," *Azure* 38 (2009): 82–127.

recourse to the idea which Habad shared with Schelling—the unification of opposites, *ahdut ha-hafakhim*. [16]

Yet, in his innovative reworking of these doctrines, the opposites being united are not only metaphysical categories, or facets of the soul, but concrete, and antagonistic, social groups and ideologies; the raising of fallen sparks proceeds through engagement in a very secular politics and a very modern conception of historical change. All the while, he developed an increasingly ecstatic spirituality of *devequt*, glimmers of which we have seen in the later passages of *'Eyn Ayah* and his last spiritual diary from Boisk.

Sixth, and speaking of the diary, his having, after experimenting with a range of genres, finally found his most distinctive voice in the spiritual diary, seems of a piece with this ecstatic *devequt*. Moshe Idel has written: "If the Gaon of Vilnius is the most accomplished paragon of Jewish literacy and writing, the Besht is the great oral teacher."[17] It seems to me that Rav Kook's moving towards Hasidut was of a piece with his finding in the spiritual diary a genre which resembles the spontaneity and vitality of orality; indeed his concluding his meditations with Biblical verses, charged in his readings with newly revelatory energy, highlights the quasi-oral character of this sort of writing.[18] And this arching towards literature was also of a piece with his own quest for the revival of prophecy.

In a related vein, we have seen him writing in two distinct registers in his early works—exoteric and esoteric—as, for instance, the explicitly Kabbalistic discussions of *Metziot Qatan* enunciated in the philosophical tones of *Midbar Shur*. In the journals of his Palestine years, the two registers are fused—as he writes without explicit reference to Kabbalistic sources, and in a seemingly exoteric, literary idiom, which on closer inspection is utterly suffused with Kabbalistic ideas and his own reworkings of Kabbalistic terminology.[19]

---

16 On the place of Habad teachings in his metaphysics, see Dov Schwartz, "Me-'Eyn Sof' le-'Or Eyn Sof': be-Hagut Ha-Re'ayah: Li-Meqorotehah shel Ha-Havhanah Be-Hasidut Habad," in *Ruah Hadashah be-Armon Ha-Torah: Sefer Yovel likhvod Professor Tamar Ross*, ed. Ronit Ir-Shai and Dov Schwartz (Ramat Gan: Bar-Ilan University Press, 2018), 119–165. On the unification of opposites in classic Habad teachings, see Elior, *Torat Ahdut Ha-Hafakhim*.

17 Idel, *Kabbalah and Interpretation*, 475.

18 See Weisbard, *Parshanut* and Krumbein, "El Ha-Maqor." I am, for my understanding of the place of orality in religion, deeply indebted to William A. Graham, *Beyond the Written Word: Oral Aspects of Scripture in the History of Religion* (Cambridge: Cambridge University Press, 1987).

19 Explicating this at length is much of the burden of Yosef Avivi's recent, remarkable *Qabbalat Ha-Re'ayah*, 4 vols. (Jerusalem: Yad Ben-Tzvi, 2018). Elliot Wolfson powerfully unpacks the meaning of Rav Kook's fusion of these two registers in his "Secrecy, Apophasis and Atheistic Faith in the Teachings of Rav Kook," in *Negative Theology as Jewish Modernity*, ed. Michael Fagenblat (Bloomington: Indiana University Press, 2017), 131–160.

Seventh, we see his increasingly immanentist orientation, which some have described as panentheism, the idea that all is contained within God.[20] With time, this immanentism became a full-blown theology of culture.[21]

Correspondingly, if the leitmotif of his earlier work is *yosher*, the "straightening out," if you will, of the created world, the leitmotif of his mature thought is *qodesh*, the sacred, which is the saturation of creation with the divine light radiated on it from above and below.[22] Indeed, his constant use, not of the familiar adjectival form, *qedushah*, sacrality which is always predicated of something, but rather the noun *qodesh*, signifies his sense that there is in a deep way no existence outside the sphere of the sacred.

Taken together, we see a large shift in the vectors of the religious life, from top-down to bottom-up, from structure to antistructure, from objectivity to subjectivity, from reason to passion, from disclosure from above to self-expression from below. Yet, he also emerges as an acutely dialectical thinker, for whom these various moments are held together in dynamic, creative tension, en route to resolution in and beyond historical time.

If his early writings reflect a view of the world and of the individual as a hierarchically ordered structure governed by the comparatively impersonal sway of the mind, in his later writings the picture is rather one of a yearning upward from below and of a whole self—and whole world—which vibrates with spiritual energy. Yet as we have shown this later immanentism emerges out of the former structures through a complex process of development in his own thinking and in his dialogue with his times.

And it is via this immanentism that he finds the renewal of prophecy, not in the rationalistic Maimonidean terms with which he explored prophecy in his earlier years, but out of the depths of his and the Jewish people's subjectivity. And it is this kabbalistically minded exploration of his own inner life that becomes the key to his experience of modernity. The dialectical understanding of his own subjectivity expanded, concentrically, to encompass the Jewish people as a whole, conceived of as a nation, humanity, and God's cosmos.

Philosophy, Mysticism, Experience

As I discussed in the introduction, there was lively debate for decades as to whether Rav Kook ought to be seen as philosopher or mystic, debate apparently settled, once and for all, by the publication of his journals.

---

20 As noted in the introduction, I believe the first to use this phrase to characterize Rav Kook's thinking was Samuel Hugo Bergmann.

21 I explore this at length in my article, "'From Every Heresy, Faith, and Holiness from Every Defiled Thing': Towards Rav Kook's Theology of Culture," in *Developing a Jewish Perspective on Culture*, ed. Yehuda Sarna (New York: Ktav and Yeshiva University Press, 2013), 103–142.

22 It seems to me that it is this point which reflects his indebtedenss to Habad, inasmuch as God's "surrounding all worlds" in some sense dissolves the hierarchical distinction between above and below.

Yet these need not be conceived of as mutually exclusive categories. Indeed, one need look no farther than the commingling of Sufi and philosophical terminology in Ha-Levi's *Kuzari*, Abraham Abulafia's uses of Maimonides, and the neo-Platonic strains in Maimonides himself, not to mention the philosophical heritage of, say, German Idealism, to see that a rigid use of that dichotomy can regularly obscure more than it reveals. In the case of Rav Kook, we have seen him deeply engaged with very technical Kabbalah from early on. At the same time, we have seen him both drawing on the philosophical tradition and its program of self-perfection, and engrossed by some technical philosophical problems, such as the intellect's cognition of particulars, whether primordial darkness is a void or an existent, the ability or inability of the human mind to cognize things in themselves, and, of course, the respective roles of intellect and imagination in constituting the self. Clearly, his writings of this period which were intended for public consumption explicitly draw on the philosophical tradition, but so do his private writings, and we have seen how his philosophical engagements yielded much of the infrastructure for his mystical life.

In her study of Bahya's *Hovot Ha-Levavot*, Diana Lobel draws a valuable distinction between what she calls "Intellectual Mysticism," along the lines of the Aristotelians "who hold that the essence of the human being is reason . . . [such that] the goal of intellectualist mysticism is conjunction of the human intellect with the divine Active Intellect," and what she calls "Philosophical Mysticism," by which she means "thinkers for whom intellect is a key component in connecting with the divine but for whom other elements are also important: feeling, imagination, heart and spirit." Under this heading she locates Bahya.[23] And under that heading I would similarly locate Rav Kook.

Jonathan Cohen has traced three broad arcs of the history of Jewish thought in the respective writings of Harry Wolfson, Leo Strauss, and Julius Guttman.[24] Of the three approaches, that of Guttman, for whom, as Cohen puts it, "philosophy is the speculative and contemplative version of the religious orientation" and by whose lights the formal content of religious philosophy is the expression of an underlying spiritual quest, seems the most fruitful for understanding Rav Kook.[25] At the same time, as a deeply modern thinker, that quest was marked by disruption as much as by continuity, was collective as much as personal, and, for all its being a quest towards the heavens was no less a quest within.

---

23   Diana Lobel, *A Sufi-Jewish Dialogue: Philosophy and Mysticism in Bahya ibn Paquda's Duties of the Heart* (Philadelpia: University of Pennsylvania Press, 2007), 24.

24   See his *Tenuvah u-Temurah: Panim be-Heqer Ha-Filosofiyah Ha-Yehudit ve-Toldotehah* (Jerusalem: Mossad Bialik, 1997); Cohen's thesis is given in summary form in his "Yesodot Shitatiyyim be-Heqer Ha-Filosofia Ha-Yehudit be-Zemanenu: Wolfson, Gutman, and Strauss," *Da'at* 38 (1997): 105–126.

25   This is not necessarily to argue for Guttman's view across the board; after all, Strauss and Wolfson's approaches have the traction they do precisely because they offer great insight into various thinkers, most obviously Maimonides. But Guttman's approach does recommend itself precisely for a thinker like Rav Kook who while he makes use of, and contact with, the philosophical tradition, does so only as part of a spiritual quest that is in many ways about different sorts of problems.

To be sure, much of the burden of this work has been an attempt to show the extent to which Maimonides provided much of the infrastructure of Rav Kook's thought, including his mystical thought.[26] His reworking of Maimonides's positions, "pushing them to their limits to make room for subjective truth," continued in the Land of Israel.[27] Yet what gives Rav Kook's thought its electricity is precisely the tension between the ordered structures of Maimonidean philosophy—and Maimonidean halakhah—and the lyrical, ecstatic exploration of imagination, feeling, and ecstasy, as moments in the inner life and as elements of the life of the world, historical and metaphysical both.

Aqiva Ernst Simon once noted that Rav Kook is one of those thinkers who, like Buber and Pascal, believed that "God has truth, but not a system." Moreover, Simon writes, like other nonsystematic thinkers he accepts the given, created world as a reality in itself, whereas the systematic theologians seek to create an alternative world free of paradox and contradiction.[28] Rav Kook did indeed accept the world, the drama of his early years has been his struggle to accept his own inner world, and the world of his turbulent times, in all its paradox and contradiction. He did have, as Avivi suggests, a system, but it was a system that in its own self-exploration seeks to transcend itself and dissolve the very idea of system in the eternal unfolding of God.

The ongoing publication in recent decades of Rav Kook's spiritual diaries in their original form has driven home the extent to which so much of his thinking was grounded in experience, a kind of self-phenomenology, bearing in mind that, like all great phenomenologists, he was also creating new forms of experience.[29] The interpretive act of looking at his writing in experiential terms seems to militate in the direction of mysticism, and indeed much of his writing takes place squarely within the framework of mystical traditions. But it also takes place in the framework of philosophical traditions, as indeed much of what he tries to do is a double mediation, between the various spiritual traditions to

---

26 I suspect that David Cohen (Ha-Nazir) saw things in somewhat the same way, given how he edited *Orot Ha-Qodesh*, in particular in volume one where a lengthy section on "the supernal imagination" is followed by one on "the unity of feeling, intellect and will," in turn followed by "the elevation of prophecy." Thus, inasmuch as prophecy, in the Maimonidean scheme, proceeds downward through intellect towards the imagination, the converse preparation for prophecy, which was a chief preoccupation of Ha-Nazir, proceeds upwards from imagination to the intellect—which in Rav Kook's thinking, as we have seen, moves in tandem with imagiantion's higher register, feeling—towards the prophetic summit itself.

27 Diamond, *Maimonides and the Shaping of the Jewish Canon*, 233. Diamond devotes a chapter to Rav Kook's commentary to Maimonides's *Sefer Ha-Madda'* and accepts my dating of it in my article in *'Iggud* 1 (2008): 399n9 to shortly after his arrival in Jaffa.

28 See Aqiva Ernst Simon, *Ye'adim, Tzematim, Netivim: Haguto shel Mordechai Martin Buber* (Tel Aviv: Po'alim and Kibbutz Ha-Meuhad, 1985), 164–165; this is from an essay on Buber he wrote in 1963. Simon's brand of religious humanism was famously well-removed from and critical of Rav Kook's nationalism; yet see his letter to Buber on his use of Rav Kook's *Orot Ha-Teshuvah* in a sermon on Yom Kippur in 1954, in his *Sechzig Jahre gegen den Strom: Briefe von 1917–1984* (Jerusalem/Tübingen: Leo Baeck Institute/Mohr Siebeck, 1998), 145.

29 My thanks for this observation to Prof. Moshe Idel.

which he was heir, and between his own inner life, and its fluid boundaries, and the far more structured teachings and disciplinary boundaries of the traditions.[30]

Yes, Rav Kook's mature theological writing was deeply experiential. But there is no such thing as "pure" religious experience, and his experience was composed of multiple layers, and no less a search for insight into different sorts of problems. His experiences were both philosophical and mystical—and much else besides.[31]

The historical roots of what we moderns call "religious experience" go very, very deep. In his magisterial study *The Great Shift*, James Kugel has shown that the first stirrings of individuation, of an inward focus and extension of consciousness in search for an increasingly elusive God, are to be found not only in Second Temple Apocalyptic literature and the later Hekhalot, but in layers of scripture itself, not only in Ezra, Nehemiah, and Daniel, but in later prophets and even some of the Psalms.[32] This in turn helps us better understand Scholem's enduring insight that Kabbalah emerged to meet the eclipse of myth in rabbinic Judaism, shifting the immediacy of the mythic divine-human encounter to the inner life. And also reminds us of the wisdom of the observation of Shmuel Noah Eisenstadt, that modernity is not all of one piece.

Philosophy and mysticism each represent a kind of search from within our complicated inner and outer worlds, for the absolute, the deepest truths, at the farthest edges of the mind, as idea and as lived reality.[33] And this brings me to reflection on the study of religion.

Theology as Autobiography?

George Lindbeck has argued that theology be reconceived as sustained reflection on the concrete linguistic and ritual practices of religious traditions and communities.[34] This reframing seem particularly apposite for Jewish theology—and especially for entering the

---

30 In talking about "mediation" I have in mind the marvelous work of Ann Taves, *Fits, Trances and Visions: Experiencing Religion and Explaining Experience from Wesley to James* (Princeton: Princeton University Press, 1999). The "mediation" she describes is the effort by a range of thinkers to understand religious experience neither as unvarnished sectarian truth nor as a secular phenomenon entirely captured by scientific caetgories, but as something partaking of both religion and science, existing in a middle ground of universal religion. I find this term helpfully suggestive for capturing Rav Kook's attempt to render mysticism and philosophy in terms that each could understand.

31 On the impossibility of "pure" religious experience ungrounded in some prior framework and tradition, see Wayne Proudfoot, *Religious Experience* (Berkeley: University of California Press, 1985).

32 James Kugel, *The Great Shift: Encountering God in Biblical Times* (Boston: Houghton Mifflin Harcourt, 2017).

33 This point is made throughout Leszek Kolakowski's brief, marvelous, if forbiddingly titled, *Metaphysical Horror* (Chicago: University of Chicago Pres, 2001).

34 George A. Lindbeck, *The Nature of Doctrine: Religion and Theology in a Postliberal Age* (Louisville: Westminster and John Knox Press, 1984).

thought-worlds of people who don't slot neatly into obvious (and regularly Christian) categories. Eliezer Schweid has written that a distinctive feature of Jewish thought—and, indeed, part of why it may better be designated "thought" than "philosophy"—is that it is the application of philosophical tools to a range of thought-worlds which arose prior to, or distinct from, philosophy, such as scripture, midrash, or halakhah.[35] By the same token, one might say that theology represents the theologian's reflection on their own religious life, one which in significant respects took shape before the thinker's formal engagements with philosophy as such.

Indeed I would suggest taking Lindbeck's insight one step further and thinking of theology as a kind of autobiography. I do not mean to reduce thinkers' ideas to the sociopolitical and psychological circumstances of their lives. Rather, I mean to suggest that theology be read as the attempt of thinkers to understand themselves and their own religious ideas, practices, and experiences, working with the various traditions and questions to which they are heir, in tandem with other inheritors of those traditions, and in the context of a time and place with its own distinctive social, political, cultural and intellectual contours.

Religious traditions have multiple dimensions: the ideational, that is, their specific doctrines, texts, and internal grammars; the practical, that is, the sorts of religious practices they encourage, such as study, prayer, interpersonal ethics, dietary and purity practices, and so forth; the affective, such as the religion of the mind in counterpoint to the religion of the heart; the social, by which I mean the sorts of social organization they engender, such as, at the macro level, the nation, kingdom, or the state, and at a more ramified institutional level, the traditional *beit midrash*, the Mussar yeshiva, or the mystic's cell;[36] and the systemic, in particular, those that tend towards structure and those that tend towards antistructure.[37]

We have seen Rav Kook inheriting a range of traditions—Talmudism, medieval philosophy, Lithuanian Kabbalah, Hasidism—and synthesizing these different elements in different ways and at different times, and in response to social and intellectual developments in his own time and place. Thus, at times he emphasized prayer, at others study; at times the life of the mind, at others feeling and imagination; at times legal texts, at others philosophy; and at others still, aggadic or mystical texts; and so on—and all in varying

---

35 Eliezer Schweid, *Toldot He-Hagut Ha-Yehudit bi-'Et Ha-Hadashah: Ha-Me'ah Ha-19* (Tel Aviv/Jerusalem: Ha-Kibutz Ha-Meuhad/Keter, 1978), 8. This statement of Schweid's requires some qualification in light of recent decades' research into the interactions, at times oblique but real, between rabbinic and philosophic literature; but I believe that his basic observation still stands.

36 As is clear, I have here in mind Troeltsch's classic tripartite distinction between church, sect, and mystic, elaborated at length in his *The Social Teaching of the Christian Churches* [1912], trans. Olive Wyon (New York: Harper & Row, 1960).

37 See Victor W. Turner, *The Ritual Process: Structure and Anti-Structure* (Chicago: Aldine, 1969), as well as Shmuel N. Eisenstadt, "The Order-Maintaining and Order-Transforming Dimensions of Culture," in *Theory of Culture*, ed. Richard Munch and Neil J. Smelser (Berkeley: University of California Press, 1992), 64–87.

combinations. Holding this together is his own attempt to make sense of these traditions. His receptivity to the multiple traditions and trends passing through him while working to integrate them into some sort of whole is much of what makes his life and teachings so very riveting.

Rav Kook may in many ways have been one of a kind, but I do believe that the biographic mode of theology he invites becomes, if you will, a more dialogic reading, an invitation to readers to reflect on their own positions as they engage the subjects of their readings' reflections on their own time and place.

His Political Legacy

Much ink has been, and will be, spilled on the role played by Rav Kook's teachings in contemporary religious Zionism in Israel (and especially in the ideological vanguard of its settler movement) since the 1970s and to the present day. In the light of all this one of our more striking findings has been the absence of the Land of Israel in Rav Kook's early writings. It is not that the Land of Israel does not appear at all, but that it does not figure as a category that frames his preoccupations or expresses his ideas, unlike, for instance, Jewish peoplehood, to which we have seen him recur again and again throughout, be it in the framework of self-cultivation, nationalism, or sacred historiosophy.

At the practical level, from the day of his arrival in Jaffa until his death in 1935, he was a major public figure. His arrival in Palestine thrust him into leading communal, administrative, and even frequently political roles—roles for which his first thirty-eight years had, frankly, left him somewhat unprepared. In fairness, Palestine in the early twentieth century was a remarkably complicated, indeed revolutionary, place, the dynamics and developments of which took many by surprise. To be sure, Rav Kook's having been a communal rabbi and not a *rosh yeshiva* no doubt facilitated much of his dialogue, internal and external, with the intellectual, social, and cultural currents of his time. Moreover, Boisk was no shtetl and did introduce Rav Kook to some of the cosmopolitanism he would encounter in Jaffa. Yet, as we have seen, by age thirty-eight he'd acquired little political experience, had not attended Zionist congresses or been involved in the organizational work of Hibat Tzion or other groups, and thus lacked the kind of political education that would have made his life easier in Palestine. At the same time, his oblique relation to the more straightforwardly political developments of his time helped foster his own distinctive perspective. As we have seen time and again, he was simultaneously genuinely naïve about the concrete practicalities of social and political trends and breathtakingly penetrating about those developments' underlying philosophical and spiritual foundations. This combination of qualities, I believe, characterized him throughout the remainder of his life.

He was from here on forced to rule on halakhic matters of large public significance. Though the halakhic agenda of systematization which he articulated in 'Ittur Sofrim seemed to go into eclipse, it returned in the agenda he articulated in the 1920s with the creation of the chief rabbinate. His calls in those years for the creation of new forms of halakhic literature, encyclopedias, comprehensive introductions, and so on a later elaboration of ideas he had first articulated there, decades before his involvement with Zionism.[38] But unlike in Zeimel, those ideas were now connected to profound social and political currents in which he was an active figure. At the same time, while he himself did not exactly carry out Netziv's projected agenda for rabbinic literature, he was a conduit of sorts for those of his disciples he encouraged and inspired to use the tools of modern academic scholarship in the study of Jewish texts and ideas.[39]

Who Was Rav Kook?

If nothing else, this work has unearthed and brought to academic attention the first thirty-eight years of Rav Kook's life, a period that has simply hardly been studied heretofore. I know full well the many shortcomings of this study—the things that I have omitted and, perhaps, some misinterpretations. What I have attempted here is only a beginning and in all likelihood well beyond any one researcher. I nonetheless hope that others will pick up where I have left off and further develop these and other avenues in Rav Kook studies and avail themselves of the materials in my footnotes.

Moreover, casting a brighter light on the young Rav Kook has served to illuminate his milieu, and I hope I have provided material here that can help complicate our picture of the fascinating panorama of Jewish Eastern Europe in modern times. For instance, two conclusions emerging from this work are that the neat division between Maskilim and traditionalists does not capture, and perhaps obscures, the rabbinic milieu of Eastern Europe; and that a striking degree of engagement with medieval philosophy persisted in

---

38 I am thinking here of the agenda he famously laid out in a lecture on 20 Tevet 5681/December 31, 1920, subsequently reprinted under the title "Hartzaat Ha-Rav" (Jerusalem: Degel Yerushalayim, 1921) and thereafter as an appendix to *Orot Ha-Torah*. I am at this stage unable to advance an opinion as to the precise role of these early ideas in his creation of the chief rabbinate in the 1920s.

39 For instance, he had substantial influence on Saul Lieberman, with whom he had a havruta in *Tur*. For Lieberman's reminiscences of Rav Kook, see Moshe Zvi Neriah, *Liqutei Ha-Re'ayah*, vol. 2 (Kfar Ha-Ro'eh: Hai Ro'i, 1991), 337–341. Missing from there is Lieberman's story of his first meeting with Rav Kook, which is to be found in Neriah, *Bi-Sdeh Ha-Re'ayah* (Kfar Ha-Ro'eh: n.p., 1991), 275–276. Moshe Zeidel, his disciple in Boisk, became a scholar of the Bible and Semitics and a leading editor of the *Da'at Miqra* series which wed traditional Bible study to academic scholarship. To take another example, Samuel K. Mirsky's scholarly agenda, including his lifelong work on the *Sheiltot*, as well as his many other projects, took shape very much under the impress of Rav Kook's influence; I discuss this in "The New Heavens in the New World: The Religious Hebraism of Samuel Mirsky," in *The Paths of Daniel, Studies in Judaism and Jewish Culture in Honor of Rabbi Professor Daniel Sperber*, ed. Adam S. Ferziger (Ramat Gan: Bar-Ilan University Press, 2017), 101–128. On Rav Kook's attitude towards academic Jewish studies in general see the comprehensive article by Ari Shvat, "Hokhmat Yisrael bi-Qedushatah," *Talelei Orot* 13 (2007): 309–40, and his wonderfully detailed study of a number of Rav Kook's scientifically minded disciples, "Mivhanim Ma'asiyim ha-Mevatim et Ahadat Ha-Rav Kook le-Limud Torah Biqorti-Mada'i," *Asif* 4 (2017): 297–329.

Eastern European rabbinic culture. Another conclusion is that the schematic categories of Orthodoxy and ultra-Orthodoxy are nowhere near supple enough to capture the full depth and range of traditionalist Jewish thought.[40]

In terms of Rav Kook himself, this work has illustrated a number of differences between Rav Kook's persona in his youth and later in his career and life. In some respects, he shows great continuities, exhibiting from childhood, as his parents noted early on, the characteristics both of a Mitnagdic Talmudist and Hasidic pietist. At the same time, in these pages he is more polemical and more systematically oriented than we are used to seeing him. In his youth, he was self-confident to the point of brashness—out to conquer the world. He seems to have been humbled by his first wife's death and having to take up a rabbinical post in an obscure shtetl. In response, he seems to have drawn inward, and he writes movingly of the temptations of arrogance.[41] His publication of *Hevesh Pe'er*, and subsequent period of anonymous preaching was, as we have discussed, a complex gesture of self-abnegation and self-assertion. Proper observance of tefillin was, for him, central to the religious life, the proper focus of which is the mind, exercised in study, as practiced by Lithuanian Talmudism, valorized by the philosophical tradition and, more esoterically, Lithuanian Kabbalism, as the point of contact with the divine. His introspective turn was deepened by reflection on the Mussar movement and his move to Boisk, where he was challenged by more cosmopolitan horizons. It was in those years that he first began to internalize Kabbalistic concepts and use them as maps for his own soul. Once he moved to Jaffa, that map would increasingly broaden to chart the topography of the Jewish people and world history in their movement towards God.

A central drama of his life in these years was a struggle to accept himself and his own distinctive personality and passions. His acceptance that he loved aggadic study, notwithstanding the comparatively low esteem in which it was held in yeshiva circles, and admission to himself that his most distinctive contributions were to be made in theology rather than halakhah as such, seem particularly central to his moving towards subjectivity. This inward turn and concomitant process of self-acceptance, and his linking it to Luzzatto's vision of *tiqqun* and to the larger processes at work in his times, seem very much of a piece with the neo-Augustinian tradition that Charles Taylor describes as central to modern thought. And, as noted by Alain Touraine, this emergence of the subject can engender its own new tensions between reason and the subject, tensions which we have seen were very much alive for Rav Kook.

---

40 See, for now, my discussion in "Modernizing Orthodoxies: The Case of Feminism," 37–51.

41 I am referring here most obviously to his commentary on the Rabbah bar bar Hannah tales, discussed in chapter two, but this theme of cultivating a healthy humility is a theme throughout much of what we have seen here.

Concluding Reflection: Berdyczewsky, Rav Kook, Gordon—From Rupture to Reinterpretation and Experience

I have repeatedly cast a comparative glance at the trajectory of Rav Kook's exact contemporary and Volozhin classmate Micah Yosef Berdyczwesky. Time and again we have seen the two of them testing themselves against various currents of Talmudic scholarship, Haskalah and secular literature and thought, Hasidism, and Zionism. Time and again Berdyczewsky takes progressively critical and radical stances, be it on Talmudic scholarship, the Mussar movement, aggadic study, cultural Zionism or, finally, Nietzsche. He thinks critically about texts, champions Mussar's ecstatic rejection of conventional norms of study, rejects Israel's uniqueness, attempts various syntheses of the antinomies defining his world and, in the end, calls for radical renewal in and through an embrace of rupture as a source of new, creative possibilities. Throughout this period Berdyczewsky saw both Judaism and the world in starkly oppositional terms, which he engaged first through dialectic, until that gave way to rupture. As he wrote, "To my mind, we will be torn forever."[42]

Rav Kook out of principle, temperament or more, took a different tack. He took with utmost seriousness the very real ruptures within his personality and his times. He chose not to break with tradition, with the law, with the structures of the tradition. But rather than adopt a reactionary stance, as so many of his colleagues did, he undertook a series of complicated reinterpretations of the tradition and worked to contain these multiple antinomies in a dialectic structure to which the Kabbalah held the key.

One final way of characterizing the deep change in his thought after his arrival in Jaffa is that his parallel figure in the Zionist revolution was no longer Berdyczewsky, but Aharon David Gordon (1856–1922).[43] Like Gordon, Rav Kook was a good bit older than the revolutionaries of the Second Aliyah, and, like Gordon, his theorizing of that revolution dramatically rewrote the terms of Jewish thought and the Zionist enterprise itself. Both thinkers worked to integrate elements of the Kabbalah into perennial, distinctively modern, and decidedly universal questions of philosophy—with the crucial difference that while Rav Kook retained traditional understandings of the texts' internal hierarchies and their underlying structures of authority, Gordon radically revised them in the light

---

42 A full survey of Berdyczesky would require a volume at least as long as this one. See generally Holzman, *El Ha-Qer'a she-ba-Lev*. Therein at 72, Holzman offers an extraordinary listing of the multiple antinomies which defined Berdyczewsk's thinking in those years; he summarizes Berdyczewsky's final views at 268–289; the quote at the close of this paragraph, from 1898, is therein at 275.

43 For brief, excellent overview, see Joseph (Yossi) Turner, "Philosophy and Praxis in the Thought of Aharon David Gordon," *Journal of Jewish Thought and Philosophy* 24 (2106): 122–148. For an extended comparison of Rav Kook and Gordon, see Sarah Strassberg-Dayan, *Yahid, Umah ve-Enoshut: Tefisat Ha-Adam be-Mishnoteyhem shel A. D. Gordon ve-Ha-Rav Kook* (Tel Aviv: Ha-Kibbutz Ha-Meuhad, 1995). Scholarship on both figures has greatly advanced since that very helpful volume, and there is much more comparative work to be done.

of his avowedly anti-hierarchical, indeed anarchistic worldview.[44] And, for our purposes, above all, both found refuge from seemingly insoluble dilemmas of thought and practice in the idea and reality of experience.

It was Gordon, after all, who coined the modern Hebrew word for experience, *havayah*, linking "life," *hayim*, and "being," *havayah*, and echoing the Biblical YHWH.[45] It is experience, he says, that solves the inescapable constriction (*tzimtzum*) of the conscious mind, its tragic inability to fully know itself, and the unbearable alienation we suffer as a result. The only way out, for Gordon, is an expansion (*hitpashtut*) of consciousness towards the universal, in which individuals see themselves qua individuals as a part of a larger whole, namely, the nation, and still as individuals, as parts of the larger whole of the cosmos. And this experience is, crucially, tied to feeling:

> The movement towards the life of expansion begins with the feelings between a man and woman . . . of parents . . . of the family, and after them: national feeling, human feeling, feeling for the God of all that lives. From here—the feeling of mercy, feeling of justice, feeling of ethics. Onward—feeling in relation to nature and all its fullness, in relation to endless being. From there the feeling of beauty, feeling of greater love, feeling of truth, feeling of high holiness, the feeling of religion. . . . To be sure, no one person, flesh and blood and divine image in one, can be *shalem*, whole, but he can live in fullness, which is to say, to live oneself as one is . . . in every moment of life. And that is enough.[46]

As Gordon said,

> People investigate, or argue about God, if there is a God, or there isn't, and don't see, that God, the true God, the hidden mind, isn't something for conscious understanding, but something in relation to the self. The deep, oceanic relation to the self—that is the understanding that one has of God. . . . More than that man will not grasp, and what more that he does grasp—is not God.[47]

---

44 For Gordon's use of the Kabbalah, see Avraham Shapira, *Or Ha-Hayom be-Yom Qetanot: Mishnat A. D. Gordon u-Meqorotehah be-Qabbalah ve-Hasidut* (Tel Aviv: 'Am 'Oved, 1996). Gordon's use of mysticism, as well as that of Berdyczewsky and Yosef Hayim Brenner, is the subject of a forthcoming study by my student Yair Bar-Tsuri.

45 This is at the heart of his best-known essay, "Ha-Adam ve-Ha-Teva'," in Aharon David Gordon, *Mivhar Ketavim*, ed. Eliezer Schweid (Jerusalem: Ha-Sifriyah Ha-Tzionit, 1982), 49–171 and esp. 95–97.

46 Gordon, "Ha-Adam ve-Ha-Teva'," 104:
מתחילה התנועה לחיים של התפשטות ברגש שבין גבר לאשה . . . רגש ההורים . . . הרגש המשפחתי . . . הרגש הלאומי, הרגש האנושי, הרגש ביחס לאל כל חי. מכאן—רגש הרחמים, רגש הצדק, רגש המוסר. הלאה—הרגש ביחס אל הטבע במלואו, ביחס אל ההויה האין-סופית. מכאן רגש היופי, רגש האהבה העליונה, רגש האמת, רגש הקדושה העליונה, הרגש הדתי . . . אמנם אין אדם, בשר ודם וצלם אהים כאחד, יכול להיות שלם, אבל הוא יכול לחיות בשלמות, כלומר לחיות את כל עצמו כמות שוהא . . . בכל רגע של חיים. וזה די.

47 Aharon David Gordon, "Heshbonenu im 'Atzmenu," in *Ha-Umah ve-Ha-'Avodah*, ed. S. H. Bergmann and Eliezer Shohat (Tel Aviv: Ha-Sifriyah Ha-Tzionit, 1952), 327–374, esp. 352.

And what one finds in the depths of oneself is what Gordon elsewhere calls "the hidden mind," *ha-sekhel ha-ne'elam* of the world, that is, God.[48]

For Gordon, experience brings us to selfhood and subjectivity—and personhood, which when truest to itself seeks to expand—and to seek the expansion of all things, to infinity. Experience so understood is thus the foundation of what we call religion, the relentless—and inevitably partial, if not failed—attempt to give form to this absolute form-lessness, grounding our being from beyond the horizon of consciousness. Personhood is a unity of body and soul, which achieves union with the world, with nature, and brings forth its own expansion, through labor, through applied effort in and through the world, to build the world, one another, and ourselves. The land is crucial, as is the nation, the family concentrically enlarged, the inescapable vessel through which we receive cul-ture, and without which neither the individual nor humanity can coherently exist. Self-realization is the actualization of personhood—whose dignity is inseparably bound up with recognizing the dignity of other persons, and of other nations. To assume my own personhood is thus to assume my responsibility for the personhood of others, individual and collective.

As for Rav Kook, his explorations of experience after 1904 built on the language he had created in Eastern Europe, not least his explorations of mind, emotion, and feeling, individual and now collective:

> This is the order. One must purify and strengthen the body and all its faculties, then comes the faculty of the imagination and all its tributaries, which must be both clean and clear, and then feeling and all its branches, and them atop them will come the clear mind and all its tributaries, all of them. And the light of the higher listening, which comes from the sparkling holy spirit on high, comes atop them. This order doesn't just obtain for for lone individuals, but obtains for an entire nation, and these things relate to the different eras of its life.[49]

And building on the insights he achieved in *'Eyn Ayah*, this dynamic reflects the very structure of being:

> In the education of the lone individual, and so in the education of the person in general, the nation and humanity, one must pay heed to spiritual unification, which is to say that the mind directly flow onto feeling, and feeling onto imagination, and imagination onto actions. And when there is contradiction among these parts, destruction finds a space to happen. And atop

---

48 Ibid., 68, 77–85; also, Aharon David Gordon, *Mikhtavim u-Reshimot* (Tel Aviv: Ha-Sifriyah Ha-Tzionit, 1954), 200; and see Schweid, *Neviim le-'Amam ve-la-Enoshut*, 153–154.

49 *Shemonah Qevatzim,* 1:208–09, *Orot Ha-Qodesh,* 1:248:

כך הוא הסדר. צריך לטהר ולאמץ את הגוף וכוחותיו כולם. אחר כך בא כל הדמיון וכל סעיפיו, שצריך להיות גם כן חזק ומזוכך, ואחר כך בא הרגש וכל ענפיו, ועל גביהם יבא השכל הברור והסתעפויותיו כולן. ואור ההקשבה העליונה, שבאה מהתנוצצות רוח עליון, הוא בא על גביהם. סדר זה איננו בדין של יחידים לבדם, אלא הוא הדין באומה שלמה, והדברים מתיחסים לעומת תקופות שונות במהלך החיים שלה.

these four parts, the mind, feeling, imagination, action, arises the noble/emanative essence, which is the root of the soul of man and the community, at the source of higher being.[50]

For Gordon, as for Rav Kook, experience at its fullest is at once deeply personal and profoundly collective and universal—and it is precisely experience that slices the Gordian knots of consciousness and offers the possibility, at long last, of union. And for both of them, experience, though freely available, is not merely given, but requires conscious effort of mind, and, no less crucially, the body—for Gordon, working the land in concert with others, and for Rav Kook, working the land, and observing mitzvot, in concert with others, as part of national, cosmic, and divine rebirth.

Rav Kook, like Gordon, found the deepest realization of experience in identifying with, and working alongside, the new, rebellious, and regularly contradictory Jewish renaissance taking shape in the Land of Israel. Both sought to understand and articulate the deepest meanings of that revival in a new language that would capture and conceptualize the new experience of Jewishness, and provide its own foundation for action. Yet the differences between them were real. Rav Kook was not only committed to halakhah, but also to the hierarchical ordering of cosmic energies as understood by the Kabbalah, even as those energies strive to burst their bounds. Unlike Gordon, he thought he could grasp the deepest historical currents of the present and discern their future direction. Gordon, for all his idealism and sense of his historical moment, did not see redemption around the corner or think that Jewish politics would be inherently more peaceful than the politics on display throughout human history. He was perhaps utopian, but not Messianic.

Coda

A study of the centrality of experience for Rav Kook in his post-1904 thought would be several more volumes in itself. For now, this will suffice:

What do I see in a vision? I see the supreme thought, the thought that encompasses all, the thought that contains the force and innards of everything. I see how all the great streams splash out from it, and from the pools proceed rivers, and from the rivers brooks, and from the brooks floods, and from the floods, currents, and the currents too, divide into smaller channels, and the channels divide into a mass of thousands of multitudes of *thin-veined branches* [see BT Hullin 91a, where this means the simple people of Israel]. And if one is narrow it holds on to the current, and if the current before it is narrow it holds on to the flood, and if the flood is narrow it holds on to the stream, and if the stream is narrow it holds on to the river, and if the river is too narrow it takes hold of the God-stream filled with water, that is tied to the thought that has no narrows, and there is the place of the watercourses *great and*

---

50 *Shemonah Qevatzim,* 1:247, *Orot Ha-Qodesh,* 1:247:

בחינוך האדם היחיד, וכן בחינוך האדם הכללי, האומה והאנושיות, צריכים לשים אל לב לאחדות הרוחניות, דהיינו
שהשכל יהיה משפיע ישר על הרגש, והרגש על הדמיון, והדמיון על הפעולות, וכשיש סתירה בין אלה החלקים, אז
ההריסה מוצאת מקום לחול. ועל גבי אלה ארבעה החלקים, שהן שכל, רגש, דמיון, מעשה, מתעלה העניין האצילי,
שהוא שורש הנשמה של האיש ושל הציבור, במקור ההויה העליונה.

wide [Ps. 104:24]. And the final abundance, dripping down from the thin-veined branches, flows this way from the first source of the supreme thought, above which any eye would be too faint too look, and *God said I will dwell in mist* [1 Kings 8:12].[51]

And eventually, there will glimmer before him, the ultimate religious experience, beyond the mystical encounter, prophecy.

> And I listen and hear from the depths of my soul, from the feelings of my heart: the voice of God is calling. And I am gripped with terrible fear. Have I stooped so low as to be a false prophet, *to say "God has sent me"* [Isa. 48:16] *and the word of God has not been revealed to me?* [after 1 Sam. 3:7]. And I hear the voice of my soul stir, stubbles of prophecies sprout, and the sons of prophets awake, the spirit of prophecy is afoot in the land.[52]

Rav Kook's arrival in the Land of Israel in 1904 inaugurated what would turn out to be an extraordinary intellectual, political, and above all spiritual journey, one whose reverberations are still very much with us today. This journey, as I have tried to show, had its own rich, largely unexplored, and regularly surprising beginnings.

---

51 *Shemonah Qevatzim*, 1:315:

מה אני רואה בחזון, אני רואה את המחשבה העליונה, המחשבה הכוללת כל, המחשבה שכל העצמה וכל המילוי של כל בה הוא. רואה אני, שכל הפלגים הגדולים ממנה משתפכים, ומהפלגים יוצאים נהרים, מהנהרים נחלים, מהנחלים שטפים, מהשטפים זרמים, והזרמים מתחלקים גם הם לצינורות קטנים, והצינורות מתחלקים להמון אלפי רבבות לאין קץ של קנוקנות, מריקים שפעות רצון, חיים ומחשבה. לפעמים צר מאד המקום לשוט בין הקנוקנות, נאחזת אז הנשמה בשרשיהם של הקנוקנות הדקים, בצינורות. ואם הצנור גם הוא צר, נאחזת היא בזרם, ואם הזרם צר הוא לפניה, הרי היא נאחזת בשטף, ואם השטף הוא צר, הרי היא נאחזת בנחל, ואם צר הנחל, נאחזת היא בנהר, ואם גם הנהר יצר לה, נאחזת היא בפלג אלהים מלא מים, המחובר למחשבה של בלי מצרים, ששם הוא מקום יאורים רחבי ידים. והשפע האחרון, הנוזל מהקנוקנות, נובע בדרך זה מהמקור הראשי של המחשבה העליונה, שלמעלה מזה תלא כל עין לצפות, וד' אמר לשכן בערפל.

52 *Shemonah Qevatzim*, 4:17, *Orot Ha-Qodesh*, 1:157 (with substantial editing):

ואקשיב ואשמע מתוך מעמקי נשמתי, מתוך רגשי לבבי, קול אדני קורא. ואחרד חרדה גדולה, הככה ירדתי כי לנביא השקר אהיה, לאמר ד' שלחני ולא נגלה אלי דבר אדני. ואשמע קול נשמתי הומה, ספיחי נבואות הנה צומחות, ובני נביאים מתעוררים, רוח הנבואה הולך ושט בארץ . . . .

Acknowledgments

אודה לאל לבב חוקר

This book was very long in the making. It is a deep pleasure to record the many kindnesses from which I benefited along the way. I have been helped in ways large and small by too many people to name, but I will try.

The book's origins lie in my doctoral dissertation at Harvard University's Committee on the Study of Religion, completed in 2007.

The doctoral advisers who shepherded that project were each crucial. Professor Jay Harris read the entirety of the thesis several times; his close, erudite reading and exacting comments were invaluable. William Graham was an extraordinarily supportive, broad-minded advisor during my years of Islamic study, an incisive reader of my work here, and is for me in many ways the very model of a scholar and a gentleman. Moshe Idel shared with me his vast knowledge, broad sweep, and very limited time. His organizational suggestions, and his probing questions, which at times took me years to answer, have made me think more deeply about this work and about the study of religion in general. His encouragement has meant a great deal.

In my doctoral years, Professor Bernard Septimus both deepened my understanding of medieval Jewish poetry and philosophy and, crucially, impressed on me the importance of trying to translate what the authors of texts most likely meant rather than what I wish they would have said. Charles Hallisey greatly enriched my understanding of the deep and often surprising connections between ethical and religious practice.

It is a special pleasure to acknowledge the libraries in which much of the work was done: in the US, the Widener Library of Harvard University and the New York Public Library at 42nd Street; in Jerusalem, the Van Leer Institute, the library of Hebrew Union College, and the National Library of Israel at Givat Ram—in particular, the Gershom Scholem collection and the wondrous Judaica Reading Room (and its incredible librarians

Aliza Alon, Alona Avinezer, Zipporah Ben-Abu, and Ruth Flint). In my years at Brandeis I incurred many debts to our (now emeritus) Judaica librarian James Rosenbloom, whose understanding and learning are matched only by his humility.

I benefited immensely from scholarly conversations and exchanges with Daniel Abrams, Ari Ackerman, Uriel Barak, Avriel Bar-Levav, Hanoch Ben-Pazi, Yoel Bin-Nun, Menachem Butler, Shmuel Noah Eisenstadt z"l, Sharon Flatto, Jonathan Garb, Yosef Goldstein, Warren Zev Harvey, Shai Held, Tsippi Kaufman z"l, Marcie Lenk, Jonatan Meir, Kalman Neuman, Elhanan Reiner, Tamar Ross, Eli Rubin, Marc Shapiro, Elchanan Shilo, Shaul Stampfer, David Starr, Josef Stern, and Motti Zalkin. My thinking on a range of issues was immeasurably enriched by many conversations with the remarkable Shlomo Fischer.

My colleagues at Brandeis University's Department of Near Eastern and Judaic Studies and its Schusterman Center for Israel Studies are as committed to education and mutual encouragement as they are to scholarship and ideas. I am honored to be counted among them.

At Academic Studies Press, Gregg Stern, Alessandra Anzani, Kira Nemirovsky, and above all Stuart Allen have all been wonderfully supportive, patient, and a pleasure to work with throughout and have my deepest thanks. Avi Staiman, Adrian Sackson, Jacob Merlin, and Jacob Pesachov of Academic Language Experts were of tremendous help in preparing the Bibliography and Index.

This publication was made possible in part by a grant from the Memorial Foundation for Jewish Culture, the Norman Grant program of Brandeis University's School of Arts and Sciences, and generous research leave by Brandeis University's Schusterman Center for Israel Studies and its then director, David Ellenson.

The errors and infelicities herein are my own.

There is, to put it mildly, great wisdom and more beyond academia. I profoundly thank Ari Shvat, research director of Beit Ha-Rav Kook; Shuki Wieder, former research director there; Michael Baris, my study partner in Rav Kook's work during our yeshiva days, now an accomplished legal scholar; Ari Singer, my friend since childhood and steady conversation partner on Rav Kook and much else; Meir Ekstein, Efraim Borow, and Shimshon Yishai, friends from yeshiva days who always make me think harder.

I am blessed with having too many friends to thank, but in particular have to express my gratitude to Seth Aronson and Jody Sampson—wise, deeply supportive, and understanding friends, who make the world so much better.

I have had many teachers, and this book is dedicated to the memory of three of them.

I was first introduced to the study of Rav Kook's writings in the late 1970s by one of his most significant and independent-minded latter-day disciples, the late Rav Yehudah Amital, dean of Yeshivat Har Etzion, who himself first discovered those writings in pre-war Hungary, studied them in a Nazi labor camp, and put them into practice in manifold ways in Israel. From then until his death in 2010, and beyond, he was and remains a challenging master and a steady inspiration.

I was also blessed by the friendship and guidance of Rabbi Dr. Emanuel Rackman, chancellor of Bar-Ilan University and champion of equality. His luminous personality and unique mix of deep religious conviction, wide-ranging intellect, and profound human sympathy were a shelter and their own extraordinary teaching.

It is hard to put into words the immensity of what my father Rabbi Professor David Mirsky meant and means to me. He carried rich learning, piety, moral strength, and wisdom with humility, humor, and deep tenderness. And he put his ideals into practice every single day.

My father passed away when I was in college. My mother, Sarrah (Appel) Mirsky, of blessed memory, lived to see my doctorate, and it would not have come to be without her unstinting encouragement and love. My sister Zipporah Aviva and my brother Moshe Zvi and their families have been there for me just as much.

Yet my greatest teachers are my wife and children. My wife Tamar Biala entered my life when I was in the thick of my doctorate; the life we have built in the years since is lined with her love, insight, compassion, and courage. I pray it goes on forever.

Our daughters, Nehara Shulamit and Nofet Shira, have accompanied this book since they were born. Their faith, humor, and love have seen me through.

Finally, a confession. On a fall morning in Jerusalem in 1921, the subject of this book, Rav Kook himself, officiated as the Cohen at my father's *pidyon ha-ben*, the redemption of the first born. I have over the years wondered if something was amiss at that ceremony, inasmuch as he has indeed occupied the soul of my father's younger son for so many years now, with no end in sight. Perhaps this book is a final redemption, or I may simply have gotten myself in deeper. Only time will tell and, as always with Rav Kook, there will be much to learn along the way.

Bibliography

Works by Rav Kook

"Afiqim Ba-Negev." *Ha-Peles* 3 (1903-1904): 596-604, 655-663, 714-722; 4 (1904): 19-26, 73-80, 138-44.

"'Al Ha-Zionut." *Ha-Devir* 7-9 (1920): 29-33; 10-12 (1920): 33-38.

Be'er Eliyahu. Jerusalem: Ha-Makhon 'al shem Ha-Ratzyah Kook, 1988.

Da'at Cohen. Jerusalem: Mossad Ha-Rav Kook, 1942.

Eder Ha-Yaqar ve-'Iqvei Ha-Tzon. [1906]. Jerusalem: Mossad Ha-Rav Kook, 1967.

Eretz Hefetz. Edited by Yeshayahu Shapira. Jerusalem: Darom, 1930.

"'Etzot Me-Rahoq." *Ha-Peles* 2 (1902): 457-464, 530-532.

'Eyn Ayah. Edited by Ya'aqov Filber. Jerusalem: Ha-Makhon 'al shem Ha-Ratzyah Kook zt"l, 1995-2000/5755-5760.

Ginzei Reayah. Edited by Ben-Zion Shapira. Jerusalem: Qeren 'al-shem Ha-Ratzyah Kook, 1985.

Ha-Mahshavah Ha-Yisraelit. Edited by Elhanan Kalmanson. Jerusalem: Levi, 1920.

Hartzaat Ha-Rav. Jerusalem: Merkaz Ha-Rav/Degel Yerushalayim, 1921.

Hazon Ha-Geulah. Edited by Meir Bar-Ilan. Jerusalem: Ha-Agudah le-Hotzaat Sifrei Ha-Re'ayah Kook z"l, 1941.

Haskamot Ha-Re'ayah. Edited by Ari Shvat, Zuriel Halamish, and Yohanan Fried. Jerusalem: Beit Ha-Rav, 2017.

Hevesh Pe'er. Warsaw: Levenson, 1891. Reprinted 1924 and 1985.

'Ittur Sofrim. Vilna, 1888. Reprinted 1974.

Igrot Ha-Re'ayah. 3 vols. Jerusalem: Mossad Ha-Rav Kook, 1961-1965.

"Kelil Tiferet." *Torah Mi-Zion* 5, no. 4 (1900): 3-5.

Ma'amarei Ha-Re'ayah. Edited by Elisha Aviner [Langauer] and David Landau. Jerusalem: n.p., 1984.

Midbar Shur. Edited by David Landau and Michael Hershkovitz. Jerusalem: Makhon Ha-Ratzyah Kook zt"l, 1999.

"Mi-Pinqas 'Eyn Ayah." *Ha-Mizrah* 1, no. 6 (1903): 352-354.

Mishpat Cohen. Jerusalem: Ha-Agudah le-Hotzaat Sifrei Ha-Re'ayah Kook zt'l, 1937.

Mizvat Reayah. Appendix to *Oreah Neeman* by Menahem Auerbach. Published 1924. Reprinted by Mossad Ha-Rav Kook. Jerusalem, 1985.

Mussar Avikha. Edited by Zvi Yehudah Kook. Jerusalem: Ha-Yeshiva Ha-Mercazit Ha-Olamit, 1946. Reprinted with addition of Midot Ha-Re'ayah by Mossad Ha-Rav Kook, 1971.

'Olat Reiyah. Edited by Zvi Yehudah Kook. Jerusalem: Agudah le-Hotzaat Sifrei Ha-Reayah zt'l, 1939-1949.

Orah Mishpat. Jerusalem: Mossad Ha-Rav Kook, 1979.

Orot. 1920. Edited by Zvi Yehudah Kook. Rev. ed. 1963.

Orot Ha-Qodesh. 4 vols. Edited by David Cohen. 1st ed. Jerusalem: Mossad Ha-Rav Kook, 1935-1992; Yohanan Fried, additional editor on vol. 4 (1992).

Orot Ha-Re'ayah. Edited by Zvi Yehudah Kook. Jerusalem: Mossad Ha-Rav Kook, 1970.

Orot Ha-Teshuvah. Edited by Zvi Yehudah Kook. Jerusalem, 1925.

Orot Ha-Torah. Edited by Zvi Yehudah Kook. Rev. ed. Merkaz Shapira: Yeshivat Or Etzion, 2004. Originally published Jerusalem: Yeshivat Merkaz Ha-Rav, 1940.

Ozarot Ha-Reiyah. 5 vols. Edited by Moshe Zuriel. 2nd ed. Rishon Le-Zion: Yeshivat Ha-Hesder Rishon Le-Zion, 2001.

"Perush 'al Aggadot Rabbah bar bar Hannah." In *Ma'amarei Ha-Re'ayah*, edited by Elisha Aviner [Langauer] and David Landau, 419-448. Jerusalem: n.p., 1984.

Qevatzim mi-Ktav Yad Qodsho. Edited by Boaz Ofan. Jerusalem, 2006.

Qovetz Maamarim. Jerusalem: Ha-Yesod, 1935.

"Rosh Yeshivat Etz Hayim." In *Ma'amarei Ha-Re'ayah*, edited by Elisha Aviner [Langauer] and David Landau, 123-126. Originally published in *Knesset Yisrael* 2 (1887): 138-142.

Shemonah Qevatzim.. Rev. ed. Jerusalem: n.p., 2004. Originally published 1999.

Shemu'ot Ha-Re'ayah. Edited by Shmuel Kalmanson. Jerusalem: Agudat Ha-Sneh, 1939.

"Te'udat Yisrael u-Leumiyuto." *Ha-Peles* 1 (1901): 45-52, 82-94, 154-161, 223-228, 428-433.

Untitled Essay on the Mizrahi. In *Zikhron Ha-Re'ayah*, edited by Yitzhaq Refael, 5-14. Jerusalem: Mossad Ha-Rav Kook, 1986.

When God Becomes History: Historical Essays of Rabbi Abraham Isaac Hacohen Kook, ed. and trans. by Bezalel Naor. New York: Kodesh Press, 2016.

"Zvi la-Tzadiq." In *Ozarot Ha-Re'ayah*, vol. 2, edited by Moshe Zuriel, 139-147. 2nd ed. Rishon Le-Zion: Yeshivat Ha-Hesder Rishon Le-Zion, 2001. Originally published in *Mahaziqei Ha-Dat* 8, no. 15 (January 15, 1886/7 Shevat 5646): 6-7; 8, no. 16 (7 Adar I 5646/February 12, 1886): 6-7.

Zivhei Reayah. Jerusalem: Mossad Ha-Rav Kook, 1985. Originally published in Moshe Goldstein, *Sefer Yabi'a Omer*, 1924.

Secondary and Other Materials

Abramovich, Udi. "Ha-Shelihut, Ha-Monopol ve-Ha-Tzensurah—Ha-Ratzyah Kook ve-'Arikhat Kitvei Ha-Re'ayah," *Da'at* 60 (2007): 121-152.

Abrams, M. H. *Natural Supernaturalism: Tradition and Revolution in Romantic Literature.* New York: Norton, 1971.

Abramson, Shraga. "Tiqunim bi-teshuva Ahat shel HARY"Z Stern." *Ha-Maayan* 32, no. 1 (Fall 1991/Tishrei 5752): 49-52.

Ackerman, Ari. "The Philosophic Sermons of R. Zerahia Halevi Saladin." PhD diss., Hebrew University, 2000.

Afterman, Adam. *Devequt.* Los Angeles: Cherub Press, 2011.

Agnon, Shmuel Yosef. *Me-Atzmi el Atzmi.* Jerusalem and Tel Aviv: Schocken, 2000.

———. "Ha-Taba'at." In *Takhrikh shel Sippurim.* Jerusalem and Tel Aviv: Schocken, 1984.

———. *Temol Shilshom.* Jerusalem and Tel Aviv: Schocken, 1967.

Agus, Jacob B. *Banner of Jerusalem.* New York: Bloch, 1946.

———. "Ish Ha-Mistorin." *Talpiot* 3, no. 3-4 (1948): 528-578.

———. *The Vision and the Way: An Interpretation of Jewish Ethics.* New York: Frederick Ungar, 1966.

Ahad Ha-Am [Asher Ginsburg]. Vol. 4 of *Igrot Ahad Ha-Am.* Tel Aviv: Devir, 1958.

———. *Kol Kitvei Ahad Ha-Am.* Tel Aviv: Devir, 1959.

Ahituv, Yosef [Yoske]. "Erkei Mussar u-Leumiyut be-Hugei Merkaz Ha-Rav." In *Sefer Zikaron le-Professor Zev Falk z'l: Maamarim be-Madaeri Ha-Yahadut u-vi Sheelot Ha-Sha'ah*, edited by Rivka Horvitz, Moshe David Herr, Yohanan David Silman, and Michael Cordinali, 279-306. Jerusalem: Hebrew University/Magnes, 2005.

Albert, Shlomo. *Aderet Eliyahu.* Jerusalem: n.p., 2003.

Alexandrov, Shmuel. "Esh Dat ve-Ruah Ha-Leumi." *Ha-Maggid* 20 (May 20, 1891): 19-25, 31, 33.

———. *Mikhtavei Mehqar u-Viqoret.* Vol. 1. Vilna: Romm, 1907.

———. "Zeman Matan Toratenu." *Ha-Maggid* 9, no. 22 (May 31, 1900): 249-250.

Alfasi, Yitzhaq. "Mahzikei Ha-Dat—Ha-Shevuon Ha-Dati Ha-Rishon." In *Sefer Ha-Shanah shel Ha-Orkhim ve-Ha-'Itonaim bi-Kitvei Ha-Et b'Yisrael, 1990-1991*, 193-203. Tel Aviv-Yafo: Ha-Iggud Ha-Yisraeli le-'Itonut Tequfatit, 1991.

Alfes, Ben-Zion. *Eretz Hemdah.* Tel Aviv: Moses, 1940.

Almog, Shmuel. "The Role of Religious Values in the Second Aliyah." In *Zionism and Religion*, edited by Shmuel Almog, Jehuda Reinharz, and Anita Shapira, 237-250. Hanover: University Press of New England/ Brandeis University Press, 1998.

———. *Zionut ve-Historiyah.* Jerusalem: Hebrew University/Magnes, 1982.

Alroey, Gur. *Immigrantim: Ha-Hagirah Ha-Yehudit le-Eretz Yisrael bi-Reishit Ha-Meah Ha-'Esrim.* Jerusalem: Yad Ben-Zvi, 2004.

Altmann, Alexander. "Saadya's Conception of the Law." *Bulletin of the John Rylands Library* 28 (1944): 320-339.

Amital, Yehudah. *Ha-Ma'alot mi-Ma'amaqim.* Alon Shvut: Yeshivat Har Etzion, 1978.

———. *Ve-Ha-Aretz Natan li-Vnei Adam.* Alon Shvut: Herzog College, 2005.

———. "Mashma'utah shel Mishnat Ha-Rav Kook le-Doreynu." In *Yovel Orot: Haguto shel Ha-Rav Avraham Yitzhaq Ha-Cohen Kook*, edited by Benjamin Ish-Shalom and Shalom Rosenberg, 333-341. Jerusalem: Sifiyat Eliner, 1985.

———. *Resisei Tal.* Alon Shvut: Yeshivat Har Etzion, 2005.

Appel, Tamar Kaplan. "Crown Rabbi." In *Yivo Encyclopedia of Eastern European Jewish Life*, vol. 1. Yale University Press, 2008. https://yivoencyclopedia.org/article.aspx/Crown_Rabbi.

Arama, Yitzhaq. *Aqedat Yitzhaq.* Edited by Hayim Pollack. Warsaw: Schriftgisser, 1883.

Arieli, Menahem, ed. *Neshamah shel Shabbat: Osef Maamarim Toraniyyim le-Zikhro shel Ha-Rav Eliyahu Shlomo Ra'anan zt'ql.* Hevron: Shalmei Arieli, 1999.

Assaf, Simha. *Teshuvot Ha-Geonim.* Jerusalem: Mekizei Nirdamim, 1942.

Auerbach, Menahem. *Oreah Ne'eman.* Jerusalem: Solomon, 1924.

Avchinski, Levi. *Tolodot Yeshivat Ha-Yehudim be-Courland.* 2nd ed. Vilna: Garber, 1912.

Aviner, Shlomo. *Halikhot Ha-Re'ayah.* 4 vols. Jerusalem and Beit El: Sifriyat Beit El, 2005.

———. *Moses Hess: Prophet of Communism and Zionism.* New York: New York University Press, 1985.

Avivi, Yosef. "Aqdamot le-Qabbalat Ha-Re'ayah." In *Mah Ahavti Toratekhah*, edited by Yitzhak Recanati and Shaul Barth, 153-181. Alon Shvut: Yeshivat Har Etzion, 2014.

———. *Biynan Ariel.* Jerusalem: Jerusalem: Misgav Yerushalayim, 1987.

———. "Historiyah Tzorekh Gevohah." In *Sefer Ha-Yovel li-Khvod Mordechai Breuer*, edited by Moshe Bar-Asher, 709-771. Jerusalem: Aqademon, 1992.

———. *Qabbalat Ha-Ari.* Jerusalem: Yad Ben-Zvi, 2008.

———. *Qabbalat Ha-GRA.* Jerusalem: Kerem Eliyahu, 1993.

———. *Qabbalat Ha-Re'ayah.* Jerusalem: Yad Ben-Zvi, 2018.

———. "Meqor Ha-Orot." *Tzohar* 1 (Fall 2000): 93-111.

Avneri, Yossi. "Ha-Re'ayah Kook—Tadmit be-Tahalikhei Hitgabshut." *Sefer Bar-Ilan* 23-24 (2001): 161-187.

———. "Ha-Re'ayah Kook ke-Rabbah Ha-Rashi shel Eretz Yisrael." PhD diss., Bar-Ilan University, 1989.

———. "Ha-Rav Avraham Yitzhaq Ha-Cohen Kook, Rabbah shel Yafo (1904-1914)." *Cathedra* 37(1985): 49-82.

———. "Ha-Rav Avaraham Yitzhaq Ha-Cohen Kook ve-She'elat Yahasei Yehudim-'Aravim be-Eretz Yisrael, 1904-1935." *Proceedings of 10th World Congress of Jewish Studies* 2, no. 1 (1990): 331-338.

Bachrach, Yair Hayim. *Havot Yair.* Jerusalem: n.p., 1968 [1659].

Band, Arnold J. "The Ahad Ha-Am and Berdyczewski Polarity." In *At the Crossroads: Essays on Ahad Ha-Am*, edited by Jacques Kornberg, 49-59. Albany: State University of New York Press, 1983.

Bahya ben Asher. *Kad Ha-Qemah.* Edited by Hayim Chavel. Jerusalem: Mossad Ha-Rav Kook, 1995.

Bahya ibn Pakuda. *Hovot Ha-Levavot.* Translated by Yehudah ibn Tibbon. Warsaw: Goldman, 1875.

Barak, Aharon. *Parshanut Takhlitlt be-Mishpat.* Jerusalem: Nevo, 2003.

Barak, Uriel. "Ha-Hashpa'ah Ha-Me-Atzevet shel Tiur Madregat Ha-Nevuah Ha-Rishonah be-Moreh Nevukhim 'al Tefisat Athalta de-Geulah be-Hug Ha-Re'ayah." *Da'at* 64-66 (2009): 361-415.

———. "Kabbalah versus Philosophy: Rabbi Avraham Itzhak Kook's Critique of the Spiritual World of Franz Rosenzweig." *Journal of Jewish Thought and Philosophy* 23, no. 1 (2015): 27-59.

Bar-Eli, Tzila. *Shahar Oro: Ha-Rav Moshe Zvi Neriah zt"l.* Jerusalem and Psagot: Tzila Bar-Eli, 2002.

Baron, Salo. "The Historical Outlook of Maimonides." In *History and Jewish Historians*, 109-163. Philadelphia: Jewish Publication Society, 1964.

Bar-Sela', Shraga. *Beyn Sa'ar li-Demahah: Hayav u-Mishnato shel Hillel Zeitlin.* Tel Aviv: Ha-Kibbutz Ha-Meuhad, 1999.

Bartal, Yisrael. "Beyn Haskalah Radiqalit le-Sozialism Yehudi." In *Ha-Dat veHa-Hayim*, edited by Immanuel Etkes, 328-335. Jerusalem: Mercaz Shazar, 1993.

———. *Galut Ba'aretz: Yishuv Eretz Yisrael be-Terem Zionut.* Jerusalem: Ha-Sifriya Ha-Tziyonit, 1994.

———. "Mordechai Aaron Gunzburg: A Lituanian Maskil Faces Modernity." In *From East and West: Jews in a Changing Europe, 1750-1850*, edited by Frances Malino and David Sorkin, 126-147. Oxford: Basil Blackwell, 1990.

———. "True Knowledge and Wisdom: On Orthodox Historiography." *Studies in Contemporary Jewry* 10 (1994): 178-192

———. "Zikhron Ya'aqov le-Ya'aqov Lifshitz: Historiografiyah Ortodoksit?" *Mileit* 2 (1984): 409-414.

Bartal, Yisrael, Zvi Zahor, and Yehoshua Kaniel, eds. *Ha-'Aliyah Ha-Sheniyah*. 3 vols. Jerusalem: Yad Ben-Zvi, 1997.

Bar-Yosef, Hamutal. "Mah le-Ziyonut u-le-Geulah Meshihit? Ha-Reqa' Ha-Russi ve-Hidhudav ba-Sifrut Ha-Ivrit." In *Mehuyavut Yehudit Mithadeshet*, vol. 2, edited by Avi Sagi and Zvi Zohar, 773-799. Jerusalem and Tel Aviv: Hartman Institute/Ha-Kibbutz Ha-Meuhad, 2001.

———. "The Jewish Reception of Vladimir Solov'ev." In *Vladimir Solov'ev: Reconciler and Polemicist, Eastern Christian Studies*, vol. 2, edited by Wil ven den Bercken, Manon de Courten, and Evertvan der Zweerde, 363-392. Peeters: Leuven, 2000.

Barzilay, Yitzhaq. *Manasseh of Ilya: Precursor of Modernity Among the Jews of Eastern Europe*. Jerusalem: Magnes Press/Hebrew University, 1999.

Batnitzky, Leora. *How Judaism Became a Religion*. Princeton: Princeton University Press, 2011.

Bat-Yehudah [Refael], Geula. *Ha-Rav Maimon be-Dorotav*. Jerusalem: Mossad Ha-Rav Kook, 1979.

———. "Rabbi Shmuel Alexandrov." *Sinai* 100 (1987): 195-221.

Bauman, Zygmunt. *Postmodern Ethics*. Cambridge: Blackwell, 1993.

Baumgarten, Eliezer. "Ha-Kabbalah be-Hug Talmidei Ha-GRA." PhD diss., Ben-Gurion University, 2010.

———. "Historiyah ve-Historiosophia be-Mishnato shel Rav Shlomo Elyashiv." Master's thesis, Ben-Gurion University, 2006.

———. "Hadshanut ve-Shamranut be-Qabbalat Rabbi Naftali Herz Halevi." *Da'at* 79-80 (2015): 205-219.

———. "Samkhuto shel Ha-Ari etzel Ha-GRA ve-Talmidav." *Da'at* 71 (2011): 53-74.

Beck, Lewis White. "Philosophy as Literature." In *Philosophical* Style, edited by Berel Lang, 234-255. Chicago: Nelson Hall, 1980.

Beeri, Yehoshua. *Ohev Yisrael bi-Qedushah*. 5 vols. Tel Aviv: H. Y. KH., 1989.

Bellah, Robert N., and Hans Joas, eds. *The Axial Age and Its Consequences*. Cambridge, MA: Harvard University Press, 2012.

Ben-Artzi, Hagi. "Biqoret Ha-Dat u-Derakhim le-Hithadshutah be-Haguto Ha-Muqdemet shel Ha-Rav Kook." Master's thesis, Hebrew University, 1991.

———. "'He-Yashan Yithadesh ve-He-Hadash Yitqadesh': Biqoret Ha-Dat u-Derakhim le-Hithadshutah be-Haguto Ha-Muqdememet shel Ha-Rav Kook." Pt. 1. *Aqdamot* 3 (September 1997): 9-28; pt. 2. *Aqdamot* 6 (January 1999): 69-71, 73-75.

———. "Ha-Re'aYah Kook ke-Posek—Yesodot Hadshaniyyim bePesikato shel Ha-Rav Kook." PhD diss., Hebrew University, 2004.

Ben Avraham, N. [Natan Anshin]. "Demut Atiqah me-Qatamon." In *Sipurim Yerushalmiyim*, vol. 3, 113-136. Jerusalem: Maimei Ha-Da'at/Mish'an Menahem, 1996.

Ben Johanan, Karma. "Wreaking Judgment on Mount Esau: Christianity in R. Kook's Thought." *Jewish Quarterly Review* 106, no. 1 (Winter 2016): 76-100.

Ben-Pazi, Hanoch. *Ha-Parshanut ke-Ma'aseh Musari: Ha-Hermeneutica shel Emmanuel Levinas*. Tel Aviv: Resling, 2012.

———. "Ha-Yitzriyut eitzel Ha-Rav Kook." In *Sihot 'im Ha-Yetzer Ha-Ra'*, edited by Asa Qeidar, 155-163. Tel Aviv: Yediot/Hemed, 2007.

———. "R. Abraham Isaac Kook and the Opening Passage of 'The War.'" *Journal of Jewish Thought and Philosophy* 25, no. 2 (2017): 256-278.

Ben-Shlomo, Yosef. "'Ha-Idealim Ha-Elohiyyim' be-Torato shel Ha-Rav Kook." *Bar-Ilan Annual of Jewish Studies* 23 (1988): 73-86.

———. *Shirat Ha-Hayim: Peraqim be-Mishnato shel Ha-Rav Kook*. Tel Aviv: Misrad Ha-Bitahon/Broadcast University, 1989.

———. "Shlemut ve-Hishtalmut be-Torat Ha-Elohut shel Ha-Rav Kook." *'Iyun* 33, no. 1-2 (1984): 289-309.

Ben-Yehuda, Eliezer. *Milon Ha-Lashon Ha-Ivrit*. Tel Aviv: La'am, 1948.

Berdyczewsky, Micah Yosef, ed. *Beit Ha-Midrash: Miqdash Le-Torah u-le-Hokhmat Yisrael, Supplement to Otzar Ha-Sefarim*. Cracow: Shealtiel Gruber, 1888.

———. *Kitvei Micah Josef Berdyczewsky*. Vol. 5. Edited by Avner Holzman. Tel Aviv: Ha-Kibbutz Ha-Meuhad, 2002.

———. *Pirqei Volozhin*. Holon and Tel Aviv: Beit David ve-Emanuel/Reshafim, 1984.

———. "Yeshivat Etz Hayim." *He-Asif* 3 (1886): 237-238

———. "Yeshu ben Hanan." In *Oto Ha-Ish: Yehudim Mesaprim 'al Yeshu*, edited by Avigdor Shinan, 201-209. Tel Aviv: Yediot/Hemed, 1999.

Berger, Dov. "Mishnato Ha-Hitpathutit shel Ha-Re'ayah Kook ve-Torat Ha-Evolutzyah." PhD diss., Bar Ilan University, 2015.

Bergmann, Samuel Hugo. *Faith and Reason in Modern Jewish Thought*. Translated by Alfred Jospe. New York: Schocken, 1961.

———. *Toldot Ha-Philosophiyah He-Hadashah: Jacobi, Fichte, Schelling*. Jerusalem: Mossad Bialik, 1977.

Berkowitz, Peter. *Nietzsche: The Ethics of an Immoralist*. Cambridge, MA: Harvard University Press, 1995.

Berlin, Isaiah. *The Hedgehog and the Fox*. Princeton: Princeton University Press, 2013.

———. "Two Concepts of Liberty." In *Four Essays on Liberty*. London: Oxford University Press, 1969.

Berlin [Bar-Ilan], Meir. *Mi-Volozhin 'ad Yerushalayim*. Tel Aviv: Cohen Yalqut, 1939-1940.

———. *Rabban shel Yisrael*. New York: Histadrut Ha-Mizrahi, 1943.

Berlin, Naftali Zvi Yehudah. *Ha'ameq Davar*. Vilna: Romm, 1879. Rev. ed. Jerusalem Yeshivat Volozhin, 1999.

———. *Ha'ameq Sheelah*. Vilna: Romm, 1861-1867.

———. *Meshiv Davar*. Warsaw: Halter & Eisenstadt, 1894.

———. *Rinah shel Torah*. Warsaw: Halter & Eisenstadt, 1894.

Bernfeld, Shimon. *Da'at Elohim*. Warsaw: Schuldberg, 1899.

Bialik, Hayim Nahman. *Igrot*. Tel Aviv: Dvir, 1938.

Bin-Nun, Yoel. *Ha-Maqor Ha-Kaful: Hashra'ah ve-Samkhut be-Mishnat Ha-Rav Kook*. Tel Aviv: Ha-Kibbutz Ha-Meuhad, 2014.

Bindiger, Naamah. "Heqer Hitpathut Hagut Ha-Rav Kook—Tashtit Bibliographit ve-Temunah Mehqar 'Adqanit." *'Alei Sefer* 30 (forthcoming).

Binyomin, Rebbe [Joshua Radler-Feldman]. *Parzufim*. Vol. 1. Tel Aviv: Mizpeh, 1936.

Bitti, Yehudah. "Beyn Mussar Avikha le-Mussar Ha-Qodesh." Master's thesis, Hebrew University, 1998.

Blau, Rivkah. *Learn Torah, Live Torah, Love Torah: Ha-Rav Mordechai Pinchas Teitz, the Quintessential Rabbi*. Hoboken: KTAV, 2001.

Blidstein, Ya'aqov [Gerald]. *Samkhut u-Meri be-Hilkhot Ha-Rambam*. Tel Aviv: Ha-Kibbutz Ha-Meuhad, 2002.

———. "Torat Eretz Yisrael ve-Torat Bavel be-Mishnat Ha-Netziv Mi-Volozhin." In *Eretz Yisrael be-Hagut Yehudit be-Et Ha-Chadasha*, edited by Aviezer Ravitzky, 466-479. Jerusalem: Yad Ben-Zvi, 1998.

Bodek, Elimelekh Ozer. *Bo'u She'arav: Divrei Hatam Sofer 'al Sefer Hovot Ha-Levavot*. Brooklyn: Ohel Yehudah, 1999.

Bokser, Ben-Zion, ed. and trans. *Abraham Isaac Kook: The Lights of Penitence, Lights of Holiness: The Moral Principles, Essays, Letters and Poems*. New York: Paulist Press, 1978.

Bor, Harris. "Enlightenment Values, Jewish Ethics: The Haskalah's Transformation of the Traditional Musar Genre." In *New Perspectives on the Haskalah,* edited by Samuel Feiner, 48-63. London: Littman Library, 2001.

———. "Moral Education in the Age of Jewish Enlightenment." PhD diss., Cambridge University, 1996.

Breuer, Mordechai. *Ohalei Torah: Ha-Yeshiva: Tavnitah ve-Toldotehah*. Jerusalem: Mercaz Shazar, 2003.

———. "Maamar Rabbi Shimshon Refael Hirsch zt"l 'al Aggadot Hazal." *Ha-Ma'ayan* 17, no. 2 (Winter 1975-1976): 1-16.

———. "Review of Noah H. Rosenbloom, *Tradition in an Age of Reform*." *Tradition* 16, no. 4 (1997): 140-149.

Brill, Alan. "Auxiliary to Hokhmah: The Writings of the Vilna Gaon and Philosophical Terminology." In *The Vilna Gaon and his Disciples*, edited by Moshe Hallamish, Yosef Rivlin, and Rafael Shuchat, 9-37 [English]. Ramat Gan, Bar-Ilan University Press, 2003.

———. "The Mystical Path of the Vilna Gaon." *Journal of Jewish Thought and Philosophy* 3 (1993): 131-151.

———. "Worlds Destroyed, Worlds Rebuilt: The Religious Thought of R. Yehudah Amital." *Edah Journal* 5, no. 2 (2006): 2-19.

Brill, Alan, and Rori Picker-Neiss. "Jewish Views of World Religions: Four Models." In *Jewish Theology and World Religions,* edited by Alon Goshen-Gottstein and Eugene Korn, 41-60. Oxford: Littman Library, 2012.

Brodna, Avraham Zvi. *Quntres Liqutim u-Veurim 'al Sefer Ha-Qadosh Liqutei Amarim Ha-Niqra Tanya*. Jerusalem: n.p., 1921.

Brodt, Eliezer. "The Netziv, Reading Newspapers on Shabbos and Censorship." *The Seforim Blog* (blog), March 5, 2014. http://seforim.blogspot.com/2014/03/the-netziv reading-newspapers-on.html.

Brown, Benjamin. "'Eynnenu Shayakh li ki Eynni 'Oseq ba-Zeh': Yahaso shel Rabbi Yisrael Salanter le-Kabbalah." In *Ve-Zot li-Yehudah: Yehudah Liebes Festschrift*, edited by Maren Niehoff, Ronit Meroz, and Jonathan Garb, 420-439. Jerusalem: Hebrew University/Mossad Bialik, 2012.

Brown, Peter. *Augustine of Hippo: A Biography*. 2nd ed. Berkeley: University of California Press, 2000.

Buber, Martin. *On Zion*. Translated by Stanley Godman. New York: Schocken, 1973.

Campbell, Ted A. *The Religion of the Heart: A Study of European Religious Life in the Seventeenth and Eighteenth Centuries*. Columbia: University of South Carolina Press, 1991.

Caplan, Kimmy. *Ortodoksiyah be-'Olam He-Hadash: Rabbanim ve-Darshanut be-America, 1881-1924*. Jerusalem: Mercaz Shazar, 2002.

Chajes, Aharon. *Shishim ve-Shalosh Shanah bi-Yerushalayim*. Jerusalem: Salomon Press, 1953.

Chajes, J. H. "Accounting for the Self: Preliminary Generic Historical Reflections on Early Modern Jewish Egodocuments." *Jewish Quarterly Review*, n.s., 95, no. 1 (Winter, 2005): 1-15.

Chajes, Zvi Hirsch. *Torat Neviim*. Zolkiew: Hopfer, 1839.

Chatterjee, Margaret. "Rabbi Abraham Isaac Kook and Sri Aurobindo: Towards a Comparison." In *Between Jerusalem and Benares: Comparative Studies in Judaism and Hinduism*, edited by Hananya Goodman, 243-266. Albany: State University of New York Press, 1994.

Cohen, David [Ha-Nazir]. *Hug Ha-Re'ayah*. 2 vols. Jerusalem: Makhon Nezer David, 2015-2018.

———. *Qol Ha-Nevuah: Ha-Higayon Ha-'Ivri Ha-Shim'i*. Jerusalem: Mossad Ha-Rav Kook, 1979.

Cohen, Gerson D. "Esau as Symbol in Early Medieval Thought." In *Jewish Medieval and Renaissance Studies*, edited by Alexander Altmann, 19-48. Cambridge, MA: Harvard University Press, 1967.

Cohen, Jack. *Guides for an Age of Confusion: Studies in the Thinking of Avraham Y. Kook and Mordecai Kaplan*. New York: Fordham University Press, 1999.

Cohen, Richard I. *Jewish Icons: Art and Society in Modern Europe.* Berkeley: University of California Press, 1998.

Cohen, Shear-Yashuv, Zvi Kaplan, Ya'aqov Avigdor, and Shmuel Markovitz, eds. *Nezir Ehav.* Jerusalem, 1978.

Cohen, Yonatan. *Teunvah u-Temurah: Panim be-Heqer Ha-Philosophiyah Ha-Yehudit ve-Toldotehah.* Jerusalem: Mossad Bialik, 1997.

———. "Yesodot Shitatiyyim be'Heqer Ha-Philosophia Ha-Yehudit be-Zemanenu: Wolfson, Gutman and Strauss." *Da'at* 38 (1997): 105-126

Cordovero, Moshe. *Pardes Rimonim.* Jerusalem: n.p., 1968 [1548].

Dan, Joseph. *Jewish Mysticism and Jewish Ethics.* 2nd ed. Northvale: Jason Aronson, 2006.

———. "Kefel Ha-Panim shel Ha-Meshihiyut be-Hasidut." In *Be-Ma'agalei Hasidim:Kovetz Mehqarim le-Zikhro shel Mordechai Wilensky*, edited by Immanuel Etkes, 299-315. Jerusalem: Mossad Bialik, 2000.

Daniel, Shabtai. *Eliezer Don-Yehiya.* Jerusalem, 1932.

Danzig, Neil. "Geonic Jurisprudence from the Cairo Genizah: An Appreciation of Early Scholarship." *Proceedings of the American Academy for Jewish Research* 63 (1997-2001): 1-47.

Daum, Hayim Yehudah. "'Iyunei Halakhah be-Mussar Avikha." In *Berurim be-Hilkhot Ha-Re'ayah*, edited by Moshe Zvi Neriah, Aryeh Stern, and Neriah Gutel, 479-487. Jerusalem: Beit Ha-Rav, 1992.

Davidson, Pamela. "Vladimir Soloveev and the Ideal of Prophecy." *Slavonic and East European Review* 78, no. 4 (October 2000): 643-670.

Devarim Rabbah. Edited by Saul Lieberman. Jerusalem: Bamberger & Wharman, 1940.

de Vidas, Elijah. *Reishit Hokhmah.* Jerusalem: n.p., 1972 [1575].

Diamond, James A. *Maimonides and the Shaping of the Jewish Canon.* Cambridge: Cambridge University Press, 2014.

Dienstag, Yisrael Ya'aqov. "Ha-Rambam be-Mishnato shel Ha-Rav Kook zt"l: Bibliographiyah." In *Sefer Refael*, edited by Yosef Mowshowitz, 135-13. Jerusalem: Mossad Ha-Rav Kook, 2000.

Dison, Yonina. "Arba'ah Motivim be-Orot Ha-Qodesh." *Da'at* 24 (1990): 41-86.

Dixon, Thomas. *From Passions to Emotions: The Creation of a Secular Psychological Category.* Cambridge: Cambridge University Press, 2003.

Domb, Risa. "A Hebrew Island in the British Isles: Hayehoody and Its Editor I. Suwalski (1897-1913)." In *Jewish History: Essays in Honour of Chimen Abramsky*, edited by Ada Rapoport-Albert and Steven J. Zipperstein, 127-137. London: Peter Halban, 1988.

Don-Yehiya, Eliezer. *Even Shtiyah.* Vilna: Katzenellenbogen, 1893.

Dubnow, Simon. *Nationalism and History: Essays on Old and New Judaism.* Edited by Koppel S. Pinson. Philadelphia: Jewish Publication Society, 1958.

Dumont, Louis. *Essays on Individualism.* Chicago: University of Chicago Press, 1986.

———. *German Ideology: From France to Germany and Back.* Chicago: University of Chicago Press, 1994.

Durkheim, Emile. *Elementary Forms of the Religious Life.* Translated by Joseph Ward Swain. New York: Free Press, 1954 [1912].

Duvzevitz, Avraham Dov. *Ha-Metzaref.* Odessa: Beilinison, 1870.

———. *Lo Dubim ve-lo Ya'ar.* Berdiczew: Sheftel, 1890.

Dweck, Yaacob. Introduction to *Sabbatai Sevi: The Mystical Messiah, 1626-1676*, by Gershom Scholem, xxix-lxv. Translated by R. J. Z. Werblowsky. Princeton: Bollingen/Princeton University Press, 2017 [1973].

Eisen, Arnold M. *Rethinking Modern Judaism: Ritual, Commandment, Community.* Chicago: University of Chicago Press, 1998.

Eisenstadt, Ben-Zion. *Dor Rabbanav ve-Sofrav.* Vol. 3. Vilna: Katzenellenbogen, 1901.

Eisenstadt, Shmuel Noah. "Multiple Modernities." *Daedalus* 129, no. 1 (Winter 2020): 1-29.

Eitam, Uriel. "Sqirat Kitvei He-Hagut shel Ha-Re'ayah." *Tzohar* 18 (2004): 19-38.

Elbaum, Avishai. "Shinuyim be-Haskamot." *Ha-Ma'ayan* 38, no. 1 (Tishrei 5758): 34-38.

Elbaum, Jacob. *Beyn Petihut Le-Histagrut: Ha-Yezirah Ha-Ruhanit-Sifrutit be-Polin u-ve-Arzot Ashkenaz be-Shilhei Ha-Me'ah Ha-Shesh-'Esreh.* Jerusalem: Magnes, 1990.

———, ed. *Lehavin Divrei Hakhamim: Mivhar Divrei Mavo le-Aggadah u-Midrash mi-shel Hakhmei Yemei Ha-Beynayim.* Jerusalem: Mossad Bialik, 2000.

———. "Rabbi Judah Loew of Prague and His Attitude to the Aggadah." *Scripta Hierosolymitana* 22 (1971): 28-47.

Eleh Ezkerah. New York: Ha-Makhon Le-heker Ba'ayot Ha-Yahadut Ha-Haredit, 1956.

Eliah, Dov. *Ha-Gaon.* Jerusalem: Moreshet Ha-Yeshivot, 2002.

———, ed. *Kol He-Katuv Le-Hayim.* Jerusalem, 1988.

Eliasberg, Mordechai. *Shevil Ha-Zahav.* Warsaw: Schuldberg, 1897.

———. *Terumat Yad.* Vilna: Dvorzetz, 1875.

Eliasberg, Yonatan. *Darkhei Horaah.* Vilna: Metz, 1884.

Elijah ben Solomon of Vilna [Gaon of Vilna]. *Perush ,al Kamah Aggadot.* Vilna: Rotenberg, 1830.

———. *Sefer Mishlei ,im Perush Ha-GRA.* Edited by Yisrael Vidovsky. Jerusalem: Even Yisrael, 1994.

———. *Tiqunei Zohar ,im Beiur Ha-GRA.* Vilna: Shmuel Yosef Fuenn & Avraham Zvi Rosenkranz, 1867.

Elior, Rachel. *Herut ,al Ha-Luhot: Ha-Mahshavah Ha-Hasidit, Meqorotehah Ha-Mistiyyim ve-Yesodotehah Ha-Kabaliyyim.* Tel Aviv: Misrad Ha-Bitahon, 1999.

———. *Torat Ahdut Ha-Hafakhim: Ha-Theosophia Ha-Mistit shel Habad.* Jerusalem: Mossad Bialik, 1992.

Ellenson, David, *After Emancipation: Jewish Religious Responses to Modernity.* Cincinnati: Hebrew Union College Press, 2004.

Elman, Yaakov. "Meiri and the Non-Jew: A Comparative Investigation." In *New Perspectives on Jewish-Christian Relations*, edited by Elisheva Carlebach and Jacob J. Schachter, 266-296. Leiden: E. J. Brill, 2011.

Elyakim, Nissim. *Ha-Ameq Davar La-Neziv.* Rechovot: Moreshet Ya'akov, 2002.

Epstein, Barukh. *Meqor Barukh.* Vilna: Romm, 1928.

Ernst, S., ed. *Sefer Yavetz.* Tel Aviv: Ahiever, 1934.

Etkes, Immanuel. *Ha-Zionut Ha-Meshihit shel Ha-Gaon mi-Vilna: Hamtza'atah shel Masoret.* Jerusalem: Carmel, 2019.

———. "Immanent Factors and External Influences in the Development of the Movement in Russia." In *Toward Modernity: The European Jewish Model*, edited by Jacob Katz, 13-32. New Brunswick: Transaction Books, 1987.

———. "The Relationship between Talmudic Scholarship and the Institution of the Rabbinate in Nineteenth-Century Lithuanian Jewry." In *Scholars and Scholarship*, edited by Leo Landman, 107-132. New York: Yeshiva University Press, 1990.

———. *Rabbi Yisrael Salanter ve-Reishitah shel Tenu'at Ha-Mussar.* Jerusalem: Magnes/Hebrew University Press, 1982.

———. *Yahid Be-Doro: Ha-Gaon Mi-Vilna—Demut ve-Dimuy.* Jerusalem: Mercaz Shazar, 1998.

Etkes, Immanuel, and Shlomo Tickochinski, eds. *Yeshivot Lita: Pirqei Zikhronot.* Jerusalem: Mercaz Shazar, 2004.

Even-Hen, [Edelstein], Ya'aqov. *Rav u-Manhig: Hayav u-Demuto shel Ha-Rav Avraham Yizhak Ha-Cohen Kook.* Jerusalem: Sifriyat Eliner, 1998.

Evron, Yemimah. "Mi Kotevet et Ha-Sefarim shel Dick Francis." *Ha-Aretz*, April 1, 2004.

Eytam, Uriel. "Sqirat Kitvei He-Hagut shel Ha-Re'ayah." *Tzohar* 18 (1994): 19-38.

Faierstein, Morris M. "God's Need for the Commandments in Medieval Kabbalah." *Conservative Judaism* 36, no. 1 (1982): 45-59.

Falk, Alexander. *Sefat Emet.* Vilna: Garber, 1902.

Falukh, Moshe. "Nitsotsot she-Eyn ba-Hem Mamash: Yahaso Ha-Haguti ve-Ha-Hilkhati shel Ha-Re'ayah Kook le-Hiloni ve-la-Hilun: Keriyah Rav-Shikhvatit." In *Sefer Zikaron le-Professor Zev Falk*, edited by Rivka Horvitz, Yohanan Silman, Michael Corinaldi, and Moshe David Herr, 89-122. Jerusalem: Meisharim/ Makhon Schechter, 2005.

Faur, Jose. "Intuitive Knowledge of God in Medieval Jewish Theology." *Jewish Quarterly Review* 67, nos. 2-3 (1976-1977): 90-110.

Feiner, Shmuel, ed. *Mi-Haskalah Lohemet le-Haskalah Meshameret: Mivhar Mi-Kitvei Rashi Fuenn.* Jerusalem: Mercaz Dinur, 1993.

Feinstein, Moshe. *Igrot Moshe, Yoreh De'ah.* Vol. 1. New York: n.p., 1959.

Feldman, Seymour. "Maimonides—A Guide for Posterity." In *Cambridge Companion to Maimonides*, edited by Kenneth Seeskin, 324-359. Cambridge: Cambridge University Press, 2005.

Ferziger, Adam S. *Exclusion and Hierarchy: Orthodoxy, Nonobservance and the Emergence of Modern Jewish Identity.* Philadelphia: University of Pennsylvania Press, 2005.

Fine, Lawrence. *Physician of the Soul, Healer of the Cosmos: Isaac Luria and His Kabbalistic Fellowship.* Stanford: Stanford University Press, 2003.

Finkel, Natan Zvi. *Or Ha-Zafun.* Jerusalem: Haskel/Yeshivat Hevron, 1959-1968.

Fischer, Shlomo. "Self-Expression and Democracy in Radical Religious Zionist Ideology." PhD diss., Hebrew University, 2007.

———. "Radical Religious Zionism: From the Collective to the Individual." In *Kabbalah and Contemporary Spiritual Revival*, edited by Boaz Huss, 285-310. Beer-Sheva: Ben-Gurion University of the Negev Press, 2011.

———. "Fundamentalist or Religious Nationalist?: Israeli Modern Orthodoxy," in *Dynamic Belonging: Contemporary Jewish Collective Identities*, edited by Harvey E. Goldberg et al., 91-111. New York: Bergahan, 2012.

Fishbane, Michael A. *The Kiss of God: Spiritual and Mystical Death in Judaism.* Seattle: University of Washington Press, 1994.

Fishman [Maimon], J. L. "Rabbi Mordechai Eliasberg (z"l)." *Sinai* 6 (1940): 1-5.

———, ed. *Sefer Ha-Yovel Mugash le-Doctor Binyamin Menashe Levin le-Yovlo Ha-Shishim.* Jerusalem: Mossad Ha-Rav Kook, 1940.

———, ed. "Toldot Ha-Mizrahi ve-Hitpathhuto." In *Sefer Ha-Mizrahi*, 5-381. Jerusalem: Mossad Ha-Rav Kook, 1946.

———, ed. "Toldot Ha-Rav." In *Azkarah le-Nishmat Ha-Gaon Ha-Zadiq Ha-Re'ayah*, vol. 1, 17-167. Jerusalem: Mossad Ha-Rav Kook, 1937-1938.

Flanner, Janet. "Fuhrer." *The New Yorker*, February 29, 1936.

Fletcher, George P. *Basic Concepts of Legal Thought.* New York: Oxford University Press, 1996.

Frankel, Aryeh. "Kook, Avraham Yitzhaq." In *Encyclopedia shel ha-Tzionut Ha-Datit*, vol. 5, edited by Yitzhak Refael, with Geula Bat-Yehudah , cols. 89-422. Jerusalem: Mossad Ha-Rav Kook, 1983.

Frankel, Jonathan. *Prophecy and Politics: Socialism, Nationalism and the Russian Jews, 1862-1917.* Cambridge: Cambridge University Press, 1981.

Franks, Paul. "Inner Anti-Semitism or Kabbalistic Legacy? German Idealism's Relationship to Judaism." In *Yearbook of German Idealism, Volume VII, Faith and Reason*, edited by Fred Rush, Jürgen Stolzenberg, and Paul Franks, 254-279. Berlin: Walter de Gruyter, 2010.

Freeze, ChaeRan Y. *Jewish Marriage and Divorce in Imperial Russia.* Hanover: Brandeis University Press/ University Press of New England, 2002.

Friedman, Menahem. *Hevrah be-Mashber Legitimatzyah: Ha-Yishuv Ha-Yashan Ha-Ashkenazi, 1900-1917.* Jerusalem: Mossad Bialik, 2001.

———. *Hevrah Va-Dat: Ha-Ortodoksiyah Ha-Lo-Tsiyonit be-Eretz Yisrael, 1918-1936.* Jerusalem: Yad Ben Zvi, 1988.

———. "A Good Story Deserves Retelling—The Unfolding of the Akiva Legend." *JSIJ* 3 (2004): 55-93

Funkenstein, Amos. *Tadmit ve-Toda'ah Histori'l be-Yahadut u-ve-Sevivatah ha Tarbutit.* Tel Aviv: Am Oved, 1991.

Furstenberg, Yair. "Rabbinic Responses to Greco-Roman Ethics of Self-Formation in Tractate *Avot.*" In *Self, Self-Fashioning and Individuality in Late Antiquity: New Perspetives,* edited by Maren R. Niehoff and Joshua Levinson, 125-148. Tubingen: Mohr Siebeck, 2019.

Gallagher, Shaun. *Hermeneutics and Interpretation.* Albany: State University of New York Press, 1992.

Galinsky, Yehuda. "Darko be-Parshanut shel Yosef Zekharia Stern." Unpublished paper.

Garb, Jonathan. *The Chosen Will Become Herds: Studies in Twentieth-Century Kabbalah.* New Haven: Yale University Press, 2009.

———. "Ha-Model Ha-Politi be-Qabbalah Ha-Modernit: 'Iyun be-Kitvei Ramchal u-bi-Sevivato Ha-Ra'ayonit." In *'Al Da'at Ha-Qahal: Dat u-Politika be-Hagut Yehudit,* edited by Benjamin Brown, Avinoam Rosenak, Yedidya Stern 13-45. Jerusalem: Israel Democracy Institute and Mercaz Shazar, 2012.

———. "Ha-Re'ayah Kook—Hogeh Leumi o Meshorer Misti." *Da'at* 54 (2004): 69-96

———. *Ha-Qabbalah be-Et Ha-Hadasahah ki-Tehum Mehqar Autonomi.* Los Angeles: Cherub Press, 2016.

———. "Ketavav Ha-Amitiyyim shel Ramhal be-Qabbalah." *Qabbalah* 25 (2011): 165-222.

———. *Mequbal be-Lev Ha-Se'arah: Rabbi Moshe CHayim Luzzatto.* Tel Aviv: Tel Aviv University Press, 2014.

———. "Rabbi Kook and His Sources: From Kabbalistic Historiosophy to National Mysticism." In *Studies in Modern Religions, Religious Movements and the Babi-Baha'i Faiths,* edited by Moshe Sharon, 77-96. Leiden: E. J. Brill, 2004.

———. *Yearnings of the Soul: Psychological Thought in Modern Kabbalah.* Chicago: University of Chicago Press, 2015.

Gassenschmidt, Christoph. *Jewish Liberal Politics in Tsarist Russia, 1900-1914.* Oxford and London: St. Antony's/MacMillan, 1995.

Gaut, Greg. "Can a Christian Be a Nationalist? Vladimir Solov'ev's Critique of Nationalism." *Slavic Review* 57, no. 1 (Spring 1998): 77-94.

Genahovsky, Eliyahu Moshe, ed. *Ha-Rav Mordechai Eliasberg: Mivhar Ketavav.* Tel Aviv: Josef Srebrek, 1947.

———. *Rav Mordekchai Eliasberg: Toldotav, Mahsavotav ve-Helekh Ruho.* Jerusalem: n.p., 1937.

Gerber, Reuven. "Hitpathut Hazon Ha-Tehiyah Ha-Leumit be-Mishnat Ha-Re'ayah Kook." PhD diss., Hebrew University, 1991.

———. *Mahapekhat Ha-Hearah: Darko Ha-Ruhanit shel Ha-Re'ayah Kook.* Jerusalem: Mossad Bialik/ Ha-Sifriyah Ha-Zionit, 2005.

Gershuni, Shemarya. "'Yaldah Hakhamah ve-Tovat Sekhel' . . . 'Al Esther Kook, Bito shel Ha-Re'ayah." *Ha-Ma'ayan* 224, no. 2 (Tevet 5778/2018): 75-92.

Gershuni, Yehudah. *Sha'arei Zedeq.* Jerusalem: n.p., 1994.

Giller, Pinchas. *Reading the Zohar: The Sacred Text of the Kabbalah.* New York: Oxford University Press, 2001.

Goetschel, Roland. "Torah Lishma as a Central Concept in the Degel Mahaneh Efrayim of Moses Hayyim Ephraim of Sudylkow." In *Hasidism Reappraised,* edited by Ada Rapoport-Albert, 258-267. London: Littman Library, 1997.

Goldman, Eliezer. *Mehqarim ve-'Iyunim*. Jerusalem: Hebrew University/Magnes, 2000.

Goldstein, Moshe. *Sefer Yabia' Omer u-Shegiyot Mi Yavin*. Jerusalem: Rohadlt, 1924.

Goldstein, Yosef. *Ahad Ha-Am: Biographiyah*. Jerusaleam: Keter, 1992.

Golomb, Jacob, ed. *Nietzsche be-Tarbut Ha-'Ivrit*. Jerusalem: Hebrew University/Magnes, 2002.

Goodman, Lenn E., ed. *Neoplatonism in Jewish Thought*. Albany: State University of New York Press, 1992.

Goodman, Micah. "Beyn Mevukhat Ha-Zeman le-Limud Qorot Ha-Zeman: 'Iyun Mehudash bi-Tefisat Ha-Historiyah shel RaNaK." *Da'at* 57-59 (2006): 210-228.

Goodman-Thau, Eveline, Gerd Mattenklott, and Christoph Schulte, eds. *Kabbala und Romantik*. Tubingen: Max Niemeyer, 1994.

———, eds. *Kabbala und die Literatur der Romantik*. Tubingen: Max Niemeyer, 1999.

Gordley, James. "Humanists and Scholastics." In *Essays on Law and Religion: The Berkeley and Oxford Symposia in Honor of David Daube*, edited by Calum M. Carmichael, 13-28. Berkeley: University of California at Berkeley, 1993.

Gordon, Aharon David. "Ha-Adam ve-Ha-Teva.'" In *Mivhar Ketavim*, edited by Eliezer Schweid, 49-171. Jerusalem: Ha-Sifruyah Ha-Zionit, 1982.

———. "Heshbonenu im 'Atzmenu." In *Ha-Umah ve-Ha-Avodah*, edited by S. H. Bergmann and Eliezer Shihat, 327-374. Tel Aviv: Ha-Sifryiah Ha-Zionit, 1952.

Gordon, Abba, and Hanoch Levin, eds. *Smorgon: Mehoz Vilna: Sefer, Edut ve-Zikaron*. Tel Aviv: Irgun Yotzei Smorgon be-Yisrael, 1965.

Gorenberg, Gershom. *The Accidental Empire: Israel and the Birth of the Settlements, 1967-1977*. New York: Times Books, 2006.

Gottschalk, Yehiel Alfred (with Hillel Agranat). *Ahad Ha-Am ve-Ha-Ruah Ha-Leumi*. Jerusalem: Ha-Sifriayah Ha-Tziyonit/Mossad Bialik, 1992.

Graham, William A. *Beyond the Written Word: Oral Aspects of Scripture in the History of Religion*. Cambridge: Cambridge University Press, 1987.

Grayevsky, Pinhas. *Benot Zion vi-Yerushalayim*. Jerusalem: Yad Ben-Zvi, 2000. First published Jerusalem: Zuckerman Press, 1929-1933.

Greenberg, Moshe Zvi. *Mo'etzot va-Da'at*. Odessa: Beilinson, 1897.

Grey, Shalom. "Toldot Ha-Gaon Rabbi Zelig Reuven Bengis." *Yeshurun* 12 (Nisan 5763/Spring 2003): 150-192.

Gries, Zev. *Sifrut Ha-Hanhagot: Toldotehah u-Meqomah be-Hayei Hasidei Rabbi Yisrael Ba'al Shem Tov*. Jerusalem: Mossad Bialik, 1989.

Grodzinsky, Hayim Ozer. *Sefer Ahiezer*. Vilna: Garber, 1922-1939.

Gutel, Neriah. *Hadashim gam Yeshanim: Bi-Netivei Mishnato Ha-Hilkhatit-Hagutit shel Ha-Rav Kook*. Jerusalem: Hebrew University/Magnes, 2005.

———. *Mekhutavei Reayah*. Jerusalem: Makhon Ha-Ratzyah, 2000.

———. "Omanut ve-Aminut be-'Arikhat Ha-Ratzyah Kook et Kitvei Ha-Re'ayah." *Tarbitz* 70 (2001): 601-625.

———. "Protocol Ha-Agudah le-Hotza'at Kitvei Ha-Rav Kook." In *Moshe Hayim Halevi Katzenellenbogen Memorial Volume (Sinai Supplement)*, edited by Yosef Movhsovitz, 340-353. Jerusalem: Mossad Harav Kook, 2001.

Ha-Cohen, Hillel David, ed. *Ha-Pisgah*. Vilna: 1895-1904.

Ha-Cohen, Shimon of Mitowi. *Sha'ar Shimon*. Vilna: Garber, 1901.

Hadari, Yeshahayu. *Reayah Kook: Meah Shanah le-Holadeto: Ta'arukhat Yovel, Catalogue, Elul 5726*. Jerusalem: Jewish Agency, 1966.

Hadot, Pierre. *Philosophy as a Way of Life*. Translated by Michael Chase. Oxford: Blackwell, 1995.

Hall, David D. *Worlds of Wonder, Days of Judgment: Popular Religious Belief in Early New England*. Cambridge, MA, Harvard University Press, 1990.

Halpern, Ben, and Jehuda Reinharz. *Zionism and the Creation of a New Society*. Hanover: Brandeis University Press/University Press of New England, 2000.

Halpern, Eliyahu. *Hemdat Yisrael*. Jerusalem: Diskin Orphanage, 1950.

Halperin, Raphael. *Atlas Etz Hayim: Aharonim*. Tel Aviv: Heqdesh Ruah Ya'aqov, 1978-1987.

Hamiel, Hayim. "Yahasei RY"Z Stern ve-Rabbanei Doro be-Shu"t." In *Sefer Shragai*, vol. 4, edited by Yitzhaq Refael, 133-167. Jerusalem: Mossad Ha-Rav Kook, 1983.

Hansel, Joelle. *Moise Hayyim Luzzatto (1707-1746): Kabbale et Philosophie*. Paris: Patrimonies/Les Editions du Cerf, 2004.

Harris, Jay M. *How Do We Know This?: Midrash and the Fragmentation of Modern Judaism*. Albany: State University of New York Press, 1995.

———. "The Image of Maimonides in Nineteenth-Century Historiography." *Proceedings of the American Academy of Jewish Research* 54 (1987): 116-139.

———. *Nachman Krochmal: Guiding the Perplexed of the Modern Age*. New York: New York University Press, 1991.

———. "Rabbinic Literature in Lithuania after the Death of the Gaon." In *The Gaon of Vilnius and the Annals of Jewish Culture: Materials of the International Scientific Conference, Vilnius, Septermber 10-12, 1997*, edited by Izraelis Lempertas, 88-95. Vilnius: UNESCO/Community of Lithuanian Jews/Vilnius University Publishing House, 1998.

Harvey, Zev. "Torat Ha-Nevuah Ha-Synestheti shel RIHA"L ve-He'arah 'al Sefer Ha-Zohar." *Mehqarei Yerushalayim be-Mahshevet Yisrael* 12 (1996): 141-155.

Hayim of Volozhin. *Nefesh Ha-Hayim*. Vilna: Zimmel, 1837.

———. *Ru'ah Hayim*. Vilna: Romm, 1858.

Heilman, H. *Beis Rebbe*. Vilna: Rosenkranz, 1904.

Heinemann, Isaac. *Ta'amei Ha-Mizvot be-Sifrut Yisrael*. 2 vols. 3rd ed. Jerusalem: Jewish Agency Press, 1954.

Heller-Wilensky, Sara. *Rabbi Yitzhaq Arama u-Mishnato*. Jerusalem and Tel Aviv: Mossad Bialik/Devir, 1956.

Henkin, Eitam. "Ha-Rav Yitzhak Arieli ve-Shikhekhato be-Hug Ha-Re'ayah u-Mercaz Ha-Rav." *Assif* 4 (2017): 463-493.

———. "Li-Nevukhei Ha-Dor shel Ha-Re'ayah Kook: Mavo le-Hibur she-lo Hushlam." *Aqdamot* 25 (2010): 171-188.

———. *Ta'arokh le-Fanai Shulhan: Hayav, Zemano u-Mif'alo shel HRY"M Epstein, Ba'al 'Arukh Ha-Shulhan*. Edited by Eliezer Brodt. Jerusalem: Maggid/Koren, 2018.

Hertzberg, Arthur. *The Zionist Idea: A Historical Analysis and Reader*. New York: Atheneun, 1976. First published New York: Harper & Row, 1959.

Hervieu-Leger, Daniele. "Multiple Religious Modernities: A New Approach to Contemporary Religiosity." In *Comparing Modernities: Pluralism versus Homogeneity; Essays in Honor of Shmuel N. Eisenstadt*, edited by Eliezer Ben-Refael and Yitzhak Sternberg, 327-338. Leiden: E. J. Brill, 2005.

Heschel, Abraham Joshua. *Torah min Ha-Shamayim be-Aspaqlariyah shel Ha-Dorot*. Vols. 1 and 2. London: Soncino, 1962; Vol. 3. Jerusalem: Beit Ha-Midrash Le-Rabbanim be-America, 1995.

Hess, Moshe. *Roma ve-Yerushalayim*. Translated by David Tzemah. Warsaw: Tushiyah/Halter, 1899.

Hevlin, Rina. *Mehuyavut Kefulah: Zehut Yehudit beyn Masoret le-Hilun be-Haguto shel Ahad Ha-Am*. Tel Aviv: Ha-Kibbutz Ha-Meuchad, 2001.

Hirsch, Samson Rafael. *Horev*. 1837. Translated by I. Grunfeld. Repr. New York, London, and Jerusalem: Soncino, 1962.

Holzman, Avner. *El Ha-Qer'a She-ba-Lev: Micha Yosef Berdyczewsky, Shenot Ha-Tzemihah: 1887-1902*. Jerusalem and Tel Aviv: Mossad Bialik/Tel Aviv University, 1995.

Horodensky, Ya'aqov Meir. *Mei Sasson.* Warsaw: Halter and Eisenstadt, 1894.

———. *Quntres Hosafah Le-Sefer Mei Sasson.* Warsaw: Halter & Eisenstadt, 1898.

Horowitz, Brian. "Vladimir Solov'ev and the Jews: A View from Today." In *The Russian Jewish Tradition: Intellectuals, Historians, Revolutionaries,* 198-214. Boston: Academic Studies Press, 2017.

Horvitz, Rivka, ed. *Yitzhaq Breuer: 'Iyunim be-Mishnato.* Ramat-Gan: Bar-Ilan University Press, 1988.

Hundert, Gershon. "The Library of the Study Hall in Volozhin." In *The Gaon of Vilnius and the Annals of Jewish Culture,* edited by Israel Lempertas, 247-256. Vilnius: UNESCO/Community of Lithuanian Jews/Vilnius University Publishing House, 1998.

Huss, Boaz. *She'elat Qiyumah shel Mistiqah Yehudit.* Jerusalem and Tel Aviv: Van Leer/Ha-Kibbutz Ha-Meuhad, 2016.

Hutchinson, John F. *Later Imperial Russia, 1890-1917.* London: Longman, 2001.

Idel, Moshe. "Abraham Abulafia, Gershom Scholem ve-Rabbi David Cohen ('Ha-Nazir')." *Jerusalem Studies in Jewish Thought: The Eliezer Schweid Jubilee Volume* 19 (2005): 819-834.

———. "Beyn Ha-Kabbalah Ha-Nevuit le-Kabbalat Rabbi Menahem Mendel mi-Shklov." In *Ha-GRA u-Veit Midrasho,* edited by Moshe Hallamish, Yosef Rivlin, and Raphael Shuchat, 173-184. Ramat Gan: Bar-Ilan University Press, 2003.

———. "Beyn Kabbalat Yerushalayim le-Kabbalat Rabbi Yisrael Saruq." *Shalem* 6 (1992): 165-173.

———. *Enchanted Chains: Techniques and Rituals in Jewish Mysticism.* Los Angeles: Cherub Press, 2005.

———. *Hasidism: Between Ecstasy and Magic.* Albany: State University of New York Press, 1995.

———. *Kabbalah and Interpretation.* New Haven: Yale University Press, 2002.

———. *Kabbalah: New Perspectives.* New Haven: Yale University Press, 1988.

———. *Messianic Mystics.* New Haven: Yale University Press, 1998.

———. Preface to *Jewish Mystical Autobiographies,* translated by Morris M. Faierstein, xv-xxii. New York: Paulist Press, 1999.

———. "Yofyah shel Ishah: Le-Toldotehah shel Ha-Mistiqah Ha-Yehudit." In *Be-Ma'agalei Hasidim: Kovetz Mehqarim le-Zikhro shel Mordechai Wilensky,* edited by Immanuel Etkes, David Asaf, Israel Bartal, and Elhanan Reiner. 317-334. Jerusalem: Mossad Bialik, 2000.

Ir-Shai, Ronit, and Dov Schwartz, eds. *Ruah Hadashah be-Armon Ha-Torah: Sefer Yovel li-Khvod Professor Tamar Ross 'im Hagiah li-Gevurot.* Ramat Gan: Bar-Ilan University Press, 2018.

Irvin-Erickson, Douglas. *Raphael Lemkin and the Concept of Genocide.* Philadelphia: University of Pennsylvania Press, 2017.

Ish-Shalom, Benjamin. "Beyn Rav Kook li-Spinoza ve-Goethe." In *Qolot Rabim: Sefer Ha-Ziqaron le-Rivqa Schatz-Uffenheimer, Jerusalem Studies in Jewish Thought,* vol. 13, edited by Rachel Elior and Joseph Dan, 525-556. Jerusalem: Hebrew University Press, 1996.

———. *Ha-Rav Kook: Beyn Ratziyonalism le-Mistiqah.* Tel Aviv: Am Oved, 1990.

———. "Zionut Datit beyn Apologiyah le-Hitmodedut." *Cathedra* 90 (1999): 145-149.

Israel, Jonathan I. "Enlightenment! Which Enlightenment?" *Journal of the History of Ideas* 67, no. 1 (2006): 523-545.

Jaffe, Benjamin. *Ha-Rav mi-Yehud.* Jerusalem: Ha-Histadrut Ha-Zionit, 1958.

Jaffe, Mordechai Gimpel. *Mivhar Ketavim.* Jerusalem: n.p., 1978.

James, William. *The Varieties of Religious Experience: A Study in Human Nature.* New York: Longmans, Green & Co., 1902.

Kagan, Berl. *Yiddishe Shtet, Shtetlakh un Dorfishe Yishuvin in Lite.* New York: n.p., 1991.

Kagan, Yisrael Meir [Hafetz Hayim]. *Liqutei Halakhot.* Pietrkov: n.p., 1899.

Kagan, Zipora. "Homo Anthologicus: Micha Josef Berdyczewski and the Anthological Genre." *Prooftexts: A Journal of Jewish Literary History* 19, no. 1 (1999): 41-57.

Kahana, Maoz. *Me-Ha-Noda'-bi-Yehudah le-Hatam Sofer: Halakhah ve-Hagut le-Nokhah Etgarei Ha-Zman.* Jerualem: Mercaz Shazar, 2015.

Kahane, Simhah. *Magen Ha-Talmud.* Warsaw: Baumritter, 1901.

Kamenetzky, David. "Ha-Gaon Rabbi Menashe me-Ilya zt"l." *Yeshurun* 20 (2008): 729-781.

Kamenetsky, Nathan. *Making of a Godol.* Jerusalem: Ha-Mesorah, 2002.

Kanarfogel, Ephraim. "Rabbinic Attitudes toward Nonobservance in the Medieval Period." In *Jewish Tradition and the Nontraditional Jew,* edited by Jacob J. Schacter, 3-35. Northvale: Aronson, 1992.

Kaplan, Lawrence J. "Rav Kook and the Jewish Philosophical Tradition." In *Rabbi Abraham Isaac Kook and Jewish Spirituality,* edited by Lawrence J. Kaplan and David Shatz, 41-77. New York: New York University Press, 1995.

———. "The Love of God in Maimonides and Rav Kook." *Judaism* 43, no. 3 (1994): 227-239.

———. "Rabbi Mordechai Jaffe and the Evolution of Jewish Culture in Poland in the Sixteenth Century." In *Jewish Thought in the Sixteenth Century,* edited by Benard Cooperman, 266-282. Cambridge, MA: Harvard University Press, 1983.

Kaplan, Lawrence J., and David Shatz, eds. *Rabbi Abraham Isaac Kook and Jewish Spirituality.* New York: New York University Press, 1995.

Kaplan, Zvi, ed. *Sihot Ha-Sabba mi-Slobodka.* Tel Aviv: Avraham Zioni, 1955.

Karelitz, Avraham Yeshayahu [Hazon Ish]. *Emunah u-Vitahon.* Edited by S. Greineman. Tel Aviv, 1954.

Karlinsky, Hayim. "'Al Tekufat Limudo shel maran Ha-G'RAYAH Kook Be-Smorgon." In *Shanah Be-Shanah,* 389-398. Jerusalem: Heikhal Shlomo, 1982.

Kasher, Menahem. *Torah Shleimah.* Vol. 12. New York: Shulzinger, 1948.

Kasher, Moshe S., and Yaacov Belkhrovitz, eds. *Perushei Ha-Maharal Mi-Prague Le-Aggadot Ha-Shas.* Jerusalem: Torah Shlemah, 1968.

Katz, Dov. *Pulmus Ha-Mussar.* Jerusalem: Weiss, 1972.

———. *Tenu'at Ha-Mussar.* Tel Aviv: Beitan Ha-Sefer, 1946-1956.

Katz [Kehat], Hannah. *Mishnat Ha-Netziv.* Jerusalem: n.p., 1990.

Katz, Jacob. *Halakhah ve-Kabbalah.* Jerusalem: Magnes/Hebrew University, 1984.

———. *Leumiyut Yehudit: Masot u-Mehqarim.* Jerusalem: Ha-Sifriyah Ha-Zionit, 1979.

———. *Out of the Ghetto: The Social Background of Jewish Emancipation, 1770-1870.* New York: Schocken Books, 1978.

———. "Towards a Biography of the Hatam Sofer." In *Divine Law in Human Hands: Case Studies in Halakhic Flexibility,* 403-443. Jerusalem: Hebrew University/Magnes, 1998.

Katzenellenbogen, Aryeh. *He-Ketav ve-Ha-Derash.* Pietrkov: Rosengarten & Horovitz, 1909.

Katznelson, Gideon. *Ha-Milhamah Ha-Sifrutit beyn Ha-Haredim ve-Ha-Maskilim.* Tel Aviv: Devir, 1954.

Kaufmann, Tsippi. *Be-Khol Derakhekah Da'ehu: Tefisat Ha-Elohut ve-Ha-'Avodah be-Gashmiyut be-Reishit Ha-Hasidut.* Ramat Gan: Bar-Ilan University Press, 2009.

Kellner, Menachem. *Maimonides on Human Perfection.* Brown Judaic Studies 202. Atlanta: Scholars Press, 1990.

Kena'ani, David. *Ha-Aliyah Ha-Sheniyah Ha-'Ovedet ve-Yahasah le-Dat ve-la-Masoret.* Tel Aviv: Sifiyat Po'alim, 1976.

Kinnarati, Amihai. "Yahas Ha-Re'ayah li-Tenu'at Ha-Mussar." In *Ozarot Ha-Re'ayah,* vol. 7, edited by Moshe Zuriel, 496-517. Rishon Le-Zion: Yeshivat Ha-Hesder Rishon Le-Zion, 2015.

Kitover, Israel. *Berurei Ha-Middot: Levaer u-Levarer kol Davar Be-Sefer Aqedat Yitzhaq u-ve-Yihud Divrei Sefer Ha-Middot.* Joszefof: Zetzer & Ra'anan, 1872.

Klausner, Yisrael. *Toldot Ha-Agudah Nes Ziyonah be-Volozhin.* Jerusalem: Mossad Ha-Rav Kook, 1954.

Klein, Menahem. "Teyotah Ne'elamah mi-Kitvei Ha-Shaharut shel Ha-Rav Kook odot Ha-Zionut Ha-Hilonit." In *Masuot: Mehqarim be-Sifrut Ha-Qabbalah u-Mahshevet Yisrael Muqdashim le-Zikhro shel Professor Ephraim Gottlieb z'l,* edited by Mikhal Oron and Amos Goldreich, 395-413. Jerusalem and Tel Aviv: Mossad Bialik/Tel Aviv University, 1994.

Kleinberger, Aharon Fritz. *Ha-Mahshavah Ha-Pedagogit shel Ha-Maharal mi-Prague.* Jerusalem: Hebrew University/Magnes, 1962.

———. "The Didactics of Rabbi Loew of Prague." *Scripta Hierosolymitana* 13 (1963): 32-55.

Kluback, William. "Israel in the Thought of Vladimir Soloviev." *Midstream* 36, no. 5 (June–July 1990): 28-31.

Kolakowski, Leszek. *Metaphysical Horror.* Translated by Agnieszka Kolakowska. Chicago: University of Chicago Press, 2001.

———. *The Main Currents of Marxism.* Vol. 1, *The Founders.* Translated by P. S. Falla. New York: Oxford University Press, 1978.

Koltun-Fromm, Ken. *Moses Hess and Modern Jewish Identity.* Bloomington: Indiana University Press, 2001.

Kook, Zvi Yehudah. "Le-Verurei Devarim Yesodiyim Bi-Temimutam." *'Amudim* 24, no. 2 (Heshvan 5736/1975): 40.

———. *Li-Sheloshah be-Elul: Yom Ha-Shanah le-Histalquto shel Adoni Avi Mori ve-Rabbi Harav Avraham Yitzhaq Ha-Cohen Kook.* Rev. ed. Jerusalem: Ha-Po'el Ha-Mizrahi, 1947 [1938].

Krakowski, Eliyahu. "Between the Genius and the Gaon: Lost in Translation." *Hakirah* 16 (2013): 153-175.

Kreisel, Howard. "Imitatio Dei in Maimonides' Guide of the Perplexed." *AJS Review* 19 (1994): 169-211.

Krumbein, Elyakim. "El Ha-Maqor: Le-Darko shel Ha-GRA bi-Veiuro La-Shulhan Arukh." *Ma'aseh Hoshev* 1 (2015): 209-226.

Kugel, James. *The Great Shift: Encountering God in Biblical Times.* Boston: Houghton Mifflin Harcourt, 2017.

Lang, Berel. "Space, Time and Philosophical Style." In *Philosophical Style,* edited by Berel Lang, 144-172. Chicago: Nelson Hall, 1980.

Lanir, Michal. *Ha-Re'ayah Kook ve-Ha-Zionut—Gilgulah shel Tiqvah.* Tel Aviv: Safra, 2015.

Lederhendler, Eli. *The Road to Modern Jewish Politics: Political Tradition and Political Reconstruction in the Jewish Community of Tsarist Russia.* New York: Oxford University Press, 1989.

———. "Modernity without Emancipation or Assimilation? The Case of Russian Jewry." In *Assimilation and Community: The Jews in Nineteenth-Century Europe,* edited by Jonthan Frankel and Steven J. Zipperstein, 324-343. Cambridge: Cambridge University Press, 1992.

Lehman, James H. "Maimonides, Mendelssohn and the Me'asfim: Philosophy and the Biographical Imagination in the Early Haskalah." *Leo Baeck Institute Yearbook* 20 (1975): 87-108.

Lehman, Marjorie. *The En Ya'aqov: Jacob ibn Habib's Search for Faith in the Talmudic Corpus.* Detroit: Wayne State University Press, 2011.

Leiman, Sid Z. "R. Israel Lipschutz and the Portrait of Moses Controversy." In *Danzig Between East and West: Aspects of Modern Jewish History,* edited by Isadore Twersky, 51-63. Cambridge, MA: Harvard University Press, 1985.

Levin, Aryeh. *Toldot Ha-Gaon Ha-Kadosh Mehabber Sifrei Leshem Shevo ve-Ahlamah.* Jerusalem: Verker, 1935.

Levin, Binyamin Menashe. "Zikhronot." *Sinai* 14 (1944): 185-203.

Levin, Dov, ed. *Pinqas Ha-Qehillot: Latvia ve-Estonia.* Jerusalem: Yad Vashem, 1988.

Levin, Joseph, ed. *Antopol.* Tel Aviv: Ha-Po'el Ha-Mizrahi, 1967.

Levin, Reuven. *Rosh La-Reuveni*. Daugavpils and Riga: Bilike Bicher, 1936.

Levinsky, Hayim. *Toldot Ha-Gaon Rabbi Mordechai Weisel (Rosenblatt)*. Vilna: Garber, 1917.

Lewis, Shmuel [Richie]. *Ve-Lifnei Kavod 'Anavah: Idiyal Ha-'Anavah ki-Yesod bi-Sefatam Ha-Musarit shel Hazal*. Jerusalem: Magnes Press, 2013.

Li, Rina. *Agnon ve-Ha-Tzimhonut*. Tel Aviv: Reshafim, 1993.

Liebes, Yehudah. "Yonah ben Amitai ke-Mashiah ben Yosef." *Mehqerei Yerushalayim bi-Mahshevet Yisrael* 3, no. 1-2 (1983-1984): 269-311.

Lifshitz, Hayim. *Shivhei Ha-Re'ayah*. Jerusalem: Makhon Harry Fischel, 1979.

Lifshitz, Yehezqel [Sofer Mahir]. *Galgal Ha-Hozer*. Warsaw: Unterhandler, 1886.

———. *Ha-Midrash ve-Ha-Ma'aseh*. Pietrikov, 1901.

Lilienblum, Moshe Leib. "Divrei Zemer." *Luah Ahiasaf* 5 (1898): 19-24.

Lindbeck, George A. *The Nature of Doctrine: Religion and Theology in a Postliberal Age*. Philadelphia: Westminster, 1984.

Lintop, Pinhas. *Pithei She'arim*. Vilna: Katzenellenbogen, 1880/5641.

———. *Yalqut Avnei Emunat Yisrael*. Warsaw: Torsz, 1895.

Litvak, Olga. *Haskalah: The Romantic Movement in Judaism*. New Brunswick: Rutgers University Press, 2012.

Litwin, A. [Shmuel Leib Horowitz]. "Der Letzter 'Guter Yid.'" In *Yiddische Neshomes*, vol. 3, 385-402. New York: Folksbildung, 1917.

Lobel, Diana. *A Sufi-Jewish Dialogue: Philosophy and Mysticism in Bahya ibn Paquda's Duties of the Heart*. Philadelphia: University of Pennsylvania Press, 2007.

Lorberbaum, Yair. "Reflection on the Halakhic Status of Aggadah." *Dine Israel* 24 (2007): 29-64.

Louden, Robert B. *Kant's Impure Ethics: From Rational Beings to Human Beings*. New York: Oxford University Press, 2000.

Lovejoy, Arthur O. *Essays in the History of Ideas*. Baltimore: Johns Hopkins University Press, 1948.

———. *The Great Chain of Being: A Study of the History of an Idea*. Cambridge, MA: Harvard University Press, 1936.

Lovibond, Sabina. *Ethical Formation*. Cambridge, MA: Harvard University Press, 2002.

Luria, Samuel. "Midbar Qadmut." In *Qadmut Sefer Ha-Zohar*, edited by David Luria, 9-24. Warsaw: Halter, 1887. Reprinted Tel Aviv: Netzah, 1951, with bibliographical essay "Zohar Ha-Raqi'a," by Yeruham Leiner.

Luz, Ehud. "Beyn Hagut le-Mehqar be-Mif'alo shel Eliezer Schweid." *Jerusalem Studies in Jewish Thought: The Eliezer Schweid Jubilee Volume* 19 (2005): 39-62.

———. *Maqbilim Nifgashim: Dat u-Leumiyut bi-Tenu'ah Ha-Zionit be-Mizrah Europa be-Reishitah, 1882-1904*. Tel Aviv: Am Oved, 1985.

———. "Spiritualism ve-Anarchism Dati be-Mishnato shel Shmeul Alexandrov." *Da'at* 7 (1981): 121-138.

Luzzatto, Moshe Hayim. *Adir Ba-Marom*. Edited by Yosef Spinner. Jerusalem: n.p., 1995.

———. *Da'at Tevunot*. Edited by Hayim Friedlander. Bnei Braq: Brody-Katz, 1975.

———. *Kalah Pithei Hokhmah*. Edited by Hayim Friedlander. Bnei Braq: Sifriyati/Gitler, 1992.

———. *La-Yesharim Tehillah*. Edited by Yohah David. Jerusalem: Mossad Bialik, 1982.

———. *Maamar Ha-Geulah*. Edited by H. Touitou. Ashkelon: n.p., 2002.

———. *Mesilat Yesharim*. Edited by Yosef Avivi. Jerusalem: Ofeq, 1994.

MacIntrye, Alasdair. *After Virtue: A Study in Moral Theory*. Notre Dame: University of Notre Dame Press, 1984.

Magid, Shaul. "Allegory Unbound: Rav Kook, Rabbi Akiva, Song of Songs, and the Rabbinic (Anti) Hero." *Kabbalah* 32 (2014): 57-82.

Maharal of Prague [Judah Loew ben Betzalel]. *Netivot 'Olam*. Edited by Hayim Pardes. Tel Aviv: Makhon Yad Mordechai, 1982.

———. *Netzah Yisrael*. London: Ha-Hinukh, 1956.

Mahmood, Saba. *Politics of Piety: The Islamic Revival and the Feminist Subject*. Princeton: Princeton University Press, 2004.

Maimonides, Moses. *Guide of the Perplexed*. Translated by Shlomo Pines. Chicago: University of Chicago Press, 1963.

Malachi, Eliezer Refael. "Ha-Pulmus 'al Ha-Rav Kook ve-Sifro 'Eder Ha-Yaqar.'" *Or Ha-Mizrah* 15, no. 3 (1965): 136-144.

———. "Le-Toldot R' Yoel Moshe Salomon." In *Mi-Neged Tireh*, edited by Elhanan Reiner and Haggai Ben-Shammai, 229-248. Jerusalem: Yad Ben-Zvi, 2001

Mandelbaum, Simha, ed. *Sefer Torah Mi-Zion*. Jerusalem: Lyna, 1995.

Manekin, Charles H. "Conservative Tendencies in Gersonides' Religious Philosophy." In *Cambridge Companion to Medieval Jewish Philosophy*, edited by Daniel H. Frank and Oliver Leaman, 304-342. Cambridge: Cambridge University Press, 2003.

Mannheim, Karl. *Ideology and Utopia: An Introduction to the Sociology of Knowledge*. Translated by Louis Wirth and Edward Shils. San Diego and New York: Harcourt, 1985. First published New York: Harcourt & Brace, 1936.

Maor, Zohar. "Beyn Anti-Colonialism, le-Post-Colonialism: Orientalism, Biqoret ve-Ha-Hilun shel Brit Shalom." *Theoriyah u-Viqoret* 30 (2007): 13-38.

Margolin, Ron. *Miqdash Adam: Ha-Hafnamah Ha-Datit ve-'Itzuv Hayei Ha-Dat Ha-Penimiyim be-Reishit Ha-Hasidut*. Jerusalem: Hebrew University/Magnes, 2005.

Mark, Zvi. *Mistiqah ve-Shiga'on bi-Yezirat Rabbi Nahman mi-Breslov*. Jerusalem/Tel Aviv: Hartman Institute/'Am 'Oved, 2003.

Marsden, George M. *Jonathan Edwards: A Life*. New Haven: Yale University Press, 2003.

Mayah, Moshe. *'Olam Banuy ve-Harev u-Vanuy: Ha-Rav Yehudah Amital le-Nokhah Zikhron Ha-Shoah*. Alon Shvut: Herzog College, 2002.

Meir ibn Gabbai. 1566. *'Avodat Ha-Qodesh*. Warsaw: Levin Epstein, 1902.

Meir, Jonatan. "Al Shir Ganuz shel Ha-Rav Kook ve-Naftulei Pirsumo." *Da'at* 55 (2005): 165-168.

———. "Ha-Kabbalah Ha-Eqleqtit shel Rabbi Shimon Zvi Horowitz (He'arah Biqortit 'al Ha-Munah 'Kabbalah Lita'it')." *Kabbalah* 31 (2014): 411-420.

———. "Orot ve-Kelim: Behinah Mehudeshet shel 'Hug' Ha-Reiyah Kook ve-'Orkhei Ketavav." *Qabbalah* 13 (2005): 163-247.

———. "Teshuqatan shel Neshamot el Ha-Shekhinah': Beirur Masekhet Ha-Qesharim beyn Ha-Re'ayah Kook le-Hillel Zeitlin ve-Yosef Hayim Brenner." In *Derekh Ha-Ruah: Sever Ha-Yovel le-Eliezer Schweid*, vol. 2, edited by Yehoyada' 'Amir, 771-818. Jerusalem: Hebrew University/Van Leer Institute, 2005.

Melamed, Yitzhak. "Spinoza and the Kabbalah: From the Gate of Heaven to the 'Field of Holy Apples.'" In *Early Modern Philosophy & the Kabbalah*, edited by Cristina Ciucu. Forthcoming.

Meltzer, Yed'ael. *Be-Derekh etz Ha-Hayim*. Arzei Ha-Hen, 1986.

Menes, Abraham. "Patterns of Jewish Scholarship in Eastern Europe." In *The Jews: Their History, Culture and Religion*, vol. 1, edited by Louis Finkelstein, 376-392. New York: Harper, 1960.

Mermelstein, Eliezer. "Akhilah be-Yom Ha-Kippurim bi-Meqom Holi u-Zman Magefah—Mahalat Ha-Cholera—Hetero shel Ha-Gaon Rabbi Yisrael Salanter u-Svarat Ha-Holqim 'Alav." *Qovetz Etz Hayim—Bobov* 7 (2008/Tishrei 5769): 273-294.

Midrash Tehillim. Edited by Salomon Buber. Vilna: Romm, 1891.

Mieses, Fabius. *Qorot Ha-Filosofiya Ha-Hadashah.* Leipzig: Mortiz Schafer, 1877.

Mintz, Alan. "Ahad Ha-Am and the Essay: The Vicissitudes of Reason." In *At the Crossroads: Essays on Ahad Ha-Am,* edited by Jacques Kornberg, 3-11. Albany: State University of New York Press, 1983.

Miller, Yisrael David. *Sefer Milhemet Sofrim.* Vilna: Dvorzez, 1871.

Mirsky, David. *The Life and Work of Ephraim Luzzatto.* New York: Ktav, 1987.

Mirsky, Shmuel Kalman. *Beyn Sheqiyah li-Zerihah.* New York and Jerusalem: Sura, 1951.

———. *Eretz ve-Yamim.* New York and Jerusalem: Sura, 1953.

———. "Ha-Dor bi-Reiy Ha-Re'ayah." *Ohr Ha-Mizrah* (December 1965): 101-105.

———. *Mosdot Torah be-Europa be-Vinyanam u-ve-Hurbanam.* New York: 'Ogen/Histadrut Ivrit, 1956.

Mirsky, Yehudah. "'A Halfway Despair': Rav Kook's Critique of Christianity in World War I." Paper presented at the Association for Jewish Studies, Washington, DC, December 17, 2005.

———. Review of *The Faith of the Mithnagdim,* by Allan Nadler. *The New Republic,* April 27, 1998, 38-41.

———. "An Intellectual and Spiritual Biography of Rav Avraham Yitzhaq Ha-Cohen Kook, 1864-1904." PhD diss., Harvard University, 2007.

———. "From Every Heresy, Faith, and Holiness from Every Defiled Thing: Towards Rav Kook's Theology of Culture." In *Developing a Jewish Perspective on Culture,* edited by Yehuda Sarna, 103-142. New York: KTAV/Yeshiva University Press, 2013.

———. "Ha-Havayah Ha-Sovlanit le-Sugehah." *Aqdamot* 23 (2009): 219-228

———. "The Inner Life of Religious Zionism." *The New Leader,* December 4, 1995.

———. "Modernizing Orthodoxies: The Case of Feminism." In *To Be a Jewish Woman/Lihiyot Ishah Yehudiyah,* edited by Tova Cohen, 37-51. Kolech Proceedings 4. Jerusalem: Kolech—Religious Women's Forum, 2007

———. "Mussar Movement." In *Yivo Encyclopedia of Jews in Eastern Europe,* vol. 1. Yale University Press, 2008. https://yivoencyclopedia.org/article.aspx/Musar_Movement.

———. "Kook, Avraham Yitzchak." In *Yivo Encyclopedia of Jews in Eastern Europe,* vol. 2. Yale University Press, 2008. https://yivoencyclopedia.org/article.aspx/Kook_Avraham_Yitshak.

———. "Rav Kook's Latvia Days." *Jerusalem Post* (*Weekend Magazine*), January 7, 2005, 21.

———. "Ha-Re'ayah ve-Ha-Rambam: 'Iyun Mehudash." In *Iggud: Selected Essays in Jewish Studies,* vol. 1, edited by Baruch J. Schwartz, Abraham Melamed, and Aharon Shemesh, 397-405. Jerusalem: World Union of Jewish Studies, 2008.

———. "Kook, Abraham Isaac." In *Encyclopedia of the Bible and Its Reception,* edited by Dale C. Allison, Jr., Christine Helmer, C. L. Seow, Hermann Spieckermann, Barry Walfish, and Eric Ziolkowski, cols. 452-454. Berlin: De Gruyter, 2017.

———. "Multiple Modernity as Theory and Theology: Shmuel Noah Eisenstadt and Rav Kook." Unpublished paper, 2013.

———. "The New Heavens in the New World: The Religious Hebraism of Samuel Mirsky." In *The Paths of Daniel, Studies in Judaism and Jewish Culture in Honor of Rabbi Professor Daniel Sperber,* edited by Adam S. Ferziger, 101-128. Ramat Gan: Bar-Ilan University Press, 2017.

———. *Rav Kook: Mabat Hadash.* Tel Aviv: Dvir, 2021.

———. *Rav Kook: Mystic in a Time of Revolution* (New Haven: Yale University Press, 2014).

———. "Revelation and Redemption: Avraham Yitzhak Ha-Cohen Kook, 1865-1935." In *Makers of Jewish Modernity,* edited by Jacques Picard, Jacques Revel, Michael P, Steinberg, Idith Zertal, with Ulrich Schultz, 92-107. Princeton: Princeton University Press, 2016.

———. "Three Questions: Orthodoxy's Power and After." Unpublished paper, 2008. https://www.academia.edu/3081089/Three_Questions_Orthodoxys_Power_and_After.

———. Review of *The Kuzari and the Shaping of Jewish Identity, 1167-1900*, by Adam Shear. *Makor Rishon—Musaf Shabbat*, February 19, 2010.

Mittleman, Alan L. *Human Nature and Jewish Thought*. Princeton: Princeton University Press, 2015.

———. *A Short History of Jewish Ethics*. Oxford: Wiley Blackwell, 2012.

Moyn, Samuel. *Christian Human Rights*. Philadelphia: University of Pennsylvania Press, 2015.

Morgenstern, Arie. *Meshihiyut ve-Yishuv Eretz Yisrael be-Mahatzit Ha-Rishonah shel Ha-Meah Ha-19*. Jerusalem: Yad Ben-Zvi, 1985.

———. *Mistiqah u-Meshihiyut*. Jerusalem: Maor, 1998.

Moseley, Marcus. *Being for Myself Alone: Origins of Jewish Autobiography*. Stanford: Stanford University Press, 2006.

Myers, Jody. *Seeking Zion: Modernity and Messianic Activism in the Writings of Tsevi Hirsch Kalischer*. Oxford and Portland: Littman Library, 2003.

Nadler, Allan. The *Faith of the Mithnagdim: Rabbinic Resposnes to Hasidic Rapture*. Baltimore: Johns Hopkins University Press, 1997.

———. "The 'Rambam Revival' in Early Modern Jewish Thought: Maskilim, Mitnagdim and Hasidim on Maimonides' Guide of the Perplexed." In *Moses Maimonides: Communal Impact, Historic Legacy*, edited by Benny Kraut, 36-61. Flushing: Center for Jewish Studies, Queens College, 2005.

———. *Qana'utei de-Pinhas*. Spring Valley: Orot, 2013.

Nahman of Bratzlav. *Liqutei Moharan*. Jerusalem: Imrei Shefer, 2003 [1821].

Nahum of Chernobyl. *Meor 'Eynayim*. Jerusalem: Maor 'Eynayim, 1989 [1810].

Nathans, Benjamin. *Beyond the Pale: The Jewish Encounter with Late Imperial Russia*. Berkeley: University of California Press, 2002.

Nehamas, Alexander. *The Art of Living: Socratic Reflections from Plato to Foucault*. Berkeley: University of California Press, 1998.

Neher, Andre. *Le Puits de l'Exil: La Theologie Dialectique du Maharal de Prague*. Rev. ed. Paris: Cerf, 1991 [1966]. In Hebrew: *Mishnato shel Ha-Maharal mi-Prague*. Translated by Anna Greenfield. Jerusalem: Rubin Mass, 2003.

Nehorai, Michael Zvi. "Medinat Yisrael be-Mishnato shel Ha-Rav Kook." *'Amudim* 23, no. 12 (Elul/Fall 1975): 409-417.

Neriah, Moshe Zvi. *Bi-Sdeh Ha-Re'ayah*. Kfar Ha-Roeh: n.p., 1987.

———. *Liqutei Ha-Re'ayah*. 3 vols. Kfar Ha-Roeh: Hai Roi, 1990-1995.

———. *Mo'adei Ha-Re'ayah*. Bnei Braq: Tzela, 1991.

———. *Pirqei Volozhin*. Jerusalem: Weiss, 1964.

———. *Sihot Ha-Re'ayah ve-Orot Mishnato*. Jerusalem: Moreshet, 1979.

———. *Tal Ha-Re'ayah*. Bnei Braq: Hai Fisher, 1993.

Neuman, Kalman. *Quntres Reiyah Shelemah*. Jerusalem: Meimad, 1994.

Nissenboim, Yitzhaq. *'Alei Heldi*. Warsaw: Halter, 1929.

Nussbaum, Martha C. *The Therapy of Desire: Theory and Practice in Hellenistic Ethics*. Princeton: Princeton University Press, 1994.

———. *Women and Human Development: The Capabilities Approach*. Cambridge: Cambridge University Press, 2000.

Ofan, Boaz. *Maftehot le-Khitvei Ha-Re'ayah*. Ramat Gan: Reut, 2002.

Otto, Rudolf, *The Idea of the Holy*. Translated by John Harvey. Oxford: Oxford University Press, 1923.

Pachter, Mordechai. "Ha-Tashtit Ha-Qabbalit shel Tefisat Ha-Emunah ve-Ha-Kefirah be-Mishnat Ha-Rav Kook." *Da'at* 47 (2001): 69-100.

———. "Kabbalat Ha-GRA be-Aspaklaryah shel Shtei Mesorot." In *Ha-GRA u-Veit Midrasho*, edited by Moshe Hallamish, Yosef Rivlin, and Raphael Shuchat, 119-136. Ramat Gan: Bar-Ilan University Press, 2003.

———. "Tenu'at Ha-Mussar ve-Ha-Kabbalah." In *Yashan Mipnei Hadash: Emanuel Etkes Festschrift*, edited by David Assaf and Ada Rapoport-Albert, 223-250. Jerusalem: Mercaz Shazar, 2009.

Paras, Eric. *Foucault 2.0: Beyond Power and Knowledge*. New York: Other Press, 2006.

Parush, Iris. *Nashim Qorot: Yitronah shel Shuliyut*. Tel Aviv: Am Oved, 2001.

Pearl, CHayim. *The Medieval Jewish Mind: The Religious Philosophy of Isaac Arama*. London: Valentine Mitchell, 1971.

Pedaya, Haviva. "Eretz: Zeman u-Maqom—Apocalypsot shel Sof ve-Apokalypsah shel Hathalah." In *Eretz Yisrael be-Hagut Yehudit be-Me'ah Ha-'Esrim*, edited by Aviezer Ravitsky, 560-624. Jerusalem: Yad Ben-Zvi, 2004.

Penslar, Derek J. "Herzl and the Palestinian Arabs: Myth and Counter-Myth. *Journal of Israeli History* 24, no. 1 (2005): 65-78.

Perl, Gil S. "'Emek Ha-Neziv: A Window into the Intellectual Universe of Rabbi Naftali Zvi Yehudah Berlin." PhD diss., Harvard University, 2006.

———. "No Two Minds are Alike: Tolerance and Pluralism in the Work of Netziv." *Torah u-Madda Journal* 12 (2004): 74-98.

———. *The Pillar of Volozhin: Rabbi Naftali Zvi Yehuda Berlin and the World of Nineteenth Century Lithuanian Torah Scholarship*. Boston: Academic Studies Press, 2013.

Persico, Tomer. "Chabad's Lost Messiah." *Azure* 38 (2009): 82-127.

Pines, Shlomo. "Truth and Falsehood Versus Good and Evil: A Study in Jewish and General Philosophy in Relation to the Guide of the Perplexed, I:2." In *Studies in Maimonides*, edited by Isadore Twersky, 95-157. Cambridge, MA: Harvard University Press, 1990.

Pinkas Slonim. Edited by Kalman Lichtenstein and Yehezqel Rabinowitz. Tel Aviv: Ha-Po'el Ha-Tza'ir, 1972.

Posner, Richard A. *The Problematics of Moral and Legal Theory*. Cambridge, MA: Harvard University Press, 1990.

Preil, Yehoshua Yosef. *Eglei Tal*. 2 vols. Warsaw: Schuldberg, 1899-1901.

———. *Ketavim Nivharim*. New York: n.p., 1924.

Prospect le-Hozaat Kitvei Rabeinu Ha-Gadol, Sar Ha-Torah ve-Abir Ha-Umah, Zadiq Yesod 'Olam Maran Avraham Yitzhaq Ha-Cohen Kook z'l. Jerusalem: Lifschitz, 1937.

Proudfoot, Wayne. *Religious Experience*. Berkeley: University of California Press, 1985.

Rabin, Moshe Yitzhaq bar Shlomo. *Sefer Miluim le-Moshe*. Vilna: Pirashnikov, 1909.

Rabin, Nisan. *Der Yeshiva Buher, oder di Yiddishe Shtimme*. Vilna: Pirazhnikov, 1910.

Rabbiner, Zev Aryeh. "Boisk ve-Rabbanehah." *Sinai* 17 (1945): 16-80.

———. *Ha-Gaon Rabbi Eliezer Gordon*. Tel Aviv: Ayalon, 1968.

———. *Ha-Rav Yosef Zekharia Stern*. Jerusalem: WZO/Mossad Ha-Rav Kook, 1943.

———. *Maran Rabbeinu Meir Simha Cohen zt"l*. Tel Aviv: Ayalon, 1967.

———. *Or Mufla: Maran Ha-Rav Kook zt"l*. Tel Aviv: Ayalon, 1972.

———. "Shalosh Qehillot Qodesh." In *Yahadut Latvia: Sefer Zikaron*, edited by A. Ettingen, S. Lifshitz, M. Abramson, and M. Lavi. Tel Aviv: 'Igud Yotzei Latvia ve-Estonia be-Yisrael, 1953.

Rabinovich, Simon. *Jewish Rights, National Rites: Nationalism and Autonomy in Late Imperial and Revolutionary Russia*. Stanford: Stanford University Press, 2014.

Rabinowitz, Dov Ber, and Eliyahu Aqiva Rabinowitz. *Devar Emet*. Poltava: Rabinowitz, 1913.

Rabinow, Paul, ed. *Essential Works of Foucault 1954-1984*. Vol. 1, *Ethics: Subjectivity and Truth*. Translated by R. Hurley. New York: New Press, 1997.

Rabinowitz-Teomim, Eliyahu David. *Heshbonot shel Mitzvah*. Jerusalem: Makhon Yerushalayim, 2005.

———. *Hidushei Ha-Gaon Ha-Aderet*. Brooklyn: Makhon Kitvei Ha-Aderet be-Artzot Ha-Berit, 2003.

———. *Ma'aneh Eliyahu*. Mercaz Shapira: Or Etzion, 2003.

———. *Seder Eliyahu: Toldot Ha-Gaon Rabbi Eliyahu David Rabinowitz-Teomim (Ha-Aderet), Ketuvot bi-Yedei 'Atzmo*. Jerusalem: Mossad Ha-Rav Kook, 1983.

Rabinowitz-Teomim, Eliyahu David, and Zvi Yehudah. *Sefer Shevet Ahim*. Edited by Ya'aqov Moshe Hillel. Jerusalem: Ahavat Shalom: Yad Shmuel Franco, 2003.

Rados, Joshua Leib. *Zikhronot*. Johannesburg: n.p., 1936.

Ram, Hannah. "Mahloket bi-Qerev Hanhagat Ha-'Edah Ha-Yehudit be-Yafo." *Cathedra* 64 (1992): 103-126.

Rapoport-Albert, Ada. "God and the Zaddik as the Two Focal Points of Hasidic Worship." *History of Religions* 18, no. 4 (1979): 296-325.

Rappoport, Jason. "Rav Kook and Nietzsche: A Preliminary Comparison of their Ideas on Religions, Christianity, Buddhism and Atheism." *Torah U-Madda Journal* 12 (2004): 99-129.

Ravitzky, Aviezer. *Ha-Qetz Ha-Meguleh u-Medinat Ha-Yehudim: Meshihiyut, Zionut ve-Radcalism Dati be-Yisrael*. Tel Aviv: Am Oved, 1993.

Refael, Yitzhaq. "Binyamin Menashe Levin." *Sinai* 35 (1954): 66-73.

Reiner, Elhanan. "Byond the Realm of the Haskalah: Changing Learning Patterns in the Jewish Traditional Society." Unpublished lecture, 2006.

———. "Hon, Ma'amad Hevrati ve-Talmud Torah: Ha-Kloyz ba-Hevrah Ha-Yehudit be-Mizrah Europa ba-Meot Ha-17 ve-Ha-18." *Zion* 58, no. 3 (1993): 287-328.

Rimon, Yosef Zvi. *Atzei Hayim: Devarim 'al Gedolei Ha-Umah*. Jerusalem: Mossad Ha-Rav Kook, 1946.

Rivkin, B. "Courlander Litvaks." In *Lita*, edited by Mendel Sudarsky and Uriah Katzenellenbogen, 408-416. New York: Kulturgesellschaft fun Litvishe Yidn, 1951.

Rivkind, Yitzhaq. Review of *Toldot Ha-Agudah nes Zionah* [volume on Nes Zionah], by Yisrael Klausner . *Ha-Doar* 34, no. 35 (24 Av 5715/August 12, 1955): 673-674

Robinson, Ira. "Kabbalah and Science in Sefer Ha-Berit: A Modernization Strategy for Orthodox Jews." *Modern Judaism* 9, no. 3 (1989): 275-288.

Rosenak, Avinoam. "Ha-Filosofiyah shel Ha-Halakhah be-Mishnato shel Ha-Rav Avraham Yitzhaq Ha-Cohen Kook." PhD diss., Hebrew University, 1997.

———. *Ha-Rav Avraham Yitzhaq Ha-Cohen Kook*. Jerusalem: Merkaz Shazar, 2006.

———. "Mi Mefahed me-Kevatzim Genuzim shel Ha-Rav Kook." *Tarbitz* 69, no. 2 (2000): 257-291.

———. "Torat Eretz Yisrael Ha-Nevuit be-Mishnat Ha-Re'ayah Kook." In *Eretz Yisrael be-Hagut Ha-Yehudit be-Me'ah Ha-'Esrim*, edited by Aviezer Ravitsky, 26-70. Jerusalem: Yad Ben-Zvi, 2004.

Rosenberg, Shalom. "Mavo le-Haguto shel Ha-Re'ayah" and "Haguto shel Ha-Re'ayah Kook beyn Yahadut le-Tarbut Kelalit." In *Yovel Orot: Haguto shel Ha-Rav Avraham Yitzhaq Ha-Cohen Kook*, edited by Benjamin Ish-Shalom and Shalom Rosenberg, 27-105. Jerusalem: Sifiyat Eliner, 1988.

———. "Stirot ve-Dialectikah be-Mussar Ha-Hevrati e-Hagutam shel Ha-Re'ayah Kook ve-shel Ha-Rav A. S. Tamares." In *Hevrah ve-Historiyah*, edited by Yehezqel Cohen, 137-154. Jerusalem: Misrad Ha-Hinukh, 1980.

Rosenberg, Shalom, and Alexander Even-Hen. "Hidush Ha-Minuah Ha-Philosophiy Ha-'Ivri be-Shilhei Ha-Meah Ha-18." *'Iyun* 37 (1988): 263-270.

Rosenblatt, Mordechai. *Hadrat Mordechai*. Vilna: Romm, 1899.

Rosenbloom, Noah H. *Tradition in an Age of Reform: The Religious Philosophy of Samson Rafael Hirsch*. Philadelphia: Jewish Publication Society, 1976.

Rosenfeld, Joey. "A Tribute to Rav Shlomo Elyashiv, Author of Leshem Shevo v-Achloma: On his Ninetieth Yahrzeit." *The Seforim Blog* (blog), March 10, 2016. http://seforim.blogspot.com/2016/03/a-tribute-to-rav-shlomo-elyashiv-author.html.

Rosenfeld, Josh. "Seeing Silence: Jewish Mystical Experience Refracted through the Art of Mark Rothko." *Hakirah* 21 (2016): 155-168.

Ross, Tamar. "Between Metaphysical and Liberal Pluralism: A Reappraisal of Rabbi A. I. Kook's Espousal of Toleration." *AJS Review* 21, no. 1 (1996): 61-110.

———. *Expanding the Palace of Torah: Orthodoxy and Women*. Hanover: University Press of New England/ Brandeis University Press, 2004.

———. "Ha-Mahshavah ha-Iyunit be-Ktivei Mamshikhav shel Rabbi Yisrael Salanter be-Tenu'at Ha-Mussar." PhD diss., Hebrew University, 1986.

———. "Ha-Megamah Ha-Anti Ratziyonalit be-Tenu'at Ha-Mussar." In *'Alei Shefer: Alexander Safran Festschrift*, edited by Moshe Hallamish, 145-162. Ramat Gan: Bar-Ilan University Press, 1990.

———. "Hebeitim Feministiyyim be-Mishnato Ha-Utopit shel Ha-Rav Kook." In *Derekh Ha-Ruah: Sever Ha-Yovel le-Eliezer Schweid*, vol. 2, edited by Yehoyada' 'Amir, 717-752. Jerusalem: Hebrew University/Van Leer Institute, 2005.

———. "Musag Ha-Elohut shel Ha-Rav Kook." Pt. 1. *Da'at* 8 (1982): 109-128; pt. 2. *Da'at* 9 (1983): 39-74.

Rubin, Solomon. "Adam u-Vehemah, O, Tza'ar Ba'alei Hayim." In *Melitz Ehad Minei Alef: Measef Maamarim ve-Shrim le-Gilyon Ha-Elef me-az Hehel Ha-Melitz*, edited by Alexander Zederbaum. St. Petersburg: Zederbaum, 1884.

Ruderman, David B. *A Best-Selling Hebrew Book of the Modern Era: The Book of the Covenant of Pinhas Hurwitz and Its Remarkable Legacy*. Seattle: University of Washington Press, 2014.

———. "Jewish Preaching and the Language of Science: The Sermons of Azariah Figo." In *Preachers of the Italian Ghetto*, 89-104. Berkeley: University of California Press, 1992.

Sack, Bracha. *Be-Sha'arei Ha-Kabbalah shel Rabbi Moshe Cordovero*. Beersheva: Ben-Gurion University Press, 1995.

Safran, Bezalel. "Maharal and Early Hasidism." In *Hasidism: Continuity or Innovation?*, edited by Bezalel Safran, 47-144. Cambridge, MA: Harvard University Center for Jewish Studies/Harvard University Press, 1988.

Saiman, CHayim. "Legal Theology: The Turn to Conceptualism in Nineteenth-Century Jewish Law." *Journal of Law and Religion* 21 (2005-2006): 39-100.

Salai, Menahem. *Hayto Eretz*. Jerusalem: Shem, 1988.

Salanter, Yisrael. *Kitvei Rabbi Yisrael Salanter*. Jerusalem: Mossad Bialik, 1972.

Salmon, Yosef. *Dat ve-Zionut: 'Imutim Rishonim*. Jerusalem: Ha-Sifriyah Ha-Zionit, 1990.

———. "Ha-Pulmus 'al Etrogei Corfu ve-Etrogei Eretz Yisrael—1875-1891." *Zion* 65, no. 1 (2000): 106-175.

———. "Masoret, Modernizatziyah u-Leumiyut: Ha-Rav Ha-Maskil ke-Reformator ba-Hevrah Ha-Yehudit be-Russia." *Sefer Bar-Ilan* 28-29 (2001): 23-39. In English: "Enlightened Rabbis as Reformers in Russian Jewish Society." In *New Perspectives on the Haskalah*, edited by Samuel Feiner, 166-183. London: Littman Library, 2001.

———. "Rabbi Joshua Joseph Preil: 'Protesting at the Gate.'" *Modern Judaism* 35, no. 1 (February 2015): 66-82.

———. *Religion and Zionism: First Encounters*. Jerusalem: Magnes/Hebrew University Press, 2002.

Salomon, Mordechai. *Sheloshah Dorot ba-Yishuv*. Jerusalem: Salomon Press, 1939.

Salomon [Solomon], Yoel Moshe. *Yehudah ve-Yerushalayim*. Edited by Gedalyahu Kressel. Jerusalem: Mossad Ha-Rav Kook, 1955.

Samet, Moshe. "M. Mendelssohn, N. H. Wessely ve-Rabbanei Doram." In *Mehqarim be-Toldot 'Am Yisrael ve-Erez Yisrael le-Zekher Zvi Avneri*, edited by A. Gilboa, B. Mevorah, A. Rapoport, and E. Shohat, 233-257. Haifa: University of Haifa Press, 1970.

Schacter, Jacob J. "Facing the Truths of History." *The Torah U-Madda Journal* 8 (1998-1999): 200-276.

———. "Haskalah, Secular Studies and the Close of the Yeshiva in Volozhin in 1892." *The Torah U-Madda Journal* 2 (1990): 76-133.

———. "History and Memory of Self: The Autobiography of Rabbi Jacob Emden." In *Jewish History and Jewish Memory: Essays in Honor of Yosef Hayim Yerushalmi*, edited by Elisheva Carlebach, John M. Efron, and David N. Myers, 428-452. Hanover: Brandeis University Press, 1998.

———. "Rabbi Jacob Emden, Sabbatianism and Frankism: Attitudes Towards Christianity in the Eighteenth Century." In *New Perspectives on Jewish-Christian Relations in Honor of David Berger*, edited by Elisheva Carlebach and Jacob J. Schacter, 359-396. Leiden and Boston: Brill, 2012.

Schafer, Peter. "Bar Kokhba and the Rabbis." In *The Bar Kokhba War Reconsidered*, edited by Peter Schafer, 1-22. Tubingen: Mohr Siebeck, 2003.

Schatz, Rivka. "Ha-Tefisah Ha-Mishpatit shel Ha-Maharal—Antiteza Le-Hok Ha-Tiv'i." *Da'at* 2-3 (1978-1979): 147-157.

———. "Ha-Metafisiqah shel Ramhal be-Heksherah Ha-Eti: 'Iyun bi-Traktat Ha-Rishon shel 'Kalah Pithei Hokhmah.'" In *Mehkarei Yerushalayim be-Mahshevet Yisrael 9: Sefer Ha-Yovel le-Shlomo Pines*, vol. 2, edited by Moshe Idel, Zev Harvey, and Eliezer Schweid, with Avriel Bar-Levav, 361-396. Jerusalem: Hebrew University, 1990.

———. "Utopia u-Meshihiyut be-Torat Ha-Rav Kook." *Kivunim* 1 (1979): 15-27.

Schmidt-Biggemann, Wilhelm, ed. *Christliche Kabbala*. Ostfildern: Jan Thorbecke Verlag, 2003.

Schneersohn, Yehoshua Fischel. *Hayim Gravitzer: Sippuro shel Nofel*. Edited by Netanel Lederberg. Translated by Araham Shlonsky. Tel Aviv: Yediot Aharonot, 2013.

Schnold, Rachel. "Elijah's Face: The Portrait of the Vilna Gaon in Folk Art." In *The Gaon of Vilna: The Man and His Legacy*, 48-48 (English), 35-45 (Hebrew). Tel Aviv: Beth Hatefusoth, 1998.

Scholem, Gershom. *Briefe II, 1948-1970*. Edited by Thomas Sparr. Munich: C. H. Beack, 1995.

———. *Devarim Bi-Go: Pirqei Morashah U'Tehiya*. Tel Aviv: Am Oved, 1982.

———. *Major Trends in Jewish Mysticism*. New York: Schocken, 1946.

———. *The Messianic Idea in Judaism and Other Essays on Jewish Spirituality*. New York: Schocken, 1971.

———. *Sabbatai Sevi: The Mystical Messiah, 1626-1676*. Translated by R. J. Z. Werblowsky. Princeton: Bollingen/Princeton University Press, 2017 [1973].

Schower, Abraham. "Mi-Zikhronotai 'al Ha-Rav Avraham Yitzhaq Ha-Cohen Kook." In *Hedenu: Jubilee Publication of the Students' Organization of the Rabbi Isaac Elchanan Theological Seminary and Yeshiva College (Bernard Revel Festschrift)* [sic], edited by Hyman E. Bloom, 184-191. New York, 1936.

Schulte, Christoph. "Kabbala-Rezeption in der Deutschen Romantik." In *Mysticism, Magic and Kabbalah in Ashkenazi Judaism*, edited by Karl Erich Grozinger and Joseph Dan. Berlin: Walter de Gruyter, 1995

Schulze, Wilhelm August. "Schelling und die Kabbala." *Judaica* 13, no. 2-4 (1957): 65-99, 143-170, 210-232.

Schwartz, Daniel B. *The First Modern Jew: Spinoza and the History of an Image*. Princeton: Princeton University Press, 2012.

Schwartz, Dov. *Etgar u-Mashber be-Hug Ha-Rav Kook*. Tel Aviv: ,Am ,Oved, 2001.

———. *Ha-Zionut Ha-Datit beyn Higayon li-Mishihiyut*. Tel Aviv: 'Am Oved, 1999.

———. "Me-'Eyn Sof' le-'Or Eyn Sof': be-Hagut Ha-Re'ayah: Li-Meqorotehah shel Ha-Havhanah Be-Hasidut Habad." In *Ruah Hadashah be-Armon Ha-Torah: Sefer Yovel likhvod Professor Tamar Ross*, edited by Ronit Ir-Shai and Dov Schwartz, 119-165. Ramat Gan: Bar-Ilan University Press, 2018.

———. *The Religious Genius in Rabbi Kook's Thought: National "Saint"?* Brighton: Academic Studies Press, 2014.

Schwarz, Michael. "Remarks Concerning Maimonides' Conception of God's Knowledge of Particulars." In *Torah and Wisdom: Studies in Jewish Philosophy, Kabbalah and Halacha, Essays in Honor of Arthur Hyman*, edited by Ruth Link-Salinger, 189-197. New York: Shengold, 1992.

Scult, Mel, ed. *Communings of the Spirit: The Journals of Mordecai M. Kaplan.* Vol. 1, *1913-1934*. Detroit: Wayne State University Press/Reconstructionist Press, 2001.

Schofer, Jonathan. *The Making of a Sage: A Study in Rabbinic Ethics.* Madison: University of Wisconsin Press, 2005.

Schwarzschild, Steven. Review of *A Philosophy of Mizvot*, by Gersion Appel. *Journal of Biblical Literature* 95, no. 3 (September 1976): 519-520.

Schweid, Eliezer. *Beyn Ortodoksiyah le-Humanism Dati.* Rev. ed. Jerusalem: Van Leer Institute, 2003.

———. *Neviim le-'Amam u-le-Enoshut: Nevuah u-Neviim be-Hagut Ha-Yehudit shel Ha-Meah Ha-'Esrim.* Jerusalem: Hebrew University/Magnes Press, 1999.

———. "Sefer Hadash 'al Mishnat Ha-Re'ayah Kook." *Petahim* 28, no. 2 (1974): 36-37.

———. "Teologiyah Leumit-Tziyonit be-Reishitah—'Al Mishanto shel Ha-Rav Yitzhaq Ya'aqov Reines." In *Mehqarim be-Qabbalah, be-Filosofiyah Yehudit u-ve-Sifrut Ha-Mussar Mugashim le-Yeshayah Tishby bi-Melot Lo Shiv'im ve-Hamesh Shanim*, edited by Joseph Dan and Joseph Hacker, 689-720. Jerusalem: Hebrew University/Magnes, 1986.

———. *Toldot He-Hagut Ha-Yehudit bi-'Et Ha-Hadashah: Ha-Meah Ha-19.* Tel Aviv and Jerusalem: Ha-Kibutz Ha-Meuhad/Keter, 1978.

Seeman, Don. "Evolutionary Ethics: The Ta'amei Ha-Mitzvot of Rav Kook." *Hakirah* 26 (2019): 13-55.

———. "Violence, Ethics and Divine Honor in Modern Jewish Thought." *Journal of the American Academy of Religion* 73, no. 4 (2005), 1015-1048.

Seeskin, Kenneth. *Searching for a Distant God: The Legacy of Maimonides.* New York: Oxford University Press, 2000.

Seigel, Jerrold. "Problematizing the Self." In *Beyond the Cultural Turn: New Directions in the Study of Society and Culture*, edited by Victoria E. Bonnell and Lynn Hunt, 281-314. Berkeley: University of California Press, 1999.

Septimus, Bernard. "Yitzhaq Arama and Aristotle's Ethics." In *Jews and Conversos at the Time of the Expulsion*, edited by Yom Tov Assis and Yosef Kaplan, 1-24. Jerusalem: Shazar Center, 1999.

Sefer Ba'al Shem Tov. Edited by Shimon Vodnik. Lodz: Mesorah, 1938. Repr. Jerusalem: Horev, 1962.

Shahar, David. "Tefisato Ha-Zionit ve-Ha-Datit shel Ha-Rav Moredekhai Eliasberg (1817-1889)." *Kivvunim* 25 (1984): 93-112.

Shakh, Eleazer. *Shimushah shel Torah.* Bnei Braq: Bergman, 1998.

Shapira, Avraham. *Or Ha-Hayim be-Yom Qetanot: Mishnat A. D. Gordon u-Meqorotehah be-Qabbalah ve-Hasidut.* Tel Aviv: Am Oved, 1996.

Shapira, Ben-Zion. ed. *Igrot La-Reayah.* 2nd ed. Jerusalem: Machon Ha-Razyah, 1990.

Shapira, Zvi Hirsch. *Darkhei Teshuvah.* 1893. Repr. Brooklyn: Shraga, 1946.

Shapiro, Marc B. *Between the Yeshiva World and Modern Orthodoxy: The Life and Works of Rabbi Jehiel Jacob Weinberg, 1884-1966.* London: Littman Library, 1999.

———. *Changing the Immutable: How Orthodox Judaism Rewrites Its History.* Oxford: Littman, 2015.

Sharshevsky, Yehudah Edel. *Kur Le-Zahav.* Vol. 1. Vilna: Romm, 1858.

———. *Kur Le-Zahav.* Vol. 2. Vilna: Fuenn & Rosenkranz, 1858.

Shatz, David. "The Integration of Torah and Culture: Its Scope and Limits in the Thought of Rav Kook." In *Hazon Nahum*, edited by Yaakov Elman and Jeffrey S. Gurock, 529-556. New York: Yeshiva University Press, 1997.

Shatzkes, Moshe Aharon. *Ha-Mafteah/Hamafteach oder der Schlussel*. Vol. 1. Warsaw: Hayim Kelter, 1866.

———. *Ha-Mafteah/Hamafteach oder der Schlussel*. Vol. 2. Warsaw: Mahberet Sheniyah, 1869

Shear, Adam. "Jewish Enlightenment Beyond Western Europe." In *The Cambridge History of Jewish Philosophy*, edited by Martin Kavka, Zachary Braiterman, and David Novak, 252-279. Cambridge: Cambridge University Press, 2012.

———. *The Kuzari and the Shaping of Jewish Identity, 1167-1900*. Cambridge: Cambridge University Press, 2008.

Sherlo [Cherlow], Smadar. "Hitpathut Shitat Ha-Musssar shel Ha-Rav Kook be-Hibbur 'Eyn Ayah." *Da'at* 43 (1999): 95-123.

———. "Hug Ha-Re'ayah ke-Havurah Mystit." *Tarbitz* 74, no. 2 (2005): 261-303.

———. "Pulmus Ha-Mussar Ha-Sheni: Beyn Shitat Ha-Mussar shel Ha-Rav Kook le-Shitato shel Rabbi Yisrael mi-Salant." Masters Thesis, Touro College, Jerusalem, 1996.

———. *Zaddiq Yesod 'Olam: Ha-Shelihut Ha-Sodit ve-Ha-Havayah Ha-Mistit shel Ha-Rav Kook*. Ramat Gan: Bar-Ilan University Press, 2012.

———. "Zaddiq Yesod 'Olam - Shelihuto Ha-Mistit shel Ha-Rav Kook." *Da'at* 49 (2002): 99-135.

Sherlo [Cherlow], Yuval. *Ve'erastikh li l'Olam: Demutu Ha'Ruhanit shel Ha'Adam Mi'Yisrael B'et Ha'Tehiya B'Mishnat Ha'Rav Kook*. Hispin: Yeshivat Ha-Golan, 1996.

Sherwin, Byron. *Mystical Theology and Social Dissent: The Life and Works of Judah Loew of Prague*. Rutherford and London: Fairleigh Dickinson University Press, Associated University Presses, 1982.

Shilo, Elhanan. "Hashpa'ato shel Rabbi Yitzhak Isaac Haver 'al Parshanuto shel Ha-Rav Kook le-Qabbalah." *Da'at*, 79-80 (2005): 95-117.

———. "Ma'amad Ha-'Olam lifnei Hothavut 'Am Yisrael: Beyn Ha-Ramhal le-Rabbi Yitzhak Isaac Haver." *Qabbalah* 37 (2017): 251-270.

Shklar, Judith N. *Men and Citizens: A Study of Rousseau's Social Theory*. Cambridge: Cambridge University Press, 1969.

Shoham, Hizky. "From 'Great History' to 'Small History': The Genesis of the Zionist Periodization." *Israel Studies* 18, no. 1 (2013): 31-55.

Shohat, Shaul. *Beit Yedidyah*. Pietrkov: Tzederbaum, 1904.

———. *Tiferet Shaul*. Pietrkov: Faynsky, 1899.

Shuchat, Raphael. "Ha-Parshanut Ha-Historiosophit Ha-Kabbalit shel Ha-GRA ve-Hashpa'at Ramhal 'alav ve-'al Beit Midrasho." *Da'at* 40 (1998): 125-152.

———. *Olam Nistar be-Meimadei Ha-Zman: Torat Ha-Geulah shel Ha-GRA, Meqorotehah ve-Hashap'atah Le-Dorot*. Ramat Gan: Bar-Ilan University Press, 2010.

———. "Qabbalat Lita ke-Zerem 'Atzmai be-Sifrut Ha-Qabbalah." *Qabbalah* 10 (2004): 181-206.

———. "Yesodot Meshihiyyim u-Mystiyyim be-Limud Torah be-Veit Midrasho shel Ha-GRA: Hebet Hadash 'al Ha-Mashber be-Limud ba-Meah Ha-18 u-Musag Ha-Devequt." In *Ha-GRA u-Veit Midrasho*, edited by Moshe Hallamish, Yosef Rivlin, and Raphael Shuchat, 155-172. Ramat Gan: Bar-Ilan University Press, 2003.

Shulman, Kalman. *Havazelet Ha-Sharon*. Vilna: Romm, 1861.

Shulman, Shmuel Barukh. *Esh Dat*. Jerusalem: Eretz Yizrael Press, 1936.

Shumsky, Dmitry. *Beyond the Nation-State: The Zionist Political Imagination from Pinsker to Ben-Gurion*. New Haven: Yale University Press, 2018.

Shvat, Ari. "Hokhmat Yisraʾel bi-qedushatah." *Talelei Orot* 13 (2007): 309–40.

———. "Mivhanim Maʾasiyim ha-Mevatim et Ahadat Ha-Rav Kook le-Limud Torah Bikorti-Madaʾi." *Asif* 4 (2017): 297-329.

Sidarsky, David, ed. *Imrei Binah*. Warsaw: Yitzhaq Goldman, 1878.

Silber, Michael K. "The Emergence of Ultra-Orthodoxy: The Invention of a Tradition." In *The Uses of Tradition: Jewish Continuity Since Emancipation*, edited by Jack Wertheimer, 23-84. New York and Jerusalem: Jewish Theological Seminary/Harvard University Press, 1992.

Simon, Aqiva Ernst. *Seczig Jahre gegen des Strom: Briefe von 1917-1984*. Jerusalem and Tubingen: Leo Baeck Institute/Mohr Siebeck, 1998.

———. *Yeʾadim, Tzematim, Netivim: Haguto shel Mordechai Martin Buber*. Tel Aviv: Poʾalim, Kibutz Ha-Meuhad, 1985.

Sinkoff, Nancy. "Strategy and Ruse in the Haskalah of Mendel Lefin of Satanow." In *New Perspectives on the Haskalah*, edited by Samuel Feiner, 86-102. London: Littman Library, 2001.

Slater, Tsachi [Issac] "Those Who Yearn for the Divine: Rabbi Shmuel Alexandrov and the Russian Religious-Philosophical Renaissance." *Judaica Petropolitana* 5 (2016): 55-67.

——— [Yitzchak]. "Leumiyut Universalit: Dat u-Leumiyut be-Haguto shel Shmuel Alexandrov." Master's thesis, Ben-Gurion University, 2014.

Slezkine, Yuri. *The Jewish Century*. Princeton: Princeton University Press, 2004.

Slifkin, Natan. *Man and Beast: Our Relationships with Animals in Jewish Life and Thought*. New York: Yashar, 2006.

Sliyfoy, Mordekahi. *Ha-Gaon Rabbi Yehudah Leib Tzirelson: Hayyav u-Feʾulato*. Tel Aviv: Nezah, 1944.

Smith, Jonathan Z. *Map Is Not Territory: Studies in the History of Religions*. Leiden: E. J. Brill, 1978.

Smith, Oliver. *Vladimir Soloviev and the Spiritualization of Matter*. Boston: Academic Studies Press, 2011.

Smith, Wilfred Cantwell. *Modern Culture from a Comparative Perspective*. Albany: State University of New York Press, 1997.

———. *The Meaning and End of Religion*. New York: MacMillan, 1961.

Spencer, Colin. *The Heretic's Feast: A History of Vegetarianism*. Hanover: University Press of New England, 1995.

Sperber, Daniel. *A Commentary on Derekh Erez Zuta, Chapters Five to Eight*. Tel Aviv: Bar-Ilan University Press, 1990.

———. "Kavod Ha-Zibur u-Khevod Ha-Beriyot: Nashim u-Keriyat Ha-Torah." *Deʾot* 16 (June 2003): 17-20, 44.

Sperber, David. "Korbanot le-Atid La-vo be-Mishnat Ha-Rav Kook." In *Reayot Raiyah: Masot u-Mehkarim be-Torato shel Ha-Rav Kook*, edited by Shmuel Sperber, 97-112. Jerusalem: Beit Ha-Rav, 1992.

Stampfer, Shaul. *Ha-Yeshiva Ha-Litait be-Hithavutah*. Jerusalem: Merkaz Shazar, 2004 [1995].

———. "Inheritance of the Rabbinate in Eastern Europe in the Modern Period. *Jewish History* 13, no. 1 (1999): 35-57.

Stanislawski, Michael. *For Whom Do I Toil? Judah Leib Gordon and the Crisis of Russian Jewry*. New York: Oxford, 1988.

———. *Tsar Nicholas I and the Jews: The Transformation of Jewish Society in Russia, 1825-1855*. Philadelphia: Jewish Publication Society, 1983.

Steinsaltz, Adin. "Ha-Baʾayatiyut beʾ-Orot Ha-Qodesh." In *Ha-Reʾayah*, edited by Yizhak Refael, 102-105. Jerusalem: Mossad Ha-Rav Kook, 1966.

Stern, Eliyahu. *The Genius*. New Haven: Yale University Press, 2013.

———. *Jewish Materialism: The Intellectual Revolution of the 1870s*. New Haven: Yale University Press, 2018.

Stern, Josef. "Maimonides on the Growth of Knowledge and the Limitations of the Intellect." In *Maimonide: Philosophe et Savant*, edited by T. Levy and R. Rashed, 143-191. Louvain: Peeters, 2004.

———. "Maimonides' Epistemology." In *Cambridge Companion to Maimonides*, edited by Kenneth Seeskin, 105-133. Cambridge: Cambridge University Press, 2005.

———. *Problems and Parables of Law: Maimonides and Nahmanides on Reasons for the Commandments.* Albany: State University of New York Press, 1998.

Stern, Yosef Zekharia. *Tahalukhot Ha-Aggadot.* Warsaw: Meir Yehiel Halter & Partners, 5662/1902.

———. *Zekher Yehosef.* Vol. 1. Vilna: Dov Berish Torsch Nalkavy, 5659/1898 [sic]; vol. 2. Vilna: Lipman Metz, 1899; vol. 3. Vilna: Pyrzhnykov, 1901.

———. *Zekher Yehosef, Even Ha-'Ezer.* Jerusalem: Makhon Yerushalayim, 1994.

Storrs, Ronald. *Orientations.* London: Nicholson & Watson, 1937.

Strassberg-Dayan, Sarah. *Yahid, Umah ve-Enoshut: Tefisat Ha-Adam be-Mishnoteyhem shel A. D. Gordon ve-Ha-Rav Kook.* Tel Aviv: Ha-Kibbutz Hameuhad, 1995.

Tal, Zvi. "Shalosh Nashim Meshamshot be-Mokh: Iyun be-Ezrat Cohen." In *Berurim be-Hilkhot Ha-Re'ayah*, edited by Moshe Zvi Neriah, Aryeh Stern, and Neriah Gutel, 271-280. Jerusalem: Beit Ha-Rav, 1992.

Tamares, Aharon Shmuel. "Zikhronot." Translated by Avraham Bick [Shauly]. In *Sefer Shragai*, vol. 4, edited by Yitzhaq Refael, 162-174. Jerusalem: Mossad Ha-Rav Kook, 1993.

Tamares, Aharon Shmuel, and Ehud Luz, eds. *Pacifism le-Or Ha-Torah: Mikhtavei Ehad Ha-Rabbanim Ha-Margishim.* Jerusalem: Mercaz Dinur, 1992.

Ta-Shma, Yisrael. "Ha-GRA u-Ba'al 'Shaagat Aryeh,' 'Ha-Pnei Yehoshua' ve-Sefer 'Zion le-Nefesh Hayah': Le-Toldoteyhem shel Ha-Zeramim Ha-Hadashim be-Sifrut Ha-Rabbanit 'Erev Tenu'at Ha-Haskalah." *Sidra* 15 (1999): 181-191.

Taves, Ann. *Fits, Trances & Visions: Experiencing Religion and Explaining Experience from Wesley to James.* Princeton: Princeton University Press, 1999.

———. *Religious Experience Reconsidered: A Building-Block Approach to the Study of Religion and Other Special Things.* Princeton: Princeton University Press, 2009.

Taylor, Charles. *Sources of the Self: The Making of the Modern Identity.* Cambridge, MA: Harvard University Press, 1989.

———. *Hegel and Modern Society.* Cambridge: Cambridge University Press, 1979.

———. "Western Secularity." In *Rethinking Secularism*, edited by Craig Calhoun, Mark Juergensmeyer, and Jonathan van Antwerpen, 31-53. Oxford: Oxford University Press, 2011.

Tau, Zvi. *Le-Emunat 'Itenu.* Jerusalem: Hosen Yeshu'ot, 1994-2001.

Tchernowitz, Hayim [Rav Tzair]. *Pirqei Hayim.* New York: Bitzaron, 1954.

Tickochinski, Shlomo. *Lamdanut Mussar ve-Elitizm: Yeshivat Slabodka mi-Lita le-Eretz Yisrael.* Jerusalem: Mercaz Shazar, 2016.

Tirosh-Samuelson, Hava. *Happiness in Premodern Judaism: Virtue, Knowledge and Well-Being.* Cincinnati: Hebrew Union College Press, 2003.

Tishby, Isaiah. "Darkhei Hafatzatam shel Kitvei Kabbalah le- Ramhal be-Polin ve-Lita." *Qiryat Sefer* 45 (1970): 127-155.

———. "'Iqvot Rabbi Moshe Hayim Luzzatto be-Mishnat He-Hasidut." *Zion* 43 (1978): 201-234.

———. *Netivei Emunah ve-Minut.* Jerusalem: Hebrew University/Magnes, 1964.

———. *Torat Ha-Ra' ve-Ha-Qelippah be-Qabbalat Ha-ARI.* Jerusalem: Schocken, 1942.

Touraine, Alain. *Critique of Modernity.* Translated by David Macey. Oxford: Blackwell, 1995.

Troeltsch, Ernst. *The Social Teaching of the Christian Churches.* Translated by Olive Wyon. 1912. Repr. New York: Harper & Row, 1960.

Tropper, Amram. *Wisdom, Politics and Historiography: Tractate Avot in the Context of the Graeco-Roman Near East.* New York and Oxford: Oxford University Press, 2004.

Tsamriyon, Tsemach M. *Die Hebraische Presse in Europa,* Haifa: n.p., 1976.

Turbowicz, Zev Wolf. *Tiferet Ziv.* Warsaw: Unterhendler, 1896.

Turner, Joseph [Yossi]. "Philosophy and Praxis in the Thought of Aharon David Gordon." *Journal of Jewish Thought and Philosophy* 24 (2106): 122-148.

Turner, Victor. *Dramas, Fields and Metaphors: Symbolic Action in Human Society.* Ithaca: Cornell University Press, 1974.

———. *The Ritual Process: Structure and Anti-Structure.* Chicago: Aldine, 1969.

Tyckochinski, Shlomo. "Darkhei Ha-Limmud bi-Yeshivot Lita ba-Meah Ha-19." Master's thesis, Hebrew University, 2004.

Tziegelman, Eliezer. *Nahalei Emunah.* Lublin: Schneidmesser, 1935.

Tzirelson, Yehudah Leib. *Derekh Selulah.* Priulki: Mirov, 1902.

———. *Gevul Yehudah.* Pietrokov, 1906.

Ullman, Shalom. *Sefer Maftehot He-Hokhmah.* Jerusalem: Mesorah, 1987.

Urtan, Aigar. "Bauska: The Late 19th and Early 20th Century." Paper presented at the University of Latvia, 2004.

Uziel, Ben-Zion Meir Hai. *Mishpetei Uziel.* Tel Aviv: Levitzky, 1935-1940.

Valabregue, Sandra. "Philosophy, Heresy and Kabbalah's Counter-Theology." *Harvard Theological Review* 109, no. 2 (2016): 233-256.

Valler, Shulamit. *Nashim ve-Nashiyut be-Sippurei Ha-Talmud.* Tel Aviv: Ha-Kibbutz Ha-Meuhad, 1993.

Verses, Shmuel. "Dimuyo shel Rabbi Moshe Hayim Luzzatto be-Sifrut Ha-Haskalah." In *'Haqitzah 'Ami': Sifrut Ha-Haskalah be-'Idan Ha-Modernizatziyah,* 3-24. Jerusalem: Hebrew University/Magnes Press, 2004.

Veyne, Paul. *Did the Greeks Believe Their Own Myths?* Translated by Paula Wissing. Chicago: University of Chicago Press, 1988.

Vital, Hayim. *Sefer Etz Hayim.* 1782. Repr. Jerusalem: Yeshivat Ha-Mequbalim, 1999.

Wachs, Ron. "Peraqim be-Mishnato Ha-Kabalit shel Ha-Rav Shlomo Elyashiv." Master's thesis, Hebrew University, 1995.

Wald, Stephen G. *Pereq Eylu 'Ovrin: Bavli Pesahim Pereq Shlishi, Mahadurah Biqortit 'im Beiyur Maqif.* New York and Jerusalem: Jewish Theological Seminary, 2000.

Webster, Tom. "Writing to Redundancy: Approaches to Spiritual Journals and Early Modern Spirituality." *The Historical Journal* 39, no. 1 (1996): 33-56.

Weidemann, Naftali Hertz Ha-Levi. *Seder Ha-GRA: Yakhil Shnei Halaqim, Heleq Ha-Nigleh ve-Heleq Ha-Nistar.* Jerusalem: Yizhaq Nahum Loewy, 1895-1898.

Weinberg, Yehiel Ya'aqov. *Seridei Esh.* Jerusalem: Mossad Ha-Rav Kook, 1977.

———. *Li-Feraqim.* Jerusalem: Ha-Va-ad le-Hotzaat Kitvai Ha-Gaon Ha-Rav Yehiel Ya'aqov Weinberg zt"l, 2004.

Weisbard, Dov. "Parshanut Ha-Miqra be-Haguto shel Ha-Rav Kook." PhD. diss., Bar-Ilan University, 2020.

Wilf. Steven. *The Law Before the Law.* New York: Lexington Books, 2010.

Wineman, Zvi. *Ve-Da' Mah She-Tashiv.* Jerusalem: Vatikin, 2001.

Weinstein, Roni. *Kabbalah and Jewish Modernity.* Oxford: Littman, 2016.

Wolfson, Elliot R. "Secrecy, Apophasis and Atheistic Faith in the Teachings of Rav Kook." In *Negative Theology as Jewish Modernity,* edited by Michael Fagenblat, 131-160. Bloomington: Indiana University Press, 2017.

———. *Through a Speculum That Shines: Vision and Imagination in Medieval Jewish Mysticism.* Princeton: Princeton University Press, 1994.

Wolfson, Harry A. *The Philosophy of Spinoza*. Cambridge, MA: Harvard University Press, 1934.

———. *Studies in the History and Philosophy of Religion*. Cambridge, MA: Harvard University Press, 1973-1979.

Wozner, Shai Aqiva. *Hashivah Mishpatit bi-Yeshivot Lita:'Iyunim be-Mishnato shel Ha-Rav Shimon Shkop*. Jerusalem: Magnes, 2016.

Yavetz, Zev. "Igrot la-Rav Kook." *Sinai* 29, nos. 7-8 (1951): 109-121.

Yaron, Zvi. *Mishnato shel Ha-Rav Kook*. Jerusalem: Jewish Agency, 1974.

Yedidya, Asaf. *Le-Gadel Tarbut Ivriyah—Hayav u-Mishnato shel Zev Yavetz*. Jerusalem: Mossad Bialik, 2015.

Yifrah, Yehudah. "Ke-Domen 'al Pnei Ha-Sadeh." *Makor Rishon*, Shabbat Supplement. July 25, 2017, 10-15.

Yoseph Hayim of Baghdad [Ben Ish Hai]. *Torah Li-Shemah*. Jerusalem: Ahavat Shalom/Yad Franco, 2013.

Zakim, Michael. "Bookkeeping as Ideology: Capitalist Knowledge in Nineteenth-Century America." *Commonplace* 6, no. 3 (April 2006). http://commonplace.online/article/bookkeeping-as-ideology/.

Zalkin, Mordechai. "Between Dvinsk and Vilna: The Spread of Hasidism in Nineenth-Century Lithuania." In *Within Hasidic Circles: Studies in Hasidism in Memory of Mordechai Wilensky*, edited by E. Etkes, D. Asaf, I. Bartal, and E. Reiner, 21-50. Jerusalem and Tel Aviv: Mossad Bialik/Hebrew University/Tel Aviv University, 1999.

———. "Beyn 'Bnei Elohim' li-'Vnei Adam': Rabbanim, Bahurei Yeshivot ve-ha-Giyus La-Tzava Ha-Russi ba-Meah ha-19." In *Shalom u-Milhamah be-Tarbut Ha-Yehudit*, edited by Avriel Bar-Levav, 165-222. Jerusalem and Haifa: Mercaz Shazar/University of Haifa, 2006.

———. "Beyn Gaon le-Eglon—Morashtah Ha-Tarbutit shel Yahadut Lita." *Gesher* 43, no. 136 (Winter 1997): 73-82.

———. "Issachar and Zebulun—A Profile of a Lithuanian Scholar of the 19th Century." *Gal-Ed* 18 (2002): 125-154.

———. "'Iyr shel Torah—Torah ve-Limudah ba-Merhav Ha-'Iyroni Ha-Litai ba-Meah Ha-19." In *Yeshivot u-Vatei Midrashot*, edited by Immanuel Etkes, 131-161. Jerusalem: Mercaz Shazar, 2006.

———. "Mehqar Ha-Haskalah be-Mizrah Europa: Hash'arah be-Hash'arah ve-Dimyon be-Dimyon." In *Ha-Haskalah li-Gevanehah: 'Iyunim Hadashim be-Toldot Ha-Haskalah u-ve-Sifrutah*, edited by Yisrael Bartal and Shmuel Feiner, 165-182. Jerusalem: Hebrew University/Magnes, 2005.

———. "Social Status and Authority in Nineteenth-Century Lithuanian Jewish Communities." In *Central and East European Jews at the Crossroads of Tradition and Modernity*, edited by Jurgita Šiaučiunaitė-Verbickienė and Larisa Lempertienė, 174-187. Vilnius: The Center for Studies of the Culture and History of East European Jews, 2006.

Zaltzman, Avraham. "Munahim Philosophiyyim 'al pi Sefer 'Otzar Ha-Hokhmah' le-Julius Barasch." *'Iyun* 3 (1952): 151-168.

Zeidel, Moshe. *Hiqrei Miqra*. Jerusalem: Mossad Ha-Rav Kook, 1978.

Zevin, Shlomo Yosef. *Ishim ve-Shittot*. Jerusalem: Beit Hillel, 1956.

Zipperstein, Steven J. *The Jews of Odessa: A Cultural History, 1794-1881*. Stanford: Stanford University Press, 1985.

———. *Elusive Prophet: Ahad Ha'am and the Origins of Zionism*. Berkeley: University of California Press, 1993.

———. *Pogrom: Kishinev and the Tilt of History*. New York: Liveright/Norton, 2018.

Zoref, Efraim. *Hayei Ha-Rav Kook*. Jerusalem: M. Neuman, 1961.

Index

A

Abaye, 100, 206
Abel (Biblical), 204, 317
Abraham the Patriarch, 130-132, 273, 313
Abulafia, Abraham, 13n38, 29n94, 205n82, 336
Active Intellect, 83n182, 118, 202-3, 336
Adam, 13n38, 132, 166-67, 223-24, 332n8,
Adam Qadmon, 120-21, 167, 175n130
Arikh Anpin, 162
"Afiqim ba-Negev," 263
aggadah, 4, 49n32, 76n155, 87, 91, 101-3, 106, 170,
        173, 183n2, 188-97, 211, 217, 226, 231, 325
        commentary, 23n71, 24, 28, 83n181, 102,
                128n162, 159, 192n28, 273
        Aggadic commentary, viii, 8n20, 19n63, 83, 91,
                110n74, 148n31, 160n76, 182, 189, 193
        Aggadic study, 193, 196, 198, 276n194, 342-43
Agus, Jacob, 5, 13, 17, 18n52, 31n104, 157n62
Ahad Ha-Am, 21n65, 144, 144n10, 148n31, 194n38,
        235-37, 236n11, 237n12, 241, 244, 251, 251n70,
        259-60, 265, 272, 298, 301-2, 306n130. *See also*
        Asher Ginzberg
Albo, Joseph, 59, 59n80, 72, 123n139, 132, 148n30,
        267. *See also Sefer Ha-'Iqarim*
Alexandrov, Rabbi Shmuel, 87n199, 180-1, 252n71,
        259, 272, 301, 304n121
Aliyah, 281, 282n16, 284n25, 285n29, 285n31,
        286n32, 287n37
        First Aliyah, 284, 398
        Second Aliyah, 279, 282n16, 284-85, 286n33,
                316, 343
Alkalay, Rabbi Yehudah, 243, 257n103
Alroey, Gur, 284, 286n33
Amital, Yehudah, 271n173, 332, 349
Amon, 307
Angels, 163, 313
        Gabriel, 201
        Michael, 201
antinomianism, 26n86, 95, 303, 322, 325
antisemitism, 242n31, 271, 276, 297
Appel, Gersion, 254n90
'Aqedat Yitzhaq, 4, 72, 84n187, 94n13, 123, 129,132,
        178n143, 189n17, 216. *See also* Arama, Isaac
Arama, Isaac, 4, 21, 24, 72, 83n182, 84, 116, 118,
        123, 129, 132, 148n30, 199, 204, 216
Argentina, 328
Aristotle, 30, 192n30, 231, 293
'Arukh Ha-Shulhan, 74

asher yatzar blessing, 108, 168
Ashkenazi, Mordechai, 26
Augustine, Saint, 24n77, 231, 330
Aviner, Shlomo, 9-10
Avivi, Yosef, 13, 14n43, 21, 22n68, 110n74, 125n148,
        125n152, 140, 162, 334n19, 337
Avneri, Yossi, 6, 16, 18
'avodah be-gashmiyut, 134, 172n120, 225, 333
'avodah tzorekh gevohah, 176
'Avodat Ha-Qodesh, 321. *See also* Ibn Gabbai, Meir
Avraham, Hayim, 62
Avraham of Preil, 51
Axial Age civilizations, 34
Azikri, Elazar, 26

B

Ba'al Shem Tov (Besht), 154-56, 163
Babylonian Talmud (BT), 67, 88, 147, 183, 189-91,
        276n194, 323
Bakhrakh, Naftali, 296
Baltic Sea, 45, 93, 181, 308n133
Barak, Uriel, 349
Bar-Kokhba, 309
Bar Yohai, Rabbi Shimon, 36
Baumgarten, Eliezer, 163-65, 280
Beck, Lewis White, 28
be-derekh ha-shema, 134
Be'eri, Yehoshua, 6,
Beit Ha-Midrash, 87, 269n156
Belarus (White Russia), 48, 53, 114
Belinski, Tanhum-Gershon, 62
Ben Artzi, Hagi, 18, 233n1
Ben Avuyah, Elisha, 249
beneficence, 100
Bengis, Zelig Reuven, 71
Ben-Gurion, David, 284
be-'omeq ha-higayon, 192
Berdyczewsky, Micah Yosef, 27, 68, 69n118, 78, 87,
        153, 191, 251, 285, 301-2, 343-44
Bergmann, Samuel Hugo, 12, 16n46, 209n93,
        335n20
Bergson, Henri-Louis, 4, 92n7
Berlin, Hayim, 88, 91n3, 148n31, 282n13
Berlin, Naftali Zvi Yehudah (Netziv), 49n31, 62n90,
        66-68, 74-77, 88
Berlin, Rayna Batya, 67
Bernfeld, Shimon, 4, 92n7, 301n114
Berurei Ha-Middot, 178

Besht. *See also* Ba'al Shem Tov
Bet Din Ha-Gadol, 241, 264, 269, 290
Bialystok, 65, 237n13
Bible, 35, 44, 49n32, 57n67, 60, 67, 76n156, 93, 94n13, 123, 147, 153, 179, 257, 287, 341n39
Binah, 162-63, 204, 326
Binah le-'Ittim, 61n89, 77n157, 84. *See also*, de Figo, AzariahBindiger, Naamah, 11-12
Bin-Nun, Yoel, 9-10, 14, 329n1, 349
Birzh (Birzai), 114n94, 115
bitul ha-yesh, 225
Blazer, Isaac, 22n69, 153n49, 283n19, 327
Bnei Aqiva, 17
Bobroysk, 180
Boisk, 28, 90, 104n64, 137, 140-181, 191n25, 217, 238, 247, 255, 281, 283, 300-301, 307, 327, 334, 340, 342
Book of Amos, 266
Book of Chronicles, 228
Book of Deuteronomy, 75, 127n159, 201n66, 212, 216, 239n21, 274n186, 295, 311, 314
Book of Exodus, 83n180, 89, 96n23, 119, 122, 267n145, 270, 304
Book of Genesis, 106, 128, 130-32, 215-16, 267n145, 268, 295, 306, 312, 323n187, 324
Book of Job, 183n1, 307-8
Book of Leviticus, 268n150, 322
Book of Numbers, 122n133, 210, 326
Book of Proverbs, 77, 89, 96n24, 157n64, 168n98, 169, 207, 315, 320
Book of Psalms, 50n36, 60n85, 70, 76, 85, 127, 174, 176, 195, 197, 202n72, 211-13, 220, 222, 224, 239n21, 247, 263, 272, 311, 318, 347
Bor, Harris, 31, 141n3
Brenner, Yosef Hayim, 9n24, 16n46, 284, 319n168, 333n11
Brill, Alan, 32, 298
Brinker, Menahem, 301
BT *Avodah Zarah*, 70n122, 200
BT *Bava Batra*, 93, 223, 312
BT *Bava Metzia*, 76n154, 98, 195
BT *Bekhorot*, 117
BT *Berakhot*, 2n3, 50n36, 96n24, 100, 105, 109n71, 117, 119, 169n108, 177, 178n143, 183n1, 188, 189, 194n37, 197n48, 198, 201n66, 202, 208-9, 213, 221, 229, 231, 273-75, 304n121, 312, 327
BT *Eruvin*, 58, 133, 230n156, 264, 313
BT *Hagigah*, 96, 105
BT *Hullin*, 76, 106, 268n150, 311, 346
BT *Ketubot*, 274, 310n140
BT *Megillah*, 111n76, 119
BT *Nedarim*, 78, 310n140, 326n197
BT *Pesahim*, 271, 326
BT *Qiddushin*, 269
BT *Sanhedrin*, v, 97n26, 124, 269n156, 303, 306, 314n152, 323
BT *Shabbat*, 2n3, 62n92, 107n63, 108, 135n198, 168n102, 177, 183n1, 188nn15-16, 197, 293
BT *Sotah*, 174, 201n66, 318
BT *Sukkah*, 98

BT *Tamid*, 76
BT *Yevamot*, 173, 216
Buber, Martin, 6n12, 13n38, 21n67, 37, 39n130, 337

C
Cain (Biblical), 204, 317-18
Cave of Makhpelah, 133
Chajes, Aharon, 83n180
Chajes, Jeffrey (Yossi), 26
Chajes, Zvi Hirsch, 85n189, 85n192, 130n177
Cherqi, Yair, 10
cholera, 92
Christianity, 34, 208, 257, 291, 297, 306, 318n168, 322-23, 325
    Christian, 109n71, 318
    Christian critiques, 279, 301
    Christian ethics, 187, 317, 319
civilization, 24, 32, 34, 226, 249
Cohen (High Priest), 61, 350
Cohen, Rabbi David (Ha-Nazir), 7-8, 15n46, 21n68, 337n26
Cohen, Hermann, 4, 20n65, 70n123, 198n56, 333
Cohen, Jonathan, 336
consciousness, viii, 1, 27, 32-33, 44, 94, 116, 120, 162, 166-68, 173, 176, 250, 267, 338, 344-46
    Messianic consciousness, 9, 281
Cordovero, Rabbi Moshe ben Jacob, 162n80, 173, 177n142, 223, 320
    Pardes Rimonim, 204
cosmos, 3, 98, 121, 127, 141, 156, 185, 200, 209n93, 301, 326n196, 335, 344
Courlander Litvaks, 45
creation, 10, 30, 83-84, 99, 129, 133, 162, 173, 177, 195, 214, 217, 220, 228, 235, 249, 254, 259-60, 262-63, 267, 269, 271, 275, 285, 289, 335, 340
    primordial creation, 126
Creator (The Creator), 108, 110, 221, 224, 229, 253, 291, 297
Crescas, Hasdai ben Abraham, 76
culture, human, 38, 264-66, 270

D
Da'at (knowledge), 194,
Da'at Cohen, 103n50
Da'at Tevunot, 123
Daniel (Prophet), 338
Darkhei no'am, 106
Daugavpils. *See* DvinskDaugava River, 45
De Figo, Azariah, 84. *See also Binah le-'Ittim*
derash, 40, 95n20
Derekh 'Etz Hayim, 123. *See also* Luzzatto, Moshe Hayim
Derrida, Jacques, 302
destiny, 130, 135, 172, 227, 251n67, 252, 258, 264, 271, 275-76, 284n23, 289, 296, 303
Deus Absconditus, 209
devequt, 10, 31, 47n25, 48, 94, 96, 157, 171-72, 226, 334
    unio mystica, 48, 94, 157
Dickens, Charles, 4

Din (judgement), 228, 268, 290
disenchantment, 44, 53
Dison, Yonina, 9
divine anthropos, 120-21
divine flow, 129, 210
divine guidance, 126, 131
divine image, 155, 288, 297, 324, 344
divine intellect, 118, 121, 133, 171, 211, 223
divine light, 126, 210, 275, 296, 335
divine mind, 117-19, 159n69, 166, 170-72, 234
divine providence, 98, 118, 213, 221, 223, 273, 275
divine will, 83n182, 126-27, 135-36, 202, 209, 214, 217, 223, 227, 278
divine wisdom, 214, 217, 227, 289
divinity, 24, 37, 101, 222, 294, 333
Dixon, Thomas, 187
Dobvelen (Dubulti), 65, 93, 180
Don-Yehiya, Eliezer, 59-60, 113n89
Dostoevsky, Fyodor, 302
Drohytshyn (Turets), 50
Dumont, Louis, 25
Durkheim, Emile, 36
Dvinsk, 45, 48, 50n34, 51, 57n67, 65, 70, 180, 327

E
Eastern Europe, viii, ix, 7n16, 17-18, 19n62, 20-22, 28, 31-32, 41-45, 52n45, 54, 57, 60n84, 61n89, 66, 67n105, 68, 78, 125n150, 158n67, 166, 196n44, 232, 235-36, 241, 257, 267, 284-86, 288n41, 297n94, 341-42, 345
ecclesia, 215, 225, 308, 323
ecclesiastes, 128,
ecstatic mysticism, 3
Eden, 152, 166, 177
Eder Ha-Yaqar, 64n98, 287
Eger, Rabbi Aqiva, 70
Eisenstadt, Shmuel Noah, 24, 32-34, 44, 46n23, 206n86, 338, 349,
élan vital, 195, 210, 214, 217, 251, 318-19, 324
The Elementary Forms of the Religious Life, 36
El Hiki Shofar, 240
Eliasberg, Mordechai, 49n31, 55, 142-47, 156, 158n67, 237, 241, 259n111, 276
Elijah ben Solomon. *See* Gaon of Vilna
Elyashiv, Rabbi Shlomo, 89, 115, 125n150, 143n6, 156, 165, 281
emanation, 13n37, 15n43, 84, 118, 162, 164-65, 167, 204, 211
'Emeq Ha-Melekh, 296
Emunot Ve-De'ot, 153
Encyclopedia of Religious Zionism, 15
Enlightenment, 21, 42, 52, 54, 56, 137, 150, 189, 195, 212, 228n149, 229, 231, 269-70, 310, 324
Ephraimson, Ya'aqov, 147
Ephraimson, Yequtiel Ha-Levi, 147
epistemology, 9, 39, 219, 258n109, 304
Epstein, Barukh, 66n105
Epstein, Moshe Mordechai, 69n119, 79n166, 151n41
Epstein, Yehiel Mikhel, 74
Eretz Yisrael. *See* Land of Israel.

Esau (Biblical), 130, 132, 324, 331n7
eschatology, 24-25, 186n11, 233, 248, 263, 273, 279, 312
eschaton, 97, 117, 129-30, 132, 136-37, 195, 248, 250, 269-71, 290, 298, 313, 315, 321, 323
Esh Dat ve-Ruah Leumi, 259
esoteric study, 94, 98
esotericism, 28-29, 35, 47, 71, 76n155, 184n3, 199n56
ethics, ix, 3, 7n16, 9, 29-30, 39, 85, 88, 99, 126, 130, 186n11, 187, 196n44, 196n46, 230, 244, 258n104, 272, 276, 287, 289, 296, 300, 302, 307, 312-13, 317, 322, 339, 344
    Hellenistic -, 30
    Jewish -, 30, 31n104, 100, 261, 300-301
    Kantian -, 29, 268
    Lurianic -, 177
    Maimonidean -, 31, 177
    Maskilic -, 52
    non-Jewish -, 78, 287, 313
    philosophical -, 31, 53
    Universal -, 219, 279-80
    Western -, 29, 302-3, 307, 312
ethos, 10, 30, 95, 167, 185-86, 302, 310, 318
Etkes, Immanuel, 46n23, 47n26, 52n47, 159
eudaemonia, 31, 131, 133, 217, 268-69, 316-17. *See also shlemut*evil, 96, 100, 101, 126, 132, 166, 168, 176, 178, 186, 214-15, 219, 221, 268-69, 290, 295, 307, 312, 314-21, 324
evolution, 78, 141, 231, 248, 264, 278, 287-89, 302, 326n196
exile, 97, 144, 189, 195, 241, 243, 265, 273, 314, 324, 329
Exodus Rabbah, 313
expressivism, 21-24, 231, 307,
'Eyn Ayah, 8n20, 19n63, 25, 28, 83, 110n74, 127, 159, 182-89, 191-94, 196, 198, 201-3, 206, 209, 211, 213-14, 217-18, 220-21, 225-26, 229, 231, 251, 254, 259, 261-62, 267, 273-74, 276, 287, 293, 301, 306, 310, 313, 334, 345
Eyn Sof, 173-74
Eyn Ya'aqov, 59
Ezekiel (Biblical), 321
Ezra (Biblical), 195, 338
'Ezrat Cohen, 106

F
Fara'id al-Qulub, 123. *See also Hovot Ha-Levavot*-
Ferziger, Adam, 305
Filber, Ya'aqov, 9
Fishman, David, 279
Foucauldian rubric, 26
Foucault, Michel, 30
Frankel, Aryeh, 15, 89n210
Franklin, Benjamin, 27, 54n54
fraternity, 4, 16n46, 54, 154, 191, 220, 244-45, 253-54, 257, 272, 289, 301, 332
Freedom, 6, 24, 33, 86n197, 214, 225, 238n20, 241, 266, 269, 287-88, 299, 326-27
Fuenn, Shmuel Yosef, 52

G

Gaon of Vilna (Elijah ben Solomon), 32, 36, 46, 67, 94, 96n24, 108, 112, 125, 162, 189, 204, 235, 248

Garb, Jonathan, 13, 32, 35-36, 124, 140, 186n10, 349

garment, 76, 164, 167, 304. *See also Levushgemilut hasadim,* 130

"The Generation" (*Ha-Dor*) 316

Genocide Convention, 25

gentiles, 95-98, 127n157, 133, 135, 257, 297, 311

Geonim, 58

Gerber, Reuven, 18, 255n95

Germany, 42, 113n91

German Haskalah, 42

German Idealism, 23, 336

Germans, 146

Gersonides, 118

Gevurah, 228

Gikatilla, Yosef, 321

Giller, Pinhas, 304

Ginzberg, Asher, 236. *See also Ahad Ha-Am*

Ginzburg, Aryeh Leib of Metz, 104

glory, 75, 80n167, 110, 131, 134, 155, 228,

Golden Calf, 135-36

Goldman, Eliezer, 12, 18, 92n7, 104n52, 258

Gordley, James, 39

Gordon, Aharon David, 39n130, 286, 343-46

Gordon, Eliezer, 72n138, 153, 237, 243

Gordon, Judah Leib, 44, 49n32

Gottschalk, Alfred, 236-37
    The Great Shift, 338

Greece, 34

Griva, Latvia, 45, 48, 50-51, 60, 70, 327

Grodno, 50, 62

Gush Emunim, 332

Guttman, Julius, 336

H

Ha'ameq Davar, 66n105, 67, 75, 76n153

Ha'ameq She'elah, 67, 113n90

Habad, 43, 48, 51, 66n105, 156, 185, 209n93, 216, 221, 225, 231, 275, 313, 333-34, 335n22

Ha-dat ha-nimusit, 132

Hadot, Pierre, 30-31, 171

Hafetz Hayim (Rabbi Meir Kagan/Ha-Cohen), 50, 158n67, 243

hagiography, 15, 17n49, 50n33

halakhah, 10, 14, 19n60, 29, 55, 67, 78, 81, 84-88, 95, 98, 102, 109, 112n81, 155, 164, 170, 179, 193, 195, 197, 211, 214n106, 226, 231, 234, 241, 250, 266-67, 269-70, 276-77, 291, 301, 322, 325, 337, 339, 342

halakhic responsa, 19, 28, 90

halakhists, 58, 106, 148n32, 153

Ha-Levanon, 56n61, 62, 86n198

Ha-Levi, Yehudah, 4, 20, 83n182, 123, 148n30, 153, 201-2, 204, 216n113, 311, 336

Ha-Levi (Weidemann), Naftali Hertz, 280

Ha-Maggid, 73, 259n111

Ha-Mahshavah Ha-Yisraelit, 8

Ha-Meiri, Menachem, 291

Ha-Melitz, 56, 73, 74n147, 78n162, 86n198, 91n3, 152, 237n14

Ha-Mizrah, 183n1, 284n23, 308

Ha-Nazir, 8-9, 196n44

hanhagat ha-tov ve-ha-ra, 126

hanhagat ha-yihud, 126

Hansel, Joelle, 125

Ha-Peles, 18, 48n30, 50, 79n166, 147n27, 193n33, 233, 234n1, 245-47, 250-51, 257, 260-61, 272-73, 275-77, 287, 298, 301, 306, 312, 327

Harlap, Ya'aqov Moshe, 15n46, 21n68, 63, 108n66, 110n74, 111n80, 112n87, 179n149, 332

Ha-Shiloah, 92n7, 301n114, 318

Hasidism, 24, 29, 36, 41, 43, 45, 46n23, 47-48, 55, 81n173, 124, 140, 142, 150, 155-57, 165, 169-70, 172, 197, 209-10, 231, 244, 248, 333, 339, 343

Hasidim, 47n26, 48, 59, 68, 146, 154, 156, 163, 280, 282-83, 294

Hasidic Thought, 4, 142, 165, 209, 333

Haskalah, viii, 21, 32, 41-47, 52-56, 60, 67-70, 75n149, 236, 241, 245, 253n76, 279, 285, 343
    - literature, 4, 68
    - writings, 24

haskamot, 16n46, 79, 148

Ha-Tevunah, 150n35, 177, 178n143

Ha-Tzefirah, 49n32, 77n157, 86n198, 152-53

Hayim of Volozhin, 46-48, 55n56, 57, 62n91, 70n127, 113, 157n64

Heaven, 82n178, 98, 101, 138, 199n57, 215, 228, 262, 272, 291-92

Hegel, Georg Wilhelm Friedrich, 4, 24, 305

heresy, 100, 111n76, 223, 249, 257, 272, 279, 301, 303-4, 310-12, 315-17, 320, 323

Hervieu-Leger, Danielle, 33

Herzl, Theodore, 78n164, 235-37, 247n50, 255, 256n96, 271n168, 297, 306

Herzlian Zionism, 256, 264, 306

Heschel, Abraham Joshua, 10, 21n65, 67n107, 76n154, 269n156

hesed, 97, 136, 205, 228

heshbon ha-nefesh (soul reckoning), 169

Hess, Moses, 4, 235, 251, 258, 276

Hevesh Pe'er, 28, 109, 111, 116, 133n190, 203, 342

Hibat Zion, 244n36

Hillel (The Elder), 179n149, 225n138, 306, 313

Hirsch, Rabbi Samson Raphael, 147, 190, 255, 290-91, 305

Hod, 228

Hokhmah (wisdom), 120-21, 162-63, 166-68, 177, 204, 210

holiness, 2, 10, 31, 125, 129, 134, 136-37, 167-68, 206-7, 226, 316, 320, 344

holy of holies, 308-10

holy spirit, 84-85, 130n177, 168, 213, 345

Holzman, Avner, 22n69, 302, 343n42
    reoq ha-nimus, 131

Horev, 147, 255

Horowitz, Isaiah, 26

Hosea, Prophet, 334, 376
Hovot Ha-Levavot (Duties of the Heart), 4, 123, 139n218, 151, 153, 158n66, 169, 195-96, 201, 244, 319, 336. See also Ibn Paquda, Bahya
human agency, 33-34, 44, 162n80, 209n93
human consciousness, viii, 162, 166, 173
human dignity, 105, 109n72, 151n41, 198n55, 206-7, 287-88
human flourishing, 30-31, 127
human intellect, 130, 156, 203, 270, 275, 336
humility, 31, 40, 55n56, 108n67, 150n37, 151n41, 176-77, 181, 280, 295, 342n41, 349-50
hu shakul ke-neged kulam, 71
Huss, Boaz, 37-38

I

Ibn Gabbai, Meir 156n58, 321. See also *'Avodat Ha-Qodesh*
Ibn Habib, Jacob, 189. See also *'Eyn Ya'aqov*Ibn Paquda, Bahya, 61n89, 151, 198. See also *Fara'id al-Qulub* and *Hovot Ha-Levavot*)
Idel, Moshe, 25, 167n96, 205n82, 209, 334, 337n29, 348
ideology, 39, 44, 52n46, 234, 269n156, 277, 284, 286
idolatry, 39, 290-91, 322
Idra Rabbah, 173
'iggulim, 126, 211
illumination, 18, 28, 168, 214, 222, 268n148
imagination, 10, 20-21, 23n71, 108n69, 152, 154, 169, 185-86, 201-213, 216, 223, 245, 265, 285, 289, 293, 300, 316, 318, 327, 331, 336-37, 339, 345-46
imitatio dei, 128, 199n57, 200, 213
immanence, 33, 35, 126
Imperial China, 34
individualism, 25, 36, 144, 170, 179n149, 219, 226
interiority, 81, 83-84, 89, 97, 102, 129, 134, 139n218, 154, 165, 171, 173-74, 175n130, 195, 217, 219
'Iqarim, 72. See also Albo, Joseph
Isaac, Biblical Patriarch, 130
Isaiah, Prophet, 83n180, 242, 270
Ish-Shalom, Benjamin, 12, 14n43, 15n46, 92n7, 185n7, 206n85
Islam, 34, 244, 291, 297
    Muhammad, 297
Istanbul, Turkey, 327
'Ittur Sofrim, 28, 78, 84-88, 102n49, 109, 111, 113n90, 127n159, 143n6, 153, 173, 185, 188n15, 190, 192, 201, 241, 309, 340

J

Jacob, Patriarch, 130, 132, 215-16, 323n187, 324, 331n7
Jaffa, 6, 8, 18, 22n68, 153, 185, 188, 234, 278, 280-84, 299, 321n184, 327-30, 337n27, 340, 342-43
Jaffe, Dov Ber, 48
Jaffe, Mordechai, 48, 106, 112, 123n142. See also *Levush*

Jaffe, Mordechai Gimpel, 49, 55, 60n82, 63n92, 79n167, 327
James, William, 4, 36
    The Varieties of Religious Experiences, 36
Jaspers, Karl, 34
Jelgava (Mitoit/Mitau), 327
Jerusalem, ix, 6, 9, 18, 71, 88n209, 89n211, 110n74, 153n49, 211, 241, 247, 269, 280-82, 283n19, 284, 348, 350
Jesus, 95n18, 100-101, 297-98, 317-19, 321n184
Jewish history, 14, 52n45, 82, 113n91, 247, 252, 318
Jewish identity, 236n10, 237n12, 244, 247, 250-51, 271, 276, 285
Jewish nationhood, 3, 234, 254
Jewish peoplehood, 105, 243, 251, 266, 282, 316, 329-30, 340
Jewish radicalism, 279, 286
Jewish society, 27, 38, 44, 52-53, 140, 150, 210, 231, 279, 305
Jewish thought, ix, 11-12, 14n42, 21, 25, 32, 40, 43, 96n23, 99n32, 336, 339, 342-43
Jewish women, 147
Jews, 35, 45, 52-53, 56, 59, 62n90, 73, 78, 82n178, 99, 144, 146-47, 197, 235-36, 237n13, 244, 252, 255-57, 259, 275-76, 285, 286n35, 290-91, 294-98, 305, 311, 331n6
Jordan River, 95
Judaism, viii, 15, 34, 37, 47, 52, 67n105, 77, 80, 232, 235, 244, 247n52, 254, 265, 272, 279, 284, 286, 291, 298, 300-301, 318-19, 323, 338, 343
    traditional -, ix, 27, 52, 148n31, 244, 285, 291, 305

K

Kabbalah, ix, xv, 3-4, 11, 14n43, 20-21, 24-26, 29, 31-36, 47, 54, 67, 72, 91, 92n7, 98, 115, 119-21, 139-40, 150, 154-57, 165, 170, 173, 182, 185, 197, 199n56, 204n81, 209-10, 214, 232, 255, 280, 287, 288n41, 293, 301, 326, 331n5, 336, 338, 343, 346
    Christian -, 23
    esoteric -, 95
    Lithuanian -, viii, 3-4, 29, 89, 94, 125, 162, 165-67, 172, 203-4, 219, 221, 266, 296, 333, 339
    Lurianic -, 21, 89n212, 119, 125, 155, 294
    modern -, 32, 34-35, 124
Kabbalistic diaries, 27
Kabbalistic studies, 24, 90, 154, 156, 158, 273n180
Kabbalistic teachings, 46n23, 89n211, 155, 173
Kabbalistic tradition, 121, 143n6, 154, 171, 178, 205n82, 219, 231
Kabbalists, 36, 40–41, 120, 133, 169, 227, 316, 393
Kagan, Israel Meir, 73, 158n67, 243. See also Hafetz Hayim
Kalcheim, Uzi, 9
Kalischer, Zvi Hirsch, 235, 243, 245, 252
Kalmanson, Elhanan, 8, 9n24
Kamenetz, 149

Kant, Immanuel, 4, 30, 42, 92n7, 218, 304n121
Karo, Rabbi Yoseph, 26
kashrut, 69n122, 72n138, 102, 254
Katz, Jacob, 43n8, 44n13, 120, 235n4
Katznelson, Berl, 284
Kavod, 167n96, 211, 290
kavvanah (intentionality), 108
Kenites, 318
Keter, 120, 173, 177
Keilim. See Vessel
Kierkegaard, Søren Aaby, 302
King David (Biblical), 203, 306-7, 309, 315
Kishinev, 257, 279
Klein, Menahem, 259n112, 260
Kletzk, 149
Knesset Ha-Gedolah, 11n33, 86
Knesset Yisrael, 75n151, 77
Kolakowski, Leszek, 23, 338n33
Kook, Frayde Batya, 48
Kook, Perel Zlota, 45, 51
Kook, Shlomo Zalman, 45, 48-51, 60, 91n3, 109n73, 243
Kook, Zvi Yehudah, 7-9, 15n46, 19, 64, 77n160, 80n173, 90n1, 107n66, 122n135, 123n140, 137, 141, 153, 154n52, 158, 160, 165, 180, 188, 230n156, 246-47, 274n187, 278, 287n37, 299, 308n134, 325n194, 327n203, 328n205, 332n8, 333n11
Korah, 97
Krochmal, Nahman, 4, 236, 286-87, 299, 331
Kugel, James, 338

L
Lamentations Rabbah, 222
Land of Israel, 20, 85n190, 117, 122n136, 143, 186, 195n39, 216n113, 233, 238, 239n22, 246n49, 247, 254, 273-74, 277, 282-83, 298-99, 301, 327-29, 331n6, 337, 340, 346-47
Lang, Berel, 186
Lanir, Michal, 18, 184n3, 234n2
Lappin, Bezalel, 328
lashon haltziyi, 76
Latvia, 45, 73, 142
La-Yesharim Tehillah, 45, 61, 124n143
Lefin, Menahem Mendel, 54, 150
Lefort, Claude, 33
Lemkin, Raphael, 25
Leshem Shevo Ve-Ahlamah, 89
Lessing, Gotthold, 269
Levin, Binyamin Menashe, 142, 147, 179, 259, 307, 308n134
Levin, Rabbi Reuven of Dvinsk, 57, 62n91
Levush, 48, 76
Levush (Kabbalistic concept). *See* Garment
Lewis, Shmuel (Richie), 31
liberalism, ix, 10, 52-53, 56, 236, 299
Liebes, Yehudah, 306, 321
Lifshitz, Dov, 93
Lifshitz, Ya'aqov, 44, 56n61, 73n141, 243, 244n36

Lifshitz, Yehezqel, 145
Lilienblum, Moshe Leib, 49n31, 53, 56, 67, 244, 284n23, 310n140
limitations, 26n86, 40, 96, 133, 270, 293
Linat Ha-Tzedeq, 147
Lindbeck, George, 338-39
Li-Nevukhei Ha-Dor, 2n3, 28, 286-87, 300-301, 305, 316-17, 320, 326-27, 331n6
Lintop, Pinhas Ha-Cohen, 115, 144, 165, 282
Lipkin, Israel, 54
Liqutei Halakhot, 243
Liqutei Moharan, 94
Lithuania, 48, 53, 73, 114, 147, 189, 281
    Lithuanian Jewry, 47, 55
    Lithuanian Kabbalists, 45, 155n54, 163, 199n56
    Lithuanian Talmudism, viii, 4, 24, 41, 46, 74, 87, 101, 121, 140, 186, 226, 342
Litvak, Olga, 42, 56-57
Lobel, Diana, 336
Lomza, 149
Lovingkindness, 130, 134n192, 135, 245
Ludza, 59
Luria, Rabbi Yitzhak (ARI), 36, 82, 125-26, 143n6, 162-165, 320
lusts, 100, 132, 311
Luther, Martin, 35
Luzzatto, Rabbi Moshe Hayim, 4, 14n43, 35, 44, 61, 85n189, 89, 98n30, 121, 123-27, 136, 140-41, 143, 150, 153n47, 156-57, 159, 162-67, 171, 173, 176-77, 182, 185, 200, 204n81, 211, 213, 217, 225, 233, 269, 273, 303, 315, 320-21, 342
    Adir Ba-Marom, 94n13, 127
    Mesillat Yesharim, 45, 123-24, 151-52, 200
Lyelufa River, 146
Lyutsin, 59-62, 113n89, 190n23

M
MacIntyre, Alasdair, 29-30
Magen Avot, 51
Maharal of Prague (Judah Loew), 4, 133, 192, 198
Mahaziqei Ha-Dat, 74, 77, 84
Mahberot Qetanot Boisk, 2n3, 28, 141, 193n33, 233
Maimon, J.L. (Fishman), 17, 57n66, 63, 69n122, 92, 246, 260n113
Maimonides, 20n64, 21, 24, 29, 31-32, 35, 41, 43, 72, 76n155, 83-84, 102, 108, 116-18, 123n138, 132, 154, 171, 176-77, 192, 196, 198, 201-2, 207, 213, 216, 222, 254, 261-62, 269-70, 283n22, 287-89, 293, 297, 300, 336-37
    Guide of the Perplexed, 278, 286
    Maimonidean doctrine, 21, 201, 265
    Maimonidean philosophy, 20, 140, 155, 337
Maimonides' Code (Mishneh Torah), 57n67
    Hilkhot De'ot, 293
    Hilkhot Melakhim, 297
Malbim, Meir Libush, 61
malbushim, 167. *See also* Garment*Malkhut,* 204, 304n121

manifestation, 24, 120, 136, 209, 211, 236, 301, 315, 329
Mannheim, Karl, 277
Margolin, Ron, 210
marriage, 58n74, 72, 116, 174, 258n104
Marxism, 285
Maskilim, 42-43, 45, 49n31, 53-56, 59-61, 79n166, 113n90, 124, 141, 144, 160n74, 180, 189=90, 199n56, 240-41, 249, 267, 341
materiality, 99, 226
Mayin nuqvin (feminine waters), 173
Medievals, 34, 58, 109, 288
    medieval Jewish philosophy, viii, 29, 91, 118, 186, 192n29
    medieval philosophical tradition, 3, 20-21, 23-24, 32, 107, 127, 221, 234n1, 249, 287, 293, 313, 316
    medieval philosophy, viii, 30, 42, 52, 63, 109, 116, 121, 196-97, 233, 288, 295n78, 339, 341
    medieval Talmudists, 58
Medini, Hayim Hezekiah, 49n32, 88, 91n3
meditation, 168, 173, 334
mefursamot, 96, 132-33, 135
Megaleh 'Amuqot, 322
Meir, Jonatan, 16n46
Meisel, Rabbi Eliyahu Hayim, 50, 148n31, 243
Menachem Mendel of Shklov, 10, 164, 333
Menashe of Ilya, 54, 57, 63
Mendelssohn, Moses, 43n8, 144, 187n14, 302
Menorat Ha-Maor, 59
mercy, 80, 268-70, 296, 344
Messiah, 101, 223, 239n21, 243, 298, 300- 303, 305, 312, 319-21
    final messianic redemption, 452
    Messiah ben David, 305
    Messiah ben-Joseph, 305-6, 320-22
    Messianic awareness, 10, 25
    Messianism, 3, 11, 124, 209, 243, 279, 281, 331, 333
metaphysics, viii, 7, 9, 29, 126, 132, 150, 163, 170, 192n29, 199n58, 209, 236, 293, 302, 330n4, 333, 334n16
Metziot Qatan, 2, 28, 98-102
Midbar Qedem, 122
Midbar Shur, 2n3, 25-26, 28, 48n28, 91, 103n51, 116, 121-23, 127-28, 136-37, 155, 160n74, 160n76, 185, 192-93, 206, 240, 251, 273, 276, 287, 291, 313, 331n7, 334
Middle Ages, 26, 132, 198
middot, 128, 166
midrash, 4, 46, 59, 74, 87, 123, 146n25, 147n28, 152-54, 189, 229, 264n133, 313, 323, 339
mindfulness, 116, 208
Mir, 63, 91n3, 143n6, 148n31, 149
Mirsky, David, 125n149
Mirsky, Samuel Kalman, 5n8, 61n86, 68n117, 283n21, 341n39
Mishna, 69n122, 76, 84

Mishnaic tractates, 183
    Mishnah *Avot*, 169
    Mishnah *Sotah*, 93n10, 223, 269n156, 275, 298, 302, 312
    Mishnah *Sukkah*, 98
    Mishnah *Yadayim*, 308
Mitnagdic Kabbalah, 162
Mitnagdic Talmudic study, 229
Mitnagdim, 43, 95, 146, 154, 294
mitzvah, 104, 109-111, 113, 135-36, 245, 253
Mitzvot, 31, 79n166, 95, 108, 119, 128-31, 134, 136, 142, 155-58, 161, 163, 167-68, 175n130, 192n28, 196-97, 200, 208, 244, 246n49, 249-50, 252-55, 257, 259, 266, 270-72, 289-90, 298, 300, 313, 325, 346
Mizrahi, 237, 247n50, 259-60, 263, 271, 279, 282, 284
Moab, 307
Modern capitalism, early, 27
Modernism, 23
Mohilever, Shmuel, 55, 93n11, 237n13, 238n18
Mohin (chambers of consciousness), 120-21, 167-68
monism, 33
monotheisms, 290, 297
morality, 3, 52-53, 91, 127-28, 130 ,132, 135, 137, 142, 159n69, 194, 196n46, 219-21, 223, 236, 237n12, 250-51, 254, 257, 259, 264, 268-70, 276, 290, 293, 295-96, 302, 306, 308, 311, 313, 316-18, 322
    gentile morality, 99, 116, 122, 287, 291
Moscow, 88, 144
Moses, 97-98, 101n44, 119, 132, 167n95, 178n146, 195, 205, 210, 213, 216, 270, 273, 289, 297, 313-14, 317
Moses of Coucy, 113-14
multiplicity, 33, 100, 210, 214
Mussar Avikha, 8, 28, 141, 159-60, 165, 166n86, 194n36, 217
Mussar controversies, viii, 139, 160n76, 182, 189, 197
Mussar movement, viii, 24, 27, 29, 54, 140, 149-50, 151n41, 154, 158, 166, 175-76, 185-86, 194, 198, 261, 342-43. *See also* Salanter, Israel
mystic, 1, 12, 14, 115, 180, 210, 335
mysticism, 3, 13n37, 22n68, 24n74, 36-38, 106n62, 123-24, 335-38, 344n44

N
Nahman of Bratzlav, 94, 203, 205-6, 217
Naor, Bezalel, 10, 79n166, 93n12, 115n101, 122n136
Nathans, Benjamin, 42, 52
national identity, 3, 53, 248-49, 252, 259, 285. 294
nationalism
    Jewish -, ix, 7, 28, 56, 140, 233-35, 240-41, 243, 245, 247, 250-51, 271, 278-79, 297, 303, 305-6
    non-Jewish -, 247, 271, 306
    Romantic -, 22, 234
    secular -, 141, 247n52, 285-86, 306, 322

nationalists, 68, 79n166, 247, 250, 255-57, 263, 285, 299, 305, 326, 331n6
national love, 252-53, 256-57, 309-310
nationhood, 3, 35n118, 234, 248, 250-52, 254, 296, 330
natural law, 84, 100n36, 118-19, 130, 132-33, 135n199, 199n55, 312
natural morality, 135, 313
nefesh, 96, 118, 163, 166
Nefesh David, 64
Nehemiah, Prophet, 338
Neriah, Moshe Zvi, 6, 11n33, 17, 51n38, 57, 58n70, 60n85, 63, 69, 75n151, 90n1, 92, 146n25, 158n68, 197n48, 308n133
neshamah, 96-97, 118, 163
Netzah, 228
Netziv. *See* Berlin, Naftali Zvi Yehudah
Neumark, David, 4, 92n7
Nietzsche, Friedrich Wilhelm, 4, 92n7, 180n153, 247n54, 295-96, 301-2, 306, 317, 319, 343
nihilism, 294, 302, 320
Nimusim sikhliyim, 130, 132, 135
Niselovich, Lazar, 146
Nissenbaum, Yitzhak, xv, 93n10, 238
nivdelet, 167, 247
Noah (Biblical), 132, 323
Noahide laws, 119, 128, 133n190, 264, 313
nomos, 132
non-Jews, 3, 35, 49n31, 56, 95n15, 128, 146, 197, 251, 290, 297-98
Nordau, Max, 255, 271n168
Novaredok, 149
nuqva (feminine supernal principle), 174
Nussbaum, Martha, 30

O
obedience, 31, 136, 157n62, 201, 204, 279, 290
Odessa, Russia, 144, 327
Ofan, Bezalel, 248
Olam Ha-Herut, 326
Olam Ha-Nequdim, 315
Olat Re'ayah, 8
Orah Mishpat, 104-5
Oral Torah, 56, 80, 97-98, 241, 289, 299-300
Or La-Yesharim, 237n14, 243-44
Orot, 2n3, 7-9, 19n62
Orot Ha-Qodesh, 2n3, 8-9, 19n62, 21n68, 196n44, 337n26
Orot Ha-Teshuvah, 7, 19n62, 337n28
Orot Ha-Torah, 8, 341n38
Orthodoxy, 42, 44n13, 52, 56, 115, 305, 331, 342
Oshmany (Asmina), 114
Ostropoler, Samson, 321
Otto, Rudolf, 36
    The Idea of the Holy, 36
Otyan, 49
Otzar Ha-Ge'onim, 179

P
Pachter, Mordechai, 12-14, 89n211
Palestine, viii-ix, 2, 5, 12, 15, 19, 35, 48n30, 49n31, 56, 75n149, 78, 81n173, 86, 93n11, 106n62, 122n135, 137, 144, 148n32, 153n49, 154n52, 158n67, 160n75, 164, 167, 179, 183n2, 184n4, 232, 235-36, 244, 278-87, 306, 316, 327-28, 340
Palestinocentrism, 19
Paris, 281n10, 327
Pascal, Blaise, 337
Patah Eliyahu, 120
pathos, 126, 284
peace, 64, 100, 110, 133-34, 144-45, 154, 156, 206-7, 215, 230, 238, 245, 253-54, 274, 289, 295, 313, 317, 332
Pedaya, Haviva, 13
penim, 76
Pereq Heleq (of Tractate Sanhedrin), 76
perfection, 3, 62, 83, 96-97, 121, 126-36, 145, 154-57, 166, 168, 170-71, 174, 176-77, 185, 198-210, 213, 216-17, 224, 226, 240, 242, 248, 251-52, 256, 258, 268. 273. 275-76, 288, 311-12
Perl, Gil, 68, 189
personhood, 20, 39, 163, 203, 345
peshat, 40, 95n20
Petah Tiqva, 281, 283
Philosophical Mysticism, 336
philosophical tradition, 3, 14, 20-21, 23-24, 31-32, 72, 107, 116, 127, 139, 157n64, 178n145, 185, 198, 221, 249, 267, 287, 293, 313, 316, 336-37, 342
Picker-Neiss, Rori, 298
piety, 50, 61, 64-65, 70, 74, 77, 85, 104, 108, 144, 152, 156, 158, 165, 170-71, 175, 193, 198, 200, 206-7, 212, 215, 226, 257, 259, 262, 280, 310, 350
Pines, Yehiel Mikhel, 55-56, 283n22
pinqas, 26
Pinqas 15, 2, 28. 98-102
Pinqas 16, 2, 28, 172-179
Pinqas Aharon be-Boisk, 2, 28, 278, 301-327
Pinqasei Ha-Re'ayah, 248
Pinsker, Leon, 297
Pirqei Avot, 30
polemics, 42-43, 56, 75, 81n175, 103, 121n132, 156, 180, 189, 190n22, 241, 245n45, 274, 293, 295, 305
Poltava, 68, 245
Ponevezh, 63, 65, 72, 143n6
Porush, Iris, 60
Postmodernism, 231
prayers, 50n36, 109n72, 147, 152, 188n16
Preil, Yosef Yehoshua, 79n165, 92n7, 192
Pressburg, 65
primordial darkness, 336
Primordial Man, 167
primordial shattering, 168, 223, 275, 318
Primordial Torah, 167

Priulki, 257
prophet, 26, 82-84, 164, 202-3, 204n81, 216, 218-19, 289, 297, 347
Protestant ethic, 35
Proto-Zionism, 46n23, 88, 140
Puritans, 28
purity, 62n92, 101-2, 131, 144, 208, 215, 268, 291, 307, 316-17, 321, 339

Q

Qabbalat Ha-Gra, 162
qarqafta de-tefillei, 120
qav ha-emtza'i, 98
qedushah, 198, 335
qelippah, 76, 101, 317, 319-21
  Qelippat Nogah, 320-22
  qelippot, 76, 126, 295, 316, 320-22
Qidmat Ha-'Emeq, 67

R

Rabbah bar bar Hannah, 93-94, 95n16, 117, 317, 342n41
Rabbinate, 43, 73-74, 88, 91, 93, 142n6, 146, 148-49, 153n49, 281, 340, 341n38
Rabbiner, Benjamin,
Rabbiner, Mordechai, 71
Rabbiner, Zev Aryeh, 146, 153, 180
rabbinic culture, viii, 24, 30, 43, 56, 172-73, 342
rabbinic Judaism, 37, 47, 52, 77, 232, 300, 338
rabbinic literature, 4, 16n46, 28, 43, 64, 67, 78, 156n62, 190, 341
rabbinic Maskilim, 54
rabbinic tradition, 49n32, 62, 120n124, 153, 191, 194-95, 267, 302, 305, 314
Rabbi of Zeimel, 93 (we should double check this, I think it's how somebody once referred to Rav Kook in a conversation with him, and if so doesn't need its own entry)
Rabin, Moshe Yitzhak, 72
Rabin, Nisan, 72
Rabinowitz, Alexander Ziskind, 8
Rabinowitz, Shaul Pinhas, 77
Rabinowitz, Ya'aqov, 60, 65n103, 190n23
Rabinowitz, Eliyahu Aqiva, Rabbi, 48n30, 245
Rabinowitz-Teomim, Bat Sheva Alta, 90
Rabinowitz-Teomim, Bat Sheva Raiza Rivka, 88
Rabinowitz-Teomim (Aderet), Eliyahu David, Rabbi, 63-64, 280
Radom, 149
Rahmani, Shahar, 286-87, 288n39
Rahmistrivka, 80
Ramhal. *See* Luzzatto, Rabbi Moshe Hayim
Rashi, 86
rationalism, 41-42, 43n8, 89, 159n69, 184n3, 185n6, 198, 231
rationalist, 24, 200
Ratzon (Will), 177
Ravitzky, Aviezer, 243
Rav Ruvele. *See* Levin, Rabbi Reuven of Dvinsk

Razhiche, 48
Rebecca, Matriarch, 130
Recanati, Menahem, 123
reconciliation, 143, 145, 154, 295
rectification, 165
redemption, 2, 28, 95-96, 128, 137n203, 140, 170n115, 185, 242, 244, 271, 303, 305, 313, 322, 346, 350
Red Sea, 174-75
Reform movement, 241
regesh, 135
Reiner, Elhanan, 43, 349
Reines, Yitzhak Ya'aqov, 55, 68, 79n166, 87, 237, 259, 276
religious experience, ix, 36-38, 47n25, 104, 120, 184, 338, 347
religious practice, 38, 46, 121, 339, 348
religious tradition, 37, 218, 236, 291, 298, 338-39
Religious Zionism, 9n27, 10, 17, 184n3, 234n1, 340
remez, 40, 95n20
repentance, 7, 95, 136, 252, 258, 270, 326
resurrection, 192n28, 248, 289
revelation, 28, 36-37, 39, 83n180, 107, 113n91, 121n132, 129, 137, 155, 161-64, 167, 192n28, 193n33, 194-95, 197, 198n55, 203, 204n81, 217-18, 223, 261, 289, 294, 311, 313, 331
Ricci, Emanuel Chai, 164
Riga, 65, 73n141, 74, 93, 327
righteous, 60n85, 75, 96, 124, 132, 135, 195, 261, 275, 296, 318, 320, 322
righteousness, 72n136, 100, 127, 130-32, 176, 197, 199, 201, 203, 211-12, 225, 252, 258, 265-66, 268, 275, 288, 297, 318-19
Rinah shel Torah, 128
ritual, 38, 210
Rokah, Shimon, 282, 327n203, 328
Romanticism, 23, 42, 43n8, 231, 308
Rosenak, Avinoam, 13, 16n48, 18, 19n60, 92n7
Rosenberg, Shalom, 14, 239n20
Rosenblatt, Mordechai, Butener Tzadiq, 114, 115nn98-100, 121n132, 282n13
Rosh Amanah, 99
Ross, Tamar, 13, 333n9, 349
Rotenstreich, Nathan, 12
Rothschild Family, 143n6, 257n103, 284, 327n203
Rousseau, Jean-Jacques, 23, 28n90, 42, 220, 225, 252, 306
ruah, 96, 118, 163, 167, 198
Russia, 27, 43, 52n46, 53, 56, 210, 286, 327
  Russian Empire, 42n4, 45, 52, 236, 258, 279, 305
  Russian Haskalah, 52
  Russian Jewry, 52-53, 146n24, 232, 236
Ruzhinai, 49, 55n58

S

Sabbath, 51, 58n70, 73, 81, 83n180, 254, 270
Sabbatianism, 26n86, 82, 279, 297n94, 303n119, 320, 322

sages, 59n80, 63n94, 76, 111, 155, 170, 183n2, 188n16, 192, 230, 243
Salant, Shmuel, Rabbi, 49n31, 280, 282
Salanter, Israel, Rabbi, 24, 54, 63, 92, 93n8, 150, 152, 154, 158-59, 166, 177-78, 194, 198, 327
Salomon, Yoel Moshe, 281, 284, 328
Salonika, 189
Sanctity, 119-20, 134, 152, 168, 228, 269, 291, 297, 309, 311
Sanhedrin, 73n144, 76, 241-43, 253n76, 272, 303n119, 318
Sarah, (Biblical Matriarch), 133
Saruq, Israel, 164, 167
Schatz, Rivka, 258, 278n1
Schelling, Friedrich Wilhelm Joseph, 4, 23n73, 92n7, 218, 221, 313, 334
Schneersohn, Menahem Mendel, 10, 333
Schofer, Jonathan Wyn, 30
Scholem, Gershom, 6n12, 13, 21n67, 37, 155n57, 209, 278n1, 303n119, 338, 348
Schopenhauer, Arthur, 4, 92n7, 301n114
Schower, Avraham, 61
Sclar, Davis, 124
Schwarzschild, Steven, 254
Sdei Hemed, 88, 91n3
secularism, 252
secularization, 32, 42, 187
Seder Eliyahu, 64, 109n73
Sefer Ha-'Iqarim, 132
Sefer Ha-Kuzari , 4, 20, 35n118, 72, 123, 153, 167n95, 201-2, 261, 336
Sefer Ha-Middot, 123
Sefer Ha-Mitzvot, 104
Sefer Mizvot Gadol, 113
Sefer Yetzirah, 162, 167
sefirah, 120, 204, 326
sefirot, 136, 162, 204, 228, 266n141, 304, 333
sekhel, 121, 166
self-awareness, 32-34, 40
self-consciousness, 33, 44, 98, 102
self-cultivation, viii, 3, 24, 29-31, 53-54, 89, 108-9, 139, 150, 159, 185-86, 198n55, 276, 340
selfhood, 3, 23, 99, 101, 141, 170, 182, 231, 307, 345
self-love, 187, 225, 252, 256, 265, 268, 275, 306-7, 313
self-perfection, 121, 124, 127, 135, 174, 198, 200, 209n93, 269, 313, 336
sermonics, 25, 98, 110n74
serpent, 135n198, 166, 168
Seth (Biblical), 317, 349
Sha'agat Aryeh, 104
Sha'arei Orah, 321
Sha'arei Qedushah, 124
Sha'ar Ha-Sofer, 80
Sha'atnez, 290
Shabtai Zvi (Sh"Z), 306, 317, 319-20. See also Sabbatianism
shalom bayit (domestic tranquility), 105

Shalom be-Shem (Peace in G-d's Name), 138n209, 144, 238n19
Shalom la-'Am (Peace to the People), 145
Shapira, Hayim Avraham, 62
Shapira, Natan, 321-22
Shapira, Yehudah Leib, 57
Sharabi, Shalom, 36
shattering of the vessels, 164, 267, 275, 296, 318
Shavil, 49, 84, 89n210, 105
Shear, Adam, 35n118, 42
Shekhinah, 174, 204, 223, 311
Shemonah Qevatzim, 2n3, 12n34
Sherlo (Cherlow), Yuval, 184
Sherlo, Smadar, 10, 13, 16n46, 18n52, 158, 184nn3-4, 185n6, 301n113
Shevet Ahim, 64
Shevil Ha-Zahav (The Golden Mean), 143n8, 144
Shevirat Ha-Kelim. See shattering of the vessels
Shilo, Elhanan, 164n83, 296, 349
Shimeathites, 318
shlemut, 127, 170, 175-76, 198-99. See also eudaemoniaShnei Luhot Ha-Berit, 26, 123
Shneur Zalman of Liady, 86n196, 112n87, 163, 296
Shtei Terufot (Two Remedies), 251n68, 257
Shulhan 'Arukh, 28, 50, 58, 107-8, 222n131
Shurin, Yoel, 68
Sifra to Parashat Shemini, 317
sikhliyot, 130n176, 135-36, 296
Simon, Aqiva Ernst, 337
sin, 47, 106, 135-36, 159n69, 166-68, 171, 187, 206, 258, 283, 303, 322, 326
Sinai, 83n180, 97, 107, 130, 135n198, 297, 311
Sitra Ahra, 121, 315
Slabodka, 149, 151
Smorgon, 57, 59, 62-63, 114
socialism, 52, 72n138, 316
sociology, contemporary political, 11
sod, 40, 95n20
Soloveitchik, Hayim, 62n91, 70, 148n31, 176n132, 243, 276n194
Soloviev, Valdimir, 4, 82, 218, 251, 252n71
Song of Songs, 67, 128, 183n1, 307-310
soul-mate, 15n46
Spektor, Yitzhak Elhanan, 50n33, 59n80, 72, 73n141, 79nn166-67, 106n62, 122n134, 148n31
Spinoza, Baruch, 4, 42n1, 92n7, 177, 204n80, 267n146, 293-94
spiritual diary, 7, 25-26, 28, 92, 98, 137, 185, 321n184, 334
spirituality, 112, 225-26, 276, 279, 334
spiritual tradition, 23, 121, 140-43, 154, 182, 197, 201, 232, 337
Srednik, 93
statecraft, 10, 136, 235, 241, 299
Stern, Eliyahu, 42
Stern, Josef, 31
Stern, Nathan Hayim David, 84
Stern, Yosef Zechariah, 49, 55, 73n143, 85, 89n210, 105, 123n140, 191, 237n14, 349

Strauss, Leo, 28, 35n117, 198n56, 336
Suchathites, 318
Suvalski, Yitzhak, 86, 280n6

T

ta'amei ha-mitzvot, 254-55, 295
tallit, 68, 91
talmid hakham, 29
Talmud, 31, 47, 58, 60, 64, 67, 71, 87-88, 91, 93, 119, 123, 146, 147, 153, 156-58, 171, 174, 183-84, 189-91, 197, 212, 228, 230, 241, 261, 270, 276, 301, 309, 323, 325
Talmud study, 60, 71, 153, 156, 261, 276, 301
Talmudic novellae, 19, 80, 81n175, 86, 90, 106, 257n103
Talmudism, viii, 4, 24, 41, 46, 56, 63, 74, 87, 101-2, 121, 140, 186, 200, 226, 339, 342
Tau, Zvi, 9-10, 184n3, 331n7
Taves, Ann, 36-37, 338n30
Taylor, Charles, 22, 24, 27, 34, 44, 187, 210, 225, 231, 258n109, 302, 342
tefillah ve-'avodah murgeshet, 156
tefillin, 28, 68, 91, 109-113, 116-17, 119-123, 282, 342
    phylacteries, 4, 91, 109
Telos, 30n99, 99-100, 117, 125-28, 135-36, 157, 176-78, 200, 208, 212-14, 225, 230, 250-51, 256, 275, 313, 316, 322, 332n7
    takhlit, 128, 131, 251
Telz, 72n138, 147n28, 149, 153, 179, 180, 237, 283
Temple, 136, 211, 216, 239, 241, 270, 319n168, 338
    Temple sacrifices, 71, 99, 243, 290, 315
Ten Commandments, 109n71, 257
Teshuvah, 270
Te'udah, 251n67, 257
Te'udat Yisrael u-Leumiyuto (Israel's Mission and Its Nationhood), 251
theology, ix, 3-4, 9-10, 14n41, 21, 24, 32, 37, 72, 82n178, 98, 101, 103, 153, 163-64, 170, 182, 192n29, 225, 261-62, 264, 308, 323, 330n4, 333, 335, 338-40, 342
theosophy, 11, 37-38, 185, 209
Tiferet, 317
Tiferet Bahurim, 203, 332
tikkun 'agunot, 86
Tiqqun (restoration), 80, 99, 125-26, 136, 140-42, 155-56, 160, 168-69, 171, 185, 207, 217, 223, 289, 295-96, 315, 342
    cosmic tiqqun, 159, 177
    tiqqun ha-yetzer, 178
Tiqqun 'Olam, 129, 131, 226, 317
Tiqqunei Zohar, 61n89, 120, 162n80
Tirathites, 318
Tirosh-Samuelson, Hava, 31
Tolstoy, Leo, 180n153, 267
Torah Li-Shemah, 157
Torah study, 8, 47, 54-55, 68, 71, 80, 85-86, 99, 128, 142, 152, 154-55, 157, 163-64, 166-67, 169, 171, 200, 229, 239, 323

Touraine, Alain, 22n71, 206, 232, 242
traditionalism, 30n100, 44, 46n23, 52, 56, 257n103
traditionalist, 39, 42, 52, 77, 141, 236, 257n103, 280, 341
transcendence, 33-35, 206, 258, 302
Tree of Knowledge, 168, 312
Tropper, Amram, 30
Twersky, Zev, 80-81
tzadiq, 94, 97n26, 199n60, 225, 248, 275, 333
tzimtzum (divine contraction), 165, 167, 169, 294, 344
Tzirelson, Yehudah Leib, 251n68, 257-58

U

Ultra-Orthodoxy, 15, 342
unification, 129, 210, 221, 230-31, 306, 313-14, 334, 345
unio scholastica, 48
unity, 1, 92n7, 115, 126, 145, 216, 221, 227, 232n162, 240, 244, 246, 253, 255, 265, 296, 337, 345
universalism, viii-ix, 33, 166, 253, 278, 286
universal morality, 128, 130, 137, 317
universe, 31, 39, 62, 94, 121, 126, 154, 163-64, 167, 169, 171, 186, 209-10, 221, 228, 234, 270, 274, 289, 296, 315
utopia, 33, 233, 276-77

V

vegetarianism, 242, 267, 287, 290
Vessel, 71, 95, 101, 110, 116-17, 126, 129, 137, 156, 164, 168-69, 175-77, 208, 223, 234, 248, 251, 266-67, 275, 295-96, 299, 316, 318, 333, 345. See also shattering of the vessels)
Vienna, 65
Vilna Haskalah, 52, 55
virtue, 17, 29, 97, 107-8, 128, 134-36, 145, 157, 170-71, 174, 176, 200-201, 211, 215, 217, 226, 229, 231, 241, 252, 291-93, 314
Vital, Rabbi Hayim, 26-27, 35, 125n152
Volozhin, 22, 46-51, 54-57, 65-70, 78, 87, 112-14, 143, 149, 189, 191, 343

W

Warsaw, xv, 65, 112
Weber, Max, 35, 44, 81
Webster, Tom, 26, 27n87
Weisgal, 151
Weizmann, Chaim, 237
Wessely, Naftali Herz, 43n8, 123
Western Dvina River, 45
Western Europe, 56, 257, 305
Westernization, 33
Western Jews, 236
Whitman, Walt, 218
Wildman, Yizhak Isaac Haver, 94n13, 164, 204n82
Wisdom of Truth, 157, 165
Wissenschaft, 60
Wolfson, Elliot, 28-29, 334n19
Wolfson, Harry, 83n182, 336

world history, 5, 184, 211, 279, 291, 342
world of emanation, 162, 165
World War I, 308n134, 319, 331
Worship, 78, 99, 128, 156-57, 176, 178, 200-201,
    207-8, 224, 245, 248, 289, 333
Written Torah, 98, 164, 241, 300

Y
Yanover, Yehezqel, 51
yashar, 128, 135, 199n60
Yavetz (Javitz), Zev, 260n113, 283-84, 308
yedi'at Ha-Shem, 176
yirah, 156n62, 198
Yom Kippur, 92, 238n16, 239n21, 337n28
Yosef, Ovadia, 10
yosher, 119, 126-27, 131, 176, 192n28, 199, 211, 288,
    319n171, 335

Z
Zalkin, Mordechai, 49n32, 73n143, 149n33, 150,
    153

Zalman, Shlomo, of Kapust (Kopst), 51
Zeidel, Moshe, 147, 179-80, 341n39
Zeimel, 73-74, 83n180, 85, 90-91, 93, 98, 105, 114,
    122, 139-140, 142, 145-146, 148, 182-83, 238,
    317, 341
Ze'ir Anpin, 164
Zeitgeist wars, 261
Zeitlin, Hillel, 13, 16n46, 92n7, 225n138, 301, 318-
    19
Zion, 142, 247, 257, 278
Zionists, 5n10, 146n24, 235, 238, 243, 245n45,
    246n50, 247, 253, 255-60, 266, 276-77, 281, 285,
    299, 331n6
Zivhei Re'ayah, 106
Zohar, 36, 51, 67, 94n13, 123, 126, 153, 162-64, 307,
    317
Zoref, Avraham Shlomo Zalman, 281
Zuriel, Moshe, 6n13, 154n52, 188n16, 270n162
Zvi Le-Tzadiq, 75